MANAGING ORGANIZATIONAL BEHAVIOR

WILEY SERIES
IN MANAGEMENT

WILEY

JOHN WILEY & SONS
NEW YORK / CHICHESTER / BRISBANE / TORONTO / SINGAPORE

THIRD EDITION
MANAGING ORGANIZATIONAL BEHAVIOR

JOHN R. SCHERMERHORN, JR.
SOUTHERN ILLINOIS UNIVERSITY AT CARBONDALE

JAMES G. HUNT
TEXAS TECH UNIVERSITY

RICHARD N. OSBORN
WAYNE STATE UNIVERSITY

Copyright © 1982, 1985, 1988, by John Wiley & Sons, Inc.

All rights reserved. Published simultaneously in Canada.

Reproduction or translation of any part of
this work beyond that permitted by Sections
107 and 108 of the 1976 United States Copyright
Act without the permission of the copyright
owner is unlawful. Requests for permission
or further information should be addressed to
the Permissions Department, John Wiley & Sons.

Library of Congress Cataloging in Publication Data:

Schermerhorn, John R.
   Managing organizational behavior / John R. Schermerhorn, Jr.,
James G. Hunt, Richard N. Osborn.
        p.   cm.—(Wiley series in management)
   Bibliography: p.
   Includes indexes.
   ISBN 0-471-85772-6
   1. Organizational behavior.   2. Management.   I. Hunt, James G.,
1932–   . II. Osborn, Richard.   III. Title.   IV. Series.
HD58.7.S34   1988   87-27370
658—dc19   CIP

Printed in the United States of America

10 9 8 7 6 5 4 3 2

For Ann, continuing love and gratitude.
John

For Donna, Doug, Holly, and Robin.
Jerry

To Judy with Love.
Dick

ABOUT THE AUTHORS

JOHN R. SCHERMERHORN, JR., is professor of management in the College of Business and Administration at Southern Illinois University at Carbondale, where he has served as chairperson of the department of management and as associate dean. John holds a Ph.D. in organizational behavior from Northwestern University, and previously taught at Tulane University, the Chinese University of Hong Kong, and the University of Vermont. He has prior work experience in personnel and hospital administration, and is most concerned with helping the field of organizational behavior serve the needs of practicing managers. He is professionally active in management training and consultation with organizations in the United States and abroad, is past chairperson of the Management Education and Development Division of the Academy of Management, and publishes regularly in scholarly journals. John is the author of *Management for Productivity, Second Edition,* a popular introduction to management textbook also published by John Wiley and Sons in 1986.

JAMES G. (Jerry) HUNT is Paul Whitfield Horn Professor of Management and co-ordinator of the management area at Texas Tech University. Jerry's Ph.D. in business administration is from the University of Illinois, and he has taught at Southern Illinois University at Carbondale, West Virginia Tech, Millikin University, the University of Illinois, and the University of Texas. He was also a distinguished visiting scholar at the University of Aston in Birmingham, U.K. He has written nearly a hundred articles and papers, is coeditor of eight state-of-the-art scholarly leadership books, and has recently coedited a book on leadership on the future battlefield. As a scholar, he is committed to increasing the rigor and usefulness of organizational research. Jerry is a Fellow of the Academy of Management, former editor of the *Journal of Management,* has been an officer in several divisions of the Academy of Management, and is coauthor of *Organization Theory: An Integrated Approach* (Krieger, 1984).

RICHARD N. OSBORN is professor of management and organization in the School of Business Administration at Wayne State University, where he has also served as department chairperson. While a senior research scientist at The Battelle Memorial Institute's Human Affairs Research Centers in Seattle, Washington, he headed a series of studies to improve the management of safety in nuclear power plants. Dick has taught strategic management, organization theory, and/or the strategic management of advanced technologies at Southern Illinois University (Carbondale), the University of Washington, and Wayne State University. He is author or coauthor of over one hundred articles, papers, and monographs.

A graduate of Kent State University's DBA program, he is active in the Academy of Management, having been president of the Midwest Division and program chairperson for The R&D/Technology/Innovation interest group. Dick has served on the editorial review boards of *The Academy of Management Review* and *The Journal of Management,* as well as being a consultant for the Advisory Committee on Reactor Safeguards of the Nuclear Regulatory Commission and for several large U.S. based corporations.

PREFACE

Welcome to the third edition of *Managing Organizational Behavior*. A thorough revision has resulted in what we believe is a most timely and substantive textbook that retains its unique identity. Most college textbooks are written for the instructor. This book is different. While we don't neglect the instructor, the book's emphasis is on getting the student in an introductory course in organizational behavior (OB) involved as he or she completes the assigned reading. *Managing Organizational Behavior* is written in a conversational manner that incorporates a number of special features designed to help students interact with the contents of the textbook. These features are explained in detail in our memo to the students that precedes Chapter 1.

While we use a conversational writing style, we have not sacrificed rigor or content. You will find this third edition of our text includes the well-known models in the field, some of the controversies (though without overwhelming the student), and a reasonable review of significant empirical work. In other words, we've tried to strike a balance between readability and scholarship for the introductory student.

We invite you to peruse the contents of this latest edition. As before, the book covers both micro and macro OB topics. In addition to major sections on individuals, groups, and processes, there are three chapters on the organization and its environment, as well as supplementary modules on research methods, the history of OB, and performance appraisal. A final integrating chapter looks at current trends in the environment and briefly reviews the book as a whole with a view toward personal career planning and development.

The third edition of *Managing Organizational Behavior* has been revised to reflect recent developments in the discipline, and respond to constructive feedback from our many satisfied adopters. The text is updated throughout in terms of both illustrative material and content. Some of the more significant changes in chapter substance include expanded attention to the following topics: managerial networks, skills, and competencies; values and personality; learning; managerial aspects of group process; creative work group designs; organizational culture; decision making; organizational politics and ethics; current thinking on leadership; and major trends in the managerial environment. In addition, we have selected cases, examples, and newslines whenever possible to highlight the increasing importance of high technology and the international dimensions of management.

Even with its rich array of content, however, *Managing Organizational Behavior* is still designed for instructional flexibility in the sequencing of topics. While the book follows an individual-group-organization sequence, it is written so that other patterns may be used without sacrificing understanding. Furthermore, the four chapters on processes in Part Five and the chapter on change and stress in Part Six may be used individually at any point in the course according to your preferences.

We have made the book as self-contained as possible. Special features designed to elicit reader involvement include chapter openers, Management Application Questions, Checkpoints, Newslines, and frequent examples of practical applications. In addition, each chapter concludes with a Case and Exercise, The Manager's Vocabulary (which is a glossary of important terms and names), and a set of thought questions.

To further enhance the learning experience for the student and to make the instructor's job easier, we've provided an extensive instructor's manual and support package. The manual includes, among other things, a number of different course schedules using alternative topic sequencing, chapter highlights and teaching suggestions, supplementary lectures, transparency masters, additional cases, and sample assignments for individual and group projects. A complete test bank of objective and essay questions accompanies the text. This test bank is available on a floppy disk for the IBM PC and IBM-compatible computers. Instructors can select specific questions or have the program randomly choose questions to make up exams. You can also build new versions of the same test by scrambling questions, adding your own questions, or editing existing test questions. A phone-in test service is available for those instructors who do not have access to computer facilities.

Finally, we have made some additions to the outstanding instructional support package. A separate book of over 100 transparencies is available to adoptors. The unique and creative supplement, AIM, Advanced Instructional Modules, provides complete instructional materials for the introduction of special course segments of up to one week duration on four timely OB topics. All have been substantially revised. The subject matter specialists who have authored these modules are as follows:

International Issues and Organizational Behavior
  William Stratton
  Idaho State University

Career Dynamics in Organizational Life
  Samuel Rabinowitz   Jeffrey H. Greenhaus
  Rutgers University at Camden   Drexel University

Ethical Issues and Organizational Behavior
  Anthony Buono
  Bentley College

The Impact of Computer Technology on Organizational Behavior
  Andrea Warfield   Jerry Miller
  University of Michigan   University of Michigan

Entirely new to this package for the third edition are two videos produced by Wilson Learning Corporation, an acknowledged leader in the field of management and sales training. These creative video programs present dramatized case scenarios of managers facing motivation and leadership challenges in the contemporary workplace. A separate instructor's guide to the programs has been prepared by Sid Nachman of Drexel University, fully describing the video segments and offering a wide variety of options for using them in class and as focal points in lectures and discussions. A truly unique supplement, these videos allow you to bring into the classroom the same tools management consultants are using in Fortune 500 corporations.

For our acknowledgments we remain indebted to those colleagues who carefully reviewed the first and second editions, as well as to those who so ably assisted us by critiquing developmental drafts of the new edition. Their many comments and suggestions have been most helpful. To these scholars and educators we extend sincere thanks: Robert Barbato, Rochester Institute of Technology; Bonnie Betters-Reed, Boston College; Gerald Biberman, University of Scranton; Dale Blount, Southern Illinois University at Edwardsville; Joseph F. Byrnes, Bentley College; Paul Collins, Purdue University; Delf Dodge, Corporate Strategic Planning, General Motors Corporation; Dalmar Fisher, Boston College; Cynthia V. Fukami, University of Denver; Joe Garcia, Western Washington University; Frederick Greene, Manhattan College; William Hart, University of Mississippi; David Hunt, Miami University; Harriet Kandelman, University of Portland; Donald Latham, University of Mississippi; Kathy Lippert, University of Cincinnati; David Luther, University of Mississippi; James McFillen, Bowling Green State University; Herff L. Moore, University of Central Arkansas; Paula Morrow, Iowa State University; Richard Mowday, University of Oregon; Linda Neider, University of Miami; Robert F. Pearse, Rochester Institute of Technology; Lawrence Peters, Texas Christian University; Joseph Porac, University of Illinois; Steven Ross, Marquette University; Anson Seers, University of Alabama; Walter W. Smock, Rutgers University; Sharon Tucker, Washington University; Joyce Vincelette, University of South Florida; David Vollrath, New York University; Andrea F. Warfield, Ferris State University; Joseph W. Weiss, Bentley College; Barry L. Wisdom, Southwest Missouri State University; Raymond Zammuto, University of Colorado.

In addition to this very fine help from colleagues, we were most fortunate to have the secretarial assistance of Lisa Stearns at Southern Illinois University at Carbondale, Nadene Ped at the Battelle Human Affairs Research Centers, and Dawn Harvard at Wayne State University. Gary South was also indispensable as a graduate research assistant.

As always, the staff at John Wiley & Sons was most helpful in the various stages of production. We thank Karin Gerdes Kincheloe, Suzanne Ingrao, Katharine Rubin, Gilda Stahl, Ann Boles, and Safra Nimrod for their support. Our editor Cheryl Mehalik deserves special recognition for her emphasis on quality and distinction. Rick Leyh has our continuing appreciation for his original determination to produce this book.

Finally, we recognize our families. *Managing Organizational Behavior,* though exciting to write and revise, continues to take more time from them than we care to remember. Thanks to Ann Schermerhorn, Donna Hunt, Judy Osborn, and the children for their forbearance.

John Schermerhorn
Jerry Hunt
Dick Osborn

CONTENTS

PART FOUR **MANAGING ORGANIZATIONS**   **291**

10. BASIC ATTRIBUTES OF ORGANIZATIONS   **295**

11. ORGANIZATIONAL DYNAMICS   **323**

SUPPLEMENTARY MODULES   573

MEMORANDUM

TO: The Reader
FROM: John Schermerhorn, Jerry Hunt, Dick Osborn
SUBJECT: You and *Managing Organizational Behavior, Third Edition*

Most people, whether they like it or not, have to work for a living. They must produce or provide goods or services of value to someone else if they are to obtain the basic requirements of life, and a few luxuries as well. Oh yes, there are alternative lifestyles that downplay the economic necessity implied in this argument. Some people join communes, others just "drop out," while some simply rely on the goodwill of parents or friends for their support. But for you, probably, and for us, certainly, work is the basis of our livelihoods. We spend a large part of our lives working, and we should, therefore, know as much as possible about it.

ON BECOMING A MANAGER

This book is about people at work in organizations. Reading it should help you to understand the many events that give meaning to your day-to-day work experiences. Sooner or later you will probably become a particular type of worker—a **manager**— a person in a work organization who is responsible for the performance of one or more other people.

Being a manager is a special type of personal challenge. Think about your own work experiences. Can you remember a time when you felt especially uncomfortable because you had to ask someone to do a rather unpleasant task, or a task that you knew they just did not want to do? Such anxiety or discomfort is typical in situations where one person must direct the work activities of others. This is a leadership challenge faced by all managers. What is your style of leadership? How effective is it? What should your style of leadership be? The learning experiences in this book will help you to answer these and other related questions.

THE BOOK IN PERSPECTIVE

Two points about this third edition of *Managing Organizational Behavior,* and our purpose in writing it for you are especially important. First, please recognize that people act as managers in many different types of organizations. The issues, concepts, theories, and insights of this book are relevant to work activities in organizations of all types. Thus, there is a useful learning experience contained in these pages, regardless of where you plan to work—be it in business, education, government, health services, or social services. We have written for people who are going to work and be managers in any of these occupational settings.

Second, we are committed to providing you with an active learning experience that will leave you with insights and knowledge that will help you in actual practice. This is not just a theory book. There is a lot of theory in it. But, the theory is explained and then applied to help you perform more effectively in an actual managerial capacity. To take full advantage of the learning experiences offered in this book, however, you must read carefully and stay involved. When we ask you to do something, such as complete an inventory of your leadership style, please do it. Such requests are designed to ensure learning outcomes that are as closely tailored to your own needs as possible.

Simply put, we have written this book

1. For people who will serve as managers in all types of organizational and occupational settings.
2. To emphasize the practical application of theory, and to help you to perform more effectively as a manager.
3. As a self-contained learning experience that uses your active participation as a way of increasing comprehension.

KEY FEATURES OF THE BOOK

A number of practical reference points and learning aids help make this a reader-oriented book. Consider each feature carefully so that you can take full advantage of the learning opportunities represented by each when they appear throughout the text.

Practical Reference Points

We want you to know what is happening in the real world of management. Four specific features in this book are designed to help you make these important theory-into-practice transitions. These features include

Chapter Opener: A brief vignette or article excerpt that focuses attention and interest on subject matter to be covered in the chapter.

Management Applications Question: A question posed at the beginning of each chapter to highlight a practical managerial issue underlying the topics presented in the chapter.

Newsline: Excerpts from recent newspapers and news magazines that give examples of the application of text material and of the current ''problems'' or ''opportunities'' that challenge managers to act effectively.

In-text Examples: Examples of actual responses by managers to specific problems or opportunities.

When you encounter these features in reading, consider them carefully. Some may prove useful as topics for term papers or special projects. Others may become topics for class discussion. It would be interesting, for example, to learn if anyone has experienced events described in a *Newsline* or example, or to find out if your professor agrees or disagrees with the practical applications being described. Asking questions can lead to a richer learning experience and help to draw forth an informative dialogue with your instructor.

Learning Aids

We want you to use this book to enrich the overall intellectual experience of your OB course. You must read to expand your knowledge and to build personal theories that will apply to a wide variety of managerial situations. Neither this nor any other book can anticipate *all* work situations and provide the action guidelines to solve *all* of your future problems. Thus, our task is to help you develop a knowledge base that can be used to analyze any situation, develop a set of feasible responses, and choose and implement the best response systematically. This capability requires you to be familiar with the concepts and theories that most textbooks merely present to the reader. We will do more, with the help of the following learning aids.

Planning Ahead: Specific statements at the beginning of each chapter that describe the key topics to be discussed.

Checkpoints: Periodic places in the text where we ask you to pause to consider the meaning of key terms and concepts or to work on a special case or example.

Summary: A review at the end of each chapter that briefly outlines the key theories and concepts introduced in the reading.

The Manager's Vocabulary: A listing at the end of each chapter of key terms and their definitions, as well as important names.

Once again, each of the features just described is specially chosen to help you to learn more when reading this book. Please take full advantage of them. Planning Ahead will give you a feel for the most important learning outcomes in each chapter. This should be especially useful when you read a chapter for the first time. Checkpoints will keep you involved with key terms and concepts as they are inntroduced. The Summary and The Manager's Vocabulary are additional chances to review a chapter and to consider whether you have understood it sufficiently. These features should be of special help when you study for exams.

A FINAL COMMENT

Managing Organizational Behavior, Third Edition, is more than a textbook. It is a learning instrument. It actively involves you in a learning process. You must think as you read. Think about yourself, the experiences you have had, and your aspirations. Think about other people, such as coworkers, classmates, and your instructor. Ask about their feelings and experiences and try to compare them with your own. Above all, read enthusiastically. These many special features provide ''interactive'' aspects that make this book different from other texts. For true learning to occur along with a sense of practical application, however, you must work as hard at using the book as we have in writing it. If you do this, we think you'll enjoy the reading and learning every bit as much as we did the writing!

PART ONE
INTRODUCTION

A **manager** is a person in an organization who is responsible for the performance of one or more subordinates. Being a manager is a special type of challenge. People are key resources of organizations and managers must ensure that these human resources are well utilized. Simply put, a manager's job is to get things done through people.

Organizational behavior is the study of individuals and groups in organizations. This body of knowledge is important to all practicing managers. Good managers plan ahead to foresee human resource problems and opportunities and to direct individual and group behavior toward productive results. They use a knowledge of organizational behavior to understand work situations and then to predict and control their consequences.

This book is designed to familiarize you with organizational behavior as a knowledge base and to introduce you to this understanding–prediction–control discipline. What follows is a case written in a prediction format. It is presented in a series of segments that end with prediction questions asking you to think about what you expect to find in the next segment. The case involves an individual at work in an organization with which you should be quite familiar—a university. Read the case and answer the questions we ask. Compare your responses to our viewpoints on the case. This is a chance to explore your awareness of the key elements of organizational behavior that will be examined in this book.

THE CASE OF THE MISSING RAISE

It was late February, and John Lloyd had just completed an important long-distance telephone conversation with Professor Fred Massie, head of the Department of Management at Central University.[1] During the conversation, John accepted an offer to move from his present position at Private University, located in the East, to Central in the Midwest as an assistant professor. John and his wife Marsha then shared the following thoughts.

John: "Well, it's final."

Marsha: "Oh, hon, it's been a difficult decision, but I know it will work out for the best."

John: "Yes, however, we're leaving many things we like here."

Marsha: "I know, but remember, Professor Massie is someone you respect a great deal, and he is offering you a challenge to come and introduce new courses at Central. Besides, he will surely be a pleasure to work for."

John: "Marsha we're young, eager, and a little adventurous. There's no reason we shouldn't go."

Marsha: "We're going, dear."

---

[1]"Prepared by Dr. John R. Schermerhorn, Jr., as a basis for class discussion rather than to illustrate either effective or ineffective handling of an administrative situation.

EARLY FALL   John Lloyd began the fall semester eagerly. The points discussed in his earlier conversations with Fred were now real challenges and John was teaching new undergraduate and graduate courses in Central's curriculum. Overall, the transition to Central had been pleasant. The nine faculty members were warm in welcoming him, and John felt it would be good working with them. John also felt comfortable with the performance standards that appeared to exist in the department. Although it was certainly not a "publish or perish" situation, Fred had indicated to John during the recruiting process that research and publications would be given increasing weight along with teaching and service in future departmental decisions. This was consistent with John's personal belief that a professor should live up to each of these responsibilities. Although there was some conflict in evidence among the faculty over what weighting and standards should apply to these performance areas, John sensed some consensus that the multiple responsibilities should be respected.

QUESTIONS

1. Fred Massie is the "manager" so far in the case. What type of a "boss" do you feel he will be for John? What type of a relationship will they have?

2. What level of work performance do you predict for John? Why?

high   medium   low

OUR VIEWPOINT

The field of organizational behavior recognizes the importance of the joining-up process, that is, the events that result in a choice by an individual to join the organization as a place of employment. In this case, John and his wife each felt they were giving up some positive things in the move to Central, but they also anticipated certain benefits. Although John and Marsha seem to have adapted well, we might wonder if the trade-offs between the losses and gains may affect John's behavior in the new job.

CONTINUING ON   It was April and spring vacation time. John was sitting at home reflecting upon his experiences to date at Central. He was pleased. Both he and Marsha had adjusted very well to life in the Midwest. Although there were things they both missed from their prior location, Marsha was teaching in a very pleasant school, and both John and Marsha found the rural environment of Central very satisfying. John had also received positive student feedback on his fall semester courses, had presented two papers at a recent professional meeting, and had just been informed that two of his papers would be published by a journal. This was a good record and John felt satisfied. He had been working hard and it was paying off.

MAY   The spring semester had ended and John was preoccupied. It was time, he thought, for an end-of-the-year performance review by Fred Massie. This anticipation had been stimulated, in part, by a recent meeting of the college faculty in which the dean indicated that a 7 percent pay raise pool was now available for the coming year. He was encouraging department chairpersons to distribute this money differentially based on performance merit. John had listened closely to the dean and liked what he heard. He felt this meant that Central was really trying to establish a performance-oriented reward system. Such a system was consistent with John's personal philosophy and, indeed, he taught such reasoning in his courses.

Throughout May, John kept expecting to have a conversation with Fred Massie on these topics. One day, the following memo appeared in his faculty mailbox.

MEMORANDUM

TO: Fellow Faculty
FROM: Fred
RE: Raises for Next Year

The Dean has been most open about the finances of the College as evidenced by his detail and candor regarding the budget at the last faculty meeting. Consistent with that philosophy I want to provide a perspective on raises and clarify a point or two.

The actual dollars available to our department exclusive of the chairman total 7.03%. In allocating those funds I have attempted to reward people on the basis of their contribution to the life of the Department and the University as well as professional growth and development. In addition, it was essential this year to adjust a couple of inequities that had developed over a period of time. The distribution of increments was the following:

| 5% or less | 3 | 7+ %−9% | 3 |
| 5+ %−7% | 2 | More than 9% | 2 |

QUESTIONS

Think about Fred's memo:

1. What effect will it have on the faculty?
2. What effect will it have on John?
3. What does it tell you about Fred's "style" as a manager?

CONTINUING ON   John read the memo with mixed emotions. Initially, he was upset that Fred had obviously made the pay raise decisions without having spoken first with John about his performance. Still, John felt good because he was sure to be one of those receiving a 9+ % increase. "Now," he mused to himself, "it will be good to sit down with Fred and discuss not only this past year's efforts but my plans for next year as well."

John was disappointed when Fred did not contact him for such a discussion. Furthermore, John found himself frequently involved in informal conversations with other faculty members who were speculating over who received the various pay increments.

JUNE   One day Carla Block, a faculty colleague, came into John's office and said she had asked Fred about her raise. She received a 7+ % increase and also learned that the two 9+ % increases had been given to senior faculty members. John was incredulous. "It can't be," he thought, "I was a top performer this past year. My teaching and publications records are strong, and I feel I've been a positive force in the department." John felt Carla could be mistaken and waited to talk the matter out with Fred.

A few days later another colleague reported to John the results of a similar conversation with Fred. This time John exploded internally. He felt he deserved just reward.

The next day John received a computerized notice on his pay increment from the Accounting Office. His raise was 7.2%. That night, after airing his feelings with Marsha, John telephoned Fred at home and arranged to meet with him the next day.

QUESTIONS

1. What do you expect to happen at this meeting between Fred and John?
2. How would you begin the meeting if you were Fred?
3. What is your prediction about John's reaction to the meeting? Why?
   positive   negative   mixed

CONTINUING ON   Fred Massie knocked on the door to John's office and entered. The greetings were cordial. John began the conversation. "Fred, we've always been frank with one another and now I'm concerned about my raise," he said. "I thought I had a good year, but I understand that I've received just an average raise." Fred Massie was a person who talked openly and responded to John in this way.

Yes, John, you are a top performer. I feel you have made great contributions to the Department. The two 9+ % raises went to correct "inequities" that had built up over a period of time for two senior people. I felt that since the money was available this year that I had a responsibility to make the adjustments. If we don't consider them, you received one of the three top raises, and I

consider any percentage differences between these three very superficial. I suppose I could have been more discriminating at the lower end of the distribution, but I can't give zero increments. I know you had a good year. It's what I expected when I hired you. You haven't let me down. From your perspective I know you feel you earned an "A," and I agree. I gave you a "B + ." I hope you understand why.

John sympathized with Fred's logic and felt good having spoken with him. Although he wasn't happy, he understood Fred's position. His final comment to Fred was this. "You know, it's not the absolute dollar value of the raise that hurts. It's the sense of letdown. Recently, for example, I turned down an extensive consulting job that would have paid far more than the missing raise. I did so because I felt it would require too many days away from the office. I'm not sure my colleagues would make that choice."

QUESTIONS

1. What do you now predict in terms of John's behavior?
2. What do you predict for other faculty in the department?
3. Think ahead to the coming academic year. Will John be a higher performer? Why or why not?

CONTINUING ON   In the course of a casual summer conversation, Carla mentioned to John that she heard two of the faculty who had received 4+ % raises had complained to Fred and the dean. After lodging the complaints, they had received additional salary increments. "Oh great," John responded to himself, "I thought I had put this thing to rest." He knew that this information would bother him and rekindle some of the irritation he had felt earlier.

About three weeks later, John, Fred, Carla, and another colleague were in a meeting with the dean. Although the meeting was on a separate matter, something was said that implied that Carla had also received an additional pay increment. John confronted the dean and learned that this was the case. Carla had protested to Fred and the dean and they raised her pay on the justification that an historical salary inequity had been overlooked. Fred was visibly uncomfortable as a discussion ensued on how salary increments should be awarded and what had transpired in the department in this respect.

Fred eventually excused himself to attend another meeting. John and the others continued to discuss the matter with the dean, and the conversation became increasingly heated. Finally, they each rose to terminate the meeting and John felt compelled to say one more thing. "It's not that I'm not making enough money," he said to the dean, "but I just don't feel I received my fair share, especially in terms of your own stated policy of rewarding faculty on the basis of performance merit."

With that remark, John left the meeting. As he walked down the hall to his office, he said to himself, "Next year there will be no turning down consulting jobs because of a misguided sense of departmental responsibility."

OUR VIEWPOINT

Now the dean is in the act too. Disgruntled faculty are complaining to the department head and taking the issue up with his supervisor, the dean. And then there's John.

He's back to his consulting agenda again. We hear him say that he can spend any extra time in one of two ways: (1) for the university or (2) in private consulting. We also hear him say that his choice is to consult. He seems to feel that the payoffs for doing "extra duty" for the university just aren't there. As a result, he is opting to reduce his university-oriented work efforts in the future.

The dean will evaluate and reward Fred on how well the Department of Management performs. Fred's challenge is to meet his responsibility by creating a work environment within which faculty members, as human resources, want to and are able to achieve high performance. Obviously, Fred is currently feeling the full weight of this managerial challenge. He will experience even greater pressure if John and the other faculty really do reduce their work efforts.

If Fred had been more sensitive to the developing dynamics of the situation and more capable of analyzing them in a systematic fashion, he might have predicted the resulting feelings and behaviors of his faculty. Once predicted, appropriate action could have been taken to facilitate desirable outcomes and minimize undesirable ones.

MANAGING ORGANIZATIONAL BEHAVIOR

Organizational behavior (let's call it OB from now on) is a body of knowledge that addresses many of the issues in "The Case of the Missing Raise." Simply put,

$$\text{OB is a knowledge base} \xrightarrow[\text{by}]{\text{used}} \text{managers} \xrightarrow[\text{accomplish}]{\text{to}} \text{good human resource utilization}$$

Managers face a wide variety of dilemmas similar to Fred's on a daily basis. Every manager's day is filled with problems to be solved and opportunities to be explored. Although these problems and opportunities will vary in magnitude and immediacy, they all have the potential to impact organizational performance and affect the satisfactions of the people who do the work. What Fred lacked, and what all managers need, is a systematic means of analyzing work situations and un-

derstanding their consequences for people at work. Learning about OB will help you to develop this capability. As you proceed now with the study of OB, remember

1. OB provides managers with a way of systematically thinking about the behavior of people at work.
2. OB provides managers with a vocabulary of terms and concepts that allow work experiences to be clearly analyzed, shared, and discussed.
3. OB provides managers with techniques for dealing with the problems and opportunities that commonly occur in work settings.[2]

---

[2]See Larry L. Cummings, "Towards Organizational Behavior." *Academy of Management Review,* Vol. 3 (January 1978), pp. 90–98.

CHAPTER 1
ORGANIZATIONAL BEHAVIOR AND THE MANAGER

The key to success in today's competitive world is a working environment in which each and every employee can make a difference.

Pacificorp Annual Report

WHAT DO WE REALLY KNOW ABOUT MANAGERS AND MANAGING?

Professor Fred Luthans of the University of Nebraska began his presidential speech to the Academy of Management on the occasion of its 50th anniversary with this question—"What do we really know about managers and managing?" In response, he reported a study of over 300 managers working at all levels in a variety of organizations. The study identified four major sets of activities that were emphasized by *effective* managers.

- *Routine communication*—processing paperwork and exchanging information with others.
- *Human resource management*—motivating, reinforcing, disciplining, punishing, staffing, and developing.
- *Traditional management*—planning, decision making, and controlling.
- *Networking*—interacting with outsiders, as well as socializing, and politicking.

Based upon related research sponsored by the Center for Creative Leadership, Robert Kaplan describes *effective* general managers as persons who:

- Have vision, think long-term, set direction.
- Are good communicators and good listeners.
- Understand operations.
- Know where to spend time and how to prioritize.
- Don't resist change.
- Delegate well.
- Act confidently.
- Accept responsibility and admit mistakes.
- Are motivating, curious, honest, credible and decisive.[1]

Management Applications Questions

Think about what it means to be a manager. What special challenges do managers face? How can a knowledge of organizational behavior help you master these challenges in your future career?

After reading this chapter and participating in the recommended learning experiences, you will be thoroughly familiar with the following topics.

Organizations
Managers in Organizations
The Nature of Managerial Work
Managerial Skills and Competencies
Scientific Thinking and the Manager
Learning about Organizational Behavior
The Manager's Challenge, OB, and this Book

Good managers are problem solvers. They continually analyze work situations to locate problems to be solved, develop solutions to these problems, and implement the solutions.[2] The importance of this three-step process was evident in the Case of the Missing Raise discussed in the Part One introduction. If Fred Massie had noticed sooner that potential problems existed in his department, he could have addressed the problems and, it is hoped, solved them before undesirable consequences occurred.

Good problem solvers know what to look for in work situations and how to understand what they find. This, for example, is a process for which physicians are carefully trained. During a physical exam, the doctor systematically asks questions and is quick to note where one condition (such as a recurrent sore on a finger) may be symptomatic of a problem that requires further medical attention (e.g., treatment for a small skin cancer). Further diagnostic work and possible medical treatments follow.

Managers need similar diagnostic and action abilities. Instead of such things as sores and headaches, the manager's problem indicators include absenteeism, turnover, tardiness, negative attitudes, poor-quality work, and declining work quantity on the part of employees. These and many other symptoms of potential problems confront all managers on a regular basis. Successful managers are able to recognize the symptoms, understand their significance in terms of problems to be solved or opportunities to be explored, and take constructive action as a result of this insight.

Regardless of the occupation you eventually pursue, it is highly likely that someday you will be responsible for serving as a manager of other people. It is precisely in this respect that the field of organizational behavior can contribute to your career success. This book presents OB as a useful knowledge base that can be applied by managers to improve their decision making and problem solving in respect to human behavior in organizations. When the inevitable managerial responsibilities come your way, we want you—in the spirit of the chapter opening example—to successfully master them. Specifically, our goal is to help you learn how to utilize individuals and grousp as the human resources of organizations. This first chapter formally introduces the concepts of "organization" and "manager," discusses managerial work, and shows how the many topics covered throughout the book combine into a meaningful study of organizational behavior and its managerial implications.

ORGANIZATIONS

An **organization** is a collection of people working together in a division of labor to achieve a common purpose. This definition fits a wide variety of fraternal groups, clubs, voluntary organizations, and religious bodies, as well as entities such as businesses, schools, hospitals, government agencies, and the like. We are most interested in the work organizations people belong to as employees.

Why Do Organizations Exist?

Organizations exist because individuals are limited in their physical and mental capabilities. This logic may be as old as time itself. Consider the following example as reported in the Bible.[3]

> Some time after leading his people out of Egypt, Moses camped at the base of the Mountain of God. His days were consumed by making the many decisions required to maintain the tribe. Moses took care that his people had proper food and clothing. He listened to their concerns, settled their disputes, and responded to all those who came before him inquiring about God.
>
> Moses was fortunate to be joined in this camp by his father-in-law, Jethro. After observing Moses' daily routine, the wise counsel Jethro commented, "thou wilt surely wear away, both thou and this people that is with thee; for this thing is too heavy for thee; thou are not able to perform it thyself alone."
>
> Jethro went on to give Moses the following advice. He counseled Moses to select other persons to assist him in these many managerial chores. He further suggested that these people be given the responsibility to rule over groups of thousands, hundreds, fifties, and tens. Finally, he encouraged Moses to let them judge the small matters for the people under their control and to only bring the large matters to him.

Jethro, in effect, gave Moses a way to organize his people. Moses' "organization" involved the appointment of certain people as managers and the grouping of the other members of the tribe under these managers. The result found Moses in a new position of managerial responsibility, as shown in Figure 1.1.

Experiences similar to Moses' occur over and over again as organizations emerge in many different settings. In most cases the situation lacks the benefit of consultation

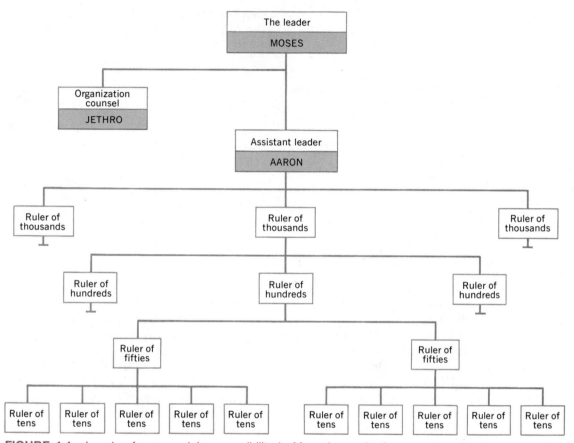

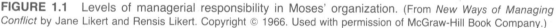

FIGURE 1.1 Levels of managerial responsibility in Moses' organization. (From *New Ways of Managing Conflict* by Jane Likert and Rensis Likert. Copyright © 1966. Used with permission of McGraw-Hill Book Company.)

such as that provided by Jethro. Inevitably, though, organizations develop to accomplish work tasks that are beyond individual capabilities.

Organizations as Open Systems

One way in which to analyze organizations is to view them as open systems as well as social systems. Because organizations involve people and ultimately depend upon the efforts of people to accomplish performance results, they are true social systems. But even though people are the human resources of organizations, organizations are more than people. They also include the machinery, equipment, raw materials, facilities, and money that allow people to produce some good or service. These are the physical or material resources of organizations.

As **open systems,** organizations transform human and physical resources received

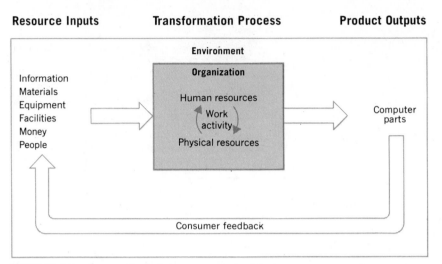

FIGURE 1.2 A manufacturing company depicted as an open system.

as inputs from their environments into goods and services that are then returned to the environment for consumption. The goods or services are created by work activities that transform resource inputs into product outputs. All this is made possible by the direct interaction of the organization with its environment.

Take, for example, a company producing electronic parts for computers. Figure 1.2 views this organization as an open system. People are human resource inputs that become part of a transformation process. They work with and combine various physical resource inputs to create a finished product. Both the physical and human resources are obtained from the external environment. Together, these resources are transformed by the organization into computer parts that are consumed by members of the environment. In this business example, the price paid by the consumers for the computer parts becomes an important monetary resource input to the organization. The company's ability to sell components today is what enables it to obtain the resources required to produce more components tomorrow.

It is often useful to view organizations and their subunits as open systems that transform resource inputs into outputs. A key contribution of the open-systems perspective is awareness that organizational survival depends on an ability to satisfy environmental demands. This input–output interdependency between a system and its environment is an important influence on organizations and the people who work within them.

Ingredients of Organizations

Organizations are working combinations of physical and human resources. Beyond that, they involve a purpose, division of labor, and hierarchy of authority. We briefly introduce each of these ingredients in the paragraphs that follow. They are discussed in greater detail later, in Part Four of the book—Managing Organizations.

NEWSLINE 1.1 / McWORLD?

McDonald's, king of the fast-food franchises, is prospering in the far corners of the world. The ''Big Mac'' and other familiar treats can be found from New York to Hong Kong, Mexico City to Sao Paulo, and Tokyo to Paris. Nearly 40 percent of new McDonald's are located outside of the United States. And, as the new locations open, the company's success is being exported.

Through careful selection of foreign partners, McDonald's seems to fit well in diverse countries. A key lies with giving international franchises the freedom to adapt to local cultures and needs, while still retaining the company's mainstay—a tradition of high-quality foods, squeaky clean operations, and friendly fast service. Robert Kwan, managing director of McDonald's Restaurants Singapore Pte. Ltd., says: ''It's the perfect partnership . . . The message that comes out from Chicago [the home office] is 'What can we do for you?'.'' Norman Sinclair, owner of a Mc-Donald's in Perth, Australia, agrees. As a McDonald's manager, he feels ''an enormous responsibility to live up to their standards.'' He said, ''You won't be in business making a profit unless you give value.''

Reported in *Business Week*.

Purpose

The **purpose of an organization** is to produce a good or service. Nonprofit organizations, for example, produce services with public benefits, such as health care, education, judicial processing, and highway maintenance. Businesses produce consumer goods and services such as automobiles, appliances, recreational opportunities, gourmet dining, and accommodations.

The following are the stated purposes found in recent annual reports of four familiar businesses. Note that each defines a domain or intended arena of operations for each organization in the broader society.

CBS, Inc.   To serve as a broad-based entertainment and communications company.

Apple Computer, Inc.   To bring technology to individuals through computers.

Chesebrough-Pond's   To serve as a diversified worldwide manufacturer and marketer of branded consumer products for the health and well-being of the entire family.

Wal-Mart   To offer quality name brand merchandise at an everyday low price.

One company familiar to most everyone is featured in Newsline 1.1—McDonald's. A giant among fast-food companies, McDonald's has been very successful in pursuing its business around the world. It is a good example of the increasing significance of the international dimension to managers and the field of OB.

Division of Labor

The essence of any organization is human effort. The process of breaking work into small components that serve the organization's purpose and to be done by individuals or groups is called the **division of labor.** It is through the division of labor that organizations mobilize the work of many people to achieve a common purpose.

Going back to the McDonald's example again, the division of labor is quite clear in any of the company's restaurants. What do you see upon entry? There are certain people waiting on customers, others cooking hamburgers, others cooking french fries, and still others cleaning up. By dividing up the labor and training employees to perform highly specialized tasks, the company strives for excellence in task accomplishment and high operating efficiency.

Hierarchy of Authority

Authority is the right to act and to command other persons. Managers have authority over their subordinates. When organizations divide labor into small components, something must be done to coordinate the efforts to ensure that work results accomplish the organization's purpose. A **hierarchy of authority,** wherein work positions are arranged in order of increasing authority, facilitates this coordination. Persons of higher authority are able to make decisions that result in the proper coordination and direction of work activities at lower levels.

The hierarchy of authority is well defined in a McDonald's restaurant. Supervisors wear different color uniforms and have special name tags. It is also quite clear that they make the big decisions when problems or special situations arise.

Synergy in Organizations

A well-defined division of labor results in **means–end chains** that link the work efforts of individuals and groups to an organization's purpose. Think of the organization's purpose as an end sought by the chief executive officer (CEO). In the division of labor, those managers directly reporting to the chief executive each have a set of performance goals. These are the means for accomplishing the ends represented by the CEO's view of the organization's purpose. Such a division of labor should flow clearly throughout an organization so that performance goals at any one level of responsibility become the means for accomplishing ends at the next higher level.

There is something more, however, to the organization as a collection of means–end chains. **Synergy** is the creation of a whole that is greater than the sum of its parts. You might think of it as the potential to make $2 + 2$ equal something greater than 4. Synergy in organizations occurs when people work well together to use available resources and pursue a common purpose. It is facilitated by the division of labor, hierarchy of authority and effective managerial behavior. Synergy results when

Organizational accomplishments	$\xrightarrow[\text{than}]{\text{are more}}$	group accomplishments	$\xrightarrow[\text{than}]{\text{are more}}$	individual accomplishments

MANAGERS IN ORGANIZATIONS

Now that we share an understanding of organizations and their basic ingredients, it is possible to speak more precisely about what it means to be a manager. Earlier, we identified a **manager** as a person in an organization who is responsible for the performance of one or more subordinates. Managers are identified by various job titles: Supervisors, principals, deans, general managers, presidents, and group leaders are a few examples. All managers, regardless of their titles, require a knowledge of organizational behavior to perform successfully. This includes an initial understanding of the manager's work setting and the basic challenge it represents.

The Manager's Work Setting

The manager is in charge of a work unit. A **work unit** is a task-oriented group in an organization that includes the manager and his or her immediate subordinates. Examples include departments in a retail store, divisions of a corporation, branches of a bank, and wards in a hospital. Even the college classroom can be considered a work unit, with the instructor as its manager.

A manager's immediate concerns are work unit **task performance,** the quality and quantity of work produced, and **human resource maintenance,** the attraction and continuation of a viable work force. This last notion focuses a manager's attention on individual job satisfaction, job involvement, commitment, absenteeism, and turnover, as well as work performance. Without proper maintenance of the people who do the work, no work unit or organization will be able to perform at consistently high levels over time. One potential sign of improper human resource maintenance is ''job burnout,'' a term commonly used to describe the feelings of mental exhaustion sometimes experienced by people facing too many demands and pressures in their work.

This book treats task performance and human resource maintenance as key results sought by a manager. Indeed, the **effective manager** we first introduced in the chapter opener is now defined as someone whose work unit achieves high levels of *both* task accomplishment *and* human resource maintenance. Figure 1.3 shows how these key results relate to work outcomes at the individual, group, and organizational levels.

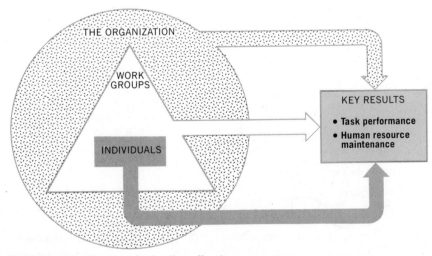

FIGURE 1.3 Key results for the *effective* manager.

The Manager's Challenge

Most managers are simultaneously subordinates and superiors. Think about this statement and what it can mean. As subordinates, managers are held accountable by their superiors (or ''bosses'') for the task performance and human resource maintenance of their work units.

This creates what we refer as the *manager's challenge*: At the same time that they are held accountable by their superiors for work unit results, managers are dependent upon the efforts of their subordinates to make these results possible. This challenge, in turn, is what makes managerial work very demanding and interesting.

This last sentence says a great deal. Assume that you are the production supervisor of a department making components for an electronic computer. Look at the diagram in Figure 1.4. This diagram depicts your manager's challenge. At the same time that you are held accountable by the plant manager for the production of electronic computer components, you depend upon the contributions of 15 subordinate employees to make this performance possible. You are responsible for work that is in large part produced by someone else! This reality is most evident on those days when the unit fails to meet its production quota. When this happens, the plant manager does not ask the employees what went wrong; he or she goes directly to you and asks the questions! You cannot say, in return, ''but my subordinates are the ones who did not do the work.'' It is the manager's job to ensure that work unit performance and human resource maintenance are successfully accomplished.

THE NATURE OF MANAGERIAL WORK

Organizational behavior, as stated earlier, is the study of individuals and groups in organizations. This book shows how, why, and where a knowledge of OB can help you to master the manager's challenge shown in Figure 1.4. Before moving further

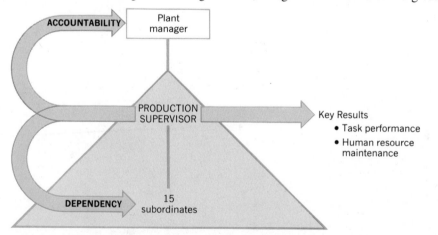

FIGURE 1.4   The manager's challenge for a production supervisor in an electronics firm.

into the substance of the book, it will be helpful for you to reflect a bit on the nature of managerial work. That is, you should understand what managers in general are called upon to do.

What Managers Do

Henry Mintzberg is a management researcher who has systematically studied what managers actually do on a daily basis. His classic book, *The Nature of Managerial Work,* reports an in-depth exmaination of the daily activities of corporate chief executives. One insightful excerpt from his observations regarding an executive's workday follows.[4]

> There was no break in the pace of activity during office hours. The mail (average of 36 pieces per day), telephone calls (average of five per day), and meetings (average of eight) accounted for almost every minute from the moment these executives entered their offices in the morning until they departed in the evenings. A true break seldom occurred. Coffee was taken during meetings, and lunchtime was almost always devoted to formal or informal meetings. When free time appeared, ever-present subordinates quickly usurped it. If these managers wished to have a change of pace, they had two means at their disposal—the observational tour and the light discussions that generally preceded scheduled meetings. But these were not regularly scheduled breaks, and they were seldom totally unrelated to the issue at hand: managing the organization . . .
>
> Why do managers adopt this pace and workload? One major reason is the inherently open-ended nature of the job. The manager is responsible for the success of the organization. There are really no tangible mileposts where one can stop and say, ''Now my job is finished.'' The engineer finishes the design of a casting on a certain day; the lawyer wins or loses a case at some moment in time. The manager must always keep going, never sure when he or she has succeeded, never sure when the whole organization may come down because of some miscalculation. As a result, the manager is a person with a perpetual preoccupation. The manager can never be free to forget the job, and never has the pleasure of knowing, even temporarily, that there is nothing else to do.

Clearly, a manager's job in any organization will be busy and demanding. The results of considerable research on managerial work can be summarized as follows.[5]

- *Managers work long hours.* A workweek of at least 50 hours is typical, and up to 90 hours is not unheard of. The length of the workweek tends to increase as one advances to higher managerial levels. Heads of organizations often work the longest hours.
- *Managers are busy.* Their work is intense activity that involves them in many different things each workday. The busy day of a manager includes up to 200 separate incidents or episodes in an eight-hour period at supervisory levels and at least 20 to 30 for chief executives.

- *Managers are often interrupted*. Their work is fragmented and variable. Interruptions are frequent and many tasks are completed quickly. The work itself involves many different types of activities ranging from scheduled meetings and telephone calls, to answering mail and writing reports, to conducting walk-around tours of the organization.
- *Managers work mostly with other people*. They spend little time working alone. Time spent with others includes working with bosses, peers, subordinates, subordinates of their subordinates, as well as outsiders such as customers, suppliers, and the like.
- *Managers are communicators*. Much of their work is face-to-face verbal communications during formal and informal meetings. They spend a lot of time getting, giving, and processing information. Higher-level managers spend more time in scheduled meetings than do lower-level managers.

These characteristics give managerial work a unique and special character. The following quotations reinforce our earlier conclusion that managers face a most challenging set of responsibilities.[6]

My day always ends when I'm tired, not when I am done. A manager's work is never done: There is always more to be done, more that should be done, always more that can be done. —Andrew Gove, president of Intel Corporation and author of *High Output Management*.

No matter what kind of managerial job, managers always carry the nagging suspicion that they might be able to contribute just a little bit more. Hence they assume an unrelenting pace in their work.—Henry Mintzberg, management scholar and author of *The Nature of Managerial Work*.

In this intense and dynamic work setting, a knowledge of OB can improve managerial decision making and problem solving. It can help you to learn what to look for in work situations and how to correctly interpret what you see. Beyond this, however, you must be able to turn this acquired understanding into effective managerial action. This involves success in enacting key managerial roles, fulfilling the basic managerial functions, and maintaining managerial networks.

Managerial Roles

Another useful aspect of Mintzberg's research is the identification of 10 action roles that managers must be prepared to enact. Each role derives from a manager's position of formal authority within the organization and defines action responsibilities of an interpersonal, informational, or decisional nature. The 10 roles falling into these three action categories follow.[7]

Interpersonal Roles

Figurehead   To attend ceremonies and represent the organization/ work unit to external constituencies.

| Leader | To motivate subordinates and integrate the needs of subordinates and the needs of the organization/work unit. |
| Liaison | To develop and maintain contacts with outsiders to gain benefits for the organization/work unit. |

Informational Roles

Monitor	To seek and receive information of relevance to the organization/work unit.
Disseminator	To transmit to insiders information relevant to the organization/work unit.
Spokesperson	To transmit to outsiders information relevant to the organization/work unit.

Decisional Roles

Entrepreneur	To seek problems and opportunities and to take action in respect to them.
Disturbance handler	To resolve conflicts among persons within the organization/work unit or between insiders and external parties.
Resource allocator	To make choices allocating resources to various uses within the organization/work unit.
Negotiator	To conduct formal negotiations with third parties such as union officials or government regulators.

Managerial Functions

The historical foundations of OB, described in Supplementary Module A at the end of the book, include a recognition of four functions of management—planning, organizing, leading, and controlling. These are considered basic action responsibilities shared by managers working in any occupational setting. As described here by definition and example, the four functions are another important aspect of the nature of managerial work.

Planning is the process of setting performance objectives and identifying the actions needed to accomplish them.

Example: The president of a small but growing fast-food chain senses the need for a new product line in order to stay competitive with the industry leaders. After talking things over with the company's top management team, a decision is made to have a new breakfast item ready for field testing within six months.

Organizing is the process of dividing up the work to be done and then coordinating results to achieve a desired purpose.

Example: The president convenes a special task force to create the new product. People with various skills are selected and assigned to the task force. A budget, clerical support, facilities, and equipment are also made available. Someone is appointed to "head" the task force and is assigned under the direct supervision of the president.

Leading is the process of directing the work efforts of other people to successfully accomplish their assigned tasks.

Example: At the first task force meeting, the president states the performance objective, answers questions, and explains why the new product is so important to the firm. The task force head is introduced as someone with whom the president has complete confidence. Before leaving, the president encourages everyone to be enthusiastic and work hard to accomplish the objective.

Controlling is the process of monitoring performance, comparing actual results to objectives, and taking corrective action as necessary.

Example: The president holds frequent conversations with the task force head to stay informed on efforts to create the new product. Sometimes the president attends task force meetings to ask and answer questions with the group as a whole. When it appears the timetable is slipping, additional personnel are assigned and the budget increased slightly. At last, all task force members are present when the new breakfast item is offered for the first time in one of the company's restaurants.

Managerial Networks

Managers enact roles and fulfill their functional responsibilities while maintaining a complex set of relationships with other persons inside and outside of the organization. These interpersonal "networks" of managers are depicted in Figure 1.5 and are further illustrated by this action description taken from John Kotter's book *The General Managers.*[8]

B.J. Sparksman had a good working relationship with his four bosses and a close mentor–protege relationship with one of them. He had cordial-to-good relations with his peers, some of whom were friends and all of whom were aware of his track record . . . He also had a good working relationship with many of the subordiantes of his peers (hundreds of people) based mostly on his reputation. B.J. had a close and strong working relationship with all but one of his main direct reports because they respected him, because he was the boss, and the fact that he tried to treat them fairly and with respect. Outside the firm, B.J. maintained fairly strong relationships with dozens of top people in firms that were important clients for his organization . . . He also had relationships with dozens of other important people in the local community.

What this example shows very well is a manager who used a complex set of interpersonal *networks,* many falling outside the formal chain of command, to help

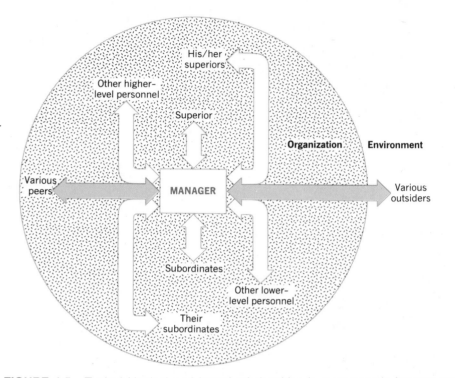

FIGURE 1.5   Typical Vertical and lateral relationships in a manager's Interpersonal networks.

get the job done. Inside the organization Sparksman's networks included both vertical relationships with a variety of superiors and subordinates, and lateral relationships with peers. They also included relationships with many outsiders such as customers and suppliers.

Such interpersonal networks are highly significant to any manager. The ability to develop, maintain, and work well within them is increasingly recognized as an important aspect of managerial work. Effective general managers, for example, have been observed to "allocate significant time and effort when they first take their jobs to developing a network of cooperative relationships among those people they feel are needed to satisfy their emerging agendas." Later on—"their attention shifts toward using the networks to both implement and help in updating the agendas."[9]

How would you estimate a typical manager would allocate time to the various interpersonal relationships shown in Figure 1.5?

_____%   with subordinates

_____%   with superiors

_____%   with peers and outsiders

  100%   = total time in contacts

You probably allocated most of al manager's time to contacts with subordinates. After all, they are the human resources upon whom the manager is most dependent for work-unit performance. Actually, research on managerial behavior suggests, on the average, that managers spend about 45 percent of their time with subordinates, 10 percent of their time with their superiors, and 45 percent of their time with peers and outsiders.[10]

The highly interpersonal nature of managerial work contributes to the fact that managers are busy people whose jobs are never really done. Even though networks are time consuming to establish and maintain, they enable managers to gain and transfer the information needed to make good decisions while fulfilling many responsibilities. As a result, OB is very concerned with interpersonal relationships and their managerial implications.

Managerial Skills and Competencies

A **skill** is an ability to translate knowledge into action that results in the desired performance. It is a *competency* that allows someone to achieve superior performance in one or more aspects of their work. Robert L. Katz classifies the essential managerial skills into three categories: technical, human, and conceptual.[11]

A **technical skill** is an ability to apply specialized knowledge or expertise to perform a job. This involves being highly proficient at using select methods, processes, and procedures to accomplish tasks. Good examples are the work of accountants, engineers, and attorneys whose technical skills are acquired through formal education. Most jobs have some technical skill components. Some require preparatory education (e.g., the staff accountant), while others allow skills to be learned through appropriate work training and on-the-job experience (e.g., a salesperson).

Human skill is the ability to work well in cooperation with other persons. It emerges as a spirit of trust, enthusiasm, and genuine involvement in interpersonal relationships. A person with good human skills will have a high degree of self-awareness and a capacity to understand or empathize with the feelings of others.

All good managers ultimately have the ability to view the organization or situation as a whole and solve problems to the benefit of everyone concerned. This ability to analyze and diagnose complex situations is a **conceptual skill.** It draws heavily on one's mental capacities to identify problems and opportunities, gather and interpret relevant information, and make good problem-solving decisions that serve the organization's purpose.

The relative importance of various skills tends to vary across levels of management. Technical skills are more important at lower management levels where supervisors are dealing with concrete problems. Broader, more ambiguous, and longer-term decisions dominate the manager's concerns at higher levels, where conceptual skills gain in importance. Human skills remain fairly consistent in their importance across the managerial levels.

Managers should be competent in a variety of skills distributed among these three categories. Table 1.1 summarizes some current thinking on the requisite skills and personal characteristics of an effective manager. You should find that this introductory

TABLE 1.1   Selected Skills and Personal Characteristics Considered Important for Managers

Analytic thinking.   The ability to identify fundamental ideas, concepts, themes or issues that help integrate, interpret, and/or explain patterns in a set of information or data.

Behavioral flexibility.   The ability to modify personal behavior to reach a goal; to adapt personal behavior to respond to changes in a situation or in the environment.

Decision making.   The ability to use logic and information to choose among alternative courses of action; to form judgments and make commitments in complex situations.

Leadership.   The ability to stimulate and guide individuals or groups toward goal and/or task accomplishment.

Oral communication and presentation.   The ability to effectively express ideas to others in individual or group situations.

Personal impact.   The ability to create a good early impression; to command attention and respect; to show confidence through verbal and nonverbal presentations.

Planning and organizing.   The ability to establish a course of action to accomplish specific goals; to properly assign personnel and allocate supporting resources.

Resistance to stress.   The ability to maintain work performance even while experiencing significant personal stress.

Self-objectivity.   The ability to realistically assess personal strengths and weaknesses; to gain insight into personal motives, skills, and abilities as applied to a job.

Tolerance for uncertainty.   The ability to maintain work performance under uncertain or unstructured conditions.

Written communication.   The ability to clearly express ideas in writing and in appropriate grammatical form.

Source: Developed from the *Outcome Measurement Project of the Accreditation Research Committee, Phase II: An Interim Report* (St. Louis: American Assembly of Collegiate Schools of Business, 1984), pp. 15–18.

study of OB is an especially useful foundation for developing competencies in the many skills needed to achieve success in today's dynamic and demanding work environments. Consider Newsline 1.2 for example. It offers a commentary on managing in what can be called the "new industrial revolution."

SCIENTIFIC THINKING AND THE MANAGER

Given the complexity of their jobs, managers frequently look for ways of simplifying and doing them better. Advice comes from many sources and includes written materials available in bookstores and libraries as well as the suggestions of friends and recognized "experts." The informed manager will be discriminating and selective in accepting such advice and implementing it in actual practice. Consider, for example, the following case.

NEWSLINE 1.2 / MANAGING IN THE "NEW" INDUSTRIAL REVOLUTION

The first industrial revolution led to a mechanization of the workplace and simpler tasks for many workers. The *new* industrial revolution involves computer-driven information technologies that require workers' mental commitments and responsibility for broader tasks. People and machines must now be successfully integrated in "sociotechnical" systems that match workers' needs and skills with technological requirements. Integrating the work of people and computer-controlled machines requires what Harvard professor Richard E. Walton calls a "collection of people to manage a segment of technology and perform as a team." New work arrangements focus on teamwork in semiautonomous groups where workers actively participate in decisions affecting them and their jobs. Old-fashioned "control-oriented" management methods are on their way out, while more innovative approaches are coming in.

Companies like GE, Xerox, IBM, and Polaroid are achieving productivity gains in new plants designed to get the best from advanced technologies and the people who must employ them. Worker involvement is essential in such work settings. At Westinghouse's Furniture Systems plant, for example, 65 percent of the 850 workers are involved in committees and task forces that address things ranging from business strategies to the redesign of work areas. Shop workers even consult regularly with customers who telephone or visit the plant to check on their orders.

Reported in *Business Week*.

Illustrative Case: Better Management, Inc.

Joan Brady, a representative of Better Management, Inc., was telling Don Black, the director of personnel for Osdo Corporation, about a new management training package her firm was offering. It was based, she said, on lengthy interviews with five outstanding company presidents whose combined work experience comprised more than 150 years.

The interviews had taken over a year to complete. They were analyzed to create a set of assessment materials that firms could use to determine the strengths and weaknesses of their managers. Better Management, Inc., was prepared to conduct the assessments and then to offer a training program capable of correcting any weaknesses so identified.

The assessment procedure begins by identifying the personal traits of a firm's managers. It then compares them with a profile of successful managers developed from interviews with the renowned chief executive officers. Don noticed that the traits were neatly listed and carefully defined. He was also impressed that each of his managers could be profiled against this list to identify their strengths and weaknesses. He worried, though, whether or not Better Management's assessment and training package really had all the answers.

1. What do you think about the assessment ideas? Why?
2. Would you purchase these materials and the training program for Osdo? Why or why not?

As impressive as Joan's proposal may seem, the manager skilled in scientific thinking would scrutinize it very carefully. Table 1.2 evaluates Joan's proposal on a checklist of scientific thinking. The ideal profile is shaded, and you can readily see that the training program of Better Management, Inc. must be questioned for its lack of adequate scientific foundations. What follows is a brief comparison of scientific versus commonsense thinking.

Characteristics of Scientific Thinking

Start by considering the source of the data used by Better Management. It makes common sense that successful executives are in a position to identify the traits of a good manager. However, this source of data is anecdotal; that is, the executives are simply reminiscing and using recollections to identify the desirable managerial traits. Although this may appeal to our common sense, the sophisticated student of OB and the informed manager would insist on a more *systematic and controlled process of data collection*. This is the first basic characteristic of scientific thinking.

Second, scientific thinking is concerned with *systematically testing proposed explanations* and in systematically examining relationships among variables. This includes considering more than one possible explanation for a given question or event and trying to locate the most feasible one and rule out the less feasible alternatives.

In our example, none of these things was done. The only explanation given for managerial success was selected personal traits. Other variables with the potential to also affect success, such as the availability of resources, economic conditions, nature of the organization, and so on were completely neglected. Because of this, even if we find a relationship between the selected traits and managerial success, we cannot be sure that there are not other factors with at least as good and perhaps better explanations for success.

Finally, scientific thinking is *unwilling to accept metaphysical explanations*. These are arguments that cannot be subjected to scientific proof. "It is God's will" is one example of metaphysical reasoning. In Better Management, Inc., attributing success

---

TABLE 1.2   Checklist for Scientific Thinking

	Yes	No
1. Systematic and controlled data collection?	■	X
2. Systematic testing of alternative explanations?	■	X
3. Metaphysical explanations avoided?	■	X

■ = Ideal response for scientific theory.
X = Evaluation for Better Management, Inc., assessment and training package.

to such traits as "charisma" or "gutsiness" are basically metaphysical arguments since these traits are hard to measure and test.

As you proceed with your studies and with the practice of management, give special attention to the need to discriminate scientific from commonsense thinking. When in doubt, use the checklist in Table 1.2 to test the rigor of your thoughts and those being offered to you by others.

OB as Scientific Thinking

As a manager, you will be better able to consume the advice and recommendations of others if you develop your scientific thinking. The same argument holds true as you consume the theories, concepts, and advice of organizational researchers. Fortunately, the field of OB is founded on insights developed by scholars who apply scientific methods to study human behavior in organizations.

As discussed in Supplementary Module B at the end of the book, OB is firmly rooted in other scientific disciplines such as psychology, sociology, anthropology, economics, and political science.[12] It has emerged as an interdisciplinary bridge among these related areas of study that endeavors to expand upon and apply their insights to increase our understanding of human behavior in organizations. This historical base in the allied behavioral and social sciences has helped make OB a developing body of knowledge with the following special characteristics.

1. *Scientific foundations.* Researchers in the field of OB use scientific methods to develop and test empirically generalizations about behavior in organizations. Commonsense explanations and "armchair speculations" are not accepted without scientific justification.

2. *Contingency orientation.* Rather than assume that there is "one best" or a universal approach to management, OB researchers recognize that behavior in organizations may vary systematically depending upon the nature of the circumstances and people involved. Through a **contingency approach,** they seek to identify how situations can be understood and managed in ways that respond appropriately to their unique characteristics.

3. *Applied focus.* OB is an applied scientific discipline that seeks answers to practical questions. An important criterion of OB research is relevancy. The body of knowledge made available as the field of OB is ultimately designed to help people achieve high performance and experience satisfaction through their work in organizations.

LEARNING ABOUT ORGANIZATIONAL BEHAVIOR

Learning is a change in behavior that occurs as a result of experience. Your learning about OB only begins with the pages of this book and your formal education. It will

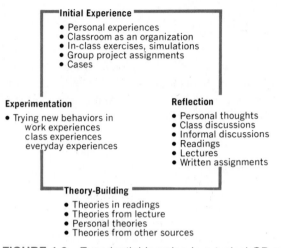

Initial Experience
- Personal experiences
- Classroom as an organization
- In-class exercises, simulations
- Group project assignments
- Cases

Experimentation
- Trying new behaviors in
  work experiences
  class experiences
  everyday experiences

Reflection
- Personal thoughts
- Class discussions
- Informal discussions
- Readings
- Lectures
- Written assignments

Theory-Building
- Theories in readings
- Theories from lecture
- Personal theories
- Theories from other sources

FIGURE 1.6   Experiential learning in a typical OB course.

continue in the future as you benefit from actual work experiences. The challenges of learning from both types of experiences are substantial enough that we take time now to consider them systematically.

Experiential learning is a means of initially learning and then continuing to learn about OB.[13] The learning sequence invovles an initial experience and subsequent reflection. Theory building follows to explain what took place, and this theory is tested thrugh experimentation at the next opportunity.

This book is a formal opportunity for you to learn more about OB. It is also written to capitalize on the values of experiential learning. Your other course activities will complement the book to help you to take full advantage of the experiential learning cycle. Figure 1.6 shows how the various aspects of a typical OB course facilitate learning.

Figure 1.6 assigns to you a substantial responsibility for learning. Along with your instructor we can offer special cases and exercises to provide you with initial experience. We can even stimulate your reflection and theory-building by presenting theories and discussing their practical implications. Sooner or later, however, you must become an active participant in the learning process. You, and only you, can do the active experimentation required to complete the learning cycle.

For example, we have already asked you to stop at two different points in this chapter to respond to our questions. This form of action inquiry can improve your understanding of key OB concepts. We hope you will stay actively involved as you read. We hope you will extend this commitment to the variety of learning activities made available through your course. And, we hope you will remain active, aware, and inquiring so as to achieve continued learning from your lifelong work and organizational experiences.

THE MANAGER'S CHALLENGE, OB, AND THIS BOOK

Having concluded Chapter 1, you are now well prepared to address the many fundamental topics in the study of OB. Chapter 2 continues our discussion of managers and organizations with a special focus on people at work. As you proceed through Chapter 2 and beyond, remember that

Once you have completed Chapter 2, the final chapter in this introductory part of the book, you will find our approach to OB next concentrates on the four major elements summarized in Figure 1.7—managing individuals, groups, organizations, and the processes of OB. Each of these becomes the focus of a separate book part, which presents insights that can help you to achieve managerial success.

Part Two focuses on understanding individuals in organizations. Chapter 3 reviews individual differences, including abilities, values, attitudes, and personalities. Chapter 4 introduces various motivation theories, and Chapters 5 and 6 acquaint you with how managers can use these theories to allocate rewards and design jobs to achieve high levels of task performance and human resource maintenance in work units.

Part Three shifts attention to understanding the group as a human resource of organizations. Chapters 7, 8, and 9 discuss dimensions of group behavior, explore group and intergroup dynamics, and identify various means of effectively managing groups.

Part Four focuses on understanding the organization as a total system. Chapter 10 presents basic attributes of organizations including goals, culture, and bureaucratic features, among others. Chapter 11 reviews organizational dynamics in respect to coordination and control, and the influences of environment, technology, and size. Chapter 12 extends these concepts to explore ways of designing organizations to best achieve their performance purposes and properly maintain human resources.

Part Five treats the important processes of OB through which managers transfer a knowledge of individuals, groups, and organizations into action. Chapters 13 and 14 deal with perception, decision making, communication, and conflict. Chapter 15 treats power and politics. Chapter 16 examines various leadership theories and develops a comprehensive model that emphasizes various dimensions of leadership as key aspects of managerial behavior.

Part Six contains two concluding chapters on managing in a dynamic environment. Chapter 17 examines the challenges of change and stress as they are bound to impact the manager. Chapter 18 reviews the major elements in the study of OB and suggests some of the critical issues that you will face in planning for a future managerial career. This final chapter both summarizes this *initial* study of OB and points you toward *continued lifelong learning* about OB in the future.

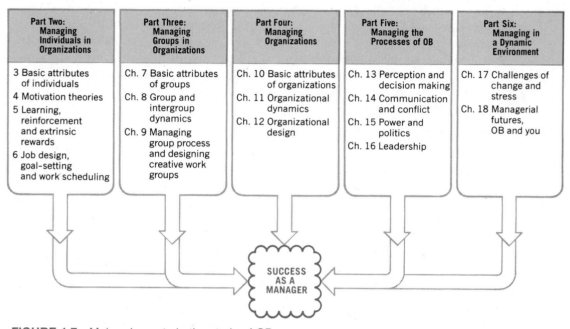

FIGURE 1.7   Major elements in the study of OB.

Finally, three modules at the end of the book broaden your study in terms of the special foundations of OB. Supplementary Module A introduces the history of OB as an academic discipline; Supplementary Module B examines its roots in scientific research; and, Supplementary Module C reviews the elements of performance appraisal.

SUMMARY

Managers are the hearts of organizations and organizational behavior is a knowledge base that enables managers to help their organizations perform. Organizations rely on both human and physical resources for their continued functioning. To successfully combine resource inputs into product or service outputs, managers must understand organizations as work settings. The components of an organization include its purpose, a division of labor, and the hierarchy of authority.

The manager heads a work unit staffed by one or more immediate subordinates. The manager is held accountable by a higher-level supervisor for how well the work unit functions as an essential component in the means–end chains of the total organization. Key results sought by managers are task performance and human resource maintenance at the individual, group, and organizational levels.

Managers share a common challenge. On the one hand, they are held accountable by superiors for work-unit performance. On the other hand, they are largely dependent upon their subordinates to do the required work. Thus, managers need special skills to implement the management functions and achieve success in their required interpersonal relationships. Ultimately, every good manager is able to understand, predict, and influence human behavior in organizations. Studying, thinking about, and applying the many insights made available in the field of organizational behavior will help you to achieve this important capability.

THINKING THROUGH THE ISSUES

1. The manager is often described as a "person in the middle" or as someone having "two masters—the organization and subordinates." Are these descriptions truly appropriate? Why or why not?
2. What is an *effective* manager? Describe what the concepts of task performance and human resource maintenance mean to a manager who wants to be effective in his or her work.
3. Draw a diagram of the "manager's challenge" faced by your instructor. Explain its implications for the instructor as a manager of the OB class as a learning organization.
4. Choose an organization with which you are familiar. Diagram it as an open system such as the one shown in Figure 1.2. Explain how the concepts of purpose, division of labor, and hierarchy of authority apply to this organization.
5. Name and define the three categories of managerial skills identified by Katz. Give examples that show why each set of skills is essential to managerial success.
6. Name and define the three categories of managerial roles identified by Mintzberg. Give examples that show why the ability to fulfill each set of roles is essential to managerial success.
7. Choose a managerial job with which you are familiar, or consider the job of university bookstore manager. List the four managerial functions and give examples showing how they might apply to someone working in this job.
8. State the three characteristics of scientific thinking. Explain why scholars contributing to the field of OB should be held responsible for the quality of the scientific thinking that underlies their work.

CASE: MICHAEL RICHARDSON— GENERAL MANAGER

Michael Richardson, president of an investment management firm, is a general manager. Here are some actual events from one day in his work.[14]

Part I: During the morning.

7:35 A.M. He arrives at work, unpacks his briefcase, gets some coffee, and makes a "to do" list for the day.

7:45 A.M. He talks with Bradshaw (an assistant) about several things and shows him some family photographs. By 8:00 A.M. they are talking about the day's schedule and priorities, including issues relating to customers and subordinates.

8:20 A.M. Wilson, another subordinates, drops in and asks about a personnel problem. She joins the rapid and sometimes humorous discussion.

8:30 A.M. Holly, the chairperson of the firm and his boss, drops in to ask about an upcoming appointment. He joins the conversation and brings up some other topics.

(Later . . .)

9:52 A.M. Richardson's secretary brings in several items of work.

9:55 A.M. Bradshaw comes in, asks a question, and leaves.

9:58 A.M. Wilson comes in with one of her people, delivers a memo, and urges Richardson to change a recent decision. After a 20 minute discussion they agree on action scheduled for the next day.

(Later . . .)

10:50 A.M. Richardson gets a phone call and does desk work.

11:03 A.M. Holly comes in as Richardson gets another call. After the call he gives his secretary instructions.

11:05 A.M. Holly raises some issues and then Bradshaw comes in. They talk about a personnel problem with Phillips, an employee. Richardson and Holly ask questions. Richardson takes notes and they eventually agree on a next step.

Part II: During the afternoon.

12:00 P.M. Richardson orders lunch for himself and Bradshaw, who comes in to discuss some things. Wilson also stops by to follow up on an earlier conversation.

12:10 P.M. Another staffer stops by with some data and leaves after a short, friendly conversation.

12:20 P.M. Lunch arrives. Richardson and Bradshaw eat in the conference room while discussing various business and nonbusiness subjects. They laugh a lot and end by talking about a potential customer.

(Later . . .)

1:55 P.M. Thomas, one of Richardson's subordinates, comes in to discuss some performance appraisals they will do together. They talk briefly about how they will handle the meetings to be held in Richardson's office.

2:00 P.M. Jacobs, a subordinate of Thomas, comes in for his appraisal. Thomas runs the meeting. He states Jacobs's bonus for the year and the reasons for it. All three discuss Jacobs's work in the coming year.

2:30 P.M. Kimble, another of Thomas's subordinates, comes in for her appraisal. The meeting follows the same format. Richardson asks questions and gives praise at times. The discussion ends in friendly agreement.

(Later . . .)

    3:45 P.M. Richardson gets a phone call. His secretary and Bradshaw come in with several requests.

    3:50 P.M. Phillips, the subject of the personnel problem discussed earlier in the morning, telephones in. They talk back and forth, often emotionally, for a long time. By the end of the call, they both agree on the next steps.

(Later . . .)

    5:30 P.M. Richardson packs his briefcase. Five people stop in one or two at a time.

    5:45 P.M. He leaves the office.

Questions

1. Which of the managerial (a) roles, (b) functions, and (c) skills, discussed in Chapter 1, are displayed by Michael Richardson in this excerpt from his work day? Give examples from the case to support your answers.
2. Is interpersonal "networking" important to Michael Richardson? Does he appear to use it well to help get his job done? Why or why not?
3. Is Michael Richardson doing things that one would expect an "effective" manager to be doing? Be specific and use examples from the case to clearly explain your answer.

EXERCISE: "MY BEST MANAGER"

Purpose:

To help you reflect seriously on the attributes of a good manager; to allow you to share your views with others and compare their thoughts with yours; and to provide an opportunity for you to get to know other participants in the course and learn about their work experiences.

Time:

30 to 40 minutes.

Procedure:

1. Make a list of the attributes that describe the **best** manager you have ever worked for. If you have trouble identifying with an actual manager, make a list of the attributes you would like the manager in your next job to have.
2. Convene as a member of a small group composed of four to eight other persons who have also completed step 1. Go around the group with everyone sharing his or her list. Discuss any points of special interest, similarity, dissimilarity, disagreement, and so on.
3. Create one list that combines all the unique attributes of the "best" managers represented in your group. Make sure that you have all attributes listed, but list each only once. Place a checkmark next to any that were reported by two

or more members. Have one of your members prepared to present the list in general class discussion.

4. After all groups have finished step 3, spokespersons should report to the total class. The instructor will make a running list of the ''best'' manager attributes as viewed by the class.

5. Feel free to ask questions and discuss the results.

THE MANAGER'S VOCABULARY

Authority   The right to act and to command other persons.

Conceptual Skill   The ability to view the situation as a whole and solve problems for the benefit of everyone concerned.

Contingency Approach   The attempt by OB scholars to identify how situations can be understood and managed in ways that respond appropriately to their unique characteristics.

Controlling   The process of monitoring performance, comparing actual results to objectives, and taking corrective action as necessary.

Division of Labor   The process of breaking work into small components that serve the organization's purpose, and to be done by individuals or groups.

Effective Manager   A manager whose work unit achieves high levels of *both* task performance *and* human resource maintenance.

Hierarchy of Authority   The arrangement of work positions in order of increasing formal authority.

Human Resource Maintenance   The attraction and continuation of a viable work force.

Human Skill   The ability to work well in cooperation with other persons.

Leading   The process of directing the work efforts of other people to successfully accomplish their assigned tasks.

Learning   A change in behavior that occurs as a result of experience.

Manager   A person in an organization who is responsible for the performance of one or more subordinates.

Means–End Chains   The linking of the work efforts of individuals and groups to an organization's purpose.

Planning   The process of setting performance objectives and identifying the actions needed to accomplish them.

Open Systems   Transform human and physical resources received as inputs from their environments into goods and services that are then returned to the environment for consumption.

Organization   A collection of people working together, in a division of labor, to achieve a common purpose.

Organizational Behavior   The study of individuals and groups in organizations.

Organizational Purpose   The goal of producing a good or service.

Organizing   The process of dividing up the work to be done and then coordinating results to achieve a desired purpose.

Skill   The ability to translate knowledge into action that results in the desired performance.

Synergy   The creation of a whole that is greater than the sum of its parts.

Task Performance   The quality and quantity of work produced.

Technical Skill   The ability to use a special proficiency or expertise relating to a method, process, or procedure.

Work Unit   A task-oriented group in an organization that includes the manager and his or her immediate subordinates.

NOTES

[1] Fred Luthans, "Fifty Years Later: What Do We Really Know About Managing and What Managers Do?," *Academy of Management Newsletter,* Vol. X (1986), pp. 3, 9–10; Robert E. Kaplan, *The Warp and Woof of the General Manager's Job,* Technical Report No. 27 (Greensboro, N.C.: Center for Creative Leadership, 1986).

[2] Harold J. Leavitt, "Future Directions in Organizational Behavior," *The Teaching of Organizational Behavior,* Vol. 1 (December 1975), pp. 9–13.

[3] Adapted from "The Second Book of Moses, Called Exodus," Chapter 18, *The Holy Bible.* (Philadelphia: A. J. Holman Company, 1942), pp. 88–89.

[4] Abridged and adapted from p. 30 in *The Nature of Managerial Work* by Henry Mintzberg (New York: Harper & Row, 1973), p. 30. Copyright © 1973 by Henry Mintzberg. Reprinted by permission of Harper & Row, Publishers, Inc.

[5] See Morgan W. McCall, Jr., Ann M. Morrison, and Robert L. Hannan, *Studies of Managerial Work: Results and Methods,* Technical Report No. 9 (Greensboro, N.C.: Center for Creative Leadership, 1978), pp 7–9; John P. Kotter, *The General Managers* (New York: Free Press, 1982a); and Kaplan, op. cit.

[6] Andrew Grove, *High Output Management* (New York: Random House, 1983); Mintzberg, op cit.

[7] Developed from Mintzberg, op cit., pp. 92–93.

[8] Kotter, op cit., (1982a) pp. 67–69.

[9] John P. Kotter, "What Effective General Managers Really Do," *Harvard Business Review,* Vol. 60 (November–December 1982b), p. 161. See also Robert E. Kaplan, "Trade Routes: The Manager's Network of Relationships," *Organizational Dynamics,* Vol. 12 (Spring 1984), pp. 37–52.

[10] Based on research reported by Mintzberg, op cit.; McCall, et al., op cit.; Kotter, op cit. (1982a; 1982b).

[11] Robert L. Katz "Skills of an Effective Administrator," *Harvard Business Review,* Vol. 52 (September–October 1974), p. 94. See also Richard E. Boyatzis, *The Competent Manager: A Model for Effective Performance* (New York: John Wiley, 1982).

[12] See Paul R. Lawrence, "Historical Development of Organizational Behavior," pp. 1–9 in Jay W. Lorsch (Ed.), *Handbook of Organizational Behavior* (Englewood Cliffs, N.J.: Prentice-Hall, 1987).

[13] David A. Kolb, "On Management and the Learning Process," in David A. Kolb, Irwin M. Rubin, and James M. McIntyre, eds., *Organizational Psychology: A Book of Readings,* 2nd ed. (Englewood Cliffs, N.J.: Prentice-Hall, 1974), pp. 27–42.

[14] Developed from Kotter, op cit. (1982b), pp. 156–158.

CHAPTER 2
PEOPLE AT WORK

IBM's
prospects rest
with our
people,
who have
confirmed
once again
that they are
remarkably
energetic,
resourceful
and dedicated.

**IBM Annual
Report**

STUDS TERKEL LOVES HIS
WORK BUT HE SAYS YOU DON'T

The following excerpt is from an interview with Studs Terkel, a noted contemporary author.[1] It raises interesting issues about people at work.

MBA: We've heard you say—on several occasions—that work as we know it is an instrument of violence against the individual. That's a strong charge. How do you know it's true?

Terkel: I ride the bus, the Michigan Boulevard bus in Chicago, and I look at people's faces. I see the bank teller, the elevator operator, the secretaries, the guys who work on the assembly lines, when they come home at night. They're tired. They're beaten. There's a fatigue. It isn't the satisfying tiredness of a day well spent, but the fatigue of another day killed.

MBA: What about their bosses?

Terkel: I look down in the cars alongside the bus, and I see the managers and the executives. They sit behind their wheels with their teeth gritted, smoking one cigarette after another, looking as though they were furious. If getting caught on one little stoplight makes them *that* furious, there's something else going on: violence to the spirit—as well as the body. These execs, they *think* they have control, but they don't. They're always worried about being taken over by a comglomerate or a bigger company, or about having to fire someone they don't want to fire, or about being fired themselves.

MBA: In your book *Working,* you interviewed 150 or so workers, blue and white collar, and it seemed that none of them liked their jobs.

Terkel: Oh, the great majority of people don't get any satisfaction from their work. Now, when I'd interview, very often, at the beginning, people would say, "Oh, I like my job." There was one woman, a switchboard operator at a Holiday Inn, she started out, "I like my work . . . I like it." And then, she started talking: "You know, they don't even know me. People take me for granted. I'm the center of this huge communications hub, but they talk to me like I'm nothing. You know what I'd like to do sometime? I'd like to take all of those plugs out and goof 'em and switch 'em around. And one night, when people ring I'd like to say, 'Marriott Inn. Marriott.' " So I asked her why she wanted to do that, and she answered, "I don't know. To make the night go faster."

Management Applications Questions

What is the meaning of work—to people in general? . . . to those persons who may serve as your future subordinates? . . . to you?

PLANNING AHEAD

This chapter explores the meaning of work and its implications for individual job satisfaction and task performance. The learning activities of the chapter address the following topics.

The Psychological Contract
Perception and the Meaning of Work
Job Satisfaction
Herzberg's Two-Factor Theory
The Satisfaction–Performance Controversy
Work and Nonwork

The quality of life is everyone's concern, and the quality of work is an important component in the quality of life for most of us. This reality makes Studs Terkel's observations on the quality of work in America most ominous. Indeed, his book *Working* (which we highly recommend for reading) will leave you with a rather pessimistic view of work and the contribution it makes to people's lives. Because people at work are your concern as a manager, we need to think through carefully some basic issues relating to the quality of work.

Work is an activity that produces value for other people. It is what people do in exchange for things they value but cannot provide for themselves. Work is a transaction that results in a mutually beneficial linkage between an individual and an organization. Managerial work involves influencing the activities of subordinates so that the performance goals of the work unit and organization are best served and so that the subordinates are adequately maintained as human resources. This chapter discusses a number of issues that will help you better understand the relationship between people and their work. We begin by focusing on the psychological contract.

THE PSYCHOLOGICAL CONTRACT

You are probably familiar with the word "contract" as it reflects on relations between labor unions and organizations employing their members. Such a contract is written and formal. Contract negotiations may cover such items as pay, work hours, vacations, and seniority rights, among others.

There is another, less formal contract that relates every employee to his or her work organization. A **psychological contract** is the set of expectations held by the individual and specifying what the individual and the organization expect to give to and receive from one another in the course of their working relationship. This contract represents the expected exchange of values that causes the individual to work for the organization and causes the organization to employ that person. During the time when the individual is being recruited by the organization, this exchange is an anticipated one. Later, during actual employment, expectations are either confirmed or not. Needless to say, part of the manager's job is to ensure that both the individual and the organization continue to receive a fair exchange of values under the psychological contract.

Inducements and Contributions

Figure 2.1 depicts the reciprocal character of this individual–organization exchange relationship. The individual offers **contributions** or work efforts of value to the organization's production purpose. These contributions make the individual a true resource to the organization. We can say at this point that these contributions are valued by the organization because of the various needs that it has. In fact, one important measure of organizational success is its ability to attract and maintain high-quality contributions from its members. Newsline 2.1 highlights this issue in a direct comparison of Japanese and American workers—one of the continuing sources of debate about the productivity and global competitiveness of U.S. industries.

Those things that the organization gives to the individuals in return for contributions are called **inducements.** The term means exactly what it implies. To induce participation, the organization offers the individual things of value. As with the organization, individuals value these inducements in accord with their responsiveness to one or more individual needs.

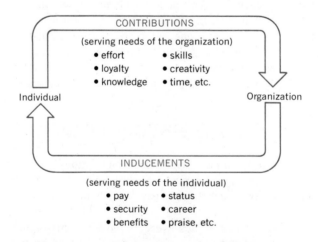

FIGURE 2.1 The inducements–contributions exchange between the individual and the organization.

NEWSLINE 2.1 / CAN U.S. WORKERS COMPETE?

When *U.S. News & World Report* asked 10 leading scholars to rate Japanese and American workers on a variety of qualities, there was reasonable consensus. The results include these comparisons.

Hard Work Both countries are strong on the work ethic, but the experts give the Japanese a slight edge. They routinely put in extra hours and the employing organization is central to their lives.

Initiative American workers are more willing to stand out as individuals and take the lead. They are concerned about getting personal credit for extra work. An indi-vidualistic culture encourages workers to strive to get ahead.

Loyalty The average Japanese worker is very loyal to the employer, often expecting to spend an entire career with one organization. Employers, in turn, are viewed as more paternalistic toward employees.

Advanced Skills The experts see this as a close call, but give Americans the edge due to a higher percentage of college graduates and white-collar professionals. Workers in both countries are well educated.

Reported in *U.S. News & World Report.*

When the individual and the organization both feel the exchange is fair, a state of inducements–contributions balance exists. Imbalance occurs in the individual's favor when inducements are greater than contributions; it occurs in the organization's favor when contributions are greater than inducements. This concept of balance, or imbalance, is important to the manager. In the Case of the Missing Raise discussed in the Introduction to Part One, for example, John Lloyd felt that the expectations of his psychological contract were not being fulfilled with Central University. His actual inducements seemed less than his contributions. Apparently, too, he felt that this imbalance could be resolved by reducing his contributions. For John's manager, Fred, this is not a desirable outcome, as Central would lose some of John's potential as a major contributor in organization.

Managing Psychological Contracts

In a sense, the rest of this book is designed to increase your ability to manage successfully the psychological contracts of your subordinates. Fred, the manager in the Case of the Missing Raise, could have benefited from similar ability. Many of his problems with John might have been avoided if Fred had done a better job of addressing the expectations in John's psychological contract with Central University.

The importance of realistic and healthy psychological contracts for yourself and for people who work for you should not be underestimated. In fact, some organizations hire consultants to help achieve this goal. An example follows.[2]

> Three new college engineering graduates were hired as junior managers in a manufacturing plant of a large corporation. For three months they participated in a training program. A senior manager was concerned that the trainees ''get up to speed'' as quickly as possible and that they be prepared to negotiate and explore expectations with their ''first bosses.'' He also wanted to receive feedback from them on the training program, to acquaint the other top managers with the trainees, and to help the trainees feel a part of the management team. A consultant was hired to conduct a 12-hour session designed to accomplish these goals. Four senior managers, three supervisors, and the three trainees participated in the sessions, which were held over three days and involved the following activities:

> - Questionnaires were completed beforehand by each participant to summarize their expectations regarding the give and take between the trainees, their eventual first bosses, and the organization.
> - The first session began with a contract-setting exercise that resulted in the participants setting goals for the session, establishing individual roles, and making an agenda.
> - The consultant gave a brief lecture on the concept of the psychological contract. Participants were divided into subgroups of senior managers, supervisors, and trainees to share experiences and expectations.
> - After subgroups shared results with one another, the session closed with problem solving on the issue ''What can we do better concerning our joining-up process?''

PERCEPTION AND THE MEANING OF WORK

Work can certainly be more than a source of pure economic livelihood for people. It can and should be a source of personal satisfaction as well. But it is the inability of work to always achieve this broader level of meaning that is being condemned by Terkel in the comments used to introduce this chapter. There are data in support of his concerns. Take Table 2.1 for example. It shows that, in one sample at least, most of the employees in other than professional occupations would not choose the same work again. A majority of both white-collar and blue-collar workers felt this way. Findings such as this have led to some concern for what is at times referred to as the prevalence of ''white-collar woes'' and ''blue-collar blues'' in our society.

TABLE 2.1 Percentages in Occupational Groups that Would Choose Similar Work Again

Professional and Lower White Collar		Working Class	
Occupations	%	Occupations	%
Urban university professors	93	Skilled printers	52
Mathematicians	91	Paper workers	42
Physicists	89	Skilled autoworkers	41
Biologists	89	Skilled steelworkers	41
Chemists	86	Textile workers	31
Lawyers	83	Blue-collar workers	24
Journalists	82	Unskilled steelworkers	21
White-collar workers	43	Unskilled autoworkers	16

Source: Reprinted from *Work in America: Report of a Special Task Force to the Secretary of Health, Education and Welfare,* (Cambridge, Mass.: MIT Press, 1973).

The debate over whether people are really alienated from their work is likely to continue. For the manager, the key fact is that some workers achieve a sense of identification and self-worth from their jobs, while others do not. A key task is to discover what work means to other people at any given point in time and to strive to make this meaning as positive as possible. Part of the issue in all this is perception.

Perception

Perception, the mechanism through which people receive, organize, and interpret information from their environments, is an important element in this process through which work takes meaning for the individual. An important viewpoint shared among most OB scholars is that people respond to situations and other people in terms of their perceptions. Indeed, the "perceived" meaning of the same work situation may vary significantly from one person to the next.

Perceptual Differences Between Managers and Subordinates

The data in Figure 2.2 show perceptual differences that existed between managers and subordinates in one work setting. At issue is the frequency with which recognition is allocated as a work reward. Managers perceive that they give recognition frequently; subordinates perceive recognition as being less frequently available as a work reward.

Differences like these are often caused by the fact that each party lacks full and complete information on the situation. And, the consequences of these differing perceptions can be severe. Since perception links information with behavior, we might expect the managers' and subordinates' reactions to the same situation to be inconsistent with one another. One possible result is described in Figure 2.3. As you can

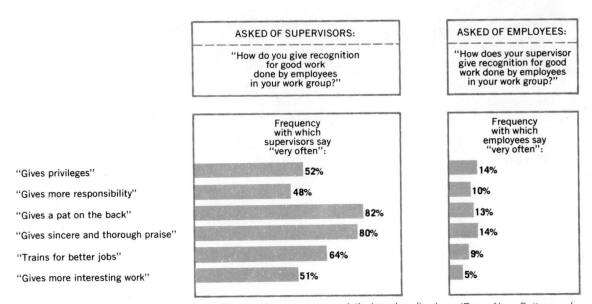

FIGURE 2.2 Perceptual differences between managers and their subordinates. (From *New Patterns of Management* by Rensis Likert, p. 91. Copyright © 1961, McGraw-Hill. Used with the permission of McGraw-Hill Book Company.)

see, the perceptual differences could lead to problems if the managers reduce their attention to subordinates' needs for recognition and focus instead on other concerns. The subordinates' desires would remain frustrated and the unfortunate outcome could well be declining job performance and satisfaction.

Managerial Implications of Perception

To help the manager master situations such as this, the field of OB gives significant attention to perception and its influence on various affairs of the workplace. Extensive research recognizes that the ultimate meaning of work for an individual will be influenced by a person's perceptions of such things as the nature of tasks performed, types and amounts of rewards received, structure of the organization and work unit, and relationships with coworkers, supervisors, and subordinates. A manager, in turn, must be aware and sensitive to perceptions when trying to perform effectively in such capacities as "leader" (i.e., someone who encourages other people to work hard in support of organizational goals) and "change agent" (someone who facilitates constructive change and development of the organization and its human resources).

We will remain sensitive throughout this book to how perceptions affect the behavior and feelings of people at work and the responses of managers to them. In Chapter 13, the perception process will be analyzed in detail to further establish and summarize its managerial implications. For the moment, one related issue of immediate importance is the concept of "job satisfaction."

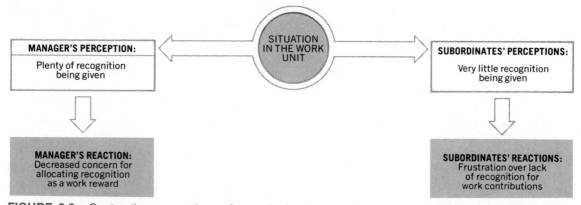

FIGURE 2.3 Contrasting perceptions of a work situation and their consequences for managers and subordinates.

JOB SATISFACTION

Formally stated, **job satisfaction** is the degree to which an individual feels positively or negatively about the various facets of the job tasks, the work setting, and relationships with co-workers. It is an underlying belief or feeling that conveys someone's evaluation of their overall job and its separate aspects. It also reflects the degree to which the expectations of a psychological contract are being fulfilled. Job satisfaction is likely to be higher for the person who senses a balance in the inducements–contributions exchange, than for someone who feels their realized inducements are less than their work contributions. Later in Chapter 3 we include job satisfaction among the important *attitudes* that can and do influence human behavior in organizations. As a result, OB researchers are interested in accurately measuring job satisfaction and understanding its consequences for people at work.[3]

Measuring Job Satisfaction

Researchers go to great lengths to create good measures of job satisfaction. One straightforward approach is simply to ask people to respond orally or in writing to a question such as this.

How satisfied are you with your present job?

not at all   somewhat   extremely

1   2   3   4   5

Let's measure your ''job'' satisfaction. Circle the response in the previous question that best reflects your feelings so far about one of your courses.

Assume that everyone else in your class also answers the prior question for the same course. Suppose, too, that your instructor collects and summarizes the responses. What would the instructor know if the average of all responses to the question was 3.5? Is this a good, bad, or in-between satisfaction score? Actually, it is very hard to say if the 3.5 is good or bad as a satisfaction score. It is hard to know whether or not people share the same meanings for the terms "somewhat" and "extremely." Furthermore, it is likely that there are some aspects of the course that you find to be more satisfying than others. Perhaps you had a hard time deciding how to respond to the course satisfaction question because of this.

Your instructor would really like to know what he or she can do to improve the course and the average satisfaction score. Once again, the single-question measure of job or course satisfaction proves deficient, since it gives the instructor no insight into what facets of the course could be improved upon. It is also deficient because it is not as reliable as multiple items in measuring the same concept. That is, single-item measures are answered less consistently than those with more items. Because of problems such as these, researchers try to use more sophisticated measures of the various facets of work that can become sources of job satisfaction and dissatisfaction.

Two widely used questionnaire measures of job satisfaction are the Job Descriptive Index (JDI) and the Minnesota Satisfaction Questionnaire (MSQ).[4] A popular version of the JDI measures satisfaction with five facets of a job: the work itself, quality of supervision, coworkers, promotion, and pay. The MSQ measures a number of similar facets including satisfaction with working conditions, chances for advancement, freedom to use one's own judgment, praise for doing a good job, and feelings of accomplishment, among others. Any one or all of these job facets can be a source of specific meaning for people at work. Instruments like the JDI and MSQ are important to managers interested in assessing the job satisfaction among subordinates, and developing ideas for improving things. For example, Table 2.2 lists some implications of the facets of satisfaction measured by the JDI.

Job Satisfaction Trends and Issues

The extent of job satisfaction experienced by people in the labor force is a topic of continuing social interest. Over the years, a number of studies and opinion polls have addressed the issue in the United States.[5] Even though there is always concern that most workers are unhappy with their jobs, the empirical evidence generally indicates that most American workers are moderately satisfied with their jobs. At worst, job satisfaction has declined slightly on the average since the early 1960s. Among workers in various occupational groups, managerial and professional workers seem most satisfied and unskilled workers least satisfied; older workers (over the age of 30) seem more satisfied than their younger counterparts. Furthermore, a person's level of job satisfaction seems relatively consistent, even when jobs and occupations are changed.[6] Someone who is unhappy in one work setting is likely to feel the same in another.

These and related issues continue to attract the attention of researchers and watchers of public opinion. "Loyalty," for example, was earlier identified as one of the contributions individuals make to organizations. One *Business Week*/Harris Poll of middle

TABLE 2.2 Sample Implications of High and Low JDI Satisfactions of Employees		
JDI Facets	High Satisfaction	Low Satisfaction
Work itself	Come early; stay late; stay on job	Seek transfer; be absent or late; quit
Supervision	Seek company of; accept demands and advice; stay on job	Avoid; complain and argue; reject demands and advice; file grievance; quit
Co-workers	Approach; conform to norms; stay on job	Avoid; argue with; be absent; quit
Promotion	Increase effort; raise aspirations; stay on job	Decrease effort; lower aspirations; quit
Pay	Modify effort depending on pay-performance connection; stay on job	Complain; modify effort depending on pay-performance connection; quit

Source: Abridged from E. A. Locke, "Job Satisfaction and Job Performance: A Theoretical Analysis," *Organizational Behavior and Human Performance,* Vol. 5 (1970), p. 496.

managers reported 65 percent as saying they were less loyal to their employers than they were 10 years earlier. This decline may be explained, in part, by basic changes in the way managers view their jobs. For example:[7]

- We live at a time when firms in many industries are experiencing acquisitions, mergers, and staff cutbacks in the quest for increased productivity—employee security and loyalty may be suffering as a result.
- As the workforce grows more "professional" in nature, these employees may identify more with their professions and external reference groups than with their employers—thus reducing loyalty.
- Values may be shifting toward greater emphasis on the importance of family, leisure, and other aspects of one's nonwork life—loyalty to the employer may be losing ground in competition with loyalty to personal affairs.

On the other hand, the nature of the work itself is changing in many occupations. For many years we have used the terms "blue collar blues" and "white collar woes" to signify displeasures with jobs that are routine and boring. The growing presence of computers and related high technologies in the workplace is adding a new dimension to such concerns. Take the machinist who once prepared all the settings on a machine tool and did the required work. Now the settings are likely to be controlled through a computer that also operates the machine. This machinist is now more of a "helper" and "observer," and less of a "doer." Or, think of the airline reservation clerks whose work is done via a computer that also closely monitors their performance. After suffering a nervous breakdown brought on in part by job pressures, one clerk said: "Management is acting as if I am supposed to have a digital clock in my head. I'm not a machine."

Consequences of Job Satisfaction

The job satisfaction of a manager's subordinates is important because of the various consequences with which they may be associated. Here we are especially concerned to establish what these consequences may mean in terms of the manager's ability to take full advantage of people as a human resources of organizations. In effect, managers must be concerned with two decisions individuals make about their work and work organizations: the decision to belong and the decision to perform.

Job Satisfaction and the Decision to Belong

One response of people whose psychological contracts are unconfirmed is to withdraw from organizations either temporarily, through absenteeism, or permanently, through turnover. Such situations sometimes develop because unrealistic expectations are created during the recruiting process. In contrast to traditional recruiting which tries only to "sell" job candidates on the organization, **realistic recruitment** is the preferred approach. This method gives prospective employees as much pertinent information— both good and bad—as is possible and without distortion.[8] It communicates a greater sense of reality and helps keep any initial expectations reasonable. When early job satisfaction is then experienced as a result of a fulfilled psychological contract, costly premature turnover is avoided as the new member is more likely to remain with the organization.

Thus, it is not enough for a manager to induce people to join the organization or work unit, they must also be induced to stay. One way of doing so is to increase job satisfaction by creating a work environment that is perceived as meeting expectations.[9] Job satisfaction influences **absenteeism,** or the failure of people to attend work. Satisfied workers are more regular in attendance and less likely to be absent for unexplained reasons than their more dissatisfied counterparts. Job satisfaction can also affect **turnover,** or decisions by workers to terminate their employment. Satisfied workers are less likely to quit; dissatisfied ones are more likely to leave when they can.

Both absenteeism and turnover are of major concern to managers. When people fail to show up for work or quit, human resources that would otherwise contribute to the work unit's production purpose are missing. The resulting loss in performance and the need to replace the missing personnel, permanently or temporarily, can be expensive. The costs of turnover are especially high. They include the expenses of recruiting, selecting, and training replacements, as well as productivity losses caused by any operational disruptions and low morale that may occur.

Still, a manager must be careful when dealing with these issues. For someone who is "burned out" or highly stressed in their work, a day or more of absence might be beneficial—for both the individual and the organization. Turnover, too, is sometimes of value to the organization. It can, for example, be an opportunity to bring replacements with creative ideas and new energy into the work unit. It may also reduce conflict by removing a dissatisfied employee from the work setting and/or increase morale by providing position vacancies into which continuing employees may advance.[10] Thus, neither absenteeism nor turnover should be viewed as entirely negative phenomena. Rather, they should always be addressed contingently and with adequate consideration for potential positive as well as negative consequences.

Job Satisfaction and the Decision to Perform

Somewhere near a Ford Motor Company plant in Dearborn, Michigan, a tavern displays the sign

> I SPEND FORTY HOURS A WEEK HERE—AM I SUPPOSED TO WORK TOO?

This sign communicates a simple but potent message to the manager. It is one thing for people to decide to report to work regularly and stay with an organization; it is quite another for them to work hard to perform well while they are there! High performance by individuals and groups throughout an organization, furthermore, is the basic building block of accomplishments such as those highlighted in Newsline 2.2.

Performance is defined as a summary measure of the quantity and quality of work contributions made by an individual or group to the accomplishment of the organization's purpose. High performance occurs when these contributions are made in a superior manner that complies with job and organizational requirements.

Supplementary Module C at the end of the book is devoted to "Performance Appraisal Foundations of Organizational Behavior." It contains useful insights on performance appraisal methods and the management issues associated with them. For now, our specific focus is on the creation of high-performance outcomes by people at work. In this respect, it seems logical that job satisfaction and work performance should be related to one another. The presumption, however, raises the question that is central to the field of OB: **"What causes high levels of individual work performance?"** We know that job satisfaction is one possible cause of employee absenteeism and turnover. Can we also say that job satisfaction *causes* individual work performance?

HERZBERG'S TWO-FACTOR THEORY

Frederick Herzberg is a psychologist whose work suggests that job satisfaction *is* a cause of work performance. He has developed one of the most frequently praised and criticized theories in OB, the two-factor theory.[11] Herzberg began his research by asking workers two straightforward questions:

NEWSLINE 2.2 / MOST ADMIRED CORPORATIONS

Fortune magazine annually publishes a list of America's most admired corporations. Over 300 companies in various industries are rated by more than 4000 senior executives, outside directors, and financial analysts. The following eight attributes are used to create the corporate scorecards.

- Quality of management.
- Quality of products or services.
- Innovativeness.
- Long-term investment value.
- Financial soundness.
- Ability to attract, develop, and keep talented people.

- Community and environmental responsibility.
- Use of corporate assets.

Two companies that consistently score in the top 10 overall are IBM, the office equipment and computer giant, and Merck, a large pharmaceutical firm. Others who have scored well recently are Boeing (aerospace), Liz Claiborne (apparel), J.P. Morgan (commercial banking), Rubbermaid (rubber and plastics products), Johnson & Johnson (pharmaceutical), Dow Jones (publishing and printing), and Herman Miller (furniture).

Reported in *Fortune*.

1. "Tell me about a time when you felt expectionally good about your job."
2. "Tell me about a time when you felt exceptionally bad about your job."

After analyzing almost 4000 responses to these questions, Herzberg and his associates developed the two-factor theory. They noticed that persons responding to the two questions identified different things as sources of satisfaction and dissatisfaction in their work. A summary of the actual data is presented in Figure 2.4.

Hygiene Factors

Items appearing as sources of **job dissatisfaction** in Herzberg's research were found to be associated with the **job context.** That is, job dissatisfaction was linked more to the work setting than to the work itself. Herzberg refers to the sources of job dissatisfaction as **hygiene factors.**

The hygiene factors are shown on the left side of Figure 2.4. They include such things as working conditions, interpersonal relations, organizational policies and administration, supervision, and salary. "Salary," you say? Yes, Herzberg views salary as a hygiene factor. The implications of this classification are most important. You may think, for example, that paying people more by raising their base salaries will create job satisfaction and increase performance. You might make a similar argument that improved work conditions (e.g., special offices, air conditioning) will do the

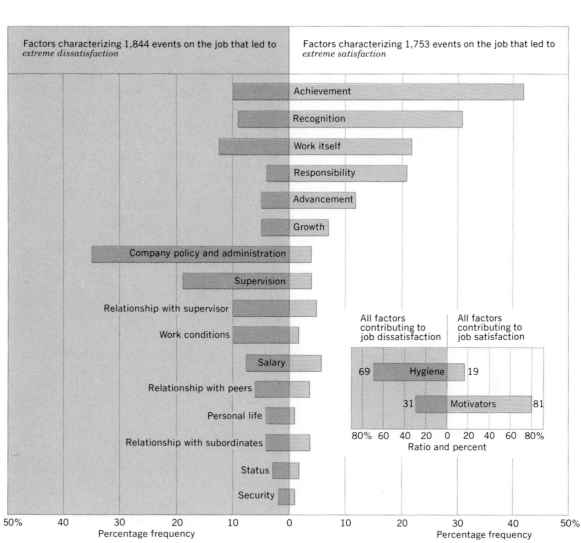

FIGURE 2.4   Sources of satisfaction and dissatisfaction as reported in 12 investigations. (Adapted from Frederick Herzberg, "One More Time: How Do You Motivate Employees?" Harvard Business Review, Vol. 46, January–February, 1968, p. 57. Copyright © 1968 by the President and Fellows of Harvard College. All rights reserved.)

same. Herzberg disagrees. The essence of this disagreement establishes the two-factor logic upon which his theory is based.

In the two-factor theory, job satisfaction and dissatisfaction are considered totally separate dimensions. Hygiene items only affect job dissatisfaction. Improving hygiene factors in the workplace can reduce the level of dissatisfaction felt by workers, but the improvement will not contribute to job satisfaction. The hygiene factors should be viewed by managers as follows:

$$\text{Hygiene factors} \xrightarrow[\text{in}]{\text{exist}} \text{job context} \xrightarrow[\text{affect}]{\text{and}} \text{job } \textit{dis}\text{satisfaction}$$

Table 2.3 gives examples of hygiene factors found in many work settings. Two current developments in U.S. society are also quite relevant. One relates to the Surgeon General's report on the adverse health effects of involuntary smoking, and the increasing restriction of smoking in the workplace. The other relates to employer concerns for drug abuse among people at work, and the growing use of drug testing of job applicants and even employees in some organizations. Both are controversial trends representing ''job context'' issues with potential legal as well as organizational implications.

Satisfier Factors

Remember, Herzberg argues that improving a hygiene factor such as working conditions cannot make people satisfied with their work. It will only prevent them from being unhappy. To improve **job satisfaction,** the manager's attention must shift to **satisfiers.** These satisfiers are listed on the right side of Figure 2.4, and they are part of **job content;** that is, they relate to what people actually do in their work.

Adding satisfiers to people's jobs is the link to performance in Herzberg's theory. He argues that managers can create opportunities for subordinates to experience such things as a sense of achievement, recognition, responsibility, advancement, and growth in the course of their performance. When these opportunities are absent from work, Herzberg feels that workers will neither experience job satisfaction nor perform

TABLE 2.3 Sample Hygiene Factors Found in Work Settings	
Hygiene Factors	Examples
Organizational policies, procedures	Attendance rules
	Vacation schedules
	Grievance procedures
	Performance appraisal methods
Working conditions	Noise levels
	Safety
	Personal comfort
	Size of work area
Interpersonal relationships	Co-worker relations
	Customer relations
	Relationship with boss
Quality of supervision	Technical competence of boss
Base salary	Hourly wage rate or salary

their best. According to the logic of the two-factor theory,

$$\text{Satisfier factors} \xrightarrow[\text{in}]{\text{exist}} \text{job content} \xrightarrow[\text{affect}]{\text{and}} \text{job satisfaction}$$

Two-Factor Dynamics

Two principles summarize the two-factor dynamics:

1. Improvements in hygiene factors can prevent and/or help eliminate job dissatisfaction; they cannot increase job satisfaction.
2. Improvements in satisfier factors can create job satisfaction; they cannot prevent job dissatisfaction.

You may be uncomfortable with these principles, especially the last one. It implies that a person can simultaneously experience job satisfaction and dissatisfaction. Because Herzberg considers job satisfaction and dissatisfaction to be separate dimensions, this is, in fact, possible under the theory. People at work can fall into any one of the four possibilities shown below.

Job Satisfaction	**Job Dissatisfaction**
High	High
High	Low
Low	High
Low	Low

The most appealing situation for the manager is to have subordinates experiencing high satisfaction and low dissatisfaction. The manager's goal under the two-factor theory is to minimize job dissatisfaction by improving hygiene factors and maximize job satisfaction by improving satisfier factors.

Research and Practical Implications

OB scholars debate the merits and demerits of the two-factor theory.[12] Herzberg's continuing research and that of his followers support the theory. Some researchers have used different research methods and find they are unable to confirm the theory. It is therefore criticized as being method-bound, that is, as being supportable only by applying Herzberg's original methodology. This is a serious criticism, since the scientific approach requires that theories be verifiable when different research methods are used.

With all this debate, you may ask if the two-factor theory is of any value. We think it is because of the discipline it adds to managerial thinking. Many managers allocate considerable time, attention, and other resources to things that Herzberg would consider hygiene factors. Special office fixtures, piped-in music, fancy lounges for breaks, and even high-base salaries are examples. The two-factor theory suggests caution in expecting too much performance impact from these investments. Herzberg's theory is perhaps even more useful because it is associated with a specific technique for building satisfiers into job content. This approach is called **job enrichment,** and we give it special attention in Chaper 6.

THE SATISFACTION–PERFORMANCE CONTROVERSY

One offshoot of the debate over the two-factor theory is a more fundamental controversy illustrated by the following conversation.[13]

> As Ben walked by smiling on the way to his office, Ben's boss remarked to a friend: ''Ben really enjoys his job and that's why he's the best damn worker I ever had. And that's reason enough for me to keep Ben happy.'' The friend replied: ''No, you're wrong! Ben likes his job because he does it so well. If you want to make Ben happy you ought to do whatever you can to help him further improve his performance.''

The core issue here is, does job satisfaction cause performance? Will managerial efforts designed to increase a person's job satisfaction cause that person's work performance to improve? Will a decline in job satisfaction cause a corresponding decrease in individual performance?

These questions introduce the satisfaction–performance controversy, a debate that involves three alternative points of view:[14]

1. Satisfaction causes performance (S→P).
2. Performance causes satisfaction (P→S).
3. Rewards cause both performance and satisfaction (R→P, S).

Argument: Satisfaction Causes Performance (S→P)

If this argument is true, managers should try to improve the job satisfaction of subordinates to increase their work performance. Herzberg's two-factor theory is consistent with this tradition. The position is a legacy of early research studies (e.g., the Hawthorne studies described in Supplementary Module A) and is typically associated with the ''human relations movement.'' A classic example is the following quotation taken from a book published in 1951.[15]

> Management has at long last discovered that there is greater production, and hence greater profit *when* workers are satisfied with their jobs.

The Research

Reviews of research on the S→P hypothesis consistently indicate that there is no simple and direct relation between individual job satisfaction at one point in time and work performance at a later point in time. This conclusion is well respected among OB scholars, even though some continue to suggest that the S→P relationship may exist to various degrees depending upon the exact situation. These alternative views continue to be debated and justify our use of the qualifiers ''simple'' and ''direct'' in summarizing the research evidence.

Current Thinking

As researchers and as managers, we should recognize that job satisfaction alone is probably not a consistent predictor of individual work performance. It may well be, however, an important component of a larger set of variables that together can predict performance—and it may predict performance for certain persons. Finally, regardless of whether or not job satisfaction causes work performance, it is a part of human resource maintenance and is, therefore, an important work result in its own right. Managers should seek to create job satisfaction among their subordinates as something desirable in and of itself.

Argument: Performance Causes Satisfaction (P→S)

If this argument is true, managers can promote job satisfaction by helping subordinates to achieve higher levels of work performance. Rather than trying to create job satisfaction first, the manager's attention under this argument would be shifted directly to performance. Given performance, job satisfaction and its positive contribution to human resource maintenance are assumed to follow.

Typical reasoning in support of the performance-causes-satisfaction argument follows. When high performance is followed by a valued reward, satisfaction occurs. Thus, a manager can create satisfaction by first establishing conditions under which a person can achieve high performance, and then by properly rewarding the person for performance accomplishments. Figuratively speaking,

$$\text{Work performance} \xrightarrow{\text{followed by}} \text{valued rewards} \xrightarrow{\text{will create}} \text{job satisfaction}$$

The Research

Research studies report an empirical relationship between individual performance measured at one time and later job satisfaction. This relationship is typically stronger than the one between initial job satisfaction and later work performance. The most provocative line of present inquiry is an attempt to examine the role of rewards as an intervening variable in the P→S hypothesis.

Figure 2.5 summarizes a model of the P→S relationship offered by Edward E. Lawler and Lyman Porter.[16] In the figure, performance accomplishment leads to re-

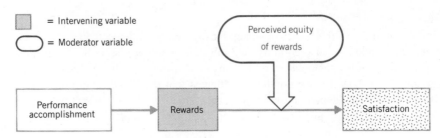

FIGURE 2.5   Simplified model of the relationship of performance to satisfaction.

wards that, in turn, lead to satisfaction. Rewards intervene between performance and satisfaction; that is, they constitute the essential ''link'' that causes the P→S relationship to happen. A moderator variable, perceived equity of the reward, further affects whether or not performance-based rewards will lead to satisfaction. The moderator relationship implies that when an individual perceives the reward for performance as being equitable or fair, satisfaction will be forthcoming; when a perceived inequity exists, however, it is predicted that the reward will not lead to satisfaction. This figure highlights two open questions that must be answered in regard to managing the P→S relationship: (1) How should rewards be best allocated? and (2) Do variables other than rewards also intervene in the P→S relationship?

Current Thinking

The P→S hypothesis is important to OB, not because it resolves the satisfaction–performance controversy, but because of the provocative research and managerial implications with which it is associated. This hypothesis appropriately focuses a manager's attention on how he or she rewards performance and how these rewards are perceived by the people doing the work. Rewards are within a manager's capability to control. As inducements to work, they are also fundamental to the individual's psychological contract.

Argument: Rewards Cause Both Satisfaction and Performance (R→S, P)

This final argument suggests that a proper allocation of rewards can influence both individual job satisfaction and work performance. While research seems to question that satisfaction can cause performance, the potential for rewards to cause performance has captured the attention of scholars.

The Research

The evidence on the R→S, P hypothesis is encouraging. Researchers note that people receiving higher rewards for performance report greater job satisfaction. Furthermore, rewarding subjects on a ''performance contingent'' basis (i.e., high rewards for high performance, low for low) is positively associated with later work performance. While giving a low performer a small reward may lead to initial dissatisfaction, research indicates that such action is also likely to lead to higher performance in the future.

The managerial implications are straightforward. If you are only interested in creating high job satisfaction, pass out high rewards. If you are interested in high work performance as well, allocate rewards in proportion to performance.

Current Thinking

This final argument in the satisfaction–performance controversy is the most compelling. From a practical point of view, it focuses the manager's attention on work rewards as things that can affect both the job satisfaction and work performance of subordinates. In terms of theory, the hypothesis also raises useful research questions such as

- What determines the values individuals will attach to various work-related rewards?
- What else in addition to rewards will or can affect work performance?

These and related questions will be examined in the four chapters in Part Two on ''Managing Individuals in Organizations.'' As you read on, remember that empirical research does suggest that job satisfaction is not alone a good predictor of work performance, but performance-related rewards can influence both job satisfaction and future work performance.

WORK AND NONWORK

Throughout this chapter we have discussed work and its meaning for the individual. Our concern has been to examine the meaning of work so that you, as a manager, can better assist subordinates to achieve high levels of *both* task performance and job satisfaction. Before leaving this topic, however, it is important to remind you that people's work and nonwork lives are intertwined. Managers must understand that what happens to people at work can affect how they feel and what they do outside work, and vice versa. Someone who is having a ''bad day'' on the job, for example, may be responding to worries about family responsibilities or other pressures in their nonwork life.

Furthermore, the central importance of work in the total life experience varies from one person to the next—and, this centrality may change over the course of a career. Work may mean quite different things to the young single adult, to the mid-career adult with a working spouse and school-age children involved in a variety of sports and activities, and to the late-career adult making retirement plans. Indeed, the very nature of the inducements–contributions balance required to maintain ''healthy'' psychological contracts for different individuals and for the same individual at different life and career stages, will vary significantly. More is said on this issue in our discussion of developmental aspects of the adult personality in Chapter 3, and of career planning and development in Chapter 18.

In concluding this discussion of people at work, we want you to realize that there is a broader social value associated with work that makes any manager's responsibilities even more complex. We said earlier that the "quality of work is an important component in the quality of life." Consider the following words of a steelworker.[17]

> When I come home, know what I do for the first 20 minutes? Fake it.
> I put on a smile. I got a kid three years old. Sometimes she says, "Daddy, where've you been?" I say, "Work." I could have told her I'd been in Disneyland. What's work to a three-year-old kid? If I feel bad, I can't take it out on the kid. Kids are born innocent of everything but birth. You can't take it out on your wife either. That is why you go to a tavern. You want to release it there rather than do it at home. What does an actor do when he's got a bad movie? I got a bad movie every day.

These comments show quite tragically how negative work experiences can affect a person's nonwork life. It may even be that a contributing cause of some worrisome social ills—alcoholism, drug abuse, spouse and child abuse, and the like—may in part trace to the adjustment problems of people unable to find meaning and self respect in their work. To the extent that this is true, the social importance of managers as major influences on the quality of work life experienced by other people in organizations is certainly magnified.

Thus, the field of OB recognizes that every employee of a work organization lives two overlapping lives, a work life and a nonwork life. The environment created by managers for people at work may have consequences that extend beyond the time an individual spends in the work setting. Managers should be fully aware that the quality of any individual's life, even their own, can be heavily influenced by the quality of life at work. Poor management can decrease the quality of overall life, not just the quality of work life. Hopefully, good management can increase both.

SUMMARY

Two themes dominate this chapter. The first is the concept of work and what it means to people. We have defined work, discussed it as a form of exchange between the individual and the organization, and identified how it can affect the overall quality of people's lives. We hope this chapter has left you with the feeling that being a good manager is of value not only to you and the organization, but also to society.

The second theme of the chapter centered around job satisfaction and its relationship to job performance. We have defined job satisfaction and have found dissatisfaction to be one cause of employee turnover. Herzberg's two-factor theory of job satisfaction focused your attention on hygiene factors as sources of dissatisfaction and on satisfier factors as sources of satisfaction. In going on to examine the satisfaction–performance controversy, we concluded that job satisfaction alone is probably not a good predictor of work performance. Rather, managers should consider satisfaction and performance as two separate but equally important work results affected by the allocation of work-related rewards. In Part Two, which follows, we will further address these issues from the individual's point of view. For now, remember that

1. Well-allocated rewards can increase job satisfaction and encourage people to seek high levels of performance.
2. The quality of people's work lives is an important component in the overall quality of their lives in general.

THINKING THROUGH THE ISSUES

1. Explain the concept of a "psychological contract." What significance does it hold for managers of people at work?
2. Define "perception." Why is perception an important element in the relationship between a manager and other people and events in organizations?
3. We have argued that "as the performance of individual subordinates rises or falls, work unit performance will also be affected." Explain how "synergy" affects this relationship.
4. If researchers are correct in their current tendency to think that job satisfaction is *not* a good predictor of work performance, why should managers be interested in the job satisfaction of their subordinates at all?
5. Why should Studs Terkel enjoy his work, if, as he claims, other people don't enjoy theirs?
6. Use Herzberg's two-factor theory to identify possible sources of dissatisfaction–satisfaction in a job with which you are familiar.
7. Explain and defend a managerial strategy for increasing the satisfaction and performance of persons employed in the job described in number 6.
8. Choose a current newspaper or magazine article that reports on the quality of work life. Summarize and explain the managerial significance of the report.

CASE: THE SILENT SUPERVISOR

"Big Brother Is Watching" read the buttons donned by some employees of the *New York Times*.[18] What's the issue? Something new to the workplace—electronic supervision. For as many as 4 million American workers, with the number growing each day, the computer is taking over as their manager. Some examples—

- A maid cleaning rooms in a Washington hotel starts and finishes the task by entering a code number in the bedside push-button telephone. The computer on the other end records the work time.
- A trucking firm uses computers to monitor drivers and ensure they adhere to

speed limits. The practice is credited with saving wear and tear on vehicles and increased fuel efficiency.

- At an airlines reservations office, computers track how long clerks spend on calls. Negative points are assigned for using more than an average of 109 seconds on calls. Earning more than 37 negative points in a year, may result in loss of one's job.
- Many grocery stores are installing computerized price scanning equipment. The scanners not only ring up prices, they also tell a central computer how many items per minute a clerk is handling. One chain claims to have saved $15 million in one year due to increased efficiency at the checkout counter.

All this is what leads these workers to feel like "big brother is watching." Many employees claim computerized monitoring systems take the human touch out of work and manager–subordinate relationships. Comments one, "If I'm ever slow, the company will know. It means I can't have a bad day." Employers claim the use of computerized monitoring systems increases productivity and brings new opportunities. Some have eliminated managerial personnel as the need for direct supervision is reduced. Others use the built-in record keeping to develop pay-for-performance programs. Whereas some employees are motivated by such incentives, others resent the implicit pressure for increased performance. They suggest work quality may suffer in the quest for quantity. One union official says, "Telephone operators used to be a voice with a smile, but automation has depersonalized their jobs." Perhaps the ultimate concern is expressed by Karen Nussbaum, director of *9 to 5,* a national group of working women. She says, "The potential for corporate abuse is staggering. It puts you under the gun in the short run and drives you crazy in the long run."

Questions
1. Which of the OB concepts developed in Chapters 1 and 2 are illustrated by the situation described in this case? Use specific examples to support your answer.
2. What is the desired "human touch" in the relationship between a person and his or her employing organization? What is the manager's role in establishing and maintaining this relationship?
3. Can the "human touch" be maintained as computers and related technologies become a part of more and more jobs? Why or why not?

EXERCISE: VIEW FROM THE EXECUTIVE SUITE

Purpose:
To explore the meaning of managerial work, both for yourself and for other people; and, to examine the implications of these findings.

Time:
50 to 75 minutes in class; no outside preparation.

Procedures:

1. Consider these *Wall Street Journal* news reports on managers and their jobs.[19]

   - "Federal executive morale is on the skids." Out of 1364 government managers responding to a survey by the Federal Executive Institute, 61% said they would *not* recommend a federal career to young people. A year earlier, 51% felt this way.
   - "The large number of corporate restructurings is making it more difficult to have a managerial career." Hay Group surveys of middle managers report the following: In 1975–77 slightly over 70% of respondents held favorable views of their opportunities for advancement; in 1983–85 only about 38% felt favorably.
   - "If you were now starting over, what career would you pursue?" This question is asked in Korn/Ferry International's surveys of executives. In 1985, 60% of respondents said they would choose the same career; in 1987, only 47% said they would do so.

2. Convene in small groups and discuss the meaning and significance of these reports. What do you offer as plausible explanations for the apparent decline in managerial job satisfaction evidenced by these data? What are the implications—a) to society as a whole? . . . and, b) to you and your future career?

3. Select a spokesperson to summarize, for the benefit of the class as a whole, key points and conclusions from your group discussion.

4. When class reconvenes, spokespersons will present their reports. Everyone should participate in class discussion led by the instructor to examine the results and develop their managerial implications.

THE MANAGER'S VOCABULARY

Absenteeism   The failure of people to attend work on a given day.

Contributions   Individual work efforts of value to the organization.

Hygiene Factors   Sources of job dissatisfaction that are found in the job context.

Inducements   Things that the organization gives to the individual in return for contributions.

Job Enrichment   A technique for building satisfier factors into job content.

Job Satisfaction   The degree to which an individual feels positively or negatively about the various facets of the job tasks, the work setting, and the relationships with co-workers.

Perception   The mechanism through which people receive, organize, and interpret information from their environments.

Performance   A summary measure of the quantity and quality of task contributions made by an individual or group to the work unit and organization.

Psychological Contract   The set of expectations held by the individual and specifying what the individual and the organization expect to give and to receive from one another in the course of their working relationship.

Realistic Recruitment   Recruiting that gives job candidates as much pertinent information, both good and bad, as is possible and without distortion about the job and the organization.

Satisfier Factors   Sources of job satisfaction that are found in the job content.

Turnover   Decisions by workers to terminate their employment.

Two-Factor Theory   A theory separating hygiene or job context factors as sources of job dissatisfaction from satisfier or job content factors as sources of job satisfaction.

Work   An activity that produces value for other people.

IMPORTANT NAMES

Frederick Herzberg   Author of the two-factor theory.

Edward E. Lawler and Lyman W. Porter   Researchers who developed a useful model of the performance-satisfaction relationship.

NOTES

[1]From "Studs Terkel Loves His Work, But He Says You Don't," an interview in *MBA,* Vol. 10 (June 1976), pp. 41–44. Used by permission. See also, Studs Terkel, *Working* (New York: Avon Books, 1975).

[2]Adapted from a case described by John P. Kotter, "The Psychological Contract: Managing the Joining-up Process." Copyright © 1973 by the Regents of the University of California. Reprinted from *California Management Review,* Volume XV, No. 3, pp. 96 and 97 by permission of the Regents.

[3]For a good review see Edwin A. Locke, "The Nature and Causes of Job Satisfaction," in Marvin D. Dunnette, ed., *Handbook of Industrial and Organizational Psychology* (Chicago: Rand McNally, 1976), pp. 1267–1349.

[4]The Job Descriptive Index (JDI) is available from Dr. Patricia C. Smith, Department of Psychology, Bowling Green State University; the Minnesota Satisfaction Questionnaire (MSQ) is available from the Industrial Relations Center and Vocational Psychology Research Center, University of Minnesota.

[5]For major summaries see *Work in America: Report of a Special Task Force to the Secretary of Health, Education and Welfare* (Cambridge, Mass.: MIT Press, 1973); George H. Gallup, *The Gallup Poll, 1972–77*

(V.1) (Wilmington, Del: Scholarly Resources, 1978); and, Charles N. Weaver, "Job Satisfaction in the United States in the 1970s's," *Journal of Applied Psychology,* Vol.65 (1980), pp. 364–367. For an example of the frequent polls and surveys see "Most Workers Don't Trust Their Bosses, Study Finds," *The Wall Street Journal* (February 10, 1987), p. 1.

[6]Barry M. Staw, "Organizational Psychology and the Pursuit of the Happy/Productive Worker," *California Management Review,* Vol. XXVIII (Summer 1986), pp. 40–53.

[7]These and following examples are from "The End of Corporate Loyalty," *Business Week* (August 4, 1986), pp. 42–49, and "The Boss that Never Blinks," *Business Week* (July 28, 1986), pp. 46–47.

[8]John P. Wanous, *Organizational Entry* (Reading, Mass.: Addison-Wesley, 1980).

[9]See K. Dow Scott and G. Stephen Taylor, "An Examination of Conflicting Findings on the Relationship Between Job Satisfaction and Absenteeism: A Meta-Analysis," *Academy of Management Journal,* Vol. 28 (1985), pp.599–612.

[10]Barry M. Staw, "The Consequences of Turnover," *Journal of Occupational Behavior,* Vol. 1 (1980), pp. 253–273.

[11]The complete two-factor theory is well explained by Herzberg and his associates in Herzberg, Bernard Mausner, and Barbara Bloch Synderman, *The Motivation to Work,* 2nd ed. (New York: John Wiley, 1967); and Frederick Herzberg, "One More Time: How Do You Motivate Employees?" *Harvard Business Review,* Vol. 46 (January–February 1968), pp. 53–62.

[12]See Robert J. House and Lawrence A. Wigdor, "Herzberg's Dual-Factor Theory of Job Satisfaction and Motivation: A Review of the Evidence and a Criticism," *Personnel Psychology,* Vol. 20 (Winter 1967), pp. 369–389; and Steven Kerr, Anne Harlan, and Ralph Stogdill, "Preference for Motivator and Hygiene Factors in a Hypothetical Interview Situation," *Personnel Psychology,* Vol. 27 (Winter 1974), pp. 109–124.

[13]Charles N. Greene, "The Satisfaction–Performance Controversy," *Business Horizons,* Vol. 15 (1972), p. 31.

[14]See Michelle T. Iaffaldano and Paul M. Muchinsky, "Job Satisfaction and Job Performance: A Meta-Analysis," *Psychological Bulletin,* Vol 97 (1985), pp.251–273; Greene, op cit., pp. 31–41; Dennis Organ, "A Reappraisal and Reinterpretation of the Satisfaction-Causes-Performance Hypothesis, *Academy of Management Review,* Vol. 2 (1977), pp.46–53; Peter Lorenzi, "A Comment on Organ's Reappraisal of the Satisfaction-Causes-Performance Hypothesis," *Academy of Management Review,* Vol. 3 (1978), pp.380–382.

[15]Willard E. Parker and Robert W. Kleemeier, *Human Relations in Supervision: Leadership in Management* (New York: McGraw-Hill, 1951), p. 10, as cited in Donald P. Schwab and Larry L. Cummings, "Theories of Performance and Satisfaction: A Review," *Industrial Relations,* Vol. 7 (1970), pp. 408–430.

[16]See, for example, Lyman W. Porter and Edward E. Lawler, III, *Managerial Attitudes and Performance* (Homewood, Ill.: Richard D. Irwin, 1968).

[17]Terkel, *Working,* p. 7.

[18]Developed from Gene Gibbons, "The Silent Supervisor," Reuters news release, Washington, January 1986; and, "The Boss that Never Blinks," *Time* (July 28, 1986), pp.46–47.

[19]These data are reported in *The Wall Street Journal* (May 19, 1987), p. 1 and (May 26, 1987), p. 29.

PART TWO
MANAGING INDIVIDUALS IN ORGANIZATIONS

CHAPTERS IN THIS PART OF THE BOOK

Now that you are sensitive to the need for managers to be good at understanding, predicting, and controlling behavior in organizations, the following case is most appropriate. This case involves people working in a manufacturing situation. It is presented in a prediction format so that you can further develop your analytical capabilities. The case introduces the full range of issues we will discuss in Part Two on individuals in organizations.

THE HOVEY AND BEARD COMPANY CASE

The Hovey and Beard Company manufactures a variety of wooden toys, including animals, pull toys, and the like.[1] The toys were manufactured by a transformation process that began in the wood room. There, toys were cut, sanded, and partially assembled. Then the toys were dipped into shellac and sent to the painting room.

In years past, the painting had been done by hand, with each employee working with a given toy until its painting was completed. The toys were predominantly two-colored, although a few required more than two colors. Now in response to increased demand for the toys, the painting operation was changed so that the painters sat in a line by an endless chain of hooks. These hooks moved continuously in front of the painters and passed into a long horizontal oven. Each painter sat in a booth designed to carry away fumes and to backstop excess paint. The painters would take a toy from a nearby tray, position it in a jig inside the painting cubicle, spray on the color according to a pattern, and then hang the toy on a passing hook. The rate at which the hooks moved was calculated by the engineers so that each painter, when fully trained, could hang a painted toy on each hook before it passed beyond reach.

The painters were paid on a group bonus plan. Since the operation was new to them, they received a learning bonus that decreased by regular amounts each month. The learning bonus was scheduled to vanish in six months, by which time it was expected that they would be on their own—that is, able to meet the production standard and earn a group bonus when they exceeded it.

QUESTIONS

1. Assume that the training period for the new job setup has just begun. What change do you predict in the level of output of the painters? Why?

increase   decrease   stay the same

2. What other predictions regarding the behavior of these painters do you make based upon the situation described so far?

CONTINUING ON   By the second month of the training period, trouble developed. The painters learned more slowly than had been anticipated and it began to look as though their production would stabilize far below what was planned. Many of the hooks were going by empty. The painters complained that the hooks moved too fast and that the engineer had set the rates wrong. A few painters quit and had to be replaced with new ones. This further aggravated the learning problem. The team spirit that the management had expected to develop through the group bonus was not in evidence except as an expression of what the engineers called "resistance." One painter, whom the group regarded as its leader (and the management regarded as the ringleader), was outspoken in taking the complaints of the group to the supervisor. These complaints were that the job was messy, the hooks moved too fast, the incentive pay was not correctly calculated, and it was too hot working so close to the drying oven.

OUR VIEWPOINT

"Problems"—this is what you should have predicted! This is a perfect example of a case in which "management" institutes a change in people's jobs without consulting those to be affected and without thinking ahead to anticipate the consequences of the change for the people involved. The actual work performance of the individual painters and the work unit as a whole has decreased. In addition, the workers are complaining about the new job arrangement. Some have even quit. Productivity and employee satisfaction are down.

QUESTION

1. What would you recommend that the responsible manager do now? Why?

CONTINUING ON   A consultant was hired to work with the supervisor. She recommended that the painters be brought together for a general discussion of the working conditions. Although hesitant, the supervisor agreed to this plan.

The first meeting was held immediately after the shift was over at 4 o'clock in the afternoon. It was attended by all eight painters. They voiced the same complaints again: the hooks went by too fast, the job was too dirty, and the room was hot and poorly ventilated. For some reason, it was this last item that seemed to bother them most. The supervisor promised to discuss the problems of ventilation and temperature with the engineers, and a second meeting was scheduled. In the next few days the supervisor had several talks with the engineers. They, along with the plant superintendent, felt that this was really a trumped-up complaint and that the expense of corrective measures would be prohibitively high.

The supervisor came to the second meeting with some apprehensions. The painters, however, did not seem to be much put out. Rather, they had a proposal of their own to make. They felt that if several large fans were set up to circulate the air around their feet, they would be much more comfortable. After some discussion, the supervisor agreed to pursue the idea. The supervisor and the consultant discussed the idea of fans with the superintendent. Three large propeller-type fans were purchased and installed.

The painters were jubilant. For several days the fans were moved about in various positions until they were placed to the satisfaction of the group. The painters seemed completely satisfied with the results, and the relations between them and the supervisor improved visibly.

The supervisor, after this encouraging episode, decided that further meetings might also prove profitable. The painters were asked if they would like to meet and discuss other aspects of the work situation. They were eager to do this. Another meeting was held and the discussion quickly centered on the speed of the hooks.

The painters maintained that the engineer had set them at an unreasonably fast speed and that they would never be able to fill enough of them to make a bonus.

The discussion reached a turning point when the group's leader explained that it wasn't that the painters couldn't work fast enough to keep up with the hooks but that they couldn't work at that pace all day long. The supervisor explored the point. The painters were unanimous in their opinion that they could keep up with the belt for short periods if they wanted to. But they didn't want to because if they showed they could do this for short periods then they would be expected to do it all day long. The meeting ended with an unprecedented request by the painters: "Let us adjust the speed of the belt faster or slower depending on how we feel." The supervisor agreed to discuss this with the superintendent and the engineers.

The engineers reacted negatively to the suggestion. However, after several meetings it was granted that there was some latitude within which variations in the speed of the hooks would not affect the finished product. After considerable argument with the engineers, it was agreed to try out the painters' idea.

With misgivings, the supervisor had a control with a dial marked "low, medium, fast" installed at the booth of the group leader. The speed of the belt could now be adjusted anywhere between the lower and upper limits that the engineers had set.

QUESTIONS

1. What changes do you now expect in the level of output of the painters? Why?
   increase   decrease   stay the same
2. What changes do you expect in the feelings of the painters toward their work situation? Why?
   more positive   more negative   no change
3. What other predictions do you make about the behavior of the painters?

CONTINUING ON   The painters were delighted and spent many lunch hours deciding how the speed of the belt should be varied from hour to hour throughout the day. Within a week the pattern had settled down to one in which the first half hour of the shift was run on a medium speed (a dial setting slightly above the point marked "medium"). The next two and a half hours were run at high speed, and the half hour before lunch and the half hour after lunch were run at low speed. The rest of the afternoon was run at high speed with the exception of the last 45 minutes of the shift, which was run at medium.

The constant speed at which the engineers had originally set the belt was actually slightly below the "medium" mark on the control dial; the average speed at which the painters were running the belt was on the high side of the dial. Few, if any, empty hooks entered the oven, and inspection showed no increase of rejects from the paint room.

Production increased, and within three weeks (some two months before the scheduled ending of the learning bonus) the painters were operating at 30 to 50 percent above the level that had been expected under the original arrangement. Naturally, their earnings were correspondingly higher than anticipated. They were collecting their base pay, earning a considerable piece-rate bonus, and still benefiting from the learning bonus. They were earning more now than many skilled workers in other parts of the plant.

OUR VIEWPOINT

The supervisor's meeting with the painters appears to have been worthwhile. Productivity is up, satisfaction is up, and, for the individual painters, earnings are up. These three results suggest an ideal work situation in which individuals perform at high production levels, are satisfied, and are well rewarded.

QUESTIONS

1. How do you feel about the situation at this point?
2. Suppose that you were the supervisor. What would you expect to happen next? Why?

CONTINUING ON   Management was besieged by demands that the inequity between the earnings of the painters and those of other workers in the plant be taken care of. With growing irritation between the superintendent and the supervisor, the engineers and supervisor, and the superintendent and engineers, the situation came to a head when the superintendent revoked the learning bonus and returned the painting operation to its original status: the hooks moved again at their constant, time-studied, designated speed. Production dropped again and within a month all but two of the eight painters had quit. The supervisor stayed on for several months, but, feeling aggrieved, left for another job.

OUR VIEWPOINT

It seems that a manager's job is never done! Do you remember Chapter 1, when we discussed how managers spend their time? They spend a lot of it *outside* of the work unit, and they do so for a purpose—to gain support for the unit within the larger context of the total organization. The Hovey and Beard case is a good example of how the rest of the organization interfered with what seemed to be a very satisfied and productive work unit. Perhaps this interference could have been prevented through astute managerial action. The fact that it did occur reinforces the manager's need to be very aware of the total organization as a work setting.

SUMMARY

There are numerous issues in the Hovey and Beard Company case that highlight the challenges of managing individuals as human resources of organizations. The four chapters in Part Two of this book will give you many insights into how to deal with these challenges. Specifically, you may look forward to studying about individual attributes, motivation theories, rewards, learning, reinforcement principles, job designs, goals, and work schedules, among other related topics. As you

move through these chapters, you will find an increasing emphasis on applications that can help you to become a better manager of individuals as human resources of organizations.

---

[1]Abridged and adapted from Chapter 10, Group Dynamics and Intergroup Relations, by George Strauss and Alex Bavelas (under the title "The Hovey and Beard Case"). From *Money and Motivation,* edited by William F. Whyte. Copyright © 1955 by Harper & Row, Publishers, Inc.

CHAPTER 3
BASIC ATTRIBUTES
OF INDIVIDUALS

The nation is best served by holding no one back. Let us use our resources—technological and human—to the fullest.

Nynex
Annual
Report

PERSONALITY TESTS ARE BACK

A sign on the desk of an accountant at a Dallas computer firm reads *"ESFJ Spoken Here."* Another sign on the controller's desk states that he speaks *"ISTJ."* What's at issue is a theory that suggests people with different ways of perceiving the world and making decisions have a hard time working together. To the extent they become more aware of their and others' personalities, the theory says, interpersonal communication and work performance can be improved. And that's just what a growing number of counselors and management trainers are trying to achieve at the computer firm and other companies like AT&T, Apple, Exxon, GE, and many more.[1]

The theory is based on combinations of personality traits first identified by the Swiss Psychologist Carl Jung, and later refined and popularized by Katherine Briggs and Isabel Briggs Myers, an American mother–daughter team. An instrument called the Myers–Briggs Type Indicator identifies a persons tendencies toward being extroverted or introverted (E or I), sensing or intuitive (S or N), thinking or feeling (T or F), and perceiving or judging (P or J). Someone who is extroverted focuses outwardly on other people and things; the introvert focuses on inner feelings and ideas. Sensing types like detail, while intuitive types look for the big picture. Thinkers want to make logical decisions; feelers make more subjective ones. Perceiving types are flexible, while judging types want to get things done.

Type theorists classify people into different combinations of these traits. The *ESFJ* accountant, for example, is expected to be warm-hearted, talkative, conscientious, and cooperative, while also needing harmony and working best with encouragement. Her *ISTJ* boss, on the other hand, is expected to be serious, quiet, practical, orderly, logical, realistic, and dependable, while believing success is earned by concentration and thoroughness.

When applied in management development programs, the theory is supposed to help participants better understand their personalities and how they relate to other people who may see things quite differently. David Carpenter, chief executive of Transamerica's Occidental Life Insurance Co., says, "We've used the theory to help us change our corporate culture; it has turned out to be one of the most meaningful things we have done."

Skeptics worry that people become stereotyped by the process and complain that the theory is just another "fad" using yet another set of "labels" to oversimplify the nature of human behavior at work. Proponents say the Myers–Briggs Type Indicator should only be used to improve someone's self awareness and must always be kept in perspective. In the midst of it all, use of the test continues to grow . . . and the corporate community is the biggest consumer of all.

Management Applications Questions

How do personality characteristics and other personal attributes affect people's work performance and job satisfaction? What can a manager do about them?

The reading and other learning experiences in this chapter will familiarize you with the following topics.

The Individual Performance Equation
Demographic Differences among Individuals
Competency Differences among Individuals
Values and Attitudes
Personality
Managing Individual Differences

People are different! Accordingly, it is important for you to stop and ask how individual differences may influence performance and satisfactions at work. Specifically, what things must a manager be concerned about when attempting to influence individual performance? This question introduces the concerns addressed in this chapter. Our discussion begins with an individual performance equation that identifies major influences on job performance. The rest of the chapter looks in some detail at each component of the equation and gives special attention to several of the more talked about basic attributes of individuals.

THE INDIVIDUAL PERFORMANCE EQUATION

The individual performance equation is

$$\text{Performance} = \frac{\text{individual}}{\text{attributes}} \times \frac{\text{work}}{\text{effort}} \times \frac{\text{organizational}}{\text{support}}$$

This equation views performance to be the result of the personal attributes of individuals, the work efforts they put forth, and the organizational support that they receive. The multiplication signs indicate that all three factors must be present for high performance to be achieved. This means that each factor should be maximized for each person in a work setting if the desired levels of accomplishment are to be realized. Every manager should understand how these three factors, acting alone and in combination, can affect performance results.

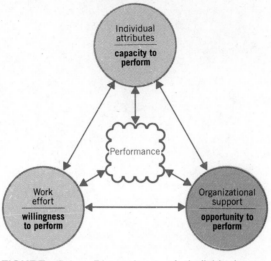

FIGURE 3.1 Dimensions of individual performance factors.

As shown in Figure 3.1, it helps to recognize that[2]

- Individual attributes relate to a *capacity* to perform.
- Work effort relates to a *willingness* to perform
- Organizational support relates to the *opportunity* to perform.

Individual Attributes

Three broad categories of attributes create individual differences relevant to our study of OB: demographic characteristics (age, for example), competency characteristics (i.e., aptitude/ability), and psychological characteristics (e.g., values, attitudes, and personality). These characteristics are the major topics of study in this chapter. Each has the potential to influence performance by its impact on a person's capability to accomplish assigned tasks. Of course, the importance of the various attributes depends on the nature of a job and its task requirements. Managerially speaking:

$$\text{Individual attributes} \xrightarrow[\text{match}]{\text{must}} \text{task requirements} \xrightarrow[\text{facilitate}]{\text{to}} \text{job performance}$$

Work Effort

Suppose that a manager has a subordinate whose individual characteristics fit the task requirements as closely as possible. Can we predict that the individual will be a high performer? The answer is ''no,'' and the reason traces to the important variable we call work effort.

To achieve high levels of performance, even people with the right individual attributes must have the willingness to perform; that is, they must put forth adequate work effort. Consider the college classroom. In your present course, for example, the chances are that the actual abilities, ages, and social backgrounds of you and your colleagues are quite similar. Does that mean that your instructor can expect the same level of performance from everyone? "Certainly not," is our reply, and the typical end of the course grade distribution supports our position. But why, as you look around the class, does performance vary when the individual characteristics of students are pretty much the same? Part of the answer rests with effort. Some students work harder at their learning tasks than do others.

Instead of using the term "effort," your response to our question may have been different. Perhaps you said, "performance will vary because some students are more motivated than others." **Motivation to work** is a term used in OB to describe the forces within a individual that account for the level, direction, and persistence of *effort* expended at work. A highly motivated person works hard. But, notice that this definition links motivation to work effort, not to performance results. The distinction is important. Motivation predicts effort. Effort combines with individual attributes and organizational support to predict performance.

The concept of motivation is a most significant addition to our study of individual work performance. Earlier, we described people who had the requisite individual attributes to perform but did not put forth the effort required to achieve high-performance results. They were not motivated to do so. The converse is just as real. Some people are very motivated, meaning they work very hard, but still do not achieve high levels of performance. The performance equation suggests this might occur because of a lack of fit between individual attributes and task requirements, or inadequate organizational support, or both.

Managers must develop good ways of positively influencing other people's motivations to work. Willingness to exert effort is an individual prerogative. A manager cannot do someone else's work. This is the essence of the manager's challenge—being held accountable for work that someone else has to do. As a manager therefore, you should be very interested in understanding individual motivation. Chapters 4, 5, and 6 offer many insights in this regard.

Organizational Support

The third component of the individual performance equation is support from the organization. Even the person whose individual characteristics satisfy job requirements and who is highly motivated to exert work effort may not be a good performer because of inadequate support in the workplace. OB researchers refer to such inadequacies as **situational constraints** and include among them[3]

- Lack of time.
- Inadequate budgets.
- Inadequate tools, equipment, supplies.
- Unclear instructions, job-related information.

- Unfair levels of expected performance.
- Lack of job-related authority.
- Lack of required services and help from others.
- Inflexibility of procedures.

You have probably experienced how a lack of organizational support can intrude on work performance. Having to rush a job because of a short deadline, not having the best tools, or not receiving clear instructions are common examples. In fact, you might argue that such failures of support are often found in the college classroom. They can include unrealistic due dates for assignments, inability to get library reference material, and not getting a clear statement of what the instructor is looking for in the first place.

All such problems share a common theme. They direct a manager's attention to the question, "How well is the motivated and capable individual supported as he or she seeks to perform assigned tasks?" They challenge all managers to ensure that organizational support for performance exists in their areas of supervisory responsibility. Chapter 6 will examine such support in terms of alternative job designs and work schedules. In Part Three we discuss how the work group can provide or withhold support for individual task performance and similarly influence human resource maintenance. Part Four deals with organizational size, structure, and technology, all of which are additional sources of support. Finally, Part Five includes a treatment of leadership and other interpersonal processes that, when provided by the manager and other key persons in the work setting, become additional and very significant support mechanisms.

A Manager's Viewpoint on Work Performance

Table 3.1 summarizes the action implications associated with each major variable in the individual performance equation. To ensure the presence of capable people, a manager must do a good job of recruiting, selecting, and training subordinates. Motivating workers to put forth maximum effort is accomplished by creating enthusiasm and through a good allocation of rewards. Proper planning, organizing, leading, and controlling the affairs of the workplace are ways of ensuring necessary support.

The remainder of this chapter reviews three sets of individual differences—demographic, competency, and psychological characteristics. The discussion can help you better understand the individualities of people at work and also recognize their managerial implications.

DEMOGRAPHIC DIFFERENCES AMONG INDIVIDUALS

Demographic characteristics are background variables that help shape what a person has become. Some are current, such as a person's socioeconomic status; others are

TABLE 3.1   **Management Implications for Variables in the Individual Performance Equation**

Variable	Key Factors	Managerial Implications
Individual attributes	Demographic, competency, and psychological characteristics	Increase *capacity* to perform by doing a good job of recruiting, selecting, and training employees
Work effort	Motivation to work	Increase *willingness* to perform by creating enthusiasm and doing a good job of allocating work-related rewards
Organizational support	Resources, tools, technology, organization structure, job designs, and task goals	Increase *opportunity* to perform by doing a good job of planning, organizing, leading, and controlling affairs of the workplace

historical, such as where and how many places a person lived while growing up, size of family, family socioeconomic status, and the like.

Two such characteristics of considerable significance in the workplace are age and sex. As Newsline 3.1 shows, the profile of the U.S. labor force is changing significantly. The proportion of men in the civilian labor force is on the decline, while the proportion of women is increasing. There is also an ''aging'' of the population overall, with proportionately more people falling into the 65 and over category.

These two demographic variables are often the source of inappropriate generalizations and decision-making by managers. The following actual headlines from items in *The Wall Street Journal* give you a feel for the issues.

> Younger Employees Appear to Have Much Less Need
>   to Lead or Succeed
> A Man among Women Often Makes More Money

You, too, may be party to mistaken general impressions. How often have you commented, for example, that ''women are so emotional,'' ''men are so cold and insensitive,'' or ''older people just aren't creative?''

The point of these illustrations is simply that managers who fall prey to such misperceptions are losing sight of individual differences among people. As a result, they tend to make erroneous decisions in their daily dealings with them. Someone who believes older people aren't creative may mistakenly decide not to assign a very creative 60-year-old person to an important task force; someone who believes women are too emotional to make good managers may fail to hire a very capable woman for a supervisory job. In fact, this problem is so serious that the U.S. government has enacted Equal Employment Opportunity legislation to protect people from such un-

NEWSLINE 3.1 /
WHAT'S AHEAD FOR THE LABOR FORCE?

A growing proportion of work in America is done by women. By 1995 more than 60 percent of all women of working age will be employed. Many of these will be married women with children. Families with the husband as sole wage earner are now in the minority among married couples.

The average age of the workforce is increasing with the number of persons aged 65 or older also on the rise. By 2025 up to 50 percent of the U.S. federal budget may be needed to support the elderly. New laws protect the elderly and ban mandatory retirement in many occupations.

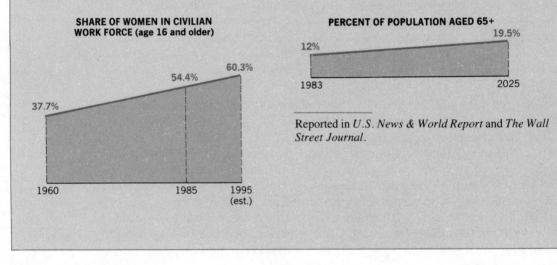

SHARE OF WOMEN IN CIVILIAN WORK FORCE (age 16 and older)

37.7%   54.4%   60.3%

1960   1985   1995 (est.)

PERCENT OF POPULATION AGED 65+

12%   19.5%

1983   2025

Reported in *U.S. News & World Report* and *The Wall Street Journal*.

founded discrimination in their work. It prohibits employment discrimination on the basis of such things as race, sex, age, or religion.

Male–female differences, in particular, remain a timely and much talked about issue. Yet, there are far fewer performance-relevant differences between the sexes than many people think. For example, researchers find no consistent male–female differences in sociability, suggestibility, self-esteem, learning ability, and analytical skills. There are also no differences in vocational interests, leadership and problem-solving capabilities, cooperation, competition, motivation, or job satisfaction.

Demographic factors can be used to broadly classify differences among people. However, these factors should be assessed very carefully and always with an awareness of the more specific characteristics they represent. More on these and related issues is found in the discussion of stereotypes and other perceptual distortions in

Chapter 13. For now, we can say that even if certain generalizations about differences between men and women, younger and older people, and the like should ever be proven to hold up, it must still be recognized that they will not describe the specific performance potential in any one situation for any one individual. The essential managerial issue frequently becomes more a question of "competency" than "demography."

COMPETENCY DIFFERENCES AMONG INDIVIDUALS

Competency is central to the aptitude and ability characteristics so important to individuals at work. **Aptitude** represents the capability to learn something. **Ability** reflects an existing capacity to perform the various tasks needed for a given job.[4] Aptitudes, in fact, are potential abilities. Abilities are skills that an individual already possesses.

Competency is an important consideration when a manager is initially hiring or selecting individuals to do a job. Once people with the appropriate aptitudes or abilities have been selected, then on-the-job and continuing education or training activities can be used to develop or enhance the required job skills. These are important investments in the human resources of an organization or work unit, since competency is a motivational force that can stimulate work efforts. Psychologists call this the **effectance motive** and relate its impact to the sense of mastery it gives a person over the environment.[5] People who feel competent in their work can be expected to work harder at it. In this sense, competency becomes an internal force that stimulates and encourages people to work hard. Both mental and physical competencies are at issue here.[6]

Each of us is acquainted with various tests used to measure mental aptitudes and abilities. Some provide an overall "IQ" score (e.g., the Stanford–Binet IQ test). Others provide measures of more specific competencies required of people entering various educational programs or career fields. Surely you have taken the ACT or SAT college entrance tests. Perhaps you plan to take a test for graduate study in law, medicine, or management. All such tests seek to measure mental aptitude or ability and thereby facilitate the screening and selection of applicants. Of course, there is controversy over the validity of such tests and the significance accorded to test score trends over time. The same holds true for college grades and class rank, which are often used by potential employers as indicators of a person's mental competencies and performance potential.

Table 3.2 presents sample mental and physical or motor competencies recognized by industrial psychologists for their job relevance. It is important to remember that this relevancy varies from job to job and it should always be confirmed before becoming a part of the selection process. A manager should always know the exact requirements of jobs to be done and be able to clearly document why particular competencies are essential to master them. An important social issue in this regard relates to the hiring of handicapped workers. Such people deserve full respect for their

TABLE 3.2   Sample Mental and Motor Competencies Used in the Job Recruitment and Selection Processes

	Description	Example
Mental Competencies		
Numerical ability	To be speedy and accurate in arithmetic computations such as adding, subtracting, multiplying, dividing	Making change at a cash register
Verbal comprehension	To understand the meanings of words and comprehend readily what is read or heard	Understanding and answering customer inquiries
Inductive reasoning	To be able to discover a principle and apply it in solving a problem	Determining what is wrong when a machine fails to function
Motor Competencies		
Response orientation	To make correct and accurate movements in relation to a stimulus under highly speeded conditions	Flicking a switch to halt a machine when a warning horn sounds
Manual dexterity	To make skillful arm and hand movements in handling objects under speeded conditions	Adding parts to items moving rapidly on an assembly line
Finger dexterity	To manipulate skillfully small objects with the fingers	Screwing a nut on a small bolt in a tight space

Source: Summarized from a discussion in Marvin D. Dunnette, ed., *Handbook of Industrial and Organizational Psychology* (Chicago: Rand McNally, 1976), pp. 473–520.

competencies and should not be denied jobs for which their skills and capabilities are appropriate.[7] The key is to focus on what people can do and determine whether or not that provides a good match with job requirements.

VALUES AND ATTITUDES

The third category of individual attributes in which we are interested is **psychological characteristics.** While there is a wide range of these characteristics, they share a common tendency to predispose an individual to behave in predictable ways. These predispositions can have a substantial influence on behavior. Extroverted salespersons, for example, are likely to see things differently from introverts and to be seen differently by others. These differences will influence their behavior and perhaps the sales they are able to generate. Our treatment of psychological differences looks first at values and attitudes, and then at personality.

Values

The noted psychologist Milton Rokeach defines **values** as global beliefs that guide actions and judgments across a variety of situations.[8] The study of values has an important place in OB because values are individual attributes than can affect such things as the attitudes, perceptions, needs, and motivations of people at work.

Sources and Types of Values

Parents, friends, teachers, and external reference groups can all influence individual values. Indeed, a person's values develop as a product of learning and experience in the cultural setting in which he or she lives. As learning and experiences vary from one person to the next, value differences are the inevitable result.

Rokeach classifies values into two broad categories. **Terminal values** reflect a person's beliefs about "ends" to be achieved; **instrumental values** reflect beliefs about the "means" for achieving desired ends. Among the values Rokeach places in each category are

Terminal Values ("ends")	Instrumental Values ("means")
• Comfortable life	• Ambition
• Sense of accomplishment	• Courage
• Family security	• Honesty
• Mature love	• Helpfulness
• Self-respect	• Independence
• Wisdom	• Imagination

Another classification of human values was developed in the early 1930s by Psychologist Gordon Allport and his associates. They categorized values into six major types.[9]

1. *Theoretical*.   Interest in the discovery of truth through reasoning and systematic thinking.
2. *Economic*.   Interest in usefulness and practicality, including the accumulation of wealth.
3. *Aesthetic*.   Interest in beauty, form, and artistic harmony.
4. *Social*.   Interest in people and love as a human relationship.
5. *Political*.   Interest in gaining power and influencing other people.
6. *Religious*.   Interest in unity and understanding the cosmos as a whole.

Patterns and Trends in Values

Values are important to managers and the field of OB because of their potential to influence behavior in the workplace. When values differ among people, conflicts over such things as goals and the means to achieve them is a likely result. Take a professional like Hank here, as a case in point.[10]

Jim, the marketing manager, approaches Hank, the engineering project leader. "Hey Hank. When can we get this model ready for display? You know that sales convention is coming up in two weeks and Jane claims that if we don't show, the competition is really going to close in.''

"Sorry Jim," Hank explains. "We're just not satisfied with the speed of this computer. We need at least six weeks; before that there is just no way. My people won't tolerate getting it out earlier if it's not perfect. They've worked too hard to do that.''

"O.K. Hank," Jim continues. "How about just a prototype for people to look at with a promise of the increased speed to come later?''

"Forget it, Jim," Hank insists. "Engineers don't work that way. You can't just promise, you have to deliver. Besides, sending the prototype would be dishonest. Tell Jane to come down here and I'll explain it to her.''

This real situation illustrates the potential for conflict between salaried professionals—such as engineers and scientists, who have chosen to practice their crafts within organizations—and their managers. The professional is apt to view things from an independent and technical perspective, as did Hank, whereas the generalist manager is likely to view things from a more conforming enterprise perspective, as did Jim. Things are further complicated in this case because Hank grew up and went to college in the U.S. during the "60's generation," a group identified with the following four cultural values that contrast at times with the realities of organizational life.

- *Defiance of authority.* A willingness to challenge the status quo, to exercise self-control, and to reject imposed structure and authority.
- *Participation in decision making.* A willingness and desire to get involved, exercise individual autonomy, be responsible, and use one's competencies.
- *Service.* A willingness to serve society by advancing the quality of life and to demand personal treatment and a high quality of life inside an organization.
- *Social justice.* A willingness to set aside "careerism" per se and seek the "right" and socially responsible things in one's work, not just the easy ones.

Another interesting perspective on values is offered by Geert Hofstede who has studied how work-related values vary across national cultures.[11] In research on personnel from a large multinational corporation operating in 40 countries, he concludes that cross-cultural variations on the following four value dimensions can have significant managerial implications.

1. *Power distance.* The degree to which a society accepts a hierarchical or unequal distribution of power in organizations.
   Example: U.S. managers reflected a moderate tolerance of unequal power distribution; those from Singapore and Hong Kong showed more tolerance.
2. *Uncertainty avoidance.* The degree to which a society perceives ambiguous and uncertain situations as threatening and as things to be avoided.
   Example: U.S. managers reflected above-average tolerance for uncertainty; those from France and Italy showed a greater tendency toward uncertainty avoidance.

3. *Individualism–collectivism*. The degree to which a society focuses on individuals or groups as resources for work and social problem solving.

    Example: The United States ranked as the most individualistic country in the sample; Columbia and Venezuela ranked among the least individualistic.

4. *Masculinity*. The degree to which a society emphasizes such stereotyped ''masculine'' traits as assertiveness, independence, and insensitivity to feelings as dominant values.

    Example: The United States ranked as generally strong on ''masculine'' values; Sweden and Norway fell substantially to the other extreme.

A final example of applied research on values relates to trends that are observed over time. Daniel Yankelovich, for example, is known for his informative public opinion polls.[12] Among American workers, he notes trends away from valuing economic incentives, organizational loyalty, and work-related identity and sees trends toward valuing meaningful work, pursuit of leisure, and personal identity and self-fulfillment. Yankelovich beieves that the modern manager must be able to recognize value differences and trends among people at work. He reports, for example, finding higher productivity among younger workers employed in jobs that match their values and/or who are supervised by managers who share their values.

Values and the ''Corporate Culture''

One theme shared by recent best selling books about management (*In Search of Excellence* and *Corporate Cultures* to name but two) is emphasis on the role of *shared* values in creating a climate for success. **Corporate culture** is a term used to describe systems of shared values (what is important) and beliefs (how things work) that create behavioral norms (the way we do things around here) to guide the activities of organization members. The popular argument found in the best-sellers is that strong corporate cultures facilitate high performance. Thomas J. Peters and Robert H. Waterman, Jr., authors of *In Search of Excellence* state, for example: ''Every excellent company we studied is clear on what it stands for, and takes the process of value shaping seriously.''[13]

As a system of shared values, the corporate culture reflects a climate within which people value the same things and apply these values to benefit the corporation as a whole. One example is the dominant value of customer service at IBM. This value helps keep everyone from top management down to persons on the factory floor pulling in the same direction. Other examples are found in corporate slogans or creeds such as

General Electric: ''Progress is our most important product''
Delta Airlines: ''The Family Feeling''
Sears: ''Quality at a good price''

The strength of such slogans in communicating values lies in the basic premise that values can influence behavior. To the extent employees understand and share values such as those reflected in the slogans, their behavior should be more uniform and consistent. Performance of individuals, groups and the organization as a whole should benefit as a result. Research shows that managers who sense a compatibility between their personal values and those of the organization experience feelings of success in their lives, show high regard for organizational objectives and significant stakeholders, and have a healthy assessment of the values and ethics of their colleagues, subordinates, and bosses.[14]

The concept of "corporate culture" and its companion notion of shared values is important in the field of OB. Researchers recognize that organizations develop different cultures, that these cultures have different performance implications, and that they can be changed.[15] *Strong* cultures that fit the needs and challenges of the situation are "in," whereas *weak* or poorly matched cultures are "out." The case of AT&T, the telecommunications giant, is a good example. For many years the company operated as a regulated monopoly and created what many observers felt was the best phone system in the world. All this was achieved in a highly structured corporate culture where "universal service at reasonable cost" was the predominate value. Things are different for AT&T today. The culture is changing, albeit slowly, as the company trys to instill in itself the new sense of innovation and competition that is necessary to prosper in a deregulated environment.

Attitudes

Attitudes constitute another psychological attribute of individuals. Formally defined, an **attitude** is a predisposition to respond in a positive or negative way to someone or something in one's environment. When you say, for example, that you "like" or "dislike" someone or something, an attitude is being expressed. One important work-related attitude we previously discussed in Chapter 2 is job satisfaction. This attitude expresses someone's positive or negative feelings about various aspects of their job and/or work environment.

Components of Attitudes

It is useful to classify three primary components of an attitude. These are[16]

1. *Cognitive component.*   Beliefs and values representing information and observations regarding the object of a person's attention. These are antecedent conditions to the actual attitude itself.
2. *Affective component.*   A specific feeling regarding the personal impact of the antecedent conditions. This is the actual attitude in respect to the object of attention.
3. *Behavioral component.*   An intention to behave in a certain way in response to the feelings. This is a result of the attitude; it is a predisposition to act in a specific way.

Figuratively speaking, the components of attitudes systematically relate to one another in the following way:

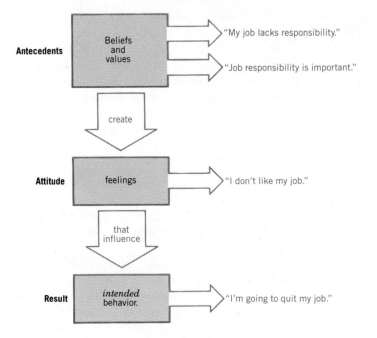

FIGURE 3.2 A work-related example of the three components of attitudes.

$$\text{Beliefs and values} \xrightarrow{\text{create}} \text{attitudes} \xrightarrow[\text{predispose}]{\text{that}} \text{behavior}$$

Thus, another way to view an attitude is as a variable that intervenes between beliefs and values as antecedent conditions, on the one hand, and intended behavior that is a result, on the other. Figure 3.2 presents this logic in the context of a work-related example.

Attitudes and Behavior

Look again at Figure 3.2. It is essential to recognize that the link between attitudes and behavior is tentative. An attitude results in *intended* behavior. This intention may or may not be carried out in any given circumstance. Take a person with a favorable attitude toward labor unions. Other things being equal, this attitude would predict such intentions as saying nice things about labor unions and buying union-made products. Practically speaking, however, other factors in a given situation may override the intentions. Hearing a good friend say negative things about a union, for example, may lead to the suppression of the tendency to say something nice about them in the same conversation. The person's favorable attitude in this case, has not changed, but its associated intention to behave was not carried out.

Even though attitudes do not always predict behavior, the link between attitudes and potential or intended behavior is important for managers. Think about your work experiences and/or conversations with other people about their work. It is not uncommon to hear concerns expressed about someone's "bad attitude." These concerns are expressed for a reason, and that reason is usually displeasure with the behavioral consequences with which the poor attitude is associated. In Chapter 2, we noted that unfavorable attitudes in the form of job dissatisfaction can result in costly labor turnover. They may also result in absenteeism, tardiness, low productivity, and even impaired physical or mental health. One of a manager's responsibilities, therefore, is to recognize attitudes and understand both their antecedents and potential implications.

Attitudes and Attributions

Thus, we are reminded once again that an attitude is a hypothetical construct. One never sees, touches, and/or actually isolates an attitude. What actually happens is that attitudes are *inferred* from things people say and do. To this effect, we often "attribute" the reasons for things happening the way they do to the presence of certain attitudes held by the people involved.

Attribution theory is a specific attempt to (1) understand the cause of a certain event, (2) assess responsibility for outcomes of the event, and (3) assess the personal qualities of people involved in an event.[17] These attempts frequently involve the inference of attitudes that seem to explain the event or things in question. From the manager's perspective, a subordinate's behavior may be observed (e.g., increased absenteeism) and an attempt made to explain it based on the person's attitude (e.g., job dissatisfaction). The problem is that the attribution of the attitude may or may not be accurate. Accordingly, the manager's response to the situation may or may not be correct.

We will encounter other applications of attribution theory in later discussions of motivation, group dynamics, and various approaches to leadership. We will also discuss the concept itself in further detail along with our treatment of perception in Chapter 13.

Attitudes and Cognitive Consistency

One additional avenue of research on attitudes is interest in cognitive consistency, that is, in the consistency between a person's expressed attitudes and his or her actual behavior. Let us go back to the example in Figure 3.2. The person in this illustration has an unfavorable attitude toward a job. She knows and recognizes this fact. Now assume that her intentions to quit are not fulfilled and she continues to work at the same job day-in and day-out. The result is an inconsistency between the attitude (job dissatisfaction) and the behavior (continuing to work at the job).

Leon Festinger, a noted social psychologist, uses the term **cognitive dissonance** to describe a state of inconsistency between an individual's attitudes and behavior.[18] He predicts that the discomfort experienced by someone experiencing such an inconsistency results in a desire to reduce or eliminate it. This is achieved by changing the underlying attitude, changing future behavior, and/or developing new ways of explaining or rationalizing the inconsistency.

Festinger's cognitive dissonance theory offers yet another perspective on attitudes as special attributes of people at work. Among the work-related implications of the theory are

1. A recognition that behavior may influence attitudes, as well as that attitudes may influence behavior.

   Work example: a person who actually tries a new task and likes it may change a previously held negative attitude toward the task.

2. A recognition that attitudes may develop consistent with a person's initial emotional response to a new person or object.

   Work example: a person who has a quick negative reaction to the unshaven appearance of a new co-worker may develop the attitude that the person is untrustworthy.

PERSONALITY

The preceding discussion of values and attitudes provides an initial look at the special psychological characteristics of individuals. Now, we will add one more dimension to this set of individual difference factors: personality. A frequently heard term, **personality** is specifically used to represent the overall profile or combination of traits that characterize the unique nature of a person. Think about it. You regularly refer to the "personalities" of other persons. A friend may be viewed as "introverted"; a boss may be seen as very "Machiavellian"; you may see yourself as a "compulsive" worker.

Each of these labels leaves a particular impression of the person being talked about. And, just as with values and attitudes, such attempts to classify personalities are significant to OB because of the expectation that personality may influence behavior in certain predictable ways. It follows that a knowledge of personality as an individual difference factor can help managers understand, predict, and even influence the behaviors of other people.

Personality Theories and Personality Development

Within the field of OB, it is recognized that a good understanding of personalities can help in understanding behavior in organizations—whether that behavior is individual, interpersonal, group, or organizational.[19] Among the "theories" of personality are

- *Psychoanalytic theory.* Based on the work of Sigmund Freud and Carl Jung, emphasizing the contributions of the "unconscious" as a component of personality.

- *Trait theory*. Popularized by Gordon Allport and Raymond Cattell, using observable traits such as values, abilities, and temperament to describe personalities.
- *Humanistic theory*. Represented in the work of Abraham Maslow and Carl Rogers, emphasizing the importance of individual growth, improvement, and the self-concept to personality.
- *Social learning theory*. Well described by Albert Bandura, recognizing the importance to personality of learning from other people and person–situation interactions.

In addition to using these theories of personality, scholars also study personality development and its implications. One approach is to view an individual's personality as developing in a series of "stages" over time. Freud, for example, viewed the important stages as a progression of one's psycho*sexual* development; Erik Erikson, a child psychologist, viewed them as a progression of psycho*social* development. Two other developmental perspectives with more direct managerial implications follow.

Figure 3.3 shows various stages in the adult life cycle. This age-based view of personality development is described by Daniel Levinson.[20] It includes four key transitions—age-30, mid-life, age-50, and late adult—that may have significant impact on a person's relationship with their job, career, and employing organization. As we will further discuss in a section on careers in Chapter 18, people at various adult life stages may have different work needs and thus require quite different managerial responses. The interests of a single person taking his or her first job, for example, may be quite dissimilar to those of a married manager with a family and substantial personal responsibilities.

Another developmental view is offered by Chris Argyris, a management scholar who is concerned about possible conflicts between individuals and organizations.[21] He notes that people develop along a continuum of dimensions from immaturity to maturity. A person progresses during life

From Immaturity	To Maturity
• Passivity	• Activity
• Dependence	• Independence
• Limited behavior	• Diverse behavior
• Shallow interests	• Deep interests
• Short-time perspective	• Long-time perspective
• Subordinate position	• Superordinate position
• Little self-awareness	• Much self-awareness

Argyris believes the nature of the mature adult personality can sometimes be inconsistent with work opportunities. Organizations and their managers may neglect the "adult" sides of people. They may use close supervision and control more typically needed by "infants" whose personalities are still immature.

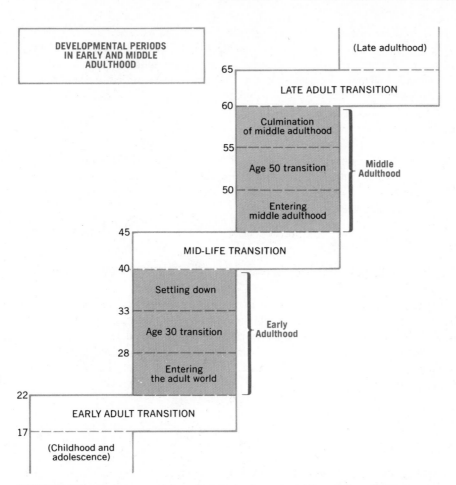

FIGURE 3.3 Developmental periods in early and middle adulthood. *Source:* From *The Seasons of a Man's Life,* by Daniel J. Levinson, et al., copyright © 1978 by Daniel J. Levinson. Reprinted by permission of Alfred A. Knopf, Inc.

What follows is an introduction to four dimensions of personality that have special relevance in work settings. These include locus of control, problem-solving style, Machiavellianism, and Type A–Type B behavior. As you read on, think about yourself as someone with a particular ''personality'' that may well affect what you do and how you respond to things that happen to you at work. Think, too, about the ''personalities'' of other persons and how these personality factors may influence their behavior and accomplishments in the work setting.

Locus of Control

Locus of control measures the internal–external orientation of a person, that is, the extent to which a person feels able to affect his or her life.[22] People have general conceptions about whether events are controlled primarily by themselves, which indicates an internal orientation, or by outside forces, characteristic of an external orientation. "Internals," or persons with an internal locus of control, believe they control their own fate or destiny. "Externals," or persons with an external locus of control, believe that much of what happens to them is uncontrolled and determined by outside forces.

Consider these items from a much longer questionnaire that has been used to separate internals from externals.

1. a. Many of the unhappy things in people's lives are partly due to bad luck.
   b. People's misfortunes result from the mistakes they make.
2. a. As far as world affairs are concerned, most of us are the victims of forces we can neither understand nor control.
   b. By taking an active part in political and social affairs, the people can control world events.

Answers 1a and 2a reflect an external orientation; 1b and 2b show an internal orientation.

In general, externals are more extroverted in interpersonal relationships and oriented toward the world of people and things around them. Internals are more introverted and oriented toward their inner world of feelings and ideas. Other ways in which externals and internals have been found to differ are summarized in Table 3.3. As you look at the table, ask yourself how these differences might be of importance in various jobs that people may hold.

Problem-solving Style

Another personality characteristic is **problem-solving style,** the way in which a person goes about gathering and evaluating information in solving problems and making

TABLE 3.3 Some Ways in Which Internals Differ from Externals	
Information processing	Internals make more attempts to acquire information, are less satisfied with the amount of information they possess, and are better at utilizing information.
Job satisfaction	Internals are generally more satisfied, less alienated, and less rootless.
Self-control and risk	Internals exhibit greater self-control, are more cautious, engage in less risky behavior.
Expectancies and results	Internals see stronger relationship between what they do and what happens to them, expect working hard leads to good performance, feel more control over their time.
Response to others	Internals are more independent, more reliant on their own judgment, and less susceptible to the influence of others; they are more likely to accept information on its merit.

decisions. In this process, information gathering and evaluation are separate activities. Information gathering involves getting and organizing data for use. Styles of information gathering vary from sensation to intuitive. Sensation-type individuals prefer routine and order, and emphasize well-defined details in gathering information. Intuitive-type people prefer the big picture, like solving new problems, and dislike routine.

Evaluation involves making judgments about how to deal with information once it has been collected. Styles of information evaluation vary from an emphasis on feeling to an emphasis on thinking. Feeling-type individuals are oriented toward conformity and try to accommodate themselves to other people. They try to avoid problems that might result in disagreements. Thinking-type people use reason and intellect to deal with problems. They downplay emotional aspects in the problem situation.

When these two dimensions of information gathering and evaluation are combined, the matrix of problem-solving styles shown in Table 3.4 results. The table contains descriptions of four basic problem-solving styles: sensation–feeling (SF), intuitive–feeling (IF), sensation–thinking (ST), and intuitive–thinking (IT).

These styles were first introduced in the chapter opener, which illustrated how the Myers–Briggs Type Indicator instrument for measuring these aspects of personality is being used in management development. The table also suggests some occupational pairings based upon research in this area also using the Myers-Briggs approach. This summary may give added insight into your predispositions toward problem-solving and their potential career implications.[23] The basic point is that some styles may be

---

TABLE 3.4   Four Problem-Solving Styles and Their Occupational Match-ups

Sensation–Thinking: decisive, dependable, applied thinker, sensitive to details	**Sensation–Feeling:** pragmatic, analytical, methodical, and conscientious
Accounting	Direct supervision
Production	Counseling
Computer programming	Negotiating
Market research	Selling
Engineering	Interviewing
Intuitive–Thinking: creative, progressive, perceptive thinker, with many ideas	**Intuitive–Feeling:** charismatic, participative, people oriented, and helpful
Systems design	Public relations
Systems analysis	Advertising
Law	Personnel
Middle/top management	Politics
Teaching business, economics	Customer services

Source: Developed in part from Don Hellriegel, John W. Slocum, Jr., and Richard W. Woodman, *Organizational Behavior,* 4th ed. (St. Paul, Minn.: West P, 1986), pp. 126–134.

better suited to certain jobs than others. Given a fit between the problem-solving style and the information processing and evaluation requirements of a job, a person should be more productive and satisfied than when there is a lack of fit.

Machiavellianism

Niccolo Machiavelli! Why the very name itself evokes visions of a master of "guile," "deceit," and "opportunism" in interpersonal relations. This sixteenth-century author earned his place in history by writing a nobleman's guide to the acquisition and use of power—*The Prince*.[24] From its pages emerges the personality profile of a **Machiavellian,** someone who views and manipulates others for purely personal gain.

The subject of Machiavelli's book is manipulaton as the basic means of gaining and keeping control of others. Among his admonitions to the princes of his day were

"It is far better to be feared than loved if you cannot be both."

"Princes should delegate to others the enactment of unpopular measures and keep in their own hands the distribution of favors."

From just these two short examples it is easy to see why Machiavelli's ideas have been so avidly read *and* heavily criticized over the years.

Psychologists have developed a series of instruments (called Mach scales) to measure a person's Machiavellian orientation.[25] A *high-Mach* personality is someone with tendencies to behave in ways consistent with Machiavelli's basic principles.

Additional predispositions of the high-Mach personality are: tendencies to approach situations logically and thoughtfully; capability of lying to achieve personal goals; they are not easily swayed by loyalty, friendships, past promises, or the opinions of others; and they are skilled at influencing others.

Research using the Mach scales has led to a number of predictions regarding the way high and low Machs behave in various situations. A "cool" and "detached" high-Mach personality can be expected to take control and try to exploit loosely structured situations, but will perform in a perfunctory, even detached manner in highly structured situations. Low Machs tend to accept direction imposed by others in loosely structured situations, and to work hard to perform well in highly structured ones.

Type A and Type B Behavior

Let's switch gears for the moment and focus a bit more directly on *you*. Take the following quiz, and then read on.[26]

Personal Quiz. Circle the number that best characterizes you on each of the following pairs of characteristics.

| Casual about appointments | 1 2 3 4 5 6 7 8 | Never late |
| Not competitive | 1 2 3 4 5 6 7 8 | Very competitive |

Never feel rushed	1	2	3	4	5	6	7	8	Always feel rushed
Take one thing at a time	1	2	3	4	5	6	7	8	Try to do many things
Do things slowly	1	2	3	4	5	6	7	8	Do things fast
Express my feelings	1	2	3	4	5	6	7	8	Hold in my feelings
Many outside interests	1	2	3	4	5	6	7	8	Few outside interests

A fourth personality dimension that has attracted a lot of interest from medical and organizational researchers alike includes the Type A and Type B behavior profiles. **Type A behavior** is a personality profile characterized by impatience, desire for achievement, and perfectionism; **Type B behavior** is a profile of someone more easygoing and less competitive in relation to daily life events.[27]

The point of the quiz you just completed is really Type A/Type B behavior. Now score the quiz and determine how strong your orientation is toward Type A behavior. Total your points for the seven items in the quiz. Multiply this total by 3 to arrive at a final score. Use this total to locate your suggested personality profile on the following list.

Final Points	**Personality Type**
Below 90	B
90–99	B +
100–105	A −
106–119	A
120 or more	A +

Think about the accuracy of your Type A/Type B behavior profile and its implications—both in terms of your work and nonwork behaviors and your personal health. Type A personalities are prone to the behavior patterns listed in Table 3.5. For example, they tend to work fast on task performance, and in interpersonal relations they tend to be impatient, uncomfortable, irritable, and aggressive. Such tendencies indicate ''obsessive'' behavior, a fairly widespread—but not always helpful—trait of

---

TABLE 3.5 Characteristics of the Type A Personality

- Always moves, walks, and eats rapidly
- Feels impatient with the pace of things; hurries others, dislikes waiting
- Does several things at once
- Feels guilty when relaxing or doing nothing for several hours or days
- Tries to schedule more and more in less and less time
- Uses ''Type A'' nervous gestures (such as clenched fist, banging hand on table)
- Does not have time to enjoy life

Source: Based on Meyer Freidman and Ray Roseman, *Type A Behavior and Your Heart* (New York: Alfred A. Knopf, 1974).

many managers. These are hard-driving, detail-oriented people who have high-performance standards and thrive on routine. But when such work obsessions are carried to the extreme, they may lead to greater concerns for the details than the results, resistance to change, an over control of subordinates, and difficulties in interpersonal relationships. Persons with Type A personalities create a lot of stress for themselves in situations other persons find relatively stress free. This aspect of personality deserves serious thought. More on this issue and its important implications for behavior in organizations is discussed in Chapter 17 on change and stress.

MANAGING INDIVIDUAL DIFFERENCES

Newsline 3.2 illustrates once again the need to achieve a good fit between individual attributes and job requirements. This example of the importance of the "human factor" is especially timely given the rapid technological advancements taking place in today's workplace. Researchers report being able to predict as much as 30 to 50 percent of the variation in performance by individual attributes alone.[28] Achieving the desired "fit" between the person and the job, however, involves giving special managerial attention to individual differences in such things as employee communications, recruitment, selection, new employee orientation, training and development programs, and reward systems. Let's take the important case of values as one example. Among the things that can be done to help develop strong and desired values among organization members are[29]

- *Programs to clarify and communicate values*. In order for values to provide the "rules of the road" for employees, they must be stated, shared, and understood by everyone in an organization. Formal programs to clarify and communicate important values can help accomplish this objective.
- *Proper attention to employee recruitment, selection, and orientation*. The values of prospective employees should be examined and discussed, and the results used in making selection decisions. A person's first encounters with an organization and its members also "say" a lot about key beliefs and values. Every attempt should be made to expose new hires to the "correct" values and expectations, and to teach them "the way we do things here."
- *Appropriate training and development programs*. Any organization should offer a variety of training and development opportunities to establish and maintain the skills of members. Values can and should be emphasized along with other important individual attributes.
- *Progressive reward systems*. Rewards in the form of monetary compensation, employee benefits, and special recognition can reinforce individual values and maintain enthusiasm in support of organizational values. Creative managers can find many ways to reward people for displaying the values that are considered essential to organizational success.

These and other strategies can be used by managers to achieve the best continuing

NEWSLINE 3.2 /
TECHNOLOGY AND
THE HUMAN FACTOR

Success isn't automatic when mixing autos and automation in Detroit. The U.S. automobile industry has been spending billions on robots for welding and installing parts, laser systems for inspecting, and computer systems for integrating assembly operations. But even though these "factories of the future" are supposed to help the companies compete with their Japanese and other foreign rivals, the automakers admit they may have underestimated the importance of pairing technology and people. Today's complex technologies are running into problems with workers who don't have the skills to operate them. This "human factor" has delayed startups and caused production interruptions at General Motors where some 15 percent of hourly employees, up to 30 percent in some plants, can't read or write. Consider a job like inventory control. Workers used to simply check stock lists for whether the right type and quantity of items were on hand. At one of GM's highly automated plants, this is now done by computer and the workers must punch the right keys and log in several codes.

Although the big three automakers are spending millions on training, they also feel pressure to increase production quickly for payback on the investments. Japanese automakers use technology more selectively, start up production more slowly at new plants, and simultaneously train workers. GM has scaled back its automation timetable and revised plans for its state-of-the-art Saturn plant in Tennessee. CEO Roger Smith says that GM has concluded "technology alone can't get the job done."

Reported in *The Wall Street Journal*.

match between job demands and the personal attributes of the individuals who must master them. The specific individual differences covered in this chapter are illustrative rather than exhaustive. We have simply tried to familiarize you with some of the important ones and with the related issues. Remember, high-performance foundations are first established when a manager achieves a good match between the requirements of a job and the individual attributes of any person asked to do it.

SUMMARY

This chapter introduced the individual performance equation:

$$\text{Performance} = \frac{\text{individual}}{\text{attributes}} \times \frac{\text{work}}{\text{effort}} \times \frac{\text{organizational}}{\text{support}}$$

The equation focuses your attention on individual attributes, work effort, and organizational support as three important determinants of individual performance at work.

The study of motivation, defined as the forces within the individual that account for the level and direction of work effort, and organizational support were largely reserved for the coming chapters. The bulk of our discussion has dealt with individual attributes and how managers can take them into account in seeking to develop desirable work behaviors among their subordinates.

Three categories of basic individual attributes have been specified: demographic, competency, and psychological characteristics. Demographic characteristics include age and sex, among others. Our discussion emphasized how these factors may be incorrectly assumed to be a source of performance variations at work. Competency has been defined to include ability and aptitude factors. We have looked at mental characteristics and motor/physical competencies in this regard. Psychological characteristics include values, attitudes, and personality. Each of these is a major potential influence on individual behavior at work. Values are basic beliefs that guide actions and judgments in a variety of situations; attitudes are predispositions toward people and/or things in one's environment. Personality is the overall set or profile of characteristics and predispositions that make a person unique. Someone's stage of personality development as well as their personal traits in respect to locus of control, problem-solving style, Machiavellianism, and Type A/B behavior each have potential managerial implications.

The chapter concludes with a reminder that managers should use a knowledge of individual differences to obtain a proper fit between individuals and their jobs. Doing so is an important first step in managing individuals at work. Given this preliminary understanding, Chapter 4 next directs your attention to various motivation theories with managerial implications for work effort, as a second key variable in the individual performance equation.

THINKING THROUGH THE ISSUES

1. Describe the individual performance equation. Use examples to show how each of the three major variables must be present if high performance is to be truly facilitated in the work setting.
2. List some forms of organizational support. Describe how a lack of organizational support might inhibit the otherwise capable and motivated person from doing a good job.
3. State and defend a list of competency characteristics that might be associated with high performance as (a) a market researcher, (b) personnel specialist, and (c), assembly-line worker.
4. Find an example from a newspaper or magazine of age, sex, or other improper discrimination in employment. Analyze and explain why such discrimination occurs and state how it might be eliminated.
5. Do you believe that entrance tests (e.g., SAT, GMAT) are useful and fair as screening devices for selecting applicants to colleges and various professional schools? Why or why not?

6. Make a list of the values and attitudes you expect to be associated with success as a manager. Defend your list.
7. Make a list of the personality characteristics that you expect to be associated with success as a manager. Defend your list.
8. Describe the basic characteristics of a Type A personality. Discuss the challenges likely to be encountered as the supervisor of someone with strong Type A tendencies.

CASE: REVERSE DISCRIMINATION

At a meeting of all management personnel, the legal advisor to the Rampart Insurance Company spoke on the subject of employee discrimination with special emphasis on subjects relating to employees of minority groups and female employees.[30] Essentially the message was that there should be no discriminatory decisions by managers relating to the selection and hiring process, promotion policies, seniority, recognition, vacations, work loads, and so forth.

The managers of the company accepted the advice seriously, and under a climate established and implemented by the president, administered the philosophy vigorously. In some cases, women who had good performance records, equal seniority with men, and other minimal qualifications were promoted to supervisory positions, even though they might be married, have several children, and could not work overtime when needed. In other cases, employees who were classed as members of minority groups were purposely rated high on employee evaluation reports so a basis could be established for justifying a forthcoming promotion.

After about a year had passed, other nonmanagement employees gave signs that they were upset, dissatisfied, and angry about the newly introduced managerial philosophy. When no attention was given to their statements that they were now being discriminated against, and when no action came forth when they requested a hearing with the president, the informal leaders of the group posted a notice on all bulletin boards which read as follows:

All employees who are dissatisfied with present management practices and who desire to meet and discuss the organization of an independent union or discuss the possibility of affiliating with a national union, please sign below.

Questions
1. Where and how does the individual performance equation apply to this case? Give specific examples of the individual attributes that appear to be of special issue.
2. In view of your response to the prior question, has Rampart's president done a good job on the issue of employee discriminaton? Why or why not?
3. What would you do now as president of Rampart Insurance Company? Why?

EXERCISE: ALLIGATOR RIVER STORY

Purpose:
To help you realize the different perceptions, values, and attitudes that people have on common, everyday happenings.

Time:
50 minutes plus out-of-class preparation.

Procedure:
1. Read the "Alligator River Story," which follows.[31] After reading the story, rank the five characters in the story beginning with the one whom you consider as the most offensive and end with the one whom you consider the least objectionable. That is, the character who seems to be the most reprehensible to you should be entered first in the list following the story, then the second most reprehensible, and so on, with the least reprehensible or objectionable one being entered fifth. Of course, you will have your own reasons as to why you rank them in the order that you do. Very briefly note this too. Bring this material to class with you.
2. Form groups as assigned by your instructor (at least four persons per group, at least one female per group and as close to an equal mix of males and females, if this is possible).
3. Each group should
   a. Elect a spokesperson for the group.
   b. Tabulate how your group members ranked each of the characters that appear in the story.
   c. Examine the reasons as to why the characters got the rankings that they did. That is, what was the primary reason why each member of the group ranked individuals in the order that they did.
   d. Try to arrive at a group consensus on the rankings.
      (1) If you can, be prepared to tell the class later the basis on which you arrived at the agreement and what the final rankings were.
      (2) If you cannot, what were the main reasons that blocked a consensual ranking? Be prepared to discuss this with the class later and share the final rankings of your group with the class.
4. Reassemble for debriefing at the time specified by your instructor. The spokesperson for each group should first indicate the group's outcomes during the debriefing session. There will be a general discussion thereafter.

The Alligator River Story

There lived a woman named Abigail who was in love with a man named Gregory. Gregory lived on the shore of a river. Abigail lived on the opposite shore of the same river. The river that separated the two lovers was teeming with man-eating alligators. Abigail wanted to cross the river to be with Gregory. Unfortunately, the bridge had been washed out by a heavy flood the previous week. So she went to ask Sinbad, a riverboat captain, to take her across. He said he would be glad to if she would consent to go to bed with him prior to the voyage. She promptly refused and went to a friend named Ivan to explain her plight. Ivan did not want to get involved at all in the situation. Abigail felt her only alternative was to accept Sinbad's terms. Sinbad fulfilled his promise to Abigail and delivered her into the arms of Gregory.

When Abigail told Gregory about her amorous escapade in order to cross the river, Gregory cast her aside with disdain. Heartsick and rejected, Abigail turned to Slug with her tale of woe. Slug, feeling compassion for Abigail, sought out Gregory and beat him brutally. Abigail was overjoyed at the sight of Gregory getting his due. As the sun set on the horizon, people heard Abigail laughing at Gregory.

Rank	Name	Reasons
First	_____	_____
Second	_____	_____
Third	_____	_____
Fourth	_____	_____
Fifth	_____	_____

Character	Frequency of Being Ranked				
	First	**Second**	**Third**	**Fourth**	**Fifth**
Abigail	_____	_____	_____	_____	_____
Gregory	_____	_____	_____	_____	_____
Sinbad	_____	_____	_____	_____	_____
Ivan	_____	_____	_____	_____	_____
Slug	_____	_____	_____	_____	_____

THE MANAGER'S VOCABULARY

Ability   The capacity to perform the various tasks needed for a given job.

Aptitude   The capability to learn something.

Attitude   A predisposition to respond in a positive or negative way to someone or something in one's environment.

Attribution Theory   The attempt to understand the cause of an event, assess responsibility for outcomes of the event, and assess the personal qualities of people involved.

Cognitive Dissonance   A state of perceived inconsistency between a person's expressed attitudes and actual behavior.

Corporate Culture   A system of shared values and beliefs which guides the activities of organization members.

Demographic Characteristics   Background variables (e.g., age, sex) that help to shape what a person becomes over time.

Effectance Motive   The stimulation to work hard based on a feeling of competency or mastery over one's environment.

Instrumental Values   Values that reflect a person's beliefs about the ''means'' for achieving desired ends.

Locus of Control   The internal–external orientation that is the extent to which people feel able to affect their lives.

Machiavellian   A person who views and manipulates others for purely personal gain.

Motivation to Work   The forces within an individual that account for the level, direction, and persistence of effort expended at work.

Personality   The overall profile or combination of traits that characterizes the unique nature of a person.

Problem-Solving Style   The way in which a person goes about gathering and evaluating information in solving problems and making decisions.

Psychological Characteristics   Psychological factors that predispose an individual to behave in predictable ways.

Situational Constraints   Factors in the workplace which give inadequate support to individual performance.

Terminal Values   Values that reflect a person's beliefs about ''ends'' to be achieved.

Type A Behavior   A personality profile characterized by impatience, desire for achievement, and perfectionism.

Type B Behavior   A personality profile characterized by being easy-going and less competitive in daily life.

Values   Global beliefs that guide actions and judgments across a variety of situations.

IMPORTANT NAMES

Chris Argyris   A management scholar who sees a potential conflict between the mature adult personality and the organization as a work environment.

Leon Festinger   A social psychologist who emphasized the importance of cognitive dissonance in explaining and predicting human behavior.

Milton Rokeach   A social scientist who has contributed pioneering work in the area of human values.

NOTES

[1]Developed from Thomas Moore, ''Personality Tests Are Back,'' *Fortune* (March 30, 1987), pp. 74–82.

[2]Melvin Blumberg and Charles D. Pringle, The Missing Opportunity in Organizational Research: ''Some Impli-

cations for a Theory of Work Performance,'' *Academy of Management Review*, Vol. 7 (1982), pp. 560–569.

[3]See Lawrence H. Peters, Edward J. O'Connor, and Joe R. Eulberg, ''Situational Constraints: Sources, Con-

sequences, and Future Considerations,'' in Kendreth M. Rowland and Gerald R. Ferris, eds., *Research in Personnel and Human Resources Management,* Vol. 3 (Greenwich, Conn.: JAI Press, 1985).

[4]Larry L. Cummings and Donald P. Schwab, *Performance in Organizations: Determinants and Appraisal* (Glenview, Ill.: Scott, Foresman, 1973) p. 8.

[5]See Jay W. Lorsch and John J. Morse, *Organizations and Their Members* (New York: Harper & Row, 1974). See also Marilyn E. Gist, ''Self-Efficacy: Implications for Organizational Behavior and Human Resources Management,'' *Academy of Management Review,* Vol. 12 (1987), pp. 472–485.

[6]See Marvin D. Dunnette, ''Aptitudes, Abilities, and Skills,'' in Marvin D. Dunnette, ed., *Handbook of Industrial and Organizational Psychology* (Chicago: Rand McNally, 1976).

[7]See Sara M. Freedman and Robert T. Keller, ''The Handicapped in the Workforce,'' *Academy of Management Review,* Vol. 6 (1981), pp. 449–458.

[8]Milton Rokeach, *The Nature of Human Values* (New York: Free Press, 1973).

[9]Gordon Allport, Philip E. Vernon, and Gardner Lindzey, *Study of Values* (Boston: Houghton Mifflin, 1931).

[10]This incident and related research is reported by Joseph A. Raelin, ''The '60's Kids in the Corporation: More than 'Daydream Believers','' *Academy of Management Executive,* Vol. 1 (1987), pp. 21–30; and, Joseph A. Raelin, *Clash of Cultures* (Cambridge, Mass.: Harvard University Press, 1986).

[11]Geert Hofstede, *Culture's Consequences: International Differences in Work-Related Values* (Beverly Hills, Calif.: Sage Publications, 1980).[12]Daniel Yankelovich, *New Rules! Searching for Self-fulfillment in a World Turned Upside Down* (New York: Random House, 1981); and Daniel Yankelovich, Hans Zetterberg, Burkhard Strumpel and Michael Shanks, *Work and Human Values: An International Report on Jobs in the 1980's and 1990's* (Aspen, Co.: Aspen Institute for Humanistic Studies, 1983).

[13]Thomas J. Peters and Robert H. Waterman, Jr., *In Search of Excellence* (New York: Harper & Row, 1982). See also Terrence E. Deal and Allan A. Kennedy, *Corporate Cultures: The Rites and Rituals of Corporate Life* (Reading, Mass.: Addison-Wesley, 1982).

[14]Barry Z. Posner, James M. Kouzes and Warren H.

Schmidt, ''Shared Values Make a Difference: An Empirical Test of Corporate Culture,'' *Human Resource Management,* Vol. 24 (Fall 1985), pp. 293–309.

[15]See Ralph H. Kilmann, Mary J. Saxton, Roy Serpa, and Associates, *Gaining Control of the Corporate Culture* (San Francisco: Jossey-Bass, 1985).

[16]See Martin Fishbein and Icek Ajzen, *Belief, Attitude, Intention and Behavior: An Introduction to Theory and Research* (Reading, Mass.: Addison-Wesley, 1975).

[17]See Robert G. Lord and Jonathan E. Smith, ''Theoretical, Information Processing and Situational Factors Affecting Attribution Theory Models of Organizational Behavior,'' *Academy of Management Review,* Vol. 8 (January 1983), pp. 50–60.

[18]Leon Festinger, *A Theory of Cognitive Dissonance* (Palo Alto, Calif.: Stanford University Press, 1957).

[19]Harry Levinson, ''Psychoanalytic Theory in Organizational Behavior,'' pp. 51–61, in Jay W. Lorsch, ed., *Handbook of Organizational Behavior* (Englewood Cliffs, N.J.: Prentice-Hall, 1987).

[20]Daniel J. Levinson, *The Seasons of a Man's Life* (New York: Alfred A. Knopf, 1978).

[21]Chris Argyris, *Personality and Organization* (New York: Harper & Row, 1957).

[22]J. B. Rotter, ''Generalized Expectancies for Internal versus External Control of Reinforcement,'' *Psychological Monographs,* Vol. 80 (1966), pp. 1–28.

[23]About the Myers–Briggs instrument, see Isabel B. Myers, *Manual for the MBTI* (Palo Alto, Ca.: Consulting Psychologists Press, 1985), and Isabel B. Myers and Mary McCaulley, *Gifts Differing* (Palo Alto, Ca.: Consulting Psychologists Press, 1980).

[24]Niccolo Machiavelli, *The Prince,* George Bull, trans. (Middlesex: Penguin, 1961).

[25]Richard Christie and Florence L. Geis, *Studies in Machiavellianism* (New York: Academic Press, 1970).

[26]Adapted from R. W. Bortner, ''A Short Scale: A Potential Measure of Pattern A Behavior,'' *Journal of Chronic Diseases,* Vol. 22 (1969). Used by permission.

[27]See Meyer Freidman and Ray Roseman, *Type A Behavior and Your Heart* (New York: Alfred A. Knopf, 1974). For another view see Walter Kiechel III, ''Attack of the Obsessive Managers,'' *Fortune* (February 16, 1987), pp. 127–128.

[28]J. P. Campbell, M. D. Dunnette, E. E. Lawler III,

and K. E. Weick, *Managerial Behavior, Performance and Effectiveness* (New York: McGraw-Hill, 1970).

[29]See Posner, et al., op cit.

[30]John M. Champion and John H. James, *Critical Incidents in Management,* 5th Ed. © Richard D. Irwin, Inc., 1985, pp. 218–219. All rights reserved. Used with permission.

[31]From *VALUES CLARIFICATION: A Handbook of Practical Strategies for Teachers and Students* by Sidney Simon, Leland Howe, and Howard Kirschenbaum, Copyright 1972 Hart Publishing Co., Inc. Used with permission. This story is with 78 other thought-provoking situations in Sidney Simon, Leland Howe, and Howard Kirschenbaum, *Values Clarification* (New York: Hart, 1972). Used with permission.

CHAPTER 4
MOTIVATION
THEORIES

We shall maintain an attractive and supportive work environment contributing to employee well-being and job effectiveness.

Squibb Corporation Annual Report

WHEN EMPLOYEES GIVE
SOMETHING EXTRA

The 480 employees of Piggly Wiggly Carolina, a Charleston, South Carolina, grocery store and distributing business, threw a party for their bosses early last May.[1] Held out in front of the loading docks, the chain store's TV spokesperson stood on the back of a flatbed trailer and sang the company's commercial jingle. Soon, everyone was singing along. Some of the chorus were truckers and some were secretaries and some were executives; some were dressed in greasy overalls and some in pants suits and some in coats and ties. Most wore big buttons that said "I'm Piggly Wiggly PROUD!"

At a choreographed moment, four beefy truckers started to tug at a black plastic tarpaulin hiding something big and rectangular. "Here it is, folks. The Rig for the Pig!" the TV spokesperson cried as a brand-new refrigerated semitractor trailer was revealed, bearing the inscription "Thanks, Piggly Wiggly—This trailer donated by your proud employees." Hundreds of balloons carried the same message, "Thanks, Piggly Wiggly," up into the air.

In the months preceding this special event, the employees of Piggly Wiggly Carolina had seen the economic malaise made manifest in a wave of local business closures, in friends and family suddenly out of work. In contrast, they were secure in their jobs. They enjoyed a wide range of benefits. They liked their bosses, Joseph T. Newton III and his brother-in-law, Burton R. Schools. Most of all, they liked it that there had never been a layoff at the two-generation family business. Not one.

But in the current turndown, even their company was feeling the pinch. So when a large corporation made a buyout offer, it was considered, then rejected. "If we'd sold," explained Newton, "we would have just been a couple of other millionaires walking down the street."

Relieved employees conceived and organized the $40,000 "Rig for the Pig" campaign. Ninety-eight percent of them participated, voluntarily contributing two days' pay. In the end, they raised $7000 more than they needed.

"When you can work for a company as good to you as this one, you jus' feel like doing good for them," said Marion "Smitty" Smith, a 10-year mechanic, at the gala in the parking lot.

Management Applications Questions

Surely, any manager would like a workforce as positive and "turned on" as this store's employees seem. What do people value as work rewards? How should rewards be allocated by managers to achieve the desired levels of individual performance and job satisfaction?

The following topics in the present chapter offer learning opportunities that will help you to respond to the Management Applications Questions.

Types of Motivation Theories
Maslow's Hierarchy of Needs Theory
McClelland's Acquired Needs Theory
Questions and Answers on the Content Theories
Equity Theory
Expectancy Theory
Predicting Performance and Satisfaction

The Management Applications Questions ask what managers must know and do if they are to be successful at using rewards to promote high performance and job satisfaction in the work unit. This chapter is an opportunity for you to examine motivation theories that respond to this question. These theories are an important foundation for the ideas to be developed throughout the rest of this book. Before looking at the separate theories, it is worthwhile to recall the definition of motivation given in Chapter 3. **Motivation to work** refers to the forces within an individual that account for the level, direction, and persistence of effort expended at work.

TYPES OF MOTIVATION THEORIES

Theories of work motivation are largely grounded in the field of psychology. Psychologists, in turn, rely substantially upon the philosophical tradition of hedonism, that is, the view that people seek to maximize pleasure and minimize pain in their daily lives, in their theory-building efforts. Two categories of motivation theories evolve from this point that are of immediate concern to us: content theories and process theories.

Content and Process Theories

The **content theories** of motivation offer ways in which to profile or analyze individuals to identify their needs or motives. We use **needs and motives** interchangeably to mean physiological or psychological deficiencies that an individual feels some compulsion to eliminate. Content theories lend insight into people's needs and, thus, help a manager to understand what people will and will not value as work rewards. The theories of Maslow and McClelland are singled out later as two of the better known representatives of the "content" orientation.

Content theories are sometimes criticized as being static and descriptive. The **process theories** offer a more dynamic alternative. They strive to provide an understanding of the thought or cognitive processes that take place within the minds of people and that act to influence their behavior. We will discuss two process theories that offer significant managerial implications: the equity theory and the expectancy theory.

The content and process motivation theories complement rather than compete with one another. While the content theories are less directly linked with work efforts than job satisfactions, the process theories are directly concerned with work efforts and their performance implications. Together they address both performance and satisfaction as key work outcomes. Ultimately, we will use expectancy theory to combine the insights of the content and process theories in a way that is most useful to the practicing manager.[2]

Mastering Motivation Theories

As we turn now to examine selected theories of motivation, remember that you must not only master the pure theories but also recognize their implications for managerial thought and action. No one theory has yet been proven to dominate all others. Thus, every theory must be carefully studied to derive its implications for predicting and controlling behavior in organizations. Accordingly, we have organized this chapter to help you successfully master the three following goals in studying motivation theories.

Goals	Chapter Support
1. To examine each theory in its pure form (e.g., to learn about Maslow's theory).	Each theory will be described with an emphasis on managerial usefulness.
2. To critically evaluate each theory (e.g., to identify the limitations of Maslow's theory).	A summary will be provided to detail key research results and scholarly opinions on each theory.
3. To create a personal theory of work motivation (e.g., to create a theory that seems useful to you for understanding individuals at work).	The theories will be compared for their similarities and differences. Then we offer an integrative theory.

INTRODUCING THE CONTENT THEORIES

Content theories use individual needs to help in the understanding of job satisfaction and work behaviors. Needs reflect either physiological or psychological deficiencies. Hunger, for example, is a physiological need; desire for emotional support is a psychological need. Needs are an additional aspect of individual attributes that complement the demographic, competency, and psychological characteristics, which we discussed in Chapter 3. Because needs are so important to individuals at work, we give them separate and detailed attention here.

Although content theorists disagree somewhat concerning the exact nature of these needs, they do agree that

$$\text{Individual needs} \xrightarrow{\text{activate}} \text{tensions} \xrightarrow[\text{influence}]{\text{that}} \text{attitudes and behavior}$$

Stated even more precisely, content theorists suggest that the manager's job is to create work environments that respond positively to individual needs. Such things as poor performance, undesirable behaviors, and/or decreased satisfactions can be partially explained in terms of "blocked" needs or those that are not satisfied on the job. Also, the motivational value of rewards can be analyzed in terms of "activated" needs to which a given reward either does or does not respond.

Take, for example, the situation depicted in the following parable.[3]

> Once upon a time there was a donkey standing knee-deep in a field of carrots, contentedly munching away. A wise farmer wanted the donkey to pull a loaded wagon to another field, but the donkey would not walk over to the wagon. So the wise farmer stood by the wagon and held up a bunch of carrots for the donkey to see. But the donkey continued to contentedly munch away on carrots in the field.

The farmer in the parable failed to allocate the reward (carrots) in a way that responded to a corresponding need (hunger) of the donkey. The moral of this story is that neither donkeys nor human beings are motivated to work for rewards when their needs for them are already satisfied!

To allocate rewards successfully, the content theorists argue that managers must

1. Understand how individuals differ in what they need from their work.
2. Know what can be offered to these individuals in response to their needs.
3. Know how to create work environments that give people the opportunity to satisfy their needs by contributing to the task performance of the work unit and organization.

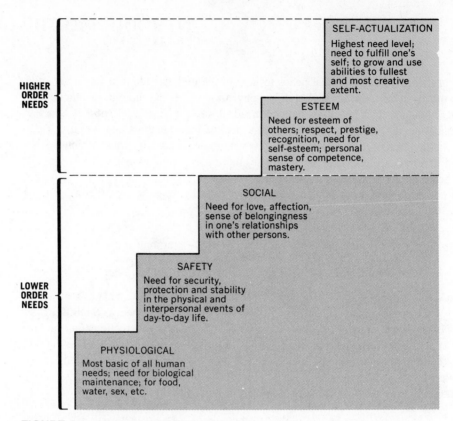

FIGURE 4.1   Maslow's hierarchy of needs.

MASLOW'S HIERARCHY OF NEEDS THEORY

Abraham Maslow developed a hierarchy of needs theory as shown in Figure 4.1.[4] The *higher-order needs* are self-actualization and esteem; the *lower-order needs* are social, safety and physiological. His formulation suggests a prepotency of these needs. Some are assumed to be more important (potent) than others and must be satisfied before the other needs can serve as motivators. Thus, according to the figure, the physiological needs must be satisfied before the safety needs are activated and the safety needs must be satisfied before the social needs are activated, and so on.

Maslow has argued that he would expect his theory to hold for most people though not necessarily for everyone. Furthermore, Figure 4.1 implies that a lower-order need, such as safety, must be entirely fulfilled before the next level (social) need is activated; however, that is too rigid an interpretation. It is more accurate to argue simply that the greater the fulfillment of a specific need, the less it serves as a motivator and the more the next higher-level need becomes activated.

The Research

Research identifies some tendency for higher-order needs to increase in importance over lower-order needs as individuals move up the managerial hierarchy.[5] Other studies report that needs vary according to a person's career stage,[6] organization size,[7] and even geographical location.[8]

However, there is no consistent evidence that the satisfaction of a need at one level will decrease its importance and increase the importance of the next higher need.[9] As a result, some theorists have tried to modify Maslow's theory and make it more realistic in terms of daily individual behavior. One of the most promising among these latter efforts is the ERG (existence, relatedness, growth) theory of Clayton Alderfer.

Alderfer's Modification

ERG theory differs from Maslow's theory in three basic respects.[10] First, the theory collapses Maslow's five need categories into three: **existence needs** relate to people's desires for physiological and material well-being; **relatedness needs** represent desires for satisfying interpersonal relationships; **growth needs** are desires for continued personal growth and development. Second, while Maslow's theory argues that individuals progress up the hierarchy as a result of the satisfaction of lower-order needs (i.e., a satisfaction–progression process), ERG theory includes a ''frustration–regression'' principal whereby an already satisfied lower-level need can become activated when a higher-level need cannot be satisfied. Third, while Maslow's approach has a person focusing on one need at a time, ERG theory contends that more than one need may be activated at the same time.

Let us look at Kim Blair to illustrate ERG theory. A newly hired engineer at Texas Instruments (TI), Kim is concerned about pay, security, and working conditions (existence needs). After being at TI a while, Kim achieves satisfaction on these matters (existence need satisfaction) and becomes concerned with developing good interpersonal relations with co-workers (satisfaction–progression). After satisfying these relatedness needs, Kim's concerns increasingly deal with the desire for advancement to a more challenging job in another department (growth need). However, after learning that this job requires considerably more experience (need frustration), Kim's disappointment causes a renewed emphasis on good interpersonal relations with co-workers (frustration–regression). Kim continues to emphasize high performance on the present job.

Research on the ERG theory is relatively limited and includes some disclaimers.[11] A supportive article provides evidence for the ERG need categories and reports additional findings.[12] Among the more interesting of these are: (1) blacks had greater existence need strength than whites, (2) growth needs were greater for those with more highly educated parents, and (3) women had lower strength of existence needs and higher strength of relatedness needs than men. Even though future research is

The Thematic Apperception Test (TAT) asks people to view pictures and write stories about what they see.

needed to shed additional light on is validity, the supporting evidence on ERG theory is stronger than for Maslow's theory. For now, the combined satisfaction–progression and frustration–regression principles provide the manager with a more flexible and useful approach to understanding human needs than does Maslow's strict hierarchy.

McCLELLAND'S ACQUIRED NEEDS THEORY

In the late 1940s, the psychologist David I. McClelland and his co-workers began experimenting with the Thematic Apperception Test (TAT for short) as a way of measuring human needs.[13] The TAT asks people to view pictures and write stories about what they see.

One TAT picture is presented in the accompanying photograph. What short story would you write about it?

Three Types of Acquired Needs

In one case, McClelland tested three executives using a similar photograph. One wrote of an engineer who was daydreaming about a family outing scheduled for the next day. Another described a designer who had picked up an idea for a new gadget from remarks made by his family. The third saw an engineer who was intently working on a bridge-stress problem that he seemed sure to solve because of his confident look.[14] Compare your response with those of the executives. Do you note any similarities?

McClelland distinguishes three themes that appear in such TAT stories. Each theme corresponds to an underlying need that he feels is important for understanding individual behavior. These needs are:

Need for Achievement (nAch):   The desire to do something better or more efficiently, to solve problems, or to master complex tasks.

Need for Affiliation (nAff):   The desire to establish and maintain friendly and warm relations with other persons.

Need for Power (nPower):   The desire to control other persons, to influence their behavior, to be responsible for other people.

Let's go back to the picture of the man sitting at his desk. McClelland scored the stories given by the three executives as follows:

Person dreaming about family outing: nAch = +1

Person pondering new idea for gadget: nAch = +2

Person working on bridge-stress problem: nAch = +4

Think back to your own story. To what degree does it reflect needs for achievement, affiliation, and power?

McClelland's basic theory is that these three needs are acquired over time and as a result of life experiences. People are motivated by the needs, and each can be associated with individual work preferences. The theory encourages managers to learn how to identify the presence of nAch, nAff, and nPower in themselves and other people and to be able to create work environments that are responsive to the respective need profiles.

The Research

McClelland's research supports the work preferences associated with each need type as described in Table 4.1. This research lends considerable insight into nAch and includes some particularly interesting applications in developing nations. Recent studies have examined the relationship between the nAch of farmers and persons running small businesses to economic growth in their countries, and also examined the effects of selected psychological factors on nAch and the vocational aspirations of women.[15]

Two practical applications of the theory are very relevant to you as a manager. First, nAch, nAff, and nPower complement the needs identified in Maslow's hierarchy and Alderfer's ERG theory. Thus, they can help you to understand people in their work settings. Acquired needs theory is especially useful, since each need is directly associated with a set of individual work preferences as summarized in Table 4.1.

TABLE 4.1   Work Preferences of Persons High in Need for Achievement, Affiliation, and Power

Individual Need	Work Preferences	Example
High need for achievement	Individual responsibility Challenging but doable goals Feedback on performance	Field sales person with challenging quota and opportunity to earn individual bonus
High need for affiliation	Interpersonal relationships Opportunities to communicate	Customer service representative; member of work unit subject to group wage bonus plan
High need for power	Control over other persons Attention Recognition	Formal position of supervisory responsibility; appointment as head of special task force or committee.

Second, if these needs are truly acquired, it may be possible to acquaint people with the need profiles required to be successful in various types of jobs. One interesting avenue of McClelland's personal research, for example, seeks to identify the need profiles typical of successful managers. Working with what he calls the "leadership motive pattern," McClelland has found that the combination of moderate to high need for power and lower need for affiliation enables people to be effective managers at higher levels in organizations. High nPower creates the willingness to have influence or impact on others; lower nAff allows the manager to make difficult decisions without undue worry of being disliked.[16] This finding, however, appears to be true at the general management level, it does not seem to hold at lower levels where technical expertise is more important.[17]

QUESTIONS AND ANSWERS ON THE CONTENT THEORIES

The content theories focus on human needs as a way to understand and predict work attitudes and behaviors. Even though the terminology differs, there is a substantial similarity in what the theories offer as a frame of reference for understanding these needs. Let us look at some questions you may have regarding the content theories and their managerial implications.[18]

1. *How many different individual needs are there?*   Research has not yet defined the complete listing of work-related individual needs. Each of the needs we have discussed has been found to be especially useful by OB scholars. As a manager, you can use these needs as a point of departure for understanding the many different needs that people may bring with them to the work setting.

2. *Can one work outcome satisfy more than one need?*   Yes, some work outcomes or rewards can satisfy or block more than one need. Pay is a good example. It is a source of performance feedback for the high need achiever. Pay can also be a source of security as well as a way of satisfying physiological and social needs.

3. *Is there a hierarchy of needs?*   Research evidence fails to support the existence of a precise five-step hierarchy of needs as postulated by Maslow. Rather, the evidence seems to suggest that it is more legitimate to picture needs operating in a more flexible hierarchy, such as the one in ERG theory. Also, it appears useful to distinguish between lower-order and higher-order needs in terms of motivational properties.

4. *How important are the various needs?*   Research is inconclusive as to the importance of various needs. Individuals probably vary in this regard. Also, they may value needs differently at different times.

5. *What is the manager's responsibility as defined by the content theories?*   Although their details vary, each content theory generally suggests that the manager is responsible for creating a work environment within which individual subordinates find opportunities to satisfy their important needs. To the extent that some needs are acquired, the manager's responsibility may also include acquainting subordinates with the value of needs to which the work setting can positively respond.

6. *What lies beyond the content theories of motivation?*   The process theories offer further insights to the manager. They focus on individual thought processes as influences on behavior. Let us turn our attention to two of them—equity theory and expectancy theory.

EQUITY THEORY

Do you remember the parable introduced earlier in this chapter? It said something about farmers, donkeys, and carrots, if you recall. Let us spin the parable around another time.

Second Parable[19]
Once upon a time there were six donkeys hitched to a wagon pulling a heavy load up a steep hill. Two of the donkeys were not achievement oriented and decided to coast along and let others do most of the pulling. Two others were relatively young and inexperienced, and had a difficult time pulling their share. One of the remaining two suffered from a slight hangover from consuming fermented barley the night before. The sixth donkey did most of the work.

The wagon arrived at the top of the hill. The driver got down from his seat, patted each of the donkeys on the head, and gave six carrots to each. Prior to the next hill climb, the sixth donkey ran away.

An equity dynamic operates in the new parable, and it has affected the behavior of the sixth donkey. From a donkey's perspective, the moral is never be the high per-forming donkey if everyone get six carrots! From a manager's point of view, similar equity dynamics can affect people's behavior in the work unit whenever rewards are being allocated. How would you like to lose your best worker under conditions such as those described in the parable? Fortunately, a manager can use equity theory to help avoid such undesirable consequences.

The Equity Comparison

Equity theory is a process motivational theory whose origins lie in studies of social comparison. We know it best through the writings of J. Stacy Adams.[20] He argues that when people gauge the fairness of their work outcomes in comparison with others, felt inequity is a motivating state of mind. That is, when people perceive inequity in their work, they will be aroused to remove the discomfort and restore a sense of felt equity to the situation. Inequities exist whenever people feel that the rewards or inducements received for their work inputs or contributions are unequal to the rewards other persons appear to have received for their inputs. For the individual, the equity comparison or thought process that determines such feeling is

$$\frac{\text{Individual rewards}}{\text{Individual inputs}} \xleftrightarrow[\text{with}]{\text{compared}} \frac{\text{Others' rewards}}{\text{Others' inputs}}$$

Resolving Felt Inequities

A **felt negative inequity** exists when an individual feels that he or she has received relatively less than others in proportion to work inputs. **Felt positive inequity** exists when an individual feels he or she has received relatively more than others. Both felt negative and felt positive inequity are motivating states. When either exists, the in-dividual is predicted to engage in one or more of the following behaviors (shown with examples for perceived negative inequity) to restore a sense of equity.

1. Change work inputs (e.g., reduce performance efforts).
2. Change rewards received (e.g., ask for a raise).
3. Leave the situation (e.g., quit).
4. Change the comparison points (e.g., compare self to a different co-worker).
5. Psychologically distort the comparisons (e.g., rationalize that the inequity is only temporary and will be resolved in the future).
6. Take actions to change the inputs or outputs of the comparison person (e.g., get a co-worker to accept more work).

Equity theory predicts that people who feel under-rewarded or over-rewarded for their work will act to restore a sense of equity. The research of Adams and others, largely accomplished in laboratory settings, lends tentative support to this prediction.[21] People who feel overpaid (felt positive inequity) have been found to increase the quantity or quality of their work, while those who are underpaid (felt negative inequity) do the

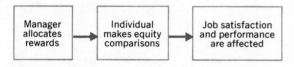

FIGURE 4.2   The equity comparison as an intervening variable in the rewards, satisfaction, and performance relationship.

opposite. The research is most conclusive in respect to felt negative inequity, it appears people are less comfortable when underrewarded than when overrewarded.

Managing the Equity Dynamic

Figure 4.2 shows that the equity comparison actually intervenes between a manager's allocation of rewards and his or her impact on the work behavior of subordinates. Managing the equity dynamic thus becomes quite central to the manager who strives to maintain healthy psychological contracts, that is, fairly balanced inducements and contributions, among subordinates. Rewards that are received with feelings of equity can foster job satisfaction and performance; rewards received with feelings of negative inequity can damage these key work results. The burden lies with the manager to take control of the situation and make sure that any negative consequences of the equity comparison are avoided, or at least minimized, when rewards are allocated. Newsline 4.1 shows that some organizations try to avoid misperceptions of pay, for example, by maintaining ''open'' as opposed to ''secret'' pay plans.

The following guidelines can help you to maintain control of the equity dynamic in your work unit.

1. Recognize that an equity comparison will likely be made by each subordinate whenever especially visible rewards such as pay, promotions, and so on are being allocated.
2. Anticipate felt negative inequities. Carefully communicate to each individual your evaluation of the reward, an appraisal of the performance upon which it is based, and the comparison points you consider to be appropriate.

Remember, feelings of inequity are determined solely by the individual's interpretation of the situation. Thus, the assumption that every employee in a work unit will view their annual pay raise as fair is incorrect. It is not how a manager feels about the allocation of rewards that counts; it is how the individuals receiving the rewards feel or perceive them that will determine the motivational outcomes of the equity dynamic. Indeed, this whole area of perception is so important that we devote a large part of Chapter 13 to it.

EXPECTANCY THEORY

In 1964, a book by Victor Vroom covering an expectancy theory of work motivation made an important contribution to the OB literature.[22] The theory seeks to predict or

NEWSLINE 4.1 / KNOWING WHAT CO-WORKERS EARN: SOME SAY OFFICE OPENNESS CAN BE HELPFUL

How much money does your neighbor at the office make?

Do you wish you knew? Or are you a little afraid to find out?

Edward Lawler, a professor of management at the University of Southern California, who recently completed a study of wage secrecy, maintains that businesses would do better to open up on the subject of who earns what, or at least what job category earns what.

How much people earn is an emotionally charged issue, Professor Lawler agrees. "Salary tends to be tied up with the worth or value of a person. I may be afraid to know what you make because if it's more than I do, that means you're a better person than I am."

But pay secrecy tends to make people overestimate the earnings of their co-workers, Lawler reasons.

"In the absence of factual data, people go on rumors and innuendoes," he says. "Even with pay secrecy, employees are inclined to tell others that they got a raise following positive evaluations of their performance."

Some companies have gone so far as to post names and salaries on the bulletin board behind the office water cooler, says Lawler, but that is going to extremes. Other companies have posted charts on which each employee is a dot, and each dot is marked with an indication of salary. Each employee, knowing his or her own salary, can then find out where they are in relation to other employees.

Lawler estimates that half of U.S. workers operate under open-pay policies—government workers, union members, top management of major companies, and employees of businesses that have adopted open pay scales.

Reported in *The Christian Science Monitor*.

explain the task-related effort expended by a person. The theory's central question, and one of both theoretical and managerial relevance, is "What determines the willingness of an individual to exert personal effort to work at tasks that contribute to the production purposes of the work unit and the organization?"

The Theory

Expectancy theory argues that work motivation is determined by individual beliefs regarding effort–performance relationships and the desirabilities of various work outcomes that are associated with different performance levels. Simply put, the theory is based on the logic: "People *will do* what they *can do* when they *want to*."[23] It may help you to keep expectancy theory in proper managerial perspective by remembering that

People exert
work effort $\xrightarrow{\text{to achieve}}$ task
performance $\xrightarrow{\text{and receive}}$ work-related
outcomes

Recall that the theory asks, "When and under what conditions will people put forth maximum work efforts in support of the organization's production purposes?" To answer this question, Vroom argues that managers must know three things.

1. The person's belief that working hard will enable various levels of task performance to be achieved.
2. The person's belief that various work outcomes or rewards will result from the achievement of the various levels of work performance.
3. The value the individual assigns to these work outcomes.

Example

Figure 4.3 presents a schematic example of the expectancy theory. The individual is pictured as making a decision on how much effort to expend at work. In the figure, the individual may elect to follow path A (working hard to achieve a high-performance level) or path B (working less hard and achieving a low- or minimal-performance level). Obviously, a manager would like to encourage, that is, motivate, this person to choose path A.

Under the theory, the first question the individual asks is, "Can I achieve different performance levels as a result of my work efforts?" Once this question is answered, attention shifts to the work outcomes that may be associated with each performance level. In the example, a high merit pay raise and social ostracism by co-workers follow the achievement of high performance. By contrast, a lower-performance level results in an average pay raise and strong group support from co-workers. Finally, the person must evaluate each work outcome, such as considering a high merit raise as very desirable and social ostracism as very undesirable.

FIGURE 4.3   An example of individual thought processes as viewed by expectancy theory.

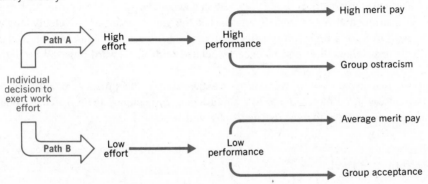

Given what you know about expectancy theory, do you expect the person in this example to elect the high-performance path or the low-performance path? We will return to examine your answer in a moment.

Key Terms

The previous example clarifies the thought process as a foundation of expectancy theory. Individuals are viewed as making conscious decisions to allocate their behavior toward work efforts and serve self-interests. The example helps you to anticipate the three key terms in expectancy theory.

Expectancy: The probability assigned by an individual that work effort will be followed by a given level of achieved task performance. Expectancy would equal "0" if it was felt impossible to achieve the given performance level; it would equal "1" if a person were 100 percent certain that the performance could be achieved.

Instrumentality: The probability assigned by the individual that a given level of achieved task performance will lead to various work outcomes. Instrumentality also varies from "1," meaning the reward is 100 percent certain to follow performance, to "0," indicating there is no chance that performance will lead to the reward.[24]

Valence: The value attached by the individual to various work outcomes. Valences form a scale from -1 (very undesirable outcome) to $+1$ (very desirable outcome).

Multiplier Effect

To predict which work path would be pursued by the individual in the example, you need to know how these three components of expectancy theory interrelate to affect motivation. Vroom posits that motivation (M), expectancy (E), instrumentality (I), and valence (V) are related to one another by the equation.

$$M = E \times I \times V$$

The equation states that motivation to work results from expectancy times instrumentality times valence. This multiplicative relationship means that the motivational appeal of a given work path is drastically reduced whenever any one or more of expectancy, instrumentality, or valence approaches the value of zero. Conversely, for a given reward to have a high and positive motivational impact as a work outcome, the expectancy, instrumentality, and valence associated with the reward must all be high and positive.

Suppose that a manager is wondering whether or not the prospect of earning a merit pay raise will be motivational to a subordinate. Expectancy theory predicts that motivation to work hard to earn the merit pay will be *low* if

1. Expectancy is low—a person feels that he or she cannot achieve the necessary performance level.

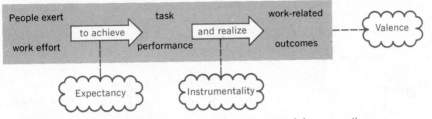

FIGURE 4.4   Expectancy theory terms in a managerial perspective.

2. Instrumentality is low—the person is not confident a high level of task performance will result in a high merit pay raise.
3. Valence is low—the person places little value on a merit pay increase.
4. Any combination of these exists.

The multiplier effect requires managers to act to maximize expectancy, instrumentality, and valence when seeking to create high levels of work motivation among subordinates through the allocation of certain work rewards. A ''zero'' at any location on the right side of the expectancy equation will result in ''zero'' motivation. Figure 4.4 puts the expectancy theory terms into such a managerial frame of reference.

Multiple Expectancies

Expectancy theory is able to accommodate multiple work outcomes in predicting motivation. Going back to the earlier case (see Figure 4.3), merit pay was not the only work outcome affecting the individual's decision to exert high or low levels of work effort. Relationships with co-workers were also a part of each work path. Expectancy theory takes multiple outcomes into consideration in the following expanded version of the expectancy equation.

$$M_i = \sum_j [(E \times I)_{ij}(V)]$$

$i = 1, n$ work effort paths

$j = 1, n$ effort–performance–outcome chains

This equation states that motivation to exert effort along a given work path (e.g., high effort) is determined by the combined sum of the values of all effort–performance–outcome chains related to that path. For example, recall the high-effort path A from Figure 4.3. Two effort–performance–outcome chains appear for this path: a merit pay chain and a group ostracism chain. These chains are reproduced in Figure 4.5. Sample numerical values of the expectancies, instrumentalities, and valences for each chain are indicated by parentheses.

Now, let us apply the prior equation to Figure 4.5 and compute the motivational force assigned by the individual to this high effort work path. The equation basically

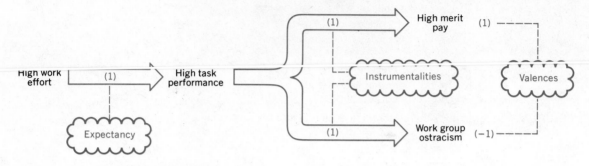

( )--Numbers in parentheses represent values in
the example for expectancy, instrumentalities, valences

FIGURE 4.5   High-effort work path in the expectancy example.

means that the motivation to exert high effort equals the value of the pay chain plus the value of the group chain.

In mathematical notation, this reduces to

$$M_{\text{high effort}} = (E \times I \times V)_{\text{pay}} + (E \times I \times V)_{\text{group}}$$

By substituting in the numerical values of E, I, V, we get

$$M_{\text{high effort}} = (1 \times 1 \times 1)_{\text{pay}} + (1 \times 1 \times -1)_{\text{group}}$$

$$M_{\text{high effort}} = (1)_{\text{pay}} + (-1)_{\text{group}}$$

$$M_{\text{high effort}} = 0$$

Thus, because of the multiplier effects and multiple expectancies, individual motivation to pursue this high-performance path is zero! Is this result consistent with your initial prediction back in the earlier discussion? Even though merit pay was both highly valued and considered accessible to the individual, its motivational power was canceled out by the countervailing negative effects of high performance on the individual's social relationships with his or her co-workers. One of the advantages of expectancy theory is its ability to help managers to take into account such multiple consequences when trying to determine the motivational value of various work rewards to individual subordinates.

When the expectancy equation is applied to the low-effort path from the example in Figure 4.3, a different result occurs. You should be able to verify that $M_{\text{low effort}} = 1.5$. Work this example through using the same methods we chose for the high-effort path. Remember, on this path the valence of an average merit pay increase is 0.5; the valence of group acceptance is 1.

When we compare the motivational value of the low-effort path (1.5) with the high-effort motivational value of 0, it is quite clear that the individual in this example would be motivated toward low performance. Concern for group acceptance and the perception that achieving minimal performance standards will still result in an average

TABLE 4.2 Managerial Implications of Expectancy Theory		
Expectancy Term	The Individual's Question	Managerial Implications
Expectancy	"Can I achieve the desired level of task performance?"	Select workers with ability Train workers to use ability Support ability with organizational resources Identify performance goals
Instrumentality	"What work outcomes will be received as a result of the performance?"	Clarify psychological contracts Communicate performance → reward possibilities Confirm performance → reward possibilities by making actual rewards contingent upon performance
Valence	"How highly do I value the work outcomes?"	Identify individual needs or outcomes Adjust available rewards to match these

merit raise (rather than no raise at all) contribute to this result. Expectancy theory, therefore, predicts this person to be a low performer based upon the available work outcomes and their individual consequences.

Managerial Applications

We have summarized the managerial implications of Vroom's expectancy theory in Table 4.2. Basically, expectancy logic argues that a manager must try to understand individual thought processes and then actively intervene in the work situation to influence them. This includes trying to maximize work expectancies, instrumentalities, and valences that support the organization's production purposes. Said differently, a manager should strive to create a work environment so that work contributions serving the organization's needs will also be valued by the individual as paths toward desired personal outcomes or rewards.

Table 4.2 shows that a manager can influence expectancies by selecting individuals with proper abilities, training people to use these abilities, supporting people with abilities by providing the needed resources, and identifying desired task goals. Instrumentality is influenced by clarifying performance reward relationships in the psychological contract, by communicating revised performance → reward relationships specific to a given situation, and by confirming performance → reward expectations through direct action, that is, by actually rewarding desirable performance once it occurs. Finally, managers can influence valence by being sensitive to individual needs. This is where the content theories can be of great benefit to you. Once these needs are understood, rewards can be adjusted to respond more adequately to them.

The Research

The research on expectancy theory is voluminous, and good review articles are available.[25] Although the theory has received substantial support, specific details, such as the operation of the multiplier effect, remain subject to question. Rather than charging that the underlying theory is inadequate, however, researchers indicate that their inability to generate more confirming data may be caused by problems of methodology and measurement. Thus, while awaiting the results of more sophisticated research, OB scholars seem to agree that expectancy theory is a useful source of insight into work motivation.

One of the more popular modifications of Vroom's original version of the theory distinguishes between extrinsic and intrinsic rewards as two separate types of possible work outcomes.[26] **Extrinsic rewards** are positively valued work outcomes that are given to the individual by some other person in the work setting. An example is pay. Workers typically do not pay themselves directly; some representative of the organization administers the reward. **Intrinsic rewards,** on the other hand, are positively valued work outcomes that are received by the individual directly as a result of task performance. They do not require the participation of another person. A feeling of achievement after accomplishing a particularly challenging task is one example of an intrinsic reward. This distinction is important because each type of reward demands separate attention from a manager seeking to use rewards to increase motivation. We discuss these differences very thoroughly in Chapters 5 and 6.

PREDICTING PERFORMANCE AND SATISFACTION

Each of the theories presented in this chapter has potential usefulness for the manager. Although the equity and expectancy theories have special strengths, current thinking argues forcefully for a combined approach that develops and tests contingency-type models that point out where and when various motivation theories work best.[27] Thus, before leaving this discussion, we should pull the content and process theories together into one integrated model of individual performance and satisfaction.

Background

We will begin with the individual performance equation (see Chapter 3) and then proceed in building-block fashion. The equation directs our attention to individual attributes, work effort, and organizational support as three variables that influence individual performance. Simply put,

Recall, too, that we went on to say that because the individual alone controls his or her work effort, the manager attempts to influence effort through the concept of motivation. Thus, the foregoing relationships can be modified to

$$\text{Motivation} \longrightarrow \begin{array}{c} \text{Attributes} \\ \text{Effort} \\ \text{Support} \end{array} \longrightarrow \text{Performance}$$

Note further, however, that managers are also interested in promoting high levels of individual satisfaction as a part of their concern for human resource maintenance. Remember, too, that we concluded our Chapter 3 review of the satisfaction–performance controversy by noting that when rewards are allocated on the basis of past performance (i.e., when rewards are performance-contingent) they can cause both future performance and satisfaction. Figuratively speaking,

$$\begin{array}{c} \text{performance} \\ \text{contingent} \\ \text{rewards} \end{array} \xrightarrow{\text{influence}} \begin{array}{c} \text{performance} \\ \textit{and} \\ \text{satisfaction} \end{array}$$

Integrated Model

We have used the logic of expectancy theory to integrate these latter ideas with insights of the other motivational theories and create the predictive model of individual performance and satisfaction shown in Figure 4.6. In the figure, performance is determined by individual attributes, work effort, and organizational support. Individual motivation directly determines work effort, and the key to motivation is the manager's ability to create a work environment that positively responds to individual needs and goals. Whether or not a work environment provides motivation depends on the availability of rewards. When the individual experiences intrinsic rewards for work performance, motivation will be directly and positively affected. Motivation can also occur when job satisfactions result from either extrinsic or intrinsic rewards that are felt to be equitably allocated. When felt negative inequity results, satisfaction will be low and motivation reduced.

Figure 4.6 is an extension of Vroom's original expectancy theory that is based on the foundation of the individual performance equation. It includes a key role for equity theory and recognizes job performance and satisfaction as separate, but potentially interdependent, work results. The content theories enter the model as the manager's guide to understanding individual attributes and identifying the needs that give motivational value to the various work rewards allocated by the manager.[28]

Illustration

Let us consider an illustration of the integrated model summarized in Figure 4.6 as it might be applied in the work setting. Assume that you are the regional manager of a group of salespersons selling sophisticated computer equipment. The salespersons all

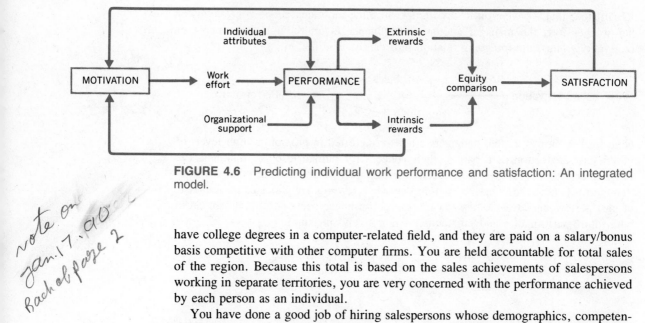

FIGURE 4.6 Predicting individual work performance and satisfaction: An integrated model.

note on Jan. 7. 90 Back of page 2

have college degrees in a computer-related field, and they are paid on a salary/bonus basis competitive with other computer firms. You are held accountable for total sales of the region. Because this total is based on the sales achievements of salespersons working in separate territories, you are very concerned with the performance achieved by each person as an individual.

You have done a good job of hiring salespersons whose demographics, competencies, and psychological characteristics match quite well with job demands. As a followup, new hires also undergo thorough training and orientation that help to develop their aptitudes into abilities and skills and shape their values and attitudes around the firm's way of doing business. At the same time, all salespersons are provided with the latest equipment and best of modern facilities, and are given all necessary resources. In short, the individual attributes and organizational support variables are such that each salesperson has the capability and opportunity to achieve high performance in the assigned job territories.

As manager, you can now devote most of your energy toward creating the desire or willingness of each salesperson to exert maximum work efforts. The firm's compensation system is important because it uses a combination of a fixed salary plus a performance-related bonus. The fixed component helps to attract highly educated people to the job; the bonus is a good performance incentive. But the bonus system rewards performance, not effort. To develop and enhance the willingness to exert effort, you thus hold formal review sessions with each salesperson twice a year and provide informal feedback on a week-to-week and sometimes more frequent basis. You also work with each person to show how effort can generate sales. This means spending time in the field and providing lots of praise as progress and accomplishments are made. For example, salespersons who make the most calls each month (a good effort indicator) get their names listed in the company newspaper and posted in the regional sales office.

Of course, you are extremely fair when doing performance reviews, and try hard to ensure that each person is treated equitably and correctly perceives the equity. This applies both to the intrinsic rewards of the job itself and to extrinsic rewards such as pay and recognition. You also understand that people have different needs and may

well seek things other than just money and recognition from their work. This m
you very sensitive to treating each salesperson as a unique individual.

In short, as the progressive manager in this illustration, you have carefully a
the work situation and have made good use of the integrated insights offered i
4.6.

Let us close with some additional considerations to keep in mind. Our example
provided conditions where use of the integrated model by you as a manager was
particularly appropriate. There are, however, some conditions where such a model
may not be feasible to use.[29]

1. Where the reward system is rigid and inflexible (e.g., it covers large groups
   of employees and is based on seniority).
2. Where it is difficult to observe what people are actually doing on the job
   (e.g., a research and development scientist).
3. Where a person's behavior is heavily dependent on that of others.
4. Where there are lots of changes in people, jobs or expected behavior.
5. Where social pressures are the major determinants of what people are doing
   on the job (e.g., there are strong group pressures).

Our point here is simply to note that even as comprehensive as this model is, a
good manager will need to recognize its limitations. Coming discussions in Chapters
5 and 6, as well as in Part Three on ''Managing Groups in Organizations,'' will add
to your abilities to deal with the complexities of human behavior in the workplace.

SUMMARY

This chapter introduces selected content and process theories of work motivation.
Although the theories differ, each is useful in offering implications for management
practice. They are likely to be especially useful when integrated into a personal theory
that can best meet your needs as a manager. We have described one example of our
integrated theory in Figure 4.6.

The management of work motivation begins with an ability to identify and understand individual needs. The content theories of Maslow, Alderfer, and McClelland
are helpful in this regard. The process theories go further in helping you learn still
more about what motivates people to apply their work efforts to support the organization's production purpose. Equity theory introduces the important dynamic of social
comparison. Expectancy theory focuses our attention on the role of expectancies,
instrumentalities, and valences in determining motivation to work.

Expectancy theory proves of special value as a way of integrating the multiple
insights of the content and process theories. Thus, our final discussion has specified
an integrated theory that can be used by managers to predict individual job performance and satisfaction, and to generate ideas on how to achieve these two key
work results.

As we have shown, a manager must try to create a work setting that is a motivating stimulus to its individual members. One of the key aspects of any work setting is the pool of available work rewards. As a manager, you will need to be good at allocating these rewards. Chapters 5 and 6 build on this theme as it applies to rewards in both their extrinsic and intrinsic forms. Before you press on, though, consider a final parable.

Final Parable[30]

Once upon a time a farmer had six donkeys and a barn full of carrots, which she kept under lock and key. At the end of a day of wagon pulling, the farmer looked back over the day's performance of each donkey. To one of the donkeys she said, "You did an outstanding job; here are six carrots." To four of the others, she said, "Your performance was average; here are three carrots." To the remaining donkey she said, "You didn't pull your share of the load; here is one carrot."

Another day of wagon pulling dawned. The top donkey, having been properly rewarded, began the day in high spirits. The thoughts of the remaining donkeys were consumed with how they might earn more carrots through their efforts that day. The farmer had carrots available, but they had to be earned.

THINKING THROUGH THE ISSUES

1. What is the key difference between the approaches taken by the content and process theories concerning their explanations of work motivation.
2. Two OB theorists are discussing the topic of work motivation. One says "motivation can never come from the boss," while the other states "if people aren't motivated, managers are to blame." How can each position be defended? How can the two positions be reconciled with one another?
3. Suppose that you are a manager and find yourself with one group of subordinates who apparently seek higher-order need satisfactions at work, and another group that seems concerned only with lower-order needs. What would you do to motivate each group of subordinates? Why?
4. Refer back to the chapter opening example, "When Employees Give Something Extra." Make a needs profile for Piggly Wiggly employees based on evidence presented. Explain why they acted as they did and what the management staff of Piggly Wiggly should do now to maintain their motivation to work.
5. If David McClelland is right, and it is possible to stimulate certain needs in people, what is the managerial significance of this finding?
6. Choose an example of how the equity dynamic has affected your behavior as a student. What guidelines would you suggest to instructors that could help them to minimize the negative consequences potentially associated with this equity dynamic?

7. Explain the managerial significance of the final parable.
8. What is one major modification that you would make to the model of motivation to work presented in Figure 4.6 to increase its usefulness to practicing managers?

CASE: PERFECT PIZZERIA

Perfect Pizzeria in Southville, in deep southern Illinois, is the second largest franchise of the chain in the United States.[31] The headquarters is located in Phoenix, Arizona. Although the business is prospering, employee and managerial problems exist.

Each operation has one manager, an assistant manager, and from two to five night managers. The managers of each pizzeria work under an area supervisor. There are no systematic criteria for being a manager or becoming a manager trainee. The franchise has no formalized training period for the manager. No college education is required. The managers for whom the case observer worked during a four-year period were relatively young (ages 24 to 27) and only one had completed college. They came from the ranks of night managers or assistant managers, or both. The night managers were chosen for their ability to perform the duties of the regular employees. The assistant managers worked a two-hour shift during the luncheon period five days a week to gain knowledge about bookkeeping and management. Those becoming managers remained at that level unless they expressed interest in investing in the business.

The employees were mostly college students, with a few high school students performing the less challenging jobs. Since Perfect Pizzeria was located in an area with few job opportunities, it had a relatively easy task of filling its employee quotas. All the employees, with the exception of the manager, were employed part time and were paid the minimum wage.

The Perfect Pizzeria system is devised so that food and beverage costs and profits are computed according to a percentage. If the percentage of food unsold or damaged in any way is very low, the manager gets a bonus. If the percentage is high, the manager does not receive a bonus; rather, he or she receives only his or her normal salary.

There are many ways in which the percentage can fluctuate. Since the manager cannot be in the store 24 hours a day, some employees make up for their paychecks by helping themselves to the food. When a friend comes in to order a pizza, extra ingredients are put on the friend's pizza. Occasional nibbles by 18 to 20 employees throughout the day at the meal table also raise the percentage figure. An occasional bucket of sauce may be spilled or a pizza accidentally burned. Sometimes the wrong size pizza may be made.

In the event of an employee mistake or a burned pizza by the oven operator, the expense is supposed to come from the individual. Because of peer pressure, the night manager seldom writes up a bill for the erring employee. Instead, the establishment takes the loss and the error goes unnoticed until the end of the month when the inventory is taken. That's when the manager finds out that the percentage is high and that there will be no bonus.

In the present instance, the manager took retaliatory measures. Previously, each employee was entitled to a free pizza, salad, and all the soft drinks he or she could drink for every 6 hours of work. The manager raised this figure from 6 to 12 hours of work. However, the employees had received these 6-hour benefits for a long time. Therefore, they simply took advantage of the situation whenever the manager or the assistant was not in the building. Although the night manager theoretically had complete control of the operation in the evenings, he did not command the respect that the manager or assistant manager did. This was because he received the same pay as the regular employees, he could not reprimand other employees, and he was basically the same age or sometimes even younger than the other employees.

Thus, apathy grew within the pizzeria. There seemed to be a further separation between the manager and his workers, who started out as a closely knit group. The manager made no attempt to alleviate the problem, because he felt it would iron itself out. Either the employees that were dissatisfied would quit or they would be content to put up with the new regulations. As it turned out, there was a rash of employee dismissals. The manager had no problem in filling the vacancies with new workers, but the loss of key personnel was costly to the business.

With the large turnover, the manager found that he had to spend more time in the building, supervising and sometimes taking the place of inexperienced workers. This was in direct violation of the franchise regulation, which stated that a manager would act as a supervisor and at no time take part in the actual food preparation. Employees were now placed under strict supervision with the manager working alongside them. The operation no longer worked smoothly because of differences between the remaining experienced workers and the manager concerning the way in which a particular function should be performed.

Within a two-month period, the manager was again free to go back to his office and leave his subordinates in charge of the entire operation. During this two-month period, the percentage had returned to the previous low level, and the manager received a bonus each month. The manager felt that his problems had been resolved and that conditions would remain the same, since the new personnel had been properly trained.

It didn't take long for the new employees to become influenced by the other employees. Immediately after the manager had returned to his supervisory role, the percentage began to rise. This time the manager took a bolder step. He cut out any benefits that the employes had—no free pizzas, salads, or drinks. With the job market at an even lower ebb than usual, most employees were forced to stay. The appointment of a new area supervisor made it impossible for the manager to "work behind the counter," since the supervisor was centrally located in Southville.

The manager tried still another approach to alleviate the rising percentage problem and maintain his bonus. He placed a notice on the bulletin board, stating that if the percentage remained at a high level, a lie detector test would be given to all employees. All those found guilty of taking or purposefully wasting food or drinks would be immediately terminated. This did not have the desired effect on the employees, because they knew if they were all subjected to the test, all would be found guilty and the manager would have to dismiss all of them. This would leave him in a worse situation than ever.

Even before the following month's percentage was calculated, the manager knew it would be high. He had evidently received information from one of the night managers about the employees' feelings toward the notice. What he did not expect was that the percentage would reach an all-time high. That is the state of affairs at the present time.

Questions

1. Consider the situation where the manager changed the time period required to receive free food and drink from 6 to 12 hours of work. Try to apply each of the motivational approaches discussed in this chapter to explain what happened. Which of the approaches offers the most appropriate explanation? Why?
2. Repeat Question 1 for the situation where the manager worked beside the employees for a time and then later returned to his office.
3. Repeat Question 1 for the situation as it exists at the end of the case.
4. Establish and justify a motivational program based on one or a combination of motivation theories to deal with the situation as it exists at the end of the case.

EXERCISE: EXECUTIVE PAY: HOW MUCH IS TOO MUCH?

Purpose:
To facilitate discussion and reflection on the subject of motivation to work, particularly in terms of pay-for-performance contingencies, and to increase your sensitivities to the broader issues surrounding motivation and compensation in the workplace.

Time:
50 minutes.

Procedure:
1. Working alone, read and think about the following statements.[32]
    a. Recently Lee Iacocca, chief executive of Chrysler Corporation, headed the list in *Business Week's* executive compensation survey. He earned $20.5 million in salary, bonus and stock options. The CEO of Ford earned $4.3 million. Owen Beiber, then head of the United Autoworkers Union which represents both Chrysler and Ford workers, earned $84,721 for the same period.
    b. A Louis Harris poll for *Business Week* reported 76 percent of the American public believed top corporate executives were *not* worth the compensation they received. Only 14 percent felt the top executives were worth what they were paid; 10 percent felt they were underpaid or were not sure.
2. Still working alone, take a position now on the following question.

Question: Does top executive pay make sense?

3. Convene in your assigned work groups. Share and discuss your perspectives on the prior statements and the question. Analyze one another's perspectives in terms of the various motivation theories discussed in Chapter 4. Be sure to look at things from the perspective of lower-level managers and workers at companies like Chrysler, Ford and others. How does top executive pay affect them, if at all?

4. Have someone in the group prepared to summarize the results of this analysis for the class as a whole.

5. The instructor will ask for the group reports and lead a further discussion on the motivational implications of top executive pay.

THE MANAGER'S VOCABULARY

Content Theories   Offer ways to profile or analyze individuals to identify the needs that motivate their behavior.

Esteem Needs   Desires for ego gratification in the forms of self-esteem and reputation.

Existence Needs   Desires for physiological and material well-being.

Expectancy   The probability assigned by the individual that work effort will be followed by a given level of achieved task performance.

Extrinsic Rewards   Positively valued work outcomes that are given to the individual by some other person in the work setting.

Felt Inequity   A work situation in which the individual feels that his or her rewards received in return for work contributions made are relatively less (felt negative inequity) or relatively more (felt positive inequity) than those received by others.

Growth Needs   Desires for continued personal growth and development.

Higher-Order Needs   Esteem and self-actualization needs in Maslow's hierarchy.

Instrumentality   The probability assigned by the individual that a given level of achieved task performance will lead to various work outcomes.

Intrinsic Rewards   Positively valued work outcomes that are received by the individual directly as a result of task performance.

Lower-Order Needs   Physiological, safety, and social needs in Maslow's hierarchy.

Motivation to Work   Forces within the individual that account for the level, direction, and persistence of effort expended at work.

Need   A physiological or psychological deficiency which the individual feels some compulsion to eliminate.

Need for Achievement (nAch)   The desire to do something better, to solve problems, or to master complex tasks.

Need for Affiliation (nAff)   The desire to establish and to maintain friendly and warm relations with other persons.

Need for Power (nPower)   The desire to control other persons, to influence their behavior, to be responsible for other people.

Physiological Needs   The basic desire for biological maintenance.

Process Theories   Seek to understand the thought processes that take place in the minds of people and that act to motivate their behavior.

Relatedness Needs   Desires for satisfying interpersonal relationships.

Safety Needs   The desire for security, protection, and stability in daily life.

Self-actualization Needs   The desire to fulfill one's self, to grow, and to use one's abilities to their full and most creative extent.

Social Needs   The desire for love and affection and a sense of belongingness in one's relationships with other persons.

Valence   The value attached by the individual to various work outcomes.

IMPORTANT NAMES

Abraham Maslow   Created the hierarchy of needs theory.

Clayton Alderfer   Modified Maslow's work to create the ERG theory.

David McClelland   Developed the managerial applications of acquired needs theory.

J. Stacy Adams   Applied equity theory to work situations.

Victor Vroom   Introduced the expectancy theory of motivation.

NOTES

[1]Excerpted from Michael VerMeulen, "When Employees Give Something Extra," *Parade Magazine,* November 6, 1983, p. 14. Used by permission of Wendy Weil, Julian Bach Literary Agency, Inc. Copyright © 1983 by Michael VerMeulen.

[2]For a good review article that identifies the need for more integration among motivation theories, see Terence R. Mitchell, "Motivation—New Directions for Theory, Research and Practice," *Academy of Management Review,* Vol. 7 (January 1982), pp. 80–88.

[3]Adapted from Dale McConkey, "The 'Jackass Effect' in Management Compensation," *Business Horizons,* Vol. 17 (June 1974), pp. 81, by the Foundation for the School of Business at Indiana University. Reprinted by permission.

[4]This discussion on Maslow's theory is reported in Abraham H. Maslow, *Eupsychian Management* (Homewood, Ill.: Richard D. Irwin, 1965); Abraham H. Maslow, *Motivation and Personality,* 2nd ed. (New York: Harper & Row, 1970).

[5]Lyman W. Porter, "Job Attitudes in Management: II. Perceived Importance of Needs as a Function of Job Level," *Journal of Applied Psychology,* Vol. 47 (April 1963), pp. 141–148.

[6]Douglas T. Hall and Khalil E. Nougaim, "An Examination of Maslow's Need Hierarchy in an Organizational Setting," *Organization Behavior and Human Performance,* Vol. 3 (1968), pp. 12–35.

[7]Lyman W. Porter, "Job Attitudes in Management: IV. Perceived Deficiencies in Need Fulfillment as a Function of Size of Company," *Journal of Applied Psychology,* Vol. 47 (December 1963), pp. 386–397.

[8]John M. Ivancevich, "Perceived Need Satisfactions of Domestic Versus Overseas Managers," *Journal of Applied Psychology,* Vol. 54 (August 1969), pp. 274–278.

[9]Mahmoud A. Wahba and Lawrence G. Bridwell, "Maslow Reconsidered: A Review of Research on the Need Hierarchy Theory," *Academy of Management Proceedings* (1974), pp. 514–520; Edward E. Lawler III and J. Lloyd Suttle, "A Causal Correlational Test of the Need Hierarchy Concept," *Organizational Behavior and Human Performance*, Vol. 7 (1973), pp. 265–287.

[10]See Clayton P. Alderfer, "An Empirical Test of a New Theory of Human Needs," *Organizational Behavior and Human Performance*, Vol. 4 (1969), pp. 142–175; Clayton P. Alderfer, *Existence, Relatedness, and Growth* (New York: Free Press, 1972); Benjamin Schneider and Clayton P. Alderfer, "Three Studies of Need Satisfaction in Organization," *Administrative Science Quarterly*, Vol. 18 (1973), pp. 489–505.

[11]Lane Tracy, "A Dynamic Living Systems Model of Work Motivation," *Systems Research*, Vol. 1 (1984), pp. 191–203; John Rauschenberger, Neal Schmidt, and John E. Hunter, "A Test of the Need Hierarchy Concept by a Markov Model of Change in Need Strength," *Administrative Science Quarterly*, Vol. 25 (1980) pp. 654–670.

[12]Clayton P. Alderfer and R. A. Guzzo, "Life Experiences and Adults' Enduring Strength of Desires in Organizations," *Administrative Science Quarterly*, Vol. 24 (1979), pp. 347–361.

[13]Sources pertinent to this discussion are David C. McClelland, *The Achieving Society* (New York: Van Nostrand, 1961); David C. McClelland, "Business, Drive and National Achievement," *Harvard Business Review*, Vol. 40 (July–August 1962), pp. 99–112; David C. McClelland, "That Urge to Achieve," *Think* (November–December 1966), pp. 19–32; and G. H. Litwin and R. A. Stringer, *Motivation and Organizational Climate* (Boston: Division of Research, Harvard Business School, 1966), pp. 18–25.

[14]George Harris, "To Know Why Men Do What They Do: A Conversation with David C. McClelland," *Psychology Today*, Vol. 4 (January 1971), pp. 35–39.

[15]S. Singh, "Relationships Among Projective and Direct Verbal Measures of Achievement Motivation," *Journal of Personality Assessment*, Vol. 43 (1979), pp. 45–49; and F. Salili, "Determinants of Achievement Motivation for Women in Developing Countries," *Journal of Vocational Behavior*, Vol. 14 (1979), pp. 297–305; David C. McClelland, *Human Motivation*, Glenview, IL, Scott, Foresman, 1985.

[16]David C. McClelland and David H. Burnham, "Power Is the Great Motivator," *Harvard Business Review*, Vol. 54 (March–April 1976), pp. 100–110; and David C. McClelland and Richard E. Boyatzis, "Leadership Motive Pattern and Long-Term Success in Management," *Journal of Applied Psychology*, Vol. 67 (1982), pp. 737–743.

[17]Edwin T. Cornelius III and Frank B. Lane, "The Power Motive and Managerial Success in a Professionally Oriented Service Industry Organization," *Journal of Applied Psychology*, Vol. 69 (1985), pp. 32–39.

[18]This section is based, in part, on a discussion by Edward E. Lawler III in *Motivation in Work Organizations* (Monterey, Calif.: Brooks/Cole, 1973), pp. 30–36.

[19]McConkey, "The 'Jackass Effect' in Management Compensation," p. 82.

[20]See, for example, J. Stacy Adams, "Toward an Understanding of Inequity," *Journal of Abnormal and Social Psychology*, Vol. 67 (1963), pp. 422–436; and J. Stacy Adams, "Inequity in Social Exchange," in L. Berkowitz, ed., *Advances in Experimental Social Psychology*, Vol. 2 (New York: Academic Press, 1965), pp. 267–300.

[21]For an excellent review, see Richard T. Mowday, "Equity Theory Predictions of Behavior in Organizations," in Richard M. Steers and Lyman W. Porter (eds.), *Motivation and Work Behavior* (4th Ed.) (New York: McGraw-Hill, 1987), pp. 89–110.

[22]Victor H. Vroom, *Work and Motivation* (New York: John Wiley, 1964).

[23]Gerald R. Salancik and Jeffrey Pfeffer, "A Social Information Processing Approach to Job Attitudes and Task Design," *Administrative Science Quarterly*, Vol. 23 (June 1978), pp. 224–253.

[24]Strictly speaking, Vroom's treatment of instrumentality would allow it to vary from −1 to +1. We use the probability definition here and the 0 to +1 range for pedagogical purposes. This connection remains consistent with the basic notion of instrumentality.

[25]Terrence R. Mitchell, "Expectancy Models of Job Satisfaction, Occupational Preference and Effort: A Theoretical, Methodological, and Empirical Appraisal," *Psychological Bulletin*, Vol. 81 (1974), pp. 1053–1077; Mahmoud A. Wahba and Robert J. House, "Expectancy Theory in Work and Motivation: Some Logical and Methodological Issues," *Human Relations,*

Vol. 27 (January 1974), pp. 121–147; Terry Connolly, "Some Conceptual and Methodological Issues in Expectancy Models of Work Performance Motivation," *Academy of Management Review,* Vol. 1 (October 1976), pp. 37–47; and Terence Mitchell, "Expectancy–Value Models in Organizational Psychology," in N. Feather (ed.), *Expectancy, Incentive and Action* (New York: Erlbaum and Associates, 1980).

[26]Lyman W. Porter and Edward E. Lawler III, *Managerial Attitudes and Performance* (Homewood, Ill.: Richard D. Irwin, 1968).

[27]Mitchell, "Expectancy–Value Models in Organizational Psychology."

[28]An earlier model by Porter and Lawler provided useful insights for Figure 4.6 and the integrated model in the figure is also consistent with the kind of comprehensive approach suggested in a recent review by Evans. See, Lyman W. Porter and Edward E. Lawler, III, *Managerial Attitudes and Performance,* (Homewood, IL: Richard D. Irwin, 1968) p. 17; Martin G. Evans, "Organizational Behavior: The Central Role of Motiva-

tion," in J. G. Hunt and J. D. Blair (Eds.), *1986 Yearly Review of Management of the Journal of Management,* Vol. 12 (1986) pp. 203–222.

[29]Terence R. Mitchell, "Motivation: New Directions for Theory, Research and Practice."

[30]McConkey, "The 'Jackass Effect' in Management Compensation," p. 91.

[31]Adapted from a case assignment prepared by Lee Neely for Professor James G. Hunt, Southern Illinois University at Carbondale. The case appears in John E. Dittrich and Robert A. Zawacki, eds., *People and Organizations: Cases in Management and Organizational Behavior,* pp. 126–128. © Business Publications, 1981. All rights reserved. Used by permission.

[32]"Executive Pay: Who Got What in '86," *Business Week* (May 4, 1987), pp. 50–58; "How Much Top Labor Leaders Made in 1986," *Business Week* (May 4, 1987), p. 96; "Top Executive Pay Peeves the Public," *Business Week* (June 25, 1984), p. 15.

CHAPTER 5
LEARNING, REINFORCEMENT, AND EXTRINSIC REWARDS

Innovative provisions, such as an incentive plan for non-management employees, will let these employees share in the success of our business.

Ameritech Annual Report

A&P FATTENS PROFITS
BY SHARING THEM

It wasn't long ago that the Great Atlantic & Pacific Tea Company, the grocery chain we know as A&P, was being called "the worst in the business" by its rivals. After four straight years of losses, the company had only 1016 stores in 1982 compared to 3468 in 1974. But then A&P turned to an important but neglected resource—its employees.[1]

Beginning in the Philadelphia area, an experimental plan designed to boost productivity *and* employees' earnings was worked out with the United Food & Commercial Workers (UFCW) Union. Workers were asked to take a 25 percent cut in pay in exchange for the opportunity to earn percentage bonuses whenever they could boost sales revenues, or keep labor costs in a store at or below 11 percent of sales. This was a risky venture in a low-margin business . . . but it worked. A&P credits the incentive program with doubling its market share.

Philadelphia area workers now earn more than their counterparts in other stores when their bonuses are combined with wages. The local union president, Wendell W. Young III, says, "It has been very successful." Workers having a vested interest in the way stores are run make useful suggestions in their bimonthly meetings with management. Yet local union officials admit the program isn't a panacea. It involves putting part of workers' wages at risk, something they don't usually volunteer to do.

On the company side, the innovative plan for giving workers a bonus for raising productivity has spread to nearly 300 stores. Each has trimmed wages, and allowed workers a say in running the business plus the chance to earn bonuses. Indeed, in the Philadelphia area alone A&P has paid out about $2 million per year in bonuses since the program was started.

Chairman James Wood credits the practice with a big share of the company's 81 percent increase in operating profits. Part of A&P's prior woes, he says, were due to an absence of "the motivation you find at a family business." Even though his rivals thought him crazy to attempt the approach, Wood clearly feels differently. "The idea of people getting a piece of what they are trying to achieve has always appealed to me enormously," he says.

Management Applications Question

This case illustrates how creative incentives are used in one company. How will you manage learning, reinforcement, and rewards to achieve similar positive results in your work?

The learning activities in this chapter will help you answer the Management Applications Question. Important topics of study include the following.

Learning
Reinforcement
Positive Reinforcement
Extinction
Punishment
Reinforcement Accolades and Criticisms
Managing Pay as an Extrinsic Reward

Good managers try to promote high levels of work performance and human resource maintenance among their subordinates. One key to effective action is allocating rewards in such a way that desired work behaviors are encouraged and facilitated, rather than discouraged and inhibited. The management of A&P, at least for the stores discussed in the chapter opener, appears to have done just that. But the issues are complicated and challenging. Managers have access to many different kinds of rewards. Some managers, furthermore, are clearly better than others at using them to create high performance and satisfaction in the workplace.

LEARNING

Learning, previously defined in Chapter 1 as a relatively permanent change in behavior resulting from experience, is an important part of rewards management. It is the process through which people acquire the competencies and beliefs that affect their behavior in organizations. An understanding of basic learning principles will deepen your perspectives on the concepts and theories of motivation already studied in Chapter 4. Managers with such an awareness are well positioned to help other persons "learn" the behaviors necessary to achieve maximum positive outcomes from their work.

There are four general approaches to learning—classical conditioning, operant conditioning, cognitive learning, and social learning. Each offers insights of potential value to managers and the field of OB.[2]

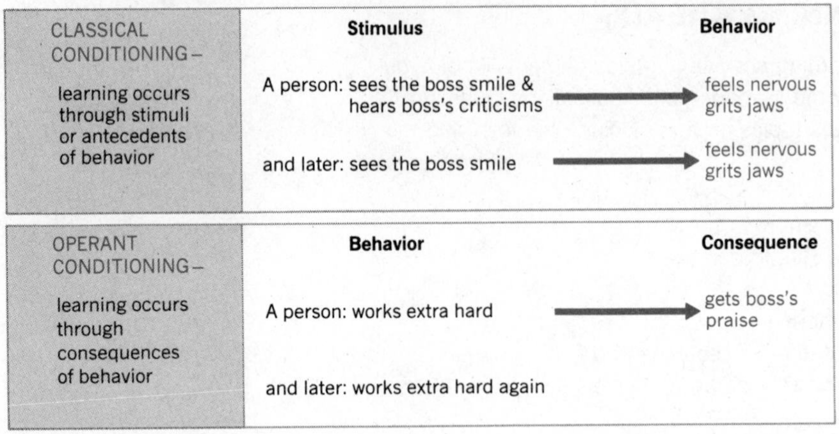

CLASSICAL CONDITIONING— learning occurs through stimuli or antecedents of behavior	**Stimulus**	**Behavior**
	A person: sees the boss smile & hears boss's criticisms ⟶	feels nervous grits jaws
	and later: sees the boss smile ⟶	feels nervous grits jaws

OPERANT CONDITIONING— learning occurs through consequences of behavior	**Behavior**	**Consequence**
	A person: works extra hard ⟶	gets boss's praise
	and later: works extra hard again	

FIGURE 5.1   Differences between the classical and operant conditioning approaches to learning.

Classical Conditioning

Classical conditioning is a form of learning through association. As shown in Figure 5.1, it involves the manipulation of *stimuli* to influence behavior. Classical conditioning associates a previously neutral stimulus, one having no effect on behavior, with another stimulus that does affect behavior. The former thus becomes a *conditioned stimulus* which, upon its occurrence, also draws forth the now *conditioned response*. This process is illustrated in the well-known experiments by Ivan Pavlov, the Russian psychologist, who "taught" dogs to salivate (conditioned response) at the sound of a bell (conditioned stimulus). He did so by ringing the bell when feeding the dogs, something that caused them to salivate. The dogs eventually "learned," through the association of the bell with the presentation of meat, to salivate by the ringing of the bell alone. Reflexive behaviors of humans are also susceptible to classical conditioning. Someone who is verbally reprimanded on several occasions after being "asked to step into the boss's office," for example, may become conditioned to display apprehensiveness and nervous reactions whenever "asked" to come into the office in the future.

Operant Conditioning

Operant Conditioning is learning achieved when the *consequences* of behavior lead to changes in the probability of its occurrence. You may think of it as learning through reinforcement. Figure 5.1 clarifies how this operant or behaviorist approach contrasts with classical conditioning. It views behavior as "operating" on its environment to produce consequences that affect its future occurrence. The noted psychologist B. F. Skinner has popularized operant conditioning as a way of controlling behavior by manipulating its consequences.[3] It has rather substantial applications in the workplace.

Take the earlier example of innovations at A&P. One explanation for the favorable results is that workers receiving bonuses (positive consequences) for their cost reduction efforts (behaviors) proved willing to repeat the desired behaviors over and over again. That is, they "learned" through the positive consequences of their behaviors to continue to do the right things. Whereas classical conditioning works only on behaviors that are reflexive in nature, operant conditioning has a broader application to almost any human behavior.

Cognitive Learning

Cognitive learning is learning achieved by thinking about the perceived relationship between events and individual goals and expectations. The process motivation theories reviewed in Chapter 4 are good examples of how this approach is applied to the work setting. They are concerned with explaining "why" people decide to do things. They do so by examining how people come to view various work activities as perceived opportunities to satisfy needs, pursue desired rewards, and eliminate felt inequities. These cognitive explanations of learning differ markedly from the cognitive or behaviorist explanations of operant conditioning. Take the example of a person walking down the street and finding a $10 bill on the pavement.[4] Thereafter, this person is observed to spend more time looking down when walking. The question is, "why?"

The Cognitive Learning Explanation: The person does so with the goal of finding more money, something held in high value. The person *reasons* that more money may be lost in the streets, and thus *decides* to look down more frequently when out walking in the future.

The Operant Conditioning Explanation: When the initial behavior of "looking down" occurred, it was positively reinforced by the consequence of finding the $10 bill. Having been positively reinforced, the behavior is then repeated when the person is out walking in the future.

Social Learning

Social learning is learning achieved through the reciprocal interactions between people, behavior, and their environment. Social learning theory, as introduced in Chapter 3 and well expressed in the work of Albert Bandura, integrates the cognitive and operant approaches to learning.[5] It recognizes the importance of consequences as determinants of behavior. But, it also emphasizes that people acquire new behaviors by observing and imitating others in the social setting. Learning is not a case of enviromental determinism (classical and operant views) or of individual determinism (the cognitive view). Rather, it is a blending of both.

Social learning theory places special emphasis on three aspects of the learning process—modeling or vicarious learning, symbolism, and self-control. Through **vicarious learning** or **modeling,** people acquire behaviors by directly observing and imitating others. When the "models," such as the manager or a coworker, demonstrate desirable behaviors, this can have major impact on a person's work efforts.

"Mentors," or senior workers who befriend younger and more inexperienced proteges, can also be very important models. In fact, a shortage of mentors for women in management is sometimes cited as a major constraint to their progression up the corporate ladder.

Symbolic behavior can also help people learn. Words and other symbols used by managers and people at work can help communicate values, beliefs, and goals, and thereby become guides to behavior. Finally, people can learn to exercise self-control over their behavior. By observing things that happen, thinking about them, and then trying to manage them to better achieve goals, humans are capable of self-regulation and able to influence their own behavior.

REINFORCEMENT

Reinforcement plays a key role in the learning process. The foundation for this relationship is the "law of effect" as stated by E. L. Thorndike.[6]

Law of Effect: Behavior that results in a pleasant outcome is likely to be repeated; behavior that results in an unpleasant outcome is not likely to be repeated.

The implications of the law of effect for the management applications question that introduced this chapter are straightforward. Those outcomes or environmental consequences that are considered by the reinforcement orientation to determine individual behavior are rewards. Thus, one way in which to increase your ability to successfully manage rewards is to understand the nature of rewards and the principles of reinforcement as they apply to the work setting. Some creative applications are illustrated in Newsline 5.1.

Reinforcement and Rewards

You should remember the distinction between extrinsic and intrinsic rewards as clarified in Chapter 4. The relationship between reinforcement and extrinsic rewards is especially important here.

Extrinsic rewards are positively valued work outcomes that are given to the individual by some other person. They are important reinforcers or environmental consequences that can substantially influence people's work behaviors through the law of effect. Table 5.1 presents a sample of extrinsic rewards that can be allocated by managers to their subordinates. Some of these are *contrived* rewards, which have direct costs and budgetary implications—examples are pay increases and cash bonuses. Others are *natural* rewards, having no cost other than the manager's personal time and efforts—included here are such things as verbal praise and recognition.

NEWSLINE 5.1 / CORPORATE REINFORCEMENTS PUSH SAFE WORK AND HEALTHY HABITS

John Brenda earns about 15 ''Live for Life'' dollars a week for running and lifting weights. His benefactor is also his employer, Johnson & Johnson Company. The innovative program rewards company employees for taking care of their health. The ''dollars'' can be used to buy small commodities like clocks and fire extinguishers. For someone like Brenda it all helps create an incentive to ''work out when I might not feel up to it.''

Similar creative uses of rewards are increasingly common as managers in many organizations try to combat the increasing costs of employees' medical insurance and lost work time due to illness, work-related accidents, and tardiness. City workers in Bellevue, Washington are awarded ''points'' with a monetary value based on the cost of their health insurance—one point must be given up for each dollar of health benefits they use, and the value of the points increases as the number of claims filed by all workers goes down. At Scherer Brothers Lumber Company in Minneapolis, the vice president says: ''We have no sick pay, we have well pay.'' A worker receives an extra two hours of salary for each month he or she is neither late for work nor out ill—annual bonuses of up to $300 can also be earned by losing no more than three work days due to on-the-job injuries.

Employees who don't have an industrial or automotive accident for a month are eligible for lottery drawings at Boston Gas Company—winners get $25 gifts from a catalog. Another lottery at William Byrd Press in Richmond, Virginia rewards employees for containing the cost of health insurance. A person receives a lottery ticket for each $5 of unused premium in their account for the year—cash awards of up to $5000 are available in the annual drawing.

Source: Reported in *Business Week, Time,* and *The Wall Street Journal.*

TABLE 5.1   A Sample of Extrinsic Rewards Allocated by Managers

Contrived Rewards: Some direct cost		Natural Rewards: No direct cost
refreshments	promotion	smiles
piped-in-music	trips	greetings
nice offices	company car	compliments
profit-sharing	pay increase	special jobs
office parties	gifts	recognition
cash bonuses	paid insurance	feedback
sport tickets	stock options	asking advice

Source: Developed from Fred Luthans and Robert Kreitner, *Organizational Behavior Modification and Beyond* (Glenview, Ill.: Scott, Foresman, 1985), p. 126–130.

Reinforcement Strategies

Organizational behavior modification, or ''OB Mod,'' is the systematic reinforcement of desirable work behavior and the nonreinforcement or punishment of unwanted work behavior. It includes four basic reinforcement strategies: positive reinforcement, negative reinforcement, punishment, and extinction. Let us look at these in some detail.[7]

- **Positive reinforcement:** Increasing the frequency of or strengthening a desirable work behavior by making it contingent with the occurrence of a desirable consequence.
  Example—A manager nods to express approval to a subordinate after she makes a useful comment during a staff meeting.
- **Negative reinforcement** or **Avoidance:** Increasing the frequency of or strengthening a desirable work behavior by making it contingent with the removal of an undesirable consequence.
  Example—A manager who has been regularly nagging a worker about his performance, stops nagging when the daily production quota is met one day.

Make sure you understand the difference between positive and negative reinforcement. Both reinforcement strategies seek to encourage *desirable* behavior. They just go about it differently.

- **Punishment:** Decreasing the frequency of or weakening an undesirable behavior by making it contingent with the occurrence of an undesirable consequence.
  Example—A manager docks an employee's pay when he reports late for work one day.
- **Extinction:** Decreasing the frequency of or weakening an undesirable behavior by removing desirable consequences previously contingent with its occurrence.
  Example—A person's disruptive behavior is receiving social approval from co-workers. The manager counsels co-workers to stop giving this approval.

Notice the common goal shared by punishment and extinction as reinforcement strategies. Each seeks to discourage *undesirable* behavior.

The four strategies are further illustrated in Figure 5.2. This example shows how a supervisor uses each of the strategies to direct employee work behavior toward desirable practices. Notice once again that both positive and negative reinforcement are used to strengthen desirable behavior when it occurs; both punishment and extinction are applied to undesirable behaviors in an attempt to decrease the frequency of their occurrence.

The reinforcement strategies may be used in combination with one another, as well as alone. The following discussion places special emphasis on the managerial significance of positive reinforcement, extinction and punishment.

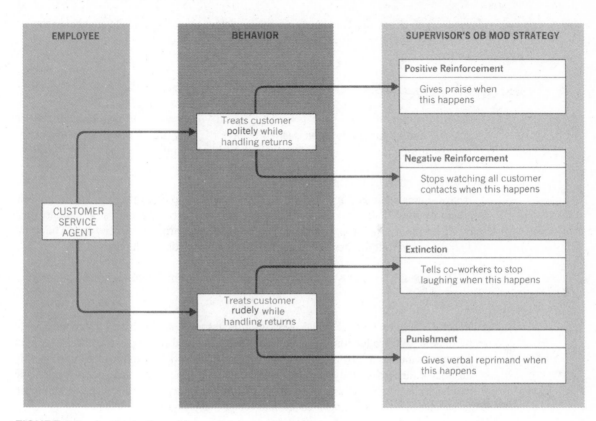

FIGURE 5.2   An illustration of four reinforcement strategies.

POSITIVE REINFORCEMENT

Positive reinforcement is advocated by B. F. Skinner and his followers. To do positive reinforcement well in the work setting you must first be aware of the wide variety of things in the organization that have potential reward value. Table 5.1 introduced a number of such possibilities. Once you know what extrinsic rewards may be available to you as a manager, however, you must then know *how* to allocate them to achieve the desired effects. Two laws guide managerial action in this regard:[8]

The Law of Contingent Reinforcement: For a reward to have maximum reinforcing value, it must be delivered only if the desired behavior is exhibited. This law indicates that rewards given indiscriminately by managers, that is, noncontingently, will not act as positive reinforcers.

The Law of Immediate Reinforcement: The more immediate the delivery of a reward after the occurrence of a desirable behavior, the greater the reinforcing effect on behavior. The longer a manager delays in rewarding a desired behavior, the less likely the reward will act as a positive reinforcer.

A Case of Positive Reinforcement

Taken together, the two prior laws require that you give rewards as immediately as possible and contingently upon desired behavior if they are to serve as positive reinforcers in the work setting. Try your hand in this example.

The Assembly-Line Supervisor

A new young manager finds herself in charge of a group of workers on an automobile assembly line[9] This work unit is expected to produce components at a standard rate of 72 per hour. Actual performance has been running around 45 per hour. The manager's boss is holding her accountable for the production discrepancy.

> How would you analyze and approach this case from a reinforcement point of view?

In actual fact, the manager called her subordinates together and asked them what could be done to get production up to standard. They decided that an extra "break" might justify the increased effort. A deal was made; *if* the workers produced 72 units within an hour's time, *then* they could use the remaining time in the hour as a break. The results were immediate and positive. Within a week the work unit was producing up to standard and was taking a 25 minute break every hour!

> Check your understanding of reinforcement terminology. For the workers, the possibility of an hourly break was a (1) _____. When the break was provided as a result of the production standard being met, it became a (2) _____. Because the break was given only when the production standard was met, the law of (3) _____ was satisfied; because the break closely followed the accomplishment of the production standard, the law of (4) _____ was also satisfied.
>   The correct answers are (1) extrinsic reward, (2) positive reinforcer, (3) contingent reinforcement, (4) immediate reinforcement.

To resume the case, after these results were realized, it became obvious to both the manager and her subordinates that the situation could not continue. Higher management and the other work units would not tolerate this group taking a 25-minute break every hour. Another deal was made: when the group reached 92 units an hour, the remaining time in the hour could be used as a break. As a result of this agreement, the work unit was soon able to take a 10-minute break almost every hour.

This manager used her reinforcement theory well. The result was that she was able to associate a desirable consequence—the work break—with behavior appropriate to organizational goal attainment—exceeding the desired production rate. It is also significant that the break was only one of a number of possible rewards the manager may have tried to use as a positive reinforcer. Wisely, she obtained information from the workers before choosing among the alternative rewards. As a result, the break was highly valued by the workers and proved to be a powerful positive reinforcer of a key work result.

Shaping

The supervisor in the previous example could also have used another form of positive reinforcement to achieve the desired level of production. **Shaping** is the creation of a new behavior by the positive reinforcement of successive approximations to the desired behavior. Recall that the work unit was originally producing 45 units per hour, while 72 per hour was the desired goal. A shaping strategy would be to reward the subordinates with verbal praise and recognition each time they produced more than 45 units in an hour. As production increased, reinforcement would then be given only when production surpassed the previous highest level. Eventually, this rewarding of successive approximations to the desired production goal, that is, shaping, should lead to the accomplishment of the goal. Once production arrived at the standard level, continued positive reinforcement would then be used to stabilize behavior at this new performance.

Scheduling Positive Reinforcement

Positive reinforcement can be given according to continuous and intermittent schedules. **Continuous reinforcement** administers a reward each time a desired behavior occurs. **Intermittent reinforcement** rewards behavior only periodically.

These alternatives are important since the two schedules may have significantly different impacts on behavior. In general:

1. Continuous reinforcement draws forth a desired behavior more quickly than intermittent reinforcement; but continuous reinforcement is more costly in the consumption of rewards.
2. Behavior acquired under intermittent reinforcement lasts longer upon the discontinuance of reinforcement than does behavior acquired under continuous reinforcement.

These differences are relevant in the prior example of the assembly-line supervisor. To succeed with the shaping strategy, positive reinforcement should be given on a continuous basis until the desired behavior is achieved. Then, an intermittent schedule should be used to maintain the behavior at the desired new performance level.

Intermittent reinforcement, as shown in Table 5.2, can be given according to fixed or variable schedules. The variable schedules are considered to result in more consistent patterns of desired behaviors than are fixed reinforcement schedules. *Fixed interval schedules* provide rewards at the first appearance of a behavior after a given

TABLE 5.2 Four Ways to Schedule Intermittent Positive Reinforcement	
Reinforcement Schedule	Example
Fixed interval—Give reinforcer after specific time passes	Weekly or monthly paychecks
Fixed ratio—Give reinforcer after specific number of responses	Piece rate pay or sales commissions
Variable interval—Give reinforcer at random times	Occasional praise by boss on unscheduled "walk arounds"
Variable ratio—Give reinforcer after a random number of responses	Random quality checks with praise for zero defects

time has elapsed; *fixed ratio schedules* result in a reward each time a certain number of the behaviors has occurred. A *variable interval schedule* rewards behavior at random times, while a *variable ratio schedule* rewards behavior after a random number of occurrences.

Guidelines for Positive Reinforcement

To ensure that the allocation of extrinsic work rewards has the desired positive reinforcement effects, a manager should[10]

1. Clearly identify the desired behaviors. That is, determine what specific behaviors will result in positive contributions to organizational goal attainment by each person in the work unit.
2. Maintain an inventory of rewards that have the potential to serve as positive reinforcers for these people.
3. Recognize individual differences as to which rewards will actually have positive value for each person.
4. Let each person know exactly what must be done to receive a desirable reward. Set clear targets, and give performance feedback.
5. Allocate rewards contingently and immediately upon the appearance of the desired behaviors. Make sure that the reward is given only if the desired behavior occurs.
6. Allocate rewards wisely in terms of scheduling the delivery of positive reinforcement.

EXTINCTION

Extinction is the withholding of reinforcement for a behavior that has previously been positively reinforced. Whereas positive reinforcement seeks to establish and maintain desirable work behaviors, the goal of extinction as a reinforcement strategy is to weaken and eliminate undesirable ones. How would you apply this new strategy to the following case?

A Case of Extinction

The president of Alpha Company is worried.[11] One of her bright young assistants is developing a problem behavior that could eventually erode his credibility. At the weekly staff meeting, Jason has started acting more like a comedian than an aspiring executive. He interjects "one-liners" and makes "wisecracks" with increasing frequency during discussions. As a result, the meetings are often disrupted. The president is becoming annoyed and is especially concerned because Jason's behavior has gotten worse during the last month.

> If you were the president of Alpha, how would you use reinforcement theory to analyze this situation?

The president decided not to reprimand Jason. Rather, she tried to analyze his behavior in terms of the environmental consequences that it produced for him. She reasoned that his behavior must be receiving some sort of positive reinforcement. At the next two meetings, she closely observed Jason's disruptive behavior and its results. She noticed that two other staff members usually acknowledged Jason's remarks with smiles and by nodding approval. In fact, the president noticed that Jason immediately looked to these persons each time after making one of his disruptive comments.

In terms of reinforcement theory, the president has found that Jason is being positively reinforced by these two persons for a behavior that is organizationally undesirable. Given this diagnosis, the president decided on a strategy of extinction. She went to Jason's two colleagues and asked them to avoid approving his disruptive behavior. They did so. In future meetings the frequency of his "joking" decreased dramatically.

Extinction and Positive Reinforcement

Extinction can be especially powerful when combined with positive reinforcement. In fact, this is what actually occurred in the previous case. Extinction caused Jason to stop making disruptive comments. However, the president was still concerned that Jason maintain and even increase his useful contributions. Whenever such a valuable comment was made, therefore, she provided him with immediate acknowledgment and approval. These extrinsic rewards had a positive reinforcing effect on desirable behavior. Thus, the combined strategy of extinction and positive reinforcement is a most useful tool for managers.

PUNISHMENT

Another reinforcement strategy that managers use to eliminate undesirable behavior is **punishment.** This involves delivering an unpleasant consequence contingent upon the occurrence of an undesirable behavior. To punish an employee, a manager may deny the individual a valued reward, such as praise or even merit pay; or the manager may administer an adversive or obnoxious stimulus, such as reprimand or monetary fine. It is just as important to understand punishment as a reinforcement strategy as it is to understand the principles of positive reinforcement. Punishment can be done poorly, or it can be done well. Your goal, of course, is to know when to use this strategy, and then to know how to do it right.

Problems with the Punishment Strategy

Problems may accompany a manager's use of punishment. Three deserve special mention.

1. *Although a behavior may be suppressed as a result of punishment, it may not be permanently abolished.*   An employee, for example, may be reprimanded for taking unauthorized work breaks. The behavior may stop, but only when the manager is visible. As soon as the threat of punishment is removed from the situation, such as when the manager is no longer present, the breaks may occur once again.
2. *The person who administers punishment may end up being viewed negatively by others.*   A manager who frequently punishes subordinates may find that he or she has an unpleasant effect on the work unit even when not administering punishment. This manager has become so associated with punishment that his or her very presence in the work setting is an unpleasant experience for others.
3. *Punishment may be offset by positive reinforcement received from another source.*   A worker may be reinforced by peers at the same time that punishment is being received from the manager. Sometimes the positive value of such peer support may be strong enough to cause the individual to put up with the punishment. Thus, the undesirable behavior continues. As many times as a student may be verbally reprimanded by an instructor for being late to class, for example, the "grins" offered by other students may well justify the continuation of the tardiness in the future.

Does all of this mean that you should never punish? No. The important things to remember are to do punishment selectively, and then do it right. Consider the following case.

A Case of Punishment

Peter Jones is a forklift operator in a warehouse.[12] This is the highest paid nonsupervisory job in the firm. It is considered a high-status job, and it took Peter five and a half years to work himself into the position. Unfortunately, he is prone to "show off" by engaging in a variety of unsafe driving habits that violate federal safety codes. Pete's manager "chews him out" regularly, but the unsafe driving continues.

Pete's boss analyzed the situation from a reinforcement perspective. He sought to determine what environmental consequences were associated with Pete's unsafe driving habits. As you may have predicted, he found that the undesirable behavior was typically followed by laughter and special attention from the other warehouse workers. He decided that it would be impossible to enlist their aid to implement a strategy of extinction similar to the one followed by the president of Alpha.

The next time Pete was observed to drive unsafely, Pete's boss took him off the forklift truck, explained what he was doing wrong and what was desired, and reassigned him to general warehousing duties for a period of time. When allowed back on the forklift, Pete drove more safely. Finally, a true punishment had been found.

Punishment and Positive Reinforcement

Punishment can also be combined with positive reinforcement. Pete, for example, could now be positively reinforced when observed to drive safely. Then he would know exactly what was wrong and the unpleasant consequences associated with it, and what was right and the pleasant consequences with which it may be associated. This combined strategy is advantageous in that it may help a manager to avoid the first problem identified: having an undesirable behavior suppressed for a period of time but not abolished.

Guidelines for Punishment

The following guidelines are useful for managers using punishment as a reinforcement strategy.[13]

1. *Tell the individual what is being done wrong.*   Clearly identify the undesirable behavior that is being punished.
2. *Tell the individual what is right.*   Identify clearly the desirable alternative to the behavior that is being punished.
3. *Punish in private.*   Avoid public embarrassment by punishing someone in front of others.
4. *Punish in accord with the laws of contingent and immediate reinforcement.*   Make sure that the punishment is truly contingent upon the undesirable behavior and follows its occurrence as soon as possible.
5. *Make the punishment match the behavior.*   Be fair in equating the magnitude of the punishment with the degree to which the behavior is truly undesirable.

REINFORCEMENT ACCOLADES AND CRITICISMS

The effective use of reinforcement strategies can assist in the management of human behavior at work. Testimony to this effect is found in their application in formal OB Mod Programs used by many substantial corporations, including General Electric, B.F. Goodrich, Emery Airfreight, and many others.[14] It is also supported by the growing number of consulting firms who specialize in reinforcement techniques. However, we must also recognize that managerial use of these approaches is not without criticism. Some reports on the "success" of specific OB Mod programs, for example, are single cases analyzed without the benefit of scientific research designs. It is hard to conclude definitively that the observed results were "caused" by reinforcement dynamics. In fact, one critic argues that the improved performance may well have occurred only because of the goal-setting involved—that is, because specific performance goals were clarified and workers were individually held accountable for their accomplishment.[15]

Another criticism rests with the potential value dilemmas associated with the use of applied operant conditioning techniques to influence human behavior at work. For example, there is expressed concern that the systematic use of reinforcement strategies[16]

1. Leads to a demeaning and dehumanizing view of people that stunts human growth and development
2. Results in managers abusing the power of their position and their knowledge by exerting external control over individual behavior

Advocates of OB Mod attack the problem straight on. They agree that behavior modification involves the control of behavior. But they also argue that behavior control is an irrevocable part of every manager's job. "Managers manipulate people all the time," they might say. The real question is, "How are we to ensure that this manipulation is done in a positive and constructive fashion"?

Each of us must consider these dilemmas and express *our* values in the process. It is inevitable that a manager influences the behavior of other people—and it must be done well if the manager's challenge is to be met successfully. Thus the real question may not be whether it is ethical to control behavior, but whether it is ethical *not* to control it well enough so that the goals of both the organization and all of its members are served.

In sum, we expect that continuing research will mainly refine our knowledge of the reinforcement strategies rather than dramatically change existing insights. Their worth in application to work settings seems clearly established. Future research will probably tell us how, as managers, to better use the various reinforcement strategies. That we should be using them already seems well established.

MANAGING PAY AS AN EXTRINSIC REWARD

Pay is one of the important extrinsic rewards made available to people through work-ing. It can help organizations attract and retain highly capable workers, and it can help satisfy and motivate these workers to work hard to achieve high performance. But, as suggested in Figure 5.3, it doesn't always work that way. Indeed, pay is a very complex reward whose many facets make it a good example for us to use in this inquiry into reinforcement and the management of extrinsic rewards.

Multiple Meanings of Pay

To begin, a manager must understand why pay is important to people if he or she is to use it effectively as a reward. Various OB theories recognize multiple meanings of pay and the potential of these meanings to vary from one person or situation to the next. When it comes to the relationship between pay and job satisfaction, for example, each of the following theories with which you are already familiar offers a slightly different perspective.

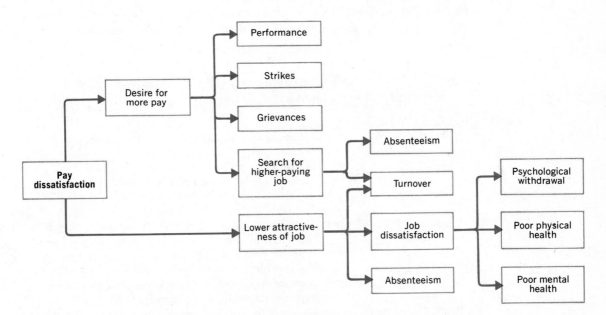

FIGURE 5.3   The consequences of pay dissatisfaction. (From *Pay and Organizational Effectiveness: A Psychological View* by Edward E. Lawler III, p. 233, Copyright © 1971 Edward E. Lawler, III. Used with permission.)

Under Maslow's hierarchy of needs theory   pay is a unique reward that can satisfy many different needs. It is used directly to satisfy lower-order needs, such as the physiological; and it is of symbolic value in satisfying higher-order needs, such as ego fulfillment.

Under McClelland's acquired needs theory   pay is important as a source of performance feedback for high-need achievers; it can be attractive to persons with high needs for affiliation when offered as a group bonus; it is valued by the high need for power person as a means of buying prestige or control over others.

Under Herzberg's two-factor theory   pay in the form of base wage or salary is a hygiene factor which may cause dissatisfaction when the amount is too low. Merit pay raises given as special rewards for jobs done well can cause increased satisfaction and motivation.

The expectancy and equity theories as well as the reinforcement orientation give additional insight into the multiple meanings of pay and their potential relationships to job performance. These ideas are summarized in Table 5.3, and they each show that pay can serve as a good motivator of work effort . . . *when properly managed*. The highlighted phrase is the real key to the issue. For pay to prove successful as a reward that is truly motivational to the recipient, it must be given (1) contingent with the occurrence of specific and desirable work behaviors and (2) in a manner consistent with the positive aspects of the equity dynamic. Merit pay and a variety of emerging creative pay practices are applications that deserve your special consideration.

TABLE 5.3   The Multiple Meanings of Pay as Viewed from a Performance Perspective

Theory	The Meaning of Pay
Equity theory	Pay is an object of social comparison. People are likely to compare their pay and pay increases with those received by others. When felt inequity occurs as a result of such comparisons, work effort may be reduced in the case of negative inequity or increased in the case of positive inequity.
Expectancy theory	Pay is only one of many work rewards that may be valued by individuals at work. When valence, instrumentality, and expectancy are high, pay can be a source of motivation. The opportunity to work hard to obtain high pay will, however, be viewed in the context of other effort–outcome expectancies and the equity dynamic.
Reinforcement theory	Pay is one of the extrinsic rewards that a manager may use to influence the work behavior of subordinates. Through the techniques of operant conditioning, pay can be used as a positive reinforcer when the laws of contingent and immediate reinforcement are followed.

Merit Pay

Edward Lawler is a management scholar and consultant whose work has contributed greatly to our understanding of pay as an extrinsic reward. His research generally concludes that, for pay to serve as a source of work motivation, high levels of job performance must be viewed as the path through which high pay can be achieved.[17] **Merit pay** is defined as a compensation system that bases an individual's salary or wage increase on a measure of the person's performance accomplishments during a specified time period. That is, merit pay is an attempt to make pay contingent upon performance.

Although research supports the logic and theoretical benefits of merit pay, it also indicates that the implementation of merit pay plans is not as universal or as easy as we might expect. One study, in fact, found only 22 percent of surveyed American workers reporting a direct link between how hard they worked and how much they were paid. The same study also reported 73 percent of the workers felt that the absence of merit pay resulted in a decrease in their work efforts. This data is discouraging in light of evidence that pay can be a powerful incentive to work when used properly. To work well, a merit pay plan should

- Be based on realistic and accurate measures of individual work performance.
- Create a belief among employees that the way to achieve high pay is to perform at high levels.
- Clearly discriminate between high and low performers in the amount of pay reward received.
- Avoid confusing ''merit'' aspects of a pay increase with ''cost-of-living'' adjustments.

Creative Pay Practices

Managers can use a variety of approaches to increase the positive value and minimize the negative consequences of pay plans.[18] Newsline 5.2 reports on the renewed popularity in American industry of pay incentives as a means of encouraging high productivity. The chapter opening example of pay bonuses at A&P is yet another. A number of important developments in the area of creative pay practices deserve your attention. They include ''skill-based pay,'' ''gain-sharing plans,'' ''lump-sum pay increases,'' and ''cafeteria benefits plans.''

''Skill-Based'' Pay

Skill-based pay rewards people for acquiring and developing job-relevant skills. Pay systems of this sort pay people for the mix and depth of skills they possess, not for the particular job assignment they hold. In a typical manufacturing plant, for example, a worker may know how to perform several different jobs, each of which requires different skills. He or she would be paid for this ''breadth'' of capability, even though working primarily in one job assignment. Of course, this person must be willing to

NEWSLINE 5.2 / PAY FOR PROFITS

American Can is doing it. Bell Atlantic, American Express, Equitable Life, and Tektronix are too. Those are some of the big ones. You may not recognize the names of Soft-Switch and Riley Gear, but they and many other small firms like them are also doing it. What is *it*? Pay for profits, that's what. More and more companies are turning to incentive pay schemes to boost profits and achieve objectives.

At American Can, a new pay scheme allows 40 top managers in the packaging sector to benefit when the success of the whole group goes up. Douglas Moul, a general manager, says he feels like "an entrepreneur" and "an owner" now that he stands to gain if one of his plant's new products is a big seller. Seventy key employees at Soft-Switch are eligible for an annual bonus pool tied to the achievement of specific sales and profit targets. How much an individual gets, depends on measured contributions to the company's success. For the vice president of operations, this means improving customer satisfaction ratings and shortening the time needed to install products. Gain sharing at Riley Gear gives all employees a financial stake in the company's performance. How well the group as a whole does in reaching monthly productivity targets determines the size of the bonus pool. Company President Tom Lowry says, "There's a lot of peer pressure. People know that if we get cost reductions, everyone gets something." He's thinking of expanding the program to include extra vacation time and other nonfinancial rewards.

About 16 percent of blue-collar workers in the United States are covered by pay-for-performance schemes—and the numbers are growing. The average value of the plans comes to about 9 to 10 percent of an hourly worker's annual earnings. Ford's profit sharing plan, being tried in cooperation with the United Auto Workers Union, resulted in an average bonus of $2100+ per worker for the company's banner 1986 performance. A 19-year veteran at one of Ford's plants remarked: "I feel really good about it . . . I'll do my part for the company because they deserve it. They're giving us these profits."

Source: Reported in *The New York Times* and *The Wall Street Journal*.

---

use any of the compensated skills in other assignments and at any time in accordance with the company's needs.

Such skill-based pay systems are rather experimental, but promising. They offer flexibility to the organization in making work assignments and thus offer the potential for increased productivity. The opportunities to master skills and be rewarded for it can also be a source of motivation and satisfaction for workers. One of the difficulties is that the measurement of skill acquisition can sometimes be difficult and even controversial.

"Gain-Sharing" Plans

Cash bonuses, or extra pay for performance above standards or expectations, have been common practice in the compensation of managers and executives for a long time. Top managers in some industries earn annual bonuses of 50 percent or more of their base salaries. This is a substantial ''bonus,'' indeed, and it can be highly motivating. Growing in number and significance today are attempts to extend such opportunities to all employees. Popular among them is **gain-sharing,** an approach which links pay and performance by giving workers the opportunity to share in productivity gains through enhanced earnings.

The Scanlon Plan is probably the oldest and best known gain-sharing plan. Others you may hear or have heard about are the Lincoln Electric Plan, the Rucker Plan, IMPROSHARE, or more generally, profit-sharing plans. All build from a common premise that workers having an impact on productivity increases and improved operating results should share in the benefits. For example, the basic Scanlon Plan operates as follows:

1. A business unit (e.g., plant, division, or department) is defined for purposes of performance measurement.
2. Some concrete measure of costs is agreed upon for this business unit, as well as appropriate time periods for performance measurement.
3. Employee bonuses are paid to all members of the business unit according to a predetermined formula relating the size of bonuses to realized cost savings.

The intended benefits of gain-sharing plans include increased worker motivation, due to the pay-for-performance incentives, and greater sense of personal responsibility for making performance contributions to the organization. Because they can be highly participative in nature, gain-sharing plans may also encourage cooperation and teamwork in the workplace. Although more remains to be learned about gain-sharing, it is being used by a growing number of large and small organizations. They are doing so to achieve benefits such as those just described.

''Lump-Sum Pay Increases''

Do you know what an annual pay raise of $1200 is worth when spread over 52 pay checks? It means exactly $23.08 per week! This figure is even further reduced when taxes and other deductions are made. Most of us don't have any choice in such matters. Our ''annual'' pay increases are distributed in proportionate amounts as part of weekly, biweekly, or monthly paychecks. And, as a result, they may lose considerable motivational impact in the process.

An interesting alternative is the **lump-sum pay increase** program, which lets people elect to receive an increase in one or more lump-sum payments. The full increase may be taken at the beginning of the year and used for some valued purpose (e.g., a down payment on a car or a sizable deposit in a savings account). Or, a person might elect to take one-half of the raise early and get the rest at the start of the winter holiday season. In either case, the motivational significance of the pay increase is presumably enhanced by allowing the individual to receive it in larger doses and realize the most personal significance out of its expenditure as possible.

Another related, but more controversial development in this area is the lump-sum *payment* as differentiated from the lump-sum *increase.* The former is an attempt by employers to hold labor costs in line and still give workers more money—if corporate earnings allow. It involves giving workers a one-time lump-sum payment, often based upon a gain-sharing formula, instead of a yearly percentage wage or salary increase. In this way a person's base pay remains fixed, while overall monetary compensation varies according to the bonus added to this figure by the annual lump-sum payment. American labor unions, in particular, are somewhat resistant to this approach.

"Cafeteria Benefits" Plans

The total compensation package of an employee includes not only direct pay but also any fringe benefits that are paid by the organization. These fringe benefits often add an equivalent of 10 to 40 percent to a person's salary. It is argued that organizations need to allow for individual differences when developing such benefit programs. Otherwise the motivational value of this indirect form of pay incentive is lost. One popular approach is to let individuals choose their total pay package by selecting benefits from a range of options made available by the organization. These **cafeteria benefits plans** allow workers to select benefits according to needs. A single worker, for example, may prefer quite a different combination of insurance and retirement contributions than a married person. The predicted result is increased motivational benefit from pay as an extrinsic work reward.

Cafeteria benefits plans are popular with employers and with many employees. It offers flexibility to both parties in the employment relationship, but they can also contain some disadvantages. Some plans shift costs to the employee by raising the required co-payments and deductibles on such things as medical and dental coverage. Then, too, the Internal Revenue Service continues to monitor the plans in an attempt to determine which benefits may actually be taxable. Yet the plans are growing in number and offer workers new opportunities to tie more closely this form of monetary compensation to their personal needs.

SUMMARY

The significance of extrinsic work rewards can be summed up this way. Every manager will want to make sure that his or her use of extrinsic rewards promotes individual job performance and human resource maintenance as desirable work results. There are many types of extrinsic rewards. Thus, a manager must know which extrinsic rewards are available for allocation and how to allocate them to achieve the desired impact on performance and satisfaction.

The predominant themes of this chapter have been learning and reinforcement. We began with a review of learning as a concept and as it is approached from the classical conditioning, operant conditioning, cognitive learning, and social learning perspectives. This led into a detailed look at several basic strategies and principles of reinforcement, something that lies at the heart of learning. We have discussed them with special emphasis on positive reinforcement, extinction, and punishment.

Pay is an especially important extrinsic reward because of the multiple meanings with which it is associated. Previous theories of motivation are valuable in helping a manager identify these meanings. Yet there will be many challenges to be met when a manager actually seeks to use pay to help promote satisfaction and performance in the workplace. Our discussion of creative pay practices demonstrates the lengths to which some organizations and their managers have gone to try to realize motivational gains from their investments in rewards. This special case of pay illustrates quite well the multifaceted challenge of managing extrinsic rewards. Remember,

> money is one tool among many for managing motivation. It is a treacherous tool because it is deceptively concrete, tempting many managers to neglect other variables in the work situation and climate that really affect productivity. In the near future, there will be less and less excuse for neglecting these variables. . . .

David I. McClelland[19]

THINKING THROUGH THE ISSUES

1. How do "operant conditioning" and "cognitive learning" differ from one another? Of what significance to managers are these differences?
2. What is "social learning theory"? How does it integrate the operant and cognitive approaches to learning and human behavior?
3. Explain "OB Mod." Describe how one or more reinforcement strategies could be used to deal with an employee who is consistently late for work, but very productive once present.
4. Do you believe in the power of positive reinforcement when rewards other than pay are used as the potential reinforcers? Defend your answer.
5. When do you feel a manager is justified in using punishment as a reinforcement strategy? What guidelines should be followed when administering punishment?
6. Do you agree or disagree with those critics who claim that the systematic use of reinforcement strategies by managers is an unethical control of human behavior? Why or why not?
7. What is an "extrinsic" work reward? What are some examples of extrinsic rewards that managers might use to encourage high performance by subordinates? What does it mean to say that these rewards are best given on a "performance-contingent" basis?
8. Choose two of the creative pay practices discussed in this chapter. Do you feel the practices are valuable from the perspectives of (1) the managers who must implement them, and (2) their subordinates who participate in them? Explain your answers.

CASE: HIGHVIEW STORES

Highview Stores is a convenience chain operating 14 small retail outlets in an eastern state.[20] Specializing in groceries, each store is run by a store manager (SM) during the day and night manager during the evening. Of the two, the night manager has little authority over decision-making and is mainly an evening "care-taker." The store manager employs one or two clerks, assisted once a week by an extra clerk, who stock shelves and handle bulk shipments and inventories.

The firm is headed by the president to whom a vice president and general manager (VP) reports. The VP directs the SMs of four stores, a day regional manager (RM) responsible for five stores, and night regional manager (NRM) responsible for another five.

At first, SMs were paid a flat salary that was adjusted by "headquarters" only when something significant had been done to improve store operations. There were no regular performance reviews, and salary adjustments were actually based more on length of service than performance accomplishments. In addition to base salary, the SMs were eligible for annual cash bonuses. These were distributed by the VP based on his personal evaluation of an SM's years of experience, overall value to the firm, and inventory shrinkage at the SM's store (i.e., the difference between actual inventory and projected inventory based on sales receipts). Most stores experienced shrinkage of one-half to one percent, and it was always discussed at what they called the VP's "regular weekly punishment" meetings. Nevertheless, the SM's jobs were quite secure and they had little fear of discharge.

One April, top management concluded the company was in trouble. Inventory shrinkage was high, 3.42 percent of sales, and growing; sales were down; stores looked sloppy; SMs were unhappy with their pay; SMs seemed unconcerned about supervising clerks and fulfilling management expectations. It was decided to test a new reward system in 10 of the 14 stores.

The plan was to pay the SMs on a commission plus annual bonus basis. The commission was negotiated with the VP and averaged 7 percent of a store's weekly sales. But, they had to pay a number of direct expenses out of this figure, including the clerk's wages, long distance phone calls, bad checks, and the like. Whatever was left after these expenses were deducted from the commission was the weekly income of the SM. The company covered things felt to be outside of the SM's control, such as insurance and electricity. The annual bonus was based on years service and inventory shrinkage. Another bonus based on store appearance was paid semiannually.

The SM's average weekly income rose 8.41 percent under the new system. The average store payroll for clerks dropped 3.33 percent. For the company as a whole, the new annual bonuses cost $4000 more than before, payroll expenses overall increased 3.56 percent, inventory shrinkage decreased an amazing 80.73 percent, and sales increased 5.3 percent. Although top management continued to make other organizational and operational improvements during the period, the new pay system was credited with a substantial portion of these positive results.

Questions

1. Before the new pay system was introduced, what incentives existed for the SMs to improve store performance? Should these incentives have been sufficient to guarantee high-performance results? Why or why not?
2. Analyze the new pay system in reinforcement terms. What reinforcement strategies did it involve? Why do you feel they apparently worked so well?
3. What is your evaluation, based on information available in the case, of the

VP's effectiveness as a manager? What suggestions would you offer, and why, to further enhance this effectiveness?

EXERCISE: ANNUAL PAY RAISES

Purpose:

This exercise will allow you to experience the choices faced by managers when they make pay raise decisions. It will help you to review some of the theoretical issues involved in attempts to use pay as a motivator and to apply these issues in a realistic and practical work setting.

Time:

50 minutes.

Procedure:

1. Read the instructions on the accompanying "Employee Profile Sheet," and decide on a percentage pay increase for each of the eight employees.[21]
2. Make salary increase recommendations for eight managers that you supervise. There are no formal company restrictions on the size of raises you give, but the total for everyone should not exceed the $7000 (a 4 percent increase in the salary pool) which has been budgeted for this purpose. You have a variety of information upon which to base the decisions, including a "productivity index" (PI), which Industrial Engineering computes as a quantitative measure of operating efficiency for each manager's work unit. This index ranges from a high of "10" to a low of "1." Indicate the percentage increase *you* would give each manager in the blank space next to their names. Be prepared to answer "why."

_____ *A. Alvarez*   Alvarez is new this year and has a tough work group whose task is dirty and difficult. This is a hard position to fill, but you don't feel Alvarez is particularly good. The word around is that the other managers think so too. PI = 3. *Salary* = $21,000.

_____ *B.J. Cook*   Cook is single and a "swinger" who enjoys leisure time. Everyone laughs at the problems B.J. has getting the work out, and you feel it certainly is lacking. Cook has been in the job two years. PI = 3. *Salary* = $22,500.

_____ *Z. Davis*   In the position three years, Davis is one of your best people even though some of the other managers don't agree. With a spouse who is independently wealthy, Davis doesn't need money, but likes to work. PI = 7. *Salary* = $24,600.

_____ *M. Frame*   Frame has personal problems and is hurting financially. Others gossip about Frame's performance, but you are quite satisfied with this second year employee. PI = 7. *Salary* = $22,700.

_____ *C.M. Liu*   Liu is just finishing a fine first year in a tough job. Highly respected by the others, Liu has a job offer in another company at a 15 percent increase in salary. You are impressed and the word is that the money is important. PI = 9. *Salary* = $22,000.

_____ *B. Ratin*   A first-year manager who you and the others think is doing a good job. This is a bit surprising since Ratin turned out to be a "free spirit" who doesn't seem to care much about money or status. PI = 9. *Salary* = $21,800.

_____ *H. Smith*   A first-year manager recently divorced and with two children to support as a single parent. The others like Smith a lot, but your evaluation is not very high. Smith could certainly use extra money. PI = 5. *Salary* = $21,000.

_____ *G. White*   White is a big spender who always has the latest clothes and a new car. In the first year on what you would call an easy job, White doesn't seem to be doing very well. For some reason, though, the others talk about White as the "cream of the new crop." PI = 5. *Salary* = $21,000.

3. Convene in a group of four to eight persons. Share your raise decisions with them. As a group, decide on a new set of raises and be prepared to report them to the rest of the class. Make sure that the group spokesperson can provide the rationale through which each person's raise was determined.

4. The instructor will call on each group to report its raise decisions. After some discussion, your instructor will give you the "expert's" decisions. More discussions will follow.

THE MANAGER'S VOCABULARY

Classical Conditioning   A form of learning through association that involves the manipulation of stimuli to influence behavior.

Cognitive Learning   A form of learning achieved by thinking about the perceived relationship between events and individual goals and expectations.

Continuous Reinforcement   This schedule administers a reward each time a desired behavior occurs.

Extinction   Decreasing the frequency of or weakening an undesirable behavior by making it contingent upon the removal of a desirable consequence.

Extrinsic Rewards   Positively valued work outcomes that are given to the individual by some other person in the work setting.

Gain-Sharing   A pay system that links pay and performance by giving workers the opportunity to share in productivity gains through increased earnings.

Intermittent Reinforcement   This schedule rewards behavior only periodically.

Law of Contingent Reinforcement   The view that for a reward to have maximum reinforcing value, it must be delivered only if the desired behavior is exhibited.

Law of Effect   Thorndike's observation that "behavior that results in a pleasing outcome will be likely to be repeated; behavior that results in an unpleasant outcome is not likely to be repeated.''

Law of Immediate Reinforcement   The more immediate the delivery of a reward after the occurrence of a desirable behavior, the greater the reinforcing effect on behavior.

Learning   A relatively permanent change in behavior resulting from experience.

Lump-Sum Pay Increase   A pay system in which people elect to receive their annual wage or salary increase in one or more ''lump-sum'' payments.

Merit Pay   A compensation system that bases an individual's salary or wage increase on a measure of the person's performance accomplishments during a specified time period.

Modeling (or Vicarious Learning)   Learning new behaviors by directly observing and imitating their demonstration by others.

Negative Reinforcement   Increasing the frequency of or strengthening a desirable work behavior by making it contingent upon the avoidance of an undesirable consequence.

Operant Conditioning   The process of controlling behavior by manipulating its consequences.

Organizational Behavior Modification (OB Mod)   The systematic reinforcement of desirable organizational behavior and the nonreinforcement or punishment of unwanted organizational behavior.

Positive Reinforcement   Increasing the frequency of or strengthening a desirable work behavior by making it contingent upon the occurrence of a desirable consequence.

Punishment   Decreasing the frequency of or weakening an undesirable behavior by making it contingent upon the occurrence of an undesirable consequence.

Shaping   The creation of a new behavior by the positive reinforcement of successive approximations to the desired behavior.

Skill-Based Pay   A pay system that rewards people for acquiring and developing job-relevant skills in number and variety relevant to organizational needs.

Social Learning   Learning that is achieved through the reciprocal interaction between people and their environments.

Vicarious Learning (or Modeling)   Learning new behaviors by directly observing and imitating their demonstration by others.

IMPORTANT NAMES

Albert Bandura   Psychologist who provided a useful description of social learning theory and its applications.

Edward Lawler III   Management scholar and consultant specializing in pay and reward systems.

B. F. Skinner   Popularized the use of operant conditioning to modify animal and human behavior.

E. L. Thorndike   Expressed the ''law of effect,'' which became a foundation for reinforcement theory.

NOTES

[1]Developed from "How A&P Sharpens Profits by Sharing Them," *Business Week* (December 22, 1986), pp. 44–45; and, "Worker Participation at Some A&P Stores Gives the Chain a Boost," *The Wall Street Journal* (January 1, 1987), p. 1.

[2]For good overviews see W. E. Scott, Jr. and P. M. Podsakoff, *Behavioral Principles in the Practice of Management* (New York: John Wiley, 1985); and, Fred Luthans and Robert Kreitner, *Organizational Behavior Modification and Beyond* (Glenview, Ill.: Scott, Foresman, 1985).

[3]For some of B. F. Skinner's work see *Walden Two* (New York: Macmillan, 1948), *Science and Human Behavior* (New York: Macmillan, 1953), and *Contingencies of Reinforcement* (New York: Appleton-Century-Crofts, 1969).

[4]Edward L. Deci, *Intrinsic Motivation* (New York: Plenum Press, 1975), pp. 7–8.

[5]See Robert Kreitner and Fred Luthans, "A Social Learning Approach to Behavioral Management: Radical Behaviorists 'Mellowing Out'," *Organizational Dynamics,* Vol. 13 (Autumn 1984), pp. 47–65.

[6]E. L. Thorndike, *Animal Intelligence* (New York: Macmillan, 1911), p. 244.

[7]See Fred Luthans and Robert Kreitner, *Organizational Behavior Modification* (Glenview, Ill.: Scott, Foresman, 1975).

[8]Both laws are stated in Keith L. Miller, *Principles of Everyday Behavior Analysis* (Monterey, Calif.: Brooks/Cole, 1975), p. 122.

[9]Adapted from Harry Wiard, "Why Manage Behavior? A Case for Positive Reinforcement," *Human Resource Management* (Summer 1972), pp. 15–20. Used by permission.

[10]Adapted in part from W. Clay Hamner, "Using Reinforcement Theory in Organizational Settings," in Henry L. Tosi and W. Clay Hamner, eds., *Organizational Behavior and Management: A Contingency Approach* (Chicago: St. Clair Press, 1977, pp. 388–395.

[11]Adapted from *Organizational Behavior Modification,* by Fred Luthans and Robert Kreitner. © 1975 Scott, Foresman and Company, pp. 125–126. Reprinted by permission.

[12]Ibid, pp. 127–129.

[13]Developed in part from Hamner, "Using Reinforcement Theory in Organizational Settings."

[14]See Luthans and Kreitner, op cit., 1985.

[15]Edwin A. Locke, "The Myths of Behavior Mod in Organizations," *Academy of Management Review,* Vol. 2 (October 1977), pp. 543–553. For a counterpoint see Jerry L. Gray, "The Myths of the Myths about Behavior Mod in Organizations: A Reply to Locke's Criticisms of Behavior Modification," *Academy of Management Review,* Vol. 4 (January 1979), pp. 121–129.

[16]Robert Kreitner, "Controversy in OBM: History, Misconceptions, and Ethics," in Lee Frederiksen, ed., *Handbook of Organizational Behavior Management* (New York: John Wiley, 1982, pp. 71–91.

[17]For complete reviews of theory, research, and practice, see Edward E. Lawler III, *Pay and Organizational Effectiveness* (New York: McGraw-Hill, 1971); Edward E. Lawler III, *Pay and Organization Development* (Reading, Mass.: Addison-Wesley, 1981); and, Edward E. Lawler III, "The Design of Effective Reward Systems," pp. 255–271, in Jay W. Lorsch (Ed.), *Handbook of Organizational Behavior* (Englewood Cliffs, N.J.: Prentice-Hall, 1987).

[18]This discussion draws on Lawler, op cit., 1981 and 1987. Both books are excellent sources for a background on performance-based pay plans and developments in creative pay practices.

[19]David C. McClelland, "Money as a Motivator: Some Research Insights," *The McKinsey Quarterly* (Fall 1967), p. 41.

[20]Developed from Stuart C. Feedman, "Performance-Based Pay: A Convenience Store Case Study," *Personnel Journal,* Vol. 64 (July, 1985), pp. 30–34.

[21]Suggested by an exercise "Motivation through Compensation" in Douglas T. Hall, Donald D. Bowen, Roy J. Lewicki, and Francine S. Hall, *Experiences in Management and Organizational Behavior,* 2nd ed. (New York: John Wiley, 1982).

CHAPTER 6
JOB DESIGN, GOAL SETTING, AND WORK SCHEDULING

In order to sustain Apple's high level of innovation, we must give the people within Apple every opportunity to work creatively—unafraid to experiment, to dare the impossible.

Apple Computer, Inc. Annual Report

JOB ROTATION KEEPS SWISSAIR FLYING HIGH

Swissair sets many of the standards in the air travel industry. It is consistently rated by travelers as one of, if not *the* best of the world's airlines. And it makes money too. The company has turned a profit consistently now for over 30 years. Among the many innovations that collectively keep Swissair on top of the competition is a job rotation program in which managers periodically shift among various departments.

Peter Graf, general manager of North American Operations, says: "Probably the greatest fear that any company has is that employees will become too complacent . . . morale and motivation can diminish, and productivity will most likely drop." Board Chairperson Armin Baltensweiler adds, "We are very concerned with the happiness of our staff . . . We put a great deal of time and money into human resources—we want to ensure that our employees remain productive and stimulated."

The job rotation program broadens managers' viewpoints by giving them expanded knowledge in the full range of company operations. A typical manager will be rotated several times in the course of a career. This often means being assigned to unfamiliar areas, but a person won't be sent into a position without some qualifications. The major determining factors in who gets chosen and who doesn't are—overall job performance and demonstrated initiative.

Being selected for job rotation is a source of individual pride. It is a signal that Swissair wants to invest in someone's future by giving them hands-on experience in different areas. Managers who do it get to know people in various divisions, and learn about others' unique problems and priorities. Individual capabilities are stretched as managers are forced to respond to new and unfamiliar challenges, and to rely on the assistance of others along the way. They gain valuable experience, become more well-rounded, and feel a greater sense of loyalty to the company in the process.

Job rotation at Swissair has helped create a group of managers who work more closely together and are better able to understand the needs of one another's departments. As Graf notes, "If you've had experience in several different areas, you'll understand the needs of other managers better."

Management Applications Question

People at all levels of work responsibility deserve the opportunity to satisfy personal needs in the pursuit of productivity. How will you, as a manager, design jobs to facilitate high levels of task performance and human resource maintenance within your work unit?

PLANNING AHEAD

After reading and participating in the learning activities provided in this chapter, you will develop new and creative responses to the management applications question. The topics you will study include the following:

Intrinsic Work Rewards
Job Design in Theory
Job Design in Practice
A Diagnostic Approach to Job Enrichment
Goal Setting
Alternative Work Schedules

This chapter continues our study of rewards and their impact on individual performance and job satisfaction. The opening example introduces a new and important element into the study of motivation and work behavior—the nature of the job itself. Our interest here begins with the subject of intrinsic work rewards, proceeds by examining a number of useful job design strategies, and ends with a look at alternative ways of scheduling work.

INTRINSIC WORK REWARDS

Intrinsic rewards are those rewards received by an individual directly as a result of task performance. One example is the feeling of achievement that comes from completing a challenging project. Such feelings are individually determined and integral to the work itself. They are self-regulated in that a person is not dependent on an outsider, such as the manager, to provide them. This is in direct contrast to the nature of extrinsic rewards such as pay, which, you should recall, are externally controlled. The following comments from people at work further highlight this unique nature of intrinsic rewards.[2]

Teacher:	"The money I earn as a teacher is nothing; but I really enjoy teaching a student a new idea."
Machinist:	"The company doesn't give me a darn thing; but I take pride in producing a quality product."

Social worker: "My working conditions are bad and my co-workers are boring; but I get a real sense of satisfaction out of helping my clients."

When we discussed extrinsic rewards, the conclusion was that they should be given contingent upon work performance. The manager was viewed as an agent of the organization; as a person responsible for allocating extrinsic rewards such as pay, promotion, and verbal praise to employees. To serve in this capacity, a manager must be good at evaluating performance, maintaining an inventory of valued work rewards, and giving these rewards to employees in proportion to their performance contributions.

The management of intrinsic work rewards is an additional challenge for the manager. The manager still acts as an agent of the organization. Now, however, he or she must design jobs for individual subordinates so that intrinsic rewards become available to them as a direct result of working on assigned tasks. There is a natural tendency at this point to assume that every manager should design every job to provide every employee maximum opportunity to experience intrinsic work rewards. This is not a good assumption. Indeed, this chapter will help you to understand

- When people may desire intrinsic work rewards.
- How to design jobs for people who desire greater intrinsic work rewards.
- How to motivate those people who do not desire intrinsic work rewards.

JOB DESIGN IN THEORY

Our investigation of the intrinsic sources of motivation begins with the job itself. What, really, is a "job"? We all have them, but can we define the term? A **job** is one or more tasks that an individual performs in direct support of the organization's production purpose. The key word in this definition is "tasks." In fact, **intrinsic motivation** is essentially task motivation, that is, a desire to work hard solely for the pleasant experience of task accomplishment. When a job is properly designed, both task performance and job satisfaction should be facilitated. Additional human resource maintenance aspects, such as absenteeism, commitment, and turnover, may also be influenced.

Job design is the planning and specification of job tasks and the work setting in which they are to be accomplished. This definition encompasses both the specification of task attributes and the creation of a work setting for these attributes. The manager's responsibility is to design jobs that will be motivational for the individual employee. Figuratively speaking, this is properly done when

$$\text{Individual needs} + \text{task attributes} + \text{work setting} \xrightarrow[\text{to}]{\text{lead}} \text{performance and satisfaction}$$

The history of scholarly interest in job design traces in part to Frederick Taylor's work with "scientific management" in the early 1900s. As described in Supplementary Module A at the end of the book, Taylor and his contemporaries sought to increase the efficiency of people at work. Their approach was to break a job into its basic components, and then estabish exact time and motion requirements for each task to be done. These early efforts were forerunners of the industrial engineering approaches to job design that attempt to determine the best processes, methods, work-flow layouts, output standards, and person-machine interfaces for various jobs. The Hawthorne studies of the 1920s, also described in Supplementary Module A, and the subsequent human relations movement of the 1950s and 1960s, further broadened job design issues to include other social and human factors. It is out of this historical context that the modern and comprehensive approaches to job design have emerged.

JOB DESIGN IN PRACTICE

We can surely agree that job designs are important to the individual employee. Two questions, however, remain to be answered. What are some of the alternative strategies of job design? And which of these strategies provides more intrinsic work rewards for the employee? Let us answer these questions by example.

A Case in Job Design

Charles Krug is a competent person who is motivated by social satisfactions.[3] He likes to participate in interesting conversations and feels good when being helpful or stimulating to other persons. How do you think Charles will react to each of the following job designs?

The Assembly-Line Job

Charles reports to a work station on an assembly line. The product is electric toasters. A partially assembled toaster passes in front of Charles on a conveyor belt every 2½ minutes. Charles puts plastic handles on each toaster and then lets the conveyor take the unit to the next work station. Everyone gets a 10-minute break in the morning and afternoon. There is a ½-hour lunch period. Charles works by himself in a rather noisy and cluttered setting.

> Note below your predictions for Krug's performance and satisfaction in this work setting.

Job satisfaction: low   moderate   high

Job performance: low   moderate   high

The Modified Assembly-Line Job

Charles reports to work on the same assembly line. Now, however, a toaster comes to Charles' station every 12 minutes and he performs a greater number of tasks. He adds the sides to the assembly, puts on the two handles, and installs the "light–dark" selection switch. Periodically, Charles changes stations with one of the other workers and does a different set of tasks. In all other respects, the work setting is the same as in the first job described.

Mark your predictions once again.

Job satisfaction: low   moderate   high

Job performance: low   moderate   high

The Team Assembly Job

Charles is part of a team responsible for assembling electric toasters. The team has a weekly production quota, but it makes its own plans for the speed and arrangement of the required assembly processes. The team is also responsible for inspecting the quality of the finished toasters and for correcting any defective units. These duties are shared among the members and are discussed at numerous team meetings. Charles has been selected by the team as its plant liaison. In addition to his other duties, he works with people elsewhere in the plant to ensure a smooth supply of component parts to his team.

Make a final set of predictions for Krug in this last job.

Job satisfaction: low   moderate   high

Job performance: low   moderate   high

Now, we can identify the following categories of job design strategies that are available to managers: job simplification, job enlargement and rotation, and job enrichment. Each of these strategies has its merits and demerits. A manager must learn when and how to employ each to its proper advantage.

Job Simplification

Job simplification involves standardizing work procedures and employing people in very clearly defined and specialized tasks. Charles Krug's first assembly-line job was simplified. The machine-paced automobile assembly line is a classic example of this job-design strategy. One person's description of what it can be like to work on such a job follows.[4]

For eight hours every day, says Henry Belcher, a 40-year old welder, "I am as much a machine as a punch press or a drill motor is." . . .

Promptly at 6 AM, the assembly line begins sending cars past his work station, and from then on Belcher is a part of the line, like the well-oiled gears and bearings. The noise is deafening; Belcher could not talk to the men at the next stations three feet away even if there were time. There never is.

Partially assembled cars move past him at the rate of 62 an hour; in less than one minute he is expected to look over each auto, pound out a dent in a fender or reweld an improperly joined seam. Cars that cannot be fixed that quickly are taken off the line. In the winter, drafts from ill-caulked windows chill Belcher's chest, while hot air blasts from rust-proofing ovens 30 feet away singe his back. After two hours of standing on the concrete floor his legs ache, but the whistle does not blow for lunch until 10 AM. . . .

The potential advantages of simplified job designs include increased operating efficiencies. Jobs can be staffed by low-skill and low-cost labor, they require little training, and production quantity is easily controlled. Possible disadvantages, on the other hand, include loss of efficiency due to low-quality work, high rates of absenteeism and turnover, and the need to pay high wages to get people to do unattractive jobs. Some of these are quite consistent with the experience described by Henry Belcher. These negative aspects are prone to emerge when a simplified job fails to satisfy individual needs. In the earlier example of Charles Krug, an important social need was thwarted by his first assembly-line job. Thus, we would predict that his job satisfaction would be low and that he would be frequently absent. Boredom may lead to a high error rate, and his overall performance will probably be just good enough to prevent him from being fired!

Simplified jobs are highly specialized and usually require an individual to perform repetitively a narrow set of tasks. In today's "high technology" age, a natural direction is complete **automation**—allowing a machine to do the work previously accomplished through human effort. This increasingly involves the use of robots, as illustrated in Newsline 6.1.

Job Enlargement and Job Rotation

The job enlargement and job rotation strategies seek to increase the "breadth" of a job by adding to the variety of tasks performed by a worker. Task variety is assumed to offset some of the disadvantages of job simplification and thereby increase job performance and satisfaction for the individual.

Job enlargement increases task variety by combining into one job two or more tasks that were previously assigned to separate workers. The only change in the original job design is that a worker does more different tasks than previously. **Job rotation,** as illustrated in the chapter opener, increases task variety by periodically shifting workers among jobs involving different tasks. Job rotation can be arranged according to almost any time schedule, such as hourly, daily, or weekly.

Charles Krug's second job on the modified assembly line is an example of job enlargement with occasional job rotation. Rather than doing only one part of the toaster assembly task, he did three. Furthermore, he occasionally changed jobs with another worker to complete a different phase of the assembly process.

Because job enlargement and rotation reduced some of the monotony of Krug's original assembly-line job, we would expect an increase in both his satisfaction and

NEWSLINE 6.1 / "STEEL-COLLAR" WORKERS

It used to be you could only see robots on automobile assembly lines in some progressive plants. Now they are breaking out of Detroit and starting to show up in more and more places. Visit a custom upholstery factory and you might find a robot slicing carpeting to fit inside vans; at a novelties company look for robots to be stretching balloons flat so slogans can be printed on them; at a jewlery factory don't be surprised if a robot is positioning class rings while they are engraved by laser.

Yes, robots aren't just for the automobile industry any more, and prospects for the robotics industry are looking up. As robots are becoming lighter, faster, and more intelligent, their range of applications is rapidly increasing. Many of the more successful robot makers are focusing their machines on basic operations that can be fine tuned or "customized" to fit a number of alternative jobs. Some concentrate on robots that handle small components, for example, while others specialize in those that dispense liquids. One of the problems of the past has been robot "breakdowns," which can be very costly in most manufacturing settings. The newer models are more reliable than some of their predecessors. Companies to watch in this developing market for "steel-collar" workers are Adept Technology, American Cimflex Corporation, and Intelledex, Inc., among others.

Reported in *Business Week*.

performance. Satisfaction should remain at a moderate level, however, since the job still does not provide a strong response to Krug's social needs. In addition, although quality should increase as boredom is reduced, low intrinsic motivation and lingering absenteeism are also likely to keep job performance at a moderate level.

Job Enrichment

Frederick Herzberg, whose two-factor theory was discussed in Chapter 2, feels that it is illogical to expect high levels of motivation from employees whose jobs are designed according to the rules of simplification, enlargement, or rotation. "Why," he asks, "should a worker become motivated when one or more 'meaningless' tasks are added to previously existing ones or when work assignments are rotated among equally 'meaningless' tasks?"[5] Rather than pursuing one of these job design strategies, therefore, he recommends that managers practice job enrichment.

Job enrichment is the practice of building motivating factors into job content. This job design strategy differs from the previous ones in that it seeks to expand job content by adding some of the planning and evaluating duties normally performed by

TABLE 6.1 Herzberg's Principles of Job Enrichment	
Principle	Motivators Involved
1. Remove some controls while retaining accountability	Responsibility and achievement
2. Increase the accountability of individuals for own work	Responsibility and recognition
3. Give a person a complete natural unit of work (module, division, area, and so on)	Responsibility, achievement, and recognition
4. Grant additional authority to an employee in his or her activity; provide job freedom	Responsibility, achievement, and recognition
5. Make periodic reports directly available to the worker rather than to the supervisor	Recognition
6. Introduce new and more difficult tasks not previously handled	Growth and learning
7. Assign individuals specific or specialized tasks, enable them to become experts	Responsibility, achievement, and recognition

Source: Copyright © 1968 by the President and Fellows of Harvard College; all rights reserved. Reprinted by permission of the *Harvard Business Review,* ''One More Time: How Do You Motivate Employees?'' by Frederick Herzberg, January–February 1968.

the manager to the subordinates' job. These changes, which increase the ''depth'' of a job, are referred to by Herzberg as a **vertical loading** of the job tasks.

Charles Krug's final job in the team assembly situation contains elements of job enrichment. The team became responsible for doing some of the planning and evaluating work, typical managerial tasks, as well as for the actual assembly of toasters. Charles should find this arrangement especially satisfying for the intrinsic rewards it provides in response to his strong social needs. He should get added satisfaction from acting as the team's plant liaison because his assigned tasks bring him into regular contact with other people. This increase in intrinsic motivation should result in high levels of both job satisfaction and performance.

The seven principles guiding Herzberg's approach to job enrichment are listed in Table 6.1. Note that each principle is an action guideline designed to increase the presence of one or more motivating factors in the content of a job. Remember, too, that in the job enlargement and rotation strategies managers retain all responsibility for work planning and evaluating. The job enrichment strategy, by contrast, involves vertical loading that allows subordinates to share in these planning and evaluating responsibilities, as well as to do the actual work.

A Continuum of Job Design Strategies

The various strategies of job design are summarized on a continuum in Figure 6.1. This figure shows how the strategies differ in degree of task specialization and as sources of intrinsic work rewards. The availability of intrinsic rewards is lowest for task attributes associated with simplified jobs, and highest for enriched jobs. Task specialization, in turn, is higher for simplified jobs and lower for enriched ones.

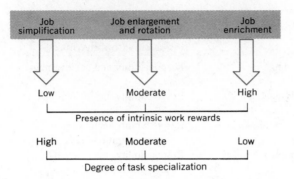

FIGURE 6.1 A continuum of job design strategies.

A DIAGNOSTIC APPROACH TO JOB ENRICHMENT

Herzberg's thinking implies that everyone's job should be enriched in order to improve job satisfaction and motivation to work. Although intrigued by the concept of job enrichment, OB scholars were uncomfortable with job enrichment being universally applied to all types of people working in all types of jobs and settings. The diagnostic approach developed by Richard Hackman and his colleagues offers a popular alternative way to address job design in a contingency fashion.[6]

The Theory

The current version of this "job characteristics" theory or model is shown in Figure 6.2. Five core job characteristics are identified as being task attributes of special importance to job designs. A job that is high in the core characteristics is said to be enriched. The core job characteristics and their definitions are

Skill variety: The degree to which a job requires a variety of different activities in carrying out the work and involves the use of a number of different skills and talents of the employee.

Task identity: The degree to which the job requires completion of a "whole" and identifiable piece of work, that is, one that involves doing a job from beginning to end with a visible outcome.

Task significance: The degree to which the job is important and involves a meaningful contribution to the organization or society in general.

Autonomy: The degree to which the job gives the employee substantial freedom, independence, and discretion in scheduling the work and determining procedures used in carrying it out.

Feedback from the job itself: The degree to which carrying out the work activities results in the employee obtaining direct and clear information on how well the job has been done.

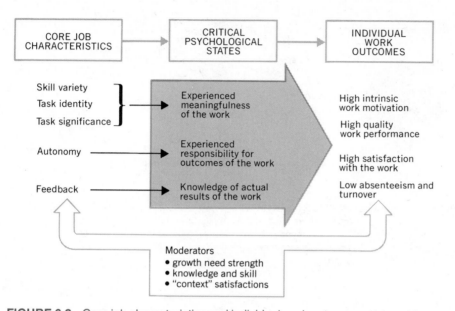

FIGURE 6.2 Core job characteristics and individual work outcomes. (Adapted from J. Richard Hackman and Greg R. Oldham, "Development of the Job Diagnostic Survey," *Journal of Applied Psychology,* Vol. 60, 1975, p. 161. Used by permission.)

Hackman and his colleagues state further that three critical psychological states must be realized for people to develop intrinsic work motivation: (1) experienced meaningfulness in the work, (2) experienced responsibility for the outcomes of the work, and (3) knowledge of actual results of the work activities. These psychological states represent intrinsic rewards that are believed to occur, and influence later performance and satisfaction, when the core job characteristics are present in the job design.

Consider the case of Christine Szczesniak who used to perform one job repetitively as a check processor for a bank.[7] Her job has been redesigned to include nearly all the tasks relating to checks received from the bank's clients. This includes receiving the checks, depositing them, calling customers with account information, and mailing reports to them. About the new job design, Christine says: "I think it's exciting and different . . . it has cut down on the error ratio . . . I like it . . . you see the package from beginning to end . . . it's better to be part of the whole thing."

This theory recognizes that the five core job characteristics do not affect all people in the same way. Growth need strength, one of the moderators shown in Figure 6.2, is considered an important source of individual variation. The theory predicts that people with strong growth needs will respond positively to enriched jobs, whereas people low in growth need strength will have negative reactions and find enriched jobs a source of anxiety. These relationships are summarized in Figure 6.3.

Other variables that may have similar moderating effects are an individual's knowledge and skill, and degree of satisfaction with job context. The point about knowledge and skill once again highlights how important a sense of competency can be to people

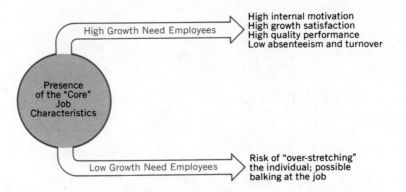

FIGURE 6.3   Growth needs and the core job characteristics. (From J. Richard Hackman, Greg Oldham, Robert Janson, and Kenneth Purdy, "A New Strategy for Job Enrichment." Copyright © 1975 by the Regents of the University of California. Reprinted from *California Management Review*, Vol. 17, p. 60 by permission of the Regents.)

at work. People whose capabilities match the requirements of an enriched job are likely to experience positive feelings and perform well; people who are or who feel inadequate in this regard are likely to have difficulties. By the same token, people who are satisfied with such things as the hygiene factors in job context are likely to respond more positively to a newly enriched job than are persons who are dissatisfied with them.

This diagnostic approach to job enrichment has been examined in a variety of work settings, including banks, dentists' offices, corrections departments, and telephone companies, among others. The results are promising, but additional research is needed to refine and more completely support the concept.[8] At the moment, researchers generally agree that job enrichment is not a universal panacea for job performance and satisfaction problems. They also recognize that job enrichment can fail when job requirements are increased beyond the level of individual capabilities and/or interests. In this regard, it is important to remember that

- Growth need strength is a key variable that may influence how different people will react to jobs high in the core characteristics.
- Jobs high in the core characteristics are likely to increase job satisfaction, especially among high growth need employees.
- Jobs high in the core characteristics may lead to improved work performance by the people who do them.

Implementing the Diagnostic Approach

A diagnostic approach to job enrichment holds promise for the practicing manager. To make sure that you fully understand the concept, let's work through the following case.

Travelers Insurance Company

The company depends heavily on computerized information processing.[9] This information is generated from keypunched cards that serve as input to the computer. The keypunch operators' job is to transfer data onto punched cards from printed or written documents supplied by user departments.

Requests for keypunching come from many departments within the company. These requests are received in the keypunch unit by assignment clerks who review the requests for accuracy, legibility, and so on. Rejected requests are sent to the unit supervisor, who corrects the problems through direct contact with the user departments. Accepted requests are parceled out to keypunch operators in batches requiring approximately one hour of punching time.

The operators are supposed to punch exactly the information on the input documents, even when obvious coding mistakes exist. A verifier then checks all punching for accuracy as measured against the supporting documents. Any punching errors are randomly assigned back to the operators for correction.

1. Use the following scale to assess the keypunch operator's job on each of the five core job characteristics.

Skill variety	low	high
Task identity	low	high
Task significance	low	high
Autonomy	low	high
Feedback	low	high

2. Based on your analysis of the job, what do you predict in terms of the operators' job performance and satisfaction?

Job satisfaction:	low	moderate	high
Job performance:	low	moderate	high

Continuing On

Travelers Insurance Company became concerned because the keypunch operators were apathetic and sometimes hostile toward their jobs. Error rates were high and absenteeism was frequent. If you predicted low performance and satisfaction, you were right.

The company next hired a professional consulting firm to look into the situation. The consultants concluded that the motivating potential of the keypunch job was low. Specifically, they identified the following weaknesses.

Skill variety: There was none. Only a single skill was involved, the ability to punch the data recorded accurately on input documents.

Task identity: It was virtually nonexistent. Keypunch batches were assembled to provide an even work load in the unit, but this did not create whole and identifiable jobs for the operators.

Task significance: None was apparent. The keypunching operation was a necessary step in providing service to the company's customers. The individual operator, however, was isolated by an assignment clerk and a supervisor from any knowledge of what the operation meant to the user department let alone its meaning to the customers of the company.

Autonomy: There was none. The operators had no freedom to arrange their daily tasks to meet production schedules, or to resolve problems with the user departments, or even to correct, while punching, information that was obviously wrong.

Feedback: There was none. Once a punching batch left the operator's hands, he or she was not guaranteed feedback on its quality, since punching errors were randomly assigned back to the operators.

Continuing On

The consultants ultimately decided to enrich the job design. Initially, however, they did so only for some operators. The jobs of the others were left unchanged to serve as a control group. This quasi-experimental procedure was followed to provide evaluative data as to whether or not the enriched job was beneficial for the company and the operators. Thus, a decision could be made to abandon the program if it was not working or to revise it in a constructive fashion.

The actual changes made by the consultants to enrich the keypunch operator's job illustrate five implementation concepts central to the diagnostic approach to job enrichment. These concepts indicate that, to improve upon the five core job characteristics, a manager must be skilled at combining tasks, forming natural work units, establishing client relationships, vertical loading, and opening feedback channels. The relationship between these implementation concepts and the core job characteristics is shown in Figure 6.4. Their use in the present case included:

1. *Forming natural units of work:*   The random assignment of work batches was discontinued. Instead, each operator was assigned continuing responsibility for certain accounts, either user departments or specific recurring jobs. Now all work for a given account always goes to the same operator.
2. *Combining tasks:*   Some planning and evaluating duties were included along with the central task of keypunching. These changes are elaborated upon as we discuss the additional changes undertaken.
3. *Establishing client relationships:*   Each operator was allowed direct contact with keypunch clients. The operators, not the assignment clerks, now inspect input documents for correctness and legibility. When problems arise, the operator, not the supervisor, takes them up with the client.
4. *Opening feedback channels:*   The operators are provided with a number of additional sources of data about their performance. The computer department now returns incorrect cards to the operators who punched them and operators correct their own errors. Each operator also keeps a personal file of punching errors. These can be reviewed to determine trends in the frequency and types of errors being made. Each operator receives a weekly computer printout

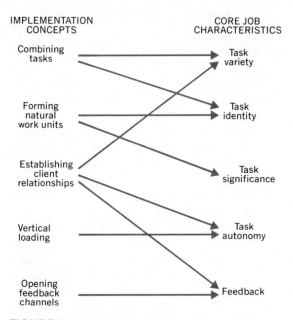

IMPLEMENTATION
CONCEPTS

CORE JOB
CHARACTERISTICS

FIGURE 6.4   Implementation concepts and the core job characteristics. (Adapted from J. Richard Hackman et al., "A New Strategy for Job Enrichment." Copyright © 1975 by the Regents of the University of California. Reprinted from *California Management Review*, Vol. 17, p. 62 by permission of the Regents.)

summarizing errors and productivity. This report is sent directly to the operator rather than to the supervisor.

5. *Vertical loading:*   Operators now have the authority to correct obvious coding errors on input documents. They also set their own punching schedules and plan their daily work, as long as they meet deadlines. Some competent operators have been given the option of not having their work verified.

Questions and Answers on Job Enrichment

The far-ranging, indeed world-wide, appeal of job design as an important focus for productivity development and performance improvement in organizations is illustrated in Newsline 6.2. Before we leave this discussion, however, there are probably a number of questions still in your mind. Answering these questions gives us a way of summarizing previous points and orienting you to the remaining issues to be covered in this chapter.

Question: "Is it expensive to do job enrichment?

NEWSLINE 6.2 / A SOVIET MANAGER STARTS THINKING FOR HIMSELF

Vadim Zavyalov is the general director of Sibelectroterm, a Siberian company making high-temperature metallurgical furnaces in the USSR. By most western standards his job is still fairly well constrained. The state determines prices for the firm's products, sets basic pay scales, and sets profit margins. Until recently, the director even had to await detailed instructions from a government ministry before drawing up his business strategy. But things are loosening up a bit. Reforms, stimulated by pressures for better Soviet economic performance, have granted him more management autonomy and created new worker incentives. "Initiative can be taken, and we're taking it," he says.

Zavyalov now prepares his business plan and then submits it to the ministry for approval.

"We work directly with the customers," he says, "and we know better what we need." He has authority to spend more money than in the past for such things as new technology and restructuring of plant operations. Monetary bonuses also allow workers to increase monthly wages, with the extra pay tied to specific performance accomplishments. They are encouraged to divide bonuses in work teams whose members switch tasks and provide greater job flexibility in plant operations.

Future plans call for adding robots to replace welders, and a new computer which will give the director daily performance data for each shop and work team. Zavyalov's enthusiasm isn't shared by all managers in Soviet industry. Accustomed to running their plants according to state plans and substantial external controls, many are expected to have trouble coping with the new increase in job responsibilities.

Reported in *Business Week*.

Job enrichment can be very costly. It is unlikely that the enrichment of the keypunch operator's job costs very much. But a job enrichment project can get expensive when it requires major changes in work flows, facilities, and/or equipment.

Question: Can job enrichment apply to groups as well as individuals?"

Yes. In Chapter 9 we discuss creative work group designs. These include the innovative efforts that redesigned and enriched work groups on the automobile assembly line at a Volvo plant in Sweden. The application of job design strategies at the group level is growing in many types of settings.

Question: "Will people demand more pay for doing enriched jobs?"

Herzberg argues that if employees are being paid a truly competitive wage or salary (i.e., if pay dissatisfaction does not already exist), then the intrinsic rewards of performing enriched tasks will be adequate compensation for any increased labor required. Other researchers are more skeptical. One study reports that 79 percent of the people whose jobs were enriched in a company felt that they should have been paid more.[10] A manager must be cautious on this issue. Any job enrichment program should be approached with due consideration given to pay as an important program variable.

Question: "What do the unions say about job enrichment?"

It is hard to speak for all unions. Suffice it to say that the following comments made by one union official sound a note of caution for the manager.[11]

> better wages, shorter hours, vested pensions, a right to have a say in their working conditions, the right to be promoted on the basis of seniority, and all the rest. That's the kind of job enrichment that unions believe in. And I assure you that that's the kind of job enrichment that we will continue to fight for.

Question: "Should everyone's job be enriched?"

No, not everyone's job should be enriched. The informed manager will make very careful decisions when considering job enrichment as a way of promoting satisfaction and performance in the work unit. The logic of individual differences suggests that not everyone will want an enriched job. The people most likely to have positive reactions to job enrichment will be those who need achievement, those who hold middle-class working values, and/or those seeking higher-order growth need satisfactions at work. It also appears that job enrichment will be most advantageous when workers are not dissatisfied with hygiene factors found in the job context and have the levels of ability required to do the enriched job. Costs, technological constraints, and work group or union opposition, furthermore, may make it difficult to enrich some jobs.[12]

Question: "What are some summary guidelines for doing job enrichment?"

The guidelines for implementing a program of job enrichment include:

1. Consider a job to be a candidate for job enrichment only when evidence exists that job satisfaction and/or performance is either deteriorating or open for improvement.
2. Use a diagnostic approach and proceed with actual job enrichment only when each of the following conditions is met:
   a. Employees view their jobs as deficient in one or more of the core job characteristics.
   b. Extrinsic rewards and job context are not causing dissatisfaction.
   c. Cost and other potential constraints do not prohibit the types of job design changes necessary to result in enrichment.

     d. Employees view the core job characteristics with high and positive valences.

     e. Employees have needs and capabilities consistent with the new job designs.

3. Whenever possible do a careful evaluation of the results of job enrichment. This gives the manager an opportunity to discontinue the job design strategy or to make constructive changes to increase its value.

4. Expect that enrichment will also affect the job of the supervising manager. He or she will normally be asked to delegate duties to subordinates. Some managers are threatened by this requirement, and they can become anxious or feel frustrated. These managers may need help to make the required personal work adjustments.

Question: ''What lies beyond job enrichment as additional aspects of job design that should receive a manager's attention?''

Other aspects of the work setting are also important job design variables. In the remainder of this chapter, we will examine two characteristics of work settings that are especially subject to managerial control: task goals and work schedules. Proper attention to these variables can extend a manager's job design activities beyond job enrichment.

GOAL SETTING

Without proper goals, employees may suffer a direction problem. Some years ago, for example, the Minnesota Vikings' Defensive End Jim Marshall gathered up an opponent's fumble. Then, with obvious effort and delight, he ran the ball some 50 yards into the *wrong* end zone. Clearly, Jim Marshall did not lack intrinsic motivation. Unfortunately, though, he failed to channel his work energies toward the right goal. Similar problems are found in many work settings. They can be eliminated, or at least reduced, by the proper setting and clarification of task goals.

Goal Setting Theory

Goal setting is the ''process of developing, negotiating, and formalizing the targets or objectives that an employee is responsible for accomplishing.''[13] Incorporating goal setting into job designs results in specific task objectives for each individual. The presence of these objectives is important because of the motivational consequences with which they may be associated.

Edwin A. Locke has developed a set of assertions as to the motivational properties of task goals. Locke's research, and that of others, tends to support his predictions that[14]

1. Difficult goals are more likely to lead to higher performance than less difficult ones.

2. Specific goals are more likely to lead to higher performance than vague or very general ones (such as ''do your best'').
3. Task feedback, or knowledge of results, is likely to motivate people toward high performance when it leads to the setting of higher performance goals.
4. Goals are most likely to lead to higher performance when people have the abilities required to accomplish them.
5. Goals are most likely to motivate people toward higher performance when they are accepted.

This last finding is of special interest to managers. Unless your subordinates accept their task goals, you can't expect to receive a motivational advantage. Research suggests that people will be more inclined to accept goals when they have had the chance to participate in the goal-setting process. Goal acceptance is also enhanced when people feel that the goals are reasonable (i.e., expectancy is high) and when they see a clear relationship between goal attainment and desirable work outcomes (i.e., high instrumentality). Once again, as you can see, the basic tenets of expectancy theory prove useful in explaining work behavior.

Goal Setting and MBO

When we speak of goal setting and its potential to influence individual performance at work, the concept of **management by objectives** (or **MBO**) comes immediately to mind. The essence of **MBO** is a process of *joint* goal setting between a supervisor and a subordinate.[15] It involves managers working with their subordinates to establish performance goals that are consistent with higher-level work unit and organizational objectives. When this process is followed throughout an organization, MBO helps to clarify the hierarchy of objectives as a series of well-defined means–end chains.

The concept of MBO is consistent with the notion of goal setting and its associated principles just discussed. There is a basic element of participation in MBO that offers opportunity to mobilize the potential benefits of goal setting for maximum positive impact on the individual and the organization.

Figure 6.5 depicts a comprehensive view of MBO. It shows how joint discussions between supervisor and subordinate can extend the element of participation from the point of initial goal setting to the point of evaluating performance results in terms of goal attainment. This comprehensive approach to participation and goal setting can offer individuals greater opportunity to find intrinsic rewards from their work and increase their capacity for self-management. MBO, therefore, fits nicely with Locke's emphasis on goal setting as part of a manager's overall job design responsibilities.

ALTERNATIVE WORK SCHEDULES

Another way that work settings may be modified is to rearrange employee work schedules. The requirements of balancing work shifts with family and other personal demands, for example, can make work a difficult endeavor for many people. A manager should recognize at least five alternatives to the traditional 8-hour per day/5 days

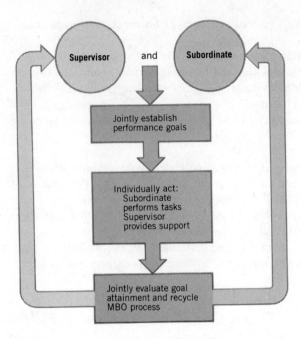

FIGURE 6.5   The management by objectives (MBO) process.

per week work schedule: the compressed workweek, flexible working hours, job sharing, telecommuting, and part-time work. Each of these approaches shares a common concern for making the work day and its time requirements more compatible with individual needs and nonwork activities.

The Compressed Workweek

A **compressed workweek** is any scheduling of work that allows a full-time job to be completed in fewer than the standard five days.[16] The most common form of the compressed work week is the "4–40," that is, 40 hours of work accomplished in four 10-hour days. A 4–40 schedule for a work unit of two employees is shown in Table 6.2. As the table shows, one result of the 4–40 is that employees have three consecutive days off from work each week.

This added time off is the source of most benefits associated with compressed work

TABLE 6.2 A Sample "4–40" Work Schedule						
Employee	Mon.	Tues.	Wed.	Thurs.	Fri.	Sat.	Sun.
Smith	*On*	*On*	*On*	*On*	Off	Off	Off
Jones	Off	*On*	*On*	*On*	*On*	Off	Off

week plans. The individual often benefits from increased leisure time, more 3-day weekends, free weekdays to pursue personal business, and lower commuting costs. The organization can benefit, too, in terms of reduced energy consumption during 3-day shutdowns, lower employee absenteeism, improved recruiting of new employees, and having extra time available for building and equipment maintenance.

The disadvantages may include increased fatigue from the extended workday and family adjustment problems for the individual, and increased work scheduling problems and possible customer complaints due to breaks in work coverage for the organization. Possible constraints on utilization of compressed workweek schedules include occasional union opposition and laws that require some organizations to pay overtime for work that exceeds 8 hours of individual labor in any one day.

Overall, researchers report generally favorable worker attitudes toward the compressed workweek and find that it has the potential to positively influence job attitudes and behavior. This is particularly true for workers who see the alternative work schedule as a way to compensate for negative job and work setting factors. It is also pointed out that organizations shifting to compressed workweeks might be enriching some jobs as well. If the schedule extends the workday but keeps the organization open for business the same number of days as previously, the number of people at work on a given day may be reduced. This may provide for job enrichment by changing key job characteristics such as autonomy and task responsibility.

Flexible Working Hours

Would you believe that there is a work schedule loaded with advantages, but with few reported disadvantages? Examine these lists of potential benefits then read on.

Organizational Benefits	**Individual Benefits**
Lower absenteeism	More leisure time
Reduced tardiness	Less commuting time
Reduced turnover	Higher job satisfaction
Higher work commitment	Greater sense of responsibility
Higher performance	Easier personal scheduling

The work schedule to which these benefits are assigned is called **flexible working hours,** defined as ''any work schedule that gives employees daily choice in the timing between work and nonwork activities.''[17] A sample flexible working hour schedule is depicted in Figure 6.6. Employees are required to work four hours of ''core'' time.

FIGURE 6.6 A sample flexible working hours scheme.

Flexible time	Core time	Flexible time	Core time	Flexible time

7 A.M.   10 A.M.   12 noon   2 P.M.   4 P.M.   6 P.M.

They are then free to choose their remaining four hours of work from among flexible time blocks.

Flexible working hours, or "flextime," increases individual autonomy in work scheduling. Early risers may choose to come in early and leave at 4 P.M.; late sleepers may choose to start at 10 A.M. and leave at 6 P.M. In between these two extremes are opportunities to attend to such personal affairs as dental appointments, home emergencies, visiting the bank, and so on. Proponents of this scheduling strategy argue that the discretion it allows workers in scheduling their own hours of work encourages them to develop positive attitudes and increase commitment to the organization. Research tends to support this position. The reason for such positive impact may well trace to the ability of flexible working hours to help workers adjust themselves to the demands and opportunities of both work and nonwork involvements.

Among the possible disadvantages of flextime approaches are difficulty in scheduling multiple persons on the system, problems of interdepartmental communication during worker absences, and the potential for employees to become frustrated when problems occur in the absence of their supervisors.

Job Sharing

Another alternative work schedule is **job sharing.** This occurs when one full-time job is assigned to two persons who then divide the work according to agreements made between themselves and with the employer.[18] Job sharing often occurs where each person works one-half day, although it can also be done on such bases as weekly or monthly sharing arrangements.

Organizations can benefit from job sharing when they are able to attract talented people who would otherwise be unable to work. An example is the qualified school-teacher who is also a parent. This person may feel unable to be away from the home a full day, but able to work a half-day. Through job sharing, two such persons can be employed to teach one class. Many other opportunities for job sharing exist.

Telecommuting

Yet another impact of high technology on the workplace has been to make it easier for people to work at home. **Telecommuting** is work done at home and using a computer with linkages to a central office or other employment location.[19] More than 7 million Americans are already doing telecommuting, which is especially popular among computer programmers and growing in frequency in other areas including marketing, financial analysis, and secretarial support services.

Telecommuting provides the potential advantages of flexibility, the comforts of home, and choice of locations consistent with one's preferred life-style. Among the possible disadvantages are a sense of isolation from coworkers, decreased identification with the "team" or work group, and lack of contact with key power and influence networks in the office. Managers, in particular, may find it difficult at times to "supervise" telecommuting workers who they rarely see.

Part-Time Work

There is another work schedule of increasing prominence and controversy in the United States. **Part-time work** is done on a schedule that classifies an employee as "temporary" and requires less than the standard 40-hour work week. It is estimated that as many as 12 million people, or 13 percent of American workers do part-time work.[20] Some 70 percent of them are females.

Part-timers are usually easy to release and hire as needs dictate. Because of this, many organizations use part-time work to hold down labor costs and help smooth out peaks and valleys in the business cycle. This alternative work schedule can be a benefit to people who also hold full-time jobs, or want something less than a full work week for a variety of personal reasons. For someone who is holding two jobs, including at least one part-time, the added burdens can be stressful and may affect performance in either one or both work settings. Furthermore, part-timers often fail to qualify for fringe benefits such as health care, life insurance, and pensions, and they may be paid less than their full-time counterparts. Nonetheless, part-time work schedules are of growing practical importance. They are likely to command additional attention from researchers in the future.

SUMMARY

We can now pull together the accumulated insights of this second part of the book. Your learning objective has been to develop a capability for systematically analyzing the behavior of individuals at work and to identify action alternatives for relating them more productively and with greater satisfaction to their jobs.

The capability to analyze individual behavior at work was established in the first two chapters of Part Two. Chapter 3 looked in detail at basic attributes of individuals, while Chapter 4 discussed various motivation theories. These theories led into Chapter 5, which introduced learning and reinforcement, and their insights for managing extrinsic rewards. In the present chapter, we have looked in depth at intrinsic rewards as a means of promoting individual job performance and human resource maintenance through proper job design.

More specifically, this chaper examined job simplification, enlargement, rotation and enrichment as job design strategies. The job diagnostic model developed by Hackman and his colleagues recognizes that people high in growth, or higher-order, need strengths respond most favorably to job enrichment. To enrich a job, they argue that tasks should be altered to increase the presence of five core characteristics of job content: skill variety, task identity, task significance, autonomy, and feedback. Two characteristics of work settings that may also affect individual motivation are the presence of task goals and the nature of the work schedule. Managers are encouraged to use goal setting and to be aware of compressed workweeks, flexible working hours, job sharing, telecommuting, and part-time work as alternative work schedules for employees.

The responsibility of managers for successfully allocating work rewards is real.

Managers can either use rewards to good advantage, or use them poorly. The challenge to you is clear. To be good at using work rewards as a way of relating people more productively and with greater satisfaction to their jobs, it is important to

- Maintain an inventory of possible work rewards.
- Remain continually aware of different individual work needs.
- Allocate extrinsic rewards on a performance-contingent basis and according to reinforcement principles.
- Design jobs so that task attributes, task goals, and work schedules are properly matched with individual work needs.

Finally, consider this thought, expressed by one worker about jobs in general.

I think most of us are looking for a calling, not a job. Most of us, like the assembly-line worker, have jobs that are too small for the spirit. Jobs are not big enough for people.

Nora Watson, a worker[21]

THINKING THROUGH THE ISSUES

1. Go back to Charles Krug's assembly-line job described earlier in the chapter. Write a profile of the type of person you feel would be satisfied and productive in this job. Defend your profile and describe its managerial implications.
2. Look back to the union official's comment in the section on questions and answers about job enrichment. Why do you think the official feels this way? Do you think this opinion would be shared by most union members? Why or why not?
3. In what types of work situations would job enlargement and/or job rotation be preferred to job enrichment as job design strategies?
4. List and explain three of the conditions cited by Locke as creating motivational properties for task goals? What role should "participation" play in the goal-setting process?
5. In what ways does management by objectives (MBO) offer managers the opportunity to apply and benefit from the insights of Locke's goal-setting theory?
6. Why would (1) flexible working hours and (2) the compressed work week be attractive as alternative work schedules for some people? What difficulties might these schedules create for the managers of persons using them?
7. Extrinsic and intrinsic rewards present quite different challenges to managers who seek to make use of them. What are these differences and what are their implications for managers?
8. What does the closing quotation mean to you? What should it mean to the practicing manager? Explain your answers.

CASE: WORK REDESIGN
IN AN INSURANCE COMPANY

The executive staff of a relatively small life insurance company was considering a proposal to install an electronic data processing system.[22] The proposal to install the equipment was presented by the assistant to the president, John Skully. He had been charged with studying the feasibility of the equipment after a management consultant had recommended a complete overhaul of the jobs within the company.

The management consultant had been engaged by the company to diagnose the causes of high turnover and absenteeism. After reviewing the situation and speaking with groups of employees, the management consultant recommended that the organization structure be changed from functional to client basis. The change in departmental basis would enable management to redesign jobs to reduce the human costs associated with highly specialized tasks.

The present organization included separate departments to issue policies, collect premiums, change beneficiaries, and process loan applications. Employees in these departments complained that their jobs were boring, insignificant, and monotonous. They stated that the only reason they stayed with the company was because they liked the small company atmosphere. They believed the management had a genuine interest in their welfare but felt that the trivial nature of their jobs contradicted that feeling. As one employee said, ''This company is small enough to know almost everybody. But the job I do is so boring that I wonder why they even need me to do it.'' This and similar comments led the consultant to believe that the jobs must be altered to provide greater motivation. But he also recognized that work redesign opportunities were limited by the organization structure. He, therefore, recommended that the company change to a client basis. In such a structure each employee would handle every transaction related to a particular policyholder.

When the consultant presented his views to the executive staff, they were very interested in his recommendation. And, in fact, the group agreed that his recommendation was well founded. They noted, however, that a small company must pay particular attention to efficiency in handling transactions. The functional basis enabled the organization to achieve the degree of specialization necessary for efficient operations. The manager of internal operations stated, ''If we move away from specialization, the rate of efficiency must go down because we will lose the benefit of specialized effort. The only way we can justify redesigning the jobs as suggested by the consultant is to maintain our efficiency; otherwise, there won't be any jobs to redesign because we will be out of business.''

The internal operations manager explained to the executive staff that despite excessive absenteeism and turnover, he was able to maintain acceptable productivity. The narrow range and depth of the jobs reduced training time to a minimum. It was also possible to hire temporary help to meet peak loads and to fill in for absent employees. ''Moreover,'' he said, ''changing the jobs our people do means that we must change the jobs our managers do. They are experts in their own functional areas but we have never attempted to train them to oversee more than two operations.''

The majority of the executive staff believed that the consultant's recommendations should be seriously considered. It was at that point that the group directed John Skully to evaluate the potential of electronic data processing (EDP) as a means to obtain efficient operations in combination with the redesigned jobs. He had completed the study and presented his report to the executive staff.

"The bottom line," Skully said, "is that EDP will enable us to maintain our present efficiency, but with the redesigned jobs, we will not obtain any greater gains. If my analysis is correct, we will have to absorb the cost of the equipment out of earnings because there will be no cost savings. So it comes down to what price we are willing and able to pay for improving the satisfaction of our employees."

Questions
1. What core characteristics of the employees' jobs will be changed if the consultant's recommendations are accepted? Explain.
2. What alternative redesign strategies should be considered? For example, job rotation and job enlargement are possible alternatives; what are the relevant considerations for these and other designs in the context of this company?
3. What would be your decision in this case? What should the management be willing to pay for employee satisfaction? Defend your answer.

EXERCISE: DOING JOB ENRICHMENT

Purpose:
To allow you to practice job enrichment; to compare your results to a consultant's actual solution, and to increase your sensitivity to the many practical issues that a manager must be prepared to face when implementing job enrichment as a job design strategy.

Time:
50 minutes.

Procedure:
1. Working individually or in your assigned group, use the seven principles in Table 6.1 to develop a list of changes that could enrich the position described here. Remember that Herzberg suggests the following guidelines for approaching such a task:
   a. Approach the job with the conviction that it *can* be changed.
   b. Brainstorm a list of possible changes *without* regard to their practicality.
   c. Screen the list to *eliminate*
      (1) Suggestions involving hygiene factors.
      (2) Generalities that fail to represent substantive change directions (e.g., "give them more responsibility").
      (3) Suggestions that represent horizontal rather than vertical loading.
      (4) Technological impossibilities.

2. Once you have a list of suggestions for doing job enrichment, be prepared (or designate someone in your group) to report these ideas to the rest of the class.

3. The instructor will record your suggestions on the blackboard and use them as a basis for further discussion on the job enrichment concept. Since this is a real case, he or she will provide you with the consultant's actual recommendations. These will stimulate additional discussion.

Position Description:[23]

Title   Stockholder Correspondent

Location   Company Headquarters

Duties   Working in the assigned location, a stockholder correpondent will answer letter inquiries received from stockholders requesting information on such things as stock transfer procedures, dividend policies, purchases, or dispositions, and so on. The correspondent will

- Receive inquiries assigned by the supervisor in a quantity sufficient to meet the standard daily production quota.
- Match each inquiry with standardized responses cataloged in a loose-leaf binder according to type of request.
- Draft letter responses to the inquiries based on the standardized format.
- Submit completed letter drafts to the typing pool for final preparation and eventual transmittal to the supervisor for proofreading, signature, and mailing.
- Correct any letters previously drafted and found inappropriate or incorrect by the supervisor.
- Refer back to the supervisor for assignment to a specialist those unique inquiries that fail to fit a standardized response.
- Ask the supervisor for assistance on any especially difficult inquiries.
- Perform additional duties as assigned by the supervisor.

THE MANAGER'S VOCABULARY

Automation   A job design that allows machines to do work previously accomplished by human effort.

Compressed Workweek   Any scheduling of work that allows a full-time job to be completed in fewer than the standard five days.

Flexible Working Hours   Any work schedule that gives employees daily choice in the timing between work and nonwork activities.

Goal Setting   The process of developing, negotiating, and formalizing the targets or objectives that an employee is responsible for accomplishing.

Intrinsic Motivation   Task motivation, that is, a desire to work hard solely for the pleasant experience of task accomplishment.

Intrinsic Work Rewards   Those rewards that are received by the individual directly as a result of task performance.

Job   One or more tasks that an individual performs in direct support of the organization's production purpose.

Job Design   The planning and specification of job tasks and the work setting in which they are to be accomplished.

Job Enlargement   Increasing task variety by combining into one job tasks that were previously assigned to separate workers.

Job Enrichment   The practice of building motivating factors into job content.

Job Rotation   Increasing task variety by periodically shifting workers among jobs involving different tasks.

Job Sharing   The assignment of one full-time job to two persons who divide the work according to agreements made between themselves and with the employer.

Job Simplification   Standardizing work procedures and employing people in very clearly defined and specialized tasks.

Management by Objectives (MBO)   A process of joint goal setting between a supervisor and subordinate.

Part-Time Work   Work done on a schedule that classifies the employee as "temporary" and requires less than the standard 40-hour work week.

Telecommuting   Work done at home and using a computer with linkages to the central office or other places of employment.

Vertical Loading   Increasing job depth by adding responsibilities like planning and controlling previously done by supervisors.

IMPORTANT NAMES

Richard Hackman   Developed, along with colleagues, a diagnostic approach to job design based on five core job characteristics.

Edwin Locke   Specified a goal-setting theory of work motivation.

NOTES

[1]Developed from "Job Rotation Keeps Swissair Flying High," *Management Review*, Vol. 36 (August 1985), p. 10.

[2]Ramon J. Aldag and Arthur P. Brief, "The Intrinsic–Extrinsic Dichotomy: Toward Conceptual Clarity," *Academy of Management Review*, Vol. 2 (1977), pp. 497–498.

[3]Adapted from an example presented in Edward E. Lawler III, *Motivation in Work Organizations* (Monterey, Calif.: Brooks/Cole, 1973), pp. 154–155. Copyright

1970 Time, Inc. All rights reserved. Reprinted by permission.

[4]Reported in "The Grueling Life on the Line," *Time*, Vol. 96 (September 28, 1970), pp. 70–71. Used by permission.

[5]Frederick Herzberg, "One More Time: How Do You Motivate Employees?" *Harvard Business Review*, Vol. 46 (January–February 1968), pp. 53–62.

[6]For a complete description and review of the research see J. Richard Hackman and Greg R. Oldham, *Work*

Redesign (Reading, Mass.: Addison-Wesley, 1980).

[7]Reported in "You See the Package from Beginning to End," *Business Week* (May 16, 1983), p. 103.

[8]See Ibid. For a critical review see Karlene H. Roberts and W. Glick, "The Job Characteristics Approach to Task Design: A Critical Review," *Journal of Applied Psychology,* Vol. 66 (1981), pp. 193–217. For a further perspective see Ricky W. Griffin, *Task Design: An Integrative Approach* (Glenview, Ill.: Scott, Foresman, 1982).

[9]This case is from J. Richard Hackman, Greg Oldham, Robert Janson, and Kenneth Purdy, "A New Strategy for Job Enrichment." Copyright © 1975 by the Regents of the University of California. Reprinted from *California Management Review,* Vol. 17 (1975), pp. 51–71 by permission of the Regents.

[10]Paul J. Champagne and Curt Tausky, "When Job Enrichment Doesn't Pay," *Personnel,* Vol. 3 (January–February 1978), pp. 30–40.

[11]William W. Winpisinger, "Job Enrichment: A Union View," in Karl O. Magnusen, ed., *Organizational Design, Development and Behavior: A Situational View* (Glenview, Ill.: Scott, Foresman, 1977), p. 222.

[12]See William A. Pasmore, "Overcoming the Roadblocks to Work-Restructuring Efforts," *Organizational Dynamics,* Vol. 10 (1982), pp. 54–67; and Hackman and Oldham, op. cit.

[13]Denis D. Umstot, Terrence R. Mitchell, and Cecil H. Bell, Jr., "Goal Setting and Job Enrichment: An Integrated Approach to Job Design," *Academy of Management Review,* Vol. 3 (October 1978), p. 868.

[14]See Edwin A. Locke, Karyll N. Shaw, Lise M. Saari, and Gary P. Latham, "Goal Setting and Task Performance: 1969–1980," *Psychological Bulletin,* Vol. 90 (July–November 1981), pp. 125–152. See also, Gary P. Latham and Edwin A. Locke, "Goal Setting—A Motivational Technique That Works," *Organizational Dynamics,* Vol. 8 (Autumn 1979), pp. 68–80; Gary P. Latham and Timothy P. Steele, "The Motivational Effects of Participation versus Goal-Setting on Performance," *Academy of Management Journal,* Vol. 26 (1983), pp. 406–417; and, Miriam Erez and Frederick H. Kanfer, "The Role of Goal Acceptance in Goal Setting and Task Performance," *Academy of Management Review,* Vol. 8 (1983), pp. 454–463.

[15]For a good review of MBO, see Anthony P. Raia, *Managing by Objectives* (Glenview, Ill.: Scott, Foresman, 1974); Steven Kerr summarizes the criticisms well in "Overcoming the Dysfunctions of MBO," *Management by Objectives,* Vol. 5, No. 1 (1976).

[16]Allan R. Cohen and Herman Gadon, *Alternative Work Schedules: Integrating Individual and Organizational Needs* (Reading, Mass.: Addison-Wesley, 1978), p. 125; see also, Simcha Ronen and Sophia B. Primps, "The Compressed Work Week as Organizational Change: Behavioral and Attitudinal Outcomes," *Academy of Management Review,* Vol. 6 (1981), pp. 61–74.

[17]Cohen and Gadon, op. cit., pp. 38–46. See also, Jon L. Pierce and John W. Newstrom, "Toward a Conceptual Clarification of Employee Responses to Flexible Working Hours: A Work Adjustment Approach," *Journal of Management,* Vol. 6 (1980), pp. 117–134.

[18]Cohen and Gadon, op. cit., p. 127.

[19]See Boas Shamir and Ilan Salomon, "Work-at-Home and the Quality of Working Life," *Academy of Management Review,* Vol. 10 (1985), pp. 455–464.

[20]Information from "Part-time Workers: Rising Numbers, Rising Discord," *Business Week* (April 1, 1985), pp. 62–63.

[21]Statement by Nora Watson found in Studs Terkel, *Working* (New York: Avon Books, 1975), p. xxix.

[22]Case from James L. Gibson, John M. Ivancevich, and James H. Donnelly, Jr., *Organizations: Behavior, Structure, Processes,* 3rd ed., pp. 299–300. © Business Publications, Inc., 1973, 1976, 1979, and 1982. All rights reserved. Used by permission.

[23]Developed from ideas presented in Herzberg, "One More Time."

PART THREE
MANAGING GROUPS IN ORGANIZATIONS

In this part of the book, our focus is on the group as a human resource of organizations. Several questions to keep in mind are

What is a group?

Why do groups exist in organizations?

What makes a group successful?

How do groups affect their members?

How do groups affect organizational performance?

The following case helps to put these and related questions in a managerial perspective. Read the case and test your understanding of group behavior in organizations.

THE CASE OF THE CHANGING CAGE

The voucher–check filing unit was a work unit in the home office of the Atlantic Insurance Company.[1] The assigned task of the unit was to file checks and vouchers written by the company as they were cashed and returned. This filing was the necessary foundation for the main function of the unit: locating any particular check for examination on demand. There were usually eight to ten requests for specific checks from as many different departments during the day. One of the most frequent reasons checks were requested from the unit was to determine whether checks in payment of claims against the company had been cashed. Thus, efficiency in the unit directly affected customer satisfaction with the company. Complaints or inquiries about payments could not be answered with the accuracy and speed conducive to client satisfaction unless the unit could supply the necessary document immediately.

Nine workers staffed this unit. There was an assistant (a position equivalent to a supervisor in a factory) named Ms. Dunn, five other full-time employees, and three part-time workers.

The work area of the unit was well defined. Walls bounded the unit on three sides. The one exterior wall was pierced by light-admitting north windows. The west interior partition was blank. A door opening into a corridor pierced the south interior partition. The east side of the work area was enclosed by a steel mesh reaching from wall to wall and floor to ceiling. This open metal barrier gave rise to the customary name of the unit— "The Voucher Cage." A sliding door through this mesh gave access from the unit's territory to the work area of the rest of the company's agency audit division, of which it was a part, located on the same floor.

The unit's territory was kept inviolate by locks on both doors, fastened at all times. No one not working within the cage was permitted inside unless his or her name appeared on a special list in the custody of Ms. Dunn. The door through the steel mesh was generally used for departmental business. Messengers and runners from other departments usually came to the corridor door and pressed a buzzer for service.

The steel mesh front was reinforced by a rank of metal filing cases where checks were filed. Lined up just inside the barrier, they hid the unit's workers from the view of workers outside their territory, including Mr. Burke, the section head responsible for overall supervision of this unit according to the company's formal plan of operation.

QUESTIONS

1. What level of work performance will be produced by this group? Why?
   high   medium   low
2. What level of membership satisfaction will exist within the unit? Why?
   high   medium   low

CONTINUING ON   On top of the cabinets, which were backed against the steel mesh, one of the male employees in the unit neatly stacked pasteboard boxes in which checks were transported to the cage. They were later reused to hold older checks sent into storage. His intention was less getting these boxes out of the way than increasing the effective height of the sight barrier so the section head could not see into the cage "even when he stood up."

The clerks stood at the door of the cage that led into the corridor and talked to the messengers. The workers also slipped out this door unnoticed to bring in their customary afternoon snack. Inside the cage, the workers sometimes engaged in a good-natured game of rubberband "snipping."

Workers in the cage possessed good capacity to work together consistently, and workers outside the cage often expressed envy of those in it because of the "nice people" and friendly atmosphere there. The unit had no apparent difficulty keeping up with its work load.

OUR VIEWPOINT   The voucher–check filing unit is doing its job. The members also seem reasonably well satisfied with their work. The privacy afforded by the filing cases, opportunities to converse with messengers, afternoon snacks, and the rubberband game all appear to be sources of special enjoyment. The situation seems quite acceptable, unless something changes!

CONTINUING ON   For some time, the controller's department of the company had not been able to meet its own standards of efficient service to the clients. Company officials felt the primary cause to be spatial. Various divisions of the controller's department were scattered over the entire 22-story company building. Communication between them required phone calls, messengers, or personal visits—all costing time. The spatial separation had not seemed very important when the company's business volume was smaller, but business had grown tremendously and spatial separation appeared increasingly inefficient.

Finally in November, company officials began to consolidate the controller's department by relocating two divisions together on one floor. One was the agency audit division, which included the voucher–check filing unit. As soon as the decision to move was made, lower-level supervisors were called in to help with planning. Line workers were not consulted, but were kept informed by the assistants of planning progress. Company officials were concerned about the problem of transporting many tons of equipment and some 200 workers from two locations to another single location without disrupting work flow. So the move was planned to occur over a single weekend, using the most efficient resources available. Assistants were kept busy planning positions for files and desks in the new location.

Desks, files, chairs, and even wastebaskets were numbered prior to the move and were relocated according to a master chart checked on the spot by the assistant. Employees were briefed as to where the new location was and which elevators they should take to reach it. The company successfully transported the paraphernalia of the voucher–check filing unit from one floor to another over one weekend. Workers in the cage quit Friday afternoon at the old stand and reported back Monday at the new.

The exterior boundaries of the new cage were still three building walls and the steel mesh, but the new cage possessed only one door—the sliding door through the steel mesh into the work area of the rest of the agency audit division. The territory of the cage had also been reduced in size. An entire bank of filing cabinets had to be left behind in the old location to be taken over by the unit moving there. The new cage was arranged so that there was no longer a row of metal filing cabinets lined up inside the steel mesh obstructing the view into the cage.

QUESTIONS

1. How will this change affect work performance? Why?

   increase   no change   decrease

2. What will happen to membership satisfaction? Why?

   increase   no change   decrease

CONTINUING ON   When the workers in the cage inquired about the removal of the filing cabinets from along the steel mesh fencing, they found that Mr. Burke had insisted that these cabinets be rearranged so his view into the cage would not be obstructed by them. Ms. Dunn had tried to retain the cabinets in their prior position, but her efforts had been overridden.

Mr. Burke disapproved of conversation. Since he could see workers conversing in the new cage, he "requested" Ms. Dunn to put a stop to all unnecessary talk. Attempts by clerks to talk to the messengers brought the wrath of Mr. Burke down on Ms. Dunn, who was then forced to reprimand her workers.

Mr. Burke also disapproved of an untidy work area, and any boxes or papers that were in sight were a source of annoyance to him. He did not exert supervision directly, but would "request" Ms. Dunn to "do something about those boxes." In the new cage, desks had to be completely cleared at the end of the day, in contrast to the work-in-progress piles left out in the old cage. Boxes could not accumulate on top of filing cases.

The custom of afternoon snacking also ran into trouble. Lacking a corridor door, the food-bringers had to venture forth and bring back their snack trays through the work area of the rest of their section, bringing a hitherto unique custom to the attention of workers outside the cage. The latter promptly recognized the desirability of afternoon snacks and began agitating for the same privilege. This annoyed the section head, who forbade workers in the cage from continuing this custom.

Mr. Burke later made a rule that permitted one worker to leave the new cage at a set time every afternoon to bring up food for the rest. This rigidity irked cage personnel, accustomed to a snack when the mood struck or none at all. Having made his concession to the cage force, Mr. Burke was unable to prevent workers outside the cage from doing the same thing. What had once been unique to the workers in the cage was now common practice in the section.

Although Ms. Dunn never outwardly expressed anything but compliance and approval of superior directives, she exhibited definite signs of anxiety. All the cage workers reacted against Burke's increased domination. When he imposed his decisions upon the voucher–check filing unit, he became "Old Grandma"

to its personnel. The cage workers sneered at him and ridiculed him behind his back. Workers who formerly had obeyed company policy as a matter of course began to find reasons for loafing and obstructing work in the new cage. One of the changes that took place in the behavior of the workers had to do with their game of rubberband snipping. All knew Mr. Burke would disapprove of this game. It became highly clandestine and fraught with dangers. Yet shooting rubber bands increased.

Newly arrived checks were put out of sight as soon as possible, filed or not. Workers hid unfiled checks, generally stuffing them into desk drawers or unused file drawers. Since boxes were forbidden, there were fewer unused file drawers than there had been in the old cage. So the day's work was sometimes undone when several clerks hastily shoved vouchers and checks indiscriminately into the same file drawer at the end of the day.

Before a worker in the cage filed incoming checks, he or she measured the thickness in inches of each bundle to be filed. At the end of each day input was totaled and reported to Ms. Dunn. All incoming checks were measured upon arrival. Thus, Ms. Dunn had a rough estimate of unit intake compared with file input. Theoretically, she was able to tell at any time how much unfiled material she had on hand and how well the unit was keeping up with its task. Despite this running check, when the annual inventory of unfiled checks on hand in the cage was taken, a seriously large backlog of unfiled checks was found. To the surprise and dismay of Ms. Dunn, the inventory showed the unit to be far behind schedule, filing much more slowly than before the relocation of the cage.

OUR VIEWPOINT   The changes have led to a decline in both group task performance and human resource maintenance. New facilities and supervisory practices prevent many of the nonwork activities that were enjoyed so much. Similarly, group practices that once worked to the benefit of the organization now work to its disadvantage. Ms. Dunn is having difficulty controlling the work group and suffers considerable anxiety as a result.

SUMMARY

This change in the voucher–check filing unit's location was badly handled. It involves management decisions that could be greatly improved with a better understanding of group behavior in organizations. The following three chapters will provide you with a knowledge base that can help you to make good decisions when faced with the many challenges of managing groups in organizations. As you read through the three chapters in this part, you will find an increasing emphasis on management applications of the multiple dimensions of group behavior.

---

[1]Adapted from "Topography and Culture: The Case of the Changing Cage," by Cara E. Richards and Henry F. Dobyns. Reproduced by permission of The Society for Applied Anthropology from *Human Organization,* Vol. 16, No. 1 (1957), pp. 16–20.

CHAPTER 7
BASIC ATTRIBUTES OF GROUPS

We believe ... Delta must be staffed with people who are not only experienced and efficient ... but also dedicated to the carrier's goals.

Delta Air Lines, Inc. Annual Report

FORD PRODS DEALERS TO "INVOLVE" EMPLOYEES

DETROIT (AP)—The employees at a Pompano Beach, Fla., Lincoln car dealership helped their boss save $1000 a month by devising a time-saving system for ordering parts. The dealer also took their suggestion to put in a wheelchair ramp to help disabled customers get to a waiting area.[1]

At an Omaha Ford dealership, workers helped save an estimated $500,000 in nearly two years by suggesting reductions in parts supplies and improvements in inventory control.

In Westlake, Ohio, a Ford dealership updated and cleaned up its service department on the advice of workers.

The efforts are part of Ford Motor Co.'s push to get its dealerships around the country to implement "employee involvement" groups that allow workers to take part in running the business. They are designed to improve worker morale and product quality.

"We have everyone working together; normally, they want to stay by themselves," said Joe Chiavaroli, executive vice president and general manager of Pompano Lincoln-Mercury in Pompano Beach. "We're like a family."

At his dealership, 10 of the 105 employees meet once a month in employee involvement groups. The program, started in April, resulted in a new parts ordering system under which vehicle parts that must be obtained from outside the dealership are highlighted by a red underline on service orders.

That brings prompt attention from the parts department and saves $1000 a month in loaner car expenses because the dealership has been able to cut the number of loaners given to customers whose cars are not ready by the promised time, Chiavaroli said.

While Ford has not found these employee involvement groups to be a panacea for poor management—employee relationships among its dealers, the company and its dealers generally have been satisfied with the results. In dealerships, such as those mentioned previously, the groups have helped convince skeptics of the value of group involvement of employees.

Management Applications Question

The "employee involvement" program of Ford reflects good sensitivity to groups as important human resources of organizations. As a manager, you will be called upon to exercise similar creativity and capability. What are the basic attributes of groups that influence their success and functioning in organizations?

PLANNING AHEAD

The reading and other learning experiences offered in
this chapter will acquaint you with the following aspects
of groups in organizations

What Do We Mean by Groups?
Types of Groups in Organizations
Usefulness of Groups in Organizations
Group Effectiveness
The Group as an Open System
Key Group Inputs
Managerial Challenges of Groups

Individuals and groups are the human resource foundations of organizations. We discussed the individual in Part Two. Now it is time to study the collective behavior of individuals in the form of groups. The term "group" raises both positive and negative reactions in the minds of most people. Although it is said that "two heads are better than one," we are also warned that "too many cooks spoil the broth." "A camel is a horse put together by a committee," admonishes the true group skeptic!

The chapter opener is an example of the positive effects that groups can have. Contrast that with Jack Jones' experience.

> Jack was attending a meeting of a group of employees. Their purpose was to make recommendations to management concerning employee parking. At issue was a plant expansion which would take away half the current parking spaces. The meeting was called on short notice and the group members had not had a chance to make advance preparations. The meeting was constantly interrupted by Joe Black, a long-time company cynic. He spent most of his time explaining why various suggestions would not work. The meeting ended after two hours with very little accomplished. Even though the meeting was on company time, Jack was more fed up than ever with groups.[2]

These examples make a useful point. Groups have advantages and disadvantages for their members and for organizations. As far back as the historic Hawthorne studies (see Supplementary Module B), researchers have noted that employees can develop strong group attachments and that these attachments may prove functional or dysfunctional for the organization. In this chapter, our purpose is to introduce you thoroughly to groups in the work setting of the organization. The knowledge foundation estabished here will help you to understand and manage better the multiple and complex dynamics of group behavior.

WHAT DO WE MEAN BY GROUPS?

Suppose that there is an automobile accident and that you join a number of other people gathered around the wreck. Or suppose that you join several persons waiting for an elevator. Are these ''groups''? Not in the way most social scientists define the term. A **group** is a collection of people who interact with each other regularly over a period of time and see themselves to be mutually dependent with respect to the attainment of one or more common goals.[3]

The key elements in the definition are interaction, time, and feelings of mutual dependence for goal accomplishment. Neither the people at the wreck nor those waiting for the elevator would meet all these characteristics. They would be considered an aggregation or collection of individuals, but not a group.

Some people go further and talk about **psychological groups.**[4] These extend the definition one more step by adding the additional criterion that group members are aware of one another's needs and potential resource contributions. Just as we said that not all aggregations are groups, all groups are not psychological groups.

Keeping in mind these notions, let us look at some different types of groups found within organizations.

TYPES OF GROUPS IN ORGANIZATIONS

Groups appear in various forms within the work setting of the organization. It is especially useful to define work groups, formal groups, and informal groups clearly.

Work Groups

A **work group** is one created by the formal authority of an organization to transform resource inputs (such as ideas, materials, and objects) into product outputs (such as a report, decision, service, or commodity).[5] Indeed, it is popular to view organizations as interlocking networks of work groups, as shown in Figure 7.1. Notice the ''linking-pin'' function of the managers in such a network. Through managers, acting as superiors in one group and as subordinates in others, all work groups are interconnected to create some sense of totality for the organization.

Work groups may be permanent or temporary. Permanent groups may appear as departments (for example, market research department), divisions, (General Motors Oldsmobile Division), or units (voucher–check filing unit in the Case of the Changing Cage). Permanent work groups will vary in size. They may be as small as two or

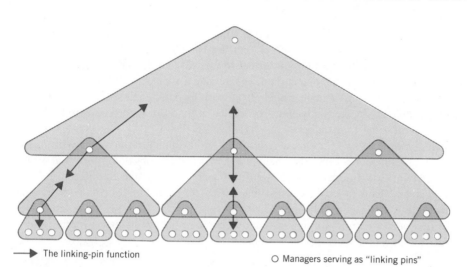

→ The linking-pin function   O Managers serving as "linking pins"

FIGURE 7.1   Likert's linking-pin model of an organization. (From *New Patterns of Management* by Rensis Likert. Copyright © 1961, McGraw-Hill. Used with the permission of McGraw-Hill Book Company.)

three members or as large as several hundred members. Regardless of size, formal work groups all share the common characteristic of being created to contribute to the organization's production purpose. It is the highest-level manager within a work group who is held accountable for this contribution. Earlier, we called this responsibility "the manager's challenge."

Committees and task forces represent temporary forms of work groups. They are created for a specific purpose and typically disband with its accomplishment. Temporary work groups will usually have a chairperson who is accountable for results. You have observed these in organizations to which you have belonged.

Formal and Informal Groups

Social psychologists use the term **formal group** as synonymous with this concept of a work group. Formal groups are created via formal authority for some purpose. They typically have rather clear-cut superior–subordinate relationships, and they often appear on formal organization charts.

It is most important for us that theorists make a distinction between formal and **informal groups.** The latter exist without being formally specified by someone in authority. These are often found as subgroups or cliques within formal groups. You may find, for example, that the same people eat together, go on breaks together, or engage in other spontaneous activities on the job. Informal groups develop across as well as within formally designed work units. For instance, secretaries from one department may eat lunch with those from another.

The key difference between the informal and formal groups is that informal groups emerge spontaneously, whereas formal ones are designated by an organizational authority. Figure 7.2 illustrates how informal groups add complexity to the linking-pin model of organization discussed earlier. They create a vast array of informal, but very real, networks that further relate people from various parts of the organization to one another. Managers, accordingly, must be skilled at working with groups in both their formal and informal forms.

There are at least two reasons why informal groups emerge to coexist with formal groups in organizations. First, they help people to get their jobs done. Informal groups offer a network of interpersonal relationships with the potential to "speed up" the work flow or "gain favors" in ways that formal lines of authority fail to provide. Second, informal groups help individuals to satisfy needs that are thwarted or left unmet in a person's formal group affiliations. Among the things that informal groups can provide in this respect are

Social satisfactions Opportunities for friendships and pleasing social relationships on the job.

Security Opportunities to find sympathy for one's feelings and actions, especially as they relate to friction with the formal organization; opportunities to find help or task assistance from persons other than one's superior.

Identification Opportunities to achieve a sense of belonging by affiliating with persons who share similar values, attitudes, and goals.

FIGURE 7.2 Informal groups and Likert's linking-pin model of organization.

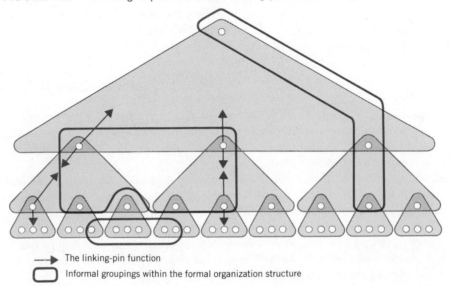

→ The linking-pin function

▢ Informal groupings within the formal organization structure

As our discussion progresses, you will learn more about how such informal arrangements and the networks they create can help and hinder organizations.

Returning to our earlier definition of psychological groups, we can see that most informal groups would probably also qualify as psychological groups. However, many formal groups might not. Just being assigned to work together in the same department does not mean that group members will share and work toward common goals. Think of group projects you have worked on in your college courses. Each project was designated as a formal group effort by an instructor. But did all these groups meet the four criteria of psychological grouping? Perhaps group success and your satisfaction would have been higher if they all had.

Managers frequently wish that their formal work groups would act and think as psychological groups. Our study of group behavior in organizations should aid you, as a manager, to help your group make this transition.

Managerial Implications

Figure 7.3 portrays several of the action settings in which managers find themselves involved with groups. With respect to the formal work group, managers can be either figures of superior authority (department head or chairperson) or of general membership (subordinate or committee member). Managers will also be involved in a variety of informal networks. In each of these action settings, the manager is challenged to help the group achieve success and thereby contribute to the achievment of organizational purposes.

FIGURE 7.3   Possible group involvements of managers.

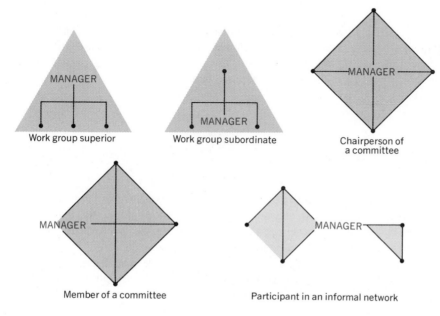

USEFULNESS OF GROUPS IN ORGANIZATIONS

Groups are good for organizations and their members. They can make important contributions to organizational task accomplishment, and as our opening vignette shows, they can also exert a strong influence on individual work attitudes and behaviors. Nonetheless, at least one prominent organizationist theorist, Harold J. Leavitt, feels that we have not taken groups seriously enough as basic building blocks of organizations. He points to the linking-pin model depicted earlier in Figure 7.1 as one notable exception. In this model, multiple groups form the basis for organizations and managers are the ''linking pins'' through which the complex network of groups is coordinated and integrated into a total system.

It is worth listening to Leavitt's arguments in behalf of the group as an essential human resource component of organizations. After all, as Leavitt says,[6]

Groups seem to be good for people.

Groups seem to be useful in promoting innovation and creativity.

Groups make better decisions that individuals in a wide variety of situations.

Groups can gain commitment of members for carrying out decisions.

Groups can control and discipline members in ways it is otherwise difficult to do.

Groups help fend off the negative effects of increasing size as organizations grow larger.

Groups are natural phenomena in organizations; their spontaneous developments cannot be prevented.

This list gives us a very positive and promising view of what groups can bring to organizations. All these issues will be developed more thoroughly as we study groups in Chapters 7, 8, and 9. Before moving on, however, several specific points on the usefulness of groups in terms of organizational task accomplishment and individual behavior should be pointed out.

Groups and Organizational Task Accomplishment

Many things in life are beyond the capabilities of one person. It takes group efforts, for example, to build a jet airplane or a multistory office building. It also takes a group to play basketball and to act out a television soap opera. The element common to each of these examples is the benefit of group synergy.

You should recall that synergy is the creation of a whole that is greater than the sum of its parts. When synergy occurs, groups accomplish more than the total of their members' individual capabilities. Research shows, for example, that[7]

NEWSLINE 7.1 / WHY TO HOLD A MEETING

Meetings have a bad name. Indeed, one school of thought considers them the curse of the manager's existence. Management guru Peter Drucker has said that managers spending more than 25 percent of their time in meetings is a sign of "malorganization." But there is another way to regard meetings.

Meetings are nothing less than the medium through which managerial work is performed. Think about it. A big part of what managers do is to pass along information and to impart a sense of the preferred method of handling things—"how we do things here at XYZ Corp"—to the people under them. Managers also make decisions and help others make

them. Both these managerial tasks require person-to-person encounters—meetings, in short. We should not be fighting their existence, but rather using the time spent in them as efficiently as possible.

Be clear about the nature of a meeting. The two basic types of managerial tasks—passing along information and making decisions—entail two different kinds of meetings. In what are called "process-oriented meetings"—they're part of, and further, the process of managing—information is exchanged in a continuing, scheduled series of encounters. The second kind of meeting—call it "mission-oriented"—is convened to solve a problem. It's an ad hoc affair, called whenever a problem arises that requires a decision.

Reported in *Fortune*.

- When the presence of an "expert" is uncertain, groups make better judgments than would the average individual.
- When problem solving can be handled by a division of labor and the sharing of information, groups are typically more successful than individuals.
- Because of their tendencies to make more risky decisions than individuals, groups can be more creative and innovative in their task accomplishments.

On the other hand, there can be social loafing, or something called the "Ringmann effect," in groups. Ringmann, a German psychologist, pinpointed this effect by asking people to pull as hard as they could on a rope, first alone and then in a group. He found that average productivity dropped as more people joined the rope pulling task.[8] Thus, the **Ringmann effect** acknowledges that people may tend *not* to work as hard in groups as they would individually. This is because their contribution is less noticeable and because they like to see others carry the work load.

Social loafing is one reason why groups can get a bad name for their value to organizational task accomplishment. But, as Newsline 7.1 shows, the usefulness of groups to managers and organizations cannot be denied. The manager's challenge is to learn when a group is the best human resource configuration for a certain task. Then the manager must know how to ensure that the full benefits of group synergy are achieved.

Groups and Individual Behavior

Formal work groups and informal networks are important aspects of an individual's work setting. Groups are social settings that offer a variety of information, expectations, and opportunities that relate to individual need satisfactions. As a result, these groups are major influences on individual work attitudes and behaviors. Figuratively speaking,

$$\text{Group involvements} \xrightarrow{\text{offer}} \begin{array}{c}\text{information,}\\ \text{expectations,}\\ \text{opportunities}\end{array} \xrightarrow[\text{influence}]{\text{that}} \begin{array}{c}\text{individual}\\ \text{attitudes and}\\ \text{behavior}\end{array}$$

Groups are mechanisms through which people learn relevant job skills and knowledge. Group members can model correct behaviors, offer feedback on performance, and provide direct instruction and assistance to one another. Often these relationships among group members assist individuals in building abilities and acquiring competencies required to do their jobs well. These group benefits often make up for deficiencies in the formal training and education practices of the organization.

Individual motivation to expend effort on group tasks can also be affected by group involvements. This can occur in two ways. First, there is the social facilitation effect whereby the mere presence of others either facilitates or inhibits performance.[9] Second, individual motivation can be affected by group involvements.

Group members communicate expectations to one another regarding work performance. They may encourage or discourage high levels of effort. Members also influence one another's beliefs and predispositions about various aspects of the work setting. A new employee soon learns, for example, who the "bad" supervisors are or whom you cannot "trust" as a co-worker. These influences may even extend to the point of communicating how the individual should feel about his or her job and the organization. For example, a co-worker may indicate that "this is a good job to have and a great place to work." We develop these notions further in Chapter 8.

Perhaps the most apparent function of groups is their ability to satisfy the needs of their members. Groups provide for obvious social interactions and interpersonal fulfillments. A group can provide individual security in the form of direct work assistance and technical advice, or emotional support in times of special crisis or pressure. Groups also give their members a sense of identification and offer opportunities for ego involvement by assisting in group activities.

Individuals can find from their group involvements the full range of need satisfactions discussed in Chapter 4. Those satisfactions that are left unfulfilled by the formal work group may be met in the informal group. Whether or not the net result of group influence on the individual is positive or negative for the organization, however, depends on many factors. This is the issue that makes our study of groups in organizations so interesting.

One example of how groups were mobilized to the benefit of both the organization and its members follows.[10] You might be thinking, as you read, of how you will act to mobilize the human resource potential of groups in your job as manager.

Rutland (Vermont) Hospital undertook a program to deter the depersonalization among employees that so often accompanies institutional growth. Having just completed a hundred-bed addition, the once-small community hospital now boasted three hundred beds and more than six hundred employees. Specifically, the management was worried that the increase in both size of physical plant and number of employees would lead to a lack of employee identification with the hospital and that patients might pick up this depersonalization to their detriment.

After a series of meetings on the subject, it became apparent that, in order to accomplish the goal, the hospital's administrative staff would have to actually get out into the hospital and meet with all of its employees, no matter how unwieldy such a system might seem on the surface.

The name of the program finally devised was as simple as the underlying concept: Employee Group Meeting Program. The mechanics of the program called for the executive vice-president and personnel director to meet on an informal basis with two groups of employees each week, joined in each instance by the appropriate department head and/or administrative officer. One meeting would be held in a nursing service area and the second in one of the other departments. The meetings were scheduled to allow for personal contact with every employee at least twice a year, for the express purpose of hearing problems, ideas, and requests for information.

Many of the early meetings were taken up with grievance-based items, such as wages, benefits, and other economic factors, and in all cases these were responded to properly. However, today's meetings are more likely to center around well-thought-out suggestions by well-prepared participants who frequently arrive with lists of concerns for consideration.

GROUP EFFECTIVENESS

Task performance and human resource maintenance are the key results of interest in our study of groups at work, just as they are with the study of individuals. In the group context, the concept of human resource maintenance represents a group's ability to maintain its social fabric as a working entity over time and includes the element of member satisfaction.

An **effective work group** is one that achieves high levels of both task performance and human resource maintenance over time. A classic list showing basic characteristics of effective groups is presented in Table 7.1. As you review this list, think about the obvious disadvantages that *in*effective groups (i.e., those with either poor performance, poor human resource maintenance, or both) can have for organizations, the groups themselves, and the individual members. Think also about the challenges of helping a group satisfy each of the criteria in the list and achieve true effectiveness.

TABLE 7.1   The Nature of Highly Effective Groups

1. The members of the group are attracted to it and are loyal to its members, including the leader.
2. The members and leaders have a high degree of confidence and trust in each other.
3. The values and goals of the group are an integration and expression of the relevant values and needs of its members.
4. All the interaction, problem-solving, decision-making activities of the group occur in a supportive atmosphere. Suggestions, comments, ideas, information, criticisms are all offered with a helpful orientation.
5. The group is eager to help members develop to their full potential.
6. The group knows the value of ''constructive'' conformity and knows when to use it and for what purposes.
7. There is strong motivation on the part of each member to communicate fully and frankly to the group all the information that is relevant and of value to the group's activity.
8. Members feel secure in making decisions that seem appropriate to them.

Source: Excerpted from Rensis Likert, *New Patterns of Management* (New York: McGraw-Hill, 1961), pp. 166–169. Copyright © 1961, McGraw-Hill. Used with the permission of McGraw-Hill Book Company.

THE GROUP AS AN OPEN SYSTEM

Every manager should act to promote work group effectiveness. This requires an ability to understand and influence many variables with the potential to affect group behavior. In Figure 7.4 we view the group as an open system transforming various inputs into two outputs—task performance and human resource maintenance—the ultimate criteria of group effectiveness.[11]

FIGURE 7.4   The work group as an open system.

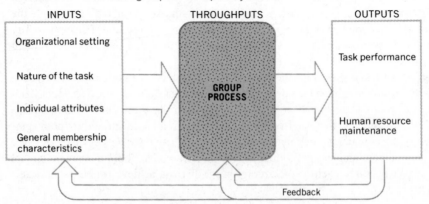

A group's ability to be effective depends, in part, on how well it transforms resource inputs into group outputs. We refer to this transformation stage as the group process and give it detailed attention in Chapters 8 and 9. For now, it is sufficient to recognize **group process** as the means through which multiple and varied resource inputs are aggregated and transformed into group outputs. Stated in other terms,

$$\text{Group process} \xrightarrow{\text{transforms}} \text{resource inputs} \xrightarrow{\text{into}} \text{group outputs}$$

KEY GROUP INPUTS

A major influence on group effectiveness is the nature of the inputs themselves. Inputs are the initial "givens" in a group situation. They set the stage for or "arm" the group for action. In this way, inputs can either enhance or impede the group in its efforts to achieve a high level of effectiveness. Even the most capable group process will be unable to achieve effective results when inadequate or inappropriate inputs are available.

We are concerned with four general categories of group inputs: the organizational setting, the nature of the task, individual attributes, and membership characteristics. The following sections look in some detail at the facets of each input category shown in Table 7.2. Our primary interest is on the implications of each for group effectiveness.

Organizational Setting

The total organization is a major component in the environment within which both formal and informal groups operate. The nature of the organization as a work setting thus becomes an important input to groups. Table 7.2 lists several aspects of the organization that are of special importance in this regard. They include such things as resources, technology, spatial arrangements, reward systems, structure, and size. Research suggests that each of these factors may influence the degree to which group members get psychologically close to one another, the extent to which they cooperate

TABLE 7.2 Important Facets of the Major Group Inputs

Input	Facets
Organizational setting	Resources, technology, spatial arrangements, reward system, goals, structure, size
Nature of the task	Simplicity–complexity of task and social components
Individual attributes	Demographic, competency, and psychological characteristics
General membership characteristics	Interpersonal compatibilities, homogeneity–heterogeneity, status congruence, number of members

or compete with one another, and the nature of the communication patterns that emerge within the group.[12] Other things equal, group task performance and human resource maintenance are enhanced by an organizational setting that includes

1. Abundant resources.
2. Technology and spatial arrangements that make it easy for group members to interact.
3. Reward and goal systems that emphasize the importance of group as opposed to individual efforts.
4. Compatibility in other aspects, including its structure and size.

Resources

Organizational resources important to the work group include such things as tools, equipment, facilities, work methods and procedures, and related items of the kind discussed in Chapter 3 as a part of the "support" variable in the individual performance equation. Just as with individuals, groups need proper resource support if they are to achieve their true potential in task performance. Furthermore, the relative scarcity or abundance of resources in the organization can affect what happens within and between groups. When resources are scarce, group members are more likely to compete with one another to access them. Similarly, resource scarcity is often an antecedent to intergroup competition.[13]

Technology

Technology is defined and described in some detail in Chapter 10. For now, you may think of it as the means through which work gets accomplished. The basic impact of technology on groups is the degree to which it facilitates or impedes interaction among group members. It is one thing, for example, for a group to work intensively on custom-crafted products tailor made to customer specifications; it is quite another to be part of a machine-paced automobile assembly line. The former technology allows for more interaction among group members and will probably create a closer-knit group that has a stronger sense of identity than the group formed around one small segment of an automobile assembly line.

Spatial Arrangements

The spatial or physical arrangements of the work setting can also influence what takes place in a group. This was demonstrated in the Case of the Changing Cage (see Part Three opening). Workers in the "cage" initially arranged their furniture in a way to increase privacy. This allowed the development of the group's social fabric and generally supported task performance as well. When the spatial arrangement was altered in the new location of the "cage," a loss in this privacy contributed to a drop in performance and loss of morale. Researchers recognize that differing spatial arrangements may affect the amount of interaction that occurs among group members, their attitudes toward their jobs and the organization itself, and their attitudes toward one another. A recent study showed that where people sit, who they sit next to and the' closeness of the seats all affected group process. Newsline 7.2 indicates how the

NEWSLINE 7.2. / MANAGERS AT HONDA'S HUB

"We don't want to have cogwheel-type people in our company."

Ten years after Soichiro Honda retired from the presidency of the motorcycle and car company he founded, his successors uphold his philosophy even as they practice a less personal, more collegial, style of management.

"Here, take a look at our board room," said Hideo Sugiura, chairman of Honda Motor Company. "Do you notice that as soon as you step from the corporate reception room to the executive office area, the quality of the carpet changes? It's not so luxurious, not so thick."

He led the way past a large office where secretaries and other workers were busy typing, or copying, or poring over documents, into a long, bright, airy room, divided into three main areas. The central feature of each area was a large round table with comfortable chairs. Beyond these tables, facing the windows, was a row of desks, four or five per area.

The central area had four of these desks, each about the size of a school desk. Only one of them was occupied. These quite plebeian desks were for the four managing directors who handle the day-to-day affairs of the company, Mr. Sugiura said. The three absent directors were probably out on the workshop floor, or in a laboratory, or somewhere in the field.

To the left of the managing director's area, in the same big room, is the area for ordinary directors. To the right is that for the chairman, the president, and three vice presidents. These five, plus the four managing directors, make up Honda's top management, responsible for all major decisions such as establishing a car factory in the United States or embarking on a joint venture with British Leyland of the United Kingdom.

"Most of the real business of the company," Mr. Sugiura said, "is conducted not at our desks but at these round tables you see in the center. Anytime one of us has something he wants to discuss, he will gather round this table with the two or three, or four or five, people he wants to talk to. At any hour during the day, you may see groups of us sitting here. It all seems very ad hoc, but each of us knows what the others are doing. And somehow the work gets done."

Reported in *Christian Science Monitor.*

spatial design of executive offices in the Honda Motor Company facilitates interaction and group decision-making.

Reward Systems and Goals

Like individuals, groups are influenced by the reward systems and goals characteristic of their work environment. Well-designed reward systems and appropriate goals help to establish and maintain proper levels and direction for group work efforts. Groups can suffer from reward systems that stress individual-level as opposed to group-level contributions and outcomes. They can also suffer from goals that are unclear or insufficiently challenging and/or appear inappropriately imposed from the outside. We examined rewards and goals in Chapters 5 and 6. Many of those insights can now be applied to the group, in addition to the individual, level of analysis.

Structure and Size

The overall structure and size of the organization surrounding a group can also influence the group's performance potential. A group that gets "lost" in a larger setting may experience confusion, loss of identity and even feel a lack of accountability for results. Similarly speaking, a group with a structure that is inconsistent or incompatible with the larger system can experience difficulties. Organizational structures and size are treated in Chapters 10, 11, and 12. You should recognize that these related parts of the book contain insights relevant to the management of groups in organizations. Rather than review the material here, we leave you the responsibility of including the total organization as an environmental input of groups.

Nature of the Group Task

We have already talked about the usefulness of group task accomplishments to the organization. The specific nature of the task as an input to the group process, however, can place special demands on a work group. To be effective, a work group must be successful at (1) assessing task demands and (2) meeting these demands by proper planning, coordination, and utilization of member resources.[15]

One useful distinction when assessing task demands is between simple and complex tasks. Complexity is a measure of how easy or difficult it is to satisfy the various demands of a particular task. This is significant from a managerial viewpoint since increasing task complexity adds to the difficulty of achieving high levels of group effectiveness. Group outcomes will be affected by how well the group process is able to accommodate the task complexity caused by social and technical demands.

Social Demands

Group task complexity is affected by social demands relating to the amount and nature of required interactions among group members. These social demands can be analyzed in terms of the following attributes.[16]

1. *Ego involvement.*   This attribute refers to members' personal investment in the group's task and its outcomes. Tasks that engage deeply rooted values or beliefs (for example, deciding whether to support legalized abortions), that affect important aspects of participants' lives (such as setting budgets for participants' respective departments), or that engage highly valued skills such that performance reflects individuals' self-concepts, can all be considered high on the ego involvement dimension.

2. *Agreement on means.*   This dimension refers to the extent group members agree on how the group should go about performing its task. For some tasks there may be high agreement on the best approach to the task and on who should do what. For other tasks, different approaches will be favored by different group members. Some sub-tasks will be more attractive than others so that decisions on who performs them become important issues subject to potential disagreement.

3. *Agreement on ends.* This attribute reflects group members' agreement on what they are trying to accomplish and what criteria will be used to define success. For some tasks, it is very clear what the group is trying to achieve, and one may expect wide agreement on the part of group members. For example, a fund-raising group can often agree that they should raise as much money as possible. For other tasks, the group may have considerable difficulty agreeing on what constitutes a satisfactory outcome. For example, a group of department heads will often disagree about which of them will receive a particular office when offices differ in desirability.

The most socially complex task demand on a group is ego involving *and* a source of disagreement over means and/or ends.

Technical Demands

The other dimension of group task complexity involves a more technical set of demands. Table 7.3 illustrates the various technical dimensions of task complexity, including the attributes of task programmability, difficulty, and information diffusion.

Simple tasks place fewer demands on the group process than do tasks of greater technical and social complexity. Managers' concerns for group process, therefore, should be enhanced in groups whose social and technical inputs evidence high task complexity. The challenges facing the supervisor of one segment of an automobile assembly line, for example, will differ greatly from the group process requirements of a research and development laboratory in a high-technology electronics firm. Or,

TABLE 7.3 Technical Dimensions of Simple and Complex Tasks

Task Attributes	Characteristics of Simple Tasks	Characteristics of Complex Tasks
Programmability	Single acceptable solution achieved via a single path and easily verified as correct.	Many alternative solutions and means to solution; any given solution not easily verified.
	People who must perform task have experience with the task.	People who must perform the task do not have experience with the task.
	Task requirements remain constant.	Task requirements vary.
Difficulty	Little effort is required. Few operations are required. Involves low-level skills.	Great deal of effort required. Many operations are required. Involves complex skills.
Information diffusion	Required knowledge is centralized.	Knowledge and skills are widely distributed.
	Involves few skills or areas of knowledge.	Several skills or areas of knowledge are necessary.

Source: Adapted from David M. Herold, "The Effectiveness of Work Groups," in Steven Kerr, ed., *Organizational Behavior* (New York, John Wiley & Sons, 1979), p. 100. Reprinted with permission from Organizational Behavior by Steven Kerr, John Wiley & Sons, Inc., New York, N.Y., 1979.

consider a group of Air Force personnel responsible for the selection of a new prototype fighter plane to be the major weapons system for the next 10 years.[17] This task clearly has complex technical demands, involving concerns such as cost, combat effectiveness, serviceability, and the like. It also has complex social demands, involving such things as use of foreign manufacturers, use of bids from firms with a cost overrun history, and so on.

Here the manager would have to make sure those assigned had the technical expertise and provide any necessary additional technical help. Also the manager would need to sensitize group members to the differing member orientations and play an active role in reconciling differences so that the task could be completed. Where either or both task or social demands were simple, less intervention would be needed on the part of the manager.

Research on Task Properties and Group Effectiveness

Tasks of different complexities demand varying amounts of competence and effort on the part of group members.[18] Increasing complexity makes it harder for a group to achieve both high-quality and high-quantity performance. Group members are required to distribute their efforts more broadly than on simple tasks, and greater cooperation and interdependence is required to achieve a common product. When the group process fails to meet these demands, performance suffers accordingly.

In general, membership satisfaction increases as the complexity of the group's task increases. This is most likely to occur when group members have the required competencies and needs appropriate to a complex task, and when the group process allows for abilities to be properly aggregated and individual needs to be fulfilled.

Individual Attributes

Chapter 3 was devoted to a discussion of the basic attributes of individuals. Although our attention focused at that time on the significance of these attributes for individual performance and human resource maintenance, these same individual attributes are an important input to any group. A group will be influenced in both its process and effectiveness by the demographic, competency, and psychological characteristics of its individual members. To the extent that the right competencies are present, for example, group performance outcomes can be directly enhanced.

To take advantage of the competencies, however, the individuals must function well in the setting of the work group and in harmony with one another. Whether they do or do not achieve this result depends in part on how well individual attributes blend into the general characteristics of the membership as a whole. Before we go on to discuss this ''blending'' in more detail, recall that the individual as a group resource is the very same individual that we studied very thoroughly in Part Two of the book.

General Membership Characteristics

The willingness of individual members to exert efforts on the group's behalf will be influenced by many factors. Among the most important are the special characteristics of the general membership itself, including interpersonal compatibilities, membership heterogeneity, status congruence, and size. They join organizational setting, nature of the task, and individual member attributes as key group inputs in our model. As a manager you will need to be sensitive to each of these classes of inputs and the variables that are included in each. The trick is to try to match and combine inputs for the most favorable group process results.

Interpersonal Compatibilities

A key element in the functioning of any group is the degree of interpersonal compatibility among its members. The FIRO-B (fundamental interpersonal orientation) theory helps to explain how people orient themselves toward one another.[19] This theory is based on how strongly people need to express and receive feelings of inclusion, control, and affection. These needs, along with descriptive statements adapted from an instrument (the FIRO-B Scale) designed to measure them, are the following.

Need for inclusion: Strive for prominence, recognition, and prestige:
        Try to be included in informal social activities.
        Like to be invited to things.
        Try to participate in group activities.
        Like to be asked to participate in discussions.

Need for control: Tendency to rebel and refuse to be controlled or
tendency to be compliant and submissive:
        Try not to let other people decide what I do.
        Try to influence strongly other people's actions.
        Try to be the dominant person when with people.
        Not easily led by people.

Need for affection: Desire to be friendly and seek close emotional ties
with others:
        Try to have close, personal relationships
        with people.
        Try to be friendly with people.
        Like people to act close and personal.
        Do not like people to act distant toward me.

Think about *your* needs for inclusion, control and affection. How strong or weak are they? How do/may they affect your participation in group activities? How may they affect your success in group situations as a manager?

The FIRO-B theory argues that groups in which members have reciprocal or compatible needs will be more effective than will groups characterized by incompatibilities. Groups of the latter type are predicted to be less likely to have their members work well together. Symptoms of harmful incompatibilities include withdrawn members, open hostilities, struggles over control, and domination of the group by a few members. As you think about what interpersonal compatibilities can mean to a work group, recall these words of advice to managers that were offered by the author of the FIRO-B theory.[20]

If at the outset we can choose a group of people who can work together harmoniously, we shall go far toward avoiding situations where a group's efforts are wasted in interpersonal conflicts.

Membership Homogeneity–Heterogeneity

People vary on other attributes in addition to their interpersonal orientations. Homogeneous groups consist of members of similar backgrounds, interests, values, attitudes, and the like. Heterogeneous groups include membership diversity on these dimensions.

Research is mixed as to the implications of membership homogeneity–heterogeneity for group effectiveness. Heterogeneity can bring a variety of skills and viewpoints to bear on problems and thus facilitate task accomplishment; but homogeneity increases the chances for harmonious working relationships among group members.

A particularly interesting experiment helps to illustrate the point.[21] A number of two-person groups were created on the basis of the homogeneity–heterogeneity of both the abilities and attitudes of members. They were then asked to perform a creative task. The most effective groups were those having homogeneous abilities and heterogeneous attitudes. Similar levels of ability formed a common base for communication; heterogeneity in attitudes provided for more creativity than where attitudes were similar. Where both attitudes and abilities were heterogeneous, there was too much diversity within the group; individuals could not reconcile their differences well enough to be creative.

As suggested in this example, the nature of the task is an important factor in determining whether membership homogeneity or heterogeneity is best for a group. Research evidence shows a tendency for homogeneity to be more functional in simple as opposed to complex task situations.[22] Managers, therefore, must exercise good judgment when selecting members for their work groups to balance the advantages of both homogeneity and heterogeneity. The more heterogeneous the membership, furthermore, the more skilled the manager will have to be in facilitating a successful group process.

Status Congruence

A person's **status** is his or her relative rank, worth, or standing on prestige and esteem within a group. This standing can be based on any number of characteristics, including age, work seniority, occupation, education, work accomplishments, or status in other groups. **Status congruence** occurs when a person's standing on each of these factors is consistent with his or her standing on the other factors. Status incongruity occurs when standings vary among the factors. When members of a group experience status incongruity (e.g., a senior member is not chosen to chair a committee, or a new and young college graduate without experience is hired to supervise a group of experienced production workers), stress, dissatisfaction, and frustration can all occur. Attempts to reconcile the status incongruity may lead to behavior detrimental to group process and effectiveness (e.g., the senior committee member tries to take control anyway, or the experienced production workers refuse to help their new boss "learn the ropes").

Group Size

Consider the implications of being in groups of various sizes. As the size of a group increases, the number of possible relationships among its members increases in a geometric progression. In a group of two members there is 1 possible mutual relationship; in a group of five, this number increases to 10.

Although it is difficult to pinpoint an ideal group size, it has been shown that for problem-solving groups[23]

1. Less than five members results in:
   - Fewer people to share task responsibilities.
   - More personal discussions.
   - More complete participation.
2. More than seven members results in:
   - Fewer opportunities to participate.
   - More member inhibitions.
   - Domination by aggressive members.
   - Tendency to split into subgroups.

Such findings argue for an ideal problem-solving group size of five to seven members. However, you need to weigh this against the fact that increasing group size offers more human resources to help achieve the desired task accomplishment. But at the same time as groups grow larger, more communication and coordination are also required to aggregate the collective potential of the membership. Thus, special efforts must be made in the group process to overcome any disadvantages that may be associated with the increasing size.

This impact of size on the resource and communication/coordination trade-off is shown in Figure 7.5. As groups become larger, more potential resources become

FIGURE 7.5 Trade-offs in group size and performance.

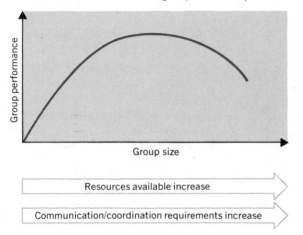

available to perform the task. However, the growth in size also increases communication and coordination requirements. The result is a trade-off as shown in the figure. The same kind of reasoning holds for other membership characteristics, including interpersonal compatibilities and homogeneity–heterogeneity as discussed earlier. Managers must be aware of the existence of these trade-offs when staffing their work groups or otherwise acting to affect the composition of the membership.

Research shows that member satisfaction increases as group size approaches five members and decreases thereafter. Turnover and absenteeism also increase with group size.[24] In general, it appears that the larger groups suffer some disadvantages in terms of the maintenance criterion of group effectiveness. Smaller groups enable members to interact more frequently and to get to know one another better. As a result, membership satisfaction is enhanced.

Another important group size issue is the odd/even character of group membership. Groups with an even number of members (e.g., four, six, eight) as compared with an odd number of members (e.g., three, five) tend to show more disagreement and conflict when performing tasks. They also tend to have lower rates of members seeking suggestions from one another. These differences appear to occur because it is easier for members in odd-numbered groups to form coalitions and take majority votes to resolve disagreements. Where speed is required, this behavior is useful. Where careful deliberations are required, as for example in jury duty or very complex problem solving, even-numbered groups can be more effective *if* they do not deadlock.[25]

Conclusions vary as to the impact of size on group performance.[26] A number of complexities may account for these inconsistencies. They include the additional effects of such things as the nature of the task and the other membership factors just discussed. The Ringmann effect also has a chance to operate as more members are added to a group and the opportunity for social loafing increases. Thus, it appears, groups of any size can achieve high performance. To do so, however, good decisions must be made on managing the group process.

MANAGERIAL CHALLENGES OF GROUPS

Work groups enable organizations and their members to accomplish things that individuals cannot do alone. This is yet another illustration of synergy, and as a result the group becomes a key human resource of organizations.

As you conclude this chapter, recall that groups are like double-edged swords. Individuals affect group outcomes by the extent to which their competencies and efforts are applied or withheld in the group's behalf. On the other hand, the group can have a strong influence on individual behavior. Among other things, the group can affect an individual's choice of performance goals, establish expectations regarding the probability of success, influence the choice of work methods, clarify which rewards are to be expected, and reinforce work values consistent with group beliefs and standards. All in all, it is important for the practicing manager to recognize that

1. Groups, both formal and informal, are important phenomena in organizations.
2. Groups can have positive and negative effects on both organizations and their members.
3. An understanding of group behavior can help to enhance the desirable consequences and reduce the undesirable consequences of groups as human resources of organizations.

This chapter has concentrated most heavily on the first of these concerns. Chapters 8 and 9 focus primarily on the second and third points.

SUMMARY

We started this chapter with a discussion of positive and negative effects of groups and how groups differ from simple aggregations or collections of people. This involves regular interactions of members who see themselves to be mutually dependent in terms of goal accomplishment. To this we have added member awareness of one another's needs and potential contributions as additional criteria of a "psychological group." We have then talked about types of groups in organizations and divided these into formal work groups of both a permanent and temporary (e.g., committees and task forces) nature. These were contrasted with various kinds of informal groups spontaneously arising from the interactions among people.

The usefulness of groups in organizations was considered next. We noted some examples of where groups can be superior to individuals in terms of task accomplishment. Once again, synergy was shown to be an important contributor in creating this superiority.

Although groups are often necessary for task accomplishment, some are more effective than others. Four basic inputs to the group process are important in this regard: the organizational setting, nature of the group task, individual attributes, and total membership characteristics. These inputs are the "givens" in a situation that initially set the stage for group action. As a result, group inputs can have an important influence on a group's potential to achieve high levels of effectiveness.

The factors in the organizational setting include rewards, technology, spatial arrangements, structure, technology, goals, and size. Individual attributes, as reviewed in Chapter 3, include demographic, competency, and psychological characteristics. To function with effectiveness, a work group requires a supportive organizational setting and competent individual members.

We went on to note that the complexity of the task also influences group effectiveness. The greater the social and technical complexity, the harder it is for a group to achieve both quantity and quality of performance. On the other hand, satisfaction tends to increase with complexity.

In terms of membership, we have shown some effects of interpersonal compatibilities and number of members on group outputs. There is a resource and communications/coordination trade-off involved in these factors, such that an optimum combination of either compatibility or size is reached when the resource and communications requirements are balanced.

Finally, we have concluded this look at formal and informal groups from a managerial perspective by directing your attention to the importance of group process as the mechanism that links group inputs and outputs. Group process and its role in facilitating group effectiveness are the subjects of the coming chapter.

THINKING THROUGH THE ISSUES

1. Define and give work examples of formal and informal groups.
2. List and explain some of the advantages and disadvantages of informal groups for (a) their members and (b) their host organizations.
3. When does a formal group become a psychological group? Should every manager want his or her work unit to become a psychological group? Defend your answer.
4. Describe some of the important characteristics that influence a group's effectiveness in terms of task performance and human resource maintenance.
5. Describe circumstances under which a group is likely to be superior to an individual in task accomplishment.
6. Describe general membership influences on group effectiveness and relate these to the resource-communications/coordination trade-off.
7. We argued that the number of potential relationships among group members grows geometrically as group size increases. Explore this argument by calculating and drawing the number of potential relationships for groups of three, six, and nine members. What implications do you see here in terms of the resource-communications/coordination trade-off?
8. What is the significance of the ''Ringmann effect'' as far as group effectiveness is concerned?

CASE: PART-TIMERS AT STUDENT TOOL RENTAL I

This case is concerned with the student tool rental unit of a large state-supported vocational-technical school.[27] To minimize the tools and equipment that students must purchase, the school has arranged to charge them a flat per term rental fee and make certain kinds of tools and equipment available to them as needed during a term. The unit has two main responsibilities. The first is to process orders from instructors concerning equipment needed for their classes. The second is to check the equipment in and out to the students as needed during the term.

The organizational hierarchy at tool rental consists of four levels. At the top is A. A. Jones who is responsible for the whole operation of the unit. Under him there are five civil service workers: four females and one male. Of the four females, two are general secretaries. One is A. A. Jones's chief assistant and the other is in charge of a number of part-time workers. The male civil service worker is responsible for a small number of highly specialized tools which are sold rather than rented. However, he also helps with other jobs, as necessary. Of the civil service workers, one has graduated from college, one has flunked out of the vocational school several times, and the others have a high school education. All these workers have lived within a few miles of the vocational school most of their lives.

Under Mrs. Johnson, who is in charge of the part-time workers, there are three part-time supervisors. Under the supervisors are the rest of the part-time workers. According to the organization chart, Mrs. Johnson should have complete control of the workers. However, this is not the case. Mrs. Lockin tries to act as the part-time worker boss. Whenever these workers are caught doing something wrong, she lets Mrs. Johnson do the ''dirty work'' in reprimanding them. Mrs. Johnson tries to overlook small faults, but Mrs. Lockin looks for the most unimportant faults. Thus, two people are watching over the part-timers most of the time. As a result, there is a conflict in the hierarchy.

There are 34 part-time workers at tool rental. All are vo-tech students. Many are married and badly need the job. The pay starts at the federal minimum wage rate. The only form of promotion present in this system is moving from worker to supervisor. Supervisor positions are kept open for married students. Ten-cent-an-hour pay increases are granted after 1500 hours of work.

Tool rental is currently housed on the fourth floor of the auto repair shop. Its storage area has been moved twice in less than a year. Originally, it was located in a temporary building behind the health sciences building. Next it was moved to the basement immediately across from the electronics repair area and, finally, to its present location. Adequate storage is very important for tool rental. There is a very large tool and equipment inventory necessary. The storage area is also used to handle tool turn-ins at the end of the term. Since all the tools are currently processed by hand, the storage area is also used for this.

Most of the remaining work is done by hand and involves physical and clerical labor by all workers. Among the most important duties of the workers are shelving tools, processing tools, checking tools in and out, finding special tools for people, and keeping accurate records. Every person is taught how to do every job. The typical working period for a part-timer is four hours per day.

The physical conditions are generally good. Since the service is located on the fourth floor, it is isolated from the rest of the building. There is not much outside traffic, except for laborers who use a freight elevator. Tool rental has a large area in which the workers can work. The area is well lighted, and it is usually neatly kept through the term. The offices are enclosed by glass windows through which the civil service workers can watch the part-timers at all times.

The working conditions are clean most of the time. Part-timers may wear casual clothes unless there is work to be done at the old warehouse. Tool rental keeps obsolete and discarded tools in this old warehouse. It is dirty most of the time. The lighting is very poor there. In the warm months, it is too hot, and in the cold months, it is too cold; however, by going to the warehouse, part-timers are out of the sight of the regular supervisors.

There are no written rules for the workers. The rules seem to have come about through the work practices rather than being formally written. Management assumes that every worker will be at work every free hour of the day. In practice this is also assured. If a worker does not show up for work, he or she is supposed to call in and tell the supervisor. Some employees have been fired for not doing this. The rule is strictly enforced. For the first offense, there is a strong reprimand. Usually, most excuses given for failure to call in are not taken into consideration. If a person misses work and does not call in, management assumes that this person does not care about his or her job.

It is also assumed that the worker will work every minute he or she is there. The only exception to this is during the worker's break. The rule for a break is that any person who works four straight hours is entitled to a 15-minute break. If a worker does not work four hours, there is not supposed to be a break; but, in reality, everyone takes a break whether they work four hours or not. However, those workers caught get a reprimand.

Management also assumes that the person is there to work, not talk. This assumption is taken for granted, but management enforces it. If a worker is caught talking too much, he or she is told to stop. If the talking continues, the worker is moved to an isolated spot away from the other workers. However, this rule is not enforced all the time. Its enforcement seems to be a function of the mood of the civil service workers. If they are in a good mood, most workers can converse during work, but if the atmosphere is bad, the worker will get reprimanded. Therefore, workers try to find out the atmosphere on a particular day.

During the beginning and end of the term, tool rental is open from 8 A.M. to 9 or 9:30 P.M. The part-timer is supposed to be at work at 7:30 A.M. and work up to 9:30 P.M., if possible. Thus the typical 4-hour work period may stretch to more than 12 hours a day during the week at the beginning and at the end of each term.

All workers are also supposed to work at least once each school break. If a person does not, the job probably will not be there when he or she gets back.

Workers are expected to conform to the job requirements and rules of tool rental with no back talk. The workers need the job, and there are few alternative jobs available for them in the area.

However, there are many things that occur in addition to those mentioned. One event is playing frisbee with the plastic top to a glue can. Games such as this are typical. They all take place in the storage area. Another game that has developed is baseball played with a frisbee. Each team has as many people as there are workers available. While one team is up to bat, the other team spreads out over the storage area. Consequently, there is a potential problem with the civil service workers. There are two ways they can enter the area. One is by the freight elevator, and the other is by the main elevator. By approaching in either of these ways, it is possible to unlock a door and sneak in behind the part-timers. This happened once, and now one worker is assigned to the door while the game is being played.

The fun of these games for the workers is that they know if they are caught they will be fired. Management knows about the games but has not been able to catch one in action. On some days when there is no work to be done, the games are played for

2 or 3 hours. The only time the game stops is when a civil service worker approaches to check up on the workers or to take a break. To keep from getting caught, each worker is assigned to a position involving some tool processing. When a civil service worker shows up, the game is stopped, and everyone acts as if some work is being done.

Everyday after work, one of the civil service workers goes upstairs to try to find the frisbees. Whenever the game is finished, the frisbees are hidden in a special place. Occasionally, the workers leave one out so the civil service worker will find it. Management is overjoyed and thinks the hiding place has been found.

As previously indicated, workers are supposed to show up for work promptly and regularly. Often, however, a worker will call or have someone else call indicating that he or she will not be in on a particular day. This happens more often during nice weather.

Workers are also not supposed to do any unnecessary talking. However, they try to see how much talking they can get away with without being caught by management. Usually someone watches the office windows to see if a civil service worker is coming to tell them to be quiet. Of course, if a member of management comes along, the part-timers act as if they are working.

Among part-timers, the part-time supervisors have the greatest amount of status and power. If a worker does not follow their orders, that person could be fired very easily. After the supervisors, there is a struggle for status. Usually the people directly under the supervisor are the workers who have been employed the longest. The people who usually get the worst jobs are those who have worked the shortest period of time or those whom the supervisors do not like.

From this description you might think performance would be low, but it meets management expectations. However, the potential for individual development is low and job satisfaction is low.

Questions

1. Use the key group inputs discussed in this chapter to classify the part-time worker tool rental unit.
2. Some of the group inputs work to enhance the task performance and human resource maintenance outputs and some work at cross purposes with these outputs. Analyze the case in terms of both sets of forces and discuss those inputs which seem to have the strongest impact.
3. Explain and justify changes in group inputs which you feel would be most feasible for management to enhance group outputs. Make sure you are sensitive to cost considerations.

EXERCISE: ANALYZING GROUP INPUTS

Purpose:
This exercise is designed to increase your awareness of group input factors and their capacity to influence group effectiveness.

Time:
50 minutes.

Procedure:
1. Form work groups as directed by your instructor.
2. Turn to Figure 7.4 and review the logic of the "work group as an open system" as summarized in the figure.
3. Focus now on your OB class as a work group, or on another group designated by your instructor. Analyze its effectiveness in terms of task performance and human resource maintenance. Rate the group on each dimension as "excellent," "good," or "poor." Be prepared to defend your ratings in general class discussion.
4. Now analyze the input factors as they relate to the group you are focusing on. Identify specific characteristics of the group as they apply to each factor.
5. Next review the input factors for their actual or potential influence on group effectiveness. Discuss and identify ideas for changing input factors as a means of improving group effectiveness in the future.
6. Have a spokesperson prepared to report in general class session on group results for items 3, 4, and 5.
7. The instructor will ask for reports from each group. General discussion on the nature of groups as open systems will follow.

THE MANAGER'S VOCABULARY

Effective Work Group   One that achieves high levels of both task performance and membership satisfaction and is able to maintain itself over time.

Formal Group   A group created by formal authority for some organizational purpose; synonymous with work group.

Group   A collection of people who interact with each other regularly over a period of time and see themselves to be mutually dependent with respect to the attainment of one or more common goals.

Group Process   The means through which multiple and varied resource inputs are aggregated and transformed by a group into product or service outputs.

Informal Group   A group that exists without being formally specified by someone in authority.

Psychological Group   A group whose members achieve a true sharing of goals and values.

Ringmann Effect   The tendency of people not to work as hard on a task in a group as they would working alone.

Status   Standing of prestige and esteem of a member in a group.

Status Congruence   When a person's standing on various status factors is congruent with his or her standing on the other factors.

Work Group   A group created by the formal authority of an organization to transform resource inputs into product or service outputs.

IMPORTANT NAMES

Harold J. Leavitt   An organization theorist who feels groups are not taken seriously enough as building-blocks of organizations.

NOTES

[1]Excerpted from "Ford Prods Dealers to 'Involve' Employees," *Chicago Tribune,* November 29, 1983. Copyright © by the Associated Press. Used by permission.

[2]This example is based on a critical incident by William J. Wasmuth and Leonard Greenhalgh, *Effective Supervision: Developing Your Skills through Critical Incidents* (Englewood Cliffs, NJ: Prentice-Hall, 1979), pp. 162–167.

[3]Kenneth N. Wexley and Gary A. Yukl, *Organizational Behavior and Personnel Psychology* (Homewood, Ill.: Richard D. Irwin, 1977).

[4]See, for example, Edgar H. Schein, *Organizational Psychology,* 2nd ed. (Englewood Cliffs, N.J.: Prentice-Hall, 1970), p. 81.

[5]David M. Herold, "The Effectiveness of Work Groups," in Steven Kerr ed., *Organizational Behavior* (New York, John Wiley, 1979), p. 95.

[6]Harold J. Leavitt, "Suppose We Took Groups Seriously," in Eugene L. Cass and Frederick G. Zimmer, eds., *Man and Work in Society* (New York: Van Nostrand Reinhold, 1975), pp. 67–77.

[7]See Marvin E. Shaw, *Group Dynamics: The Psychology of Small Group Behavior,* 2nd ed. (New York: McGraw-Hill, 1976).

[8]See Bib Latané, Kipling Williams, and Stephen Harkins, "Many Hands Make Light the Work: The Causes and Consequences of Social Loafing," *Journal of Personality and Social Psychology,* Vol. 37 (1978), pp. 822–832; E. Weldon and G. M. Gargano, "Cognitive Effort in Additive Task Groups: The Effects of Shared Responsibility on the Quality of Multiattribute Judgments," *Organizational Behavior and Human Decision Processes,* Vol. 36 (1985), pp. 348–361.

[9]C. F. Bond, Jr. and L. J. Titus, "Social Facilitation: A Meta-Analysis of 241 Studies," *Psychological Bulletin,* Vol. 94 (1983), pp. 245–292.

[10]Exerpted from Robert F. Lagasse, "Hospital Puts Employees on the Management Team," *Hospitals,* Vol. 51 (December 1, 1977), pp. 89–90. Used by permission.

[11]For further insights see J. Richard Hackman, "The Design of Work Teams," in Jay W. Lorsch, ed., *Handbook of Organizational Behavior* (Englewood Cliffs, N.J.: Prentice-Hall, 1987), pp. 343–357.

[12]Linda N. Jewell and H. Joseph Reitz, *Group Effectiveness in Organizations* (Glenview, Ill.: Scott, Foresman, 1981), pp. 149, 150.

[13]Ibid; and Joseph McCann and Jay Galbraith, "Interdepartmental Relations," in Paul C. Nystrom and William H. Starbuck, eds., *Handbook of Organizational Design,* Vol. 2 (New York: Oxford University Press, 1981), pp. 60–84.

[14]For good summaries, see Jeffrey Pfeffer, *Organizations and Organization Theory* (Boston: Pitman, 1982), pp. 265–271, and Tim R. V. Davis, "The Influence of Physical Environment in Offices," *Academy of Management Review,* Vol. 9 (1984), pp. 271–283; see also Greg R. Oldham and Nancy L. Notchford, "Relationships between Office Characteristics and Employee Reactions: A Study of the Physical Environment," *Administrative Science Quarterly,* Vol. 2 (1983), pp. 542–556.

[15]This discussion is developed from Herold, "The Effectiveness of Work Groups," pp. 99–103.

[16]Ibid, p. 101. Reprinted with permission.

[17]Based on ibid, p. 103.

[18]These conclusions are consistent with Shaw, *Group Dynamics.*

[19]William C. Schutz, *FIRO: A Three-Dimensional Theory of Interpersonal Behavior* (New York: Rinehart & Co., 1958).

[20]William C. Schutz, "The Interpersonal Underworld," *Harvard Business Review,* Vol. 36, no. 4 (July–August, 1958), p. 130.

[21]Harry C. Triandis, E. R. Hall, and Robert B. Ewen, "Member Heterogeneity and Dyadic Creativity," *Human Relations,* Vol. 18 (1965), pp. 33–55.

[22]Bernard M. Bass, *Organizational Psychology* (Boston: Allyn & Bacon, 1965).

[23]E. J. Thomas and C. F. Fink, "Effects of Group Size," in Larry L. Cummings and William E. Scott, eds., *Readings in Organizational and Human Performance* (Homewood, Ill.: Richard D. Irwin, 1969), pp. 394–408.

[24]L. W. Porter and Richard M. Steers, "Organizational, Work, and Personal Factors in Employee Turnover and Satisfaction," *Journal of Applied Psychology*, Vol. 80 (1973), pp. 151–176.

[25]Alexander P. Hare, *Handbook of Small Group Research* (New York: Free Press, 1976).

[26]R. Z. Gooding and J. A. Wagner III, "A Meta-Analytic Review of the Relationship between Size and Efficiency of Organizations and Their Subunits," *Administrative Science Quarterly*, Vol. 30 (1985), pp. 462–481.

[27]Adapted from a course assignment prepared by James T. Wallace for Professor J. G. Hunt, Southern Illinois University–Carbondale. Copyright © by J. G. Hunt, 1980. Used by permission.

CHAPTER 8
GROUP AND INTERGROUP DYNAMICS

GE is a unique set of different businesses run by a unique group of people with different talents.

General Electric Company

JIM THOMAS'S PROBLEM

Jim Thomas is manager of the Mountain Side plant of the National Alloys Company.[1] He has a tough production schedule that demands solid performance from all of his people in all areas of the plant. Jim wants to do a top-flight job and becomes concerned when production drops, problems go unsolved, or morale sags.

After his job and his family, Jim's greatest interest is pro football—particularly as played by the Dallas Cowboys. Being a native Texan, Jim has followed the Dallas team from its inception. He gets to attend an occasional game and watches the team regularly on TV or listens to games on the radio. When a game is over, Jim can give a clear, detailed accounting of the team's success or failure.

What raises Jim's boiling point higher than anything is to watch his team fail to play together. He can spot in an instant when someone misses a block, loafs on the job, fails to pass on obvious information to the quarterback, or tries to "shine" at the expense of the team. He can diagnose the Cowboys' areas of weakness, and, if the coach could only hear him, he would tell him what to do to remedy the situation. But with all his insight into teamwork and football, Jim fails to see the parallels between what is needed to improve the Dallas Cowboys and what is needed to shape up the management team at National Alloys. Many problems are the same:

- Some individuals have never really learned what their assignments are, particularly for certain plays or situations.
- Some are afraid of the coach, so they pretend to know things that they should be asking questions about.
- Some want to do things "the old way," while others feel that more modern methods are needed.
- Factions and cliques quarrel and fight among one another.
- The whole unit has not come together to develop common goals to which everyone is committed.
- Decisions are made by someone, but some people either don't "get the word" or they disagree with the decision and drag their feet.
- There is jealousy between units and a lack of playing together.
- Even when people are aware of a problem, they don't know exactly what to do about it.

Management Applications Question

The analogy between the Dallas Cowboys football team and work groups in general is most appropriate. It should lead you to ask, "What are the key forces in groups and between groups with which a manager should be concerned?"

PLANNING AHEAD

This chapter will help you to understand the following dimensions of group and intergroup dynamics in organizations:

Homans' Model of Group Dynamics
Stages of Group Development
Group Norms and Cohesiveness
Interaction Patterns in Groups
Decision Making in Groups
Group Task and Maintenance Activities
Intergroup Relations

The previous chapter introduced task performance and human resource maintenance as the ultimate criteria of work group effectiveness. Figure 8.1 places these criteria in the perspective of the group as an open system. This figure shows that the group process transforms various inputs into performance and maintenance as the two key outputs. The outputs, in turn, become sources of performance feedback that may be

FIGURE 8.1   The group as an open system.

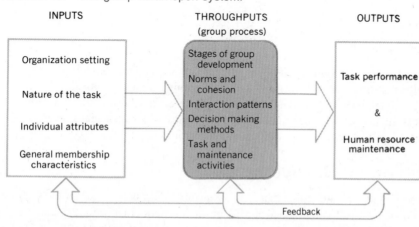

used constructively to modify input and/or throughput factors to increase group effectiveness in the future.

Sporting teams such as the Dallas Cowboys work hard in trying to understand their successes and failures and then to practice ways of improving how well members of the team work together. Work groups in organizations can benefit from similar efforts to review results, analyze group behavior, and make constructive changes. Figure 8.1 offers the manager a way of looking at groups and seeking to understand their behavior with such a purpose in mind.

When you review the work groups with which you are concerned as a manager, you will examine how the outputs relate to both inputs and group process. In respect to the input factors, you will be concerned about the support offered by the organization setting, the nature of the task demands, attributes of individual members, and the characteristics of the group membership as a whole. These were discussed in detail in Chapter 7.

When attention shifts to the group process, your concern is to ensure that it takes full advantage of the various inputs to produce the desired outputs. There are five aspects of group process that are especially important—stages of group development, group norms and cohesion, interaction patterns, decision-making methods, and task and maintenance activities. These major topics of the present chapter are highlighted in Figure 8.1. Since, together the process issues are often referred to as the basic elements of *group dynamics,* we will begin by clarifying this concept.

Group dynamics are forces operating in groups that affect task performance and human resource maintenance. They enact the transformation process through which group inputs are turned into group outputs. Naturally, an informed manager will want to facilitate group dynamics that are positive influences on group effectiveness. In the previous chapter, we discussed group attributes as if they were static. Now, the notion of group dynamics allows us to breathe life into group attributes and make the open systems model in Figure 8.1 the foundation of a truly dynamic group.

HOMANS' MODEL OF GROUP DYNAMICS

One classic view of group dynamics is offered by George Homans.[2] He feels that it is useful to distinguish among the activities, sentiments, and interactions of group members, and to examine the required and emergent forms of each. Because Homans' model can help you to conceptualize group dynamics better, especially in respect to their formal and informal sides, we briefly outline it here.

Required and Emergent Behaviors

Required behaviors are those that the organization formally requests from group members as a basis for continued affiliation and support. They may include such work-related behaviors as being punctual, treating customers with respect, and being helpful to co-workers. **Emergent behaviors** are what group members do in addition to or in place of what is asked by the organization. In "The Case of the Changing Cage" described in the introduction to Part Three, the afternoon snacks and games of rubber-band sniping were emergent behaviors. Other examples include "punching in" a late co-worker and extending the authorized coffee breaks.

What members actually do in respect to both required and emergent behaviors constitutes the basic process through which the group turns resource inputs into outputs. Whereas the required behaviors are formally designed with the group's purpose in mind, emergent behaviors exist purely as matters of individual and group choice. They essentially create an informal system of behaviors that supports the formal system defined by the required behaviors.

You might think that the required behaviors in Homans' model are desirable and functional from a managerial viewpoint, while the emergent ones are not. This is incorrect. What is important is that the behaviors specified in the required/formal system and those found in the emergent/informal system complement rather than contradict one another in contributing to group effectiveness. Indeed, supportive emergent behaviors are necessary for almost any group or organization to achieve true effectiveness. Rarely, if ever, can the required behaviors be specified so perfectly that they meet all the demands of the work situation. This is especially true in dynamic and uncertain environments where job demands change over time. Clearly, there are times when the informal or emergent work behaviors are much more efficient than are those required by formal rules. We can illustrate this point in the reverse—that is, by giving an example of what happens when postal workers work strictly by the rules and do only what is required.[3]

> The U.S. postal system has many formal rules and policies that route delivery workers are supposedly required to follow. None of these men and women can perform their work satisfactorily while following all these rules to the letter. Complete conformity is so ridiculous that postal employees have chosen to follow rules perfectly only when they wish to "strike" in opposition to federal law against "strikes." In such cases the "strike" is called a "work-by-the-rules strike." The deliverers leave in the morning, park on the opposite side of the street from their postal box (a rule), unlock their trucks, get their bags out, lock the trucks (a rule), go across the street, come back, unlock the trucks, put the mail in, lock their trucks, and so on. Thus by following rules perfectly, the deliverers come in late from their daily activities with only half the mail delivered and free from any possible prosecution.

It may help you to think of the system of emergent behaviors as a "shadow" or informal aspect of any required group behaviors. We show this shadow effect in Figure 8.2. Ideally speaking once again, the emergent behaviors (informal system) will function in support of the required behaviors (formal system), enhance a group's process, and be a positive influence on overall group effectiveness.

Homans' model also identifies the activities, interactions, and sentiments of group members as things that can have both required and emergent forms. These concepts can assist the manager to understand a group and are briefly explained next. As you

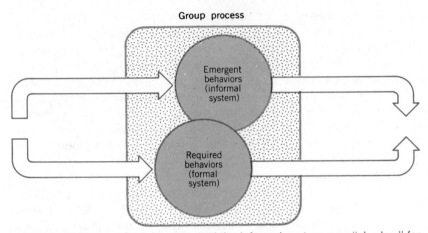

FIGURE 8.2 Emergent behaviors and the informal system as a "shadow" for required behaviors and the formal system in the group process.

read on, think back to "The Case of the Changing Cage" and see if you can apply the concepts to this case. Keep in mind that the activities, interactions, and sentiments of any group must be understood in both their required and emergent forms.

Activities

Activities are the verbal and nonverbal actions in which group members engage. They are the things people do in groups and include efforts directed toward the group task, social activities, and other forms of physical movement. The required activities of a work group member are often specified by the organization in a written job description. This document outlines the activities that the organization expects the individual to accomplish as a group member and in return for any inducements offered.

Both required and emergent activities will be found in any group. Table 8.1 gives examples of each as taken from "The Case of the Changing Cage." Many other examples can be found in that same case.

TABLE 8.1   Examples of Required and Emergent Behaviors: The Case of the Changing Cage

Group Element	Required Behavior	Emergent Behavior
Activities	Canceled checks are to be filed in numerical order.	Periodic games of rubber-band "sniping" take place.
Interactions	Clerks take orders from Ms. Dunn, the unit supervisor.	Clerks stand and "chat" with the messengers.
Sentiments	Clerks should be polite to persons from the other work units.	Clerks held negative feelings toward Mr. Burke.

Interactions

Interactions are communications and interpersonal contacts that occur between and among group members. The essence of any interaction is the sending and receiving of information. This occurs by oral conversation as well as in written (such as letters, memos, and signs) and nonverbal communication (such as facial gestures and hand signals). Table 8.1 shows examples of required and emergent interactions. As with activities, they can be positive or negative in their influence on group functioning and effectiveness.

Sentiments

Sentiments are the feelings, attitudes, beliefs, or values held by group members. These sentiments may be brought into a group from the outside by individual group members, or they may be learned as a result of becoming a group member. A new employee may value hard work and the concept of a "fair day's work for a fair day's pay." To maintain harmonious working relations with other members of the work group, however, this person may learn that it is more important to value restricted efforts and to avoid outperforming other members of the group.

Group sentiments are especially subject to emergent forces. Although it may be easy to require positive attitudes toward work such as a respect for authority and belief in company rules and procedures, it is more difficult to achieve these results in actual practice. When the goals of the emergent system support the required system, the likelihood of this occurring is greatly increased. "The Case of the Changing Cage" illustrates, however, just how tenuous this relationship between required and emergent group sentiments can be.

Managerial Implications

Homans' concepts of required and emergent group behaviors and of activities, interactions, and sentiments as key elements of group dynamics are useful in describing what takes place in groups. To the extent that required and emergent behaviors complement, rather than contradict, one another, and to the extent that the activities, interactions, and sentiments of members support organizational goals, group dynamics are also likely to support rather than hinder group effectiveness.

STAGES OF GROUP DEVELOPMENT

One key aspect of group dynamics is the stage of development of a given group. Newly formed groups show quite different behavior patterns from mature ones. A knowledge of group development can help you to predict the kinds of behavior most likely to occur and provide additional understanding of why one group acts one way and another quite differently. A synthesis of the research on small groups suggests that there are four distinct phases of group development: (1) forming, (2) storming, (3) initial integration, and (4) total integration.[4]

Forming Stage

The forming stage involves the initial entry of individual members into the group. At this point individuals ask a number of questions as they begin to identify with other group members and the group itself. What can or does the group offer its members? What will they be asked to contribute? Can individual needs be met at the same time that individual contributions serve the needs of the group?

In the forming stage, people are concerned to discover what is considered acceptable behavior and what the real task of the group is. Defining group boundaries and group rules is important. In a work group, this identification process is likely to be more complicated than in other group settings. The work setting may consist of individuals who have been in the organization for substantial time periods. Such things as multiple group memberships and identifications, prior experience with task group members in other contexts, and impressions or organization philosophies, goals, and policies may all affect newly formed work groups.

Storming Stage

This second stage of group development is a period of high emotionality. There may be periods of overt hostility and infighting. Typically, the storming period involves relatively high tension among the members.

During the storming period, changes occur in the group. Required activities are further elaborated, and attention is shifted toward obstacles standing in the way of group goals. In work groups individuals begin to clarify one another's interpersonal styles. Efforts will be made to find appropriate ways to accomplish group goals while also satisfying individual needs.

Outside demands create pressures. Coalitions or cliques may form as subgroups on an emergent and informal basis. Conflict may develop over authority as individuals compete to try to impose their preferences on the group and to achieve their desired position in the group's status structure.

Initial Integration

While the storming phase is characterized by differences among group members, the next phase of group development stresses integration. Here the group begins to become coordinated as a working unit. The probes and jockeying behaviors of the storming phase lead to a precarious balancing of forces. Group members strive to maintain this balance. The group will try to regulate individual behavior toward this end. Members are likely to develop a sense (although possibly superficial) of closeness, an interacting communication network, a division of labor, to want to protect the group from disintegration. Indeed, holding the group together may become more important than successful task accomplishment.

During initial integration, minority viewpoints may be strongly discouraged. Although a group may feel a sense of integration at this stage, it may be superficial rather than genuine.

Total Integration

Total integration characterizes a mature, organized, and well-functioning group. The integration is now completed. The group is able to deal with complex tasks and to handle membership disagreements in creative ways. Group structure is stable, and members are motivated by group goals. The primary challenges of this stage are to continue working together as an integrated unit, to remain coordinated with the larger organization, and to adapt successfully to changing conditions over time. A group that has achieved total integration will score high on the criteria of group maturity presented in Figure 8.3. Group members will also tend to be more satisfied than in earlier stages.[5]

> Choose a group to which you belong, perhaps your OB class or project group might serve as an example. Rate this group using Figure 8.3. What needs to be done to help this group achieve or maintain total integration? Students in project groups often mistake stage 3 for stage 4. Has this happened in one of your groups? If so, with what result?

GROUP NORMS AND COHESIVENESS

Stages of group development are one important aspect of group dynamics. A second important aspect, and one based on Homans' Model of group dynamics, is the relationships that come about from the interactions, activities, and sentiments of people working together in a group. Among these relationships stand two group process factors of very special managerial significance: norms and cohesiveness. Consider the following incident as an illustration.

Illustrative Case: Frank Jackson

Frank Jackson deftly soldered his last wires in the interconnection.[6] That was 18 for the morning—not bad, he thought. He moved on to the next computer and began to string out the cable for the next job.

"You're new here, aren't you?" The man was standing beside Frank, soldering iron in hand.

"Yeah. I came over from Consumer Products Division—been with the company for 10 years."

"I'm Jim Miller. Been working here in computer assembly for 5 years."

The men shook hands. Jim walked back to the last job Frank did and looked it over. "Pretty good, Frank, pretty good." He looked back down the assembly floor. "How many have you done this morning?"

"Eighteen."

"Hey, you're quite a rate-buster, aren't you?" Jim laughed. "Most of us here figure 15 interconnections a day is about par for the course."

"Well, these I'm doing are pretty easy."

A MATURE GROUP POSSESSES:

1. Adequate mechanisms for getting feedback:

| Poor feedback mechanisms | 1   2   3   4   5 Average | Excellent feedback mechanisms |

2. Adequate decision-making procedure:

| Poor decision-making procedure | 1   2   3   4   5 Average | Very adequate decision-making |

3. Optimal cohesion:

| Low cohesion | 1   2   3   4   5 Average | Optimal cohesion |

4. Flexible organization and procedures:

| Very inflexible | 1   2   3   4   5 Average | Very flexible |

5. Maximum use of member resources:

| Poor use of resources | 1   2   3   4   5 Average | Excellent use of resources |

6. Clear communications:

| Poor communication | 1   2   3   4   5 Average | Excellent communication |

7. Clear goals accepted by members:

| Unclear goals— not accepted | 1   2   3   4   5 Average | Very clear goals— accepted |

8. Feelings of interdependence with authority persons:

| No interdependence | 1   2   3   4   5 Average | High interdependence |

9. Shared participation in leadership functions:

| No shared participation | 1   2   3   4   5 Average | High shared participation |

10. Acceptance of minority views and persons:

| No acceptance | 1   2   3   4   5 Average | High acceptance |

FIGURE 8.3   Criteria of group maturity. (From Edgar H. Schein, *Process Consultation,* Copyright © 1969, Addison-Wesley Publishing Company, Inc., Chapter 6, p. 62, Figure 6.1, "A Mature Group Process." Reprinted with permission.)

Jim frowned. "Yeah, but look what happens. You do 20, maybe 25 easy ones, and the boys stuck with the hard jobs look bad. You wouldn't want that to happen, would you?"

"Well, no, of course not."

"That-a-boy!" Frank smiled. "You know, the boys here have a bowling team— kind of a company deal. Not everybody is on it—just the interconnection group. Even a few of them don't make it. You know, we like to keep it a friendly bunch." He paused. "Like to come next Wednesday?"

"Why, OK. Sure Jim, what does the foreman think about the number of jobs a day?"

"Him? He don't know the difference, and if he did, what difference would it make? You can't find good interconnection men right off the street. He goes along— the boys upstairs don't know how fast the work should go, and they don't bother him. So he don't bother us."

Frank looked over his next job. He was doing the toughest kind of interconnection, and he knew that any reasonably skilled man should be able to do at least 40 jobs a day on most of the other interconnections. Boy, this was going to be a relaxing job. He didn't like to goof off, but these people were going to be working with him every day—and he wasn't about to get off on the wrong foot with them. Besides, he liked to bowl.

"It's all cost plus anyhow," Jim said. "The company gets plenty from the government for the work. They've got nothing to worry about. Hey, come over to the latrine with me—we can have a smoke. We got plenty of time."

Norms

Previously, we discussed the proposition that group performance is largely determined by how well the competencies and other attributes of its members are aggregated. In the incident just related, a person of ability and motivation has been influenced by the group to withhold work effort. The forces at play in this example include group norms and cohesiveness.

A **group norm** is a behavior that is expected by members of a group. Norms are often referred to as "rules" or "standards" of behavior that apply to group members.[7] When violated, they may be enforced with reprimands and/or other group sanctions. In the extreme, violating group norms can result in expulsion from the group or social ostracism. In fact, it was just this concern that apparently caused Frank Jackson in the prior case to agree to the group norm of restricted performance.

Norms are among the sentiments that develop as group members interact with one another. They serve the group by allowing members to predict one another's behavior and, therefore, to be better able to select appropriate behaviors for themselves. Norms help a group to avoid chaotic behavior as the inputs of many different individuals are organized into collective group action. There are many types of norms. For a student project group, there may be norms regarding attendance at meetings, social behaviors, preparedness for meetings, willingness to challenge one another's ideas, and so on.

Of course, one of the most important norms relates to the levels of work effort and performance that members are expected to contribute to the group's task.

The performance norm is a key characteristic of work groups. It can be positive or negative in terms of its implications for organizational goals. In the case of Frank Jackson's group, the result was obviously negative. Researchers report that work groups with more positive norms tend to be more successful in accomplishing organizational objectives than are groups with more negative norms. Compare and contrast, for example, some of the following norms summarized in one study.[8]

Norms of . . .	Positive Form	Negative Form
Organizational and personal pride	It's a tradition around here for people to stand up for the company when others criticize it unfairly.	In our company they are always trying to take advantage of us.
Performance/ excellence	In our company people always try to improve, even when they are doing well.	Around here there's no point in trying harder— nobody else does.
Teamwork/ communication	Around here people are good listeners and actively seek out the ideas and opinions of others.	Around here it's dog-eat-dog and save your own skin.
Leadership/ supervision	Around here managers and supervisors really care about the people they supervise.	In our company it's best to hide your problems and avoid your supervisor.
Profitability/cost effectiveness	Around here people are continually on the lookout for better ways of doing things.	Around here people tend to hang on to old ways of doing things even after they have outlived their usefulness.

Other norms that may emerge as important sentiments in the work setting include relationships with supervisors, collegues, and customers, as well as honesty, security, personal development, and change.

Finally, a manager should not forget that norms also operate in informal groups. For example, you may meet for lunch with two or three people from work just about every day. There will be expected behaviors, or norms, operating even here. There will be expectations about time, where to meet, when to leave, and probably even topics that are in or out of bounds for discussion. As Homans' model of group dynamics reminds us, the norms of this informal group could have an impact on the formal work groups to which you and the other informal group members belong.[9]

Cohesiveness

Norms vary in the degree to which they are accepted and adhered to by group members. Conformity to norms is strongly influenced by a group's cohesiveness. **Group cohesiveness** is the degree to which members are attracted to and motivated to remain part of a group. Persons in a highly cohesive group value their membership and strive to maintain positive relationships with other group members. The work group that Frank Jackson joined was apparently cohesive. Other members of his team rallied together and restricted their work efforts. This sense of group belongingness apparently had a strong attraction for Frank. Perhaps it was a need for social affiliation that led him to accept this norm rather than to break it and run the risk of being ostracized from the group.

Cohesion is an important group property. Managers should know the answers to such questions as (1) "What creates group cohesiveness?" and (2) "What are the results of group cohesiveness?"

Sources of Cohesion

Group cohesiveness is affected by a variety of personal and situational variables.[10] Cohesion tends to be high in groups characterized by members who are homogeneous in terms of attitudes, socioeconomic backgrounds, needs, and other individual attributes. When members respect and hold one another's competencies in high esteem, cohesiveness is also likely to be high. Situational factors that enhance group cohesion include agreement on group goals, small size, tasks requiring a high degree of interdependence, physical isolation from other groups, performance success, and performance failure or crisis. We will give you a chance to explore these influences on group cohesion further in Chapter 9, after you have gained additional insights on group dynamics.

Results of Cohesion

Members of highly cohesive groups, whether formal or informal, are concerned about their group's activities and achievements. They tend, as opposed to persons in less cohesive groups, to be more energetic in working on group activities, less likely to be absent, happy about performance success, and sad about failures. Cohesive groups generally have stable memberships and foster feelings of loyalty, security, and high self-esteem among their members. They satisfy a full range of individual needs.

Cohesive groups are good for their members. But the critical remaining question is whether or not cohesive work groups are good for their host organizations. Research answers, "it all depends on the group's performance norm!" A basic rule of group dynamics is that, the more cohesive the group, the greater the conformity of members to group norms. When the performance norm is positive, high conformity has a very beneficial effect; when the norm is negative, however, substantial undesirable results can occur when conformity is high.

Table 8.2 illustrates the performance levels predicted for various combinations of group cohesion and performance norms. Performance is likely to be highest in a highly

TABLE 8.2   Group Cohesiveness, Performance Norms, and Predicted Levels of Group Performance

Cohesion	Performance Norms	
	Positive	Negative
High	High performance	Low performance
Low	Moderate performance	Moderate to low performance

cohesive group with positive performance norms. In this situation, members with the proper competencies can work hard and achieve both performance success and satisfaction with their group affiliation. The worst situation for a manager is a highly cohesive group with negative performance norms. Once again members will be highly motivated to support one another and experience personal satisfactions. However, the organization will probably suffer as the group restricts its performance to levels consistent with the negative performance norm.

Between these two extremes are mixed situations. In both cases, the lack of cohesion fails to ensure member conformity to the guiding norm. Thus the strength of the performance norm is substantially less and the level of outcome is somewhat unpredictable, but on the moderate or low side.

In summary, group cohesion is a source of member satisfaction in both formal and informal groups. Turnover and absenteeism also tend to be low in highly cohesive groups. This should be good for the group. With high cohesion comes high conformity to group norms. When there is a positive performance norm, performance will be high, with little variability among the members. When the norm is low, the performance level will be low and again little variability will occur. As an informed manager you would like to be able to influence group norms and cohesiveness to support the organization's production purposes. In the next chapter we offer specific guidelines for building positive norms and influencing group cohesion.

INTERACTION PATTERNS IN GROUPS

Up to now, we have treated groups as if they were all structured the same way in the patterns of interactions linking members to one another. That is an oversimplification. In fact, it is useful for you to think about three different patterns of interaction employed by groups. Consider, for example, a manager who calls his or her subordinates together for a problem-solving meeting, serves as an information hub for gathering opinions on a proposed new policy, and becomes caught on one side of an issue about which work group members are divided into two camps. Figure 8.4 describes each of these situations schematically. They are formally referred to as interacting, coacting, and counteracting groups, respectively.

Interacting, Coacting, and Counteracting Groups

Interacting groups involve high interdependence among members in task performance.[11] Each member interacts regularly with every other. You would expect to find this pattern in a medical team working on an emergency accident victim. Close coordination is required to manage the high level of interdependency and facilitate task performance.

Members of **coacting groups** work independently on common tasks. Members divide up the required labor and then work individually to fulfill this responsibility. A central control point is required to hold each member accountable and to accumulate the individual contributions into a final group product. Department store sales clerks work in coacting groups.

Counteracting group formations include the presence of subgroups that disagree on some aspect of overall group operations. These may be issue-specific disagreements, such as temporary debate over the best means to achieve a goal. They may also be of longer-term duration, such as labor management disputes. In either case, the interaction pattern involves polarized subgroups that contest one another's positions and, therefore, maintain restricted and sometimes antagonistic relations. Some of the implications of counteracting formations will become clearer in our later discussion of intergroup competition.

PATTERN	DIAGRAM	CHARACTERISTICS
Interacting group	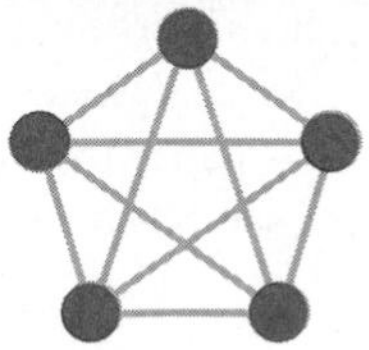	High interdependency around a common task
Coacting group	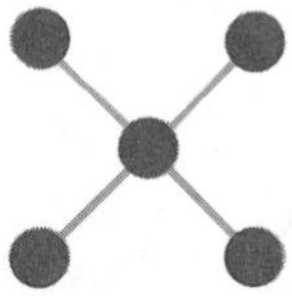	Independent individual efforts on behalf of common task
Counteracting group	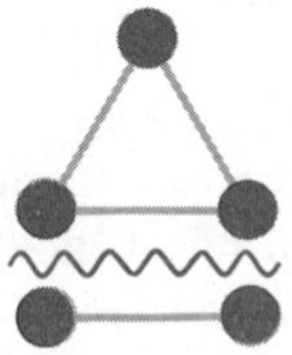	Subgroups in disagreement with one another

FIGURE 8.4 Basic patterns of group interactions.

NEWSLINE 8.1 / A PLANT WITHOUT WALLS

In keeping with company tradition, Hewlett-Packard's Waltham, Massachusetts, plant is a big bullpen with shoulder-high dividers splitting up the space. The idea is to achieve closer cooperation among workers, supervisors, and managers by eliminating physical barriers that might separate them. The arrangement helps, too, in getting product-design people and manufacturing types to work together. Production skills specialist

Idaline Henriques (standing) discusses a circuit board with her supervisor, Willie Dixon, while production section manager Jim Meek works in the background. As in other Hewlett-Packard facilities, the plant manager's office is also on the shop floor—a spartan cubicle without doors. Says manager Ron Rankin: "We don't go for the peacock alleys of executive offices with secretaries guarding the boss's door. I'm accessible to everyone here." The plant makes electronic devices to monitor patients.

Reported in *Fortune*.

Most groups will have a predominate interaction pattern, that is, one used by the group most of the time. In many cases, the possible interaction patterns will be substantially influenced by some of the group input factors. Spatial arrangements and technology are particularly important here. As Newsline 8.1 shows, the physical architecture of the workplace may prohibit certain patterns and encourage others. Work flow layout and technology can have similar effects. A manager's job is to make sure that his or her work unit adopts the interaction pattern best suited to its individual circumstances and to help the group move successfully in and out of the other patterns as required over time.

Group Communication Networks

Communication is discussed at length and defined in Chapter 14 as an interpersonal process of sending and receiving symbols with meanings attached to them. Communication is what allows group members to interact and complete their business. It enables members to get to know one another, learn norms, and distribute information required to accomplish necessary tasks.

The interaction pattern of a group at any particular point in time represents a network of interpersonal relationships through which the members can communicate with one another. Interacting groups allow all members of a group to communicate directly with one another and are, therefore, called **decentralized communication networks.** In a coacting group, by contrast, all communication flows through a central person who serves as the "hub" of a **centralized communication network.** This basic distinction is an important one in the field of OB.

Table 8.3 summarizes the key findings of research on communication networks within groups.[12] In general, people tend to be better satisfied in interacting groups or

TABLE 8.3   Interaction Patterns, Communication Networks, and Group Effectiveness

Group Effectiveness Criteria	Coacting Groups or Centralized Networks	Interacting Groups or Decentralized Networks
Member satisfaction	Low*	High
Task performance		
Simple tasks	High	Low
Complex tasks	Low	High

*Except for central person.

decentralized networks. This results from more opportunities to be involved in information flows associated with work on the group task. The table also shows that the central person in the coacting group or centralized network tends to be highly satisfied. Again, this is because of this person's access to information.

Performance results vary with the nature of the group task. Centralized networks work better on simple tasks requiring little creativity, information processing, and problem solving. Here, coacting groups will be faster and more accurate in task performance than will interacting groups. The reverse is true under more complex task conditions, where the decentralized network is the top performer.

Communication within a counteracting group will be disjointed as subgroups form around different sides of an issue. This can be a source of creativity and critical evaluation and thereby benefit the group. However, there are forces at work in the situation that make the manager's goal of achieving such benefits from counteracting group situations a most challenging one. Although the members of subgroups may relate effectively with one another, communication between subgroups can suffer as emotions, antagonisms, and other biases intervene in the situation. More will be said on this topic when intergroup relations are examined later in this chapter, and when communication and conflict are discussed in Chapter 14.

DECISION MAKING IN GROUPS

One of the key activities in which group members engage is the making of decisions. The fundamentals of **decision making** as the process of choosing among alternative courses of action are discussed in Chapter 13. Our present interest is focused on the alternative ways in which groups make decisions as they share information and work on tasks. This is an important issue since groups are sometimes criticized for their inability to make timely decisions or for making poor decisions. An interesting historical example relates to the length of time it once took the College of Cardinals in the Roman Catholic Church to elect a pope and how this problem was resolved.[13]

In the Middle Ages after an election for pope that had taken nearly three years, the people decided to expedite things. The cardinals were locked in a room until they elected a pope. This worked so well that in the next election the cardinals were sequestered, forbidden from outside contact, and allowed only two dishes of food a day. After eight days there was to be only bread, wine, and water. Ever since, or so the saying goes, the papal elections have gone much more quickly!

How Groups Make Decisions

Edgar Schein, a noted scholar and consultant, has worked extensively with groups to analyze and improve their decision-making processes. He observes that groups may make decisions through any of the following methods.[14] As you read about them, think how often you encounter these methods in your group activities. Think, too, about the consequences resulting from each.

1. *Decision by lack of response.*   One idea after another is suggested without any discussion taking place. When the group finally accepts an idea, all others have been bypassed and discarded by simple lack of response rather than by critical evaluation.

2. *Decision by authority rule.*   The chairperson, manager, or some other authority figure makes a decision for the group. This can be done with or without discussion and is very time efficient. Whether the decision is a good one, however, depends on whether or not the authority figure had the necessary information and how well this approach is accepted by other group members.

3. *Decision by minority.*   One, two, or three people are able to dominate or "railroad" the group into making a decision they agree with. This is often done by providing a suggestion and then forcing quick agreement by challenging the group with—"Does anyone object? . . . Let's go ahead then."

4. *Decision by majority rule.*   Groups can make decisions by majority rule, that is, by voting or polling members to find the majority viewpoint. This method parallels the democratic political system and if often used without awareness of its potential problems. Voting tends to create coalitions of "winners" and "losers." Those in the minority (i.e., the "losers") can easily feel left out or discarded without having a fair say. This can detract from the implementation of a decision since support is fragmented in the final result.

5. *Decision by consensus.*   Schein defines *consensus* as a state of affairs where a clear alternative appears with the support of most members, *and* even those who oppose it feel that they have been listened to and had a fair chance to influence the decision outcome. Consensus, therefore, does *not* require unanimity. What it does require is for any dissenting member to be able to say[15]

   I understand what most of you would like to do. I personally would not do that, but I feel that you understand what my alternative would be. I have had sufficient opportunity to sway you to my point of view but clearly have not been able to do so. Therefore, I will gladly go along with what most of you wish to do.

6. *Decision by unanimity.*   All group members agree on the course of action to be taken. Schein considers this a "logically perfect" group decision method that is extremely difficult to attain in actual practice.

Assets and Liabilities of Group Decision Making

The decision-making methods discussed by Schein range from very individual-oriented decisions at one extreme (e.g., authority rule) to more truly "group" decisions at the other (e.g., consensus). One of the reasons why groups sometimes turn to authority decisions, majority voting, or even minority and lack of response decisions is due to the difficulty of managing the group process to actually get consensus or unanimity. Table 8.4, for example, lists a number of guidelines for members in consensus-seeking groups. Success in achieving consensus requires discipline and support from everyone in the group. Breakdowns can and do occur in this process. As a result, there are both potential assets and liabilities to group decision making. A number of these follow.[16]

Potential Assets of Group Decision Making

1. *Greater sum total of knowledge and information.*   The involvement of more than one person increases the information that can be brought to bear on the problem.

TABLE 8.4   Guidelines for Facilitating Group Consensus

1. Avoid blindly arguing for your own individual judgments. Present your position as clearly and logically as possible, but listen to other members' reactions and consider them carefully before you press your point.
2. Avoid changing your mind just to reach agreement and avoid conflict. Support only solutions that you are able to agree with to at least some degree. Yield only to positions that have objectives and logically sound foundations.
3. Avoid "conflict-reducing" procedures such as majority vote, tossing a coin, averaging, or bargaining in reaching decisions.
4. Seek out differences of opinion. They are natural and expected. Try to involve everyone in the decision process. Disagreements can help the group's decision because a wide range of information and opinions improves the chances for the group to hit upon more adequate solutions.
5. Do not assume that someone must win and someone must lose when discussions reach a stalemate. Instead, look for the next most acceptable alternative for all members.
6. Discuss underlying assumptions, listen carefully to one another, and encourage the participation of all members—three important factors in reaching decisions by consensus.

Source: These guidelines are found in "Decisions, Decisions, Decisions," *Psychology Today* (November 1971), pp. 55, 56. Reprinted from *Psychology Today* magazine. Copyright © 1971 American Psychological Association.

2. *Greater number of approaches to the problem.*   The availability of several individuals means that more perspectives will be offered on a problem and the "tunnel vision" of a single perspective avoided.
3. *Better understanding of final decision.*   Because participants in group decision making are involved in all stages of discussion, comprehension of the decision is high.
4. *Increased accèptance of final decision.*   Participants in group decision making are more inclined to accept the final decision or feel a sense of responsibility for making it work.

Potential Liabilities of Group Decision Making

1. *Social pressure to conform.*   The desire to be a good member and go along with the group can lead people to conform prematurely to poor decisions.
2. *Individual domination.*   A dominant individual may emerge and control the group's decisions; this may be particularly true of the leader whose viewpoints may dominate group discussion.
3. *Time requirements.*   Groups are frequently slower to reach decisions than are individuals acting alone; groups can also delay decisions while individual members "play games" and/or "fight" with one another.

Group decision making is thus a complex and even delicate process. Its success depends on how well group process and individual contributions are balanced and integrated. Simply put,[17]

| Group decision effectiveness | = | sum of individual contributions | + | group process gains | − | group process losses |

In Chapter 9 we extend this discussion by looking at some specific strategies for improving group decision making. In Chapter 13 we focus on a well-known decision-making model, by Vroom and Yetton, which is useful for determining the degree to which a manager should use individual or group decision making.

GROUP TASK AND MAINTENANCE ACTIVITIES

One element critical to the group process, and thereby to the effectiveness of group decision making, is the behavior of the individual members themselves. Group members occupy different *roles* in a group. A **role** is formally defined as a set of activities expected of a person holding a particular office or position in a group or organization. "Leader/manager" or "follower/subordinate" are two common ways of differentiating membership roles in a work group. Roles may also be differentiated according to the kind of contributions a person makes to the group process. Research on the social psychology of groups suggests that two broad types of roles or activities—task and maintenance—are essential if group members are to work effectively over time.[18]

| TABLE 8.5   Sample Group Task and Maintenance Activities ||
Task Roles	Maintenance Roles
Initiating: offering new ideas or ways of defining problems, suggesting solutions to group difficulties.	*Encouraging:* praising, accepting, agreeing with other members' ideas, indicating solidarity and warmth.
Seeking information: attempting to clarify suggestions in terms of factual accuracy, asking for ideas of others.	*Harmonizing:* mediating squabbles within the group, reconciling differences, seeking opportunities for compromise.
Giving information: offering authoritative and relevant information and facts.	*Setting standards:* expressing standards for the group to achieve or use in evaluating group process.
Clarifying: clarifying relations among various suggestions or ideas, attempting to coordinate member activities.	*Following:* going along with the group, agreeing to try out the ideas of others.
Summarizing: assessing group functioning, raising questions about logic and practicality of member suggestions.	*Gate-keeping:* encouraging participation of group members, trying to keep some members from dominating.

Task Activities

Task activities of group members focus on and contribute directly to the group's production purpose.[19] They include efforts to define and solve problems relating to task accomplishment. Without relevant task activities, groups will have difficulty accomplishing their objectives. Group task performance depends on the willingness of members to fulfill task roles by contributing activities such as those described in Table 8.5.

Maintenance Activities

Maintenance activities support the emotional life of the group as an ongoing social system.[20] They help to strengthen and perpetuate the group as a social entity. These maintenance activities, listed by example in Table 8.5, help to enhance member satisfaction and thereby contribute, along with the task activities, to group effectiveness. When these activities are well performed, good interpersonal relationships should be achieved, and the ability of the group to stay together over the longer term will be ensured.

Distributing Group Task and Maintenance Activities for Group Effectiveness

The activities involved in carrying out task and maintenance roles are skills. They can and should be learned by all persons, especially managers, who wish to be successful in helping groups perform.

Both task and maintenance activities are required for groups to be effective over the long run. Every member can assist the group by performing these functions. Although a formal authority, such as chairperson or supervisor will do these activities, the responsibility for their occurrence should also be shared and distributed among all group members. For anyone involved in group dynamics, this responsibility thereby includes

1. Correctly diagnosing group dynamics and recognizing when the task and/or maintenance roles are needed.
2. Responding to this need by providing the appropriate task and/or maintenance activities.

Even though both task and maintenance roles must be fulfilled for groups to be effective over the long run, the relative emphasis of each within a group will vary. As has so often appeared in our discussion of group dynamics, group inputs will make a difference. Take the extreme example of a radar outpost in Greenland. This outpost is assigned to provide early warning of enemy aircraft or missiles flying over the North Pole. While task activities are certainly important, this group will probably need to devote an extremely heavy emphasis on maintenance activities as well. If not, the outpost may not survive as a social system ready and able to perform its task well when needed. Your local fire department provides a parallel example. Many of its activities are probably oriented toward group maintenance during prolonged waiting periods.

In contrast to these illustrations, consider a student project group. Here, a relatively heavy emphasis on task activities is probably important since the group is temporary and short term. The level of maintenance activities has to be just sufficient to keep the group together well enough and long enough to complete the projects. Thus, a good manager and group member understands the relative blend or mix of task and maintenance necessary to achieve effectiveness for different types of groups.

INTERGROUP RELATIONS

Throughout Chapters 7 and 8 we have focused on the group as an essential human resource of the organization. Now we need to look once again at the organization itself as a complex network of many interlocking groups. In this setting, **intergroup dynamics,** that is, the dynamics that take place *between* as opposed to within groups, are especially important. Newsline 8.2 conveys how intergroup relationships were involved when Procter & Gamble Company was developing a new product.

Managers should strive to establish relationships among groups so that each can attain its goal, that is, achieve effectiveness, at the same time that their combined results add up to accomplishment of the organization's goals. This creates "synergy," a subject we first talked about in Chapter 1. Unfortunately, the very nature of groups and organizations tends to create intergroup rivalries and antagonisms that can detract from rather than add to this desired synergy.

NEWSLINE 8.2 / COOKIE CONFLICT AT PROCTER & GAMBLE COMPANY

One of Procter & Gamble Co.'s most vaunted new products is Duncan Hines packaged chocolate-chip cookies, with which P&G began the battle for the fast-growing chewy-cookie market. But P&G introduced the cookies only after some disagreements that illustrate the tensions between the old and new styles at the company.

"One of our goals was to get it out to the marketplace in a big hurry," says Gordon M. Tucker, who left the company after working on the cookies team. So the team urged P&G's

management to contract some cookie production to plants outside the company. The manufacturing executives, used to a more deliberate approach to product introductions argued against outside production, citing quality control and fears of a security breach. "There was lots of internal pressure against it," says Mr. Tucker.

The cookie team finally won some outside production. Recently, the cookies entered test-marketing in Kansas City, Mo. and moved into six more states some two months later. But they're still only sold in 18 percent of the country, and the competition is heated. "They're moving so slowly they're going to get killed," says a former P&G brand manager.

Reported in *The Wall Street Journal*.

Factors Affecting Intergroup Relations

Organizations obviously require the coordination of many groups to achieve their production purposes.[21] Indeed, the lack of adequate intergroup coordination is often a problem. Take, for example, colleges and universities where numerous separate departments are responsible for teaching specialized subjects. It would be impossible for a student to get a degree if the course offerings and program requirements were not well coordinated across departments. But we all know that coordination occasionally does break down at considerable inconvenience to students, just as it does in organizations of all types. Achieving effective coordination requires an understanding of how work flow interdependencies and differences in group characteristics can affect intergroup relations.

Work-Flow Interdependencies

Figure 8.5 shows three types of work-flow interdependencies commonly found in organizations: pooled, sequential, and reciprocal. The degree to which groups are dependent on one another to achieve their respective goals varies from very low in the pooled work flow case to very high in the case of reciprocal work flow.

The amount and kind of work flow interdependencies that exist will influence the emphasis that managers need to place on intergroup relationships. This emphasis varies according to the patterns of interdependency described. Not much attention is needed

Pooled (low) interdependency:

The work of each group contributes to the mission of the total organization but is not directly related to that of the other group. The groups may not directly interact with each other but are indirectly affected by each other's actions.

Example.

Sporting goods and hardware departments in a retail store. Each is concerned with its own effectiveness and has pooled interdependence in terms of the total store profitability.

Sequential (medium) interdependency:

Outputs of one group become inputs for another group.

Example.

A foundry producing castings to be used in an assembly department for early American type wood stoves. The assembly department cannot function without castings received from the foundry.

Reciprocal (high) interdependency:

Each group has outputs that are inputs to the other group.

Example.

Manufacturing and maintenance groups in a manufacturing plant. Manufacturing cannot produce its product within cost, quality, and time specifications without the cooperation of maintenance (maintenance provides input of well-maintained machines) in keeping the machines functioning well. At the same time, maintenance is dependent on manufacturing for work to do (manufacturing provides input of machines needing servicing).

FIGURE 8.4   *Basic patterns of group interactions.*

where there is pooled interdependence since these groups will seldom, if ever, meet. As long as each is familiar with overall organizational goals and the group's role in contributing to these, there should be little concern with the activities of other groups in the pooled work flow.

The importance of managing intergroup relations increases, however, when there is sequential interdependence. Here, there are many possibilities for difficulties to arise as one group's outputs become another group's inputs. In the example from Figure 8.5, the assembly group might blame the foundry group for poor quality or for producing the stove castings late. When this happens, the foundry group will probably not be very helpful when the assembly group needs assistance in getting out a special order expeditiously, some time in the future.

Management of intergroup relations becomes even more important and challenging where there is reciprocal interdependence. In this case, multiple groups are sources of inputs and outputs for one another. Going to the figure for an example again, if maintenance is slow at handling emergency repairs, manufacturing might fall behind its schedule and blame maintenance. Manufacturing may then find a way to handle the repairs itself and cause the maintenance group to lose business and be threatened by staff cutbacks. As you can see, the potential for breakdowns in the working relationships between reciprocally interdependent groups is great.

Differences in Group Characteristics

Other factors affecting intergroup relations are found in basic differences in the characteristics of the groups themselves. These include issues of status, time and goal orientation, reward systems, and resources, among other possibilities.

We have already discussed status in terms of a person's standing on prestige and esteem in a group. Just as a person has differing status compared with others within a group, groups have differing status compared with others in the organization. Such status hierarchies are usually quite clear to the people involved, and they can influence intergroup relations. This is particularly true if the groups have sequential or reciprocal work flow interdependence. If the higher-status groups initiate the work flow, there is less likely to be a problem than where the opposite is the case.

Groups may also have different *time and goal orientations*. Time orientation is concerned with the length of time necessary to obtain information concerning task performance. A difference in time horizon can complicate intergroup relations where there is a high degree of work flow interdependence. The same is true for differences in goal orientations. One illustration follows.

> The sales manager of XYZ Company had just spent the last several weeks gearing up for increased sales during the upcoming quarter. He had carefully touched base with the manufacturing manager, and it looked as if all systems were "go" in terms of increasing production. However, at this same time, the credit manager had become increasingly concerned about excessive credit losses. She, therefore, developed a campaign to tighten up on credit at the same time as manufacturing and sales geared up for an aggressive sales campaign. Instead of sales increasing, they actually declined because of the tightening of credit. Relations between the sales and credit groups deteriorated rapidly as a result.

The *reward systems* under which groups perform can also affect intergroup relations. The sales group in the prior example was actually rewarded for increasing sales; the credit group was rewarded for holding down credit losses. Basic goal differences between the two interdependent groups were thus reinforced by the reward system. Difficulties in intergroup relations were also enhanced.

Groups differ in the amount of *resources* that have been allocated to them. If a "resource-rich" group has frequent dealings with one feeling "resource-deprived," problems in the intergroup relations may develop. In the previous example, if the credit group received or saw itself as receiving relatively fewer resources to do its job than did sales, an already potentially bad situation could become worse. Sometimes, too, groups need to share the same resources to get the job done. If resources are scarce and there is no clear agreement on how they are to be allocated, problems may develop as the groups jockey for position vis-à-vis one another.

Intergroup Competition

An ideal view of organizations depicts them as entirely cooperative systems in which people and groups work together harmoniously to achieve a common result. The practical implications of the work flow interdependencies and group differences just discussed, however, suggest a real world in which considerable room for intergroup competition exists. Groups in organizations compete for rewards, resources, status, and tasks, among other things. As they do so, some important dynamics may occur.[22]

WITHIN Each Competing Group

- Members become closer knit and evidence increased group loyalty; group cohesion increases.
- Concern for the accomplishment of the group's task grows; members become more task-oriented.
- Group members become more willing to accept a single leader.
- Activities become more highly structured and organized.

BETWEEN the Competing Groups

- Each group views the other as an enemy.
- Each group tends to develop very positive images of itself and very negative images of the other; one's own group strengths are overestimated while those of the other are underestimated.
- Hostilities increase and communications decrease between the groups.
- When forced into interaction, group members listen only to what reinforces their original predispositions toward one another.

You can imagine the organizational difficulties that may result from these latter consequences of intergroup competition. Managers walk a thin line as they try to realize some of the advantages of intergroup competition while minimizing its disadvantages. Intergroup competition may be beneficial to the organization if the dynamics result in increased effort, task focus, cohesion and satisfaction within groups, and more balance in power relationships among them. The organization may suffer, however, if intergroup competition leads to negative consequences such as the following.[23]

1. *Diversion of energy.*   Group efforts and energies are channeled toward "winning" the competition rather than task and goal accomplishment.

2. *Altered judgment.*   Judgment is lost as competition creates biased viewpoints among group members.
3. *Loser effects.*   Dissatisfaction and loss of commitment emerges in groups that actually do "lose" something as a result of intergroup competition.
4. *Poor coordination.*   An internal focus on group goals may displace important and needed attention to goals of the organization as a whole and thereby reduce the overall level of integration among multiple-group efforts.

Reducing the Disadvantages of Intergroup Competition

There are two general approaches to managing intergroup competition.[24] The first is to deal with the competition after it occurs; the second is to take action preventing its occurrence in the future.

Controlling Existing Competition

Strategies for minimizing negative consequences when groups are in a state of competition include

1. Identifying a common enemy (for example, another company to be outperformed).
2. Appealing to a common goal (for example, corporate profits).
3. Bringing representative subgroups into direct negotiations with one another.
4. Training members of the competing groups in group skills and then engaging them in structured interactions.

Preventing Future Competition

Additional guidelines for preventing future disadvantages from intergroup competition include the following:

1. Reward groups on the basis of their contribution to the total organization rather than solely on individual group task accomplishment.
2. Reward groups for the help they give one another.
3. Stimulate frequent interaction between groups; avoid tendencies for the groups to withdraw and become isolated from one another.
4. Rotate members among the various groups whenever possible.
5. Avoid putting groups in positions of win–lose competition to obtain desired organizational rewards; emphasize the sharing of resources for maximum benefit to the organization.

SUMMARY

In this chapter, we have looked intensely at group dynamics, forces present within groups that affect performance, and membership satisfaction. We began with Homans' model of group dynamics, which describes a group in terms of required and emergent behaviors, as well as activities, interactions, and sentiments. Our attention then shifted to the stages of group development, an in-depth look at group norms and cohesion, interaction patterns and communication networks, decision-making methods, task and maintenance activities, and intergroup relations.

Groups go through four stages in evolving from a newly formed group to a mature group: (1) forming stage (which involves the entry of individual members into the group); (2) storming stage (when group members are trying to establish themselves and their positions in the group); (3) initial integration stage (when the group establishes superficial integration and may try to smooth over potential differences); and (4) total integration stage (when integration is completed and the group is able to deal with disagreement in constructive ways).

Norms refer to the behavior expected of other group members. Cohesiveness refers to the degree to which members are attracted to and motivated to remain part of the group. In combination, these two concepts have a substantial influence on group effectiveness. The most advantageous situation from a manager's perspective is to have a highly cohesive work group with a high-performance norm.

There are three basic interaction patterns in groups: (1) interacting (where there is high interdependence on task performance), (2) coacting (where members perform essentially independent task functions), and (3) counteracting (where groups work at cross purposes with each other). These, in turn, influence communication networks. Interacting structures provide decentralized communication networks and coacting structures provide centralized networks. The effectiveness of the two networks varies with the nature of the task to be performed. The informed manager helps a group to choose and use interaction patterns and communication networks most appropriate to the problem or task at hand.

Groups make decisions in a wide variety of ways. These vary from lack of response and authority on one extreme to group consensus and unanimity on the other. In between are such alternatives as minority rule and majority voting.

In terms of roles played by group members, the manager is especially concerned with those involving group and task maintenance activities. The former facilitate completion of the group's task; the latter are concerned with maintaining the group over time as an ongoing social system. Although each is and should be performed by the manager, the activities should also be distributed across all group members if a group is to be successful in the long run.

Finally, a manager is not concerned with the work group alone. He or she must be sensitive to intergroup relations and their impact on the effectiveness of the total organization as a complex system of interlocking groups. A number of factors in this setting may create intergroup competition. Depending on how well it is managed, this competition can have positive or negative consequences for the organization. Once again, the manager can play a key role in determining which of these outcomes of intergroup relations is likely to occur.

THINKING THROUGH THE ISSUES

1. Apply the concepts of activities, interactions, and sentiments to ''The Case of the Changing Cage.'' Distinguish for each concept its required and emergent forms in the case.

2. Analyze a group that you have recently joined in terms of the stages of group development. Show evidence supporting your assessment.

3. What is a group norm? Give examples of norms that you think would be good for a group in which you currently participate. Defend your choices.

4. List the factors that originally fostered high cohesiveness in the voucher–check filing unit in "The Case of the Changing Cage." Which of these were disrupted after the move? With what result?

5. Explain why it is that centralized communication networks are better for simple tasks, while decentralized networks are better for more complex tasks.

6. Choose a decision-making group with which you are familiar. Identify when, why, and with what results the group made decisions by each of the methods described in this chapter.

7. Think of one of your class project groups. To what extent were task and maintenance activities performed over the life of the group? To what extent were they distributed among the members? With what net result for group effectiveness?

8. Explain why groups in sequential work flow interdependencies may end up in disagreements with one another. What options would the manager have in trying to control any competition that may result?

CASE: PART-TIMERS AT STUDENT TOOL RENTAL II

Turn to the Part-Timers at Student Tool Rental Case at the end of Chapter 7. Review the case and then answer the following questions.

Questions

1. Discuss how the group inputs for the part-time workers influence the throughputs of the open system model in Figure 8.1. Make sure you cover each separate input and throughput.

2. Discuss how the throughputs can be used to help explain the outputs in the model in Figure 8.1. How does this knowledge of throughputs aid in the explanation as compared with trying to make the explanation from knowledge of inputs alone?

3. Extend your discussion in 1 and 2 above by applying appropriate aspects of Homan's model.

EXERCISE: IDENTIFYING GROUP NORMS

Purpose:
This exercise will help you to recognize norms that develop in groups and analyze their influence on group effectiveness.[25]

Time:
50 minutes

Procedure:
1. Form into work groups as directed by your instructor.
2. As a group, clarify the definition of ''group norm'' so that everyone shares a common understanding of the concept.
3. Make a list, using the ''brainstorming'' technique, of the various norms operating in your OB class, student work group or another group designated by your instructor.
4. Review each norm on the list to develop a ''consensus'' regarding its presence in the group selected for analysis. Remove from the list those suggested norms for which no consensus can be reached.
5. Develop a statement for each norm on the final list of its actual or potential influence on group effectiveness. Make sure a spokesperson is prepared to report in general class session on the list of group norms and their implications for group effectiveness.
6. The instructor will call on each group to report. After discussion of the norms as analyzed by each group, further discussion may follow on the ''brainstorming'' process used in the work groups and experiences in trying to reach ''consensus'' on the final list of norms.

THE MANAGER'S VOCABULARY

Activities   The verbal and nonverbal behaviors in which group members engage.

Centralized Communication Network   A group communication network where all communication flows through a central person who serves as the ''hub'' of the network.

Coacting Groups   Groups whose members work independently on common tasks.

Cohesiveness   Degree to which members are attracted to and motivated to remain part of a group.

Communication   Interpersonal process of sending and receiving symbols with meanings attached to them.

Consensus   A group decision-making method wherein a clear alternative is supported by most members *and* even those who oppose it feel they have been listened to and had a fair chance to influence the decision outcome.

Counteracting Groups   Groups that include the presence of subgroups that disagree on some aspect of overall group operations.

Decentralized Communication Network   A group communication network where all members communicate directly with one another.

Decision Making   Process of choosing among alternative courses of action.

Emergent Behaviors   What group members do in addition to or in replacement of what is asked by the organization.

Group Cohesiveness   The degree to which members are attracted to and motivated to remain part of a group.

Group Dynamics   Forces operating in groups that affect group performance and member satisfaction.

Group Norms   Rules or standards that apply to group members such that when violated the standards may be enforced with reprimands and/or other group sanctions.

Interacting Groups   Groups with high interdependence among members in task performance.

Interactions   Behaviors that group members direct toward other persons.

Intergroup Relations   The dynamics that take place *between* as opposed to within groups.

Maintenance Activities   Activities that support the emotional life of the group as an ongoing social system.

Required Behaviors   Those behaviors that the organization requests as a basis for membership and support.

Sentiments   Feelings, attitudes, beliefs, or values held by group members.

Task Activities   Activities that focus directly on the group's production purpose.

IMPORTANT NAMES

George C. Homans   Offers a model of group dynamics that includes activities, interactions, and sentiments and that differentiates required and emergent behaviors.

Edgar Schein   A noted scholar and consultant who has worked extensively with groups to improve their decision-making and other group processes.

NOTES

[1]William G. Dyer, *Team Building,* copyright © 1977, Addison-Wesley Publishing Company, Inc., Chapter 4, pages 34, 36, 37, Chapter 6, pages 6, 55, 56, 64–67. Reprinted with permission.

[2]See George C. Homans, *The Human Group* (New York: Harcourt Brace, 1950).

[3]Burt Scanlan and J. Bernard Keys, *Management and Organizational Behavior,* 2nd ed. (New York: John Wiley, 1983), p. 294.

[4]J. Steven Heinen and Eugene Jacobson, "A Model of Task Group Development in Complex Organization and a Strategy of Implementation," *Academy of Management Review,"* Vol. 1 (Oct. 1976), pp. 98–111.

[5]Marilyn E. Gist, Edwin A. Locke and M. Susan Taylor, "Organizational Behavior: Group Structure, Process, and Effectiveness," in J. D. Blair and J. G.

Hunt (eds.), *1987 Yearly Review of Management of the Journal of Management,* Vol. 13 (1987), pp. 237–257.

[6]This incident was obtained from Dorothy N. Harlow and Jean J. Hanke, *Behavior in Organizations* (Boston: Little, Brown, 1975), pp. 244–245. The original source cannot be located.

[7]See Daniel C. Feldman, "The Development and Enforcement of Group Norms," *Academy of Management Review,* Vol. 9 (1984), pp. 47–53.

[8]Developed from Robert F. Allen and Saul Pilnick, "Confronting the Shadow Organization: How to Detect and Defeat Negative Norms," *Organization Dynamics* (Spring 1973), pp. 6–10.

[9]See Gist, Locke, and Taylor, (1987) for additional aspects of norms.

[10]For a good summary of research on group cohesive-

ness see Marvin E. Shaw, *Group Dynamics* (New York: McGraw-Hill, 1971), pp. 110–112, p. 192.

[11]This discussion is developed from Fred E. Fiedler, *A Theory of Leadership Productivity* (New York: McGraw-Hill, 1967).

[12]Alex Bavelas, "Communication Patterns in Task-Oriented Groups," *Journal of the Accoustical Society of America,* vol. 22 (1950), pp. 725–730; see also "Research on Communication Networks," as summarized in Shaw, *Group Dynamics,* pp. 137–153.

[13]Excerpted from "Rome's Example," *The Wall Street Journal,* August 31, 1978, p. 14.

[14]Developed from a discussion by Edgar H. Schein, *Process Consultation: Its Role in Organization Development* (Reading, Mass.: Addison-Wesley, 1969), pp. 53–57.

[15]Ibid., p. 56.

[16]Developed from Norman R. F. Maier, "Assets and Liabilities in Group Problem Solving," Psychological Review, Vol. 74 (1967), pp. 239–249.

[17]See Gayle W. Hill, "Group versus Individual Performance: Are $N + 1$ Heads Better than One?" *Psychological Bulletin,* Vol. 91 (1982), pp. 517–539.

[18]Robert F. Bales, "Task Roles and Social Roles in Problem-Solving Groups," in Eleanor E. Maccoby, Theodore M. Newcomb, and E. L. Hartley, eds., *Readings in Social Psychology* (New York: Holt, Rinehart & Winston, 1958).

[19]This discussion is developed from Schein, *Process Consultation,* and Rensis Likert, *New Patterns of Management* (New York: McGraw-Hill, 1961), pp. 166–169.

[20]Ibid.

[21]This discussion is developed from Joseph McCann and Jay R. Galbraith, "Interdepartmental Relations," in Paul C. Nystrom and William H. Starbuck, eds., *Handbook of Organizational Design,* Vol. 2 (New York: Oxford University Press, 1981), pp. 66–68. See also Clayton P. Alderfer, "An Intergroup Perspective on Group Dynamics," in Jay W. Lorsch, ed., *Handbook of Organizational Behavior* (Englewood Cliffs, N.J.: Prentice-Hall, 1987), pp. 190–222.

[22]Schein, *Process Consultation,* p. 97.

[23]Richard L. Daft, *Organization Theory and Design,* (St. Paul, Minn.: West, 1983), p. 435.

[24]Schein, *Process Consultation,* pp. 99–102.

[25]The authors are indebted to Dr. Lars Larson, Southern Illinois University at Carbondale, for suggesting this exercise.

CHAPTER 9
MANAGING GROUP PROCESS AND DESIGNING CREATIVE WORK GROUPS

Members of the Quality Circle established two years ago . . . meet periodically to solve problems in the Detroit shop. Their impact, however, is felt system-wide.

Norfolk Southern Annual Report

ONE MORE CHALLENGE: CLINICAL PSYCHOLOGIST MANAGES GM PLANT

"Everybody's favorite question" these days, Pat Carrigan concedes, is how a psychologist like herself became the first woman to manage a domestic assembly plant for General Motors Corp.[1]

The answer, she believes, is intertwined with the democratization of the American auto industry.

It's also closely tied to the fact that Carrigan, 53, the recently appointed manager of GM's Lakewood assembly plant in Atlanta can't stand "running out of challenges."

The industry, scrambling to boost quality and productivity to compete with Japanese automakers, is turning increasingly to participatory decision making, teamwork, and upgraded communication between all levels of employees.

Consequently, there's a vast need for managers who "understand what people are all about," what motivates them, what affects their productivity and their relations with their fellow workers, she says. Many of those so versed, she adds, happen to be psychologists.

"The job of any manager in our business is defined quite differently today than it would have been 10, 15 years ago," she points out. "Technical expertise is certainly important, but the job of managing people is now understood to be where it's at."

Now, workers are increasingly involved in planning and decision making, bolstering their commitment to—and pride in—a job well done.

Carrigan, who earned her doctorate in clinical psychology from the University of Michigan, sums up her own management style in one word: "open." Less than three weeks after taking over, she had already shaken hands with each of her 1800 plant employees "at least once," and manages to "get her hands dirty" regularly.

"People do the jobs in this world," she states. "Managers don't. And I find it has always worked best for me to concentrate my efforts on the development of a team and the mobilization of team members around some common goals, and certainly the development of support for the people who are involved."

Management Applications Question

Pat Carrigan is a new breed of manager that believes in the effectiveness of teamwork and groups to get work done. What challenges are involved in managing group process and designing creative work groups?

PLANNING AHEAD

A thorough understanding of the following issues can help you to better manage groups as human resources of organizations.

Managerial Challenges of Group Development
Facilitating Individual Entry
Influencing Norms and Cohesion
Improving Group Decisions
Team Building
Designing Creative Work Groups

The new breed of managers such as Pat Carrigan in the chapter opener must be able to use groups effectively. They are part of a "new era" of management in which worker participation and group-oriented arrangements such as quality circles, work teams, and the like are key ingredients. Consider this further description of operations at three firms.[2]

At the A.E. Stanley Company in Lafayette, Indiana, a food processing plant runs without supervisors. The plant's employees work in small teams and choose their own leaders. They also make their own work assignments and do their own hiring.

Abbott Laboratories regularly uses dedicated groups to develop specific new products. When the company joined the search for a new blood test, a small team of scientists was set up in an autonomous "skunkworks." They solved the problem in record time.

GE's Newark, Ohio, plant has only four job categories, compared to 21 at other GE lighting plants. Work teams have "line of sight responsibility"—anything they can see in their area is their responsibility. The teams perform many tasks previously handled by supervisors.

To achieve success in such modern work environments, managers are increasingly called upon to discard traditional styles and adopt more progressive approaches. They are challenged to understand groups as human resources of organizations. And in particular, they are challenged to both understand the various group dynamics described in Chapter 8 and to direct them toward constructive as opposed to destructive results.

To help you achieve this latter goal, this chapter returns to the stages of group development and shows how to deal with special problems encountered in each stage. The chapter concludes by showing further case examples of creative work group designs. These designs apply many of the earlier discussed group concepts. In so doing, they try to facilitate group process and enhance group task performance and human resource maintenance.

MANAGERIAL CHALLENGES OF GROUP DEVELOPMENT

Table 9.1 summarizes selected managerial problems that are fundamental to each stage of group development. These problems include the management of individual entry (forming stage), norm development (storming stage), influencing cohesiveness (initial integration stage), and decision making and team building (total integration stage). A manager's job is to take action so that these needs are satisfied and group efforts are applied in support of the organization's production purposes. The managerial implications of the table are discussed throughout this chapter.

FACILITATING INDIVIDUAL ENTRY

There are many specific issues facing the members of work groups. Some examples are presented in Table 9.2. The table also relates each specific issue to a set of questions that a concerned group member may be led to ask. The questions, in turn, summarize the many dilemmas that may puzzle individuals upon initial entry to a group. Questions regarding atmosphere and relationships, for example, may create the dilemmas of "How friendly do I want to be?" "How close?" "Will others allow that?" These dilemmas may occur during any stage of group development, but are especially likely in the forming stage or whenever a new member joins the group. We refer to these dilemmas as problems of individual entry. Their importance lies in that

$$
\text{Individual entry dilemmas} \xrightarrow{\text{may cause}} \text{operating problems} \xrightarrow{\text{that impair}} \text{group effectiveness}
$$

TABLE 9.1   The Stages of Group Development and Their Associated Managerial Challenges

Time	Stages of Group Development	Managerial Challenges
Immature group; early in its life	Forming	Facilitating individual entry
	Storming	Developing norms
	Initial integration	Influencing cohesiveness
Mature group; later in its life	Total integration	Decision making and team building

TABLE 9.2 Some Dilemmas Facing Work Groups and Their Members	
Membership Issue	Individual Questions
Participation	Do I want to participate?
	To what extent?
Goals	Do I share any goals with the group?
	Can I learn to share some?
Control	Who values the decisions?
	To what extent can I influence what takes place?
Relationships	How close will we become?
	How close do I want to get?
Processes	Can I disagree?
	How will conflict be resolved?
	Is information shared freely?

Individual Problems Upon Entering Groups

Edgar Schein, a noted scholar and consultant, offers a set of profiles of individuals who encounter difficulties upon entering groups.[3] The profiles include the "tough battler," "friendly helper," and the "objective thinker." They are associated with coping responses that individuals may adopt in response to the dilemmas described in Table 9.2. These coping responses often include self-serving activities that interfere with, rather than facilitate, group effectiveness.

Consider the profiles described here. Have you seen such people in your course projects or in other work groups? Would one of these profiles describe your behavior in a group? What do managers need to do to help individuals to overcome these entry problems and become productive and satisfied group members?

The Tough Battler: Group members frustrated by identity problems may act aggressive and tend to resist the ideas and authority of others. These "tough battlers" are seeking answers to the question, "Who am I in this group?"

The Friendly Helper: Initial entry into a group can create tensions as people try to solve problems of control and intimacy. These tensions may lead to showing support for others, acting dependent, and helping and forming supportive alliances. The "friendly helper" is trying to determine whether or not he or she will be liked by the other group members, and if he or she will be able to exert any control or influence over their behavior.

The Objective Thinker: Another anxiety that accompanies individual entry into a group is needs and goals. People join groups for various reasons and seek many types of need satisfactions from their group memberships. Initial passivity, indifference, or oneness of logic or reason in deliberations often characterize the "objective thinker." This person is trying to determine if group goals include opportunities to satisfy personal needs.

Clarifying Membership Expectations

Individuals are expected to contribute efforts to their groups, and they expect certain inducements in return. The psychological contract of membership is based on a fair and equitable exchange of these values. Problems experienced by individuals upon entering groups often reflect uncertainties regarding expected work roles and opportunities to satisfy needs. Similar problems may occur over time as a group matures or changes to meet challenges in the setting, and as individuals personally develop. There is a continuing challenge in any group to maintain clarity of membership expectations. A managerial strategy for accomplishing this both at the point of initial entry and over time is called "role negotiations."

This is a technique sometimes used by consultants whofind their client groups unable to coordinate individual efforts for the common good. Managers and concerned group members may follow the steps listed here to facilitate role negotiations.[4]

1. Individuals write lists of things they would like to see other group members (a) do more or do better, (b) do less or stop doing, and (c) keep doing or remain unchanged.
2. These lists are shared and discussed.
3. Individuals negotiate contracts with one another specifying action commitments that will help satisfy the other's needs and enhance group effectiveness.
4. The contracts are summarized in written form as a reminder to all members of their commitments.
5. The contracts are revised at regular intervals to update and further clarify group membership roles.

Sample material from an actual role negotiation is shown in Figure 9.1. Note the presence of a true "give and take" in the final written agreements among the participating group members.

INFLUENCING NORMS AND COHESION

Group norms and the level of cohesion interrelate with one another to affect the behavior of group members. As noted in Chapter 8, this effect can include positive or negative consequences for work group effectiveness. Managers should be skilled both at influencing norms and at controlling cohesion so that group task performance and member satisfaction are best served.

Building Positive Norms

Group norms are essentially determined by the collective will of group members. As such it is very difficult for organizations and their managers to dictate which norms a given work group will possess. Thus, the concerned manager must use his or her knowledge of group dynamics very wisely to help group members to adopt norms supportive of organizational goals.

In Chapter 8 we discussed various types of group norms. Table 9.3 now equates

Role Negotiations

Issue Diagnosis Form

Messages from ___*JIM*_____

to ___*DAVID*_____

1. If you were to do the following things *more* or *better*, it would help me to increase my own effectiveness:

   - *BE MORE RECEPTIVE TO IMPROVEMENT SUGGESTIONS FROM THE PROCESS ENGINEERS*
   - *GIVE HELP ON COST CONTROL (SEE 2)*
   - *FIGHT HARDER WITH THE G.M. TO GET OUR PLAN IMPROVED.*

2. If you were to do the following things *less*, or were to *stop* doing them, it would help me to increase my own effectiveness:

   - *ACTING AS JUDGE AND JURY ON COST CONTROL*
   - *CHECKING UP FREQUENTLY ON SMALL DETAILS OF THE WORK.*
   - *ASKING FOR SO MANY DETAILED PROGRESS REPORTS.*

3. The following things which you have been doing help to increase my own effectiveness, and I hope you will continue to do them:

   - *PASSING ON FULL INFORMATION IN OUR WEEKLY MEETINGS.*
   - *BEING AVAILABLE WHEN I NEED TO TALK TO YOU.*

Final agreement between Jim Farrell and David Sills

Jim agrees to let David know as soon as agreed completion dates and cost projections look as though they won't be met, and also to discuss each project's progress fully with David on a bi-weekly basis.

In return David agrees not to raise questions about cost details and completion dates, pending a trial of this agreement to see if it provides sufficient information soon enough to deal with questions from above.

FIGURE 9.1 Actual materials from a role negotiations exercise. (From Roger Harrison, "When Power Conflicts Trigger Team Spirit," *European Business* (Spring 1972), pp. 61, 63. Used by permission.)

the focus of norm-building efforts to the stages of group development. In the forming and storming stages, norms relating to membership issues such as expected attendance and levels of commitment are important. By the time a group reaches the stage of total integration, growth-oriented norms relating to adaptability and change become most relevant. Groups that are unable to build norms consistent with the operating problems faced at various stages of development may well compromise their effectiveness.

Among the means that you may use as a manager to help groups build positive norms are the following.[5]

1. Acting as a positive role model.
2. Reinforcing, via rewards, the desired behaviors.
3. Controlling results by performance reviews and regular feedback.

TABLE 9.3	Typical Sequence of Norm Development in Work Groups	
Stage of the Group	Focus of Group Norms	Illustrative Behaviors Addressed
Early	Membership	Who is and is not a member, attendance at group meetings, punctuality, commitment.
	Influence	Leadership roles, strategies for doing the work of the group, status, and dominance relations among members.
	Affection	Patterns of inter-member liking and disliking, balance between task work and interpersonal relationships.
Late	Growth	Experimentation with new behaviors, adaptation of group norms and processes to a changing environment.

Source: David A. Nadler, J. Richard Hackman, and Edward E. Lawler III, *Managing Organizational Behavior,* p. 124. Copyright © 1979 by David A. Nadler, J. Richard Hackman, and Edward E. Lawler III. Reprinted by permission of the authors and Little, Brown and Company.

4. Training and orientating new members to adopt desired behaviors.
5. Recruiting and selecting new members who exhibit the desired behaviors.
6. Holding regular meetings to discuss group progress and ways of improving task performance and member satisfaction.
7. Using group decision making methods to reach agreement on appropriate behaviors.

Influencing Cohesion

As pointed out in Chapter 8, there are advantages and disadvantages to high-group cohesiveness. Members of highly cohesive groups typically experience satisfaction from the group affiliation. When norms related to performance are positive, high cohesiveness contributes to high levels of task accomplishment. To the extent that the performance norms are negative; however, high cohesiveness can restrict task accomplishments and work to the detriment of the organization.

Given these two sides of cohesion, the positive and the negative, there will be times when a manager will want to build cohesiveness in work groups, and there may be times when the objective is to break down cohesiveness. A number of things managers can do to increase and decrease group cohesion are listed in Table 9.4.

"Groupthink"

There is another, more subtle side to group cohesion that can work to a group's disadvantage. Let us consider an example from the world of business.[6]

TABLE 9.4   Managerial Strategies for Increasing and Decreasing Group Cohesion

Actions to Increase Cohesion:
Induce agreement on group goals
Increase membership homogeneity
Increase interactions among members
Decrease group size
Introduce competition with other groups
Allocate rewards to the group rather than individuals
Provide physical isolation from other groups

Actions to Decrease Cohesion:
Induce disagreement on group goals
Increase membership heterogeneity
Restrict interactions among members
Increase group size
Allocate rewards to individuals rather than the group as a whole
Remove physical isolation
Introduce a dominating member
Disband the group

The Boardroom

The Ozyx Corporation is a relatively small industrial company. The president of Ozyx has hired a consultant to help discover the reasons for the poor profit picture of the company in general and the low morale and productivity of the R&D division in particular. During the process of investigation, the consultant becomes interested in a research project in which the company has invested a sizable proportion of its R&D budget.

When asked about the project by the consultant in the privacy of their offices, the president, the vice president for research, and the research manager each describe it as an idea that looks great on paper but will ultimately fail because of the unavailability of the technology required to make it work. Each of them also acknowledges that continued support of the project will create cash flow problems that will jeopardize the very existence of the total organization.

Furthermore, each individual indicates he or she has not told the others about his reservations. When asked why, the president says he cannot reveal his "true" feelings because abandoning the project, which has been widely publicized, would make the company look bad in the press. In addition, it would probably cause his vice president's ulcer to kick up or perhaps even cause her to quit, "Because she has staked her professional reputation on the project's success."

Similarly, the vice president for research says she cannot let the president or the research manager know her reservations because the president is so committed to it that "I would probably get fired for insubordination if I questioned the project."

Finally, the research manager says he cannot let the president or vice president know of his doubts about the project because of their extreme commitment to the project's success.

All indicate that, in meetings with one another, they try to maintain an optimistic façade so the others will not worry unduly about the project. The research director, in particular, admits to writing ambiguous progress reports so the president and the vice president can "interpret them to suit themselves." In fact, he says he tends to slant them to the "positive" side, "given how committed the brass are."

In a paneled conference room the project research budget is being considered for the following fiscal year. In the meeting itself, praises are heaped on the questionable project, and a unanimous decision is made to continue it for yet another year.

Avoiding "Groupthink"

The Ozyx group is having difficulty managing disagreement. Its members agree publicly with courses of action while privately having serious personal reservations. Simply put, its members conform to group decisions and action expectations to maintain harmony and avoid the discomforts of disagreement. They change or suppress what they really feel or believe in response to actual or perceived pressures from the group.

Social psychologist Irving Janis considers group cohesion a key force in such situations.[7] Because highly cohesive groups demand conformity from members, Janis believes that there is a tendency for members of highly cohesive groups to lose their willingness and abilities to evaluate one another's ideas and suggestions critically. As a result, desires to hold the group together and to avoid unpleasant disagreements lead to an overemphasis on concurrence and an underemphasis on realistically appraising alternative courses of action. Janis calls this phenomenon **groupthink,** a tendency for highly cohesive groups to lose their critical evaluative capabilities.

Groupthink is attributed by Janis to a variety of well-known historical fiascoes. They include the lack of preparedness of the U.S. Naval forces for the 1941 Japanese attack on Pearl Harbor, President Kennedy's handling of the Bay of Pigs, and the many roads that led to the United States' involvement in Vietnam. The study of these and other fiascoes has led Janis to identify a number of symptoms of groupthink. These are listed in Table 9.5.

The groupthink phenomenon has received wide attention. Until recently the notion was uncritically accepted even though there was very little systematic research on it. Now there is evidence that qualifies the concept a bit. One critique argues that members of groups that have passed through earlier stages of group development to arrive at total integration may be secure enough to challenge one another and still reach agreement. In other words, where group cohesiveness comes from strong group traditions, group members may be less likely to succumb to groupthink than are those in groups that are highly cohesive but less developed.[8] Janis himself has recently argued that the basis of a group's cohesiveness may make a difference. Where cohesiveness derives from a sense of the group's competent functioning, he suggests that groupthink is less likely to occur than where cohesiveness is based simply on the group's pleasant social atmosphere.[9] Further research is needed on this intriguing concept.

TABLE 9.5 Symptoms of Groupthink

Illusions of group invulnerability   Members of the group feel that it is basically beyond criticism or attack.

Rationalizing unpleasant and disconfirming data   Members refuse to accept contradictory data or to consider alternatives thoroughly.

Belief in inherent group morality   Members of the group feel that it is "right" and above any reproach by outsiders.

Stereotyping competitors as weak, evil, and stupid   Members refuse to look realistically at other groups.

Applying direct pressure to deviants to conform to group wishes   Members refuse to tolerate a member who suggests the group may be wrong.

Self-censorship by members   Members refuse to communicate personal concerns to the group as a whole.

Illusions of unanimity   Members accept consensus prematurely, without testing its completeness.

Mind guarding   Members of the group protect the group from hearing disturbing ideas or viewpoints from outsiders.

Source: Developed from Irving Janis, *Victims of Groupthink*, 2nd Ed. (Boston: Houghton Mifflin, 1982).

When and if you ever do experience groupthink as a manager, Janis suggests the following action guidelines for avoiding its negative consequences.

1. Assign the role of critical evaluator to each group member; encourage a sharing of objections.
2. Avoid, as a leader, seeming partial to one course of action.
3. Create subgroups operating under different leaders and working on the same problem.
4. Have group members discuss issues with subordinates and report back on their reactions.
5. Invite outside experts to observe group activities and react to group processes and decisions.
6. Assign one member to play a "devil's advocate" role at each meeting.
7. Write alternative scenarios for the intentions of competing groups.
8. Hold "second-chance" meetings after consensus is apparently achieved on key issues.

IMPROVING GROUP DECISIONS

Newsline 9.1 addresses the concept of a "skunkworks," a term first used in one of the opening examples in this chapter. At issue is the relationship between group decision making and innovation. Many larger companies are finding that small groups, when properly constituted and managed, can be major sources of creativity and new

NEWSLINE 9.2 / SKUNKWORKS AID INNOVATION

Contrary to what many think, a large number of new product or service innovations are developed not by large, highly organized, large budget R & D departments, but by "skunkworks." Skunkworks perform those highly innovative, fast moving activities at the corporation's edge. They function in large organizations, such as Hewlitt-Packard, 3M, and IBM as well as much smaller ones.

Skunkworks are small research groups often consisting of three to fifteen or twenty members. They are at the heart of many new product or service developments. As an example, Xerox executives speak glowingly of the East Rochester skunkworks (a ten to fifteen-person group housed since 1978 in a third floor loft of a deteriorating old building). Product after product has been developed, often after only a few weeks effort.

The secret of their success seems to be their small size, the feeling of product or service ownership and commitment of their members, and the sense of competition with other groups including large, formal R & D departments.

Most often skunkworks spring up without being officially authorized and always have a strong sponsor from within who champions the product or service being developed.

Reported in *A Passion for Excellence*.

Chapter 8 clearly suggested that groups can and do make decisions in different ways. In many respects, the goal of group decision making is to take advantage of the group as a decision resource while minimizing its potential disadvantages. Over the years social scientists have studied ways in which to avoid some of the liabilities of open group meetings as a basis for decision making and thereby take better advantage of groups as human resources of organizations. These strategies simultaneously attempt to achieve creativity in decision making by maximizing group process gains and minimizing group process losses. Three are described here: brainstorming, the nominal group technique, and the Delphi technique.[10]

Brainstorming

In **brainstorming,** group members meet to generate ideas. Four rules typically govern the process:

1. *All criticism is ruled out.* Judgment or evaluation of ideas must be withheld until the idea-generation process has been completed.

2. *"Freewheeling" is welcomed.* The wilder or more radical the idea, the better.
3. *Quantity is wanted.* The greater the number of ideas, the greater the likelihood of obtaining a superior idea.
4. *Combination and improvement are sought.* Participants should suggest how ideas of others can be turned into better ideas, or how two or more ideas can be joined into still another idea.

By prohibiting evaluation, brainstorming reduces fears of criticism or failure on the part of the individuals. Typical results include enthusiasm, involvement, and a freer flow of ideas. Researchers consider brainstorming techniques superior to open-group discussions as a basis for creative thinking and the generation of possible solutions to identified problems.

Nominal Group Technique

There will be times when group members have differing opinions and goals so that antagonistic argument can be predicted for a decision-making situation. In such cases, a nominal group technique could be more appropriate than either an open meeting or brainstorming. In a **nominal group,** the following rules apply:

1. Participants work alone and respond in writing with alternative solutions to a stated problem.
2. These ideas are then read aloud in round-robin fashion without any criticism or discussion.
3. The ideas are recorded on large sheets of newsprint as they are read aloud.
4. The ideas are then discussed individually in round-robin sequence for purposes of clarification only; evaluative comments are not allowed.
5. A written voting procedure is followed; it results in a rank ordering of the alternatives in terms of priority.
6. Steps 4 and 5 are repeated as desired to add further clarification to the process.

The final voting procedure allows alternatives to be explicitly evaluated under the nominal group technique, without risking the inhibitions, hostilities, and distorted outcomes that may accompany antagonistic or more open and unstructured meeting formats. Thus nominal grouping can improve group decision making under otherwise difficult circumstances.

Delphi Technique

A third approach, call the **Delphi technique,** was developed by the Rand Corporation to allow for the benefits of group decision making without members having to meet face to face. In fact, it allows group decision making to be accomplished over large distances and widely scattered members.

The Delphi procedure involves a series of questionnaires distributed over time to a decision-making panel. A typical approach works as follows: The first questionnaire states the problem and requests potential solutions. These solutions are summarized by the decision coordinator. The summary is returned to the panel in a second questionnaire. Panel members respond again and the process is repeated until a consensus is reached and a clear decision emerges.

One of the problems with the Delphi technique relates to the complexity and cost of administering the series of questionnaires. However, it does offer the advantage of group decision making in circumstances when it is physically impossible to convene a group meeting. Table 9.6 compares the Delphi technique, the nominal group technique and brainstorming with ordinary or unstructured group decision making. The table provides a quick way to consider the strengths and weaknesses of each procedure.

TEAM BUILDING

When we think of the word "teams," sporting teams come to mind. The Dallas Cowboys, the New York Yankees, and the U.S. Olympic team are good examples. We know, too, that sporting teams have their problems. Members slack off or become disgruntled, and some get retired or traded to other teams as a result. Even world champion teams have losing streaks, and the most highly talented players are prone to lose motivation at times, quibble among themselves, and go into slumps. When these things happen, the owners, managers, and players are apt to examine their problems and take corrective action to "rebuild the team" and restore what we have been calling group effectiveness.

Work groups are teams in a similar sense. Like sporting teams, even the most

TABLE 9.6 Comparison of Group Procedures				
Criteria	Ordinary	Brainstorming	Nominal	Delphi
Number of ideas	Low	Moderate	High	High
Quality of ideas	Low	Moderate	High	High
Social pressure	High	Low	Moderate	Low
Time/money costs	Moderate	Low	Low	High
Task orientation	Low	High	High	High
Potential for conflict	High	Low	Moderate	Low
Feelings of accomplishment	High to low	High	High	Moderate
Commitment to solution	High	NA*	Moderate	Low
Development of "we" feeling	High	High	Moderate	Low

Source: Adapted from Keith Murninghan, "Group Decision Making: What Strategy to Use?" *Management Review* (1981), pp. 61, 70.

*NA = not applicable.

mature work group is likely to experience problems over time. When difficulties do occur, or as a means of preventing them from occurring, team building activities can help. **Team building** is a sequence of planned action steps designed to gather and analyze data on the functioning of a group and implement changes to increase its operating effectiveness.[11]

There are many team building strategies, but they generally share the steps shown in Figure 9.2. The cycle begins with a sensitivity by one or more members that a group problem may exist or might develop in the future. Group members then work together to gather and analyze data so that the problem is finally diagnosed. Plans are made and corrective action implemented. Results are then evaluated and any difficulties or new problems become reasons to recycle the process. Team building is a data-based way of assessing a work group's functioning and taking corrective action to improve group effectiveness. It can be done with or without consulting assistance, and it can become a regular part of a group's continuing work routine.

The gathering and analysis of data on group functioning is a key element in the team-building cycle. This is the point, in fact, where a manager applies the knowledge of group and intergroup dynamics discussed in Chapter 8. To be successful in this stage, group outcomes in terms of task performance and member satisfaction must be carefully assessed. Then decisions can be made regarding the constructive modification of group inputs and throughputs, including any or all of the group processes previously discussed. You can see the major points of attention in this review–analysis–change cycle in Figure 9.3.

There are many ways to gather the data required to initiate team building. Structured and unstructured interviews, questionnaires, group meetings, and written records are all examples. Some data gathering approaches get highly creative and help to increase the involvement of the participants in the team building process. Consider one consultant's recommendations.[12]

FIGURE 9.2 A typical team-building cycle.

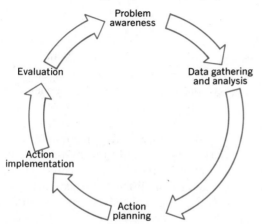

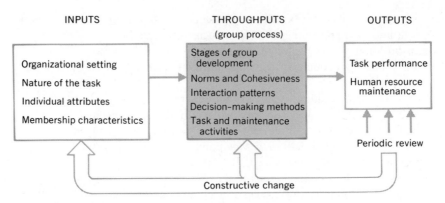

FIGURE 9.3 A group review–analysis–change cycle.

After preliminary remarks by the manager, the group members could be asked: "In order for us to get a picture of how you see our group functioning, would each of you take a few minutes to describe our group as a kind of animal or combination of animals, a kind of machine, a kind of person, or whatever image comes to mind?" Some groups in the past have been described as

a. A hunting dog—a pointer: "We run around and locate problems, then stop and point and hope that somebody else will take the action."
b. A Cadillac with pedals: "We look good on the outside, but there is no real power to get us moving."
c. A Rube Goldberg device: "Everything looks crazy and you can't imagine anything will ever happen, but, in some way, for some reason, we do get results at the end."

As people share these images and explain what elicits the image, the questions are asked: "What are the common elements in these images?" "Do we like these images of ourselves?" "What do we need to do to change our image?" The answering of these questions becomes the major agenda item of subsequent group meetings.

A frequent and convenient data gathering method is to use a standard questionnaire that has been tested and found useful in other situations. One such instrument is the team building checklist included in the end-of-chapter exercise. Regardless of the method used, the principle of team building requires that all members participate in the data gathering process, assist in the data analysis, and collectively take action to resolve and/or prevent group problems.

DESIGNING CREATIVE WORK GROUPS

We have shown some ways of improving group dynamics especially as related to dealing with problems in each of the stages of development. Now we want to focus on some very creative work-group designs that utilize many of the group process concepts discussed earlier.

These creative work groups change the nature of the job design from an individual one (as discussed in Chapter 5) to a group one. When the situation and job technology permit, these work-group designs can be powerful ways of promoting group effectiveness and enhancing organizational performance. Our discussion begins with "quality circles" and then focuses on other recent work group innovations developed in and outside of the United States.

Quality Circles

One of the most popular concepts to result from the great recent interest in Japanese management practices is the "quality circle."[13] A **quality circle** is a group of persons (usually no more than 10) who meet periodically (e.g., an hour or so once a week) to discuss and develop solutions for problems relating to quality, productivity, or cost.[14]

Quality circles (QC for short) have achieved rapid popularity in the United States and elsewhere in the world. Currently over 2500 American organizations have some level of QC activity, and there may be over 10 million Japanese participating in some form of QC. From a managerial perspective, a QC is a voluntary group whose members typically come from the same work unit. The members receive special training in information gathering and problem analysis techniques. The QC leaders are usually first-level supervisors and are responsible for training QC members and facilitating the operation of the circle. They emphasize democratic participation in identifying problems, analyzing problems, and choosing action alternatives. Proposed solutions are presented to management along with a cost–benefit analysis, and implementation is typically a joint effort between the QC and management. Newsline 9.2 conveys a good flavor for the quality circle in actual practice.

As you can see, QCs basically try to mobilize group dynamics and apply group resources to solve key problems in the workplace. They are designed to enhance an organization's creative and innovative problem-solving processes. Certainly, they receive much praise for these potential benefits. But it is wise to be cautious and not expect too much from QCs as panaceas for all of an organization's ills. Otherwise, as some of their critics charge, QCs may become just a fad viewed mainly as a panic response to Japanese success.

Indeed, a number of conditions must be met to ensure the workability of QCs and keep them from becoming merely a "gimmick." These include having an informed and knowledgeable work force, a willingness among managers to trust workers with necessary information, a true "team spirit" in the group, and a good management that ties QC goals to those of the organization.[15] The chief caveat is that QCs work

NEWSLINE 9.2 /
QUALITY CIRCLES:
ROUNDING UP
QUALITY AT USAA

"It's 9 o'clock, time for our meeting," announces one of the advertising specialists in the USAA Marketing Department. At that signal, several other employees leave their desks and head for the conference room. They start right to work on the problem they have been spending an hour a week on for the last two months. Then, regardless of how much or how little they accomplish, the meeting is adjourned exactly one hour later.

Hardly typical of a business meeting, this is a quality circle in operation. One of the first insurance companies in the country to implement quality circles as a management technique for improving quality and productivity, USAA now has 44 active circles with more planned.

Japanese companies have successfully used quality circles to promote worker involvement and improve efficiency for the past 20 years. But there are those who say that the concept is just another fad with American companies. However, USAA's success is proving that quality circles work for us and will become even more important in the future.

Bob Gaylor coordinates and directs USAA's quality circle program. "The logic behind Quality Circles is that the people who do the work know the most about it, and are the best qualified to improve it," says Gaylor. "USAA's program has been successful largely because of the support of management. With that support and the enthusiasm of our employees, there's no limit to what we can accomplish."

Reported in *AIDE Magazine*.

best where the organization as a whole reinforces participative group processes within the QCs themselves. Indeed, where such is not the case, there is evidence that quality circles can actually lead to such things as less job commitment and seeing the organization as more impersonal.[16]

Even where the organization carefully reinforces QCs, such teams can become disheartened when their projects fail in spite of their best efforts. Also, QC teams may have trouble accepting new members and there can be problems where management needs flexible work assignments. QCs need stability to function well as mature groups.[17]

Autonomous Work Groups

Now let us look at other forms of creative work group design. Take, for example, a case involving automobile assembly plants in the United States and Sweden.

Start by comparing and contrasting the accompanying photographs. The first is of an automobile assembly line somewhere in the United States; the second is

A General Motors automobile assembly line in Baltimore, Maryland (above). Inside the Kalmar plant in Sweden where teams of workers perform a variety of tasks while assembling the various components of Volvo automobiles (below).

taken in an automobile manufacturing plant in Sweden. Given a choice, which work setting would you prefer and why?

It has been said,[18]

> The auto assembly line epitomizes the conditions that contribute to employee dissatisfaction: fractionation of work into meaningless activities, with each activity repeated several hundred times each workday, and with the employees having little or no control over work pace or any other aspects of working conditions.

Indeed, the principle of the traditional automobile assembly-line process (as shown in the first photo) has changed little since introduced by Henry Ford in 1913.

But what are the alternatives? What can we do to protect workers from the alienation and frustration that often accompanies work in such settings? Answers to these questions include job designs ranging from (1) increasing the degree of production automation, that is, decreasing the use of human labor, to (2) adopting autonomous work groups as a means of expanding individual participaton in the work process.

Increasing Automation

The potential benefits of the automobile assembly-line job specialization, such as economies of scale and high production volume, must be weighed against potential social costs, which may include high wage levels and individual disenchantment with work. It was largely the goal of realizing these benefits while minimizing social costs that led General Motors in 1966 to construct the most automated automobile assembly plant in the world. It is located at Lordstown, Ohio.

Young and experienced workers were hired to work a production line that also included 26 specially designed robots. This line was capable of producing an incredible 100 cars per hour. Problems soon arose, however, and the Lordstown plant became embroiled in controversy. Poor quality of final products, including some actual sabotage, and labor-management disputes were representative of problems encountered by GM at Lordstown.

The advanced microprocessor technologies of the 1980s have renewed the interests of the automobile industry in increased automation. Most manufacturers, GM included, are now using robotics to their advantage and plan for even more applications. Complete automation remains an elusive idea, however, and for the future most manufacturing will surely remain a process that combines the benefits of increased automation with creative means of facilitating necessary human effort as well.

Creating Self-Managed Teams

An alternative or supplement to increasing the automation of assembly lines is found in the concept of **autonomous work groups.** These are self-managed teams responsible for accomplishing defined production goals, and having discretion in deciding how tasks will be distributed among individuals and at what pace work will progress to meet these goals. Members of autonomous work groups may go so far as to establish pay grades and train and certify members in required job skills.

The physical arrangement of workers and partially finished autos in the second photograph indicates the presence of autonomous work groups. The photo, taken at Volvo's Kalmar production facility in Sweden, was specially built to accommodate autonomous work group principles. The result of the Kalmar experience is described by one observer as follows:[17]

> The basic idea of Kalmar is flexibility—how people can choose the way in which they assemble a car. The facility has fewer supervisors than does a normal auto plant.
>
> Whereas assembly-line workers would be rooted in position doing a single specialized chore all day, Kalmar's workers are grouped in about 25 teams of 15 to 25 persons each. Each team handles a general area, such as door assembly, electric wiring, or fitting upholstery.
>
> Members of teams can exchange jobs or change teams when they wish. They can also vary the pace of the work, keeping up with the general flow of production but speeding up or pausing as they wish—because the car-carrying trolleys can be delayed for a while both before entering and after leaving each team's work areas.
>
> While conventional assembly-line workers must perform operations on the undercarriage by the tiring method of working from beneath, the Kalmar worker presses a button and the trolley rolls an auto 90 degrees on its side so the work can be done from a comfortable position.
>
> The resulting building differs markedly from conventional plants. While they tend to look like large rectangles, Kalmar consists of four six-sided structures—three of them two stories tall and the other single-story—that fit together, forming the general shape of a cross.
>
> The windows are big, and the workshop is compartmented so the workers, located along the outer walls, have natural light and the sensation of being in a comfortably small workshop.

The Kalmar plant is an expensive facility. To replicate it throughout the United States, literally all existing assembly-line facilities would have to be abandoned and new ones constructed. The benefits and costs of such a changeover are issues of continuing debate. A major limitation of Kalmar, for example, is that it can produce only 30,000 cars per year versus 200,000 for a typical U.S. plant and 400,000 for Lordstown! To build a Kalmar-style plant, to produce 60 cars per hour (a standard U.S. goal), a 10-mile-long facility could be required.

The disadvantages of the Kalmar approach thus include reduced production rates, increased space requirements, and the need for radically new physical plants. On the other hand, allowing the assembly process to take place under autonomous work group designs is observed to offer a number of advantages, including[19]

- Increased ease of adjusting to individual absenteeism.
- Improved quality of production.
- Lower turnover.
- Improved employee work attitudes.
- Decreased investment in supervisory personnel.

Emerging Workplace Innovations

Perhaps the ultimate question is how adaptable the Kalmar alternative is to other locations. In fact, workplace innovations (typically called quality of working life projects) in plants such as Kalmar have been receiving serious attention from U.S. automakers. Among the most active of these has been General Motors, the very same company that built the highly automated Lordstown plant described earlier.[20]

General Motors is a huge corporation. Over the past decade alone, more than 80 new operations have come into being throughout GM's worldwide organization. In addition, substantial changes have been made in old plants. All this has given GM the opportunity to use the new and changed operations as ''laboratories'' for trying out different kinds of work innovations.

A dramatic example of an old, traditional operation that underwent substantial change is GM's Tarrytown, New York, automobile assembly plant. In the late 1960s and early 1970s, the plant suffered from high labor turnover and absenteeism, and operating costs were high. The relationship between management and labor was poor (sometimes there were as many as 2000 unsettled labor grievances). The youth counterculture revolution was taking place in the late 1960s, and the workers were demanding change. A new plant manager came in and decided to work with the union to start such change. The change ultimately led to employee and management–union involvement in work teams, similar to the quality circles that we have discussed. The process of change was a long and involved one that spanned a decade. By the end of 1981, the Tarrytown plant had continued its strong performance developed during that decade. Although employee absences remained high, grievances continued at a lower level than in the past.

Some other older GM plants have followed a ''second-generation'' version of the Tarrytown model. Extensive training is given from the top to the bottom of the organization before the work teams are established. In these older plants, unlike the Kalmar plant, the traditional automobile assembly-line technology remains pretty much in place. A number of GM's newer plants such as the Delco-Remy Battery Plant in Fitzgerald, Georgia, utilize self-managing autonomous work teams. The teams select their own leaders and as a group are responsible for their own budgets, scheduling, maintenance, production, quality, discipline, EEO objectives, and other managerial aspects. All the elements in the organization fit together; that is, they are designed to create a supportive and participative climate.

Illustrative Case: General Motors Saturn Organization

General Motors is currently setting up its Saturn Organization to be on line in 1989. Saturn is an attempt to use state-of-the-art technology and autonomous work groups to develop the most modern plant in the world. It goes beyond anything GM has done up to now.[21]

Although the original Saturn proposal is being modified during the construction phases, the basic design still gives considerable attention to the autonomous work groups. They are expected to elect a counselor from among their own people and control job assignments, maintain their own equipment inventory and schedule vacations. The groups will also control their own variable costs and quality and be expected to innovate continuously. When they propose such innovations, finance and purchasing will have to arrive at a consensus with the teams. There will also be a joint labor–management work council.

The Saturn complex will be run by a manufacturing advisory committee consisting of elected United Auto Workers and company representatives plus the manager of the Saturn Complex, who is a top UAW official. That committee must reach consensus decisions on changes in salaries and benefits. It answers to the top-level strategic advisory committee. Figure 9.4 shows the proposed Saturn structure in more detail.

The UAW and company are considered to be equal partners in the Saturn operation and at least 80 percent of the workforce will have life-time job security. Seniority rules will be eliminated and pay will be based on salary, plus a performance bonus. The union will also have a say on managers' salaries.

In return for this additional management voice, the union will give GM a 20 percent reduction in guaranteed wages plus less restrictive work rules.

This is a bold plan indeed, especially for a monolithic corporation such as GM. It will be very interesting to see how successful it turns out to be.

In summary, General Motors is utilizing autonomous work groups and other creative work group designs in situations where they seem to fit. Of course, because of its size and the autonomy allowed to divisions and plants, GM still continues to have plants operated in very traditional ways as well.

Illustrative Case: General Foods in Topeka

Many other experiments are presently under way to explore possibilities for autonomous work grouping to improve productivity and employee satisfaction in a variety of other settings. As noted earlier, these are typically called quality of work life projects. One that has been evaluated most thoroughly is described in the paragraphs that follow.[22]

General Foods in 1971

General Foods Corporation was planning to construct a new dry dog food plant in Topeka, Kansas. The company's existing plant was experiencing problems. Employees were indifferent and inattentive to their work, waste was high, shutdowns frequently occurred, and there were acts of worker violence and sabotage. General Foods wanted to avoid such problems in the new plant. Richard Walton, a noted social scientist, was asked to serve as a special consultant and evaluator.

Autonomous work groups were created in the new plant. Six teams of 7 to 14 workers were formed. Each included "operators" and a "team leader." The teams

Traditional GM Plant	The Saturn Plant
Plant manager	Strategic advisory committee Does long-term planning. Consists of Saturn president and his staff, plus top UAW adviser.
Production manager	Manufacturing advisory committee Oversees Saturn complex. Includes company and elected union representatives, plus specialists in engineering, marketing, and so on.
General superintendent	Business unit Coordinates plant-level operations. Made up of company representatives and elected union adviser, plus specialists.
Production superintendent (5 per shift)	Work unit module Groups of three to six work units led by a company "work unit adviser"
General supervisor (15 per shift)	Work units Teams of 6 to 15 workers led by an elected UAW "counselor"
Supervisor/foreman (90 per shift)	

FIGURE 9.4 Proposed organization structure for GM's Saturn plant. (From Noel M. Tichy and Mary Anne Devanna, *The Transformational Leader* (New York: John Wiley & Sons, 1986) p. 231. Used by permission.

were individually responsible for a large part of the production process. Within teams, individuals were assigned work tasks by group consensus. These tasks were rotated and shared. The team was responsible for handling problems with other teams, covering of absentees, training members in equipment maintenance, product quality control, and maintenance of the work area.

In addition, pay levels and raises for team members were based on the principle of job mastery; the guiding concept was "pay for learning." Individuals first mastered all jobs within their team and then within the plant. As they did so, their pay levels increased accordingly.

Some difficulties were in evidence as workers adjusted to the ways of this plant. The compensation scheme caused problems. Decisions regarding job mastery were sometimes controversial, and tensions appeared as team members began to qualify for different pay levels. Not all workers liked the increased responsibility of team membership and the atmosphere of mutual help. Some team leaders found their roles difficult.

Still, Walton viewed the experiment positively as of 1971. Product quality and plant safety were high, employee attitudes were generally positive, and absenteeism was low. Prospects looked good for autonomous work groups in this facility. What would you predict?

Topeka—Six and Ten Years Later

Walton revisited the Topeka plant and reassessed the situation in 1977 and again in 1981. There were still advantages in terms of employee attitudes, safety, absenteeism, and turnover. However, Walton also noted some problems. In the 1977 evaluation, for example, he found group dynamics a key force in the plant. Some teams developed as working entities more quickly and positively than others. Different levels of group "skills" among the teams accounted for at least part of this variance. In addition, a growing minority of workers appeared dissatisfied with the position of "team leader," the use of peer evaluations, ways of making pay decisions, levels of interteam cooperation, and plantwide coordination.

Figure 9.5 describes the pattern that Walton observed in the development of member commitment in the Topeka plant from 1970 to 1981. Many of the initial or "start-

FIGURE 9.5 Pattern of development of member commitment in Topeka plant organization. (From Richard E. Walton, "The Topeka Work System: Optimistic Visions, Pessimistic Hypotheses, and Reality," in Robert Zager and Michael P. Rosow, eds., *The Innovative Organization,* Pergamon Press, Elmsford, N.Y., 1982. Reprinted by permission.)

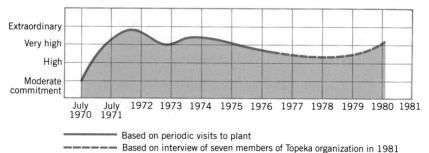

Based on periodic visits to plant
- - - - - - Based on interview of seven members of Topeka organization in 1981

Note: "Moderate commitment" is intended to describe the kind of commitment found in a conventional plant that is generally well managed and is progressive in its personnel problems and practices. A "moderate" level of commitment is below what is judged to be adequate to sustain over the long term the type of work structure employed by the Topeka plant. "Extraordinary commitment" represents the uppermost standard in my observation of innovative plants during the 1970s. "Very high" and "high" are convenient labels for intermediate points on the scale.

up'' problems were on their way to being worked out within the first year and a half, and commitment developed to an exceedingly high level by 1971. Then a significant decline and recovery took place around the third anniversary of the plant. This was followed by gradual decline until about 1978, when an upward trend set in.

Walton suggests that commitment was exceptionally high in the early stages because of four factors: design of the autonomous groups, the way in which the plan was implemented, highly favorable output results, and a positive public image (lots of good media coverage, including one 60-minute, prime-time television program). The temporary decline in commitment around the third anniversary is attributed to (1) inadequate orientation of new members, (2) inadequate interteam movements and resulting lower pay increases, and (3) temporary diversion of management attention to other matters. Once these conditions were corrected, the initial drop in commitment was halted. Moderate, long-term decline was attributed to the evolution of plant operations from uncertainty to relative certainty. In other words, the whole project gradually became less challenging to those involved. The upswing in commitment in 1978 is attributed to new products and plant expansion, as well as to well-planned organizational renewal activities of the type we will discuss in Chapter 16 under the topics of planned change and organization development.

Creative Work Group Designs in Managerial Perspective

Obviously, the success of creative work group designs depends on the ability of managers and other personnel to facilitate group effectiveness under innovative conditions. Although the proponents of workplace innovations are very enthusiastic, it is important for the manager to maintain a realistic and informed posture on them. Changing from traditional ways of work to autonomous groups, for example, will not be easy. At a minimum, it will require elaborate training of existing staff and extensive preparation of the surrounding organization to support the new ways of work. Any new staff should, of course, be selected, hired, and trained with the requirements of the new design clearly in mind. Finally, all such innovations will require lots of attention, care, and help if they are to achieve their full potential.

Think about the experiments and ideas offered in this final section of our examination of groups in organizations. Think seriously and think creatively. Perhaps these experiments to improve productivity and the quality of work life represent, among many others, the types of things that you may attempt someday in your efforts to mobilize the full potential of groups as human resources of organizations.

SUMMARY

This chapter has focused on the way in which managers may apply, in actual practice, insights from the group dynamics concepts developed in the previous two chapters. It first emphasized the key managerial problems likely to be encountered at each stage of group development. These are: (1) facilitating individual entry for the forming stage; (2) developing norms for the storming stage; (3) influencing cohesiveness for the initial integration stage; and (4) team building for the integration stage.

In terms of individual entry, the manager is concerned about resolving dilemmas that beset members unfamiliar with the group and its pattern of operations. The clarification of what members expect of one another can be done informally or by written role negotiations that managers and subordinates revise at regular intervals, as necessary.

Concerning norms and cohesiveness, a key issue is how the manager may influence them to increase the performance and human resource maintenance of a work group. The specific steps that need to be taken to affect norms and cohesiveness vary according to the group's stage of development. Cohesiveness, as noted in Chapter 8, can be a double-edged sword for the manager, depending upon the extent to which group norms encourage performance. Depending on the stage of a group's development, it can also lead to groupthink, a loss of critical evaluative capability on the part of group members.

Regardless of its stage of development, a group should be sensitive to how its decisions are arrived at and be able to improve its approach to decision making where necessary. Among the specific alternatives to making decisions in an unstructured group meeting are the brainstorming, nominal group, and Delphi techniques. Familiarity with these options is a useful component in a manager's repertoire of group skills.

Managers can also engage in team building, a sequence of planned action steps designed to gather and analyze data on group functioning and implement changes to increase its operating effectiveness. Team building is especially useful at periodic intervals to help a work group assess its progress and decide on appropriate plans for improving its future effectiveness.

In addition to the ideas just summarized, a most intriguing group management issue concerns designing creative work teams. It is sometimes possible to move job enrichment techniques (studied in Chapter 6) beyond individual jobs and apply them to work groups as a whole. Quality circles and several other applications have been discussed for their strong and weak points. Other creative approaches to group-level job design are certainly possible.

THINKING THROUGH THE ISSUES

1. Give examples from personal experience that illustrate each of the management problems summarized in Table 9.1.
2. Illustrate from personal experience each of the issues in Table 9.2.
3. Discuss groupthink and provide an example from personal experience.
4. What can a manager do to influence cohesiveness both positively and negatively? Why would a manager ever want to decrease group cohesion?
5. Use personal experience to show problems most suitable for each of the group decision-making strategies discussed in this chapter.

6. Explain the major elements in the team building process. Identify how this process relates to the open-systems model of groups that we used throughout Chapters 7, 8, and 9.

7. Think of an automobile assembly line. Compare and contrast the way in which the line might be set up to provide for individual job enrichment and group job enrichment.

8. Compare and contrast the Saturn plant with a traditional assembly line and a plant using quality circles.

CASE: A PLANT WHERE TEAMWORK IS MORE THAN JUST TALK

Life inside a Cadillac engine plant in Livonia, Mich., is worlds apart from the atmosphere of a typical auto factory.[23] Hourly workers and supervisors dress much the same and cooperate closely on "business teams" that organize the work and make other decisions normally left to management. "It makes you feel like a part of what's going on," says Gary L. Andrews, an hourly worker and assistant team coordinator (ATC). A 14-year Cadillac veteran, Andrews says he would return to a traditional auto plant "only if it was a choice between that and hitting the streets."

Livonia is one of nine General Motors Corp. plants that use the "pay-for-knowledge" team concept to make factory work less boring and more productive. This approach differs radically from the practice in most union shops, where workers perform narrow functions. At Livonia, production workers can learn all of the jobs in one section, giving management flexibility in assigning work and filling in for absent workers. Workers are paid according to the skills they acquire, giving them an incentive to learn new ones.

The system was introduced recently, when GM's Cadillac Motor Car Division closed its engine works in Detroit and moved to the western suburb of Livonia. About 95 percent of the Detroit workers transferred with Cadillac. Local 22 of the United Auto Workers was involved in planning the change from the start and even had a voice in choosing salaried employees who would function as the team coordinators. (ATCs such as Andrews, 32, are elected from the ranks.)

Livonia uses less labor per engine than the Detroit plant while producing higher-quality products. It hit the breakeven point after one year, instead of the anticipated two years. The scrap rate has fallen by 50 percent. In a recent year worker suggestions saved Cadillac more than $1.2 million.

The plant, which cranks out 1200 engines a day, is divided into 15 departments that are in turn subdivided into business teams of 10 to 20 workers each, consisting of production workers who assemble the engines and perform nonskilled maintenance duties. The engines are still produced on an assembly line, but the employees have varied routines and participate in decision making. Moreover, dress codes are passé: almost no one wears a tie, and some supervisors wear jeans. Managers and workers share the same cafeteria and compete for parking spots.

The teams meet weekly on company time to discuss issues such as safety and housekeeping. They decide when to award raises and rotate jobs, and they may even suggest redesigning the work flow. Recently, Andrews took it on himself to analyze every job on two teams that attach components to already-assembled engines. "I sat with pencil and paper and figured out how to make it easier," he recalls. His teammates accepted his idea of spreading the work more evenly along the lines. Within 15 minutes, Andrews says, the changes were made without any downtime or loss of production. His reward: election as ATC.

The 23 members of Andrews' team rotate among 12 or 13 jobs on the line, 6 engine-repair jobs, and 4 to 5 housekeeping and inspection jobs. As ATC, Andrews does a little of everything and helps the team coordinator plan work schedules.

In the old Detroit plant, there were 45 job classifications, each with its own wage rate. In Livonia, there are four wage levels for experienced workers, ranging from $9.63 an hour to a maximum of $10.08 for a "job setter"—a worker who sets up and changes tooling on the line. A worker reaches the top rate after learning all the skills on two business teams.

"In a traditional plant, you might have 90 to 100 job setters," says Peter J. Ulbrich, until recently Livonia's personnel administrator. "Here, you have the opportunity for 1200 to 1300 people to get there." This system can produce an expensive work force. "It is a neat way to get short-term productivity results," says one teamwork expert, "but you wonder what they will do when everybody reaches the top rate."

Questions

1. In what ways do the "business teams" take good advantage of basic group dynamics and mobilize the group as a human resource of the organization?
2. What potential problems with the "business teams" may occur as a result of the same or other group dynamics? To what extent could team building be used to maintain maximum advantage in the "business team" concept.
3. Do you share the concern expressed in the last sentence of the case? Why or why not?

EXERCISE: TEAM BUILDING FOR GROUP EFFECTIVENESS

Purpose:

This exercise will give you experience in the team-building process. It will help you to learn how to gather data systematically on group functioning, and use it for purposes of group development and constructive change.

Time:

50 to 75 minutes.

Procedure:

1. Complete the team building checklist in Figure 9.6 for (a) your assigned student work group or (b) your OB class as a whole. The instructor will give you directions on which to select.

Problem identification: to what extent is there evidence of the following problems in your work unit?

	Low Evidence		Some Evidence		High Evidence
1. Loss of production or work-unit output.	1	2	3	4	5
2. Grievances or complaints within the work unit.	1	2	3	4	5
3. Conflicts or hostility between unit members.	1	2	3	4	5
4. Confusion about assignments or unclear relationships between people.	1	2	3	4	5
5. Lack of clear goals, or low commitment to goals.	1	2	3	4	5
6. Apathy or general lack of interest or involvement of unit members.	1	2	3	4	5
7. Lack of innovation, risk taking, imagination, or taking initiative.	1	2	3	4	5
8. Ineffective staff meetings.	1	2	3	4	5
9. Problems in working with the boss.	1	2	3	4	5
10. Poor communications: people afraid to speak up, not listening to each other, or not talking together.	1	2	3	4	5
11. Lack of trust between boss and member or between members.	1	2	3	4	5
12. Decisions made that people do not understand or agree with.	1	2	3	4	5
13. People feel that good work is not recognized or rewarded.	1	2	3	4	5
14. People are not encouraged to work together in better team effort.	1	2	3	4	5

Scoring: Add up the score for the 14 items. If your score is between 14–28, there is little evidence your unit needs team building. If your score is between 29–42, there is some evidence, but no immediate pressure, unless two or three items are very high. If your score is between 43–56, you should seriously think about planning the team-building program. If your score is over 56, team-building should be a top priority item for your work unit.

FIGURE 9.6 Team-building checklist. (From William G. Dyer, *Team Building: Issues and Alternatives,* Addison-Wesley, Reading, Mass., 1977, pp. 36, 37. Reprinted with permission.)

2. Convene in your assigned group of four to eight persons to share responses to the team-building checklist. One member should record and summarize all responses to each item on the checklist. After all is recorded, the results should be discussed for their implications.

3. The group should then choose three items on which to focus attention. For each item, a conclusion should be reached as to (a) what the data says about the group and (b) what group members feel should be done to improve group effectiveness in the future.

4. The instructor will call on each group for a report on the results achieved in Step 3. These will be discussed and conclusions reached as to what should be done to improve group effectiveness in the future. The overall implications of the exercise for the team building process in general will also be identified.

THE MANAGER'S VOCABULARY

Autonomous Work Groups   Self-managed teams, responsible for accomplishing defined production goals, that have discretion in deciding how tasks will be distributed among individuals and at what pace work will progress to meet these goals.

Groupthink   A tendency for highly cohesive groups to lose their critical evaluative capabilities.

Quality Circle   A group of persons who meet periodically to discuss ways of improving the quality of their products or services.

Team Building   A sequence of planned action steps designed to gather and analyze data on the functioning of a group and implement changes to increase its operating effectiveness.

IMPORTANT NAMES

Irving Janis   Identified the phenomenon of "groupthink."

Edgar Schein   A noted social psychologist who has established a series of profiles characterizing people entering groups.

Richard Walton   A management consultant and scholar who helps organizations implement and evaluate creative work group designs.

NOTES

[1]Adapted from Coleen Cordes, *I/O Psychology Monitor,* (September, 1982), Copyright © 1982 by the American Psychological Association, p. 3. All rights reserved. Used with permission.

[2]These examples are found in Harry Bacas, "Who's in Charge Here?," *Nation's Business,* May 1985, pp.

57–59; and, Bill Saporto, "The Revolt Against Working Smarter," *Fortune,* July 21, 1986, pp. 58–65.

[3]This discussion is developed from Edgar H. Schein, *Process Consultation: Its Role in Organization Development* (Reading, Mass.: Addison-Wesley, 1969), pp. 32–37.

[4]This example is from Roger Harrison, "When Power Conflicts Trigger Team Spirit," *European Business* (Spring 1972), pp. 57–65.

[5]Robert F. Allen and Saul Pilnick, "Confronting the Shadow Organization: How to Select and Defeat Negative Norms," *Organizational Dynamics* (Spring 1973), pp. 13–17. See also Alvin Zander, *Making Groups Effective* (San Francisco: Jossey-Bass, 1982), Chap. 4; and Daniel C. Feldman, "The Development and Enforcement of Group Norms," *Academy of Management Review,* Vol. 9 (1984), pp. 47–53.

[6]Jerry Harvey, "Managing Agreement in Organizations: The Abilene Paradox," *Organizational Dynamics* (Summer, 1974) pp. 63–80.

[7]Irving L. Janis, "Groupthink," *Psychology Today* (November 1971), pp. 43–46; Irving L. Janis, *Groupthink,* 2nd ed. (Boston: Houghton Mifflin, 1982).

[8]J. Longley and D. G. Pruitt, "Groupthink: A Critique of Janis' Theory," in L. Wheeler ed., *Review of Personality and Social Psychology* (Beverly Hills, Calif.: Sage, 1980); see also Carrie R. Leana, "A Partial Test of Janis's Groupthink Model: The Effects of Group Cohesiveness and Leader Behavior on Decision Processes," *Journal of Management,* Vol. 11, no. 1 (1985), pp. 5–18.

[9]Janis, *Groupthink.*

[10]These techniques are well described in George P. Huber, *Managerial Decision Making* (Glenview, Ill.: Scott, Foresman, 1980); and André L. Delbec, Andrew L. Van de Ven, and David H. Gustafson, *Group Techniques for Program Planning: A Guide to Nominal Groups and Delphi Techniques* (Glenview, Ill.: Scott, Foresman, 1975).

[11]For a good discussion of team building, see William D. Dyer, *Team Building* (Reading, Mass.: Addison-Wesley, 1977).

[12]From William D. Dyer, *Team Building,* Copyright © 1977, Addison-Wesley Publishing Company, Inc., Reading, Mass., Chapter 6, pp. 55, 56. Reprinted with permission.

[13]For a good summary of quality circles, see John D. Blair and Carlton J. Whitehead, "Will Quality Circles Survive in the United States? An Analytical Perspective," *Business Horizons,* Vol. 27, no. 5 (1984), pp. 17–23.

[14]J. Bernard Keys and Thomas R. Miller, "The Japanese Management Theory Jungle," *Academy of Management Review,* Vol. 9 (1984), p. 343.

[15]Kenichi Ohmae, "Quality Control Circles: They Work and Don't Work," *The Wall Street Journal,* March 29, 1982, p. 16.

[16]Robert P. Steel, Anthony J. Mento, Benjamin L. Dilla, Nestor K. Ovalle, and Russell F. Lloyd, "Factors Influencing the Success and Failure of Two Quality Circles Programs," *Journal of Management,* Vol. 11, no. 1 (1985), pp. 99–119.

[17]J. Morvat, "The Problem Solvers: Quality Circles," In M. Robson (ed.), *Quality Circles in Action* (Aldershot, U.K.: Gorver Publishing, 1984). For additional considerations concerning quality circles, see Edward E. Lawler III and Susan A. Mohrman, "Quality Circles: After the Honeymoon," *Organizational Dynamics,* Vol. 15, no. 4 (1987), pp. 42–54.

[18]William F. Dowling, "Job Redesign on the Assembly Line: Farewell to Blue-Collar Blues," *Organizational Dynamics* (Autumn 1973), pp. 51–67.

[19]Ibid., Dowling, "Job Redesign on the Assembly Line," pp. 51–67.

[20]This discussion is developed from Robert H. Guest, "Tarrytown: Quality of Worklife at a General Motors Plant, and D. L. Landon and Howard C. Carlson, "Strategies for Diffusing, Evolving, and Institutionalizing Quality of Work Life at General Motors," in Robert Zager and Michael P. Rosow, eds., *The Innovative Organization* (Elmsford, N.Y.: Pergamon Press, 1982) Chaps. 5 and 12.

[21]This summary is based on a description in Noel M. Tichy and Mary Anne Devanna, *The Transformational Leader* (New York: John Wiley, 1986) pp. 230–232.

[22]See Richard E. Walton, "How to Counter Alienation in the Plant," *Harvard Business Review* (November–December 1972), pp. 70–81; Richard E. Walton, "Work Innovations at Topeka: After Six Years," *Journal of Applied Behavior Science,* Vol. 13 (1977), pp. 422–431; and Richard E. Walton, "The Topeka Work System: Optimistic Visions, Pessimistic Hypotheses, and Reality," in Zager and Rosow, eds., *The Innovative Organization,* Chap. 11.

[23]"A Plant Where Teamwork Is More than Just Talk," *Business Week,* May 16, 1983, p. 108. Reprinted from May 16, 1983, issue of *Business Week* by special permission. Copyright © 1983 by McGraw-Hill, Inc., New York, New York 10020. All rights reserved.

PART FOUR
MANAGING ORGANIZATIONS

The organization is every manager's work setting, and the goals of an organization provide an action context for its members. A smaller component of the organization, the work unit, is that part over which the manager is given formal authority. Both the larger organization and the work unit should be designed to take maximum advantage of the available human and physical resources. When the design of either the organization, the work unit, or both is inappropriate to meet situational demands, performance and human resource maintenance may suffer.

Thus, you as a manager must press beyond a knowledge of individuals and groups to learn about the organization as a social phenomenon. In this part of the book we will study organizations. Before getting down to business, however, let us put this interest in the organization into a true managerial perspective. Take a look at Jaccob Jaccober and Sam Ford and the dilemmas they recently faced.

THE MIDDLE STATES MANUFACTURING CASE

Jaccob Jaccober is the president of Middle States Manufacturing. The firm, while not particularly efficient, has been highly profitable, its emphasis being on innovation and maintaining the technical quality of its products at or above competitive levels. At the moment, Jaccob didn't feel much like a corporate tycoon as he sat slumped into the soft leather sidechair in his office overlooking the city. "How long will it be," he wondered, "before Susan Rice, my vice-president of finance, will call about the West Coast financing package?" The lights of the city glowed uniformly in the same neat grid of rows and columns some city planner had specified over a hundred years ago. "Oh, if only I could design such a logical, permanent structure for my rapidly growing organization," thought Jaccob.

His thoughts turned to a quick review of the hectic day of meetings. Opportunities were turning into problems. Each new piece of business seemed only to cloud further the distribution of roles and responsibilities among Middle States' managers. Orders were not getting processed promptly. Two important accounts were recently sent incomplete shipments, and both shipments were late at that! Of course, there were many new people in new jobs, and most were working long hours to overcome their inexperience. But nobody seemed able to agree with anybody on anything!

Joan Wood, vice president of production, for example, had convincingly argued that longer production runs were needed to reduce machine setup time, increase

quality control, cut wear and tear on expensive machinery, and simplify the order delivery process. To provide these longer runs, a reduction in specialized orders was the key. Pat Vincent, vice president of marketing, however, strongly resisted this recommendation. Marketing, he explained, had carefully nurtured a company image of quick delivery of quality products engineered to the unique needs of major customers. Joan's recommendations would force marketing to sell a standardized product line. Pat foresaw immediate lost sales and a longer term decline in market acceptance if this were done.

Then there was Howard Teebs, assistant to the vice president of finance. He was concerned over the financing of inventories. Howard had argued for a stricter budgeting process that stressed weekly targets for purchasing, in-process goods, and finished goods inventory. Variations over 10 percent of the plan would be subject to direct control by the assistant to the vice-president of production.

As the meeting of the executive committee droned on, it was apparent to Jaccob that the Middle States management team had numerous ideas for improving performance. Everyone seemed willing to recommend changes, particularly if the changes affected someone else's department.

As Jaccob stared out into the city lights, he argued to himself that the problems of growth had to be manageable. He reviewed things again. Business from three key customers—Chicago Distributing, Ohio Wholesalers, and Blake, Inc.—accounted for 50 percent of total sales and 75 percent of gross profits. Substantial new growth from these three appeared questionable. The potential lay with Profab. Profab was already used by the big three. It used slightly different production methods than current products and required a lot of handcrafting from a few highly skilled people. Longer production runs with a more flexible design could cut costs by 30 percent. This would increase the profitability of the existing market. Then, by starting a second shift and by using commission salespersons selling specialized lines related to Profab, new opportunities in the East and West Coast markets could be captured.

Yes, Profab was the future of the company. Yet the management staff was already overworked. Jaccob was already "passing off" direct daily relations with the "big three" to Pat. And the engineering requirements of the new direction might yield even more production problems in serving the big three. "How could Middle States capitalize on this opportunity without losing its major customers?"

Before Jaccob could try to answer his own question, the phone rang. It was an excited Susan Rice. She announced that within six months Middle States would have $2 million to market Profab and its derivatives nationally. Susan chided Jaccob that Middle States would no longer be an appropriate name. She suggested Profab National. Jaccob countered with Profab International.

Once again the grid of city lights, with neat rows and columns expanding to the horizon, caught Jaccob's eye as he congratulated Susan. It was time for a change—a change that would create the proper organization and establish the management team for Profab International.

OUR VIEWPOINT

Well, Jaccob seems to have his goals clearly in mind. He's going to reconfigure his company, that is, establish a new organizational design to meet new challenges successfully. Assuming that Jaccob has studied OB, or at least has access to an informed consultant, he should be able to develop a design that can facilitate profitable growth and still maintain the firm's technical leadership capability.

Deep down inside organizations, however, it is still people who work to perform the required tasks. We should wonder at this point what Jaccob's ideas mean to lower-level managers who are already trying hard to fulfill their current obligations and generally do a good job!

CONTINUING ON   While the future for Middle States seemed promising to Jaccob, Sam Ford's prospects didn't appear too bright at the moment. Sam was a junior executive in charge of finished goods and delivery. He reported to Joan Wood and he was on the hot seat.

For the second time in four weeks, two orders were shipped incomplete. Neither Ron Cloud, in charge of production line A, nor Sandy Rivers, in charge of production line B, had checked with each other. Chicago Distributing got only "A" items and Blake, Inc., got only the "B" items. Sam knew that the problem had been mentioned in a recent executive committee meeting, and he experienced firsthand that Joan had been livid when the error was discovered. Just switching incomplete shipments would not have been so bad, had they not also been four days late!

Now Sam sat pondering a phone message from Joan's secretary. It called for a meeting on scheduling and delivery problems, but it sure looked like it had "pink slip" potential.

Sam had to get his work unit organized to process adequately the delivery requests that called for both A and B items. These orders always came from one of the big three. But he didn't know how to proceed. He was new and both Ron and Sandy had been with the company since Jaccob Jaccober had founded it. Today was Tuesday; the meeting sealing his fate was the following Thursday. "Three months on the job and already a failure?" he thought. "How to proceed? What can be done?" Barking orders and asking for cooperation had failed. "What can be done?"

OUR VIEWPOINT

Jaccob and Sam appear to have quite different problems. But do they really? Both share the problem of experiencing the pitfalls of inappropriate organizational designs, and each must respond as a manager to the challenge of finding a better way.

Sam has yet to learn some fundamental principles of organizational structure. There are various approaches to solving problems such as incomplete deliveries. They do require, though, an understanding of different ways to divide up work. While Jaccob's prospects appear brighter, his problem is far more complex. It requires a more complete understanding of organizational design. Both Sam and Jaccob need to understand the basics, but Jaccob must also study the theory of organizational design and choose an overall strategy based on his objectives. Perhaps the design Jaccob chooses will be as neat and orderly as his grid of city lights, perhaps not.

SUMMARY

This part of the book offers a knowledge base that will help you to solve problems similar to those facing Jaccob and Sam. As you read on, keep in mind that your concern is to perform well in respect to two very specific managerial responsibilities:

1. As a manager, you must successfully link your work unit with the rest of the organization. This requires that you understand the logic of the total organizational system. Such understanding can help you take effective action to ensure that proper resource support is obtained for the work unit, and that the efforts of the work unit contribute to the purposes of the overall organization.

2. As a manager, you must also be successful in coordinating the many different activities, roles, interactions, and programs of your work unit. This is necessary if you are to achieve synergy in the combining of human and physical resource inputs into product or service outputs. To achieve such coordination, you must be familiar with alternative organization structures and recognize the special pressures imposed on these structures by differences in environment, size, and technology. Coordination also requires that you know how to design and maintain, over time, appropriate structures that provide a good fit with environmental, size, and technological factors.

The case shows clearly that both Jaccob and Sam face these two responsibilities. Jaccob faces them as the chief executive officer, while Sam faces them as a lower-level department manager. Both men could benefit from the insights that follow. Our discussion in the coming chapters will largely adopt the top manager's viewpoint, but the principles and implications are also relevant to managers like Sam whose responsibilities exist at middle and lower management levels. Remember, an organization is a collection of people working together in a division of labor to achieve a common purpose. It is time now to learn more about how to divide the labor, coordinate the results, and thereby facilitate accomplishment of the common purpose.

CHAPTER 10
BASIC ATTRIBUTES
OF ORGANIZATIONS

We can continue to make size an asset rather than a liability.

Federal Express Corporation

WPPSS (WOOPS)—WE JUST LOST ANOTHER BILLION

At one time, the Washington Public Power Supply System (WPPSS) was building five multibillion-dollar nuclear power plants for some 34 utilities in the Pacific Northwest. At its peak in the early 1980s, the five projects became one of the largest construction efforts ever attempted by a single organization, with a proposed budget of $24 billion. Before very long, the projects were millions over budget and years late. High interest rates, strikes, and changes mandated by the Nuclear Regulatory Commission were blamed. WPPSS also made at least two serious management errors early in the game. WPPSS awarded contracts to low bidders before engineering design work was completed. Low bidders were subsequently allowed to resubmit their cost estimates after the design work was completed. Critics claimed that such resubmissions were rarely competitive. Second, WPPSS tried to co-manage construction with each of the five different "lead" contractors. Millions hemorrhaged from the budget as WPPSS and "lead" contractors blamed each other for mistakes and changes.

In a desperate attempt to salvage the situation, a new top management team was brought in. The new team quickly focused the goals of the organization on completing one plant. They moved to restore both the public image of WPPSS as well as the morale of employees. For instance, executives started referring to WPPSS as the "supply system" instead of "WOOPS." The new team restructured the organization by clarifying lines of authority. They dropped less critical staff units, and instituted a whole series of computer-related controls on cost and quality.

The team did manage to save one plant, which is now producing electric power. However, WPPSS canceled or mothballed construction of the other four plants. It has declared default. The default is the largest in U.S. history.[1]

Management Applications Question

The previous example highlights an organization in trouble. What do you need to learn about organizations and organizational dynamics to help your organization avoid such operating difficulties?

PLANNING AHEAD

After reading this chapter and participating in the recommended learning experiences, you will be familiar with the following topics.

Organizational Goals
Organizational Culture
Organizations as Bureaucracies
Formal Structures of Organizations
Vertical Specialization
Horizontal Specialization

In Chapter 1 we introduced a few important characteristics of organizations. We defined an organization as a collection of people working together in a division of labor to achieve a common purpose. We suggested that organizations have a purpose to produce goods or services, and we introduced the notion of authority. In Chapter 10 we will expand upon these notions to provide a richer, more detailed, view of organizations. We will note that the goals an organization seeks, its general pattern of dividing managerial duties, and how work is assigned to different parts of the organization provide a basic understanding of even large, complex organizations. While this basic understanding is important, managers also need to recognize the forces underlying key organizational dynamics. Thus in Chapter 11 we will discuss coordination, control, centralization–decentralization, and the bureaucratic twins—standardization and formalization. We will note how the environment of the organization, its technology, and size alter what can be done and how the organization actually operates. These forces are labled organizational contingencies. Finally, in Chapter 12 we will discuss organizational design. Here the objective is to combine the basic understanding of organizations and organizational dynamics with the contingency material.

Before reading further, make sure you recall the following definitions from Chapter 1. They are fundamental to our treatment of organizations in this and subsequent chapters.

Organizational Purpose.   To produce a good or service.
Division of Labor.   The process of breaking work into small components that serve the organization's purpose and to be done by individuals or groups.

Authority. The right to command other persons.

Hierarchy of Authority. The arrangement of work positions in order of increasing authority.

ORGANIZATIONAL GOALS

Perhaps one of the most interesting characteristics of organizations is that people like to think that the organization has *a* goal or objective. Some consider huge multi-industry giants such as General Motors and TRW, Inc., to have a common, overriding objective that helps to explain their actions. For instance, GM raises or lowers prices to increase its profits. While such a simple notion may be appropriate for some analyses, as a manager you need to take a more sophisticated and realistic view.

Organizations may, indeed, be viewed as entities with goals.[2] They seek to improve themselves over time in many different ways. The goals pursued by organizations are multifaceted and often emerge in partial conflict with one another. These goals are common to individuals within the organization only to the extent that managers and other members see how their interests can be partially served by the organization. In this section we will examine two types of organizational goals. The first type centers on how the organization intends to serve society. The second focuses on its survival.

Societal Contributions of Organizations

Jim Chan, executive vice president of ZYCX Research, had a problem. Key research staff were leaving. Exit interviews suggested that pay, work challenge, and supervision were rarely problems. Instead, researchers gave some vague reference to being unable to contribute to their discipline. They said that ZYCX was only interested in growing and making a profit. Merely making money or servicing a client was not enough. They wanted to contribute to their profession. And these researchers expected ZYCX to help them to contribute to society.

As this example illustrates, societal contribution forms a basis for claims many organizations make to control resources, hire individuals, and market products. Organizations seek both support from their environments and freedom from interference. When the appearance of self-interest in this relationship dominates, however, organizations may lose legitimacy. Their actions may be challenged by others. They may lose public trust and confidence. Employees may become demoralized. Going back to our chapter opener, for instance, it will be virtually impossible for WPPSS to restart construction of its nuclear power plants without detailed scrutiny. It has lost public confidence.

Societal Goals and the Organization's Mission

Organizations that can effectively translate the character of their societal contribution for their members have an advantage. They have an additional set of motivational tools based upon a shared sense of noble purpose. Such a sense of purpose in a political party may be to generate and allocate power for the betterment of all U.S. citizens. A church attempts to instill values and protect the spiritual well-being of all. Our courts integrate the interests and activities of citizens. Finally, business firms provide economic sustenance and material well-being to society. Specifically, **societal goals** reflect the intended contributions of an organization to broader society.

In sum, organizations normally serve a specific societal function or an enduring need of the society.[3] Astute top-level managers build upon the professed societal contribution of the organization by relating specific organizational tasks and activities to higher purposes.[4] **Mission statements,** that is written statements of organizational purpose, may incorporate these corporate ideas of service to the society. Furthermore, the type of societal contribution often establishes how we evaluate an organization.

Primary Beneficiaries

While organizations may provide benefits to the society as a whole, most target their efforts toward a particular group.[5] We often expect the **primary beneficiaries** of business organizations to be stockholders, that political organizations serve the common good, that many culturally oriented organizations serve their members, and that some social service organizations serve clients or customers.

While each organization may have a primary beneficiary, its mission statement may also recognize the interests of many other parties. Thus, business mission statements often include service to customers, their obligations to employees, and their intention to support the community.

What Business Are We in?—Output Goals

Many larger organizations have found it useful to state very carefully which business they are in.[6] This statement can form the basis for long-term planning and help keep huge organizations from diverting too many resources to peripheral areas. For some corporations, answering this question may yield a more detailed statement concerning their products and services. These product and service goals provide an important basis for judging the quality of an organization's major contributions to society. In sum, **output goals** define the type of business an organization is in and begin to provide some substance to the more esoteric aspects of mission statements.

Systems Goals and Organizational Survival

Many organizations face the immediate problem of just making it through the coming years. They do not have the luxury of concentrating on societal contribution or of worrying about who their prime beneficiary should be. For instance, fewer than 10 percent of the businesses founded in a typical year can be expected to survive to reach their twentieth birthday.[7] The survival rate for public organizations is not much better. Even for organizations where survival is not an immediate problem, one can ask, "What are the types of conditions needed to minimize the risk of demise?" "What types of conditions promote survival?"

To answer these questions executives may start by developing systems goals for their organizations. **Systems goals** are concerned with conditions within the organization that are expected to increase its survival potential. The list of systems goals is almost endless, since each manager and researcher links today's conditions to tomorrow's existence in a different way. For many organizations, however, the list includes growth, productivity, stability, harmony, flexibility, prestige, and, of course, human resource maintenance. For some businesses, analysts consider market share and current profitability. Other recent studies suggest that innovation and quality also might be considered important systems goals.

In a very practical sense, systems goals represent near-term organizational characteristics that higher-level managers wish to promote. Systems goals must often be balanced against one another. For instance, a productivity and efficiency drive may cut the flexibility of an organization. Different parts of the organization may be asked to pursue different types of systems goals. As an example, higher-level managers may expect to see their production operations strive for efficiency, press for innovation from their R&D lab, and promote stability in their financial affairs.

The relative importance of different systems goals can vary substantially across various types of organizations. While we might expect a university to emphasize prestige and innovation, few would expect businesses not to emphasize growth and profitability.

ORGANIZATIONAL CULTURE

Once we were a society of small businesses. The objectives of the owner-manager were the goals of the firm. An owner-manager could individually supervise workers and only retain the ones with values consistent with these goals. But now we are also a society of complex and often very large corporations, government agencies, and unions. The work of many managers replaces that of the single owner-manager. And, it is much more difficult to make sure that the values of each individual worker are consistent with organizational goals. This situation highlights the importance of **corporate** or **organizational culture,** first introduced in Chapter 3, and defined as a system of shared values and beliefs that guide the behavior of organization members. Now is a good time to link this concept to our present interest in organizational goals.

Table 10.1 shows how two management consultants see organizational culture. Namely, organizations should have ''strong'' cultures that clearly identify and reward particular activities and that provide a distinctive competency for the organization.[8] In simple terms, there may be many corporations, but yours should be special. It should stand for something by emphasizing fundamental or core values. This idea of a ''strong'' organizational culture is closely linked to translating the societal contribution, prime beneficiaries, and a clear statement of product or service characteristics into everyday language.

Organizational culture can have substantial effects on employees. Many ''strong'' cultures may be rooted in a clear understanding of how key managers think the firm

TABLE 10.1   Elements of Strong Corporate Cultures

A widely shared philosophy.   This philosophy is not an abstract notion of the future but a real understanding of what the firm stands for, often embodied in slogans.

A concern for individuals.   This concern often places individual concerns over rules, policies, procedures, and adherence to job duties.

A recognition of heroes.   Heroes are individuals whose actions illustrate the shared philosophy and concerns of the company.

A belief in ritual and ceremony.   Management understands that rituals and ceremonies are real and important to members and to building a common identity.

A well-understood sense of the informal rules and expectations.   Employees understand what is expected of them.

A belief that what employees do is important to others.   Networking, to share information and ideas, is encouraged.

Source: Developed from Terrence Deal and Allan Kennedy, *Corporate Cultures: The Rites and Rituals of Corporate Life* (Reading, Mass.: Addison-Wesley, 1982).

serves the larger society. Thus, all aspects of the mission may not be formally stated or easily articulated by each employee. Instead, large portions of the mission may be a generally understood part of the organization, a key foundation of the organization's culture.

More systematic work on the effects of corporate culture on organizational goal attainment is just beginning to emerge. One recent study suggests that corporate culture may have a long-term payoff if three conditions are met.[9] First, the culture should enable the firm to add to the financial value of the firm. For instance, innovation could be prized (e.g., 3M—which introduces over 100 new products a year) or striving to solve customer problems (such as Nordstroms, the west coast department store chain) could be distinguishing characteristics. Second, the culture should be rare. Few if any competitors should have a similar set of values. Third, the culture should be difficult to imitate. For instance, a culture reflecting the core values of the founder (e.g., Walt Disney Co.) would be difficult for other organizations to mimic.

Another series of studies uses organizational culture more as an analogy to understand better the meanings and values organizational members hold.[10] In this perspective, stories, myths, rewriting of history, and analogies may be used to highlight what is actually happening within the organization in the eyes of the members. As yet, this line of research has not addressed questions of how or if organizational culture is associated with other factors such as the psychological contract, motivation, or job design. What it does suggest is that managers need to understand more fully the unique values, norms, meanings, and shared understandings in their organization. It also suggests that the culture of the firm, in terms of stories, myths, and ceremonies, can be employed to emphasize some systems goals over others. Subtle but important changes in goal priorities may be translated through these cultural mechanisms. For instance, consider the shift in priorities associated with changing the description of a brokerage firm from a ''main-line silk-stocking house'' to an ''aggressive growth-oriented corporation.''

ORGANIZATIONS AS BUREAUCRACIES

While many organizations have unique cultures, they also operate to some extent as bureaucracies. The concept of "bureaucracy" has crept into our common language to characterize huge, inflexible, and impersonal organizations. Another perspective of **bureaucracy** was envisioned by a German sociologist, Max Weber.[11] In his view, bureaucracies were an ideal type of organization that was based on legal authority, logic, and order. It was considered a superior way of organizing versus the other "ideal" types based either on tradition (i.e., history) or the charisma of an individual. In the traditional way of organizing, one could become a slave to history. An individual's place in the organization could be predetermined at birth. In a charismatic type, the dictates of one individual would rule. By comparison, the bureaucratic type could provide society with greater freedom and equity. The organization was to be rational (goal directed) and emphasize expertise over tradition or charisma. Weber expected that the bureaucracy would displace other forms and dominate society.

If our modern world is one of organizations, it is also one of bureaucracies. Table 10.2 summarizes the major characteristics of Weber's ideal bureaucracy. It also notes a number of dysfunctions or limitations. Much of what we call organizational design is an attempt to build upon the strengths of the bureaucractic form while minimizing its dysfunctions. Newsline 10.1 shows recent attempts by several corporations to overcome a major problem of bureaucracies—their lack of innovation.

TABLE 10.2 The Characteristics of Weber's Ideal Bureaucracy and Some Associated Dysfunctions

Characteristics of Weber's Ideal Bureaucracy	Associated Dysfunctions Identified by Critics
1. Labor is specialized so each person has clear authority and responsibility.	1. Overspecialization stimulates a divergence of interests that lead to conflict.
2. Offices and positions are arranged in a hierarchy of authority.	2. A very formal hierarchy creates inflexibility in following "official" channels.
3. Members are selected and promoted on the basis of technical competence.	3. Bureaucracies become political systems serving an elite corps of managers.
4. Members have administrative careers and work on a fixed salary.	4. Conformity to the organization's ways can be detrimental to one's mental health.
5. Members are subject to rules and controls that are strict and impersonal and are applied universally.	5. Rules become ends in themselves; rules can only specify minimum requirements.

NEWSLINE 10.1 / ESCAPING THE CONFINES OF BUREAUCRACY

Successful firms are recognizing that their large size and entrenched but effective managerial arrangements may not be appropriate for launching new innovative products or for developing more efficient ways of producing existing products. They are trying to escape their own bureaucracies by establishing quasi-independent units. Allied Corporation and 3M have established New Ventures Groups where managers can receive corporate funding to pursue ideas for new products. These managers set up their own small operations free from the constraints of the corporate bureaucracy.

Some firms, such as Lotus Development Corporation, have provided innovative engineers virtually unrestricted research and development to pursue potentially profitable ideas.

Lotus created an autonomous development entity and offered $1 million to its leader in exchange for the exclusive rights to license and market any new products coming from the venture.

In other instances, firms are establishing cooperative ventures with other firms to exploit new technologies. Included here are General Electric and Cincinnati Millicron. Many of these ventures are with leading Japanese firms. Most are small and very nonbureaucratic.

Thus, in different ways many firms are attempting to avoid the limitations of their own bureaucracies. The innovative efforts are deliberately kept small, personal, and informal with a minimum number of rules, policies, and procedures.

Reported in *The Clash of Cultures* and the *Columbia Journal of World Business*.

FORMAL STRUCTURES OF ORGANIZATIONS

As bureaucracies, organizations have a **formal structure** that shows the intended configuration of positions (jobs), job duties, and the lines of authority among different parts of the enterprise. We emphasize the word "formal" simply because the intentions of organizational designers are never fully realized. Furthermore, no formal structure can provide all the detail needed actually to show the activities within a firm. Yet the formal structure is still important because it provides the foundation for managerial action. It outlines the job to be done, who (in terms of position) is to perform specific activities, and how the total task of the organization is to be accomplished. It is the skeleton of the organization.

Organization charts are diagrams that depict the formal structures of organizations. A typical chart shows the various positions, the position holders, and the lines of authority linking them to one another. Figure 10.1 is a partial organization chart

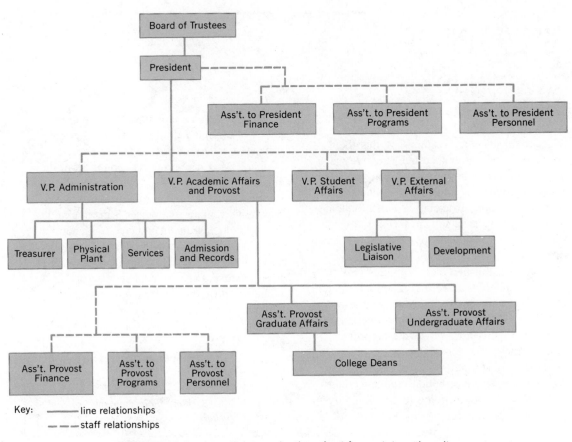

FIGURE 10.1   A partial organization chart for a state university.

for a large university. The total chart allows university employees to locate their positions in the structure and to identify the lines of authority linking them with others in the organization. For instance, in this figure the treasurer reports to the vice presidential administration who in turn reports to the president.

The most visible aspects of formal structure are the patterns of vertical and horizontal specialization. Vertical specialization deals with the question of formal authority or the authorized power to decide and act. Horizontal specialization is the division of work among those with roughly equal formal authority. Both forms of specialization are often apparent on an organization chart.

VERTICAL SPECIALIZATION

In most larger organizations, there is a clear separation of authority and duties by hierarchical rank. This separation represents **vertical specialization,** a hierarchical division of labor that distributes formal authority and establishes where and how critical decisions will be made.

The distribution of formal authority can most easily be seen in descriptions of typical managerial duties. Top managers, or senior executives, plan the overall strategy of the organization and plot its long-term future. They also act as final judges for internal disputes and serve to certify promotions, reorganizations, and the like. Middle managers guide the daily operations of the organization, help to formulate policy, and translate top-management decisions into more specific guidelines for action. Lower-level managers supervise the actions of subordinates to ensure implementation of the strategies authorized by top management and compliance with the related policies established by middle management.

The description of managerial levels should alert you to two important considerations in vertical specialization. One, as managers move up the hierarchy the scope of responsibility expands. Managers become accountable for more individuals even though they do not directly supervise their activities. You should recognize the importance of specifying common goals and emphasizing common values to ensure that unseen subordinates act as if the senior managers were directly supervising their work. Two, as managers move up the hierarchy they generally have more discretion. We will build on the importance of discretion in our discussions of organizational politics (see Chapter 15) and leadership (see Chapter 16). For now, recognize the time aspects of discretion. In many entry-level positions time horizons are very short. You may be asked to check with your boss daily and the work you supervise may be evaluated weekly or monthly. For instance, Sam Ford, a new junior manager in Middle States (see the Part opening) is in trouble because a shipment is four days late.

Chain of Command and the Span of Control

Executives, managers, and supervisors are hierarchically connected through the "chain of command." Individuals are expected to follow the decisions of their supervisors in the areas of responsibility outlined in the organization chart. Traditional management theory suggests that each individual is to have one boss. Each unit is to have one leader. When this occurs there is "unity of command." Unity of command is considered necessary to avoid confusion, to assign accountability to specific persons, and to provide clear channels of communication up and down the organization. Without unity of command no single individual is "in charge." If mistakes occur, managers will naturally try to escape accountability and point the finger of responsibility at others. The attempted co-management of the nuclear power plant projects by WPPSS is but one example where violating the unity of command caused major problems.

The number of individuals a manager can directly supervise is obviously limited. Thus, in establishing vertical specialization the organization must limit the "span of control." While research does not suggest that there is an absolute minimum or maximum span of control, it does suggest some guidelines for establishing the average number of subordinates reporting to a manager.

The span can be very broad if, (1) the tasks are comparatively simple, (2) subordinates are experienced and well trained, and (3) the tasks to be performed do not call for a team effort. Organizations would prefer broader spans simply because they reduce overhead expenses in terms of the required number of managerial personnel.

The span can be narrower where tasks are complex and call for considerable judgment and expertise. The narrower spans of control allow greater technical involvement and special consultation by the supervisor. However, there is an alternative. The organization can separate advisors (those with specialized skill and knowledge) from supervisors. This division of labor is reflected in the designation of line (command) and staff (advisory) positions of authority. Let's take a closer look at this.

Line and Staff Units

Line units and personnel conduct the major business of the organization. The production and marketing functions are two examples. In contrast, **staff units** and personnel assist the line units by providing specialized expertise and services. Accounting and public relations are examples.

The dashed lines on the organization chart in Figure 10.1 denote staff relationships, whereas the solid ones denote line relationships. For example, the vice president of administration heads a staff unit, as does the vice president of student affairs. All academic departments in the figure are line units since they constitute the basic production function of the university.

A useful distinction to be made for both line and staff units concerns the amount and types of contacts they maintain with outsiders to the organization. Some units are mainly internal in orientation; others are more external in focus. The following description briefly summarizes the differences between them.

Line Units
Internal   → Focus on   Transforming raw material and
  (e.g., production)   information into products and/or services.

External   → Focus on   Linking clients and/or suppliers
  (e.g., marketing)   to the organization.

Staff Units
Internal   → Focus on   Assisting line units in the
  (e.g., accounting)   technical areas of budgeting and fiscal control.

External   → Focus on   Linking the organization to its
  (e.g., public relations)   environment through the conveyance of a positive public image.

The placement of staff units in the formal structure is particularly important. Grouping many staff units at the top reinforces the expertise and managerial scope of top-level decision makers. In effect, it expands top management capabilities. This tends to yield comparatively little vertical specialization. As an employee or lower-level manager, you are likely to think that formal authority is concentrated at the top.

When staff specialists are moved down into the organization, the action capacity of middle managers is expanded. Each can begin to operate more independently. Commensurate with the additional assistance available from staff specialists, we would expect middle managers to expand their range, scope, and depth of decision making.

Rarely does an organization place all staff units at the top or bury them deep within the hierarchy. Most often some are elevated to the top while others remain farther down. Where the firm needs corporate-wide action to confront a specific threat or opportunity, staff specialists may be placed toward the top. For instance, in the 1970s some firms developed an affirmative action staff to guide corporate efforts to reduce discrimination. In the 1980s, these units are being dispersed down into the hierarchy. Figure 10.2 illustrates how placement of staff changes the look of the pyramid we visualize when we traditionally think of an organizational hierarchy.

There may be secondary effects associated with staff units at the top of the organization. Staff personnel may use their high-level position to increase the attention given to their area. Top-level units may attempt to get operating managers to obtain clearances before taking action. And, of course, few top-level staff units can avoid the temptation to keep detailed written records, routinize staff work via standardized forms, and improve their performance with more staff and a larger budget. Heads of such expanding staff units may be called "empire builders." The tendency toward staff proliferation can be minimized by exploring substitutes in the form of managerial techniques.

Managerial Techniques

As we have seen, merely adding staff may not provide the organization with increased efficiency. In fact, one of the foremost trends in modern industry is to streamline

FIGURE 10.2   How placement of staff changes the look of an organization.

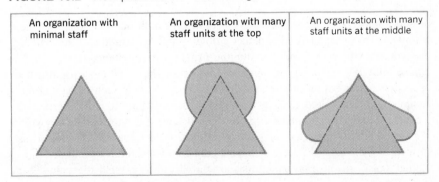

NEWSLINE 10.2 / NEW SOFTWARE MAKES THE CHOICE MUCH EASIER

For years managers have been vexed by a common problem—how to mix things together efficiently. In manufacturing a typical issue is deciding what mix of products to build at various locations; in distribution it often relates to choosing delivery routes and combinations of trucks and drivers. Getting the right mix in these and other cases often means lower costs and higher profits.

But until recently, solving these problems optimally was the province of highly specialized personnel familiar with a mathematical technique called linear programming.

Times are changing. With new software, most managers can now do many such analyses on their personal computer. A Chicago company sells a program called "What's Best." It allows users of Lotus 1-2-3 to set up a spreadsheet and then direct the computer to optimize on variables like profits, cost savings or inventory use. This makes linear programming relatively easy to do.

Therese Fitzpatrick, a nursing administrator, did just that. She used to spend up to 20 hours a month scheduling 300 nurses to get the proper mix of capabilities, wards and shifts. Her problems were complicated by vacation time and the need for special staffing for certain days. Since using "What's Best" to assist in the scheduling decisions, she has cut her time to four hours. By better scheduling of temporary nursing help she is also saving the hospital thousands of dollars per month.

Reported in *The Wall Street Journal*.

operations and reduce staff in order to lower costs and raise productivity. One way to facilitate this is to provide line managers with managerial techniques designed to expand upon their analytical and decision making capabilities. Good examples are the ever-increasing role of the computer and associated decision support software in all areas of management. Newsline 10.2 provides a brief reminder on these important developments.

In one sense managerial techniques are substitutes for both line and staff managers and staff units.[12] They may be used to detect problems and opportunities, select among alternative courses of action, and monitor the progress of implementation. For instance, those studying financial management recognize the importance of financial planning models (in detecting problems), financial decision aids such as capital budgeting models and discounted cash-flow analyses (for selecting among alternatives) and, of course budgets (to monitor progress and ensure that managers stay within financial limits). Those studying marketing, production, and personnel should also see that much of the material in these courses concerns managerial techniques.

In another sense, managerial techniques are employed to expand the volume and scope of operations a manager can administer.[13] They can allow the manager to handle more sophisticated operations. Recently, there has been intense interest in developing more sophisticated managerial techniques to aid line managers in decision making. Managers can be aided by Decision Support Systems (DSS). A DSS combines advances in computer hardware and software with the development of extensive information bases. Using judgment rules built into the computer software the manager could input the data for a given case and have the program suggest a course of action. For instance, assume you want a loan for a new car. Your financial data could be placed into a DSS to see if you qualify and to determine the level of risk the bank would be taking by giving you the loan. The DSS could be programmed to suggest rejection, acceptance, or further review. Only in the case of further review might the manager take the time to personally review your application.

The next step is to upgrade the DSS to an "expert system." Expert systems are essentially sophisticated computer programs tied to extensive information bases that simulate human thinking (also known as artificial intelligence). They can be used to duplicate the judgments of experts in areas calling for considerable skill, experience, intuition, and judgment. Some expect they will show that much of what managers call intuition is, in reality, the product of very sophisticated logical analysis. As this is recognized and simulated we expect that expert systems will become an invaluable managerial technique allowing organizations to upgrade decision making and extend the scope and depth of already skilled managers.

The mix of managers and managerial techniques adopted by a particular organization should rest on a number of factors. First are the problems and opportunities facing the system. A second is the extent to which management understands how to combine raw materials, people, and equipment to produce desired products and services. A third is the firm's consistency and range of outputs. Essentially, the more problems and opportunities, the less the available knowledge, and the greater the variation in problems and opportunities encountered, the greater the reliance on managers versus managerial techniques.

Most organizations use a combination of line and staff units, plus managerial techniques to vertically specialize the division of labor (that is, to distribute formal authority). The most appropriate pattern of vertical specialization depends on the environment of the organization, its size, its technology, and its goals. Generally, as organizations grow, vertical specialization increases. We will return to this theme in the next chapter. For now, let us turn our attention to issues relating to horizontal specialization.

HORIZONTAL SPECIALIZATION

When dividing the total task into separate duties, management attempts to group similar people and resources together.[14] **Horizontal specialization** is a division of labor that establishes specific work units or groups within an organization; it is often referred to as the process of departmentation. Let us examine three basic forms of horizontal specialization: departmentation by function, division, and matrix. For a manager, decisions regarding horizontal specialization are important because they not only define the job of the group that will be managed but also establish many opportunities and challenges.

Departmentation by Function

Grouping by skill, knowledge, and action yields a pattern of **functional departmentation.** Figure 10.3 shows the organization chart for a nuclear power plant where each department has a technical speciality considered necessary for safe and efficient op-

FIGURE 10.3 A functional pattern of departmentation for a nuclear power plant.

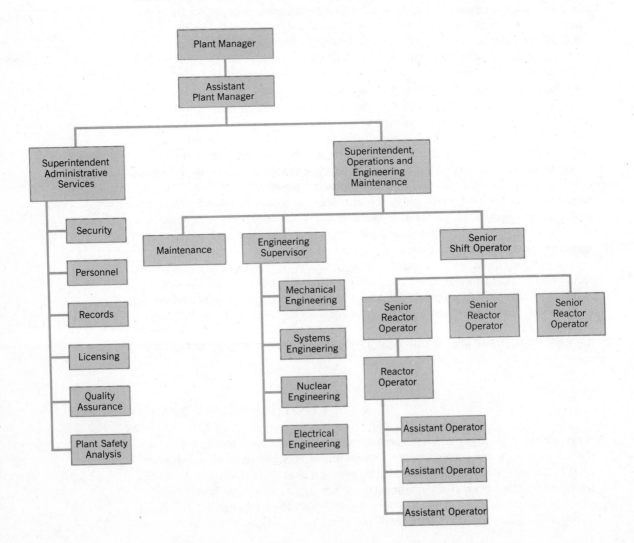

eration of the plant. In business, marketing, finance, production, and personnel are important functions. Middle States Manufacturing Company, described in the introduction to this part of the book, has a functional form of organization.

Table 10.3 summarizes the advantages of the functional pattern. With all these advantages, it is not surprising that the functional form is extremely popular. It is used in most organizations, particularly toward the bottom of the hierarchy. Of course, functional specialization also has some disadvantages, as summarized in Table 10.3.

Organizations that rely heavily on functional specialization may expect the following tendencies to emerge over time: (1) an emphasis on quality from a technical standpoint, (2) rigidity to change, particularly if change within one functional area is needed to help other functional areas, and (3) difficulty in coordinating the actions of different functional areas, particularly if the organization must continually adjust to changing external conditions. These disadvantages become challenges for the managers heading functional units.

Departmentation by Division

The pattern of **divisional departmentation** groups individuals and resources by products, services, clients, territories, and/or legal entities. Figure 10.4 shows a divisional

---

TABLE 10.3   Major Advantages and Disadvantages of Functional Specialization

Advantages	Disadvantages
1. It can yield very clear task assignments that are consistent with an individual's training.	1. It may reinforce the narrow training of individuals and lead to boring and routine jobs. Communication across technical areas is difficult and conflict between units may increase. Lines of communication across the organization can become very complex.
2. Individuals within a department can easily build on one another's knowledge, training, and experience. Facing similar problems and having similar training facilitates communication and technical problem solving.	2. Complex communication channels can lead to "top management overload." Top management may spend too much time and effort dealing with cross-functional problems.
3. It provides an excellent training ground for new managers who must translate their academic training into organizational action.	3. Individuals may look up the organizational hierarchy for direction and reinforcement rather than focus attention on products, services, or clients. Guidance is typically sought from functional peers or superiors.
4. It is easy to explain. Most employees can understand the role of each unit, even though many may not know what individuals in a particular function do.	

pattern of organization grouped around products, regions, and clients for three divisions of a conglomerate.

The divisional pattern is often used to meet diverse external threats and opportunities. Many larger, geographically dispersed organizations selling to national and international markets use departmentation by territory. The savings in time, effort, and travel can be substantial; and each territory can adjust to regional differences.

Organizations that rely on a few major customers may organize their people and resources by client. Here, the idea is to focus attention on the needs of the individual customer. To the extent that customer needs are unique, departmentation by client can also cut costs, reduce confusion, and increase synergy.

Some organizations use divisional specialization because of their history. They have acquired firms or developed new legal entities to limit their liability in new risky ventures. Organizations expanding internationally may also departmentalize by legal entity to meet host country ownership requirements. For some large organizations, the maze of subsidiaries, joint ventures, and holding agreements would confuse even the brightest lawyer. Many government agencies also have a legal form of organization, primarily because of the legislation that authorizes their activities.

FIGURE 10.4   A divisional pattern of departmentation in a conglomerate.

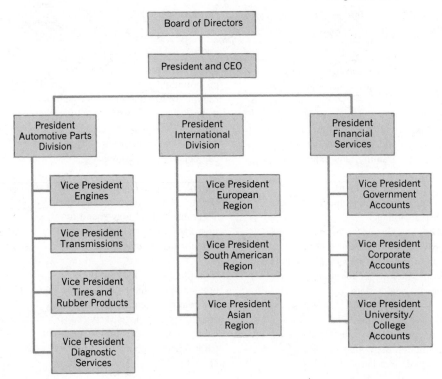

The major advantages and disadvantages of divisional specialization are summarized in Table 10.4. Organizations that rely heavily on divisional specialization can generally expect the following tendencies to occur over time: (1) an emphasis on flexibility and adaptability to the needs of important external units, (2) a lag in the technical quality of products and services vis-à-vis functionally structured competitors, and (3) difficulty in coordination across divisions, particularly where divisions must work closely or sell to each other. In organizations where satisfying the demands of outsiders is particularly important, the divisional structure may provide the desired capabilities. This pattern can help cut costs in organizations with diverse operations that operate in many territories, produce quite different products and services, or serve a few major customers. It is the most popular form among large, multinational conglomerates.

Departmentation by Matrix

From the aerospace industry we developed a third unique form of departmentation now labeled the matrix (or **matrix structure**). **Matrix departmentation** evolved from very complex projects where neither functional nor divisional forms were working.

TABLE 10.4 Major Advantages and Disadvantages of Divisional Specialization

Advantages	Disadvantages
1. It provides adaptability and flexibility in meeting the demands of important external groups.	1. It does not provide a pool of highly trained individuals with similar expertise to solve problems and train new employees.
2. It allows for spotting external changes as they are emerging.	2. It can lead to a duplication of effort as each division attempts to solve similar problems.
3. It provides for the integration of specialized personnel deep within the hierarchy.	3. Divisional goals may be given priority over the health and welfare of the overall organization. Divisional organizations may have difficulty responding to corporatewide threats.
4. It focuses on the success or failure of particular products, services, clients, or territories.	4. Conflict problems may arise when divisions attempt to develop joint projects, exchange resources, share individuals or through "transfer pricing" charge one another for goods and services.
5. To the extent that this pattern yields separate "business units," top management can pit one division against another. For instance, Procter & Gamble has traditionally promoted friendly competition among product groups.	

In aerospace efforts projects are very technically complex and they involve hundreds of subcontractors located throughout the world. Precise integration and control is needed across many sophisticated functional specialties and corporations. The solution was to use both the functional and divisional forms simultaneously. Figure 10.5 shows the basic matrix arrangement for an aerospace program. Note the functional departments on one side and the project efforts on the other. Workers and supervisors in the middle of the matrix have two bosses—one functional and one project.

The major advantages and disadvantages of the matrix form of departmentation are summarized in Table 10.5.[15] The key disadvantage of the matrix method is the loss of unity of command. Individuals are often not sure what their jobs are, who they report to for specific activities, and how various managers are to administer the effort. It can be a very expensive method since it relies on individual managers to coordinate efforts deep within the firm. Note that the number of managers almost doubles. Despite the limitations, however, it provides a dual emphasis between functional and divisional concerns. The balance between functional and divisional concerns can be resolved at the working level where the balance between technical, cost, customer, and organizational concerns can be rectified.

Many firms have adopted elements of the matrix arrangement without using the term "matrix." For example, special project teams, coordinating committees, and task forces can be the beginnings of a matrix. Yet, a firm can use these as temporary

FIGURE 10.5 A matrix pattern of departmentation in an aerospace division.

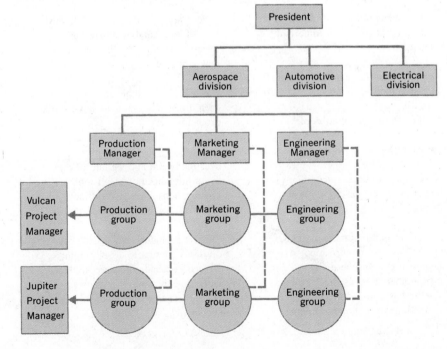

TABLE 10.5 Major Advantages and Disadvantages of a Matrix Structure

Advantages	Disadvantages
1. It combines strengths of both functional and divisional departmentation.	1. It is very expensive.
2. It helps to provide a blending of technical and market emphasis in organizations operating in exceedingly complex environments.	2. Unity of command is lost (individuals have more than one supervisor).
	3. Authority and responsibilities of managers may overlap causing conflicts and gaps in effort across units, and inconsistencies in priorities.
3. It provides a series of managers able to converse with both technical and marketing personnel.	4. It is difficult to explain to employees.

structures within a predominately functional or divisional form, and without upsetting the unity of command or hiring additional managers.

Mixed Forms of Departmentation

Which form of departmentation should be used? As the matrix concept suggests, it is possible to departmentalize by two different methods at the same time. Actually, organizations often use a mixture of departmentation forms. In fact, it is often desirable to divide the effort (group people and resources) by two methods at the same time to balance the advantages and disadvantages of each.

Take the example involving the combined use of functional and divisional departmentation. Northwest Manufacturing and Wholesale produces filters for autos and ships and, most recently, for the elimination of toxic and nuclear waste. Its plant in Tacoma, Washington, produces marine filters. The Walla Walla, Washington, works specializes in nuclear and toxic waste filters. All auto filters are manufactured in Los Angeles. The firm is active in both the new equipment market for auto filters and the replacement market. Most auto filters are sold in the replacement market via discount stores and auto supply outlets. This is a highly competitive market in which success depends on providing inventory control and restocking for hundreds of retail outlets. Filters for toxic waste, nuclear applications, and marine use must be specifically tailored to individual customers. The president also sees substantial growth opportunities in Europe. Now European sales, mainly in the United Kingdom, account for 22 percent of total sales and 29 percent of gross profits.

Using the Functional and Divisional Forms

Figure 10.6 shows a possible organization chart for this successful growing regional firm. It has three divisions, each of which is a separate legal entity. The largest division

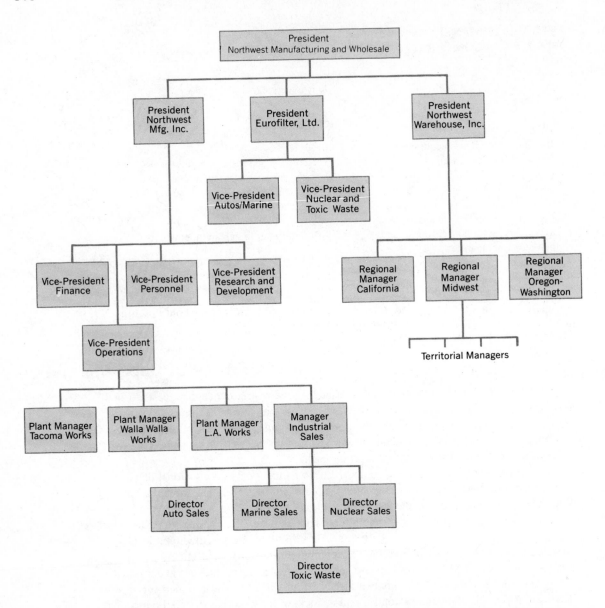

FIGURE 10.6 Partial organization chart for Northwest Manufacturing and Wholesale.

is Northwest Manufacturing, which produces all the filters and markets for industrial consumers. Note that it is functionally organized below the president with vice presidents of finance, personnel, R&D, and operations. Due to the close coordination required between manufacturing and industrial sales, both plant managers and the director of industrial sales report to the vice president of operations. As you might expect, both regional and product differences separate the plants. Note the technical thrust of this division, with its emphasis on a functional structure at the top and with product groups in sales and operations.

Eurofilter, a separate division, is structured to serve the European market. Note that the divisional form dominates. In a similar fashion, the wholesaling company is dominated by divisional departmentation, since the key to this business is service. Maintaining retailer inventories and ensuring prompt delivery are important. Thus, customers are grouped into territories, and the territories form regions headed by a regional manager.

Using the Matrix and Functional Patterns

Now let us take a look at a research organization that utilizes a matrix. The firm offers research services to a broad range of clients, but the majority of its business is with three large government agencies. Quality Research employs specialists in management, psychology, economics, sociology, law, and health care. Technical quality and responsiveness to the client are considered equally important and should be facilitated by the organization structure.

This firm solves the problem as shown in Figure 10.7. Financial and administrative functions are separated from research. This is a functional division. Within the research function, functional heads are assigned for each discipline. These individuals are charged with the responsibility of hiring qualified personnel and encouraging

FIGURE 10.7 A partial organization chart for Quality Research Associates.

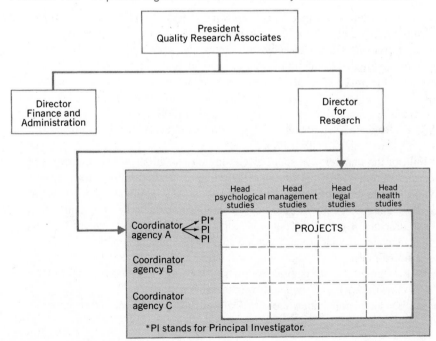

professional development. Coordinators are designated for each of the key agencies to help define client research needs, respond to client requests, and coordinate projects performed by the research staff.

For each project there is a principal investigator (PI). The PI is drawn from one of the functional areas and manages a particular project. Since individuals may work on several projects, they could be a PI on one and a researcher on another. Note that all individuals have two immediate superiors: one is the functional head; the other is an agency coordinator of PIs, or a PI for a researcher assigned to a particular project. Note also that both the coordinators and functional heads report directly to the director for research.

This use of the divisional and matrix patterns provides a structure that is more fluid and responsive to external pressures and opportunities. A pure functional pattern, on the other hand, provides a more rigid structure, often centering on technical quality.

As we will see in Chapter 12, the departmentation of an organization should fit the demands and constraints placed on it. The choice of functional, divisional, and matrix patterns will influence the organization's ability to respond to outside demands, produce high-quality products and services, and efficiently manage people and resources. No one pattern or combined form is best for all organizations. The best choice is the one in tune with the goals of the organization, technological requirements, the magnitude of its operations, and the external pressures and opportunities facing the system.

SUMMARY

This chapter has delved more deeply into what we mean by an organization. We started with the general view of an organization as a collection of people working together in a divison of labor to achieve a common purpose. In the early part of the chapter, we investigated the notion of organizational goals. Here we first centered our discussion on the mission of the organization and then moved to the question of survival. We suggested that organizations have many different types of goals. Not all of these may be compatible and the emphasis on different goals may change over time. We also revisited the concept of organization culture as it now becomes significant as a basic organizational attribute.

The bulk of the chapter was spent discussing organizations as bureaucracies. This included an examination of the formal structure and elaboration of the organization's division of labor in terms of both vertical and horizontal specialization. First, we noted that most organizations contain both line and staff components. Where staff units are placed can dramatically alter the potential capabilities of different managers. We also noted that managerial techniques are used to extend and supplement managers. We discussed horizontal specialization with a detailed analysis of different forms of departmentation–functional, divisional and matrix. It is important to remember that each form has its own unique strengths and weaknesses.

The goals and overall patterns of vertical and horizontal specialization are often enduring features of an organization. A change in goals and specialization dramatically changes the nature of an organization and its capacity to perform. In the next chapter, we will examine the more dynamic aspects of organizations. These are areas where one can expect to see both minor and major alterations in organizational attributes over time.

THINKING THROUGH THE ISSUES

1. Some argue that a major problem with government is that it is not run like a business. What problems do you see in using business logic for attaining the goals of government?
2. Would you like to be a manager in a company with a "strong" corporate culture? What disadvantages do you see?
3. As a potential management trainee, which pattern of departmentation appeals to you the most, and why?
4. From other courses in business administration, provide a list of three managerial techniques and the major goals embodied in each technique.
5. Can you devise a better pattern of departmentation for Quality Research (see Figure 10.7), given that you want to increase short-term profits?
6. Draw the organization chart of your university. Separate the line and staff units, identify the bases of departmentation, and discuss how well they work in this situation.
7. Think of an organization with which you are familiar. Classify its goals in terms of the categories developed in this chapter. Explain what you feel to be any goal deficiencies for this organization.
8. Describe the organizational culture of this same organization. How does the prevailing culture facilitate or inhibit goal attainment. Explain your answer.

CASE: EAGLE AIRLINES I

Turn to the Eagle Airlines case at the end of Chapter 12. Then answer the following questions.

Questions

1. Discuss the ideal and dysfunctional bureaucratic characteristics summarized in Table 10.2 as they apply to this case.
2. Discuss the kind of departmentation used in the case. What are its apparent advantages and disadvantages, especially in terms of top management's expressed philosophy of "decentralization"?
3. Discuss the important aspects of vertical and horizontal specialization as they are applied to both sales and service.

EXERCISE: ORGANIZATIONAL ANALYSIS—PART I

Purpose:

To apply, as clearly and thoroughly as possible, the concepts developed in Chapter 10 to a real-world organization. This will give you and your group a chance to apply the concepts and share your findings with those of your classmates.

Time:

50 minutes or more in class, plus at-home preparation.

Procedure:

1. Do the following before coming to class:
    a. Form a group of four or five people. Assume that the group is a management consulting team required to prepare a written report following the format indicated by your boss (the instructor).
    b. Select an organization for analysis. In addition to work organizations, student organizations provide another possibility. Thus, student government organizations, fraternities, sororities, professional organizations, or clubs are possibilities. So are scouting organizations, churches, and various volunteer organizations with which someone in your group may be familiar. Grocery stores, dry cleaners, or eating establishments are still other candidates. It is important to select an organization from which you can obtain observational and interview information and perhaps even some company records (such as organizational charts). If someone in your group is at least somewhat familiar with the organization, that is likely to be helpful. Finally, the organization should not be too large, since your group will be asked to discuss it from both the bottom up and the top down. If the organization is large, your instructor may want your group to focus on a major subsystem within it.
    c. Using observations, interviews, and company records as necessary, your group has been assigned to do the following for its organizational report.
        (1) Discuss the major goals and objectives of the organization and trace an example of a means–ends chain. Discuss the extent to which human resource maintenance seems to be emphasized. Tie this into a discussion of Weber's bureaucratic characteristics as they apply to the organization.
        (2) Analyze whether the organization has an identifiable culture.
        (3) Identify and discuss the organization's line and staff units.
        (4) Discuss the kind of horizontal specialization used at each level of the organization.
        (5) Discuss the kind of vertical specialization used at each level and in each department of the organization. Make sure you include details

concerning the use of line and staff managers, managerial techniques, and the trade-offs involved.

2. Be prepared to turn in this part of the group report to your instructor and to discuss the group's findings and their implications.

THE MANAGER'S VOCABULARY

Bureaucracy   An ideal form of organization whose characteristics were defined by the German sociologist Max Weber.

Departmentation   The process of dividing duties and grouping jobs and people together to form administrative units; horizontal specialization.

Divisional Departmentation   Grouping individuals and resources by product, service, client, territory, or legal entity.

Formal Structure   The intended configuration of positions, job duties, and lines of authority among the component parts of an organization.

Functional Departmentation   Grouping individuals and resources by skill, knowledge, and action.

Horizontal Specialization   A division of labor through the formation of work units or groups within an organization; the process of departmentation.

Line Units   Conduct the major business of the organization.

Managerial Techniques   The analytical methods, procedures, and tools organizations use to supplement managerial judgment.

Matrix Departmentation or Matrix Structure   A combination of functional and divisional patterns wherein an individual is assigned to more than one type of unit.

Mission Statements   Written statements of organizational purpose.

Organization Charts   Diagrams that depict the formal structures of organizations.

Organizational Culture   A system of shared values and beliefs that guide the behavior of organization members (the "corporate" culture).

Output Goals   Define the types of business an organization is in.

Primary Beneficiaries   Particular groups expected to benefit from the efforts of specific organizations.

Societal Goals   Goals reflecting the intended contributions of an organization to broader society.

Specialization   The division of labor within an organization that groups people and resources together in order to accomplish important tasks.

Staff Units   Assist the line units by performing specialized services to the organization.

Systems Goals   Goals concerned with conditions within the organization that are expected to increase its survival potential.

Vertical Specialization   A hierarchical division of labor that distributes formal authority and establishes how critical decisions will be made.

IMPORTANT NAMES

Max Weber   The German sociologist who specified the characteristics of an ideal organizational form, the bureaucracy.

NOTES

[1]Richard N. Osborn and others, *Organizational Analysis and Safety for Utilities with Nuclear Power Plants* (Washington, D.C.: U.S. Nuclear Regulatory Commission, 1984), also listed as U.S.N.R.C. NUREG/CR-3215.

[2]See Richard M. Cyert and James G. March, *A Behavioral Theory of the Firm* (Englewood Cliffs, N.J.: Prentice-Hall, 1963). A good discussion of organizational goals is also found in Charles Perrow, *Organizational Analysis: A Sociological View* (Belmont, CA.: Wadsworth, 1970) and in Richard H. Hall, "Organizational Behavior: A Sociological Perspective," in Jay W. Lorsch, ed., *Handbook of Organizational Behavior* (Englewood Cliffs, N.J.: Prentice-Hall, 1987), pp. 84–95.

[3]H. Talcott Parsons, *Structure and Processes in Modern Societies* (New York: Free Press, 1960).

[4]See, for instance, Thomas J. Peters and Richard Waterman, Jr., *In Search of Excellence: Lessons from America's Best-Run Companies* (New York: Harper & Row, 1982).

[5]Peter Blau and W. Richard Scott, *Formal Organizations* (San Francisco: Chandler, 1962).

[6]See, for instance, I. C. MacMillan and A. Meshulack, "Replacement versus Expansion: Dilemma for Mature U.S. Businesses," *Academy of Management Journal*, Vol. 26 (1983), pp. 708–726.

[7]William H. Starbuck and Paul C. Nystrom, "Designing and Understanding Organizations," in P. C. Nystrom and W. H. Starbuck, eds., *Handbook of Organizational Design: Adapting Organizations to Their Environments* (New York: Oxford University Press, 1981).

[8]Terrence Deal and Allan Kennedy, *Corporate Cultures: The Rites and Rituals of Corporate Life* (Reading, Mass.: Addison-Wesley, 1982).

[9]Jay B. Barney, "Organizational Culture: Can it be a Source of Sustained Competitive Advantage," *Academy of Management Review*, Vol. 11 (1986), pp. 656–665.

[10]For a more complete discussion, see Marianne Jelinek, Linda Smircich, and Paul Hirsch, "Organizational Culture," *Administrative Science Quarterly*, Vol. 28 (1983), pp. 331–338. This specially edited issue also contains several other interesting contributions concerning corporate cultures.

[11]Max Weber, *The Theory of Social and Economic Organization*, translated by A. M. Henderson and H. T. Parsons (New York: Free Press, 1947).

[12]See Richard N. Osborn, James G. Hunt, and Lawrence R. Jauch. *Organization Theory: Integrated Text and Cases* (Melbourne, Fla.: Krieger, 1984).

[13]For further discussion see J. Ivancevich, J. Donnelley, and J. Gibson, *Managing for Performance*, (Plano, Texas: Business Publications, 1986); and Herbert Simon, "Making Management Decisions, The Role of Intuition and Emotion," *Academy of Management Executive*, Vol. 1 (1987), pp. 57–64.

[14]This section is based on Osborn, Hunt and Jauch, *Organization Theory*, pp. 273–303.

[15]For a good discussion of matrix structures see Stanley Davis, Paul Lawrence, Harvey Kolodny, and Michael Beer, *Matrix* (Reading, Mass.: Addison-Wesley, 1977).

CHAPTER 11
ORGANIZATIONAL DYNAMICS

Brunswick Corporation manages its businesses through a decentralized form of management.

Brunswick Corporation Annual Report

THE UNCERTAIN FUTURE OF HIGH TECHNOLOGY IN A GLOBAL ECONOMY

Once steel, automobiles, detergents, and telephones were the products of the most advanced technologies. Now it is optoelectronics, biotechnology, advanced materials, and computers. Once the United States led in the development of all these areas but now it faces strong competition from Japan and Europe. In a recent assessment of developments in high technology, *Fortune* rated the competitive stature of the United States, Western Europe, Japan, and the Soviet Union. The scores were troubling for those who still think the United States dominates all phases of technological development.

Optoelectronics is the marriage of optics and electronics. Optical fiber for telephone transmissions is one example of a product from this technology. Japan holds a lead over the United States with western Europe a distant third. In biotechnology, which includes genetic engineering, the United States is the leader followed by Japan. In advanced materials, including ceramics, Japan and the United States lead. The United States leads in some areas but the Japanese are more quickly capitalizing on new developments.

In response to technological developments, U.S.- and Japanese-based firms are developing cooperative relationships. These include arrangements to share R&D, license new products, and grant access to new markets. From these cooperative arrangements new industries may form. The dominant firms may be combinations of U.S., Japanese, and European firms.[1]

Coordination and control in these multinational cooperative efforts will call for new methods and techniques that span different cultures, industries, and types of technology. Controlling these new entities and assuring coordination among members from different cultures will be a managerial challenge for the 1990s. As with other industries, managers will need to develop mechanisms consistent with technological demands, with the scope of their operations, and the nature of the competitive opportunities facing their part of the firm.

Management Applications Question

How should an organization be structured to capitalize on changing environmental opportunities and new technical developments?

PLANNING AHEAD

After reading this chapter and participating in the recommended learning experiences, you will be familiar with the following topics.

Rules, Procedures, and Policies
Formalization and Standardization
Coordination and Control
Centralization and Decentralization
Organizations as Open Systems
The Environment of Organizations
Technology and Size

If people were machines, we could expect an understanding of goals and division of labor to naturally incorporate most of the important dynamics of an organization. Of course, an essential feature of organizations is people. They no more act like machines when seen collectively than when studied individually. Thus, in this chapter we investigate selected aspects of organizational dynamics.

In Chapter 10 we provided a detailed discussion on how the organization may select different patterns of departmentation to emphasize different types of goals. There are many ways of dividing up the labor in organizations and grouping people and resources into operating departments. In terms of horizontal specialization we looked at functional, divisional, and matrix patterns of departmentation. In terms of vertical specialization we examined the elements of line and staff units, and the use of selected managerial techniques.

The process of specialization differentiates people and work units from one another. Given this differentiation, a means is then needed to integrate the multiple and varied specialized activities.[2] In respect to the various forms of departmentation, for example, there is a need to make sure that units and individuals work together when their major focus of activities is on a particular function, product, service, client, or territory. In essence, organizations ask managers and employees to concentrate their efforts and still work in harmony to reach the goals specified by management. In Chapter 1 we identified this challenge as a question of synergy.

Merely specifying the goals of the organization does not provide adequate guidance for most managers and employees. Executives must specifically link the efforts of individuals and groups to the organization's purpose. It must be able to tell employees what is expected from them, how they can contribute, and how well they are contributing to the organization. In the terms used in Chapter 1, the organization must make the means–end chains clear.

> Means-end chains and synergy are terms first introduced in Chapter 1. They are fundamental to your appreciation of organizations and for understanding important organizational dynamics. Remember the definitions:
>
> *Means-end chains.* Link the work efforts of individuals and groups to an organization's purpose.
> *Synergy.* The creation of a whole that is greater than the sum of its parts.

Organizations use a wide variety of techniques to generate synergy and clarify the desired means–end chains. First let us examine rules, procedures, and policies as three key mechanisms for achieving these results. Then we will turn to a discussion of formalization and standardization, centralization and decentralization, and coordination and control. Finally, the pressures stemming from environment, size, and technology are noted as we further examine an open-systems perspective on organizations.

RULES, PROCEDURES, AND POLICIES

While it is possible for managers to communicate verbally how synergy is to be achieved and how means and ends are linked, most organizations of any size also rely on rules, procedures, and policies.[3] They may be used to help specify the goals of a worker, indicate the best method for performing a task, show which aspects of a task are the most important, and outline how an individual will be rewarded.

Usually we think of a policy as a guideline for action that outlines important objectives and broadly indicates how an activity is to be performed. A policy allows for individual discretion and minor adjustments without direct clearance by a higher level manager. Rules and procedures, on the other hand, are more specific, rigid and impersonal. They typically describe in detail how a task or series of tasks are to be performed. They are designed to apply to all under specified conditions.

Rules, procedures, and policies are employed because they are often effective substitutes for direct managerial supervision. By carefully written rules and procedures the organization can specifically direct the activities of individual workers. It can ensure virtually identical treatment across distant locations. For example, a McDonald's hamburger and fries tastes much the same whether purchased in Hong Kong, Indianapolis, London, or New York simply because the ingredients as well as the cooking methods follow written rules and procedures.

Rules, procedures, and policies also allow organizations to practice "management by exception." Managers need not concentrate on the routine activities or decisions. They can spend their time on more important, unusual, and unique conditions that may have a more direct impact on performance and/or satisfaction. Remember

Rules, procedures, and policies $\xrightarrow[\text{seem}]{\text{may}}$ impersonal and inflexible $\xrightarrow{\text{but}}$ they free the manager for other choices

FORMALIZATION AND STANDARDIZATION

As policies work their way down the organization they are often seen as rules or procedures. This is to be expected since the zone of discretion is also reduced as one moves down the hierarchy. From the perspective of lower-level managers and workers, the use of rules, procedures, and policies may be seen in terms of the formalization and standardization of their work environment.

Formalization refers to the written documentation of rules, procedures, and policies to guide behavior and decision making. Beyond substituting for direct management supervision, formalization is often used to simplify jobs. With written instructions individuals with less training and education may be able to perform comparatively sophisticated tasks. Written procedures may also be available to ensure that a proper sequence of tasks is executed even if it is only performed occasionally. For example, operators in many nuclear power plants only have high school educations. They are instructed to follow elaborate written procedures to cope with unexpected problems in plant operations. The written procedures have also been used as a basis for simulations so that operators can experience rarely occurring plant problems. Operators who violate written procedures are subject to severe penalties to make sure that they follow what experts think should be done.

Most organizations have developed additional methods for dealing with recurring problems or situations. **Standardization** is the degree to which the range of allowable actions in a job or series of jobs is limited. It involves the creation of guidelines so that similar work activities are repeatedly performed in a similar fashion. Such standardized methods may come from years of experience in dealing with typical situations. Or they may come from outside training. For instance, managers may be trained to handle crises by setting priorities and dealing with them at all costs. Obviously, such situations call for judgment and cannot be handled by written rules—no written rules could anticipate every possible crisis. The amount of standardization that individuals experience can vary. The greater the standardization, the narrower the range of individual discretion. The less the standardization, the more discretion an individual has to decide how to perform a job.

CENTRALIZATION AND DECENTRALIZATION

So far we have discussed rules, procedures, policies, formalization, and standardization as ways in which the organization can generate synergy and link the work efforts of individuals and units to goals. These methods minimize discretion and often eliminate choice in the attempt to integrate and focus work efforts. Organizations do run on routine, but they also face unusual situations that call for responsive decisions. While neither workers nor professionals are expected to question organizational goals or means–end linkages, managers may be given limited discretion in these areas.

The farther up the hierarchy of authority the discretion to spend money, hire people, and make similar decisions is moved, the greater the degree of **centralization.** The more such decisions are delegated, or moved down the hierarchy of authority, the greaater the degree of **decentralization.** Generally speaking, greater decentralization provides higher subordinate satisfaction and a quicker response to problems. Decentralization also assists in the on-the-job training of subordinates for higher-level positions. Centralization is most often linked to consistency in decision making, short-term cost savings, and the need for greater control.

Closely related to decentralization is the notion of participation. Many people want to be involved in decisions affecting their work. Participation results when a manager delegates some authority for such decision making to subordinates. As we have discussed elsewhere, employees may want a say in both what the unit objectives should be as well as how they may be achieved. Especially in recent years and with the challenge from the Japanese forms of participation, many firms are experimenting with new ways to decentralize parts of their operations. Newsline 11.1 shows one example. Others are found in Chapter 9 where we talked about creative work-group designs.

COORDINATION AND CONTROL

Rules, procedures, and policies provide a framework for synergy and for linking units and individuals to organizational goals. While formalization and standardization translates this framework to workers and professionals, both are generally too inflexible to cope with changing circumstances. Further, neither provide for an exchange among employees, supervisors, managers, and executives. Thus, managers are expected to employ a wide variety of supplemental mechanisms to promote change and interaction. We group these into coordination and control categories.

Coordination

Coordination is the set of mechanisms that an organization uses to link the actions of its units into a consistent pattern. Much of the coordination within a unit is handled by its manager. Smaller organizations may rely on their management hierarchy to provide the necessary consistency. But as the organization grows, managers become overloaded. The organization then needs to develop more efficient and effective ways of linking work units to one another.

A mix of personal and impersonal methods of coordination are used in organizations. Some of these methods are quite obvious; some are not. They are summarized in Table 11.1. As you review the table, remember that coordination is a dynamic and

NEWSLINE 11.1 / INTRAPRENEURSHIP

In an attempt to recapture the dedication, creativity, and effort associated with entrepreneurships, some firms are experimenting with intrapreneurship (or internal entrepreneurship). In one variation the employees remain on the company payroll, but at a reduced salary. They are put in charge of identifiable activities (e.g., secretarial pools, computer programming) and are allowed to reap the full benefits of their creative efforts. If they can save money or provide new products, they share in the profits. Often such teams may be given a small start-up budget, but rarely are they asked to follow all the corporate bureaucracy. They run the business on their own. In another version, employees still keep their normal salaries but may concentrate on particular product developments. One firm uses this to keep creative programmers. Again, the team shares in the profits. It may be disbanded if success is not forthcoming. In both cases, the larger organization shares some of the risks and benefits from the experiment. Reports from participants hail the new creativity, effort, and cost savings from this new brand of capitalists.

Reported in *The Seattle Times*.

TABLE 11.1 Personal and Impersonal Methods of Coordination

Personal Methods

Common values. These are built into management through selection, socialization, training, and reinforcement. Examples are a company dress code or business philosophy.

Grapevine/informal communications. Although fast, these are often inaccurate and need to be supplemented with more formal means.

Committees. Committees allow for participation and mutual adjustment across units, are good for communicating complex, qualitative information, and are especially useful between two managers whose units must work together.

Task forces. Task forces bring individuals from different parts of the organization together to identify and solve problems cutting across departments.

Impersonal Methods

Written rules, policies, and procedures. These include schedules, budgets, and plans.

Specialized staff units. These units are often used to coordinate functions where there is divisional departmentation. An example is a personnel staff unit to ensure policy consistency across divisional units. In a matrix structure, the staff coordinating function often develops into a line decision center.

Management information systems. Originally, this included such things as suggestion systems, newsletters, and so on. Now it often refers to computerized information and record-keeping systems. These systems are particularly useful where timing of efforts is important.

continual process. The astute manager uses a mix of techniques to gain the synergy needed to accomplish assigned objectives.

Personal methods of coordination include common values, the grapevine, and committees. The key to making these techniques work to produce synergy lies in promoting dialogue and discussion among employees, managers, and executives. These personal methods allow the organization to address the particular needs of distinct units and individuals. They are often preferred in situations where individuals from different departments must act as a team by adjusting their activities to each other. In contrast, impersonal methods are mere extensions and refinements of formalization and standardization. In some cases, there are few provisions for dialogue and discussion among workers and managers. With some techniques, such as specialized staff units, the organization can promote dialogue and discussion. In general, however, organizations relying on impersonal methods become more bureaucratic and inflexible.

Control

Whereas coordination is concerned with linking together the actions of people and units throughout an organization, **control** is the set of mechanisms used to keep action and outputs within predetermined limits. Control deals with setting standards, measuring results versus standards, and instituting corrective action. As with coordination, much of the control within a unit is the responsibility of the manager. But organizations typically use a variety of impersonal control mechanisms as well.

The most popular control technique is probably the planning–budgeting process. Corporations often develop five-year rolling plans where the latest year is used to develop a detailed budget. Businesses may also employ management by objectives (MBO) (discussed earlier in Chapter 6) to ensure that managers set specific measurable goals, monitor progress toward these goals, and receive rewards based on their accomplishments. MBO is an example of output controls. Output controls focus on desired targets and allow managers to use their own methods for reacting to defined targets.[4] Organizations relying primarily on output controls can remain open to change and promote dialogue and discussion concerning how to take corrective action.

Organizations may also institute a number of process controls. Process controls attempt to specify the manner in which tasks will be performed. Process controls and procedures may be virtually identical. Where managers see attempts to gain uniform results, employees see excessive formalization and standardization. For instance, in one case we know that mail sorters were advised by the postal service to hold letters in their left hands at a 45-degree angle and sort mail with their right hands. With the aid of a prominent senator, the post office recanted and allowed employees to use either hand. Organizations relying heavily on process controls can quickly become inflexible. Process control can breed mindlessness where employees continually perform tasks without thinking. While such mindlessness may promote the efficient completion of routine tasks, it cuts the ability of the organization to detect and respond to change. Rarely is such ''process control'' applied in middle and upper management ranks.

Effective controls bring a number of potential benefits to organizations. These include providing attainable standards, accurate measurement of performance, and a means of allocating rewards or sanctions based on performance and the discretion to institute corrective action. Efforts to exert control in organizations can also yield unfortunate side effects.[5] Some of these possible problems are summarized in Table 11.2.

Organizations can have difficulty developing effective control systems. In some it may be virtually impossible to measure an individual's or unit's actual contribution. In others, institutional conditions such as union contracts may limit the use of rewards and sanctions. Thus, control in many organizations boils down to a mixture of methods and may be accompanied by negative side-effects.

You should now start to see two patterns emerging from the use of various coordination and control mechanisms. One pattern reinforces the natural tendency of organizations to use detailed rules, policies, and procedures. Organizations may emphasize the framework for synergy and linking units and individuals to organizational goals provided by the bureaucratic twins of formalization and standardization. In essence, managers direct coordination and control at individuals and units through impersonal coordination methods and process controls. In a second pattern, managers seek to involve employees by seeking dialogue and discussion. This second pattern promotes flexibility, innovation, and responsiveness to change. Here personal coordination methods and output controls are emphasized. However, before you opt for the second pattern, remember that it comes at a substantial cost. It calls for considerably more managerial time and may not ensure consistent treatment across the organization.

TABLE 11.2   Some Side Effects of Organizational Controls

Imbalance.   Concentrating on one goal neglects others. For example, rewards based on volume may lower quality. In emphasizing short-term efficiency, equipment maintenance, human resource maintenance, and research and development may be minimized.

Lack of patience.   Managers attempt a "quick fix," and when that does not work, they try one short-term fix after another without allowing time for any to be successful.

Across-the-board cuts.   Common in public institutions as politically acceptable, they don't focus on specific areas where cuts are needed most. The organization loses growth opportunities and may not reduce unnecessary expenditures.

Confusing documentation with action.   Concern for performance may lead to a stack of impressive-sounding plans but no results.

Vague and unrealistic expectations.   Chapter 6 indicated the problems of "do your best goals" in comparison with more specific ones. Also, goals asking for more than a 20 percent improvement are likely to lead to diminishing returns.

Panic.   This often ensues when controls are suddenly established over a unit. Communication accompanied by participation helps avoid panic.

Standard increasing.   Higher standards are set without increasing resources, changing methods, or giving better rewards. This often creates personnel problems.

In Chapter 12 we will return to these two patterns and discuss the conditions that might favor one over the other. Now it is important to present the factors that should be considered in favoring one pattern over another. To do so we move to an open systems view of organizations.

ORGANIZATIONS AS OPEN SYSTEMS

In the late 1950s and early 1960s, the more traditional views of management and organization such as the ''scientific management,'' ''management principles,'' and ''human relations'' schools (see supplementary Module A) were challenged by a new group of scholars. The new developments resulted in a number of innovative, insightful investigations using an open-systems view of organizations.[6]

In Chapter 1 we characterized the organization as an open system that transforms resource inputs into product outputs and human resource maintenance. One such view of a typical organization is shown in Figure 11.1. Note that the external environment is important both as a source of resource inputs and as a consumer of outputs.

When theorists recognized this interdependency between the organization and its environment, they introduced a dynamic element into our thinking about organizations. Managerial success became predicated on an ability to structure organizations in a manner best fitting a variety of environmental factors, as well as fitting the requirements of their size and production or service technologies.

Among the many different roots for this revolution in organizational theory, the work of Burns and Stalker is important.[7] They investigated 20 manufacturing firms in England and Scotland and concluded that two quite different organizational forms could be successful. A more traditional bureaucratic form thrived where the environment was stable and the firm was using a well-understood production technology.

FIGURE 11.1 An organization as an open system.

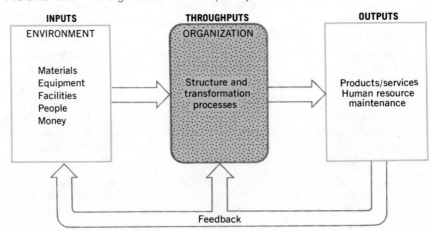

Where the environment and technology were rapidly changing, however, the vertical command structure of the more traditional bureaucratic form suffered difficulties. Here successful organizations stressed horizontal relations and managerial discretion.

Later studies in the United States and elsewhere seemed to confirm the general notions of Burns and Stalker, and the term "contingency" became part of the OB literature. That is, we now recognize that different problems and opportunities call for different organizational structures. There are many ways to run an organization, not just one. Indeed, for an organization to survive and be successful it must continuously adapt to its environment, modify its methods of production, and develop a structure that meets the opportunities and problems at hand.

While an open-systems view of an organization now appears obvious, it created a radical departure from the ways in which scholars traditionally looked at the attributes of organizations. We can summarize this revolution in two respects. First, we can examine the environment as a contingency variable; second, we can examine the context for action: that is, technology and size, in similar terms.

THE ENVIRONMENT OF ORGANIZATIONS

As open systems, organizations must obtain resources from and exchange their outputs with their external environments. *Fortune, Business Week, The Wall Street Journal,* and other popular sources of business information often place a heavy emphasis on the important role of managers in generating organizational success. Skillful, hardworking, insightful, and intelligent individuals spot an opportunity, develop an appropriate response, and reap fame, fortune, and publicity.

Recently a small group of scholars have challenged this managerial-driven theory of business success and started to seriously investigate the importance of nonmanagerial factors.[8] Chief among these is the character of the economic and institutional environment at the founding of an industry. For instance, where conditions are turbulent (with extremely high rates of technological and economic change) very specialized firms that bet correctly will outperform more generalized ones attempting to constantly adapt. Of course, the death rate of new specialized firms will be high. And survivors may be hailed as insightful managers rather than lucky guessers.

This line of research also suggests that there are periods and locations of what the popular press might call "entrepreneurial energy." Specific locations where resources are rich and existing organizations provide a training ground for potential entrepreneurs are more likely to spawn new businesses. At the turn of the century, Detroit was such a location for auto firms; in the 1970s, Silicon Valley was an incubator for the electronics industry.

The famous economist Adam Smith proposed that an invisible hand guided the competitive market to ensure efficiency. Now we are beginning to see that a host of external factors may form an invisible hand in promoting the development and survival of businesses. We think a detailed analysis of the general and specific aspects of the external environment is useful.

The General Environment

Organizations conduct most of their business within one common geographic area. This area bounds the general environment.[9] The cultural values, economic, legal–political, and educational conditions within a region comprise the general environment for organizations in that area. These conditions have a profound and often unseen effect on the internal operations and performance of organizations.

Cultural Values

The most subtle aspects of the general environment emanate from cultural values. As pointed out in Chapter 3, values tell us what actions are important, right, and proper as well as what are considered desirable. Cultural values change slowly and often come in contradictory pairs. Table 11.3 outlines some dominant and contradictory American values.

In the United States we prize individualism, initiative, democracy, the family, among other values. But we recognize that these ideals cannot always be guides for action. Organizations, as a result, have relied upon contradictory values, including collectivism, leadership, authoritarianism, and economic achievement.

Economic Conditions

While cultural values are important, organizations rely upon an economic surplus to thrive and prosper. With larger surpluses, more organizations get the resources they need to grow and develop. At the same time, economic growth means that more people have the money to buy products and services. As the economy grows, organizations not only become larger, but also more specialized.

TABLE 11.3   Selected Dominant and Contradictory American Values

Dominant Value	Contradictory Value
Individualism. The cornerstone of American greatness.	*Collectivism.* People should stand together and work for common purposes.
Initiative. People can be trusted if left alone to guide their conduct wisely.	*Leadership.* You cannot sit and wait for people to make up their minds.
Democracy. The ultimate form of living together.	*Authoritarianism.* Nothing would get done if left to a popular vote.
Goal attainment. Everyone should attempt to be successful.	*Method.* What kind of person you are is more important than success.
Family orientation. The family is the basic institution of the society.	*Economic orientation.* National welfare depends on economic organizations.
Equality of opportunity. America is the land of opportunity and all people should get a fair chance.	*Unequal opportunity.* Not everybody is equal and the best should be put in charge.

Source: Developed from R. Lynd, *Knowledge for What? The Place of Science in American Culture* (Princeton, N.J.: Princeton University Press, 1939).

Comparatively small changes in the pattern of economic growth can have a dramatic impact on financial performance of even the largest firms. For instance, in 1980, the American economy was sluggish with exceptionally high interest rates. For the first time since 1921, General Motors lost money, as did Ford and Chrysler. But, despite the huge losses in the auto industry, the U.S. economy did not collapse. By 1984 auto industry executives were cautiously optimistic, and the U.S. economy was on the rebound. By 1987 the recovery was continuing. Ford was prosperous and Chrysler had posted a third year of profits. GM, however, was not doing as well.

Economic development encourages both more specialized organizations and a wider range of products and services. Firms may be more dependent on one another, but the economy as a whole is less dependent upon one or a few major products and services.

Educational Conditions

While economic conditions may have dramatic effects on the short-term financial health of firms, organizations also need educated individuals for survival. In more developed nations, economic and educational development move hand in hand. A larger proportion of white-collar professionals reflects a more favorable climate for organizations since more complex organizations need the specialized skills provided by more educated employees. Furthermore, few organizations can afford to train individuals fully for today's complex business operations. They rely on colleges and universities to provide a pool of skilled professionals.

Historically, business analysts have downplayed the importance of educational conditions. The keys to success were most often tied to cheap abundant labor. Now analysts are recognizing that our nation as well as Japan and most of western Europe is in the post-industrial age where services provide more jobs than manufacturing. Organizations need a highly educated workforce. For example, Silicon Valley in California and Route 128 near Boston are new high-technology centers in part because they draw from prominent universities nearby.

Legal–Political Conditions

The fourth leg of the organization's general environment is the legal–political system. It allocates power among various groups in the society by developing, administering, and enforcing laws. For analyzing the general environment of organizations, three issues are particularly important. One issue concerns the range of government activity. A second deals with the capacity of the legal–political system to perform its functions. A third issue centers on stability.

There is considerable variation in the scope of government activity across nations. At one extreme sit governments that confine their activities strictly to protecting the nation from internal and external threats and establishing a few rules or laws to limit the actions of individuals and organizations. At the other extreme are governments that attempt to permeate virtually all aspects of society. The broader the domain of government, the less attractive the general environment becomes to nongovernment organizations because their freedom of action is too constrained.

Just as organizations benefit from economic success, a developed legal–political system can provide important services. As legal entities, organizations enjoy protection under the law. A government that facilitates a balanced, rational allocation of power backed by legislation with efficient administration and enforcement provides an invaluable service to organizations. For instance, U.S. corporations benefit directly from federal economic forecasts, a national banking system, and international economic treaties.

Stability in the legal–political system is also critical. Stability can reinforce a narrow scope of governmental action backed by the capacity to provide legal–political services. Constant changes in laws and their interpretations seriously undermine the efforts of organizations to provide goods and services. Organizations need to know the rules of the game and be assured they will not change dramatically.

Implications

Table 11.4 summarizes key attributes of the general environment of organizations and shows the preferred conditions for each attribute.

The Specific Environment

Organizations position themselves within one or a series of organizational networks. They buy materials, hire workers, and secure financial backing from one another. They sell their products and services under the influence of competitors and government agencies. The set of suppliers, distributors, government agencies, and competitors with which an organization must interact to grow and survive constitutes its **specific environment.**[10] Figure 11.2 highlights the distinction and linkage between the general and specific aspects of organizational environments.

An organization may have little choice about its general environment, but it can have substantial choice over its specific environment. By selecting the type of business it pursues, an organization really makes a broad choice of a specific environment. Within its industry, the organization also has some choices regarding suppliers and distributors. It has less immediate choices concerning labor unions, regulatory agencies, and competitors. Nonetheless, how the organization links itself to other organizations is partially under the discretion of top management.

TABLE 11.4 The General Environment of Organizations		
Dimension	Importance	Most Desirable Condition
Cultural values	Basis for acceptance and evaluation	Acceptance of contradictory values
Economic conditions	Source of resources for growth, survival	Rich economy with stable growth and a broad range of economic activity
Educational conditions	Source of skilled workers	Balance of white- and blue-collar workers with skills
Legal–political conditions	Provide rules of the game and the privilege to exist	A limited range of governmental activity; minimum changes in laws and regulations

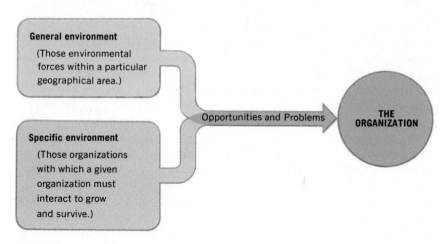

FIGURE 11.2 The general and specific environments of organizations.

Environmental Complexity

A basic question in analyzing the environment of an organization is its complexity. This is especially true of the specific environment. As the specific environment becomes more complex, it provides an organization with more opportunities and more problems. **Environmental complexity** is a measure of the magnitude of the problems and opportunities in the organization's environment as evidenced by the degree of richness, interdependence, and uncertainty.

Richness

The specific environment is richer and more developed when the firm's suppliers, distributors, competitors, and regulators are growing in numbers and resources. In a specific environment that is rich, organizations invest in each other for the future and thus help the industry grow. The opposite cycle occurs in a declining specific environment.

The richness or leanness of the environment is under only the partial control of the organization. A business firm is often driven by general economic conditions. For government agencies, the overall growth of the legal–political system appears to be a driving factor; and so it goes for educational and cultural organizations. The overall richness of the specific environment is heavily influenced by conditions in the general environment. However, each organization has some choice. It may select a richer or leaner set of specific environment organizations than the ones chosen by competitors.

Interdependence

While richness is important, equally critical is the nature and type of interdependence established by an organization with environmental elements. The critical questions become—Who does the organization need? Who has the upper hand?

Exchanges between organizations typically yield benefits to each party. But the terms of trade may favor one organization more than another. Each organization would prefer to deal with outsiders that are isolated from one another and over which it has some control. In reality, the degree of control varies. An organization may have the upper hand with distributors, be on even terms with suppliers, and play a less powerful role with financial institutions and government regulatory agencies.

Uncertainty

James D. Thompson was one of the first writers in organizational analysis to stress the importance of uncertainty.[11] He argued that organizations would avoid uncertainty if possible and that managing such uncertainty was one of the most critical tasks facing an organization. Larger organizations with rigid internal operations were considered particularly vulnerable to environmental uncertainties and external change. Investments could become outmoded, internal operations might no longer work properly, and the organization would lose the ability to direct itself.

Particularly important is the combined effect of higher interdependence and uncertainty. When most of the outsiders are changing dramatically, the environment becomes turbulent.[12] The organization can lose control or become a tool of outside interests. It can become internally frozen by constantly changing directives. Most larger organizations spend considerable resources on forecasting and planning to minimize external uncertainty. They want to anticipate changes and prepare appropriate responses.

Implications

In summary, managers need to be able to identify, understand, and relate successfully to the important elements in an organization's environment. In addition, they must recognize that

1. The greater the richness, interdependence, and uncertainty in these elements, the greater the environmental complexity.
2. The greater the environmental complexity, the more problems and opportunities the organization has to deal with and the greater the demand for a responsive organizational structure.

Chapter 12 will explain more precisely how organization structures should vary in response to environmental complexity.

TECHNOLOGY AND SIZE

In addition to the external environment, a manager must be prepared to cope with the demands and opportunities identified with size and technology. As with the environment, alterations in size and technology may call for adjustments in patterns of specialization, control, or coordination. However, within the research on size and technology, there exists a continuing controversy.

A number of scholars argue that the size of an organization is the single most important factor influencing its structure. As size increases, the organization's structure is predicted to become more complicated.[13] On the other hand, a second group argues that there is a **technological imperative.** That is, successful organizations are felt to arrange their internal structures to meet the dictates of their dominant technologies or work flows.[14] Some of the major issues in this debate are explained in the paragraphs that follow.

Technology

Technology is the combination of resources, knowledge, and techniques that creates a product or service output for an organization. The term is used in various ways in the OB literature. Thus, it will help you to become acquainted with two of the more common classification schemes used by theorists and managers to describe the technologies of organizations.

Thompson's View of Technology

James D. Thompson classifies technologies as intensive, mediating, or long-linked.[15] In the intensive technology there is uncertainty as to how to produce desired outcomes. A group of specialists must be brought together to use a variety of techniques to solve problems. There is high interdependence among the members of such teams. Examples might be found in a hospital emergency room or a research and development laboratory. Standard operating procedures are difficult to develop for this technology, and coordination is achieved by mutual adjustment among those trying to solve the problem.

The mediating technology links parties desirous of becoming interdependent. Banks, for example, link creditors and depositors, and store money and information to facilitate such exchanges. While all depositors and creditors are interdependent, the reliance is pooled through the bank. Thus, if one creditor defaults on a loan, no one depositor is injured. Wholesalers, retailers, and insurance companies are other organizations that use a mediating technology.

The long-linked technology is also called mass production or industrial technology.[16] Because it is known how to produce the desired outcomes, the task is broken down into a number of sequential and interdependent steps. A classic example is the automobile assembly line. Traditionally long-linked technology has been relatively inflexible and a high output volume was required to justify its use. Now we are entering an era of flexible manufacturing where mass production can be automated while the organization still maintains some flexibility for the future. Newsline 11.2 shows one example.

Woodward's View of Technology

Joan Woodward divides technology into three categories: small-batch, mass production, and continuous-process manufacturing.[17] These are illustrated in Figure 11.3. In small-batch production, a variety of custom products are tailor made to fit customer specifications. The machinery and equipment used are generally not very elaborate,

NEWSLINE 11.2 / THE TEXAS TWIST—A NO HANDS ASSEMBLY LINE FOR IBM

The robotic arm quickly moves to a pair of 2 by 4 inch memory boards where a camera examines the case to identify precisely where the memory boards will be located. Within a instant the robot twists the memory boards into position, snaps them into place, and moves the partially assembled component on to the next stage. From parts to the shipping box, IBM's new convertible computer is assembled completely by robots in its new Austin, Texas facility.

The automated assembly line can produce a variety of products from computers to printers to toasters merely by reprogramming the robots and altering the assembly stages. Thus, as new products emerge the line need only be modified, not junked. Of course, the product itself had to be carefully designed to be robot assembled; but the savings are enormous. For its new convertible computer, IBM estimates that it will cut production costs in half over more traditional assembly-line operations.

In many other areas of assembly robots may replace workers. The key is developing flexible robots that can perform a variety of functions. As new models and advances occur, existing facilities can be used to beat the competition to the market.

Reported in *Fortune*.

---

but considerable craftsmanship is often needed. In mass production the organization produces one or a few products with an assembly-line type of system. The work of one group is highly dependent on another, and the equipment is typically sophisticated and accompanied by very detailed instructions for workers. Mass production is similar to Thompson's long-linked technology. Organizations, using continuous-process technology produce a few products with considerable automation. Classic examples are automated chemical plants and oil refineries.

The Technological Imperative

From her studies, Woodward concluded that the combination of structure and technology was critical in the success of the organizations. When technology and organizational design were properly matched, a firm was more successful. Specifically, successful small-batch and continuous-process plants had flexible structures with small work groups at the bottom; more rigidly structured plants were less successful. Successful mass production operations, by contrast, were rigidly structured and had large work groups at the bottom. This technological imperative has since been supported by some investigations.[18]

More recent work on the role of technology in organizations has been much broader. Even though the technology may favor a particular pattern of specialization, other factors may not. The history of the firm, the attitudes of top management, and

FIGURE 11.3   Examples of Woodward's three categories of technology: *Small-batch* furniture restoration shop, *continuous process* oil refinery, and *mass production* assembly line.

a host of economic and political factors may work against organizations that attempt to follow the technological imperative.[19]

Organization Size

Several researchers challenged the notion of technological imperative. One group, the Aston researchers, found that organization size and interdependency in the environment were more important determinants of structure than is technology.[20] Another group of American sociologists, led by Peter Blau, argues that there are quite fundamental differences in the structures of small versus large organizational units.[21]

When comparing very small and very large organizations the effects of size differences are quite apparent. The larger organizations have more work to perform and, as one might expect, are structurally more complex. They generally have more levels of management with more line and staff departments and rely more on sophisticated managerial techniques. They also generally have more departments and utilize several forms of departmentation in their attempts to specialize horizontally.

However, when comparing organizations where there are comparatively minor size differences the results of prior work are not as clear. When smaller professionally managed organizations grow they do tend to become more complex structurally.[22] Such may not be the case for owner managed corporations—perhaps because owner/managers are trying to maintain complete control.

For larger organizations, growth may make it possible for a firm to have more influence over its specific environment and adopt more sophisticated technologies. But management may not use the potential for environmental influence or for adopting new technology. Further, comparatively minor differences in size among larger firms may not yield structural differences. The structural differences among larger firms that can be attributed to size alone are comparatively minor. Thus, to merely think that size alone drives the complexity of the structure is far too simplistic. There are major differences between large and small firms, but we think several factors should be examined in combination.

Both size and technology should be considered in deciding on forms of specialization, methods for control, and mechanisms for coordination. As an organization grows, it has the opportunity to increase the number and types of specialists it uses. It may substitute rules, policies, and procedures for some managers and reserve judgmental roles for only very specialized managers. Growth does cause control problems. Managers must learn to administer the system without being able to observe all activity directly. Some control problems can be eliminated by grouping units in special ways, by using sophisticated information systems, or by using administrative assignments creatively. We believe that successful organizations do change their structures as they grow to adapt to changing conditions. But there are many different ways in which they may adjust, and much of the adjustment is guided by top management.

SUMMARY

In this chapter we have introduced a number of important organizational dynamics. We started by noting that the pattern of specialization adopted by the organization calls for efforts to integrate. We noted that organizations use rules, procedures, and policies to set the stage for synergy and to link individuals and units to organizational goals. From the perspective of most employees and supervisors these rules, policies, and procedures are limits. With formalization the organization uses written directives to guide individuals. But the range of individual action may be limited in other ways such as through standardizing actions or approaches to problems. Formalization and standardization are impersonal but they do provide managers with the option to concentrate on less routine matters.

Another important organizational dynamic is centralization/decentralization of decision making. Here we noted that a number of firms are experimenting with ways to decentralize while keeping some of the benefits of centralization.

We suggested that for organizations to link units and individuals together more effectively and link their activities to organizational goals managers used coordination and control. Both coordination and control are ongoing processes. We looked at a number of personal and impersonal coordination mechanisms for meshing activities together. In the discussion of control we emphasize the use of output controls and process controls.

The open-systems perspective focuses attention beyond the internal working of the organization and asks the manager to analyze environment, size, and technology as important contingency variables. The external environment of the organization is divided into two major segments—the general environment and the specific environment. The general environment contains the cultural, economic, educational, and legal–political forces common to all organizations that operate within a given geographical area. The specific environment is unique to a particular organization and includes the other organizations with which it must interact. As an organization's environment becomes more complex, structural adaptations are required to ensure continued success.

Technology and size constitute an organization's context for managerial action. While scholars quibble over which is more important, managers must consider the impact of both on structure and outcomes. Figuratively speaking,

As context and environment $\xrightarrow[\text{complex}]{\text{become}}$ organization structures must adapt $\xrightarrow[\text{ensure}]{\text{to}}$ task performance and human resource maintenance

THINKING THROUGH THE ISSUES

1. Define coordination and control from a managerial perspective. Why must both be achieved in organizations?
2. Explain the difference between centralized and decentralized decision making. What advantages and disadvantages may surround decentralization (a) from a top manager's perspective and (b) from a lower-level manager's perspective?
3. Explain the concepts of standardization and formalization. What functions do they serve in organizations?
4. If forces in the general environment are common to all organizations in a given geographical area, why should a manager even consider them?
5. Identify those units that you think would be considered important parts of the specific environment by the president of a company in your area. See if you can assess the complexity of this environment.
6. Choose an organization with which you are familiar. Describe it as an open system. Describe in particular how interactions with the environment influence the organization and place special demands on its managers.
7. Select one of the new technologies described in the chapter opener. Describe in detail the technology. Classify the technology in Woodward's terms and in Thompson's terms. Which seems more useful and why?

CASE: EAGLE AIRLINES II

Turn to the Eagle Airlines case at the end of Chapter 12. Then answer the following questions.

Questions
1. Discuss the control and coordination methods used in Eagle Airlines.

2. Discuss centralization of decision-making authority and formalization as they apply to the case.

3. Making any necessary assumptions (and clearly identifying them), describe Eagle Airline's general and specific environments. Try to arrive at an overall assessment of complexity for each of these environmental components.

4. Discuss the technology in Dodd's and Edward's units in Thompson's terms and in Woodward's terms.

EXERCISE: ORGANIZATIONAL ANALYSIS—PART II

Purpose:
To apply, as clearly and thoroughly as possible, the concepts developed in Chapter 11 to the organization your group selected for Part I of this exercise in Chapter 10. This will give you and your group a chance to apply the concepts and share your findings with those of your classmates.

Time:
50 minutes or more in class, plus at-home preparation.

Procedure:
1. Do the following before coming to class:
   a. Form the same group used for Part I of this exercise. Assume that the group is a management consulting team required to prepare a written report following the format indicated by your boss (the instructor).
   b. Use the same organization your group selected for Part I of this exercise.
   c. Using observations, interviews, and company records as necessary, your group has been assigned to do the following for its organizational report:
      (1) Discuss the types of coordination used by different key managers.
      (2) Discuss the controls used at each level and in each department.
      (3) Specify the size of the organization and its major subunits.
      (4) Discuss the organization's dominant technology in terms of one of the categorization schemes used in this book.
      (5) Define and justify the boundaries for the organization's general environment. Briefly assess the complexity of the general environment and justify your assessment. Discuss cultural values and the impact they seem to have.
      (6) Briefly assess the complexity of the organization's specific environment and defend your assessment.
      (7) Go back to the report your group prepared in Part I. Discuss to what extent this organization seems to have adapted its formal structure to environment, size and/or technology. Do you see an environmental size, or technological imperative operating? Why or why not?
2. Be prepared to turn in this part of the group report to your instructor and to discuss the group's findings and their implications.

THE MANAGER'S VOCABULARY

Centralization   The degree to which the authority to make decisions is restricted to higher levels of management.

Control   The set of mechanisms used in an organization to keep actions and outputs within predetermined limits.

Coordination   The set of mechanisms used in an organization to link the actions of its subunits into a consistent pattern.

Decentralization   The degree to which authority to make decisions is given to lower levels in an organization's hierarchy.

Environmental Complexity   The magnitude of the problems and opportunities in the organization's environment as evidenced by the degree of richness, interdependence, and uncertainty.

Formalization   The written documentation of work rules, policies, and procedures.

General Environment   The set of cultural, economic, educational, and legal–political forces common to organizations operating within a given geographical area.

Specific Environment   The set of suppliers, distributors, competitors, and government agencies with which a particular organization must interact to grow and survive.

Standardization   The degree to which the range of actions in a job or series of jobs is limited.

Technology   The combination of resources, knowledge, and techniques that creates a product or service output for an organization.

Technological Imperative   The idea that if an organization does not adjust its internal structure to the requirements of the technology it will not be successful.

IMPORTANT NAMES

T. Burns and G. Stalker   Contingency theorists who argued that the structure of the organization should match its environment and technology.

James D. Thompson   Founder of an integrated theory of how and why organizations fear and respond to uncertainty; Thompson developed a framework for classifying technology.

Joan Woodward   Identified the technological imperative and developed a framework for classifying technology.

NOTES

[1]See Gene Bylinski, "The High Tech Race, Who's Ahead," *Fortune,* October 13, 1986, pp. 26–38 and Richard Osborn and Chris Baughn, "New Patterns in the Formation of U.S./Japanese Cooperative Ventures: The Role of Technology," *Columbia Journal of World Business,* in press.

[2]Paul Lawrence and Jay Lorsch, *Organization and Environment: Managing Differentiation and Integration*

(Homewood, Ill.: Richard D. Irwin, 1969).

[3]This section based on Richard Osborn, James G. Hunt, and Lawrence Jauch, *Organization Theory: Integrated Text and Cases* (Melbourne, Fla.: Krieger, 1984), pp. 125–215.

[4]William G. Ouchi and M. A. Maguire, "Organization Control: Two Functions," *Administrative Science Quarterly,* Vol. 20 (1977), pp. 559–569.

[5]Arlyn J. Melcher, *Structure and Process of Organizations: A Systems Approach* (Englewood Cliffs, NJ: Prentice-Hall, 1976), pp. 219–223, 252.

[6]For details, see Arthur Bedeian, *Organization: Theory and Analysis,* 2nd ed. (Hinsdale, Ill.: Dryden 1983).

[7]Tom Burns and George Stalker, *The Management of Innovation* (London: Tavistock, 1961).

[8]For a discussion of this perspective, see D. R. Wholey and J. W. Brittain, "Organization Ecology: Findings and Implications," *Academy of Management Review,* Vol. 11 (1986), pp. 513–533; and G. R. Carroll, "Organizational Ecology," *Annual Review of Sociology,* Vol. 10 (1984), pp. 71–93.

[9]This section is based on Osborn, Hunt, and Jauch, *Organization Theory* pp. 128–215.

[10]Ibid.

[11]James D. Thompson, *Organizations in Action* (New York: McGraw-Hill, 1967).

[12]For a more complete discussion, see William McKelvey, *Organizational Systematics* (Berkeley and Los Angeles: University of California Press, 1982).

[13]See Peter M. Blau and Richard A. Schoennerr, *The Structure of Organizations* (New York: Basic Books, 1971).

[14]Joan Woodward, *Industrial Organization: Theory and Practice* (London: Oxford University Press, 1965).

[15]Thompson, *Organizations in Action.*

[16]William Scott, "Organizational Structure," *Annual Review of Sociology,* (1975), pp. 1–20.

[17]Woodward, *Industrial Organization.*

[18]For a review, see Louis Fry, "Technology-Structure Research: Three Critical Issues," *Academy of Management Journal,* Vol. 25 (1982), pp. 532–552.

[19]For a comprehensive review, see L. Tornatzky, L. Eveland, M. Boylan, W. Hetzner, E. Johnson, D. Roitman, and J. Schneider, *The Process of Technological Innovation: Reviewing the Literature* (Washington, D.C.: National Science Foundation, 1983).

[20]The Aston studies include David S. Pugh, David J. Hickson, C. R. Hinings, and C. Turner, "Dimensions of Organizational Structure," *Administrative Science Quarterly,* Vol. 13 (1968), pp. 65–105; C. R. Hinings and G. L. Lee, "Dimensions of Organizational Structure and Their Context: A Replication," *Sociology,* Vol. 5 (1971), pp. 83–93; and J. Inkson, David S. Pugh, and David J. Hickson, "Organizational Context and Structure: An Abbreviated Replication," *Administrative Science Quarterly,* Vol. 15 (1970), pp. 318–329.

[21]See Blau and Schoennerr, *The Structure of Organizations;* and Peter M. Blau, C. Falbe, W. McKinley, and P. Tracy, "Technology and Organization in Manufacturing," *Administrative Science Quarterly,* Vol. 21 (1976), pp. 26–30.

[22]See Guy Geeraerts, "The Effects of Ownership on the Organization Structure in Small Firms," *Administrative Science Quarterly,* Vol. 29 (1984), pp. 903–912.

CHAPTER 12
ORGANIZATIONAL DESIGN

3M is trying to ensure that it doesn't have more layers of management than necessary to do the job and that managers' work is focused on their units' essential task.

3M Annual Report

WANTED: AN APPROPRIATE ORGANIZATION STRUCTURE!

Do you remember the Middle States Manufacturing Company case that introduced Part Four? As we left him, the president, Jaccob Jaccober, was concerned with how to redesign the structure of the firm to meet the new challenges facing the organization. He wanted a structure that was not necessarily efficient, but that would facilitate profitable growth while maintaining the firm's tradition of technical leadership at or above competitive levels.

Jaccob was feeling pressure. On the one hand, he was being counseled to reduce specialized orders and to provide longer production runs. On the other hand, it was argued that a standardized product line would hurt the company's image. There was also pressure for a tighter and more formalized budgeting and control process.

Business from three key customers accounted for 50 percent of Middle States' total sales and 75 percent of gross profits. Profab, an extremely important product, had just been developed. It used a slightly different production process than the current products and required lots of hand-crafting from a few highly skilled people. Longer production runs with a more flexible design could cut costs by 30 percent. A second shift would also be feasible. Two million dollars would be available over the next six months to market Profab.

In the midst of all this, Jaccob wondered about a number of issues relating to the redesign of the company. Specifically on his mind were

- his goals for the firm.
- the environment of the firm and industry.
- the firm's growth.
- the new technology involved in Profab.

And, he was still intrigued with the neat and orderly grid of city streets. Should the firm have a structure just as neat and orderly, or should it retain a more flexible form?

Management Applications Questions

What would you do if you were in Jaccob's shoes? What kind of structure would you design to best meet the needs of the Middle States manufacturing firm?

PLANNING AHEAD

After reading and participating in the learning
experiences offered in this chapter, you will be familiar
with the following topics

Mechanistic and Organic Organizations
A Manager's View of Organizational Design
Strategic Factors in Organizational Design
Mechanistic Designs
Organic Designs
Diverse Designs

In Chapter 10 and 11 we discussed the various attributes of organizations and then focused on organizational dynamics. We emphasized the many alternatives for accomplishing vertical and horizontal specialization, and coordination and control. It is now time to ask how managers choose among these alternatives to establish a structural configuration that best meets an organization's needs. This process of choosing and implementing a structural configuration is what we refer to as **organizational design.**

MECHANISTIC AND ORGANIC ORGANIZATIONS

Some 20 years ago, British scientists Tom Burns and G. M. Stalker introduced the notions of mechanistic and organic organizations to the field of OB.[1] The **mechanistic organizations** tend to favor what we have called vertical specialization and control. These configurations stress rules, policies and procedures; specify the techniques for decision making; and develop elaborate and well-documented control systems backed by centralized staff. In mechanistic organizations, staff units will typically be placed toward the top. This reinforces a heavy vertical emphasis. In smaller organizations, a functional form of departmentation is common.

We can describe **organic organizations** in opposite terms. Here, the design strategy emphasizes horizontal specialization and coordination, over vertical specialization and control. Rules, policies, and procedures are loose, since the organization favors personal means of coordination. When controls are used, they tend to rest heavily on socialization, training, and personal reinforcement. Staff units tend to be placed toward the middle of the organization. Divisional and matrix structures are common forms of departmentation in organic configurations.

Schematically, we can say the following to summarize the two types of organizational designs.

A mechanistic configuration $\xrightarrow{\text{involves}}$ much vertical specialization and control; tight rules, policies, procedures; a centralized staff

An organic configuration $\xrightarrow{\text{involves}}$ much horizontal specialization; personal coordination; few rules, policies, and procedures; a decentralized staff

Figure 12.1 further describes the two ideal types as opposite extremes on a continuum of organizational design strategies.

A MANAGER'S VIEW OF ORGANIZATIONAL DESIGN

These two ideal forms of structural configuration serve as the core concepts for our treatment of organizational design in this chapter. Our basic theme in this regard is quite simple. The structural configuration of the organization should be consistent with the organization's goals and the problems and opportunities posed by its environment, size, and technology. Further, it should recognize the dominant organizational culture of the firm and its history. These prescriptions address the design issues considered important by managers. There are other perspectives that give more weight to stock-

FIGURE 12.1   A basic comparison of mechanistic and organic organizations.

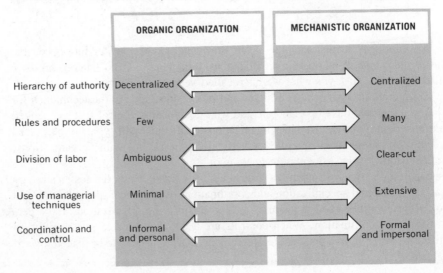

holders or employees among other constituencies of the modern organization.[2]

Although there are a vast number of ways in which organizations can be configured, we'll use ''ideal types'' to characterize a few basic patterns. As we discuss them, remember the key question in organizational design is: How should structure be adjusted to meet major problems and opportunities, and thereby allow the organization to accomplish its goals? To help you answer this question in actual managerial practice, we will rely heavily on Jaccob Jaccober's firm as our example.

The Middle States Manufacturing case will be used throughout this chapter to highlight the concepts and practice of organizational design. Make sure that you recall the case; refer back to the Part Four introduction if necessary.

Middle States Manufacturing: A Recap

A key concern for Jaccob is to exploit the new product—Profab. Customers want Profab, and lower-level managers and employees are willing to see the implementation of this new product succeed. So what's the problem? Why is Jaccob fretting so much? Why not just go ahead and schedule production, hire the needed workers, and make the appropriate sales and marketing arrangements? Some managers would simply charge ahead in this situation without seriously analyzing the structure of the organization. Let us not be so hasty.

Look at the problems and opportunities confronting Jaccob. Middle States historically stressed innovation, while maintaining the technical quality of its products at or above competitive levels. Although the firm has not been particularly efficient, innovation has provided growth and high profits. Should Jaccob continue to develop this comparative advantage? If so, how?

Currently, the new product, Profab, requires slightly different production methods than existing products. There is a lot of handcrafting, and successful production rests heavily upon the skilled work of a few key people. Profab calls for more than minor adjustments to the existing methods, and the engineers cannot yet specify how to produce it in large quantities.

Jaccob must also consider the new customers gained because of the success of Profab. Certainly the firm would be less dependent upon a few key customers. But would it be able to detect small yet important changes in a large number of customers? Currently there is a market, but will there continue to be one in the future? Also, the sale of Profab is likely to call for clearances by any number of governmental regulatory agencies.

There is the force of expanding volume. Jaccob knows that adding Profab means more than just using another production shift. Current personnel will have to cope with additional employees, and this growth will put a heavy strain on staff units. For instance, just training a new production crew might take two months. Jaccob does not want to lose the current emphasis on quality innovation.

All these issues mean that Jaccob must consider changes in specialization as well as new forms of coordination and control. He needs a means of gaining an overall perspective on this situation so that good decisions on organizational design can be made.

STRATEGIC FACTORS IN ORGANIZATIONAL DESIGN

Management must consider several competing factors in selecting an overall structural configuration for an organization. Many of these factors relate to the organization's goals, environment, size, and technology.[3] Let us review these strategic factors by starting with the bottom line: What does management really want? What are the goals for the organization?

Goals

The process of organizational design can begin with a strategic decision concerning an organization's goals. Over the long run, organizations must provide returns to society and satisfy investors, suppliers, distributors, and customers, while operating within governmental, labor, and other constraints. Over time, many organizations develop a set of goals capable of satisfying these competing groups. Some organizations operate as if flexibility and adaptability were the keys to survival. Some emphasize technical superiority. Others place the major emphasis on efficiency. Growth with consistently high profits is a common theme among U.S. corporations. Thus the relative emphasis of an organization's goals on flexibility, technical superiority, or efficiency is crucially important when its managers select an overall structural configuration for the organization.

External Environment

A second important factor, emphasized in Chapter 10, is the external environment of the organization. What is the potential for success? What other organizations must the organization rely on to reach its goals? How predictable and stable is the environment? Generally, as more opportunities arise, the structure should facilitate change and growth. Where the organization faces a few powerful outsiders, the structure should help the organization to target its responses. Conversely, where the organization faces many powerful outsiders, the structure should facilitate frequent adjustments to external demands.

Size and Technology

Managers should also recognize the important role of size and technology in selecting an overall structural configuration. Growth creates both new opportunities and problems. The structure needed for smaller organizations often becomes inadequate with the onset of growth. In high-technology firms operating on the frontiers of technical development, structure should facilitate technical problem solving and risk taking. Conversely, firms operating with more well-known and stable processes should consider structures that facilitate efficiency. As the range of products and services increases, the structure of the organization should accommodate differences across products and services.

Case Application:
Middle States Manufacturing

Table 12.1 summarizes the design issues facing Middle States Manufacturing. Since Jaccob Jaccober is president, let us take his perspective. What does Jaccob want? While only he can answer this question, the history and culture of the firm provide added insight. Specifically, Middle States has pursued innovation as a path to longer-term profits and survival. In doing so, it has placed efficiency and flexibility farther down the priority list. While the firm was small, efficiency and flexibility were not major problems since Jaccob had direct contact with most of his managers and employees. The scope of operations was small enough for him to deal with major customers and still keep tabs on internal operations.

Can Jaccob keep the existing emphasis on technological innovation and still make adequate profits to ensure long-term survival? The case description suggests that the answer is yes. But why even ask this question? Can't the skill and hard work of the chief executive and the team of managers dictate goal priorities that will ensure profits and survival? In some cases we can answer yes to this question, and in some cases no. The answer for a particular organization rests on contingencies in its environment and context, in addition to the skills of its management.

TABLE 12.1   Major Design Issues Facing Middle States Manufacturing

Strategic Factors	Case Applications
1. Goals	What does Jaccob really want?
2. General and specific environment	Possible expansion nationwide; many new customers, suppliers, distributors, government agencies, and financial backers
3. Size and technology	Anticipated growth in size; new production process required for Profab
4. Structure	
a. Horizontal specialization	Existing use of functional structure (vice presidents of marketing, finance, production, and personnel)
b. Vertical specialization	Need for new managerial levels; budgeting techniques important; assistant managers used as staff aides
c. Coordination and control	Problems occurring in product delivery and service to existing customers

In the case of Middle States, the general and specific environments are complex. The firm is small in size and may become moderately large with the planned expansion. The technology is sophisticated and makes it difficult for Jaccob to stress efficiency. The need for even more sophisticated technology to produce Profab may also restrict flexibility.

MECHANISTIC DESIGNS

We can now match the strategic factors of goals, environment, size, and technology with the major structural configurations available to managers. Remember, we will emphasize the mechanistic–organic continuum as representing the basic range of choices in organizational design.

Earlier, we described the mechanistic configuration as one emphasizing vertical specialization, the extensive use of managerial techniques, and use of top-level staff. Managers acting within such a structure would be given clear asignments, precise methods, and very specific targets. The resources available to their units would be detailed in budgets, and deviations from budgets would result in required explanations to a superior.

The mechanistic configuration is consistent with a desire for efficiency. It works best when the external environment is stable and when the organization relies on few influential suppliers, distributors, and regulatory agencies. It also presumes that the technology of the organization is well known and that only a limited range of products or services is produced. This configuration is often found in basic industries, such as steel, automobile manufacturing, and utilities.

Why They Work

Why does this configuration work in such situations? It works because it has a vertical emphasis. Procedures developed by centralized staff can be readily implemented throughout the system. Changes in standards can be used to redirect managerial effort. Careful attention to following well-defined processes allows management to plan ahead in detail and make minor corrections before they become serious problems.

There is another advantage to the mechanistic structure. When an organization faces periodic crises, such a configuration can provide the vehicle for action. Action is needed quickly in a crisis situation. The vertical emphasis of the mechanistic configuration facilitates control and generates quick responses by subordinates to top management orders. Thus, it is no wonder it is the preferred configuration in military organizations and that variations of mechanistic structure are often embodied in emergency response plans. For instance, nuclear power plants have voluminous manuals outlining formal procedures for averting disaster in the event of crisis. Of course, using this configuration in a crisis presumes that a capable person is in charge and is willing to make the required decisions.

Problems

One problem sometimes associated with mechanistic structures is low job satisfaction and poor human resource maintenance.[4] Mechanistic organizations tend to be seen by employees as rigid, centralized, nonparticipative, and very bureaucratic. Another problem is that mechanistic organizations are not very good at spotting small but potentially important variations in their environments. The attention of too many managers and their managerial techniques is directed toward vertical affairs. External communications within and outside the organization are sacrificed for responsiveness to top management.

Case Application:
Middle States Manufacturing

Table 12.2 summarizes some of the conditions that favor the mechanistic structure and contrasts them with the actual conditions facing Middle States. It is pretty obvious that a mechanistic configuration does not fit Middle States very well. Jaccob would do well to seek an alternative in his organizational design efforts.

ORGANIC DESIGNS

Now let us change the setting. Assume that an organization cannot completely engineer production operations but must rely on the judgment, craftsmanship, and professionalism of employees. Let us also assume that the quality of the major product or service is difficult to judge. Picture the environment as unstable and difficult to predict. The

TABLE 12.2   A Comparison of Selected Conditions Favoring a Mechanistic Configuration and the Conditions Facing Middle States Manufacturing

	Conditions Favoring a Mechanistic Configuration	Conditions Facing Middle States Manufacturing
1. Goals	Oriented toward efficiency	Oriented toward technical innovation
2. External environment	Generally rich in several areas; specifically reliant upon few outsiders; low in uncertainty	Generally rich in one area; specifically reliant on many outsiders; high in uncertainty
3. Size	Moderate to large	Small
4. Technology	Known means of production; extensive substitutability of capital; output quality easy to measure	Means of production not well known; little substitutability of capital; output quality moderately easy to measure

organization must rely on many different suppliers, distributors, customers, unions, and regulatory agencies, each of which places slightly different demands on it. No single opportunity appears to offer the best path toward growth and profits.

This combination of environment and technology calls for an adaptive and responsive organization. It favors the organic configuration with its emphasis on horizontal specialization and coordination. Managers in such structures are given broad objectives with only general notions of how to proceed. They are expected to work closely with fellow managers and subordinates. Although guidance from superiors would be available, there would be few written documents outlining procedures. In organic organizations, successful managers are particularly aware of minor changes in the needs and desires of outsiders. A lot of their time is devoted to external relations.

Why They Work

Why does the organic configuration work in such situations? It works because information can easily penetrate the organization and be circulated among managers. Subunits can make small adjustments to particular clients. Even though successful performance by one unit may be offset by poor performance in another, the "law of averages" produces an overall success rate. When and where success occurs, the organization can quickly add resources to exploit the opportunity. Research and development organizations, contract research firms, computer software corporations and architectural firms typically use this softer, organic structure. Employees tend to view the organic structures as decentralized, participative, and nonbureaucratic. Generally, we expect lower turnover and absenteeism and more highly committed employees than in mechanistic settings.

Problems

The organic configuration does have its disadvantages. It is not very efficient in producing large quantities of standardized products or services. It is also difficult to maintain in larger organizations. Furthermore, even if organizations with this configuration can detect changes in their environment, it may be difficult to implement an organizationwide response. Finally, the organic configuration is vulnerable to empire building when a reduction in external opportunities occurs. Few managers or employees, for example, are willing to recommend their own termination for the good of the organization.

Case Application:
Middle States Manufacturing

Table 12.3 shows that the organic configuration fits the major characteristics of Middle States pretty well. Yet the organic form does not automatically guarantee an emphasis on innovation.

TABLE 12.3 A Comparison of Selected Conditions Favoring an Organic Configuration and the Conditions Facing Middle States Manufacturing

	Conditions Favoring an Organic Configuration	Conditions Facing Middle States Manufacturing
1. Goals	Oriented toward flexibility	Oriented toward technical innovation
2. External environment	Generally rich in one narrow area; specifically reliant on many outsiders; high in uncertainty	Generally rich in one narrow area; specifically reliant on many outsiders; high in uncertainty
3. Size	Small to moderate	Small
4. Technology	Not a well-known means of production; little substitutability of capital; output quality difficult to measure	Not a well-known means of production; little substitutability of capital; output quality moderately easy to measure

DIVERSE DESIGNS

Organizations can develop a history (culture) of prosperity, growth, and long-term survival from either the mechanistic or organic structural foundations. Growth can also allow top management to slowly shift the overall configuration of the organization from mechanistic to organic, or vice versa. For example, the auto divisions of General Motors once operated under an organic structure with considerable engineering, production, and marketing autonomy. While there were strict financial controls from the top, this so-called "decentralized" approach helped General Motors to become the largest automaker in the world. In the 1970s, however, GM's structure began to become mechanistic as engineering and production decisions were made on a corporate-wide basis. While the divisions lost some autonomy, GM sought economies of scale in the attempt to take advantage of the growing market for small cars. By the mid-late 1980s, GM was struggling as its domestic and foreign rivals became ever more successful. The company responded this time by shifting part of its organization toward the organic form to try and recapture technological advantages and develop a greater market responsiveness.

In contrast, General Electric once operated under a mechanistic structure. To respond more quickly to varied market opportunities, GE decided to develop a softer structure with over 500 identifiable "businesses." Note that GE produces a much wider variety of products than do the GM auto divisions and must compete directly with a larger number of smaller, flexible manufacturers.

Selecting between the mechanistic and organic configurations would be comparatively easy if all the performance, environmental, and technological pressures of a given organization called for the same structure. Often this is not the case, and a diverse form of structural configuration is chosen. Some of the diverse configurations are weighted toward the mechanistic, while others are made more organic. Some of the more common diverse designs are described in the paragraphs that follow.

Mechanistic Core Within an Organic Shell

Perhaps the most common conflict situation occurs when an organization produces only one or a few basic products but begins to face a more uncertain environment. The technology would favor a mechanistic configuration; the changing environment calls for more flexibility and adaptability than that structure can easily tolerate. One solution is to develop a series of externally oriented, organic line and staff units to protect the mechanistic production units. Such a configuration is shown in Figure 12.2.

The line and staff units in Figure 12.2 are there to scan the environment in an attempt to provide an early warning system for top management. They can also explain the actions of internal units and convince outsiders that some of their demands are illegitimate or that the organization is already serving others. This approach is useful in protecting the basic production organization from minor changes and unwanted intrusions from external forces.

The diverse configuration of a mechanistic core and an organic shell does not meet Middle States' needs as well as the simple organic configuration does. A key reason

FIGURE 12.2   A mechanistic core wrapped by an organic shell.

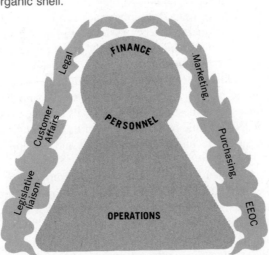

is Jaccob's desire for technical innovation and the need for a responsive production process.

Organic Core with a Mechanistic Shell

Conflicting pressures are also found in large organizations that must rely on a non-routine and intensive technology. Universities, larger research organizations, and research hospitals are examples. In such cases a possible design strategy is to allow the internal line units to maintain an organic configuration, while the staff units become mechanistic. Figure 12.3 shows such an organic core protected by a mechanistic shell. This configuration allows line managers to develop a whole series of comparatively small, quasi-autonomous departments that can detect and adjust to relevant technical developments. Each department can proceed with few internally induced rules, policies, and procedures. Staff units, on the other hand, can be designed to improve efficiency, increase the chances of immediate response, and buffer the organic core from nontechnical concerns.

There are advantages and disadvantages to this form of diverse configuration. It does allow top managers to plan and control more carefully the actions of staff units. Unfortunately, staff units in these organizations may lag their counterparts working in the more organic configuration. Attempts from the top to redirect the organic line units can also meet with resistance unless excess resources are available. The quasi-autonomous departments are likely to fight attempts to reduce their budgets, staff, or authority. Thus, these systems may be responsive and adaptable to technical matters, but may also be very resistant to other administrative changes.

This diverse configuration is likely to be preferred by Jaccob Jaccober for his Middle States Manufacturing firm. It helps provide a mix of flexibility and innovation,

FIGURE 12.3 An organic core protected by a mechanistic shell.

Legal

Finance

Marketing

R & D OPERATIONS ENGINEERING

(often grouped by product or service)

Personnel

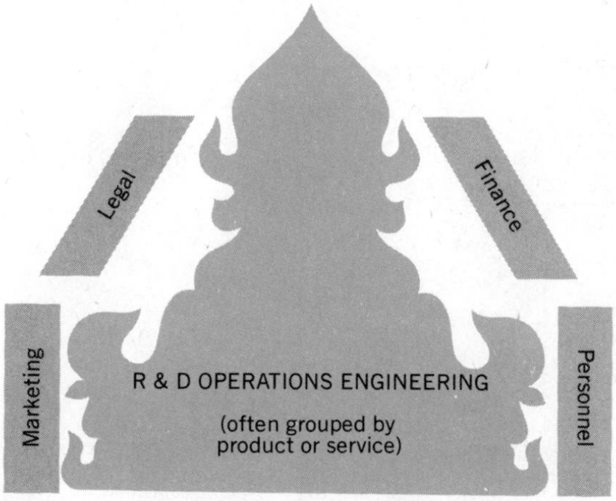

while retaining some emphasis on efficiency. Figure 12.4 shows a partial organization chart for Middle States in the new configuration with a new name—International Manufacturers.

To establish Profab as a viable product separate from existing product lines, the figure indicates that Jaccob should create two operating divisions. A new Profab division will be headed by a vice president and will have two major units within it: marketing and operations. The second division will be the old Middle States Manufacturing, with the name kept the same to maintain its identification with existing customers. Here Jaccob will place the various functional heads as subordinate to the current vice president of manufacturing. To maintain an innovative thrust, he will create the position of vice president of research and development. These three vice presidents and their units will constitute the more organic core of the new configuration.

By separating the more innovative and technically sophisticated Profab from other operations, Jaccob is able to maintain the culture and functional structure his employees are most familiar with. Although the functional departmentation within the Middle States Manufacturing division provides a mechanistic flavor, it will be moderated by the small size of the unit.

Finance and personnel staffs at the corporate level create a mechanistic shell for the organic core. They will act to protect the operating units from two problems associated with growth and expansion. First, Personnel will select and train any new employees to be added. This specialized staff unit will be able to do the job quickly, in an efficient manner, and be consistent with state and federal requirements. The

FIGURE 12.4   From Middle States Manufacturing to International Manufacturers.

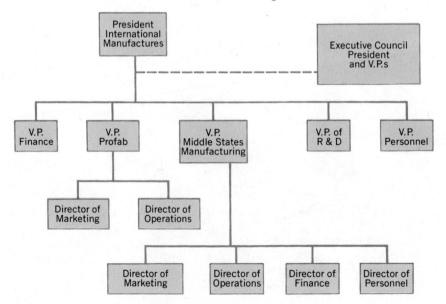

acquiring of financial resources for the expansion will be managed by the corporate vice president of finance. Again, the existence of specialized expertise will facilitate the job.

To help resolve coordination problems among subunits, and to deal with the outside regulatory agencies significant to Profab, Jaccob will create an executive council with himself as chairperson. The vice chairperson will deal with the federal agencies and act as Jaccob's chief of staff. This unit, too, will act to protect the operating divisions from outside interference.

The Conglomerate

So far we have looked at two types of compromises between the mechanistic and organic structural extremes. One had a mechanistic core surrounded by more organic units. The other had a mechanistic shell with an organic center. A third alternative is also very common. We know it as the conglomerate.

Conglomerates are typically huge businesses that produce products and services in many different industries. Some are merely large holding companies; that is, one corporation owns all or large parts of others. Each subsidiary may be structured differently. A parallel is found in the public sector in federal and state government agencies. Neither the federal nor state governments are designed to be either mechanistic or organic. Instead, they are conglomerates. Even large departments in the federal bureaucracy defy simple classification, in part because their structure is indirectly set by Congress.

SUMMARY

The key issue in organizational design is the choice of structural configuration. We have explained the mechanistic configuration and shown how it can provide profits, growth, and technical superiority under certain environmental and technological conditions. The organic configuration is also explained. It is preferred under a different combination of environmental and technological conditions. Since the pressures and opportunities from environment and technology may not be consistent, we have also analyzed a number of diverse configurations. These diverse configurations incorporated size as another important design variable. Larger organizations need more specialization, coordination, and control and may be difficult to categorize as purely mechanistic or organic in configuration.

It is also important to recognize the managerial implications of the various organizational designs. Mechanistic organizations involve tight control based on careful planning and detailed record keeping. Managers and other employees tend to experience centralization, little participation, and considerable bureaucracy. The opposite is the case with organic configurations. In the final result, you will probably manage in organizations that have diverse configurations and that offer multiple and varied challenges.

THINKING THROUGH THE ISSUES

1. Explain the basic differences between mechanistic and organic organizational designs.
2. Obtain a copy of the organization chart for your college or university. Describe the overall structural configuration and comment on its appropriateness.
3. Contrast an academic department with the registrar's office in a college or university. Which design (organic or mechanistic) is more suitable for each of these units and why?
4. Describe an actual organization or subunit that you feel should function with an organic design. Do the same for a mechanistic design. Defend your choices in both cases.
5. Describe how you as a manager might function in an organic configuration. What might your day be like? How do you think you would feel about this? Consider whether you might feel better or worse operating in a mechanistic configuration.
6. Explain the differences between a diverse configuration with a mechanistic core and organic shell, and one with an organic core and mechanistic shell.
7. Explain in your own words why an organic design is a better fit than a mechanistic design for a complex environment.
8. Discuss in some detail why a mechanistic structure has been the traditionally preferred one for the military. What about an organization such as the Catholic church? What type of design exists and why?

CASE: EAGLE AIRLINES III

Eagle Airlines was a medium-sized regional airline serving the southwest quarter of the United States.[5] The company had been growing rapidly in the last 15 years, partially as a result of dynamic company activity but also as a result of the rapid economic growth of the area it served.

The most outstanding of the areas was Bartlett City. Bartlett City's growth since the middle 1940s had rested on two primary developments. One was the very rapid growth of manufacturing and research establishments concerned with defense work. Some firms located here at the urging of government agencies to build new defense plants and laboratories away from coastal areas. Others moved to this location because of the attractive climate and scenery, which was considered an advantage in attracting technicians, engineers, and scientists for work on advanced military projects. Once some plants and research laboratories were developed, smaller, independent firms sprang up in the community for the purpose of servicing and supplying those that were established first. These developments encouraged the rapid growth of local construction and the opening of numerous attractive housing developments. The second basis for growth was the completion, also in the 1940s, of a major irrigation project that opened a large area for intensive cultivation.

While the economy of Bartlett City had grown rapidly, it was in many ways tied to coastal areas, where parent firms or home offices of many of the local establishments existed. Also, since many of its industries serviced the national defense effort, they consequently had to be closely connected with matters decided on in Washington or other places distant from Bartlett City. Finally, it had many strong financial and business ties with major coastal cities, such as San Francisco and Los Angeles. As a result, executives, engineers, and scientists in Bartlett City industries were frequently in contact with the major business, political, and scientific centers of the country, particularly those on the West Coast. In making a trip, for example, to Los Angeles from Bartlett City, one was faced with using one of three alternative modes of travel: auto, private corporate jet, or commercial jet flight. Eagle Airlines had the sole route between Bartlett City and Los Angeles, which was found to be a most lucrative run and to which it gave a great deal of attention.

Company Management

The rapid growth of Eagle Airlines was held by many to be in no small degree a result of the skill of its management. It should be pointed out that its top management had been particularly skillful in obtaining and defending its route structure and had been particularly successful in financing, at advantageous terms, the acquisition of modern aircraft, particularly jet-powered airplanes. Top management emphasized "decentralization," in which the lower members of management were given as much freedom as possible to fulfill their responsibilities in whatever way they thought best. This policy was thought to have built a dynamic, aggressive, and extremely able group of middle- and lower-level executives who had been particularly imaginative in finding ways to expand and improve the operation of the firm. This decentralization had always been accompanied by the understanding that the individual manager must "deliver." This policy, or actually philosophy, was conveyed and reinforced through letters, personal conversations, and example. Executives who increased sales or reduced costs, or in some manner made their operations more efficient, were rewarded in a number of ways. Praise, both public and private, was given to executives who improved their unit's performance. Bonuses for increased sales or cost reduction were both generous and frequent, and promotions came rapidly to those who managed outstanding units. The chairperson of the board, who was also chief executive officer during this period of growth, frequently used words that were only half-jokingly claimed by other executives to be the company motto. "This company's success rests upon expansion and efficiency."

The Local Unit

Eagle Airlines was organized as shown in Figure 12.5. The three major divisions were Operations, which was involved in scheduling and operating the planes over the entire route system; Sales, which was concerned with advertising all phases of airline service, maintaining ticket offices in all cities and airports, and also selling to institutional customers such as companies and government agencies; and Service, which was concerned with activities at the airport, maintenance, handling baggage, loading passengers, and similar functions.

For all practical purposes, operations had no local offices in that it had to operate the entire system. Sales and service had both district and local or regional offices. The sales manager in Bartlett City, for example, was responsible for the ticket sales at the airport and in maintaining a downtown ticket office, as well as for institutional sales to the local companies and agencies. Service was usually broken into a number of subdivisions at the local level, so that at Bartlett City there was a ramp service manager who was responsible for handling everything pertaining to the airplane while it was on the ground, but not while it was under maintenance. The manager would, therefore, be responsible for the loading and unloading of all baggage, mail, and passengers. That individual was also responsible for cleaning the planes between flights, having food put on board, getting baggage to the customers and picking up from them, guiding passengers on and off the aircraft, and checking their tickets when they arrived at the terminal.

FIGURE 12.5   Partial organization chart of Eagle Airlines.

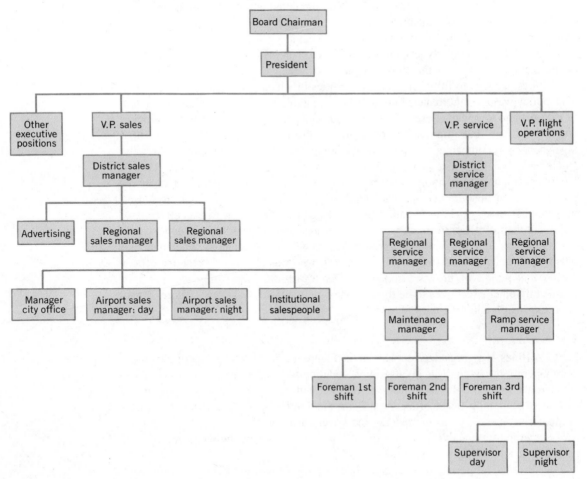

Consistent with company policy of decentralization and individual accountability, each of these local people had an individual budget and standards of performance. A sales manager, for example, was given complete authority to hire, train, and fire whatever salespeople or any other personnel he or she thought necessary. The sales manager knew what his or her budget was and was expected to stick within it and reduce it if possible. Furthermore, the sales manager knew what the standards of performance relevant to sales volume were. The company placed great emphasis on an increase in sales rather than in absolute volume of sales. Hence, the sales manager at Bartlett City, as at all other local units, knew that individual performance would be evaluated, not on matching past sales volume, but by increasing it a certain percentage. The percentage would vary from one location to another depending on the number of conditions: market potential, absolute volume, and similar terms. Although the percentage increase might vary, it was always there and was known by the company as the "ratchet." The regional service manager had no actual sales figure to be held accountable for, but that manager did have costs that were expected to be controlled and, if at all possible, reduced. While there was no similar "ratchet," such as a percentage reduction of costs expected each year, there was continual pressure on the local ramp manager in the form of exhortation, suggestions, and illustrations of managers who had successfully found ways to reduce costs.

Plan of the Sales Manager

Carl Dodds, sales manager in Bartlett City, had been with Eagle Airlines seven years, during which time he had had three promotions. Upon graduation from a western state university, he had started working for Eagle Airlines in the San Francisco office as a ticket clerk at the local airport. Within a year he had been made accounts sales representative, selling airline service to local companies and institutions. Within two years he had become a local sales manager at San Jose, the smallest of the company's sales offices. Six months ago he had received his promotion to Bartlett City, the second largest sales office and, until recently, the one growing most rapidly. Dodd's superior looked at him as a particularly dynamic, inventive salesperson and sales manager. He seemed gifted at finding spectacular ways of substantially increasing sales. In previous positions he had developed a number of attention-getting promotion packages that met with spectacular results. Higher management looked to him to again increase sales at Bartlett City, which had leveled out about a year ago with the decline in the economy. It was not known how long the decline would continue.

Some of Dodd's previous associates in the other parts of the company agreed that he had been imaginative in developing some spectacular promotion schemes but also felt that success had always been of the short-run variety—he had made sudden bursts at the expense of long-term growth. They further claimed that he had been fortunate in always being promoted out of a position before the consequences of his activity caught up with him.

The Assessment

Since coming to Bartlett City, Dodds had been intensively studying the local market situation, making contacts with the various companies and big business executives, hiring some new salespeople, and training them after having, as he called it, weeded out some deadwood. He had also increased advertising and redecorated the downtown sales office. In spite of this activity, in his own mind, he had been largely getting ready for his major effort.

Dodds defined his sales situation this way. The airline had done well attracting customers who wanted speed and convenience. However, a considerable number of business executives drove or used a company plane. He adopted and embellished a popular local image of the Bartlett City executive as a dynamic, imaginative, administrator–scientist who represented a new type of business tycoon. In Dodd's mind, what he had to do was sell this young, dynamic, new type of tycoon the comfort and gracious service that, apparently, such a person thought should come to him or her in this new role. His new plan then was to do everything possible to give the "new tycoons" this sort of service.

The Proposal

He therefore developed a plan to set up *Tycoon Specials* on certain flights carrying the greatest number of these business executives. This plan was to begin with the flight between Bartlett City and Los Angeles.

In this plan the customer–executive upon arriving at the ticket-checking counter for the *Tycoon Special* flight would be asked to select his or her own seat. This then would be reserved in the customer's name. Upon arriving at the ramp for boarding, the customer would be greeted by name by the gate attendant, usually dressed plainly but neatly in a white top, blue cap, and slacks, but now in a gold coat and a simulated turban. Stretching between the gate and the aircraft was to be a wide, rich-red carpet. Upon arrival, the customer's name would be announced through a special intercom to the plane. As the individual walked down the red carpet, the customer–executive would note that the flight hostess would appear smiling at the door, ready to greet him or her by name before being ushered to the appropriate seat, identified by a card with the executive's name, indicating, "This seat is reserved for Tycoon _____."

Once in flight this deluxe service would continue, with the hostesses changing into more comfortable and feminine-looking lounge dresses and serving a choice of champagne, wine, and cocktails along with exotic and varied hors d'oeuvres. There were other details to the plan, but this will give you some idea of its general nature. In this way, Dodds thought surely that he would be able to not only match but exceed the services and comfort some executives thought they obtained by alternative means of transportation.

The Problem

Dodds's great problem was in getting the plan operational. Almost all the service had to be provided by people who did not report to him. This would be supplied by the local ramp service manager, to whom the gate clerk reported, and who would have to provide the red carpet, the additional gold uniforms, turbans, and the other paraphernalia necessary to create the impression that Dodds had in mind. The local ramp service manager, Chris Edwards, had been particularly abrupt in rejecting this proposal, insisting that it did not make sense and that he was going to have absolutely nothing to do with it. Dodds had in several meetings attempted to "sell," persuade, pressure, and finally threaten Edwards into accepting the plan. Edwards refusal had become more adamant and pointed at every step. Relationships between the two, never close or cordial, had deteriorated until there was nothing but the most unrestrained hostility expressed between them.

Reaction of the Service Manager

Chris Edwards was a graduate engineer who had worked for the company for about 10 years. He had first started in the maintenance department of the firm and had gradually risen through several supervisory positions before being given this position as service manager with Eagle. It was the first position he had had in which he had an independent budget and was held individually accountable. After three years in this capacity, he personally felt and had been led to believe by several higher executives in the company that he had acquired as much experience in this position as was necessary. He was, therefore, looking forward to a new assignment, which probably involved a promotion in the very near future. He realized that this promotion would probably be based on his earlier proven technical competence and his more recent experience in his present position, where he had run a particularly efficient operation. This was evidenced by several reductions in his operating expenses, due to efficiencies he had installed, and by other measures of performance, such as reduction in the time necessary to service, fuel, and load aircraft.

After having met with increasingly adamant refusals by Edwards, Dodds had gone to his superior, pointing out that he was being hampered by Edwards in his effort to increase sales and advance the company. Dodds's supervisor had made a point of seeing his counterpart, in the service area, asking if something could not be done by the service people at Bartlett City to support the sales effort. Upon inquiry, Edwards's superior learned the details of the request from Edwards and the reasons for his refusal. Dodds kept insistent pressure on his superior, asking to have something done about the local service manager's obstinacy.

Management's Reaction

Eventually, word of the continued arguments between Dodds and Edwards went up the chain of command to the vice president of sales and later to the vice president in charge of service. One day while discussing this issue, their conversation was overheard by the president. Upon hearing the story, he made the comment that these personality clashes would either have to be straightened out or one or both of the men either transferred or, for that matter, fired. He emphatically insisted that the company could not operate efficiently with an unnecessary expenditure of energy going into personal disputes.

Questions

Analyze Eagle Airlines from the perspective of a consultant on organizational design.

1. Is the present design appropriate? Why or why not?
2. What design changes do you recommend? Why?

EXERCISE: ORGANIZATIONAL ANALYSIS—PART III

Purpose:

To apply, as clearly and thoroughly as possible, the concepts developed in Chapter 12 to an actual organization. This will give you and your group a chance to apply the concepts and share your findings with those of your classmates.

Time:

50 minutes or more in class, plus at-home preparation.

Procedure:

1. Do the following before coming to class:
   a. Form the same group used for Part I of this exercise. Assume that the group is a management consulting team required to prepare a written report following the format indicated by your boss (the instructor).
   b. Use the same organization your group selected for Part I of this exercise.
   c. Using observations, interviews, and company records as necessary, your group has been assigned to do the following for its organizational report:
      (1) Using relevant material from the first two parts of this analysis (which were assigned in Chapters 10 and 11) along with concepts from Chapter 12, summarize the structural configuration of this organization.
      (2) Discuss the appropriateness of this configuration in light of the material covered in Chapter 12.
      (3) Discuss one possible alternative configuration and justify your choice.
2. Be prepared to turn in this part of the report to your instructor and to discuss the group's findings and their implications.

THE MANAGER'S VOCABULARY

Mechanistic Organization   An organizational structure that emphasizes vertical specialization and control, an extensive use of managerial techniques, impersonal coordination and control, and a heavy reliance on rules, policies, and procedures.

Organic Organization   An organizational structure that emphasizes horizontal specialization, an extensive use of personal coordination, and loose rules, policies, and procedures.

Organizational Design   The process of choosing and implementing a structural configuration for an organization.

IMPORTANT NAMES

T. Burns and G. Stalker   Contingency theorists who developed the concepts of mechanistic and organic organization designs.

NOTES

[1]Tom Burns and G. M. Stalker, *The Management of Innovation* (London: Tavistock, 1961).

[2]See W. G. Astley and A. H. Van de Ven, "Central Perspectives and Debates in Organization Theory," *Administrative Science Quarterly* Vol. 30 (1983), pp. 245–273.

[3]See J. Anderson and W. Duncan, "The Scientific Significance of the Paradox in Administrative Theory," *Management International Review,* Vol. 17 (1977), pp. 99–106; Charles Perrow, *Organizational Analysis: A Sociological View* (Belmont, Calif.: Brooks/Cole, 1970); See Jeffrey Pfeffer and Gerald Salanick, *The External Control of Organizations: A Resource Dependence Approach* (New York: Harper & Row, 1978); and Richard N. Osborn, James G. Hunt, and Lawrence R. Jauch, *Organizational Theory: Integrated Text and Cases* (Melbourne, Fla.: Kreiger, 1984).

[4]Peter Blau and Richard Schoenner, *The Structure of Organizations* (New York: Basic Books, 1971); and J. Woodward, *Industrial Organization: Theory and Practice* (London: Oxford University Press, 1965).

[5]This case has been reproduced with the permission of its author, J. A. Litterer. Copyright © J. A. Litterer. Reproduced by permission of Joseph A. Litterer.

PART FIVE
MANAGING THE PROCESSES OF ORGANIZATIONAL BEHAVIOR

Hardly anyone works alone in organizations, and managers never do. As shown throughout our earlier discussions, managers maintain a complex network of interpersonal relationships as part of their daily work routines. It is through and with other people that managers get their own jobs accomplished.

This part of the book focuses your attention on the processes of organizational behavior with which every manager becomes heavily involved. Our emphasis will be on helping you understand skills that are important if you are to continue throughout your career to be successful at managing people at work.

The case that follows involves one manager who has just taken a great leap forward in his career. Read the case and think about the very demanding and complex challenges he faces.

THE JIM DONOVAN CASE

Jim Donovan, 37, the new president and chief executive officer of Famous Products, was suddenly in the roughest spot in his life.[1] Having just been selected by Omega Corporation, a huge conglomerate, to take over as president of its latest acquisition, he had been feeling very good about himself. Having grown up on "the wrong side of the tracks," worked his way through engineering college, earned an MBA from Harvard Business School, worked for 10 years as a management consultant and for two years as a successful president of a small company, he felt that he had arrived. The company he was going to manage was known throughout the world, had a good reputation, and would provide a good opportunity for visibility in the parent company. The pay would be the highest he had ever earned, and while the money itself was not that important (though he'd be able to assure his wife and four children financial security), he enjoyed the indicator of success a high salary provided. And Jim was eager to manage a company with over a thousand employees; the power to get things done on such a large scale was very attractive to him.

When Omega had selected him, he was told that Don Bird, the current president of Famous Products, was close to retirement and would be moved upstairs to chairperson of the board. Bird had been president of Famous for 22 years and had done reasonably well, building sales steadily and guarding quality. The top management group was highly experienced, closely knit, very loyal to the company, and its members had been in their jobs for a long time. As long-term employees, they all were reported to be good friends of Don Bird. They were almost all in their early sixties and quite proud of the record of their moderate-sized but successful company. Famous had not, however, grown in profits as rapidly as Omega expected of its operating companies, and Omega's president had told Jim that he wanted Jim to "grab a hold of Famous and make it take off."

With this challenge ringing in his ears, Jim flew out to Milwaukee for his first visit to Famous Products. He had talked briefly with Don Bird to say that he'd be arriving Thursday for half a day, then would be back for good after 10 days in New York at Omega. Bird had been cordial but rather distant on the phone, and Jim wondered how Bird was taking Jim's appointment. "I've only got a few hours here," thought Jim. "I wonder how I should play it."

QUESTIONS

1. How would you "play it" if you were Jim?
2. How do you anticipate the current top management staff of Famous Products will react to the real Jim Donovan?

OUR VIEWPOINT

Jim exemplifies a "fast-track" pattern of success for the young executive. At 37, he is named to the top-management post at Famous Products. He had worked hard, achieved performance levels highly valued by Omega and is now being well rewarded.

If we were Jim, this prior work and educational experience would lend considerable confidence to our facing up to the tasks ahead. Being brought into Famous

Products from the outside, he also has the advantage of not being intertwined in company politics, rumor mills, or social cliques. He is starting "fresh," and this can be to his distinct advantage.

Of course, Jim has a lot to learn about Famous Products and its people. Many of his early efforts will probably be devoted to this end. If he's smart, he'll learn quickly and act carefully.

Jim should also remember that his early actions and efforts will largely determine how people will think about and react to him in the future. This first staff meeting, therefore, can't be taken too lightly. People will be watching him very closely!

CONTINUING ON   When Jim pulled up to Famous Products headquarters in his rented car, he noticed the neat grounds and immaculate landscaping. To his surprise, Don Bird met him at the door. Bird had on a very conservative blue business suit, black tie, black shoes, and white shirt. He peered out at Jim through old-fashioned steel-rimmed glasses and said, "Welcome to our plant. You're just in time for our usual Thursday morning executive meeting; would you like to sit in on that and meet our people?" Jim thought that the meeting would give him a chance to observe the management group in action, and he readily agreed, planning to sit back and watch for as long as he could.

Jim was ushered into the most formal meeting room he could remember ever having seen. The dark-paneled room was dominated by a long, heavy table, with 12 high-backed chairs around it. Seven of the chairs were filled with unsmiling executives in dark suits.

Bird led Jim to the front of the room, indicated an empty chair to the left of the seat at the head of the table, then sat down in the place that was obviously his. Turning to the group, he said:

> Gentlemen, I want you to meet Mr. Donovan, but before I turn the meeting over to him, I want you to know that I do not believe he should be here; I do not believe he's qualified and I will give him no support. Mr. Donovan . . .

OUR VIEWPOINT

Zap! Jim is on the griddle and he has to come up with a solution to this problem fast. "Why," he is probably saying to himself, "didn't I anticipate this thing? Why wasn't I prepared?" Surely Jim could have expected some resistance and perhaps even some resentment to his appointment. Not once did he stop and try to see things through the eyes of the "old guard" at Famous Products.

Now he is in a situation where he has to learn quickly to deal with the perceptions of these people, to communicate with them, and to be able to work with them to make decisions, handle conflict, and implement change. This is where his knowledge of individual and group behavior in organizations will be put to the true test! Can he, Jim Donovan, come out of this crisis and emerge as a true source of leadership for these and all other operating personnel at Famous Products? This is the ultimate managerial question.

SUMMARY

Jim Donovan's dilemma clarifies the direction which our study of OB now takes. Managers must be able to achieve success in the interpersonal processes through which individual and group behavior is mobilized in support of an organization's purpose. The four chapters in this part delve deeply into the topics of perception, decision making, communication, conflict, power, politics, and leadership. You will find an emphasis in each chapter on understanding the concepts and learning how to apply them in actual managerial practice.

---

[1]This case is a synthesis of Jim Donovan (A) and (B) written by Allan R. Cohen and Michael Merenda, University of New Hampshire, for purposes of classroom discussion. Copyright 1979, Whittemore School of Business and Economics, University of New Hampshire. Reproduced with permission.

CHAPTER 13
PERCEPTION AND DECISION MAKING

At Morgan, research and analysis are integral to decision making. Accurate and scrupulously evaluated information is the underpinning of every aspect of our business.

J. P. Morgan & Co., Inc. Annual Report

ORIGINAL IDEAS ARE SCARCE WHEN MBAs TRY TO SAVE KOOL-AID

Six teams of business-school students came from all over the country to participate in a contest as guests of General Foods Corporation.[1] They were each secluded in a Connecticut hotel and given this task: create a marketing plan to stop the steeply declining sales of Sugar-Free Kool-Aid. The students worked for a full day. Then, neatly attired in dark business suits, they logically and articulately presented their solutions to the company's very real problem.

The University of Pennsylvania team wanted to promote the product to young teens as well as to children, its existing target market; Northwestern's wanted to target parents and stress increased parent–child interaction as a result of drinking the same beverage; Columbia's also wanted to promote the product as a "great drink for the whole family"; the University of Chicago's wanted to change the packaging to a cardboard container that could be filled with water; and Stanford's suggested developing a new low-calorie product to be called Super Kool that would serve the teen market. The University of Michigan team won with a plan to target adults and change part of the product label from "sugar-free" to "low-calorie."

These results, however, didn't really impress the judges who were from General Foods, advertising agencies, and a consulting firm. "There were a couple of ideas that were of interest," said a marketing manager, "but nothing we haven't looked at before." In fact, what was most striking about the presentations was their similarity . . . and their lack of originality. The marketing manager summed it up this way: Business schools "deal with the left side of the brain—with analysis and facts, but they don't help people much to use the other side, which is judging and intuitive."

Management Applications Question

Good management depends, in part, on a person's abilities to deal accurately and creatively with information available in the environment. How well prepared are you to handle the processes of perception and decision making as a manager?

PLANNING AHEAD

This chapter is designed to help you respond to the Management Applications Question just posed. The topics to be discussed include

The Perception Process
Perceptual Distortions
Perception and Attribution
Managing the Perception Process
Decision Making
Decision Making in a Managerial Perspective
Managing Participation in Decision Making

Managers make a wide variety of decisions in the course of their day-to-day work. They must be able to look at a situation, analyze it correctly, and make a good decision to solve the problem or explore the opportunity at hand. Two essential ingredients of managerial success in this regard are perception and decision making, the topics of this chapter.

THE PERCEPTION PROCESS

To make good decisions that actually promote job performance and human resource maintenance, a manager must be capable of drawing accurate impressions of the work situation. But, it is not always easy to do this, especially in situations that are some-what ambiguous. The Kool Aid case described in the chapter opener is one example. Team success in this situation depended on several people pooling their insights and knowledge in order to arrive at a unique solution. A team's ability to be creative depended in part on how well the members brought different perspectives and vantage points to bear on the issues. In the contest, apparently, this was a weakness rather than a strength of the MBA students. They all seemed to perceive things in a rather similar way; they also ended up with marketing plans that were quite similar to one another, and not very distinctive. The perception process is an important influence on behavior in organizations, and any manager must be skilled at dealing with it when trying to make good decisions and take effective action.

What Is Perception?

Perception is the process through which people select, receive, organize, and interpret information from their environment. Through perception, people process information inputs into decisions and actions. It is a way of forming impressions about yourself, other people, and daily life experiences. It is also a screen or filter through which information passes before having an effect on people. The quality or accuracy of a person's perceptions, therefore, has a major impact on the quality of any decisions made or actions taken in a given situation.

Clearly, perception is an important dynamic for the manager who wants to avoid making errors when dealing with other people and events in the work setting. This problem is made even more complicated by the fact that different people may perceive the same situation quite differently. A manager's response to a situation, for example, may be misinterpreted by a subordinate who perceives the situation quite differently.

We originally discussed this point in Chapter 3. The data presented in Figure 13.1 help remind you that people may perceive the same situation quite differently. At issue in the figure are viewpoints regarding what transpires during performance appraisal interviews in one organization. The data show rather substantial differences

FIGURE 13.1 Contrasting perceptions between managers and their subordinates regarding performance appraisal interviews. (*Source:* Data reported in Edward E. Lawler III, Allan M. Mohrman, Jr., and Susan M. Resnick, "Performance Appraisal Revisited," *Organizational Dynamics,* Vol. 13 (Summer 1984), pp. 20–35.)

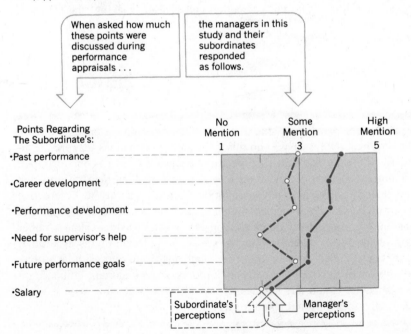

between the perceptions of the managers and those of their subordinates. Successful managers recognize that perceptions may vary in such circumstances and try to take them into account. This involves the ability to understand one's own perceptions as well as those of other people. To achieve these capabilities, you need to know more about the process of perception and how it applies to managers in their work settings.

Factors Influencing Perception

An individual's perception process is influenced by many forces.[2] These include a number of situational factors as well as tendencies for organizing perceptual data.

Situational Factors Influencing Perception

A number of situational factors have the potential to influence a person's perceptions. Consider the following incident involving former U.S. President Richard Nixon and one of his aides.[3]

> The president was working alone, very late at night, in a hotel room while on a trip. He opened the door, beckoned to a waiting aide, and ordered, "Get me coffee." The aide immediately responded to the request. Most of the activities of the hotel including the kitchen were not operating at such a late hour. Hotel personnel had to be called in and a fresh pot of coffee brewed. All of this took time and the president kept asking about "coffee" while waiting. Finally a tray was made up with a carafe of coffee, cream, sugar, and some sweet rolls and was rushed to the president's suite. It was only at this point that the aide learned that the president did not want coffee to drink, but rather wanted to talk to an assistant whose name was Coffee.

The misperceptions of the president's aide may be accounted for as follows. The situation took place late at night, and the president's physical appearance suggested a person who was getting sleepy while working alone. Through past experience, the aide had learned that the president disliked being questioned and liked immediate service. The aide wanted to please the president. These various factors affected the aide's perception of the situation. His decision was to order the president coffee to drink. Unfortunately for both parties, the decision was wrong!

Among the situational variables active in the prior case were the characteristics of the perceiver, the characteristics of what was being perceived (in this case the person of the president), and the situational context within which the incident occurred. Figure 13.2 includes these situational factors as multiple influences on the perception process.

Characteristics of the Perceiver: A person's needs, past experience, habits, personality, values, and attitudes may all influence the perception process. Someone with a strong need for ego satisfaction, for example, may select from a situation and emphasize signals that either tend to satisfy or deny the desire for self esteem. By the same token, negative attitudes toward unions may cause

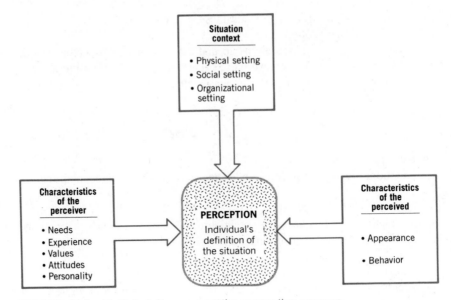

FIGURE 13.2   Multiple influences on the perception process.

a manager to look for antagonisms even during routine visits by local union officials to the organization. These and other personal factors will impact what a person gives attention to in a situation and how these cues are interpreted as a basis for decision making and action responses.

Characteristics of the Perceived: The physical attributes, appearance, and behavior of other persons in the situation also influence how that situation is perceived. We tend to notice the physical attributes of a person in terms of age, sex, height, and weight, for example. A person attempting to exert authority in a situation, but also identified as very young, may be viewed quite differently from an older person doing exactly the same thing. Personal attire and appearance are also relevant factors. Characteristics of the perceived can and do influence how one person perceives another and the situation in which they are involved.

Characteristics of the Situation: The physical, social, and organizational settings of the situation or event in question can also influence perceptions. Hearing a subordinate call his or her boss by a first name may be perceived quite differently when observed in an office hallway as opposed to an evening social reception. By the same token, a conversation with the ''boss'' may be perceived differently when taking place in a casual reception area than when held in the boss's office with the door closed. Such background characteristics of the situation context are additional factors that can affect how the situation is perceived by the different persons involved.

Tendencies for Organizing Perceptual Data

The way in which we organize information received from our environment further influences perception and affects the meaning assigned to people and events. Four organizing tendencies that influence the perception process are figure and ground, set, Gestalt, and attribution. Definitions and work-related examples of each device follow.

Figure and ground: The tendency to distinguish a central object from its surroundings.

Example: Some people "stand out" more than others in work situations. As performance appraisal time approaches, the actions of your boss may become "accented," or especially visible, in daily office routines.

Set: The tendency to respond to a situation in terms of anticipations rather than in terms of what actually exists.

Example: While preparing to interview a job applicant, a manager reads a note from the personnel department. The note says the candidate lacks interpersonal skills. Throughout the interview, the manager notices where these skills are deficient. A decision is made not to hire the applicant.

Gestalt: The tendency to avoid the discomfort of unorganized information by assigning it overall meaning.

Example: A number of people are observed lingering around the coffee machine in the company cafeteria. You see this not as a random event, but as a "meeting" of a group of people, all from your office.

Attribution: The tendency to try to understand behavior or events by interpreting them as *caused* by certain factors.

Example: In the previous example, the manager notes a "meeting" of his subordinates. Now, he concludes, they are griping about his decision to require overtime work for the coming weekend.

Everyone's perceptions are affected by organizing devices such as those just noted. As a manager, you will want to recognize when and how these devices affect your interpretation of key events. Care must be exercised to ensure accurate rather than inaccurate impressions. Managers should also recognize that these devices affect the perceptions of other people in the work setting. The astute manager, for example, may take special care to make her behavior appear nonthreatening and positive as performance appraisal time approaches for subordinates. In this way, the potentially negative effects of subordinates' figure and ground tendencies (as noted in the earlier example) may be avoided.

PERCEPTUAL DISTORTIONS

The complexity of the perception process should not deny its significance to the manager. Perception influences a manager's view of people and events, and it influences the manager's responses to them. Other people, in turn, draw their impressions of the manager from *their* perceptions of how the manager behaves in these same daily situations. It is thereby essential for managers to understand the perception process and recognize how it can affect both themselves and other persons in the work setting. A better understanding of the common perceptual distortions can help you to succeed in mastering this challenge. We will examine five perceptual distortions of special managerial significance: stereotypes, halo effects, selective perception, projection, and expectancy.

Stereotypes

Cognitive limitations prevent us from attending to more than a small portion of the infinite stimuli made available to us by the environment. To reduce the complexity of the environment we often try to classify people and events into already known categories. Prior experience with the category then tells us what we need to know about the person or event in question. This is a process of generalization from the category to the specific event or person. It results in a stereotype.

A **stereotype** occurs when an individual is assigned to a group or category, and then the attributes commonly associated with the group or category are assigned to the person in question. Common stereotypes are of young people, old people, teachers, students, union members, males, and females, among others. The phenomenon in each case is the same. A person is classified into a group on the basis of one piece of information (for example, youth). Then characteristics commonly associated with the group ("young people dislike authority") are assigned to the individual. The problem is that what may be true about the group as a whole may or may not be true about the individual.

Stereotypes obscure individual differences. When this happens in a manager's perceptions of a subordinate, for example, erroneous decisions can result. A person's race and ethnicity are often the source of unfortunate stereotypes. Two other common stereotypes to which the manager may fall prey are those of age and sex. They deserve our special attention.

Sex-Role Stereotypes

The following conversation, excerpted from a *Wall Street Journal* article, illustrates a classic sex-role stereotype.[4]

"Your secretary came outside to inspect the no-parking signs we put up at the drive-in teller," the police lieutenant told Martin Hartmann, an assistant branch manager for Continental Bank.

"Hey, that was no secretary," objected Mr. Hartmann, "that was my boss."

The article goes on to describe how Challis Lowe had to "prove" herself as the branch manager of a bank. It illustrates the sex-role stereotype evolving from the traditional perspective that managerial work is the domain of males, not females. Any female at work, therefore, may be automatically stereotyped as someone who works *for* and not *as* a manager.

The use of sex-role stereotypes is often justified by untested explanations, such as women are too emotional or too submissive to perform well as managers. Although there is research evidence showing that both women and men view successful managers as having primarily masculine traits, recent studies also show that women do *not* differ from men in key aspects of their behavior as managers. Especially important is the lack of any concrete evidence to suggest that women and men cannot be equally successful as leaders and managers.[5]

The question that remains, though, is whether or not the continuation of inappropriate sex-role stereotypes will prevent qualified women from achieving that success. We have equal employment opportunity legislation designed to protect the rights of females and other minorities against discrimination in their occupational pursuits. But we also have evidence that male managers may favor male over female employees when personnel decisions are made,[6] and we know that the pay of women still lags behind men in many comparable jobs. Thus, while we acknowledge that the negative effects of sex-role stereotypes continue to exist in society at large, we must also recognize that the responsibility rests with each of us to debunk such stereotypes and minimize their impact in those work situations over which we have some control.

Age Stereotypes

Age is another basis for stereotypes that affect people at work. Research suggests that negative stereotypes can bias managers against older workers.[7] Table 13.1 summarizes how age stereotypes can place the older worker at a disadvantage in various problem situations.

TABLE 13.1 Potential Effects of Age Stereotypes on Older Workers

Problem	Older Worker Stereotype	Biased Decision by Manager
Individual work performance is declining.	Older workers are resistant to change.	Reassign the older worker rather than encourage job improvement.
Who should be promoted to fill an important, challenging job?	Older workers lack creativity, are cautious, and tend to avoid risk.	Do not promote the older worker.
Individual requests reassignment to a job requiring substantial physical strength.	Older workers are weak; their physical strength has declined with age.	Ask the older worker to withdraw the request for transfer.

Any stereotype can prevent a manager from getting to know people and from accurately assessing individual differences at work. When this happens in a situation, stereotypes may compromise viewpoints and contribute to biased or erroneous decision making. Stereotypes based on race, ethnicity, sex, and age, in particular, are most unfortunate in a modern society that places high value on civil rights and equal employment opportunities. Yet, lest you forget the potential for stereotypes and other perceptual distortions to affect our thinking, decisions, and actions, be sure to read the descriptions in Newsline 13.1.

Halo Effects

A **halo effect** occurs when one attribute of a person or situation is used to develop an overall impression of the individual or situation. This is a process of generalization from one attribute to the total person or event. Halo effects are common in our everyday lives. When meeting a new person, for example, one trait such as a pleasant smile can lead to a positive first impression of an overall ''warm'' and ''honest'' person. The result of a halo effect, however, is the same as with a stereotype; individual differences are obscured.

Halo effects are very significant in the performance appraisal process since they can influence a manager's evaluations of subordinates' work performance. People with good attendance records, for example, tend to be viewed as intelligent and responsible; those with poor attendance records are considered poor performers.

The halo also works in reverse. A senior vice president in charge of executive recruitment for Booz, Allen & Hamilton, Inc., a Chicago-based management consulting firm, for example, contends that there is a ''high correlation between executive success and early arrival at the office.'' He also says he uses arrival time as one criterion in judging an executive's qualifications.[8] Such conclusions may or may not be true. It is the manager's job to get true impressions rather than allow halo effects to result in biased and erroneous evaluations.

Halo effects may operate among a manager's subordinates as well. A subordinate's reaction to one unique trait may affect his or her overall perspective of the manager. By the same token, halo effects can affect an employee's view of the organization as a workplace. The fact that sales are declining or resources are shrinking may create a tendency to picture all aspects of the work environment as equally grim. The astute manager will be alert to such tendencies and will take action to reduce their negative impact on the situation.

Selective Perception

Selective perception is the tendency to single out those aspects of a situation or person that reinforce or emerge consistent with existing beliefs, values, and needs. This perceptual distortion is identified in a classic research study involving executives in a manufacturing company.[9] When asked to identify the key problem in a comprehensive business policy case, the executives tended to select problems consistent with their functional area work assignments. Most marketing executives viewed the key

NEWSLINE 13.1 / JUDGING BY LOOKS ISN'T JUST UNFAIR—IT'S UNPROFESSIONAL

Yes . . . it can and does happen. Christine Craft knows it. She says she resigned from a job as newsanchor at a Kansas City television station when told she was "too old and too ugly." Mary Cunningham knows also. She says she had to resign as a Bendix Corporation Executive because she was "too young and too pretty." Gloria Steinem also knows it all so well. She has long been told she can't be taken seriously as a feminist because she is too attractive. What "it" is, is the plague of a classic sex-role stereotype all too often faced by women seeking success in areas heretofore considered by many to be a man's domain.

Social scientists recognize that "looks" count in people's perceptions of one another. In respect to personnel decisions, for example, attractive people are more likely to get hired, paid well and promoted than their less attractive peers . . . except for women that is. They do well competing for jobs, like newsanchor, which are in the public eye. But, when it comes to managerial work the old stereotype can still work against them. The more attractive a woman is, the argument goes, the more feminine she appears. The more feminine she appears, the more likely she will be perceived as being weak, emotional, and passive—all things managers, they say, aren't supposed to be. Thus in the common *mis*perception, good looking women shouldn't be managers. Steinem sums it up well in commenting "we're all being identified by our outsides rather than our insides."

Reported in *The Chicago Tribune* and *Fortune*.

problem area as sales; production people tended to see it as a problem of production and organization. These differing viewpoints would certainly affect how the executives would approach the problem; they may also have created difficulties once these persons tried to work together.

Managers can encounter problems by either being inappropriately locked into a selective perception or by being unable to handle the "clash" between alternative selective perceptions in situations such as the research case just described. In any event, a manager must test whether or not situations and individuals are being selectively perceived. The easiest way to do this is to gather additional opinions from other people. When these opinions are contradictory, an effort should be made to check the original impression. This tendency toward selectivity is one that a manager must be able to control in terms of his or her own behavior as well as recognize in the behavior of others.

Projection

Projection is the assignment of personal attributes to other individuals. You have heard the familiar admonition: "Do unto others as you would have them do unto you.'' In all due respect to its enduring wisdom, managers should be cautious in applying this maxim in the work setting. The reason is the fallacy of projection.

A classic projection error is the manager who assumes that the needs of subordinates are the same as his or her own. Suppose, for example, that you enjoy responsibility and achievement in your work. Suppose, too, that you are the newly appointed manager of subordinates whose work seems dull and routine. You might move quickly to redesign these jobs and help your subordinates to achieve higher-level satisfactions. Why? Because you want them to experience things that you personally value in work.

This may not be a good decision. By projecting your needs on subordinates, individual differences are lost. Rather than designing the subordinates' jobs to fit their needs best, you have designed their jobs to fit yours. The problem is that they may be quite satisfied and productive doing jobs that, to you, seem dull and routine.

Projection is a perceptual distortion that compromises a manager's ability to respond to individual differences in the work setting. It can be controlled through a high degree of self-awareness and by a willingness to enter the frame of reference of the other person and come to see the situation through their eyes. This is called empathy.

Expectancy

Another perceptual distortion is **expectancy.** This is the tendency to create or find in another situation or individual that which you expected to find in the first place. Expectancy is sometimes referred to as the ''pygmalion effect.''[10] Pygmalion was a mythical Greek sculptor who created a statue of his ideal mate and then made her come to life. His expectations came true! Through expectancy, you may also create in the work situation that which you expect to find.

Expectancy can have both positive and negative results for the manager. Let us consider an example. Suppose a manager assumes that his or her subordinates basically prefer to satisfy most of their needs outside the work setting and want only minimal involvement with their jobs. This manager is likely to provide simple, highly structured jobs designed to require little involvement.

Can you predict the response of the subordinates to this situation? Their most likely response is to show the lack of commitment that the manager assumed in the first place. Thus, the manager's initial expectations are confirmed as a self-fulfilling prophecy.

Is this result positive or negative? For those workers wanting challenging jobs and a lot of workplace need satisfaction, the result is clearly negative. For those who like narrow, simplified jobs, the result is positive. Whether positive or negative, though, the example demonstrates how initial expectancies can have self-fulfilling prophecy effects.

Some additional research on the positive side of expectancy may further stimulate your thinking. Psychologists, for example, have found that rats introduced to their handlers as ''maze bright'' run mazes more quickly than do rats introduced to their handlers as being ''dumb''; students identified to their teachers as ''intellectual bloomers'' do better on achievement tests than do counterparts who lack such a positive introduction; job trainees pointed out to their supervisors as having "special potential" have higher job performance than do trainees not so identified.

The expectancy effects in these cases argue strongly for mangers to adopt positive and optimistic as opposed to negative and pessimistic approaches to people at work. It also appears that certain conditions may facilitate the confirming of positive expectancies.[19] Managers, for example, who perceive their subordinates under conditions of positive expectancy may

- Create a warmer interpersonal climate between themselves and subordinates.
- Give more performance feedback to subordinates.
- Spend more time helping subordinates to learn job skills.
- Give subordinates more opportunities to ask questions.

We have just discussed five perceptual distortions that can have a significant impact on the quality of a manager's decisions. For the following columns, match each type of distortion on the left with its correct description from the list on the right. Check your answers by referring back to the preceding pages.

_____ Halo effect

_____ Projection

_____ Stereotype

_____ Expectancy

_____ Selective perception

a. Using one trait to create a total evaluation of the individual.

b. Anticipating the presence of something and then creating it by a self-fulfilling prophecy.

c. Drawing a self-reinforcing conclusion from an ambiguous situation.

d. Attributing personal needs to someone else.

e. Generalizing attributes of a group to an individual group member.

PERCEPTION AND ATTRIBUTION

Attribution is an element of the perception process that can have substantial impact on a person's attitudes and behavior. You should recall from Chapter 3 that attribution theory seeks to explain how people interpret and assign causes to events. This attempt is relevant to the present chapter since an **attribution** is really the process of inferring causality; that is, it is the attempt to explain "why" something happened as it did. Since attribution is one of the means people use to organize perceptual data, the key from a managerial perspective is to make decisions and take action on the basis of accurate and appropriate attributions rather than inaccurate ones.

The Attribution Process

Let us turn to an example to illustrate the importance of this relationship between perception and attribution. Assume you are the recipient of a promotion. Depending on the perceived cause to which the promotion is attributed, your future behavior may vary. Figure 13.3 displays this example vis-à-vis various components in the attribution process. The individual illustrated in Figure 13.3 "attributes" his or her promotion to high performance. Attribution theory predicts that this perception will enhance the likelihood of continued high performance in the future. If, by contrast, the person attributed the promotion to a "special" relationship with a higher-level manager, predicted future behavior would more likely include attempts to enhance this relationship than to achieve high task performance.

Attribution and Performance

There is an important linkage between attributions and managerial responses to perceived performance problems and opportunities. Look at Table 13.2. Obtained from a group of health care managers, these data are consistent with predictions of attribution theory.[11] When supervisors were asked to identify or *attribute* causes of poor performance by subordinates, they more often chose internal deficiencies of the individual—ability and effort—than external deficiencies in the situation—support. This shows a possible **attribution error,** or the tendency to underestimate the influence of situational factors and overestimate the influence of personal factors in evaluating someone else's behavior. When asked to identify causes of their own poor performance, however, the supervisors overwhelmingly chose lack of support—an ex-

FIGURE 13.3 Components in the attribution process and an example. (Developed from an example in Abraham K. Korman, *Organizational Behavior,* Prentice-Hall, Englewood Cliffs, N.J., 1977, p. 273.)

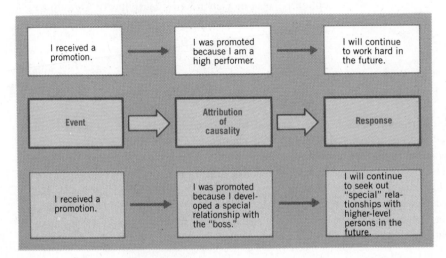

TABLE 13.2 Health Care Managers' Attributions of Causes for Poor Performance		
Cause of Poor Performance by Their Subordinates	Most Frequent Attribution	Cause of Poor Performance by Themselves
7	Lack of *ability*	1
12	Lack of *effort*	1
5	Lack of *support*	23

Source: Data reported in John R. Schermerhorn, Jr., ''Team Development for High Performance Management,'' *Training & Development Journal,* Vol. 40 (November 1986), pp. 38–41.

ternal or situational deficiency. This shows a **self-serving bias,** an attributional tendency to deny personal responsibility for performance problems but accept it for performance success.

The managerial implications of attribution theory and data such as these trace back to the fact that perceptions influence behavior. A manager who feels subordinates are *not* performing well and perceives the reason to be lack of effort is likely to respond with attempts to ''motivate'' them to work harder. The possibility of changing situational factors to remove job constraints and provide better organizational support may be largely ignored. This oversight could sacrifice rather major performance gains, given the importance of support as a variable in the individual performance equation. It is also an interesting oversight since, when it comes to evaluating their own behavior, the supervisors indicated that *their* performance would benefit from having better support. This implies that *their* abilities or willingness to work hard were not at all felt to be at issue. ''Why,'' you can and should ask, ''if the supervisors only needed more support to improve their work performance, couldn't the same be said for their subordinates?''

It is in these and related ways that attributions of causality can influence the attitudes and behavior of people at work. The informed manager understands the attribution process as an important perceptual event with potential not only to influence self-perceptions, but also to influence perceptions of and responses to others. Another illustration lies with performance appraisals as discussed in Supplementary Module C. We have already seen that performance problems on the part of a subordinate may be dealt with quite differently by a supervisor depending upon the ''causes'' to which the poor performance is attributed. Research also shows that formal performance appraisals tend to be lower when supervisors attribute poor performance to the failure of the individual to exert sufficient effort as opposed to lacking essential abilities. As you can guess, a manager's advice to the subordinate may prove more or less helpful in terms of improving future performance depending on the accuracy of such attributions.

MANAGING THE PERCEPTION PROCESS

Successful managers understand the importance of perception as an influence on behavior, and they act accordingly. They are aware of perceptual distortions, and they know that perceptual differences are likely to exist in any situation. As a result they try to make decisions and take action with a true understanding of the work situation as it is viewed by all persons concerned. A manager who is skilled in the perception process will

1. *Have a high level of self-awareness.*   Individual needs, experience, and expectations can all affect perceptions. The successful manager knows this and is able to identify when he or she is inappropriately distorting a situation because of such perceptual tendencies.

2. *Seek information from various sources to confirm or disconfirm personal impressions of a decision situation.*   The successful manager minimizes the biases of personal perceptions by seeking out the viewpoints of others. These insights are used to gain additional perspective on situations and the problems or opportunities they represent.

3. *Be empathetic—that is, be able to see a situation as it is perceived by other people.*   Different people will define the same situation somewhat differently. The successful manager rises above personal impressions to understand problems as seen by other people.

4. *Avoid common perceptual distortions that bias our views of people and situations.*   These distortions include the use of stereotypes and halo effects, as well as selective perception and projection. Successful managers are self-disciplined and sufficiently self-aware that the adverse impacts of these distortions are minimized.

5. *Avoid inappropriate attributions.*   Everyone has a tendency to try and explain why events happened the way they did or why people behaved as they did. The successful manager is careful to establish the real reasons why things happen and avoid quick or inappropriate attributions of causality.

6. *Influence the perceptions of other people.*   The successful manager is able to influence the perceptions of others so that work events and situations are interpreted as accurately as possible and to the advantage of all concerned. Closely related to this point is the concept of **impression management,** the systematic attempt to behave in ways that create and maintain desired impressions of oneself in the eyes of others.[12] Impressions, especially first impressions, can count in how other people evaluate and respond to us. They can be managed through such things as choice of manners, dress, appearance, and use of verbal and nonverbal communications.

DECISION MAKING

The essential linkage between perception and decision making is an obvious and critical one. To make good decisions, a manager must first get good information from his or her setting and then interpret it accurately via the perception process. Picture yourself receiving information from many sources, including such people as your boss, subordinates, and other people in the organization. This information is needed if you are to make good decisions about the management of your work unit. Perception, as a screen or filter, may work to your advantage or disadvantage as you interpret this information for decision-making purposes.

Decision making is the process of identifying a problem or opportunity and choosing among alternative courses of action. The basic steps in the formal or systematic decision-making process are shown in Figure 13.4. Perception has the potential to impact the decision-making process in any of these steps. It can influence the way in which problems are defined, which action alternatives are identified, which action alternative is chosen for implementation, the manner in which action is taken, and how results are evaluated.

There are additional characteristics of decision making that further highlight the potential for perception to influence the nature and operational success of various decision outcomes. Briefly, let us clarify the various types of decisions in which managers become involved and the different decision environments that also may exist. Then we will discuss the role of intuition and escalating commitments in decision making.

Types of Decisions

The two basic types of managerial decisions trace to the presence of both routine and nonroutine problems in the work situation.[13] Routine problems arise on a regular basis and can be addressed through standard responses. Called **programmed decisions,** these responses implement specific solutions determined by past experience as appropriate for the problem at hand. These are decisions whose perceptual foundations have been tested and found acceptable through past experience. Examples of programmed decisions are to reorder inventory automatically when stock falls below a predetermined level and to issue a written reprimand to someone who violates a certain personnel procedure.

Nonroutine problems are unique and new. Because standard responses are not available, they call for a creative process of problem solving specifically tailored to the situation at hand. Since they have not been encountered before, nonroutine problems have no set solutions and are very dependent on immediate perceptions to generate successful decision outcomes. Nonroutine problems call for **nonprogrammed decisions** capable of implementing creative solutions. Higher-level managers generally spend a greater proportion of their decision-making time on nonroutine problems; lower-level managers are more involved with routine problems.

FIGURE 13.4 Steps in the decision-making process.

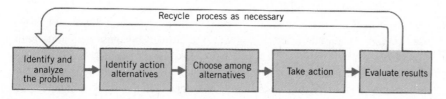

Decision Environments

Problem-solving decisions in organizations are typically made under three different conditions or environments: certainty, risk, and uncertainty.[14] As managers tackle more complex and nonroutine problems, the degree of uncertainty associated with decision making increases. This further enhances the importance of the perception process as an essential input to the decision-making process.

Certain Environments

Certainty exists in the decision environment when information is sufficient to predict the results of each alternative in advance of implementation. When one invests money in a savings account, absolute certainty exists about the interest that will be earned on that money in a given period of time. Certainty is an ideal condition for managerial problem solving and decision making. The challenge is simply to locate the alternative offering a satisfactory or even ideal solution. Unfortunately, certainty is the exception instead of the rule in managerial decision environments.

Risk Environments

Risk involves a lack of complete certainty regarding the outcomes of various courses of action but does require an awareness of the probabilities associated with their occurrence. A probability, in turn, is the degee of likelihood that an event will occur. Probabilities can be assigned through objective statistical procedures on through managerial intuition. Statistical estimates of quality rejects in various size production runs can be made; a senior production manager, on the other hand, can make similar estimates based on past experience. Risk is a fairly common decision environment faced by managers.

Uncertain Environments

Uncertainty exists when managers are unable to even assign probabilities to the outcomes of various problem-solving alternatives. This is the most difficult of the three decision environments. Uncertainty forces managers to rely heavily on individual and group creativity to succeed in problem solving. It requires unique, novel, and often totally innovative alternatives to existing patterns of behavior. Responses to uncertainty are often heavily influenced by intuition, educated guesses, and hunches, all of which are heavily influenced by perception.

DECISION MAKING IN A MANAGERIAL PERSPECTIVE

Ford's Edsel automobile, RCA's SelectaVision video player, and IBM's PCjr are among the "gallery of goofs" representing well-intentioned business decisions gone astray. Coca Cola's now infamous switch to New Coke is yet another. Each of these marketing miscues illustrates that things can, indeed, go wrong when decisions are made in environments of risk and uncertainty. Managers can further compound such

NEWSLINE 13.2 / "DECISIONAL QUICKSAND"— WHY BUSINESSES OFTEN SINK

Gavilan Computer Corporation was founded to develop a portable computer. With $31.7 million in investment capital as backing, the company did so. Its executives touted the machine even before it left the lab. But there was one piece left to fall into place—Lotus Development Corp., which sells the popular business software Lotus 1–2–3, wouldn't sell them the code for the program to run on the new machine. Gavilan's top management just couldn't accept that the answer from Lotus Development was "no." They made many visits to Lotus, begged and pleaded for the code, and even offered a million dollars for it. After each refusal they regrouped and tried again. Lotus never gave in and Gavilan never gave up. The new computer appeared. A few hundred were sold. Then Gavilan went bankrupt.

"Good management consists of knowing when to call it quits," say Professors Barry Staw and Jerry Ross. But many companies fall into a "decisional quicksand" when managers can't pull out. For some, the momentum of big decisions just overwhelms judgment. One suggestion for minimizing the cost of such mistakes is to separate the people who originate the ideas from those who make the decisions to continue on with them.

Reported in *The Wall Street Journal*.

costly mistakes by falling prey to what OB researchers call **escalating commitment** to a previously chosen course of action.[15] This is a tendency for people to continue with an action plan even when feedback suggests that it is failing. Those who do so try to resolve their experienced difficulties not by giving up or reversing the initial decision, but by working harder at the plan and increasing investments of time and energy. Newsline 13.2 shows how escalating commitments contributed to the failure of a small computer firm.

These examples highlight the complex nature of decision making applied in a managerial perspective. Managers working at all levels, in all areas, and in all types and sizes of organizations aren't supposed to just make decisions. They are supposed to make *good* ones. Sometimes this means being willing to override previous commitments and discontinue a course of action that just isn't working out the way it should. Successful managers make the right decisions in the right way at the right time. When it comes to managing the decision making process, we can say that an effective manager is one able to answer the following three questions for each and every problem situation he or she encounters.[16]

1. Is a decision really required?
2. How should the decision be made?
3. Who should be involved in the decision?

Deciding *to* Decide

Managers are too busy and have too many valuable things to do with their time to respond personally by making decisions on every problem situation that comes their way. The effective manager knows when to delegate decisions to others, how to set priorities, and when not to act at all. When confronted with a problem, therefore, it is recommended that managers ask themselves the following questions.[17]

1. *Is the problem easy to deal with?*   Small and less significant problems should not get as much time and attention as bigger ones. Even if a mistake is made, the cost of decision error on small problems is also small.
2. *Might the problem resolve itself?*   Putting problems in rank order leaves the less significant for last . . . if any time remains. Surprisingly, many of these will resolve themselves or be solved by others before the manager gets to them. One less problem to solve leaves decision making time and energy for other uses.
3. *Is this my decision to make?*   Many problems can be handled by persons at lower levels in the hierarchy. These decisions should be delegated. Other problems can and should be referred to higher levels. This is especially true for decisions that have consequences for a larger part of the organization than under a manager's immediate control.

Deciding *How* to Decide

OB theorists identify two alternative approaches to decision making, classical and behavioral. A discussion of each will help you to understand further the important relationship between perception and the processes through which managers make decisions.[18]

Classical Decision Theory

Classical decision theory views the manager as acting in a world of complete certainty. The manager faces a clearly defined problem, knows all possible action alternatives and their consequences, and then chooses the alternative giving the best or ''optimum'' resolution of the problem. Clearly, this is an ideal way to make decisions. Classical theory is often used as a model for how managers *should* make decisions.

Behavioral scientists are cautious regarding classical decision theory. They recognize that the human mind is a wonderful creation, capable of infinite achievements. But they also recognize that we each have cognitive limitations. The human mind is limited in its information processing capabilities. Information deficiencies and overload both compromise the ability of managers to make decisions according to the classical model. As a result, it is argued that behavioral decision theory gives a more accurate descripton of how people make decisions in actual practice.

Behavioral Decision Theory

Behavioral decision theory says that people act only in terms of what they perceive about a given situation. Furthermore, such perceptions are frequently imperfect.

Rather than facing a world of complete certainty, the behavioral decision maker is seen as acting under uncertainty and with limited information. Managers make decisions about problems that are often ambiguous, have only a partial knowledge about the available action alternatives and their consequences, and choose the first alternative that appears to give a satisfactory resolution of the problem. This is referred to by Herbert Simon, who has since won a Nobel Prize for his efforts, as a **satisficing** style of decision making. Simon and a colleague state,[19]

> Most human decision making, whether individual or organizational, is concerned with the discovery and selection of satisfactory alternatives; only in exceptional cases is it concerned with the discovery and selection of optimal decisions.

The key difference between a manager's ability to make an optimum decision in the classical style and the tendency to make a satisficing decision in the behavioral style is the presence of cognitive limitations and their impact on our perceptions. Cognitive limitations impair our abilities to define problems, identify action alternatives, and choose alternatives with ideal and predictable consequences. Figure 13.5 shows how these limitations differentiate between the two decision-making approaches.

Decision Making and Intuition

Planning is a form of managerial decision making, and a debate among scholars regarding how managers really plan nicely introduces the importance of intuition to our current discussion. On one side of the issue are those who believe planning can be taught and done in a systematic step-by-step fashion along the lines earlier illustrated in Figure 13.4. On the other side are those who believe the very nature of managerial work makes this hard to do in actual practice. The ideas of Henry Mintzberg, whose research on managerial behavior was first introduced in Chapter 1, are illustrative here. He argues as follows.

FIGURE 13.5   Decision making in the classical and behavioral perspectives.

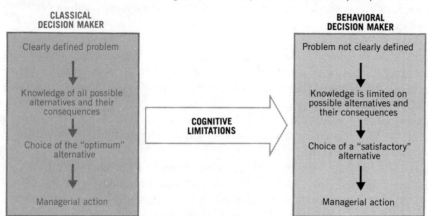

- *Managers favor verbal communications.* Thus, they are more likely to gather data and make decisions in a relational or interactive way, than in a systematic step-by-step fashion.
- *Managers often deal with impressions.* Thus, they are more likely to synthesize than analyze data as they search for the "big picture" in order to make decisions.
- *Managers work fast, do a variety of things, and are frequently interrupted.* Thus, they do not have a lot of quiet time alone to think, plan, or make decisions systematically.

This reasoning leads Mintzberg and others to stress the role of personal "hunch" and "judgment" in decision making. A key element is **intuition,** or the ability to know or recognize quickly and readily the possibilities of a situation. Intuition adds an element of spontaneity to managerial decision making, and it offers the potential for greater creativity and innovation as a result. Especially in risk and uncertain environments, successful managers are probably using a good deal of intuition in problem solving. It is a way of dealing with situations where precedents are unclear, "facts" are limited or tenuous, and time is of the essence.

One criticism of the MBA teams in the chapter opening example, in fact, was their lack of imagination in dealing with the Kool-Aid problem. Although very systematic and logical in their approaches, they were not very creative. Many executives argue that these students and others like them need help during their years of formal education to better develop their intuitive or "right brain" skills. A major and still lingering question at this point in time relates to how this can be done best. Suggestions like those listed in Table 13.3 should be considered as only a first-step toward developing your intuitive skills.

Deciding *Who* Should Decide

The actual choice of a particular problem solution can be arrived at through individual, consultative, or group decision methods. In practice, these methods result in decisions of the following types.

1. *Individual decisions.* The manager makes the final choice alone based on information that he or she possesses, and without the participation of other persons. This choice often reflects the manager's position of formal authority in the organization.
2. *Decisions via consultation.* The manager solicits inputs on the problem from other persons. Based on this information and its interpretation, the manager then makes a final choice.
3. *Group decisions.* The manager not only consults with other persons for information inputs but also asks them to participate in problem-solving discussions and in making the actual choice. Although sometimes difficult, the group decision is the most participative of the three methods of final choice.

TABLE 13.3   Suggested Ways to Activate Your Intuition

Relaxation Techniques
- Drop the problem for a while.
- Take some quiet time by yourself.
- Try to clear your mind.

Mental Exercises
- Use images to guide your thinking.
- Let your ideas run without a specific goal in mind.
- Practice accepting ambiguity and lack of total control.

Analytical Exercises
- Discuss problems with people having different viewpoints.
- Address problems at times of maximum personal alertness.
- Take creative pauses before making final decisions.

Source: Developed from Weston H. Agor, ''How Top Executives Use Their Intuition to Make Important Decisions,'' *Business Horizons,* Vol. 29 (January–February 1986), pp. 49–53.

Managers use each of these approaches to decision making. The key is to know when to use each method and then to be able to implement it well. The basic goal, of course, is to make a *good* decision, that is, one that is high in quality, timely, and understandable and acceptable to those whose support is needed for implementation. Good decisions can be made by each of the three methods: individual, consultative, and group. The successful manager achieves this by knowing when and how to use each in a manner that maximizes its advantages and minimizes its disadvantages in a given situation.

Figure 13.6 highlights the potential assets and liabilities found at both extremes of this continuum of decision-making methods. These were initially discussed in our review of group decision making in Chapter 8. Now we must use this insight as a

FIGURE 13.6   A continuum of decision-making methods.

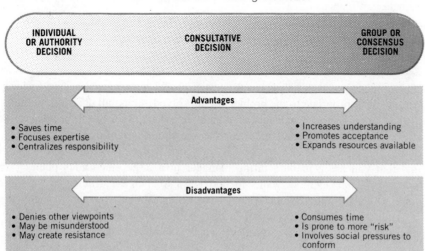

basis for helping managers to choose among these methods to ensure that good decisions are made. At issue is the degree of participation to be sought in any problem solving and decision making situation. Should a manager act alone? consult others? or seek group consensus?

MANAGING PARTICIPATION IN DECISION MAKING

Victor Vroom and Phillip Yetton have developed a framework for helping managers choose which of the three decision-making methods is most appropriate for the various problem situations encountered in their daily work efforts.[22] Their framework begins by expanding the three basic decision-making methods into the five forms that follow:

AI *(first variant on the authority decision):* Manager solves the problem or makes the decision alone using information available at that time.

AII *(second variant on the authority decision):* Manager obtains the necessary information from subordinate(s) or other group members, then decides on the problem solution. The manager may or may not tell subordinates what the problem is before obtaining the information from them. The subordinates provide the necessary information but do not generate or evaluate alternatives.

CI *(first variant on the consultative decision):* Manager shares the problem with relevant subordinates or other group members individually, getting their ideas and suggestions without bringing them together as a group. The manager then makes a decision that may or may not reflect subordinates' influence.

CII *(second variant on the consultative decision):* Manager shares the problem with subordinates or other group members, collectively obtaining their ideas and suggestions. The manager then makes the decision that may or may not reflect subordinates' influence.

G *(the group or consensus decision):* Manager shares the problem with subordinates as a total group and engages the group in consensus seeking to arrive at a final decision.

The central proposition in the Vroom and Yetton model is that the decision-making method should be appropriate to the problem being solved. Thus, all decision methods are useful and important to a manager and each should be used over time. The task is to know when and how to implement each as the situation requires.

Assume that you are a manufacturing manager in a large electronics plant.[23] The company's management wants to find ways to increase efficiency. New machines and a simplified work system have been installed, but the expected rise in productivity has not occurred. In fact, both production and quality have dropped, and employee turnover has risen. There is evidence that there is nothing wrong with the machine.

You suspect that some parts of the new work system may be responsible for the change, but your immediate subordinates do not generally agree. They are four first-line supervisors and a supply manager. The drop in production has been attributed to (1) poor operator training, (2) lack of financial incentives, and (3) poor morale. There is considerable depth of feeling and potential disagreement among your subordinates.

This morning, you received a phone call from the division manager. He just saw your production figures. He indicated that you could solve the problem however you wanted, but to let him know within a week the steps you plan to take.

Both you and your subordinates share your boss's concern. How should you proceed in making a decision regarding the production problem? Would you make your decision via

AI?   AII?   CI?   CII?   G?

Choosing a Decision-Making Method

Vroom and Yetton argue that a proper choice of decision-making method will depend on the basic attributes of the problem facing the manager. Extensive research on decision making has led them to develop the decision-process flow chart shown in Figure 13.7. They offer the chart as a way for managers to analyze the attributes of problem situations and choose the most appropriate decision method.

To use the chart in Figure 13.8, start at the left and sequentially answer each of the diagnostic questions (A through G) for the problem at hand. Highlighted in the figure is the path most appropriate for the problem that we asked you to analyze in the preceding Checkpoint. It shows that the problem would be best handled via a G method. That is, you should share the problem with your subordinates and arrive at a group consensus decision.

The "ideal" decision methods shown at the ends of the various paths in Figure 13.7 are the most time efficient methods. For each ideal solution of the A and C type, a feasible set also exists. The A set includes the C and G options; the C set includes G as an option. To the extent that sufficient time is available, Vroom and Yetton suggest that choosing another option in the set allows for subordinate development by increasing opportunities to learn through participation in the problem solving process.

Managerial Implications

The Vroom and Yetton model has been criticized as being complex and cumbersome.[24] We would agree, and certainly we do not expect you to work through Figure 13.7 for every problem faced. Yet there is a basic discipline in the model that is most useful. When you face decision situations in the future, a familiarity with this model will help you recognize how time, quality requirements, information availability, and subordinate acceptance issues can affect decision outcomes. Furthermore, the model helps

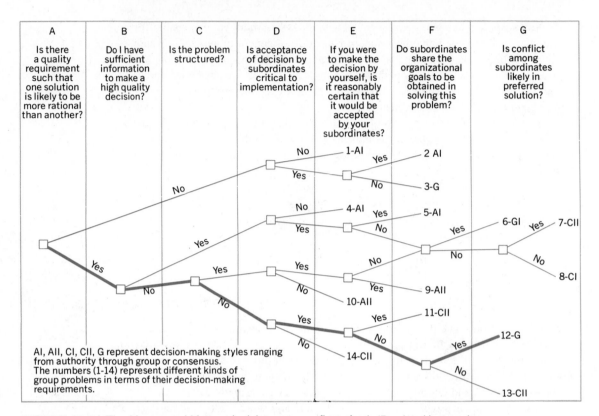

A	B	C	D	E	F	G
Is there a quality requirement such that one solution is likely to be more rational than another?	Do I have sufficient information to make a high quality decision?	Is the problem structured?	Is acceptance of decision by subordinates critical to implementation?	If you were to make the decision by yourself, is it reasonably certain that it would be accepted by your subordinates?	Do subordinates share the organizational goals to be obtained in solving this problem?	Is conflict among subordinates likely in preferred solution?

AI, AII, CI, CII, G represent decision-making styles ranging from authority through group or consensus. The numbers (1–14) represent different kinds of group problems in terms of their decision-making requirements.

FIGURE 13.7 The Vroom and Yetton decision-process flow chart. (Reprinted by permission of the publisher from "A New Look at Managerial Decision-Making," Victor H. Vroom. *Organizational Dynamics,* Spring 1973, Copyright © 1973, by AMACOM, a division of the American Management Association, pp. 68–70. All rights reserved.)

you understand that all of the decision methods are important and useful. The key is to implement each in situations for which it is most suited, and then to do it well.

SUMMARY

Managers depend on information received from their environment to make decisions. Much of this information is gathered through interpersonal relationships with the manager's boss, subordinates, and other persons inside and outside of the work unit. Perception is the process through which a manager receives, organizes, and interprets information from these sources. As the accuracy of the perception process increases or decreases, the quality of a manager's decisions and actions will be affected accordingly. Perception is affected by a variety of situational variables as well as certain organizing tendencies shared by all people. Important situational variables are the characteristics of the perceiver, the social setting, and what is being perceived. The organizing tendencies include the dynamics of Gestalt, figure and ground, set, and attribution.

Several perceptual distortions pose special threats to decision makers. They include stereotypes, halo effects, selective perception, projection, and expectancy. Each distortion, once recognized, can be controlled by the informed manager. A manager who is aware of the influence of these forces on perceptions can recognize when they are contributing to inaccurate perceptions of people or situations. The relationship between attributions and behavior is especially important here.

Perception influences the way in which people make decisions. The significance of this influence is enhanced by the fact that managers must make both programmed and unprogrammed decisions and make these decisions in certain, risky, and uncertain environments. Successful managerial decision making requires answers to three questions when a problem situation is encountered: (1) Is a decision really required? (2) How should the decision be made? (3) Who should be involved in the decision? Limited cognitive abilities to receive and process information result most often in a behavioral style of decision making. Only a limited number of action alternatives are considered, and the first satisfactory, rather than optimum one, is selected for action. The use of a behavioral style of decision making reminds all managers that their perceptions must be especially accurate to ensure that good results are achieved.

Finally, we examined issues involved in a manager's choice of individual, consultative, or group decision methods in a given situation. The Vroom–Yetton model as used to lend insight into managing participation in decision making with due consideration to the quality and acceptance required as well as the time available. This model helps to show how effective managers successfully employ each of the decision-making methods.

THINKING THROUGH THE ISSUES

1. Describe why perception is a key variable in the manager's attempt to meet his or her work responsibilities.
2. Identify the situational variables that may have influenced your perceptions of a work experience. What could be done to control these perceptions and possibly change your attitudes or behavior toward this work situation?
3. What is the major difference between the stereotype and the halo effect? Give an example of how each might have a negative effect on a manager's relationships with his or her subordinates.
4. Explain how expectancy effects may account for the behavior of students in the classroom. Be sure to include examples of where an instructor's use of initial assumptions about students may create self-fulfilling prophecies.
5. Define and give an example of ''attribution error'' and ''self-serving bias'' as perceptual tendencies that can interfere with managerial decision making.
6. Summarize the importance of the perception process to the manager who seeks to take full working advantage of the various motivational models discussed in Chapter 4.

7. What are the key differences between the classical and behavioral decision theories? How does perception contribute to these differences?

8. Some people argue that it is "good" to have subordinates participating in decision making and "bad" for the boss to be making decisions alone. React to this in terms of the chapter discussion and the Vroom–Yetton model.

CASE: THE LESSER OF TWO EVILS

When Liz Porter arrived at State U., she had a one-year contract and was assigned to teach the introductory economics course.[25] Since there were many sections, all instructors worked as a team planning the course, making up exams, and so on.

Liz had trouble from the beginning. She was insecure, acted over-controlling with students, and failed to bring in relevant examples. More important, she could not relate to students or colleagues.

During the second semester, one of her teammates, Ned Martin, took over a section of a special elective that developed a strong following among students. Since this was the first time he taught it, he had to do a lot of work in addition to the time-consuming introductory course. The special elective was in his area of expertise, however, and he did an outstanding job. He fully expected to be assigned only to the elective the following semester. This would mean moving "up" a bit in the hierarchy since teaching electives was viewed as more desirable and higher status than was teaching the introductory course.

Later in the semester, the department head met with faculty to discuss course assignments for the following year. The coordinator for the Intro course begged to have Liz reassigned. Liz admitted that the experience had been an unhappy failure for her. Ned asked to teach the elective again, but he did not push the matter, assuming it was a natural assignment given his experience and expertise. Besides, he would be coming up for promotion and didn't want to appear too aggressive.

When the course assignments were posted, people were shocked to learn that Liz would be back teaching three sections of the special elective. Ned would teach only the Intro course. Several faculty went to the department head to voice their concerns:

1. Liz had no knowledge of the area and admitted she was scared to death of it.
2. Ned had worked hard to prepare to teach the elective and had excellent ratings.
3. Ned had seniority over Liz.
4. It appeared Liz was being "rewarded" for failing.
5. The reputation of the course and number of students enrolling would be affected by putting a "bad" teacher in three sections out of four.

The department head listened and explained that this was the "lesser of two evils." Besides, he believed in the importance of supporting women and helping them develop their competencies. He was proud that he had recruited another woman for the department when Liz came, and he didn't want to let her go.

Questions

1. Look at things through Liz's eyes. How do you react to the department head's decision? Why?
2. Look at things through Ned's eyes. How do you react to the department head's decision? Why?
3. How has ''perception'' influenced events in this case? What recommendations do you have on how things should have been handled by the department head? Defend your answer.

Exercise: Choosing a Decision Making Method

Purpose:

This exercise will give you further experience working with the Vroom and Yetton decision model, and it will help you to become more familiar with the logic of choosing among individual, consultative, and group, or consensus methods for making decisions in groups.

Time:

50 minutes.

Procedure:

1. Read each of the problem situations described.[26]
2. Convene in a group of six to eight persons. Analyze each situation by plotting it on the Vroom–Yetton decision tree depicted in Figure 13.7.
3. Arrive at a final choice in your group as to which decision method is best for each problem situation. Make sure a spokesperson is prepared to explain how and why the group arrived at these choices.
4. The instructor will call on each group to report. After discussion, the Vroom–Yetton solutions to the same problems will be presented. More discussion will follow.

Situation 1. The Oil Pipeline Gang

You are general superintendent in charge of a large gang laying an oil pipeline. It is now necessary to estimate your expected rate of progress to schedule material deliveries to the next field site.

You know the nature of the terrain you will be traveling, and you have the historical data needed to compute the mean and variance in the rate of speed over that type of terrain. Given these two variables, it is a simple matter to calculate the earliest and latest times at which materials and support facilities will be needed at the next site. It is important that your estimate be reasonably accurate. Underestimates result in idle supervisors and workers, and an overestimate results in tying up materials for a period of time before they are to be used.

Progress has been good, and your five supervisors and other members of the gang stand to receive substantial bonuses if the project is completed ahead of schedule.

Situation 2. The Financial Staff Unit

You are the head of a staff unit reporting to the vice president of finance. He has asked you to provide a report on the firm's current portfolio to include recommendations for changes in the selection criteria currently employed. Doubts have been raised about the efficiency of the existing system in the current market conditions, and there is a considerable dissatisfaction with prevailing rates of return.

You plan to write the report, but at the moment you are perplexed about the approach to take. Your own specialty is the bond market, and it is clear to you that a detailed knowledge of the equity market, which you lack, would greatly enhance the value of the report. Fortunately, four members of your staff are specialists in different segments of the equity market. Together they possess a vast amount of knowledge about the intricacies of investment. However, they seldom agree on the best way to achieve anything when it comes to the stock market. While they are obviously conscientious as well as knowledgeable, they have major differences when it comes to investment philosophy and strategy.

You have six weeks before the report is due. You have already begun to familiarize yourself with the firm's current portfolio and have been provided by management with a specific set of constraints that any portfolio must satisfy. Your immediate problem is to come up with some alternatives to the firm's present practices and select the most promising for detailed analysis in your report.

THE MANAGER'S VOCABULARY

Attribution   The tendency to understand behavior or events by interpreting them as caused by certain factors; the attempt to explain "why" something happened the way it did.

Attribution Error   The attributional tendency to underestimate the influence of situational factors and overestimate the influence of internal or personal factors in evaluating someone else's behavior.

Certain Environment   A decision environment in which information is sufficient to predict the results of each alternative in advance of implementation.

Decision Making   The process of identifying a problem or opportunity and choosing among alternative courses of action.

Escalating Commitment   The tendency to continue with a previously chosen course of action even when feedback suggests that it is failing.

Expectancy The tendency to create or find in another situation or individual that which one expected to find in the first place.

Figure and Ground The tendency to distinguish a central object from its surroundings.

Gestalt The tendency to avoid the discomfort of unorganized information by assigning it an overall meaning.

Halo Effect One attribute of a person or situation is used to develop an overall impression of the person or situation.

Impression Management The systematic attempt to behave in ways that create and maintain desired impressions of oneself in the eyes of others.

Intuition The ability to quickly and readily know or recognize the possibilities of a situation.

Nonprogrammed Decisions Decisions that implement new and creative solutions to problems that have not been encountered before.

Perception The process through which people receive, organize, and interpret information from their environment.

Programmed Decisions Decisions that implement specific solutions determined by past experience as appropriate for the problems at hand.

Projection The assignment of personal attributes to other individuals.

Risk Environment A decision environment involving a lack of complete certainty but that includes an awareness of probabilities associated with the possible outcomes of various courses of action.

Satisficing Choosing the first satisfactory rather than the optimal decision alternative.

Selective Perception The tendency to single out for attention those aspects of a situation or person that reinforce or emerge and are consistent with existing beliefs, values, and needs.

Self-Serving Bias The attributional tendency to deny personal responsibility for performance problems, but to accept it for performance success.

Set The tendency to respond to a situation in terms of anticipations rather than in terms of what actually exists.

Stereotype Assigning an individual or event to a group or category and then ascribing to that individual or event the attributes commonly associated with the group or category.

Uncertain Environment A decision environment in which managers are unable to assign probabilities to the possible outcomes of various courses of action.

IMPORTANT NAMES

Herbert Simon Identified the tendency of many managers to use a "satisficing" style of decision making.

NOTES

[1]Developed from Trish Hall, "When Budding MBAs Try to Save Kool-Aid, Original Ideas are Scarce," *The Wall Street Journal* (November 26, 1986), p. 31.

[2]For a discussion of these variables and related research, see Sheldon S. Zalkind and Timothy W. Costello, "Perception: Some Recent Research and Implications for Administration." *Administrative Science Quarterly,* Vol. 7 (September 1962), pp. 218–235.

[3]Dan Rather and Gary Paul Gates, *The Palace Guard* (New York: Harper & Row, 1970), p. 109.

[4]Joann S. Lublin, "Mrs. Lowe Has to Deal with Stress and Sexism as a Bank-Branch Head," *The Wall Street Journal,* April 26, 1977. p. 1.

[5]Virginia Ellen Schein, "Relationships Between Sex Role Stereotypes and Requisite Management Characteristics Among Female Managers," *Journal of Applied Psychology,* Vol. 60 (1975), pp. 340–344; Margaret Hennig and Anne Jardim, *Managerial Woman* (Garden City, N.Y.: Doubleday, 1976); Susan M. Donnell and Jay Hall, "Men and Women as Managers: A Significant Case of No Significant Differences," *Organizational Dynamics,* Vol. 8 (1980), pp. 60–77; and R. W. Rice, D. Instone, and J. Adams, "Leader Sex, Leader Success, and Leadership Process: Two Field Studies," *Human Resources Management,* Vol. 24 (1985), pp. 12–31.

[6]See Benson Rosen and Thomas H. Jerdee, "Influence of Sex-Role Stereotypes on Personnel Decisions," *Journal of Applied Psychology,* Vol. 59 (1974), pp. 9–14: "Sex Stereotyping in the Executing Suite," *Harvard Business Review,* Vol. 52 (March–April 1974), pp. 45–58; "On-the-Job Sex Bias: Increasing Managerial Awareness," *Personnel Administrator,* Vol. 16 (January 1977), pp. 15–18.

[7]Benson Rosen and Thomas H. Jerdee, "The Influence of Age Stereotypes on Managerial Decisions," *Journal of Applied Psychology,* Vol. 61 (1976), pp. 428–432.

[8]John R. MacArthur, "The Early Bird Gets Not Only the Worm But a Better Job," *The Wall Street Journal,* September 20, 1977, p. 1.

[9]Dewitt C. Dearborn and Herbert A. Simon, "Selective Perception: A Note on the Departmental Identification of Executives," *Sociometry,* Vol. 21 (1958), pp. 140–144.

[10]J. Sterling Livingston, "Pygmalion in Management," *Harvard Business Review,* Vol. 47 (July–August 1969), pp. 81–89; also Robert Rosenthal, "The Pygmalion Effect Lives," *Psychology Today,* Vol. 7 (September 1973), pp. 56–63; and, Dov Eden, "Self-Fulfilling Prophecy as a Management Tool: Harnessing Pygmalion," *Academy of Management Review,* Vol. 9 (1984), pp. 64–73.

[11]See Terrence R. Mitchell, S. G. Green and R. E. Wood, "An Attribution Model of Leadership and the Poor Performing Subordinate," pp. 197–234, in Barry Staw and Larry L. Cummings, (eds.), *Research in Organizational Behavior* (New York: JAI Press, 1981); and, John H. Harvey and Gifford Weary, "Current Issues in Attribution Theory and Research," *Annual Review of Psychology,* Vol. 35 (1984), pp. 427–459.

[12]For a good overview, see B. R. Schlenker, *Impression Management: The Self-Concept, Social Identity, and Interpersonal Relations* (Monterey, Ca.: Brooks/Cole, 1980).

[13]Subsequent discussion is adapted with permission from John R. Schermerhorn, Jr., *Management for Productivity* (New York: John Wiley & Sons, 1986), pp. 70–71. Copyright © 1986 John Wiley & Sons. Reprinted by permission of John Wiley & Sons, Inc.

[14]Ibid, pp. 76–77.

[15]Barry M. Staw, "The Escalation of Commitment to a Course of Action," *Academy of Management Review,* Vol. 6 (1981), pp. 577–587; and, Barry M. Staw and Jerry Ross, "Knowing When to Pull the Plug," *Harvard Business Review,* Vol. 65 (March–April 1987), pp. 68–74. See also, Glen Whyte, "Escalating Commitment to a Course of Action: A Reinterpretation," *Academy of Management Review,* Vol. 11 (1986), pp. 311–321.

[16]Schermerhorn, op. cit., pp. 79–81.

[17]James A. F. Stoner, *Management,* 2nd ed. (Englewood Cliffs, N.J.: Prentice-Hall, 1982), pp. 167–168.

[18]This discussion is based on James G. March and Herbert A. Simon, *Organizations* (New York: John Wiley, 1958), pp. 137–142.

[19]Ibid. See also Herbert A. Simon, *Administrative Behavior* (New York: Free Press, 1947).

[20]Henry Mintzberg, "Planning on the Left Side and Managing on the Right," *Harvard Business Review,* Vol. 54 (July–August 1976), pp. 51–63.

[21]See James Brian Quinn, "Strategic Change: Logical Incrementalism," *Sloan Management Review,* Vol. 20 (Fall 1978), pp. 7–21; and, Herbert Simon, "Making Management Decisions: The Role of Intuition and Emo-

tion," *Academy of Management Review,* Vol. 1 (February 1987), pp. 57–64. See also Weston H. Agor, *Intuitive Management* (Englewood Cliffs, N.J.: Prentice-Hall, 1984); and for a more popular viewpoint, see John Naisbitt and Patricia Aburdene, *Re-Inventing the Corporation* (New York: Warner, 1985).

[22]The material in this section is based on Victor H. Vroom, "A New Look in Managerial Decision-Making," *Organizational Dynamics* (Spring 1973), pp. 66–80.

[23]From Victor H. Vroom and Philip Yetton, *Leadership and Decision-Making* (Pittsburgh: University of Pittsburgh Press, 1973).

[24]R. H. G. Field, "A Critique of the Vroom–Yetton Contingency Model of Leader Behavior." *Academy of Management Review,* Vol. 4 (April 1979), pp. 249–257.

[25]From Douglas T. Hall, Donald D. Bowen, Roy J. Lewicki, and Francine S. Hall, *Experiences in Management and Organizational Behavior,* 2nd ed. (New York: John Wiley & Sons, 1982), p. 312–313. Copyright © 1982 John Wiley & Sons. Reprinted by permission of John Wiley & Sons, Inc.

[26]The problem situations are from Vroom and Yetton, *Leadership and Decision-Making.*

CHAPTER 14
COMMUNICATION AND CONFLICT

BellSouth people exemplify performance, service and teamwork at its best. We cannot overstate the ability of our people to work together.

Bell Southern Corporation Annual Report

KOREA'S NEWEST EXPORT
IS MANAGEMENT STYLE

The Japanese have gotten most of the recent publicity when it comes to new and alternative management styles. But there's a newcomer on the scene that's starting to have an impact—South Korea.[1] Names such as Samsung, Hyundai and Daewoo are becoming more and more familiar to American consumers. And these companies are opening their own U.S. plants. Estimates are that the Korean investment here could swell to $5 billion in the next 10 years.

Along with their financial commitments, the Koreans are also bringing an egalitarian management style that is more flexible than its Japanese counterpart. Hai Min Lee, President of Samsung U.S.A., is one example. Like other Korean managers he espouses teamwork, employee participation, minimal hierarchy, and the corporation-as-a-family idea. Managers and workers at Samsung's television assembly plant in New Jersey exchange ideas freely on the plant floor and in the lunchroom, where Lee eats rights along with everyone else. Face-to-face meetings between supervisors and subordinates are expected, as is consensus decision making. Lee says, "the person who knows the factory process best shouldn't be left out." In one meeting, workers suggested raising the height of a belt carrying TVs through the assembly process to relieve back strain—it was done. In another they asked for piped-in music to relieve boredom—it was done. In addition, they work on a "power and free" assembly line whose speed *they* can adjust.

The Korean approach has its advocates. Myrtel Sanders, a Samsung employee, sums things up well. "I used to work at an RCA plant and they took the employees for granted," she said and then continued, "You can voice your opinion here."

Management Applications Question

Managers at all levels in organizations require accurate information to make good decisions and take effective action. What will you do, as a manager, to ensure a free and open sharing of information between yourself and the other people in your work setting?

PLANNING AHEAD

The learning activities of this chapter will help you to gain insight into the interpersonal processes of communication and conflict. Key topics include

Communication and the Manager
The Communication Process
Guidelines for Effective Communication
Communication of Roles
Conflict
Conflict Situations in Organizations
Conflict Management

"Communication" is a word like "organization." Everyone knows what it means until asked to formally state its definition. It is useful to think of **communication** as an interpersonal process of sending and receiving symbols with meanings attached to them. The opening example highlights the importance of this process to managers and the people who work with them. A major challenge for everyone in organizations is handling information exchanges and the potential conflicts sometimes associated with them. This chapter will help you gain a useful managerial perspective on both communication and conflict as two important interpersonal processes affecting behavior in organizations.

COMMUNICATION AND THE MANAGER

When problems arise in organizations, their cause is frequently identified as poor communication. This is because communication is the source of information used by managers in making decisions that affect the organization. When poor decisions result, bad communication is frequently to blame.

Managers depend on their communication skills to get the information required to make decisions, and to transmit the results and intentions of these decisions to other people. Research indicates managers spend a large proportion of their time communicating directly with other people. Henry Mintzberg's study of chief executives showed, for example, that their time was distributed on the average as follows: Scheduled and unscheduled meetings (69 percent), telephone calls (6 percent), and walk-around tours (3 percent).[2] Only 22 percent of their time was spent alone doing desk work. Giving, receiving, and otherwise sharing information with people at work was obviously very important to this group of executives. The same conclusion holds true for managers in general.

Every manager is the center of an information processing network such as the one depicted in Figure 14.1. Skills required to succeed in this important capacity involve the ability to communicate with others while acting as a monitor, disseminator, spokesperson, and strategy maker. Key linkages upward, downward, and laterally tie the manager to other persons throughout the organization and its environment. In downward communications, the manager transmits job instructions, organizational goals, and performance feedback, along with a variety of other information, to subordinates. On the lateral dimension, the manager seeks to keep the activities of the work unit well coordinated with other units in the organization and with clients or consumers. Upward communications contain opportunities for the manager to transmit information on work unit activity and personal needs to higher organization levels. As we move on in our study of the communication process, keep this description of a manager's information processing responsibilities clearly in mind.

FIGURE 14.1   The manager's responsibilities as an information processor. (Abridged and adapted text from chart on p. 72 in *The Nature of Managerial Work* by Henry Mintzberg. Copyright © 1973 by Henry Mintzberg. Reprinted by permission of Harper & Row Publishers, Inc.)

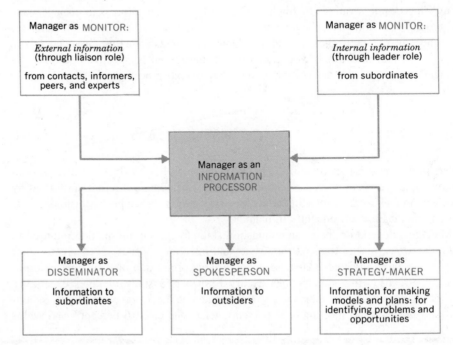

THE COMMUNICATION PROCESS

The key elements in the communication process are diagrammed in Figure 14.2. They include a source, who is responsible for encoding an intended meaning into a message, and a receiver, who decodes the message into a perceived meaning. Feedback from receiver to source may or may not be given.

The information source is a person or group of persons with a reason for communicating with someone else, the receiver. The reasons for the source to communicate include changing the attitudes, knowledge, or behavior of the receiver. As a manager, for example, you may want to communicate with your boss to make him or her understand why your work unit needs more time to finish an assigned project.

To communicate with the receiver, the source translates his or her intended meaning into symbols. This translation is an encoding process that results in a message that may consist of verbal (such as written) or nonverbal (such as gestures) symbols, or some combination of both. The receiver decodes the message into meaning. This process of translation may or may not result in the assignment of the same meaning intended by the source.

Frequently, in fact, the intended meaning of the source and the meaning as perceived by the receiver differ. How would you react, for example, to this well-intentioned road sign advertising a combination diner and gasoline station.[3]

> EAT HERE AND GET GAS

Do not let the hilarity of this example fool you. It is a challenging task to communicate accurately. Managers, like owners of roadside diners, can make mistakes. A more

FIGURE 14.2   The communication process and possible sources of "noise."

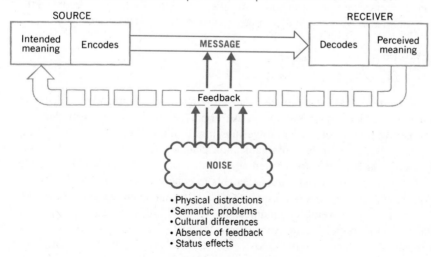

specific look at the key elements in the communication process can help us analyze the causes of such communication errors.

Effective and Efficient Communication

Effective communication occurs when the intended meaning of the source and the perceived meaning of the receiver are one and the same. This should be the manager's goal in any communication attempt. It is not always achieved. Even now, we worry whether or not you are interpreting our written words as we intend. Our confidence would be higher if we were face-to-face in class together and you could ask clarifying questions. This opportunity to offer feedback and ask questions is one way of increasing the effectiveness of communication.

Efficient communication occurs at minimum cost in terms of resources expended. Time is an important resource in the communication process. Picture your instructor taking the time to communicate individually with each student. It would be virtually impossible to do. And even if it were possible, it would be very costly in terms of time. Managers often choose not to visit employees personally to communicate messages. Instead, they rely on the efficiency of such channels as the ever-popular memo (highlighted in Newsline 14.1), posted bulletins, or group meetings.

Efficient communications are not always effective. A low-cost communication such as a posted bulletin may save time for the sender, but it does not always achieve the desired results in terms of the receiver's perceived meaning. Similarly, an effective communication may not be efficient. For a manager to visit each employee and explain a new change in procedures may guarantee that everyone truly understands the change. It may also be prohibitively expensive in terms of the required time expenditure.

Managers are busy people who depend on their communication skills to remain successful in their work. You need to learn how to maximize the effectiveness of your communications with other people and to achieve reasonable efficiency in the process. This requires an understanding of formal and informal communication channels, a special awareness of nonverbal communications, and the ability to overcome a number of communication barriers that commonly operate in the workplace.

Formal and Informal Communication Channels

Formal communication channels follow the chain of command established by an organization's hierarchy of authority. An organization chart, for example, indicates the proper routing for official messages passing from one level or part of the hierarchy to another. Because formal communication channels are recognized as official and authoritative, it is typical for written communications in the form of letters, memos, policy statements, and other announcements to adhere to them.

Although necessary and important, the use of formal channels constitutes only one part of a manager's overall communication responsibilities. You should recall that in Chapter 1 we identified interpersonal "networking" as an essential activity for effective managers.[4] In the present context, such networks represent the use of the formal

NEWSLINE 14.1 / MEMOS CAN LIFT—OR LIMIT— YOUR CAREER

Memos, Memos, Memos!! How aggravating memos can be. They're often hard to write, hard to read, and simply too time-consuming to deal with. They are also somewhat inconsistent with what the *effective* manager is really supposed to do. Harvard Professor John Kotter says, "The most effective managers tend not to be trapped in their offices reading reports and writing memos. They talk to people, sit in on meetings, and make speeches." Yet, the memo does have a legitimate place in management communications. As *Fortune* columnist Walter Kiechel, III, notes:

- The memo remains the best single device for communicating substantial chunks of detailed information to a co-worker.
- The memo is the managerial tool of choice when you want to put out work

to lots of people, more than you can conveniently assemble for an oral exhortation.

Some managers overuse memos because they are uncomfortable in face-to-face communications. Others use them for political reasons—to document something they want credit for, or to document something they want to protect themselves on. Beyond knowing *when* to use a memo, managers must also know *how* to write one well. Kiechel offers this advice.

1. Write with a well-defined purpose in mind.
2. Write clearly, whatever your motive.
3. Write the way you talk, and use short sentences.
4. Write in brief, keep it short.
5. Then hold on to it awhile, you may change your mind.

Reported in *Fortune*.

channels just described *plus* a wide variety of **informal communication channels** that do not adhere to the organization's hierarchy of authority. They coexist with the formal channels, but frequently diverge from them by skipping levels in the hierarchy and/or cutting across vertical chains of command.

The importance of informal communication channels in organizations is highlighted in the best selling book *In Search of Excellence*.[5] Thomas J. Peters and Robert H. Waterman, Jr., the book's authors, report that, "The excellent companies are a vast network of informal, open communications. The patterns and intensity cultivate the right people's getting into contact with each other." Some of the interesting examples they cite include

Walt Disney Productions. Everyone from the president on down wears a tag with only his or her first name on it.

Levi Strauss.   Management calls its open-door policy the "fifth freedom."

Corning Glass.   Management installed escalators instead of elevators in a new engineering building to increase opportunities for face-to-face contact.

3M.   The firm sponsors clubs for groups of 12 or more employees in hopes of increasing the probability of spontaneous problem-solving sessions.

Another informal channel we all know about is the "grapevine." Among the advantages of grapevines are their abilities to transmit information quickly and efficiently. Every experienced manager realizes that a message well placed in a grapevine can often travel faster and with greater impact than can the same message passed through formal channels. Grapevines also help to fulfill the needs of people involved in them. Being part of a grapevine can lead to a sense of security from "being in the know" when important things are going on. It also provides social support through the variety of interpersonal contacts involved in the give and take of communication.

The primary disadvantage of grapevines occurs when they transmit incorrect or untimely information. Rumors and prematurely released information can be dysfunctional. Astute managers get to know the grapevines operating in their work settings and try to use them to advantage. After all, one of the best ways of avoiding incorrect rumor is to make sure that key persons in a grapevine get the right information to begin with.

Nonverbal Communication

A most interesting aspect of the communication process is its nonverbal form. Look at the accompanying photograph. Notice the facial expression of the man at the left; notice, too, the arm and hand position of the man at the right. Each person appears

"Nonverbal aspects of interpersonal communication are often as important as the spoken and/or written word."

to be communicating something, but without a spoken word of their conversation being known to us!

Nonverbal communication is communication through facial expressions, body position, eye contact, and other physical gestures rather than written or oral expression. Although it is widely recognized that there is a nonverbal side to communication, we often underestimate its importance. A second look at the photograph should sensitize you to the managerial significance of this issue. Consider, too, the fact that nonverbal communication affects the impressions we make on other persons. It is known, for example, that interviewers respond more favorably to job candidates whose nonverbal cues (such as eye contact and erect posture) are positive than to those displaying negative nonverbal cues (such as looking down and slouching). Impression management, as introduced in Chapter 13, requires attention to one's nonverbal as well as verbal communications.

Nonverbal communication can also take place through the physical arrangement of space, such as that found in various office layouts. Figure 14.3 shows three different office arrangements and the messages they may communicate to visitors.

Check the diagram in Figure 14.3 against the furniture arrangement in your office, your instructor's, or that of a manager with whom you are familiar. What are you/they saying to visitors by the choice of furniture placement?

Research confirms that office designs do in fact communicate.[6] It is known that visitors tend to be uncomfortable in offices where a desk is placed between them and the person to whom they are speaking. Other things that also seem to make a difference are the selection of artwork and decorations found in an office, as well as its neatness.

Barriers to Effective Communication

Noise is anything that interferes with the effectiveness of a communications attempt. Five special sources of noise are physical distractions, semantic problems, cultural

FIGURE 14.3   Furniture placement and nonverbal communication in the office.

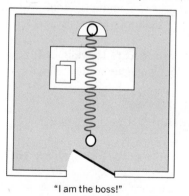

"I am the boss!"

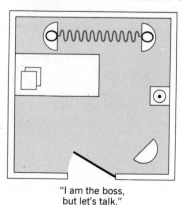

"I am the boss,
but let's talk."

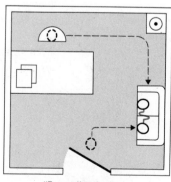

"Forget I'm the boss,
let's talk."

differences, the absence of feedback, and status effects. Each of these sources of noise should be recognized and subjected to special managerial control. They are included in Figure 14.2 (shown earlier) as potential threats to any communication process.

Physical Distractions

Any number of physical distractions can interfere with the effectiveness of a communications attempt. Some of these distractions are evident in the following conversation between an employee, George, and his manager.[7]

> Okay, George, let's hear your problem (phone rings, boss picks it up, promises to deliver the report, "just as soon as I can get it done"). Un, now, where were we—oh, you're having a problem with your secretary. She's (. . . secretary—the manager's—brings in some papers that need immediate signature, so he scribbles his name where she indicates; secretary leaves) . . . you say she's depressed a lot lately, wants to leave . . . ? I tell you what, George, why don't you (phone rings again, lunch partner drops by) . . . uh, take a stab at handling it yourself . . . I've got to go now.

Besides what may have been poor intentions in the first place, George's manager was suffering from physical distractions that created information overload. He or she was letting too many requests for information processing occur at once. As a result, the communication with George suffered.

  The mistake of processing too much information at once can be eliminated by setting priorities and planning. If George has something to say, his manager should set aside adequate time for the meeting. In addition, interruptions such as telephone calls, secretarial requests, and drop-in visitors should be prevented. All these things physically distracted both parties in their attempt to communicate in the example. Each distraction, in turn, could have been avoided by proper managerial attention.

Semantic Problems

Semantic barriers to communication occur as encoding and decoding errors and as mixed messages. They involve symbols being poorly selected by the source and the message being subsequently misinterpreted by the receiver. Communications will be effective only to the extent that the source makes good choices when creating messages.

  We generally do not realize how easily semantic errors occur. They abound, however, as this sign once posted in a University of Colorado cafeteria illustrates.[8]

**SHOES ARE REQUIRED TO EAT
IN THE CAFETERIA**

A perceptive student added to this sign the gratuitous comment: "socks can eat wherever they want."

  The following illustrations of the "bafflegab" that once tried to pass as actual "executive communications" are an additional case in point.[9]

A. "We solicit any recommendations that you wish to make, and you may be assured that any such recommendations will be given our careful consideration."

B. "Consumer elements are continuing to stress the fundamental necessity of a stabilization of the price structure at a lower level than exists at the present time."

One has to wonder why the messages weren't more simply stated as: (A) "Send us your recommendations. They will be carefully considered." and (b) "Consumers want lower prices."

Another semantic problem is the conflict between verbal and nonverbal communications. **Mixed messages** result when a person's words communicate one message while their actions or "body language" communicate something else.

Cultural Differences

We opened this chapter with an example of Koreans managing American workers. Although the reported case is a positive one, managers and other persons must always exercise caution when involved in cross-cultural communication. Newsline 14.2 indicates that some Japanese firms are now experiencing difficulties with labor–management and company–community relations at their U.S. plants. Cultural differences certainly play at least some role in these problems. Managers must understand that different cultural backgrounds between senders and receivers can cause breakdowns in the communication process. This includes communications between persons of different geographical or ethnic groupings from within one country, as well as between persons of different national cultures.

A common problem in cross-cultural communications is **ethnocentrism,** the tendency to consider one's culture and its values as being superior to others. Very often such tendencies are accompanied by an unwillingness to try and understand alternative points of view and take seriously the values they represent. This can be highly disadvantageous when trying to conduct business and maintain effective working relationships with persons from different cultures.

The difficulties with cross-cultural communication are perhaps most obvious when it comes to language differences among people. A convenient illustration is the case of advertising messages that work well in one country but encounter difficulty when translated into the language of another. Consider these international business mistakes.

Coca-Cola Company once lost sales in some Asian markets when consumers were confused over the ad, "Coke Adds Life." They translated the message to mean "Coke Brings You Back from the Dead."

General Motors' Chevrolet's "Nova" model translated into Spanish as "Chevrolet no go." This is exactly what happened to sales of the car in Latin America.

Absence of Feedback

In one-way communications like the written memo there is no direct and immediate feedback from receiver to source. Two-way communications include such feedback

NEWSLINE 14.2 / COLLISION OF CULTURES AT SOME JAPANESE PLANTS IN THE U.S.?

As Japanese investment continues to sweep across the United States, many Americans look at the positive side. They see communities gaining new sources of capital, new jobs being created in depressed areas, *and* productivity being revived in aging industries. Other Americans are concerned about possible negative sides to the trend. Some fear the Japanese are simply creating their own industrial bases in such heartland states as Kentucky, Ohio, and Tennessee where Toyota, Nissan, and Honda have large operations. "They're not creating jobs," snaps one union official, "They're stealing jobs."

Japanese management practices have generally been well received. The philosophy is to make people important, allow employees to help decide how to do their jobs, and emphasize cooperative labor–management relations. At the successful Toyota–GM joint venture in California, the United Auto Workers (UAW) local union president says: "When GM was here, we hated each other . . . Now management has given us a voice and listens to us." But, the magic doesn't always work. There's trouble at Sanyo's Arkansas television and microwave factory. A strike in which pickets carried signs reading "Japs Go Home" and "Remember Pearl Harbor" left Japanese managers and American workers openly bitter about one another. A Sanyo vice president said: "They come here for eight hours work and eight hours pay . . . As long as they get that, they don't care what happens to our production. Here, there's no sacrifice." A union official says, in contrast, "Trust really isn't there. Seniority isn't going to cause them to go broke." There's been trouble too at Sumimoto Corporation of America, which had to settle a sex-discrimination suit filed by former women workers. They complained of being restricted to clerical positions without promotions to management.

Even Japanese diplomats are worried about this potential "collision of cultures." Citing the case of a new Toyota plant being built in Kentucky, one notes that most of the people being sent in by the company "don't speak English . . . they don't know how to deal with local people, and the local people don't know how to deal with them."

Reported in *Business Week* and *Newsweek*.

and are characterized by the normal interactive conversations in our daily experiences. Figuratively speaking, two-way communication is of the form

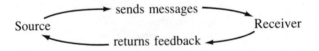

Research indicates that two-way communication is more accurate and effective than one-way; it is also more costly and time consuming.[10] Yet the more efficient

one-way forms of communication—memo, letter, posted bulletin, and the like—are frequently used in work settings. Because it avoids immediate feedback, it can be less threatening to the sender although very frustrating for the receiver. In particular, the recipient of a one-way message is often unsure of just what the sender wants done.

Status Effects

The hierarchy of authority in organizations can create another barrier to effective communication. Communication is frequently biased when flowing upward in organizational hierarchies.[11] Status differentials create special barriers between managers and their subordinates. Given the authority of their positions, managers may be inclined to do a lot of "telling" but not much "listening." Subordinates, on the other hand, may tell their superiors only what they expect the boss wants to hear. Whether the reason is a fear of retribution for bringing bad news, an unwillingness to identify personal mistakes, or just a general desire to please, the result is the same. The manager ends up making poor decisions because of a biased and inaccurate information base.

To avoid such problems, managers must develop trust in their working relationships with subordinates and take advantage of all opportunities for face-to-face communications. "Management by wandering around" is now popularly acclaimed as one way to do this. It simply means getting out of the office and talking regularly to people as they do their jobs. Managers who spend time walking around can greatly reduce the perceived "distance" between themselves and their subordinates. They can also create an atmosphere of open and free-flowing communication, which makes more and better information available for decision making, as well as increases the relevancy of decisions to the needs of lower-level personnel. Of course, the wandering around must be a genuine attempt to communicate. It should not be perceived as just another way to "check up" on employees.

GUIDELINES FOR EFFECTIVE COMMUNICATION

Being an effective communicator is a skill. Part of the skill lies in recognizing and controlling communication barriers. Another part is to simply become good at encouraging the flow of information in your direction. This involves being a good listener and also being good at giving constructive feedback to others in an unthreatening way. It is through these skills that the manager acts to take full advantage of two-way communication.

Active Listening

The ability to listen well is a distinct asset to managers whose jobs, as noted earlier, involve such a large proportion of time spent "communicating" with other people. After all, there are two sides to the communication process—sending a message or "telling," and receiving a message or "listening." There is legitimate concern, however, that too many managers may emphasize the former and neglect the latter—

especially in their relationships with subordinates.[12] One solution is for managers to develop better **active listening** skills, an ability to help the source of a message say what he or she really means. The concept comes from counselors and therapists who are highly skilled at helping people express themselves and talk about things that are important to them. You should be familiar with active listening as a technique for improving the effectiveness of communications in organizations. Five guidelines are especially useful in this regard.

1. *Listen for message content:* try to hear exactly what is being said in the message.
2. *Listen for feelings:* try to identify how the source feels in terms of the message content. Is this something pleasing or displeasing to the source? Why?
3. *Respond to feelings:* let the source know that his or her feelings, as well as the message content, are recognized.
4. *Note all cues, verbal and nonverbal:* be sensitive to the nonverbal communications as well as the verbal ones; identify mixed messages that need to be clarified.
5. *Reflect back to the source, in your own words, what you think you are hearing:* paraphrase and restate the verbal and nonverbal messages as feedback to which the source can respond with further information.

One of the two conversations below involves active listening by the supervisor. Read each and think through how you would feel as the foreman in the case.[13]

Example 1

Foreman: Hey, Al, I don't get this production order. We can't handle this run today. What do they think we are?

Supervisor: But that's the order. So get it out as soon as you can. We're under terrific pressure this week.

Foreman: Don't they know we're behind schedule already because of that press breakdown?

Supervisor: Look, Kelly, I don't decide what goes on upstairs. I just have to see that the work gets out and that's what I'm gonna do.

Foreman: The guys aren't gonna like this.

Supervisor: That's something you'll have to work out with them, not me.

Example 2

Foreman: Hey, Ross, I don't get this production order. We can't handle this run today. What do they think we are?

Supervisor: Sounds like you're pretty sore about it, Kelly.

Foreman: I sure am. We were just about getting back to schedule after that press breakdown. Now this comes along.

Supervisor: As if you didn't have enough work to do, huh?

Foreman: Yeah, I don't know how I'm gonna tell the guys about this.

Supervisor: Hate to face 'em with it now, is that it?

Foreman: I really do. They're under a real strain today. Seems like everything we do around here is rush, rush.

Supervisor: I guess you feel like it's unfair to load anything more on them.

Foreman: Well, yeah, I know there must be plenty of pressure on everybody up the line, but—well, if that's the way it is . . . guess I'd better get the word to 'em.

The supervisor in Example 2 possesses active listening skills. He responded to the foreman's communication attempt in a way that increased the flow of information. The supervisor ended up receiving important information about the work situation and should be able to use this information for constructive results. The foreman also feels better after having been able to really say what he felt, and after being heard!

The Art of Giving Feedback

Managers frequently give feedback to other people, often in the form of performance appraisals. There is an art to giving feedback in such a way that it is accepted and used constructively by the receiver. Feedback poorly given can be threatening and become a basis for resentment and alienation.

Feedback is the process of telling someone else how you feel about something they did or said, or about the situation in general. The first requirement in giving feedback is to recognize when it is intended to truly benefit the receiver and when it is purely an attempt to satisfy a personal need. A manager who berates the secretary for typing errors, for example, may actually be mad about personally failing to give clear instructions in the first place.

Given that the sender's intent is to give helpful feedback to the receiver, a manager should recognize that constructive feedback is[14]

- Given directly and with real feeling, ideally based on a foundation of trust.
- Specific rather than general, with good clear examples.
- Given at a time when the receiver appears most ready to accept it.
- Checked with others to support its validity.
- In respect to things that the receiver can really do something about.
- Not more than the receiver can handle at any particular time.

Giving criticism is certainly one of the most difficult of all communication situations faced by managers. What is intended to be polite and constructive can easily end up being unpleasant and even hostile. This risk is particularly evident in the performance appraisal process discussed in Supplementary Module C. A manager must be able to do more than complete an appraisal form and document performance for the record. In order to serve the developmental needs of the subordinate, the results of the appraisal—both the praises and the criticisms—must be well communicated. The guidelines suggested in Table 14.1 can help you make the critical parts of a performance appraisal interview more productive and beneficial for all concerned.

COMMUNICATION OF ROLES

One of the most important communications in which managers become involved is the sending and receiving of role expectations. A **role** is a set of activities expected of a person holding a particular office or position in a group or organization.[15] The various people who have these expectations regarding the behavior of someone in a role are considered members of the **role set.**

Managers are part of the role sets of their subordinates. For a subordinate, the role expectations communicated by the manager are likely to include instructions about desired behavior and behavior to be avoided, intentions regarding the allocation of rewards, and evaluations about past performance. When the communication of role

---

TABLE 14.1   How to Make Criticism Sessions Productive

Step 1. Get to the point.   Don't evade the issue. Skip the small talk and go straight to the target: "Bob, I want to talk to you about your late reports," or "Barbara, I called you in to discuss your personality conflict with the director of sales."

Step 2. Describe the situation.   Use a descriptive opening that is specific, not general. Avoid evaluative openings at all costs. Evaluative: "Bob, I can no longer deal with your late, sloppy reports." Descriptive: "Bob you've been late on three reports in the last two weeks. That caused us two shipping delays and cost us $5000."

Step 3. Use active listening techniques.   Encourage the subordinate to tell his or her side of the story. It will reduce defensiveness, clarify the situation, and provide both parties with an opportunity to think the problem through. It helps to ask open-ended questions that invite discussion and cannot be answered with a simple "yes" or "no" Begin questions with *what* or *how,* or sometimes *tell me* or *describe.* Bad: "Do you like our new computer system?" Good: "How do you feel about our new computer system?"

Step 4. Agree on the source of the problem and its solution.   It's essential that the subordinate agree that there is in fact a problem. If not, there's little likelihood the problem will be solved. Once you and the subordinate have identified and agreed on the problem, work together to identify the source, and let the subordinate get involved in coming up with a potential solution.

Step 5. Summarize the meeting.   Have the subordinate summarize the discussion and the agreed solution. Both subordinate and manager should leave the session with the same understanding of what was decided. Establish a follow-up date that allows the subordinate reasonable time to correct the situation.

Source: Excerpted from J. Stephen Morris, "How to Make Criticism Sessions Productive," *Wall Street Journal* (October 12, 1981), p. 24. Reprinted by permission of *The Wall Street Journal*. Copyright © 1981 Dow Jones & Company, Inc. All rights reserved.

expectations is distorted by barriers such as those discussed earlier, role ambiguity and role conflict may occur. These role dynamics deserve your attention as one of the many reasons why every manager should work hard at interpersonal communication skills. Remember

$$\text{The communication of role expectations} \xrightarrow{\text{creates}} \text{role dynamics} \xrightarrow[\text{affect}]{\text{that}} \text{work attitudes and behaviors}$$

Role Ambiguity

Role ambiguity occurs when the person in a role is uncertain about the role expectations of one or more members of the role set. To do their jobs well, people need to know what is expected of them. Sometimes these expectations may be unclear because the manager has not tried to communicate them to the subordinate or has done so inadequately. Or it may be a failure of the subordinate to listen that creates the lack of understanding. In either case, the resulting role ambiguity can be stressful for the individual. Research indicates that it may cause a loss of confidence in the role sender, lowered self-confidence, and/or decreased job satisfaction.

Role Conflict

Role conflict occurs when the person in a role is unable to respond to the expectations of one or more members of the role set. The role expectations are understood, but for one reason or another, they cannot be complied with. Role conflict is another source of potential tension that may result in a loss of job satisfaction, decreased confidence in one's boss, and/or a tendency to avoid the unpleasant work situation.

A common form of conflict is **role overload.** This is a situation in which there are simply too many role expectations being communicated to a person at a given time. There is too much to be done and too little time to do it. Managers may create role overload for their subordinates, especially when they rely on one-way communication. When cut off from valuable feedback, it is hard for these managers to learn when or why a subordinate is experiencing stress.

Role conflicts also occur when the expectations of one or more members of the role set are incompatible. The four basic types are intrasender, intersender, person–role, and interrole conflicts. A definition and example of each follows.

Intrasender Role Conflict: The same role-set member sends conflicting expectations.
   Example—A purchasing agent is asked by the boss to buy materials unavailable through normal channels; the boss also says company procedures should not be violated.

Intersender Role Conflict: Different role-set members send conflicting expectations.
   Example—A manager's boss expects her to be very direct and to exercise close control over subordinates; the subordinates want more freedom in their work.

Person–Role Conflict: The values and needs of the individual conflict with the expectations of the members of the role set.

Example—There is growing pressure on a senior executive to agree secretly to fix prices with competing firms; this violates the personal ethics of the executive.

Interrole Conflict: The expectations of two or more roles held by the same individual become incompatible.

Example—As work load increases, a manager spends evenings and weekends at work; the family is upset because they feel home obligations are not being met.

Role ambiguities and conflicts such as these can create tensions that reflect adversely on individual work attitudes and behaviors. The informed manager will seek to minimize these negative consequences by opening and maintaining effective two-way communications with all members of his or her role sets. This same manager will use active listening to solicit feedback from others on their understandings of any reactions to role expectations.

CONFLICT

Our review of roles and role dynamics introduces the ability to deal with conflict as another key aspect of a manager's interpersonal skills. **Conflict** occurs whenever disagreements exist in a social situation over issues of substance and/or emotional antagonisms.[16] *Substantive conflicts* involve disagreements over such things as group goals, the allocation of resources, distribution of rewards, policies and procedures, and the assignment of roles. *Emotional conflicts* result from feelings of anger, trust, dislike, fear, and resentment as well as from personality clashes.

Managers are known to spend up to 20 percent of their time dealing with conflict.[17] These include conflicts in which the manager is a principal party, one of the persons actively in conflict with one or more others. They also include conflicts in which the manager acts as a mediator, or third party, to try and resolve the conflicts between other people to the benefit of the organization and the individuals involved. In all cases, the manager must be a skilled participant in the dynamics of interpersonal conflict. He or she must be able to recognize situations that have the potential for conflict. Then the manager should be capable of diagnosing the situation and taking action through communications to ensure that the goals of the organization are best served.

Levels of Conflict

People at work encounter conflicts at each of four levels: (1) intrapersonal or conflict within the individual, (2) interpersonal or individual-to-individual conflict, (3) intergroup conflict, and (4) interorganizational conflict. The relevant question becomes, "How well prepared are you to encounter and deal successfully with each level of conflict in your experiences?"

Intrapersonal Conflict

Among the significant conflicts affecting behavior in organizations are those that involve the individual alone. We call these *intra*personal conflicts, and one example is person–role conflict previously discussed. They also often include actual or perceived pressures from incompatible goals or expectations of the following types.

Approach–approach conflict. A situation requiring a person to choose between two positive and equally attractive alternatives. An example is having to choose between accepting a valued promotion in the organization and taking a desirable new job offer with another firm.

Avoidance–avoidance conflict. A situation requiring a person to choose between two negative and equally unattractive alternatives. An example is being asked to accept a job transfer to another town in an undesirable location or have one's employment with an organization terminated.

Approach–avoidance conflict. A situation requiring a person to make a decision regarding an alternative that has both positive and negative consequences associated with it. An example is being offered a promotion carrying much higher pay but also carrying unwanted and greatly increased job responsibilities.

Interpersonal Conflict

*Inter*personal conflict occurs among one or more individuals. It can be substantive or emotional, or both. Everyone has experience with interpersonal conflict; it is a major form of conflict faced by managers given the highly interpersonal nature of the managerial role itself. We will address this form of conflict in detail when conflict management strategies are discussed in a later section of this chapter.

Intergroup Conflict

Another level of conflict in organizations occurs among groups. This topic was first introduced in our look at intergroup relations in Chapter 8. Intergroup conflict is common in organizations, and it makes the coordination and integration of task activities difficult. A classic example is the contrast in the working relationships between sales and production personnel observed in two plants of the same manufacturing company.[18] In the Elgin plant, a conflict relationship existed between the two departments; in the Bowie plant the working relationship was collaborative. These differences are most apparent in two respects to how group goals and orientation toward information handling affected decision making in each setting.

1. Differences over group goals.
   At Elgin: Each department emphasized its own needs and tasks.
   At Bowie: Each department stressed common goals and cooperation.
2. Differences over information handling.
   At Elgin: Each department ignored the other's problem and distorted its communications with the others.
   At Bowie: Each department sought to understand the other's problems and communicated accurate information to the other.

Managers stand at the interface of intergroup relationships and any conflicts they may entail. At times, the manager acts as a liaison directly linking his or her work unit with one or more others. At other times the manager is a higher level of authority to whom multiple subunits report. In each case, intergroup relations must be properly managed to maintain collaboration and avoid dysfunctional consequences from any conflicts that occur.

Interorganizational Conflict

Conflict also occurs between organizations. This conflict is most commonly thought of in terms of the competition that characterizes firms operating a private enterprise. But interorganizational conflict is really a much broader issue. Consider, for example, disagreements between unions and organizations employing their members, between government regulatory agencies and organizations subject to their surveillance, and more generally between organizations and others that supply them with raw materials. In each setting, the potential for conflict involves individuals who represent total organizations, not internal subunits or groups. Although participation in interorganizational conflict is frequently the province of higher-level managers, middle-level and lower-level managers can represent their organizations in such relationships with others. Typical examples are a purchasing agent's relationships with suppliers and a supervisor's relationships with union representatives. Again, any resulting conflicts should be managed to the benefit of the organizations and individuals concerned.

Constructive and Destructive Conflicts

Conflict in organizations can be upsetting to the persons directly involved and to others who may observe or who are affected by its occurrence. A fairly common by-product is stress, a topic we address in considerable detail in Chapter 16. It can be quite uncomfortable, for example, to be in an environment where two co-workers are continually hostile toward one another. There are two sides to conflict, however, as it relates to organizational outcomes. Conflict that results in positive benefits to the group or organization is constructive; conflict that works to the group's or organization's disadvantage is destructive.

Destructive conflict occurs, for example, when two employees are unable to work together due to interpersonal hostilities (a destructive emotional conflict) or when the members of a committee fail to act because they cannot agree on group goals (a destructive substantive conflict). Destructive conflicts reduce group effectiveness by decreasing work productivity and member satisfaction and increasing absenteeism and turnover. Managers must be alert to destructive conflicts and be quick to take action that prevents or eliminates these conflicts or at least minimizes their resulting disadvantages. But conflict can also be beneficial. *Constructive* conflict offers individuals and groups a chance to identify otherwise neglected problems and opportunities. Creativity and performance can improve as a result. Indeed, an effective manager is able to stimulate constructive conflict in situations where satisfaction with the status quo inhibits needed change and development. He or she is comfortable dealing with both sides of the conflict dynamic—the constructive and the destructive.

CONFLICT SITUATIONS IN ORGANIZATIONS

The very nature of the manager's position and responsibilities in an organization guarantees that conflict will be a part of his or her work experience. To help you better fulfill the challenges of achieving a constructive balance in conflict outcomes, we now examine the types of conflict situations experienced by managers, a way to understand these situations, and the various stages of conflict they may involve.

Types of Conflict Situations

Among the many conflict situations in organizations, four basic types exist. A good manager is able to recognize these situations for their potential to create conflict.[19]

- *Vertical conflict.* Occurs between levels in an organization's hierarchy of authority. A common example is conflict between a supervisor and subordinate over such things as task goals, deadlines, and performance accomplishments.
- *Horizontal conflict.* Occurs between persons or groups operating at the same level in the hierarchy. It may trace to such things as goal incompatibilities, resource scarcities, or purely interpersonal factors.
- *Line–staff conflict.* Occurs when line and staff representatives disagree over issues of substance in their woking relationships. Because staff personnel (e.g., an internal auditor) often have the potential for major impact on certain areas of line operations, line–staff conflict can and does appear with some frequency in organizations.
- *Role conflict.* Occurs when the communication of task expectations from role-set members proves inadequate or incompatible for the role holder. Earlier in this chapter we identified four specific types of role conflicts: intrasender, intersenter, interrole, and person–role.

Conflict becomes more likely in each of the prior situations when certain antecedent conditions exist. These include the following four characteristics of working relationships among individuals and groups in organizations.[20]

1. *Work-flow interdependence.* As discussed in Chapters 10, 11, and 12, an organization exists and must be managed as a system of interdependent parts performing distinct but coordinated functions in a division of labor. When work-flow interdependence is such that a person or group must rely on task contributions from one or more others to achieve *its* goals, the circumstances are ripe for occasional conflict.
2. *Asymmetry.* Work relationships are asymmetrical when one party differs substantially in power, values, and/or status from another with whom he or she regularly interacts. Conflict due to asymmetry is prone to occur, for example, when a low-power person needs the help of a high-power person

who will not respond, when people of dramatically different values are forced to work together on a task, or when a high-status person is required to interact with and perhaps be dependent on someone of lower status. A common example of the latter case occurs when a manager is forced to deal with another manager only through his or her secretary.

3. *Role ambiguity or domain ambiguity.* As discussed earlier, a lack of adequate direction or clarity of goals and tasks for persons in their work roles can create a stressful and conflict-prone situation. At the group or department level, this often materializes as ambiguity of domains or jurisdictions. That is, two groups are ripe for conflict when either one or both fails to understand just who is responsible for what.

4. *Resource scarcity.* Actual or perceived needs to compete for scarce resources makes working relationships among individuals and/or groups conflict-prone. This is especially relevant for individuals or groups in declining as opposed to growing organizations. Resources are usually scarce in times of decline, with the result that cutbacks commonly occur. As various persons or groups try to position themselves to receive maximum shares of the shrinking resource pool, others are likely to resist or employ countermeasures to defend their respective interests. Resources are essential to the survival and prosperity of individuals and groups in organizations. As a result, resource scarcity often breeds conflict.

Understanding Conflict Situations

Let us take an example as a way of building your sensitivity to the challenges of understanding and effectively managing conflict situations. The president of a small company is in favor of immediately introducing a new computerized record-keeping system. The head of the accounting department is quite opposed to it. There is a definite difference of opinion between the two regarding this possible change of procedures.

The president in this case is a principal party in the conflict. She is also the organizational superior of the other principal party. Although we do not know all the facts, the accountant could be quite threatened by the way the president handles the situation. He has already taken some risk to communicate his views upward, and the response of the president may well determine his willingness to do so again in the future. This is a conflict that could prove constructive in getting the best decision made for the company or become destructive by alienating a key employee.

To manage this situation, the president should begin by analyzing the various conflict ingredients. Key factors to be considered include apparent differences over facts, methods, goals, and values. Table 14.2 lists how each of these factors could be operating in the case.

Disagreement may have arisen because the president and the accountant have different data to work with, or because they are interpreting the same data differently, and/or because they feel quite different pressures in their respective organizational roles. Once the reasons for the differences are clarified and understood, steps such as the following can be taken to address them constructively and resolve the conflict.

TABLE 14.2   Key Differences of Opinion on the Computerized Record-Keeping System

	Nature of the Differences			
	Over Facts	Over Methods	Over Goals	Over Values
President	"The new system will save money."	"It should be installed at once."	"We want rapid and accurate data retrieval on demand."	"Efficiency is the key."
Head of Accounting Department	"The new system will be more expensive."	"Let's move slowly."	"We need a flexible system managed by accountants who can solve unexpected problems."	"We must consider the welfare of loyal workers."

Source: Adapted from Warren H. Schmidt and Robert Tannenbaum, "Management of Differences," *Harvard Business Review,* Vol. 38 (November–December, 1960), p. 110. Copyright © 1960 by the President and Fellows of Harvard College. All rights reserved.

Difference	**Managerial Action**
Facts	Information could be shared; steps could be taken to check the validity of the data; more data could be gathered from mutually respected outside sources.
Methods	The common goals of the company's well-being should be remembered; the current disagreement should be viewed as a difference of means, not ends; alternatives to the computerized system as proposed should be explored.
Goals	The goals of the president and the accountant should be clarified; each should be discussed and revised relative to the company's goals.
Values	The president and the accountant should share their values on the record-keeping functions; the reality of any real vlue differences should be clarified; attempts should be made to find areas where the values overlap and contain consistencies.

If steps such as these are successful, the original conflict may prove very constructive for the company. Perhaps a new computerized system will be implemented, with resulting cost savings. Or maybe the manual system will be retained and a costly "mistake" avoided. In either event, the important result is that the best interests of the company are well served.

The Stages of Conflict

It is also useful to recognize that conflict develops in stages, as shown in Figure 14.4. These stages include antecedent conditions, perceived and felt conflict, manifest conflict, conflict resolution or suppression, and conflict aftermath.[21] Some of the antecedents that establish conditions from which conflict can develop are role ambiguities,

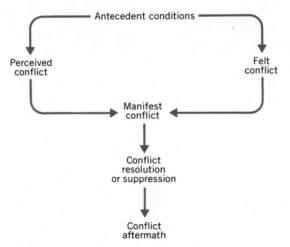

FIGURE 14.4   The stages of conflict.

competition for scarce resources, communication barriers, unresolved prior conflicts, and individual differences in needs, values, and goals. In effect, when these conditions exist, the stage is set for confict to develop. Any person who works in a situation characterized by one or more of these conditions, therefore, should be sensitive to the conflict potential they represent.

When the antecedents are viewed as a basis for substantive or emotional differences, perceived conflict exists. Of course, this perception may be held by only one of the conflicting parties. There is also a difference between perceived and felt conflict. When conflict is felt, we give it meaning in the sense that a tension exists that creates motivation to reduce feelings of discomfort. Sometimes we feel conflict, but cannot pin down its source or cause.

For conflict to be resolved, all parties should both perceive and feel the need to do something about the conflict. When conflict is openly expressed in behavior it is said to be manifest. A state of manifest conflict can be resolved in the sense that its antecedent conditions are corrected. It can also be suppressed in that, although no change in antecedent conditions occurs, the manifest conflict behaviors are controlled.

Finally, the way in which a given conflict is handled can affect future conflicts. Unresolved conflicts continue to fester and promote future conflicts over similar issues. Truly resolved conflicts may establish conditions that reduce future conflicts of a similar nature and that help other eventual conflicts to be resolved in a constructive fashion. Thus, any manager should be sensitive to the influence of conflict aftermath on future conflict episodes.

CONFLICT MANAGEMENT

Our position on conflict is that it is inevitable in managerial situations and that it should be actively and well managed. From a manager's perspective, for example, conflict can be approached from a lose–lose, win–lose, or win–win perspective.[22] Only in the latter case does true **conflict resolution** occur in the sense that the underlying reasons, substantive and/or emotional, for a conflict are eliminated.

Lose–Lose Conflict

Lose–lose outcomes occur as a result of managing conflict by avoidance, smoothing, and/or compromise. No one achieves his or her true desires, and the underlying reasons for the conflict remain unaffected. Future conflict of a similar nature is likely to occur.

Avoidance is an extreme form of nonattention. Everyone pretends that conflict does not really exist and hopes that it will simply go away. **Smoothing** plays down differences among the conflicting parties and highlights similarities and areas of agreement. Peaceful coexistence through a recognition of common interests is the goal. Smoothing may ignore the real essence of a given conflict.

''Let's compromise'' is a phrase frequently heard in a group setting. The classic example occurs whenever representatives of unions and management meet to prepare new labor contracts. **Compromise** occurs when each party gives up something of value to the other. As a result, neither party gains its full desires, and the antecedent conditions for future conflicts are established. Although a conflict may appear to be settled for a while through compromise, it may well reappear again at some future time.

Win–Lose Conflict

In win–lose conflicts, one party achieves its desires at the expense and to the exclusion of the other party's desires. This may result from **competition,** where a victory is achieved through force, superior skill, or domination. It may also occur as a result of **authoritative command** wherein a formal authority simply dictates a solution and specifies what is gained and lost by whom. When the authority is a party to the conflict, it is easy to predict who will be the winner and who the loser. Each of these strategies also fails to address the root causes of the conflict and tends to suppress the desires of at least one of the conflicting parties. As a result, future conflicts over the same issues are likely.

Win–Win Conflict

Win–win conflict is achieved by confrontation of the issues and the use of **problem solving** to reconcile differences. This positive approach to conflict involves a recognition by all conflicting parties that something is wrong and needs attention. When success is achieved in problem solving, true conflict resolution has occurred. Win–win conditions eliminate reasons for continuing or resurrecting the conflict, since nothing has been avoided or suppressed. All relevant issues are raised and openly discussed. The ultimate test for a win–win solution is whether or not the conflicting parties are willing to say to each other.[23]

''I want a solution that achieves your goals and my goals and is acceptable to both of us.''

''It is our collective responsibility to be open and honest about facts, opinions, and feelings.''

Conflict Management Styles

The five conflict management styles of avoidance, authoritative command, smoothing, compromise, and problem solving are depicted on the conflict management grid in Figure 14.5. The grid classifies each style as some combination of a person's.[24]

Cooperativeness: Desire to satisfy the other party's concerns

Assertiveness: Desire to satisfy one's own concerns

As you would expect, only the problem-solving style scores high on both dimen-

FIGURE 14.5   The conflict management grid.

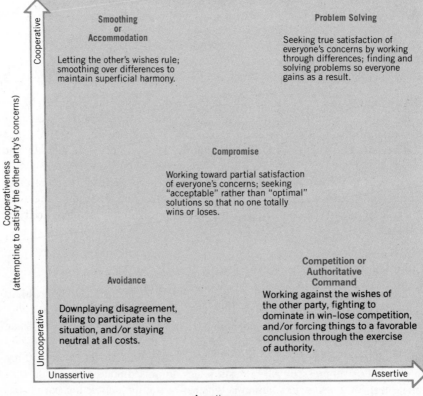

Assertiveness
(attempting to satisfy one's own concerns)

sions. This is one reason why theorists argue that only problem solving strategies lead to real conflict resolution.

Once again, it requires an attempt by the manager to locate and treat the causes of conflict, not merely to suppress them temporarily. True problem solving involves bringing conflicting parties together to discuss the situation. Through direct communication, attempts are made to identify where fact, values, methods, and/or goal differences contribute to the conflict. Then, reasons for the conflict in terms of such things as information, goals, and perceptions are identified. Once these reasons are clear, steps can be taken to eliminate or minimize them as sources of conflict.

Each of the five conflict-management styles has some potential value to the practicing manager. Although only problem solving results in true conflict resolution, there may be times when the other styles will yield adequate outcomes. The following are sample situations in which the chief executives of several organizations report using conflict-management styles other than problem solving.[25] The following are

Avoidance is used: When an issue is trivial or more important issues are pressing; and to let people cool down and regain perspective.

Authoritative command is used: When quick, decisive action is vital, e.g., in emergencies; and on important issues where unpopular actions, such as cost cutting, enforcing unpopular rules, and discipline need implementing.

Accommodating or Smoothing is used: When issues are more important to others than yourself; and to build social credits for later issues.

Compromising is used: To achieve temporary settlements to complex issues; and to arrive at expedient solutions.

Additional Conflict Management Techniques

Managers can support their problem-solving efforts by additional conflict management techniques. There are times when an *appeal to superordinate goals* can focus the attention of conflicting parties on one mutually desirable conclusion. This offers all parties a common frame of reference against which to analyze differences and reconcile disagreements. Conflicts whose antecedents lie in competition for scarce resources can also be resolved by *expanding the resources available* to everyone. Although costly, this technique removes the reasons for the continuing conflict. By *altering one or more human variables* in a situation, for example, by replacing or transferring one or more of the conflicting parties, conflicts caused by poor interpersonal relationships can be eliminated.

A final and important conflict-management approach is to *alter structural variables* in the situation. This involves rearranging the physical or material aspects of work to remove or minimize things causing conflict. The major alternatives include[26]

- *Hierarchical Referral.* Using a higher-level manager as the final authority on conflicts that have created decision "dead locks" at lower levels. This requires a major time commitment from the higher manager, may not remove the underlying causes of the conflicts, and may result in their recurence in the future.

- *Decoupling*. Redesigning the organization structure to separate the conflicting subunits from one another and provide them with independent access to needed resources. This approach can increase costs when resources and work efforts become duplicated rather than shared.

- *Buffering*. Building inventories at the interfaces between subunits that depend on one another's outputs to maintain their work flows. In manufacturing areas, for example, inventory buffers can reduce conflicts caused by work slowdowns or problems in sequentially interdependent work units. Like decoupling, this approach adds to costs through the increased inventories.

- *Linking Pins*. Assigning to designated individuals the responsibility for integrating and managing relationships between specific subunits. Such persons are expected to get to know thoroughly the operations and needs of each group, gain the respect and trust of all parties concerned, and then work with them to resolve disagreements in the best interests of the organization. Such liaison persons require special human relations skills to succeed in their "boundary spanning" positions.

- *Integrating Departments*. Creating separate departments of several members, which, like the linking pins, are formally responsible for managing relationships between two or more subunits. These departments typically have formal authority to make decisions and issue directives in response to conflicts among subunits under their supervision.

SUMMARY

This chapter has built on two basic premises. First,

$$\text{A manager's communication skills} \xrightarrow{\text{affect}} \text{the information flows} \xrightarrow[\text{which}]{\text{on}} \text{managerial decisions are based}$$

Second,

$$\text{A manager's conflict skills} \xrightarrow[\text{to}]{\text{lead}} \text{conflict that is constructive} \xrightarrow{\text{or}} \text{conflict that is destructive}$$

Simply put, good managers possess the communication and conflict skills that enable them to implement decisions in support of the organization's production purposes. The manager who is a good communicator will be effective in sending information to others and at encouraging accurate information feedback in return. To do so managers should recognize the various barriers that can threaten the effectiveness of their communication attempts. They should also be aware that efficient communications are not always effective and should practice the specific skills of active listening and the art of giving feedback.

Among the most important communications in which managers become involved are the sending and receiving of role expectations. Good communication skills can help to clarify role ambiguities and role conflicts when they occur and can minimize their negative consequences for individuals and the organization.

To manage conflicts successfully, managers need to understand the nature of the conflict process. Conflict situations must be diagnosed to locate the specific substantive and emotional differences on which they are based and to identify the reasons for these differences.

People attend to conflicts in different ways, but only a problem solving approach results in true conflict resolution. Managers should be aware of the five different interpersonal styles of conflict management, and of their personal tendencies to use each. Managers can also use additional conflict management techniques such as superordinate goals, expanded resources, and altering human and/or structural variables.

THINKING THROUGH THE ISSUES

1. Make a list of the communication barriers that might limit the effectiveness of a manager's communications with subordinates. Give examples of each barrier as they might be found in the work setting in which you expect to practice as a manager.
2. Analyze the communication skills of a person for whom you work. (Your instructor is one possible choice.) What does he or she do well as a communicator? What could he or she do to improve communications with other persons?
3. Describe the difference between formal and informal communication channels in organizations. Why are both important to managers?
4. What is "active listening"? What is its significance in terms of achieving effectiveness in managerial communications?
5. Diagram the role set for a managerial position with which you are familiar. Identify where role ambiguities and conflicts might develop in this situation. What could be done by (a) the person and (b) his or her supervisor to minimize the negative consequences of these role dynamics?
6. Select an interpersonal conflict in which you have recently been involved. Adopt a diagnostic approach to identify the reasons for this conflict. How could problem solving have been used to resolve the conflict?
7. When would a manager want to promote conflict within the work unit? How can this be done in a way that ensures a constructive rather than destructive result?
8. Identify three major alternatives for managing conflict by altering structural variables in a situation. What are the implications of each in terms of operating efficiencies?

CASE: CONFLICT OVER
A CHANGE IN JOB DESIGN

Leslie Martin was a supervisor in charge of a manufacturing operation in a medium-sized company.[27] A recent change in company procedures made it possible for employees to engage in job rotation. In a staff meeting held to discuss the possibility, Leslie became aware that two subordinates wanted to change to a job rotation schedule, when one did not. After pondering the problem, Leslie determined that four alternative approaches might be followed to manage this conflict situation:

1. Simply tell all three subordinates that job rotation will begin immediately.
2. Convince all three that their good feelings toward one another are more important than any job design, thus getting them to agree to rotate jobs or not, depending on what will maintain harmony in the group.
3. Work out an arrangement where job rotation occurs for a while, is stopped for a while, and so on, thus allowing each person to have his or her way part of the time.
4. Drop the idea about making any job design changes, thus forgetting the possibility was ever raised in the first place.

Questions
1. What conflict management styles are represented by each of the four approaches described by Leslie?
2. Which of the four approaches should Leslie choose to follow in this situation? Why? Or should an alternative approach be taken? If the latter, describe and justify the approach and label it as one of the conflict management styles.
3. What special interpersonal skills would Leslie need to succeed in this problem situation? Defend your answer.

EXERCISE: UPWARD APPRAISAL

Purpose:
To practice the art of giving feedback to an organizational superior and to observe the dynamics of status as a communication barrier; to allow the instructor to practice and demonstrate the techniques of active listening and to receive constructive feedback on the course.[28]

Time:
50 to 75 minutes.

Procedure:
1. Form work groups as assigned by your instructor.
2. The instructor will leave the room.
3. Convene in your assigned work groups for a period of 10 minutes. Create a

list of comments, problems, issues, and concerns you would like to have communicated to the instructor in regard to the course experience to date.

4. Select one person from the group to act as spokesperson in communicating the group's feelings to the instructor.

5. The spokespersons should briefly convene to decide on what physical arrangement of chairs, tables, and so forth is most appropriate to conduct the feedback session. The classroom should then be rearranged to fit the desired specifications.

6. While the spokespersons convene, persons in the remaining groups should discuss how they expect the forthcoming communications event to develop. Will it be a good experience for all parties concerned? Be prepared to observe critically the actual communication process.

7. The instructor should be invited to return, and the feedback session will begin. Observers should make notes so that they may make constructive comments at the conclusion of the exercise.

8. Once the feedback session is completed, the instructor will call on the observers for comments, ask the spokespersons for their reactions, and open the session to general discussion.

Remember:
Your interest in the exercise is twofold: (1) to communicate your feelings to the instructor and (2) to learn more about the process of giving and receiving feedback.

THE MANAGER'S VOCABULARY

Active Listening   Communication (verbal and nonverbal) that helps the source of a message articulate what he or she really means.

Communication   An interpersonal process of sending and receiving symbols with meanings attached to them.

Conflict   When two or more people disagree over issues of organizational substance and/or when they experience some emotional antagonisms with one another.

Conflict Resolution   Occurs when the reasons, substantial and/or emotional, for a conflict are eliminated.

Effective Communication   When the intended meaning of the source and the perceived meaning of the receiver are one and the same.

Efficient Communication   Communication at minimum cost in terms of resources expended.

Ethnocentrism   The tendency to consider one's culture and its values as being superior to others.

Feedback   The process of telling someone else how you feel about something they did or said or about the situation in general.

Formal Communication Channels   Communication channels that follow the chain of command established by the organization's hierarchy.

Informal Communication Channels   Communication channels that do not adhere to the organization's hierarchy.

Mixed Messages   Messages that appear mixed when a person's words communicate one message while their actions or nonverbal language communicate another.

Noise   Anything that interferes with the effectiveness of a communication attempt.

Nonverbal Communication   Communication that takes place through facial expressions, body position, eye contact, and other physical gestures.

Role   A set of activities expected of a person holding a particular office or position in a group or organization.

Role Ambiguity   When the person in a role is uncertain about the role expectations of one or more members of the role set.

Role Conflict   When the person in a role is unable to respond to the expectations of one or more members of the role set.

Role Overload   A situation in which there are simply too many role expectations being communicated to a person at a given point in time.

Role Set   The various people who hold expectations regarding the behavior of someone in a role.

NOTES

[1] Developed from "Korea's Newest Export: Management Style," *Business Week* (January 19, 1987), p. 66.

[2] Henry Mintzberg, *The Nature of Managerial Work* (New York: Harper & Row, 1973). See also Morgan W. McCall, Jr., Ann M. Morrison, and Robert L. Hannan, *Studies of Managerial Work: Results and Methods*, Technical Report No. 9 (Greensboro, N.C.: Center for Creative Leadership, 1978), and John P. Kotter, *The General Managers* (New York: Free Press, 1982).

[3] William J. Haney, *Communication and Interpersonal Communication: Text and Cases*, 4th ed. (Homewood, Ill.: Richrd D. Irwin, 1979).

[4] Kotter, op cit.

[5] Thomas J. Peters and Robert H. Waterman, Jr., *In Search of Excellence* (New York: Harper & Row, 1983).

[6] See D. E. Campbell, "Interior Office Design and Visitor Response," *Journal of Applied Psychology*, Vol. 64 (1979), pp. 648–653; and P. C. Morrow and J. C. McElroy, "Interior Office Design and Visitor Response: A Constructive Replication," *Journal of Applied Psychology*, Vol. 66 (1981), pp. 646–650.

[7] Richard V. Farace, Peter R. Monge, and Hamish M. Russell, *Communicating and Organizing* (Reading, Mass.: Addison-Wesley, 1977), pp. 97–98.

[8] Haney, *Communication and Interpersonal Communication*, p. 316.

[9] The statements are from *Business Week,* July 6, 1981, p. 107.

[10] See Harold J. Leavitt and Romald A. H. Mueller, "Some Effects of Feedback on Communication," *Human Relations*, Vol. 4 (1951), pp. 401–410; Harold J. Leavitt, *Managerial Psychology*, 3rd ed. (Chicago: University of Chicago Press, 1972).

[11] This research is reviewed by John C. Athanassiades, "The Distortion of Upward Communication in Hierarchical Organizations," *Academy of Management Journal*, Vol. 16 (June 1973), pp. 207–226.

[12] See M. P. Rowe and M. Baker, "Are You Hearing Enough Employee Concerns?," *Harvard Business Review*, Vol. 62 (May–June 1984), pp. 127–135.

[13] This discussion is based on Carl R. Rogers and Richard E. Farson, "Active Listening" (Chicago: Industrial Relations Center of the University of Chicago).

[14] Adapted from John Anderson, "Giving and Receiving Feedback," in Paul R. Lawrence, Louis B. Barnes, and Jay W. Lorsch, eds., *Organizational Behavior and Administration*, 3rd ed. (Homewood, Ill.: Richard D. Irwin, 1976), p. 109. See also John F. Kiloski and Joseph

A. Litterer, "Effective Communication in the Performance Appraisal Interview," *Public Personnel Management,* Vol. 9 (Spring 1983), pp. 33–42.

[15]See Robert L. Kahn, Donald M. Wolfe, Robert F. Quinn, and J. Diedrick Snoek, *Organizational Stress: Studies in Role Conflict and Ambiguity* (New York: John Wiley, 1964); and Daniel Katz and Robert L. Kahn, *The Social Psychology of Organizations,* 2nd ed. (New York: John Wiley, 1978).

[16]Richard E. Walton, *Interpersonal Peacemaking: Confrontations and Third-Party Consultation* (Reading, Mass.: Addison-Wesley, 1969).

[17]Kenneth W. Thomas and Warren H. Schmidt, "A Survey of Managerial Interests with Respect to Conflict," *Academy of Management Journal,* Vol. 19 (1976), pp. 315–318.

[18]Richard E. Walton and John M. Dutton, "The Management of Interdepartmental Conflict: A Model and Review," *Administrative Science Quarterly,* Vol. 14 (1969), pp. 73–84.

[19]Developed from Don Hellriegel, John W. Slocum, Jr., and Richard W. Woodman, *Organizational Behavior,* 3rd ed. (St. Paul, Minn.: West, 1983), pp. 471–474.

[20]Developed from Gary Johns, *Organizational Behavior* (Glenview, Ill.: Scott, Foresman, 1983), pp. 415–417, and Walton and Dutton, op cit.

[21]These stages are consistent with the conflict models described by Alan C. Filley, *Interpersonal Conflict Resolution* (Glenview, Ill.: Scott, Foresman, 1975); and Louis R. Pondy, "Organizational Conflict: Concepts and Models," *Administrative Science Quarterly,* Vol. 12 (September 1967), pp. 269–320.

[22]See Filley, op cit., and L. David Brown, *Managing Conflict at Organizational Interfaces* (Reading, Mass.: Addison-Wesley, 1983).

[23]Ibid., pp. 27, 29.

[24]Kenneth Thomas, "Conflict and Conflict Management," in M. D. Dunnett, ed., *Handbook of Industrial and Organizational Behavior* (Chicago: Rand McNally, 1976), pp. 889–935.

[25]Kenneth W. Thomas, "Toward Multi-Dimensional Values in Teaching: The Example of Conflict Behaviors," *Academy of Management Review,* Vol. 2 (1977), pp. 484–490.

[26]See Jay Galbraith, *Designing Complex Organizations* (Reading, Mass.: Addison-Wesley, 1973), and Rensis Likert and Jane B. Likert, *New Ways of Managing Conflict* (New York: McGraw-Hill, 1976).

[27]Developed from an example in Filley, *Interpersonal Conflict Resolution,* p. 24.

[28]Developed from an exercise reported by Eugene Owens, "Upward Appraisal: An Exercise in Subordinate's Critique of Superior's Performance," *Exchange: The Organizational Behavior Teaching Journal,* Vol. 3 (1978), pp. 41–42.

CHAPTER 15
POWER AND POLITICS

We attribute our success to our highly talented management team. We are confident because we have the qualified personnel, systems and structures in place.

American Capital Corporation Annual Report

MILLIONAIRE FIRES BILLIONAIRE

Just before Christmas in 1986 H. Ross Perot, the chairperson of Electric Data Systems (EDS) got the boot from the chairperson of General Motor's board, Roger B. Smith. About 20 years ago, Perot founded EDS with some $1000 and built it into one of the leading computer service companies. In 1984 GM purchased EDS for approximately $2.5 billion to infuse an entrepreneurial spirit and high technology into the sagging auto giant. While retaining the chair of the new GM division, Perot became the largest owner of a specialized GM stock called GME. Owners of GME stock received dividends based on the profile of the EDS division of GM.[1]

Perot is an outspoken, hard-charging, daring and decisive Texan; a self-made man accustomed to hard work and quick success. In building EDS he often took enormous risks, such as master-minding a successful plan to liberate two EDS hostages held captive by Iranian zealots. Smith was equally hardworking but a product of the GM bureaucracy. He methodically worked his way up the GM hierarchy through the finance divisions. Upon becoming CEO (chief executive officer) he initiated a series of bold moves to revitalize GM. These included a major reorganization, two multibillion dollar diversification purchases (one being EDS), and the launching of a new auto division called Saturn. Unfortunately, the bulk of the giant's operations continued to creak along in its old, stodgy ways. The clash of corporate cultures was brutal. The entrepreneurial EDS gave GM heartburn. Yet the nimble hard-charging EDS could not penetrate GM's traditions. Perot became increasingly frustrated as EDS was becoming more like GM.

In the summer of 1986 Perot started to go public with his criticisms. GM had too many highly paid top executives who were isolated from competitive reality. GM needed to change more rapidly, get managers and workers cooperating, respond more quickly to customers, and build better cars for less. His musings were widely publicized in the national press. An embarrassed Roger Smith initially refused to comment, but as Perot's criticisms became more pointed he acted through the GM board of directors.

Perot was offered $700 million for his GM shares (almost twice their value on the stock market) under the conditions that he (a) resign from the GM board, (b) leave EDS, (c) not work for a competitor or start another firm, and (d) stop publicly criticizing GM. A $7.5 million penalty was set if either party criticized the other. Perot accepted. Thus, a mere millionaire had fired a fiery billionaire who violated the first rule of organizational politics. Never go public with bad news.

Management Applications Question

Every manager must influence the behavior of people at work, and must expect to be influenced by others in return. How will you handle the processes of power and politics in organizations?

PLANNING AHEAD

This chapter offers learning activities that will acquaint
you with the following topics.

Power
Sources of Power
Power, Authority, and Obedience
Managerial Perspectives on Power and Influence
Organizational Politics
Political Action in Organizations
Ethics of Power and Politics

"**P**ower is America's last dirty word''—so begins an article in the *Harvard Business
Review*.[2] The implication is that we are uncomfortable with the concept of power,
that we are perhaps even somewhat offended by it. But the author of this provocative
sentence then goes on to explore power in organizations and to suggest how managers
can act to ensure that they have the power required to be successful in their jobs. This
theme is consistent with the case that introduced this chapter. It suggests that you
understand the concept of power and be able to see its place in organizations.

POWER

In OB, **power** is the ability to get someone else to do something you want done or
the ability to make things happen in the way you want. The essence of power is
control over the behavior of others.[3] One of the interesting things about power is that
it has no verb form. You do not ''power'' something. You can, however, ''influence''
something. Power is the force that makes things happen in an intended way.

Influence is a behavioral response to the exercise of power. It is an outcome
achieved through the use of power. People are ''influenced'' when they act in ways
consistent with the desires of someone else. Managers use power to achieve influence
over other people in the work setting. Figure 15.1 summarizes this linkage between
power and influence. It also identifies the key sources or bases of power managers
can use to influence the behavior of other people at work.

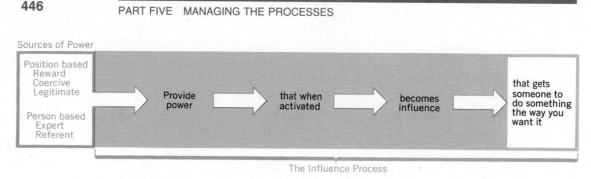

FIGURE 15.1   Power sources and the influence process.

SOURCES OF POWER

Managers derive power from both organizational and individual sources. We call these sources position power and personal power, respectively.[4]

Position Power

Three bases of power are available to a manager because of his or her position in the organization: reward, coercive, and legitimate power. **Reward power** is the extent to which a manager can use extrinsic and intrinsic rewards to control other people. Examples of such rewards include money, promotions, compliments, or enriched jobs. These types of rewards are discussed in detail in Chapters 5 and 6. Although all managers have some access to rewards, success in accessing and utilizing them to achieve influence varies according to the skills of the manager.

Power can also be founded on punishment instead of reward. A manager may, for example, threaten to withhold a pay raise or recommend the firing of a subordinate who does not act as desired. Such **coercive power** is the extent to which a manager can deny desired rewards or administer punishments to control other people. The availability of coercive power also varies from one organization and manager to another. The presence of unions and other restrictions on employee treatment can weaken this power base considerably.

The third base of position power is **legitimate power.** It stems from the extent to which a manager can use subordinates' internalized values or beliefs that the "boss" has a "right of command" to control their behavior. A classic example is in the armed forces, where officers have legitimate power over enlisted personnel.

Personal Power

Two bases of personal power are expertise and reference. **Expert power** is the ability to control another's behavior through the possession of knowledge, experience, or judgment that the other person does not have but needs. In the case of a supervisor having expert power, a subordinate would obey because the boss is felt to know more about what is to be done or how it is to be done than the subordinate. Access to or control over information is an important element in this particular power base. Access to key organizational decision makers is another. A person's ability to contact key persons informally can allow for special participation in the definition of a problem or issue, alteration in the flow of information to decision makers, and lobbying for use of special criteria in decision making.[5]

Referent power is the ability to control another's behavior because of their wanting to identify with the power source. In this case, a subordinate would obey the boss because he or she wants to behave, perceive, or believe as the boss does. This may occur, for example, because the subordinate likes the boss personally and therefore tries to do things the way the boss wants them done. In a sense, the subordinate behaves in order to avoid doing anything that would interfere with the pleasing boss–subordinate relationship.

Authority

At this point, you may be thinking that the concept of authority should fit somehow into the present discussion of power. In Chapter 1, we defined authority as the right to command. Consider once again the power bases previously described. Is there a similarity between any of them and the concept of authority?

In fact, **formal authority** and legitimate power are one and the same. The two terms represent a special kind of power that a manager has because subordinates believe it is legitimate for a person occupying the managerial position to have the right to command. In practice it is often hard to separate authority, or legitimate power, from the use of reward and coercive power. This is because persons with authority usually have special access to rewards and punishments and can thereby alter their availability to subordinates.

POWER, AUTHORITY, AND OBEDIENCE

Power is the potential to control the behavior of others, and authority is the potential to exert such control through the legitimacy of a managerial position. The chapter opener presented an example of a manager who used his or her power to end the criticisms of a potential rival. H. Ross Perot accepted Rodger Smith's "offer." Yet we also know that people who seem to have power don't always get their way. This fact leads us to the subject of obedience. Why do some people obey directives, while others do not? More specifically, why should subordinates respond to a manager's authority or "right to command"? Furthermore, given that they are willing to obey, what determines the limits of obedience?

The Milgram Experiments

These last questions point directly toward Stanley Milgram's seminal research on obedience.[6] Milgram designed an experiment to determine the extent to which people obey the commands of an authority figure, even if believing that they are endangering the life of another person. The subjects were 40 males, ranging in age from 20 to 50, representing a diverse set of occupations (engineers, sales people, school teachers, laborers, and others). They were paid a nominal fee for participation in the project, which was conducted in a laboratory at Yale University.

The subjects were falsely told that the purpose of the study was to determine the effects of punishment on learning. They were to be the "teachers," and the "learner," a confederate of Milgram's, was strapped to a chair in an adjoining room with an electrode attached to his wrist. The "experimenter," another confederate of Milgram's, was dressed in a gray laboratory coat. Appearing impassive and somewhat stern, he instructed the "teacher" to read a series of word pairs to the learner and then to reread the first word along with four other terms. The learner was supposed to indicate which of the four terms was in the original pair. This was accomplished by pressing a switch that caused a light to flash on a response panel in front of the teacher.

The teacher was instructed to administer a shock to the learner each time a wrong answer was given. This shock was to be increased one level of intensity each time the learner made a mistake. The teacher controlled switches that ostensibly administered shocks ranging from 15 to 450 volts. The voltage and degree of shock were labeled on the switches. In reality, there was no electric current in the apparatus, but the learners purposely "erred" often and responded to each level of "shock" in progressively distressing ways. A summary of the switch markings and the learner's fake responses to the various levels of shock is shown in Figure 15.2.

If a teacher proved unwilling to administer a shock, the experimenter used the following prods to get him or her to perform as requested: (1) "please continue" or "please go on," (2) "the experiment requires that you continue," (3) "it is absolutely

FIGURE 15.2 Shock levels and set learner responses in the Milgram experiment.

Switch Voltage Marking	Switch Description	"Learner's" Responses	"Teachers" Refusing to Go on
15–60	Slight	No sound	_____
75–120	Moderate	Grunts and moans	_____
135–180	Strong	Asks to leave	_____
195–240	Very strong	Can't stand the pain	_____
255–300	Intense	Pounds on wall	_____
315–360	Extreme intensity	No sound	_____
375–420	Danger: severe shock	No sound	_____
435–450	XXX	No sound	_____

essential that you continue,'' and (4) ''you have no choice, you must go on.'' Only when the teacher refused to go on after the fourth prod would the experiment be stopped.

> When do you think the ''teachers'' would refuse to go on? Write in the shaded area in Figure 15.2 the number of the 40 ''teachers'' who you think would *refuse* to obey the ''experimenter's'' order to shock the ''learner'' at each voltage level.

Milgram asked some of his students and colleagues the same question. Most felt that few, if any, of the subjects would go beyond the ''Very strong shock'' level.[7] How do your answers compare?

In actual fact, 26 subjects (65 percent) continued to the end of the experiment and shocked the ''learners'' to the XXX level! None stopped prior to 300 volts, the point at which the learner pounds on the wall. The remaining 14 subjects refused to obey the experimenter at various intermediate points.

Most people, as was Milgram, are surprised by these results. They wondered just why other people would have a tendency to accept or comply with authoritative commands under such extreme conditions. Milgram conducted further experiments to try to answer these questions. Things that appeared to make a difference in subjects' tendencies toward obedience were: the building in which the experiment took place (university laboratory or run-down office), proximity of subject and victim, proximity of subject and the experimenter, and the observed behaviors of other subjects.

Obedience and the Psychological Contract

Milgram's experiments provide a dramatic example of people's tendency to obey the directives of higher authority figures in organizational settings. A useful way to bring this issue and its implications for managers into focus lies with the psychological contract concept introduced in Chapter 2. The psychological contract, you should recall, is a set of expectations held by the individual that specify what the individual and the organization expect to give and to receive from each other in the course of their working relationship. These expectations cover how much work is to be performed for how much pay. They also summarize the broader rights, privileges, and obligations accruing to the individual–organization relationship.

Most people seek a balance between what they put into an organization (contributions) and what they get from an organization in return (inducements). Within the boundaries of the psychological contract, therefore, employees will agree to do many things in and for the organization because they think they should. That is, in exchange for certain inducements, they recognize the authority of the organization and its managers to direct their work-related behavior in certain ways.

Each of us learns to respond to authority early in our lives. You are most likely responding to your instructor's authority right now by reading this textbook. Throughout our lives, we are socialized or taught to accept orders from persons of higher status or authority. This socialization can be direct, such as that received in the instructions of parents and teachers and other authority figures. Or it can be indirect such as that received in the themes of movies, books, and television shows that depict acquiescence to authority, and through which people come to learn what is the "right" or socially acceptable behavior in various circumstances.[8] This feeling about what is "right" also sets limits beyond which people typically will not go in obeying commands or following the wishes of someone else.

Thus, within the boundaries of the exchange of values defined by the individual's psychological contract with an organization and within the boundaries of what the individual considers morally right, she or he is prone to obey the orders of authority figures in the organization. Chester Barnard, a former president of the New Jersey Bell Telephone Company and a renowned management scholar, calls this area in which directions are obeyed the "zone of indifference."[9]

Obedience and the Zone of Indifference

A **zone of indifference** is the range of authoritative requests to which a subordinate is willing to respond without subjecting the directives to critical evaluation or judgment, hence to which he or she is indifferent.[10] Directives falling within the zone are obeyed. Requests or orders falling outside the zone of indifference are not considered part of the authority relationship defined as acceptable by the terms of the psychological contract. Such "extraordinary" directives will receive critical consideration from the subordinate and may or may not be obeyed. We clarify this link between the zone of indifference and the psychological contract through the example shown in Figure 15.3.

The secretary whose psychological contract is shown in the figure may be expected to perform, in return for various inducements and with no questions asked, a number of activities falling within the zone of indifference. This response tendency will satisfy the manager most of the time. There may be times, however, when the boss would like the secretary to do things falling outside the zone. This requires efforts to enlarge the zone to accommodate additional behaviors.

It might not be difficult, for example, to broaden the zone a bit and influence the secretary to make coffee regularly and even bring in sandwiches from time to time. The secretary might even be convinced to work Saturday mornings if the boss is willing to provide extra inducements of special value. In these attempts to broaden the zone, the boss will most likely have to use power sources beyond formal authority or position power. In some instances, such as Sunday work and "fudging" expense accounts, no power base may be capable of accomplishing the desired result.

Before leaving this discussion, there is another side to power, authority, and obedience with which you should be familiar as a manager. That side is your own zone of indifference and tendency to obey. When will you say "no" to your boss? When should you be willing to say "no"?

Life in any organization will include inevitable stresses and strains between the

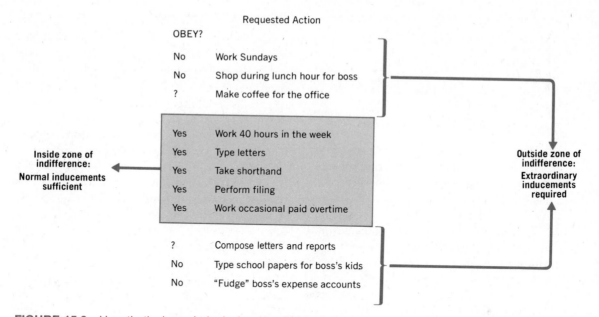

FIGURE 15.3 Hypothetical psychological contract for a secretary.

expectations of supervisors and the individual prerogatives of their subordinates. At times, this may even reach the extreme of involving ethical dilemmas where one is asked to do things that are illegal, unethical, or both. Research on ethical managerial behavior, for example, shows that supervisors are singled out as frequent causes of ethical dilemmas. They are singled out by their subordinates as sources of pressure who do such things as support incorrect viewpoints, sign false documents, overlook their wrongdoing, and do business with their friends.[11]

Most of us will face occasional ethical dilemmas throughout out careers. And history is replete with examples of loyal subordinates who failed to say ''no'' and were then led to commit socially undesirable acts. The ''Watergate'' and ''Irangate'' crimes are examples of illegalities committed by people who felt they were ''just following orders.'' Saying ''no'' can be tough and a price may have to be paid at times to protect that in which you believe. (See Newsline 15.1.)

Obedience and the Acceptance Theory of Authority

An acceptance theory of authority helps us to understand when people will and will not obey the directives of others. It holds that a manager's orders will be accepted when, and only when,[12]

1. The subordinate truly understands the directive.
2. The subordinate feels capable of carrying out the directive.

NEWSLINE 15.1 / SUMMONING MANAGERIAL COURAGE

"Courage" is the willingness to put yourself at risk in the service of some greater good. But, is there such a thing as "managerial courage"—the willingness to put your *career* at risk in similar service?

Yes there is. Courage isn't missing from the managerial ranks, but it can sometimes be hard to find. After all, it takes a bit of moxie to speak up and tell the boss one of her pet ideas is a dud, to tell a really nice subordinate that his performance isn't up to par, to act contrary to a dated standard operating procedure, and to make generally necessary but controversial decisions. In his book *Managerial Courage*, Harvey Hornstein says that many managers do take these and other risks. They tend to do so after carefully digging for facts— doing their "homework" so to speak. They also present their views in a straightforward and businesslike way. And they keep it all aboveboard.

Where does such courage come from? Hornstein's research indicates that self-respect is a major factor. Those managers who summon the courage to go against the wishes of the boss or to make an unpopular decision, do so mostly to maintain their self-respect. They're likely to say something like—"If I hadn't done it, I couldn't have lived with myself afterward."

Reported in *Fortune*.

3. The subordinate sees the directive in the organization's best interests.
4. The subordinate believes the directive to be consistent with personal values.

You will want other persons in the work setting to comply with your requests. The acceptance theory can help you to plan your communications in this regard. Ultimately, too, you should understand the psychological contracts and subsequent zones of indifference of others. Then and only then will you be complete in recognizing when position power becomes inadequate and person power becomes necessary if the desired influence is to be achieved.

MANAGERIAL PERSPECTIVES ON POWER AND INFLUENCE

A considerable portion of any manager's time will be directed toward what is called "power-oriented" behavior. This is "behavior directed primarily at developing or using relationships in which other people are to some degree willing to defer to one's wishes."[13] You will probably be surprised at how much time and energy can be expended by managers in the form of power-oriented behavior. Thus, it will serve you well to develop further familiarity with power and influence from a purely managerial perspective.

Power Demands on Managers

Up to this point in the chapter, we have tended to view power and influence from a "top down" perspective (i.e., as power exercised by a supervisor to achieve influence over the behavior of subordinates). In actual fact, the power demands on any manager will be much broader than this. A key point in our discussion of groups in organizations related to the manager's role as a linking pin in the organization as a complex network of interlocking groups. Figure 15.4 builds on this notion to show three basic

FIGURE 15.4 Three dimensions of managerial power and influence.

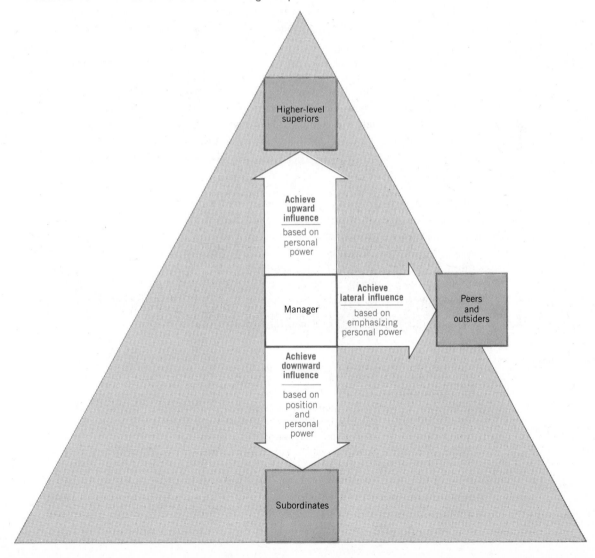

dimensions of power and influence with which a manager will become involved: downward, upward, and lateral. To fulfill their responsibilities, managers must use power to influence not only their subordinates, but also those persons outside the work unit whose support is needed to ensure its success. This requires that a manager be able to use power upward in the chain of command to achieve influence over the behavior of higher-level supervisors, and use power laterally to influence the behavior of peers within the organization and any outsiders with whom relationships are maintained.

Also shown in Figure 15.4 are some preliminary ideas on achieving success along each of these power and influence dimensions. When facing upward, managers must rely on the use of personal power to achieve influence over higher-level superiors. When facing downward, by contrast, both position and personal power can be mobilized in dealing with subordinates. In lateral relations with peers and outsiders, the manager must again emphasize personal power to achieve the desired influence.

Acquiring Managerial Power

Prior discussion and the insights of Figure 15.4 highlight the importance of both position and personal power to managers. Indeed, the effective manager is one who succeeds in building and maintaining high levels of position and personal power over time. Then and only then will sufficient power of the right types be available when a manager needs to exercise influence on downward, lateral, and upward dimensions.

Building Position Power

Table 15.1 lists five characteristics that account for and have the ability to foster power in a managerial position. As distilled from a variety of research studies, the managerial implications of Table 15.1 are basically that power is increased by greater centrality, criticality, flexibility, visibility, and relevance in a position of managerial authority.[14] Managers, accordingly, can enhance and maintain the legitimacy of their position and their capacity to administer rewards and punishments from this position by acting over time to maximize the presence of these characteristics in their jobs.

TABLE 15.1 Characteristics Enhancing the Power of a Position	
Characteristic	Description
Centrality	Relationship between positions in a communication network
Criticality	Relationship between tasks performed in a work-flow process
Flexibility	Amount of discretion vested in a position
Visibility	Degree to which task performance is seen by influential members of the organization
Relevance	Relationship between a task and organizational priorities

Source: David A. Whetten and Kim S. Cameron, *Developing Managerial Skills* (Glenview, Ill.: Scott, Foresman, 1984), p. 259. Copyright © 1984, Scott, Foresman and Company, p. 259. Reprinted by permission.

Five specific managerial guidelines for gaining position power in organizations follow:[15]

1. *Increase your centrality and criticality in the organization* by acquiring a more central role in the work flow, having information filtered through you, making at least part of your job responsibilities unique, expanding your network of communication contacts, and occupying an office convenient to main traffic flows.

2. *Increase the personal discretion and flexibility of your job* by getting rid of routine activities, expanding task variety and novelty, initiating new ideas, getting involved in new projects, participating in the early stages of the decision-making process, and avoiding "reliable performance criteria" for judging your success on the job.

3. *Build tasks that are difficult to evaluate into your job* by creating an ambiguous job description, developing a unique language or set of labels in your work, obtaining advanced training, becoming more involved in professional associations, and exercising your own judgment.

4. *Increase the visibility of your job performance* by expanding the number of contacts you have with senior people, making oral presentations of written work, participating in problem-solving task forces, sending out notices of accomplishment that are of interest to the organization, and seeking additional opportunities to increase personal name recognition.

5. *Increase the relevance of your tasks to the organization* by becoming an internal coordinator or external representative, providing services and information to other units, monitoring and evaluating activities within your own unit, expanding the domain of your work activities, becoming involved in decisions central to the organization's top-priority goals, and becoming a trainer or mentor for new members.

Building Personal Power

Personal power arises from personal characteristics of the manager rather than from the location and other characteristics of his or her position in the organization's hierarchy of authority. We discussed two primary bases of personal power as resting in expertise and reference. Three personal characteristics are singled out for their special potential to enhance these bases of personal power in organizational settings. They are[16]

1. *Knowledge and information.* A manager can enhance his or her personal power through the expertise gained by possession of special knowledge (e.g., gained by education, training, and experience) and information (e.g., gained through special access to data and/or people).

2. *Personal attractiveness.* A manager's reference power will be increased by characteristics that enhance "likability" and create personal attraction in relationships with other people. These include pleasant personality characteristics, agreeable behavior patterns, and attractive personal appearance.

3. *Effort.*   The demonstration of sincere hard work in behalf of task performance can also increase personal power by enhancing both expertise and reference. A person perceived to try hard may be expected to know more about the job and thus be sought out for advice; a person who tries hard is also likely to be respected for the attempt and even become depended on by others to maintain that effort.

Turning Power into Influence

The acquisition of power is certainly an important task for any manager. Using this power well actually to achieve the desired influence over other people, however, is yet another challenge. Consider the following examples of how some managers attempt to exercise influence.[17]

"I voice my wishes loudly."

"I offer a quid pro quo; that is, I offer to do for them if they do for me."

"I keep at it and reiterate my point over and over again until I get my way."

"I have all the facts and figures ready, and I use them as necessary."

"I go over the boss's head to higher levels when I get turned down."

What do you think of these influence attempts? How would you respond as someone on the receiving end of each, and perhaps even more important, how would you go about trying to exercise influence over someone else at work?

Strategies of Managerial Influence

Practically speaking, there are many useful ways of exercising influence. One useful classification separates them into seven general strategies of managerial influence. These strategies involve managers attempting to get their ways by[18]

1. *Reason.*   Using facts and data to support a logical argument.
2. *Friendliness.*   Using flattery, goodwill, and favorable impressions.
3. *Coalition.*   Using relationships with other people.
4. *Bargaining.*   Using the exchange of benefits as a basis for negotiation.
5. *Assertiveness.*   Using a direct and forceful personal approach.
6. *Higher authority.*   Gaining higher level support for one's requests.
7. *Sanctions.*   Using organizationally derived rewards and punishments.

This focus on strategies of managerial influence forces us to think very specifically about *how* managers get their work done—that is, how managers get things done through other people inside and outside of the organization. It is an important focus for us because a manager actually chooses *how* to attempt to achieve influence in any given situation. And, managers succeed or fail in these attempts based on the quality of these choices. In particular, they may err through force of habit, lack of adequate forethought, and/or incorrect assessment of the other person's willingness to comply with a given request.

Dimensions of Managerial Influence

Actual research on these seven strategies for achieving managerial influence suggests that reason is the most popular strategy overall but that some variation exists when the influence is directed toward a person's supervisor and subordinates.[19] Managerial attempts to influence subordinates most frequently involve reason, friendliness, and assertiveness; attempts to influence supervisors frequently include assertiveness as well as reason and friendliness. Among all the strategies, friendliness, assertiveness, bargaining, and higher authority are used more frequently to influence subordinates than supervisors. This pattern of influence attempts is consistent with our earlier contention that downward influence will generally include mobilization of both position and personal power sources, while upward influence will more likely draw on personal power.

Exercising Upward Influence

There is not much research available on the specific subject of upward influence in organizations. This is unfortunate since a truly effective manager is one who is able to influence his or her boss as well as subordinates. Each of these parties has the capability to help or hinder high levels of work-unit task performance and human resource maintenance. Thus, we should give some special attention to upward influence as a component of managerial life.

One recent study investigating success and failure in upward influence attempts reports that reason or the logical presentation of ideas is viewed by both supervisors and subordinates as the most frequently used strategy of upward influence.[20] When queried on reasons for success and failure, however, both similarities and differences are found in the viewpoints of the two groups. Table 15.2 shows that the perceived causes of success in upward influence are similar for both supervisors and subordinates. These reasons involve the favorable content of the influence attempt, a favorable manner of its presentation, and the competence of the subordinate. Where the two groups disagree is on the causes of failure. Subordinates view failure in upward

TABLE 15.2 Perceived Causes of Success and Failure in Upward Influence Attempts

	Supervisor's Views	Subordinate's Views
Causes of success	Favorable content of influence attempt; favorable manner in which attempt made; competency of subordinate	Agreement with supervisor's views
Causes of failure	Unfavorable content of influence attempt; lack of competence of subordinate; poor manner in which attempt made	Unfavorable content of influence attempt; closemindedness of supervisor; poor interpersonal relations with supervisor

Source: Developed from Warren K. Schilit and Edwin A. Locke, "A Study of Upward Influence in Organizations," *Administrative Science Quarterly,* Vol. 27 (1982), pp. 304–316.

influence due to closemindedness of the supervisor, unfavorable content of the influence attempt, and unfavorable interpersonal relationships with the supervisor. Supervisors, by contrast, view failures as due to unfavorable content of the attempt, the unfavorable manner in which it was presented, and lack of competence of the subordinate.

In interpreting these results, the growing relevance of attribution theory to the field of OB is again apparent. The researchers point out that the latter differences can be explained by the theory that each group would want to be perceived in the best light possible. To explain failure in upward influence attempts, attribution theory would expect that each group would explain failure in such a way that most likely protects its self-esteem. From the subordinates' perspective, then, failure in upward influence is more likely attributed to the "closemindedness" of a supervisor than to lack of personal competency or a poor choice of strategy.

A related set of explanations focuses on the sources of power for those attempts that failed. The data in Table 15.2 may be interpreted to show supervisors perceiving a lack of expert power in the subordinates influence attempts (i.e., unfavorable content, lack of competence, and poor manner), whereas subordinates perceive a lack of power from both expertise (unfavorable content) and reference (reflected in perceived closemindedness of supervisor and poor interpersonal relations with supervisor).

Much remains to be done before concrete guidelines on upward influence become available. Future research must examine findings such as these in a continuing framework that allows such variables as organization structure, size, and culture as well as individual differences and managerial levels to impact results. While we eagerly await the results of these inquiries, you are well advised to acknowledge the manager's need to achieve success in upward influence and use the prior insights to advantage when actually confronted with this reality in the managerial role.

ORGANIZATIONAL POLITICS

Any study of power and influence inevitably leads to the subject of "politics." This word may conjure up thoughts of illicit deals, favors, and special personal relationships in your mind. Perhaps this image of shrewd, often dishonest, practices of obtaining one's way is reinforced by Machiavelli's classic fifteenth-century work, *The Prince* (discussed in Chapter 3), which outlines how to obtain and hold power via political action. It is important, however, to adopt a perspective that allows for politics in organizations to function in a much broader capacity.[21]

Organizational Politics Defined

Organizational politics is formally defined as "the management of influence to obtain ends not sanctioned by the organization or to obtain sanctioned ends through non-sanctioned influence means."[22] A person's behavior becomes "political" when actions are taken to "acquire, develop, and use power and other resources to obtain one's preferred outcomes in a situation in which there is uncertainty or differences about choices."[23] Managers engage in political action much more than most admit.

Functions of Organizational Politics

Organizations are collections of individuals pursuing personal goals as well as common purposes. They are also networks of individuals with widely different interests attempting to deal with a host of inconsistent demands from within and outside the organization. Organizational politics helps these people to adapt and helps the organization to succeed in ways that the formal structure alone cannot guarantee. Rather than something to be avoided or denied, we argue that some aspects of "organizational politics" help give life to the skeleton of an organization. More specifically, organizational politics can serve a number of functions, including helping managers to

1. *Overcome personnel inadequacies.*   As a manager, you should expect some mismatches between people and positions in organizations. Even in the best managed firms, mismatches arise among managers who are learning, burned out, lacking in needed training and skills, overqualified, or lacking resources needed to accomplish their assigned duties. Organizational politics provides a mechanism for circumventing these inadequacies and getting the job done.
2. *Cope with change.*   Changes in the environment and technology of an organization often come more quickly than an organization can restructure. Even in organizations known for detailed planning, unanticipated events occur. To meet unanticipated problems, people and resources must be moved into place quickly before small headaches become major problems. Organizational politics can help to identify such problems and move ambitious, problem-solving managers into the breach.
3. *Channel personal contacts.*   In larger organizations, it is all but impossible to know the persons in every important position. Yet managers need to influence individuals throughout the organization. The political network of the organization can provide the necessary access.
4. *Substitute for formal authority.*   When a person's formal authority breaks down or fails to apply to a situation, political actions can be used to prevent a loss of influence. Managers may use political behavior to maintain operations and achieve task continuity in circumstances where the failure of formal authority may otherwise cause problems.

POLITICAL ACTION IN ORGANIZATIONS

Political action is a part of organizational life and it is best to view organizational politics for its potential to contribute to managerial and organizational effectiveness. It is in this spirit that we now examine several operational perspectives on political action in organizations.

Political Action and the Manager

Junior executives, especially, may gain a better understanding of political behavior by placing themselves in the positions of other persons involved in critical decisions or events. Each action and decision can be seen as having benefits and costs to all parties concerned. Where the costs exceed the benefits, the manager may act to protect his or her position.

Figure 15.5 shows a sample payoff table for two managers, Lee and Leslie, in a problem situation involving a decision whether or not to allocate resources to a special project. If both authorize the resources, project X gets completed on time and their company keeps a valuable client. Unfortunately, by doing so both Lee and Leslie will overspend their budgets. Taken on its own, a budget overrun would be bad for their performance record. Assume that the overruns will be acceptable only if the client is kept. Thus, if both act, both they and the company win. This is the upper left block in Figure 15.5. Obviously, it is the most desirable outcome for all parties concerned.

Assume that Leslie acts, but Lee does not. The company loses the client and Leslie overspends the budget in a futile effort, but Lee ends up within budget. While the company and Leslie lose, Lee wins. This is the lower left block of the figure. The upper right block shows the reverse situation, where Lee acts but Leslie does not. Leslie wins, and the company and Lee lose. Finally, if both fail to act, they each stay within the budget and therefore gain, but the company loses the client.

The company clearly wants both Lee and Leslie to act. But will they? Would you take the risk of overspending the budget, knowing that your colleague may refuse? Suppose further that Lee and Leslie will be promoted on the basis of their budgetary performance. A political analysis would presume that each will seek to maximize his or her comparative performance at minimal risk. We would predict in such an instance

FIGURE 15.5 Political payoff matrix for the allocation of resources on a sample project.

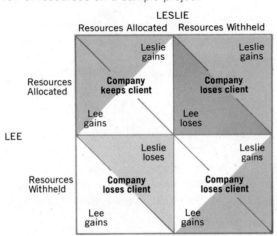

that both would fail to act. When estimating the political behavior of other managers, calculating a simple payoff matrix such as the one in Figure 15.5 may be most helpful.

Political Action and Subunit Power

The prior discussion of political action involved power and influence in person-to-person interfaces. Another level of political action links managers more formally to one another as representatives of their work units. In Chapter 8 we examined the group dynamics associated with such intergroup relationships. Now we turn our attention to the politics that occur in lateral relations among subunits.

Table 15.3 highlights five of the more typical lateral relations in which you might engage as a manager—work flow, service, advisory, auditing, and approval. The table also shows how lateral relationships among subunit representatives challenge even further the political skills of a manager. Note that each of the examples in the table requires the manager to achieve influence through some other means than formal authority.

TABLE 15.3 Typical Lateral Relations Engaged in by Managers and Their Associated Influence Requirements

Type of Relationship	Sample Influence Requirements
Work flow—contacts with units that precede or follow in a sequential production chain.	An assembly-line manager informs another line manager responsible for a later stage in the production process about a delay that must be taken.
Service—contacts with units established to help with problems.	An assembly-line manager asks the maintenance manager to fix an important piece of equipment on a priority basis.
Advisory—contacts with formal staff units having special expertise.	A marketing manager consults with the personnel manager to obtain special assistance in recruiting for a new salesperson.
Auditing—contacts with units having the right to evaluate the actions of others.	A marketing manager tries to get the credit manager to retract a report criticizing marketing's tendency to open bad-credit accounts.
Approval—contacts with units whose approval must be obtained before action may be taken.	A marketing manager submits a job description to the company affirmative action officer for approval before recruiting for a new salesperson can begin.

Source: Developed from James L. Hall and Joel L. Leidecker, "Lateral Relations in Organizations," pp. 213–223 in Patrick E. Connor, ed., *Dimensions in Modern Management* (Boston: Houghton Mifflin, 1974), which was based in part on Leonard Sayles, *Managerial Behavior* (New York: McGraw-Hill, 1964).

To be effective in political action, managers should understand the relative power of other units in the organization. Let us start with a few basics about estimating subunit power, a first step in understanding the politics of subunit relations. Line units are typically more powerful than staff groups. This is because the power of a unit is often limited by the degree to which its function is an integral part of the organization's mission. Thus, line units have more power than do staff, and units toward the top of the hierarchy are often more powerful than are those toward the bottom.

Units gain power as more of their relations with others are of the approval and auditing types. Work-flow relations are more powerful than are advisory associations, and both are more powerful than service relations. Units can also increase power by incorporating new actions into their task domains. Specifically, units that tackle and resolve difficult problems can gain power. A difficult problem is one that presents uncertainty to the organization, calls for unique skills, affects many organizational units, and requires immediate attention before it becomes a very serious matter.

Working from a more theoretical perspective, it is recognized that certain strategic contingencies often govern the relative power of subunits. For a subunit to gain power vis-à-vis others, it must increase its control over such strategic contingencies as[24]

1. *Scarce resources.*   Subunits gain in power when they obtain access to or control scarce resources needed by others.
2. *Ability to cope with uncertainty.*   Subunits gain in power when they are able to cope with uncertainty and help solve problems that uncertainty causes for others.
3. *Centrality in the flow of work.*   Subunits gain in power when their position in the work flow allows them to influence the work of others.
4. *Substitutability of activities.*   Subunits gain in power when they perform tasks or activities that are nonsubstitutable, that is, when they perform essential functions that cannot be completed by others.

Political Action and the Chief Executive

From descriptions of the 1890s robber barons such as Jay Gould to the popular JR of "Dallas," Americans have been fascinated with the politics of the chief executive suite. Biographers have glorified the individual political skills of executive heroes who are said to have established corporate political systems that outlived them.[25] An analytical view of executive suite dynamics may lift some of the mystery behind the political veil at the top levels in organizations.

Resource Dependencies

One useful view emphasizes the firm's need for resources that are controlled by others. Executive behavior can be explained in terms of these resource dependencies.[26] The resource dependence approach begins with three basic assumptions. First, executives seek to retain their jobs and increase the survival potential of their firms. Second, organizations must and should respond to outsiders who control the resources (money, labor, materials) needed for the firm's survival. Third, organizations do not maximize but, instead, "satisfice." That is, organizations and their managers do not seek the best solution or outcomes, but only workable solutions and acceptable outcomes.

These assumptions lead to an analysis of the resources needed for survival and the degree of external control over needed resources. Essentially, the resource dependence of a particular firm increases as (1) needed resources become more scarce, (2) outsiders have more control over needed resources, and (3) there are fewer substitutes for a particular type of resource controlled by a limited number of outsiders. The perspective suggests that organizations will and should adjust to resource dependencies. Thus, if capital is scarcer, under the control of fewer outsiders, and more difficult to substitute than labor, firms should adjust to serve the interests of those holding capital. However, the adjustment cannot be complete since labor must be "satisfied" and executives will seek discretion to keep their jobs. Thus, the role of chief executives is to develop a workable compromise among the competing resource dependencies facing the organization—a compromise that enhances the executive's power.

Several recent analyses suggest that there are limits on the ability of even our largest and most powerful organizations to control all important external contingencies. International competition has narrowed the range of options for managers. They can no longer ignore the rest of the world. Some may need to fundamentally redefine how they expect to conduct business. For instance, once U.S. firms could go it alone without the assistance of foreign corporations. Now they may need technically sophisticated foreign partners from Europe and Japan to revitalize their production operations and reach toward developing new products and processes in emerging technologies.[27]

To develop such a compromise, executives need to diagnose the relative power of outsiders and create strategies that respond differently to various external sources of needed resources. For larger organizations, many of these strategies may center on altering the firm's degree of resource dependence. Through mergers and acquisitions, the firm may bring key resources within its control. By changing the "rules of the game," the firm may find protection from particularly powerful outsiders. For instance, markets may be protected by trade barriers, or labor unions may be put in check by "right to work" laws.

Organizational Governance

A resource dependence perspective suggests that one of the key roles played by top management is to develop and allocate power. The question naturally arises how this is done. Analyses of organizational governance seek to understand the power development and allocation process at the top levels of organizations. Organizational governance refers to the pattern of authority, influence, and acceptable managerial behavior established at the top of the organization. The governance system of an organization establishes what is important, how issues will be defined, who should and should not be involved in key choices, and the boundaries for acceptable implementation.

Those studying organizational governance suggest that a "dominant coalition" comprised of powerful organizational actors is a key to its understanding.[28] While one expects many top officers within the organization to be members of this coalition, it occasionally includes outsiders with access to key resources. Thus, analysis of organizational governance builds on the resource dependence perspective by high-lighting the effective control of key resources by members of a dominant coalition.

This view of the executive suite recognizes that the daily practice of organizational governance is the development and resolution of issues. Via the governance system, the dominant coalition attempts to define reality. By accepting or rejecting proposals from subordinates, by directing questions toward the interests of powerful outsiders, and by selecting individuals who appear to espouse particular values and qualities, the pattern of governance is slowly established within an organization. This pattern, furthermore, rests in part at least upon very political foundations.

Political Action and Organizational Design

Although politics is common to all organizations, its nature may differ among or-ganizations adopting different structural configurations. Chapter 12 introduced you to the mechanistic, organic, and diverse forms of organizations. Now let us review the political implications of each.

Politics in the Mechanistic Structure

Organizations that emphasize vertical specialization (e.g., many levels of manage-ment), formal control, tight rules, extensive written policies, and procedures and favor a large centralized staff are often labeled "mechanistic." These organizations may find particular problems with auditing and approval relationships among subunits. The presence of many explicit rules and procedures provides these units with numerous standards for judgment and, thus, influence. Auditing groups can enforce the adher-ence to written rules, policies, and procedures to the point where lower-level managers lose the capability to make simple decisions. Here managers and employees may politically counter by manipulating the selection of applicable policies, procedures, and rules. The proliferation of rules, for instance, yields contradictory prescriptions. Thus, the astute manager acts and then finds the rule that justifies the action. This is sometimes called the "paradox of structure" since the very mechanism used to con-strain action provides a justification for political action. The manager can use the system to rationalize his or her own interests. Of course, such political games are recognized by many senior managers. They may be permitted only so long as the appearance of success continues.

Politics in the Organic Structure

Organizations are called organic when the emphasis is on personal coordination (e.g., task forces, group meetings), and there is a deemphasis on written policies, proce-dures, rules, and corporate-level staff. With less emphasis on the vertical hierarchy, organic structures put more weight on work flow and advisory relations to resolve problems among operating units. Staff units become powerful with success in selling their advice to line managers, while work-flow partners must consider the impacts of their actions when dealing with other units. Without a formal structure to resolve conflicting needs, the political games in organic organizations tend to stress trust and cooperation.

Politics in Diverse Structures

In Chapter 12 we suggested that many organizations use both mechanistic and organic aspects in their structures. Production departments, for instance, may be quite rigid whereas marketing may be quite organic. In organizations with a diverse structure, much of the political action is likely to move toward the interface between mechanistically and organically structured units. Substantial potential for conflict exists at this interface. The structural differences promote mistrust and misunderstanding. Managers in the mechanistic units see the others as loose, out of control, and needing central direction. Organic unit managers see the others as bureaucratic, inflexible, and bogged down in unnecessary paperwork.

Implications

Organizational politics flows with and supplements the design of the organization. It allows the organization to respond to a variety of changes and pressures without having to restructure. The ultimate function of organizational politics is to allow the power of different units to wax and wane while the overall design of the organization remains consistent over time. Thus, organizations need managers capable of using political action to fill the breach between subunits and formal structures over time.

ETHICS OF POWER AND POLITICS

No treatment of power and politics in organizations is complete without consideration of related ethical issues. We can begin this task by clarifying the distinction between the nonpolitical and political uses of power.[29] Power is nonpolitical in its use when it remains within the boundaries of formal authority, organizational policies and procedures, and job descriptions, and when it is directed toward ends sanctioned by the organization. When the use of power moves outside the realm of authority, policies, procedures, and job descriptions, or is directed toward ends not sanctioned by the organization, that use of power is political.

When the use of power moves into the realm of political behavior, important ethical issues emerge. It is in this context that a manager, for example, must stop and consider more than a pure ''ends justify the means'' logic. The issues are broader and involve distinctly ethical questions as the following example shows.[30] Newsline 15.2 suggests that business students may not be generally exposed to ethical questions.

> Lorna is the production manager of a noncohesive work group responsible for meeting a deadline that will require coordinated effort among her subordinates. Believing that the members of the work group will pull together and meet the deadline if they have a little competition, Lorna decides to create the impression among her subordinates that members of the sales department want

NEWSLINE 15.2 /
PROFIT AT ANY PRICE: THE MORAL FAILURE OF BUSINESS SCHOOLS

E. F. Hutton kited checks, the Bank of Boston laundered drug money, and GE falsified time sheets to overcharge the government. These moral failures and illegal activities are but examples of a disturbing disregard for business ethics that is all too frequent in modern society. University of Washington Professor William G. Scott attributes some of this disregard to business schools and their failures to sufficiently incorporate moral and ethical issues into university curricula.

Business schools preach an implicit doctrine of corrupt managerialism based on blind faith in markets, myths, and pseudo-science according to Scott. Faith in the market derives from the apparently objective and rigorous analysis of competitive forces that in reality are far from objective or clear. Faith in myths derives from the historic emphasis on manipulating employee values for the betterment of senior executives. The values of employees should and can be molded to be those desired by senior managers. The pseudo-science of statistically analyzing problems fails to recognize that as power holders, managers should be concerned with what "ought to be" not just what is currently acceptable.

Scott laments that ethical issues are rarely discussed in business schools; they have failed to establish mechanisms for moral discourse. By default, business schools have promoted a single-set value system instead of an awareness of moral choices. Moral dilemmas are at the heart of business practice. The market, popular myths, and pseudo-science are not providing insight into what managers should and should not do.

Reported in *Selections*.

her group to fail to meet the deadline so that sales can gain an edge over production in upcoming budgetary negotiations.

Think about what Lorna's behavior means. On the one hand, her action may seem justifiable if it works and the group gets its assigned job done on time. On the other hand, there may be side-effects involved. What about the possibility that the sales and production departments will lose trust in one another and thus find it difficult to work together in the future? Then, too, consider the fact that Lorna was "creating an impression" to achieve her goal. Isn't this really "lying"? And, if it is, can we accept lying as an ethical way for a manager to get his or her job done?

Recent work in the area of ethical issues in power and politics suggests the usefulness of the integrated structure for analyzing political behavior depicted in Figure 15.6. This structure suggests that a person's behavior must satisfy the following criteria to be considered ethical.[31]

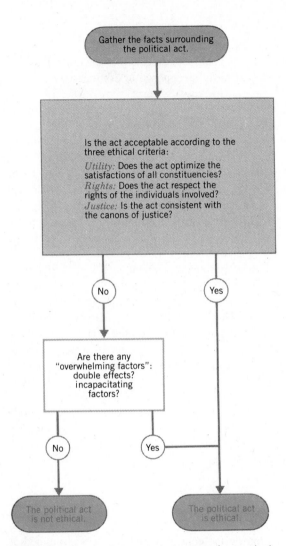

FIGURE 15.6 An integrated structure for analyzing political behavior in organizations. (*Source:* Manuel Velasquez, Dennis J. Moberg, and Gerald F. Cavanagh, "Organizational Statesmanship and Dirty Politics: Ethical Guidelines for the Organizational Politician," *Organizational Dynamics,* Vol. 11 Autumn 1983, p. 73. Used by permission.)

1. *Criterion of utilitarian outcomes.*   The behavior results in optimization of satisfactions of people inside and outside the organization; that is, it produces the greatest good for the greatest number of people.
2. *Criterion of individual rights.*   The behavior respects the rights of all affected

parties; that is, it respects basic human rights of free consent, free speech, freedom of conscience, privacy, and due process.

3. *Criterion of distributive justice.*   The behavior respects the rules of justice; that is, it treats people equitably and fairly as opposed to arbitrarily.

Figure 15.6 also indicates that there may be times when a behavior is unable to pass these criteria but can still be considered ethical in the given situation. This special case must satisfy the *criterion of overwhelming factors,* a criterion that justifies a failure to satisfy one or more of the prior criteria of ethical political behavior. This justification, however, must be based on truly overwhelming factors in which the special nature of the situation results in (1) conflicts among criteria (e.g., a behavior results in some good and some bad being done), (2) conflicts within criteria (e.g., a behavior uses questionable means to achieve a positive end), and/or (3) incapacity to employ the criteria (e.g., a person's behavior is based on inaccurate or incomplete information).

Choosing to be ethical often involves considerable personal sacrifice. Four rationalizations are often used to justify unethical choices: (1) individuals feel that the behavior is not really illegal and thus could be moral; (2) the action appears to be in the firm's best interests; (3) it is unlikely the action will ever be detected; and (4) it appears that the action demonstrates loyalty to the boss or the firm. While these rationalizations appear compelling at the moment of action, each deserves close scrutiny. The individual must ask, "how far is too far," "what are the long term interests of the corporation," "what will happen when (not *if*) the action is discovered," and "do individuals or firms that ask for unethical behavior deserve my loyalty?"[32]

All managers use power and politics to get their work done. Thus, every manager bears a responsibility to do so in an ethical and socially responsible fashion. By recognizing and confronting ethical considerations such as those just discussed, each of us should be better prepared to meet this important challenge.

SUMMARY

We started this chapter by concentrating on the concept of power. It was defined as the ability to get someone else to do what you want. Influence was introduced as the process by which power is activated. We talked about power vested in both the position and the person of the manager and of the different sources or bases of these points of power. Position power included reward, coercive, and legitimate power bases; person power included expert and referent power bases. Authority was described as a special kind of position power, one that relies on legitimacy and the right of command.

The famous Milgram experiments on obedience were reviewed to introduce a detailed look at power, authority, and obedience in organizations. We used the notion of the psychological contract to help define the zone of indifference, the arena of action within which subordinates will routinely do what they are asked to do by the boss. We discussed ways of "stretching" this zone to expand a manager's influence, and we inquired into the boundaries or limits that might characterize your personal zone of indifference as a manager.

Ultimately, our thoughts turned to the extension of power into the realm of organizational politics. Defined as the management of influence to obtain ends not sanctioned by the organization or to obtain sanctioned ends through nonsanctioned means, organizational politics was viewed as a basis for behavior that could be functional for organizations and their members. Several examples were used to clarify its implications in terms of political action and the manager, chief executives, subunit relations, and organization design.

The final segment in the chapter highlighted ethical issues relating to the use of power and politics in organizations. A basic framework for identifying when political behavior is ethical was explained. This framework involves the relationship among a person's behavior and criteria of utilitarian outcomes, individual rights, distributive justice, and overwhelming factors.

THINKING THROUGH THE ISSUES

1. Why is it that an order from a supervisor, or even someone as powerful as the president of the United States, may not be carried out?
2. Explain how the various bases of position and person power do or do not apply to a managerial situation with which you are familiar. What sources of power do lower-level participants in this situation have over their supervisors?
3. Put yourself in the shoes of one of the subjects in Milgram's experiment on obedience. Diagram a psychological contract for a typical subject, and show where you think the boundaries of the zone of indifference might be. What power bases did the experimenter have, and how did these narrow or widen the boundaries?
4. Identify and explain at least three guidelines for the acquisiton of (a) position power and (b) personal power by managers.
5. Identify and explain at least four strategies of managerial influence. Give examples of how each strategy may or may not work when exercising influence (a) downward and (b) upward in organizations.
6. Define "organizational politics" and give an example of how it operates in both functional and dysfunctional ways.
7. How does the "strategic contingencies" notion apply to political action and subunit relations?
8. Explain when political behavior in organizations can be considered ethical. Defend your answer.

CASE: POLITICAL BEHAVIOR ANALYSIS

The following two incidents involve the use of power and politics in organizations.[33] Read each incident and carefully analyze the actions being described.

Incident 1: New Product Development at General Rubber

Sam and Bob are highly motivated research scientists who work in the new product development lab at General Rubber. Sam is by far the most technically competent scientist in the lab, and he has been responsible for several patents that have netted the company nearly $6 million in the past decade. He is quiet, serious, and socially reserved. In contrast, Bob is outgoing and demonstrative. While Bob lacks the technical track record Sam has, his work has been solid though unimaginative. Rumor has it that Bob will be moved into an administrative position in the lab in the next few years.

According to lab policy, a $300,000 fund is available every year for the best new product development idea proposed by a lab scientist in the form of a competitive bid. Accordingly, Sam and Bob both prepare proposals. Each proposal is carefully constructed to detail the benefits to the company and to society if the proposal is accepted, and it is the consensus of other scientists from blind reviews that both proposals are equally meritorious. Both proposals require the entire $300,000 to realize any significant results. Moreover, the proposed line of research in each requires significant mastery of the technical issues involved and minimal need to supervise the work of others.

After submitting his proposal, Sam takes no further action aside from periodically inquiring about the outcome of the bidding process. In contrast, Bob begins to wage what might be termed an open campaign in support of his proposal. After freely admitting his intentions to Sam and others, Bob seizes every opportunity he can to point out the relative advantages of his proposal to individuals who might have some influence over the decision. So effective is this open campaign that considerable informal pressure is placed on those authorized to make the decision on behalf of Bob's proposal. Bob's proposal is funded and Sam's is not.

Incident 2: Chemical Disposal at American Semiconductor

Lee, age 61, has been director of engineering for American Semiconductor for 14 years. He is very bright and a fine supervisor, but he has not kept abreast of new developments in technology.

American Semiconductor's manufacturing process creates substantial quantities of toxic materials. Lee's casual attitude toward the disposal of these chemicals has resulted in a number of environmental citations. The firm is now tied up in court on two cases and will probably be forced to pay a considerable amount in damages. Yet Lee still does not perceive the disposal problem as urgent. For three years, Charlie, the executive vice president, has tried to persuade Lee to make this a priority issue but has failed. Charlie has reluctantly concluded that Lee must be taken out of his position as director of engineering.

Charlie recognizes that it would demoralize the other managers if he were to fire Lee outright. So Charlie decides that he will begin to tell selected individuals that he is dissatisfied with Lee's work. When there is open support for Lee, Charlie quietly sides with Lee's opposition. He casually lets Lee's peers know that he thinks Lee may have outlived his usefulness to the firm. He even exaggerates Lee's deficiencies and failures when speaking to Lee's co-workers. Discouraged by the waning support from his collegues, Lee decides to take an early retirement.

Questions

1. Can Bob's behavior in the first incident be justified on ethical grounds? Why or why not?
2. Can Charlie's behavior in the second incident be justified on ethical grounds? Why or why not?
3. What would you consider to be the most appropriate courses of action that Bob and Charlie should have taken in their respective situations? Defend your answer.

EXERCISE: POWER, POLITICS, AND MANAGERIAL SUCCESS

Purpose:
To confront the organizational realities of power and to develop a personal perspective on the implications of power and politics for managerial success.

Time:
50 minutes.

Procedure:

1. Form into groups as directed by your instructor.
2. Read the following statement.[32]

Most successful managers are successful because they understand how the system works and are willing and able to manipulate rules, regulations, and procedures to mobilize support and overcome opposition so that their ideas are accepted and their needs are met. Thus, power should not be construed as something negative but merely as a means of getting things done in a way that may or may not reflect purely rational decision making and a totally objective consideration of all the facts.

3. Decide whether you agree or disagree with this statement and why. Discuss your viewpoint with others in your work group.
4. Have a spokesperson prepare to share the results of the group discussion with the class.
5. The instructor will request group reports and a lead follow-up discussion on power, politics, and managerial success.

THE MANAGER'S VOCABULARY

Coercive Power   The extent to which a manager can deny desired rewards or administer undesirable outcomes to control other people.

Expert Power   The ability to control another's behavior due to the possession of knowledge, experience, or judgment that the other person does not have but needs.

Formal Authority   Legitimate power; the right of command vested in a managerial position.

Influence   A behavioral response to the exercise of power.

Legitimate Power   The extent to which a manager can use the internalized values of a subordinate that the "boss" has a "right of command" to control other people.

Organizational Politics   The management of influence to obtain ends not sanctioned by the organization or to obtain sanctioned ends through nonsanctioned influence means.

Power   The ability to get someone else to do something you want done; the ability to make things happen or get things done the way you want.

Referent Power   The ability to control another's behavior because of the individual's wanting to identify with the power source.

Reward Power   The extent to which a manager can use extrinsic and intrinsic rewards to control other people.

Zone of Indifference   The range of authoritative requests to which a subordinate is willing to respond without subjecting the directives to critical evaluation or judgment, hence, to which he or she is indifferent.

IMPORTANT NAMES

Chester Barnard   Famous executive and management scholar who identified the zone of indifference.

NOTES

[1] This description was compiled from a variety of popular press accounts including *The Detroit Free Press* from November 26 and 27, 1986; *Time,* December 8, 1986; and the *Wall Street Journal* December 1 and 3, 1986.

[2] Rosabeth Moss Kanter, "Power Failure in Management Circuit," *Harvard Business Review* (July–August 1979), pp. 65–75.

[3] John R. P. French and Bertram Raven, "The Bases of Social Power," in Dorwin Cartwright, ed., *Group Dynamics: Research and Theory* (Evanston, Ill.: Row, Peterson, 1962) pp. 607–623.

[4] See French and Raven, op. cit.

[5] Jeffry Pfeffer and Gerald Salancik, "The Effects of Advocacy and Information on Resource Allocations," *Human Relations,* Vol. 30 (1977), pp. 641–656.

[6] Stanley Milgram, "Behaviorial Study of Obedience," in Dennis W. Organ, ed., *The Applied Psychology of Work Behavior* (Dallas: Business Publications, Inc., 1978), pp. 384–398. Also see Stanley Milgram, "Group Pressure and Action Against a Person," *Journal of Abnormal and Social Psychology,* Vol. 69 (1964), pp. 137–143; "Some Conditions of Obedience and Disobedience to Authority," *Human Relations,* Vol. 18

(1965), pp. 57–76; *Obedience to Authority* (New York: Harper and Row, 1974).

[7]Stanley Milgram, "Behavioral Study of Obedience," *Journal of Abnormal and Social Psychology,* Vol. 67 (1963), pp. 371–378.

[8]Stephen J. Carroll and Henry L. Tosi, *Organizational Behavior* (Chicago: St. Clair Press, 1977), p. 212.

[9]Chester Barnard, *The Functions of the Executive* (Cambridge, Mass.: Harvard University Press, 1938).

[10]Richard R. Ritti and Ray G. Funkhouser, *The Ropes to Skip and the Ropes to Know* (Columbus, Ohio: Grid, 1977), p. 197.

[11]See Steven N. Brenner and Earl A. Mollander, "Is the Ethics of Business Changing," *Harvard Business Review,* Vol. 55 (February 1977), pp. 57–71; and, Barry Z. Posner and Warren H. Schmidt, "Values and the American Manager: An Update," *California Management Review,* Vol. XXVI (Spring 1984), pp. 202–216.

[12]Barnard, *The Functions of the Executive.*

[13]John P. Kotter, "Power, Success, and Organizational Effectiveness," *Organizational Dynamics* Vol. 6 (Winter 1978), p. 27.

[14]David A. Whetten and Kim S. Cameron, *Developing Managerial Skills* (Glenview, Ill.: Scott, Foresman, 1984), pp. 250–259.

[15]Ibid., p. 279. Used by permission.

[16]Ibid., pp. 260–266.

[17]See Toni Falbo, "Multidimensional Scaling of Power Strategies," *Journal of Personality and Social Psychology,* Vol. 35 (1977), pp. 537–547.

[18]David Kipinis, Stuart M. Schmidt, Chris Swaffin-Smith, and Ian Wilkinson, "Patterns of Managerial Influence: Shotgun Managers, Tacticians, and Bystanders," *Organizational Dynamics,* Vol. 12 (Winter 1984), pp. 60, 61.

[19]Ibid., pp. 58–67; and David Kipinis, Stuart M. Schmidt, and Ian Wilkinson, "Intraorganizational Influence Tactics: Explorations in Getting One's Way," *Journal of Applied Psychology,* Vol. 65 (1980), pp. 440–452.

[20]Warren K. Schilit and Edwin A. Locke, "A Study of Upward Influence in Organizations," *Administrative Science Quarterly,* Vol. 27 (1982), pp. 304–316.

[21]Although the work on organizational politics is not extensive, useful reviews include a chapter in Robert H. Miles, *Macro Organizational Behavior* (Santa Monica, Calif.: Goodyear, 1980); Bronston T. Mayes and Robert W. Allen, "Toward a Definition of Organizational Politics," *Academy of Management Review,* Vol. 2 (1977), pp. 672–677; Gerald F. Cavanagh, Denis J. Moberg, and Manual Velasquez, "The Ethics of Organizational Politics," *Academy of Management Review,* Vol. 6 (July 1981), pp. 363–374; and Dan Farrell and James C. Petersen, "Patterns of Political Behavior in Organizations," *Academy of Management Review,* Vol. 7 (July 1982), pp. 403–412.

[22]Mayes and Allen, "Toward a Definition of Organizational Politics," p. 675.

[23]Jeffrey Pfeffer, *Power in Organizations* (Marshfield, Mass.: Pitman, 1981), p. 7.

[24]See Miles, *Macro Organizational Behavior.*

[25]Thomas J. Peters and Richard H. Waterman, *In Search of Excellence: Lessons from America's Best-Run Companies* (New York: Harper & Row, 1982).

[26]See Jeffrey Pfeffer, *Organizations and Organization Theory* (Boston: Pitman, 1983); and Jeffrey Pfeffer and Gerald R. Salancik, *The External Control of Organizations* (Englewood Cliffs, N.J.: Prentice-Hall, 1978).

[27]See R. N. Osborn and C. Baughn, "New Patterns in the Formation of U.S./Japanese Cooperative Ventures," Columbia Journal of World Business, in press and I. Mitroff and S. Mohrman, "The Slack is Gone: How the United States Lost Its Competitive Edge in the World Economy," *Academy of Management Executive,* Vol. 1 (1987); pp. 65–70.

[28]James D. Thompson, *Organizations in Action* (New York: McGraw-Hill, 1967).

[29]This discussion is based on Cavanagh, Moberg, and Velasquez, "The Ethics of Organizational Politics;" and Manuel Velasquez, Dennis J. Moberg and Gerald Cavanagh, "Organizational Statesmanship and Dirty Politics: Ethical Guidelines for the Organizational Politician," *Organizational Dynamics,* Vol. 11 (1983), pp. 65–79, both of which offer a fine treatment of the ethics of power and politics.

[30]Cavanagh et al., "The Ethics of Organizational Politics," pp. 363–374. Used by permission.

[31]These criteria are developed from ibid.

[32]See Gellerman, Saul W. "Why 'Good' Managers Make Bad Ethical Choices," *Harvard Business Review* Vol. 64 (July 1986), pp. 85–97.

[33]See Keith G. Provan, "Power and Politics in Organizations," The Owen Manager (Spring/Summer 1983), pp. 11–17.

CHAPTER 16
LEADERSHIP

Patten
encourages an
entrepreneurial
management
approach.

Patten
Corporation
Annual
Report

VISIONARY LEADERSHIP
AND BEYOND

There's a new help wanted ad floating around the executive circles these days. It reads, "Wanted: Corporate Leaders—Must have vision and ability to build corporate culture. Mere managers need not apply."

What's at issue here is behind part of the business community's fascination with Lee Iacocca and his "turnaround" performance at Chrysler. It's also part and parcel of what made *In Search of Excellence* by Peters and Waterman a runaway best-seller. And it's related to the growing concern for entrepreneurism inside the large organization. Simply put, we're talking about leadership.

Yes, the recruiters are looking for leaders as they seek to fill the top jobs in industry. They're looking for executives with old fashioned charisma and with vision. Interestingly, too, much of the current thinking suggests that managers and leaders may be very different cups of tea.

The distinction boils down to issues like these. Leaders look to the future and set goals toward which they can direct the members of the organization. Managers wait for goals and then work on implementation. Leaders have a sense of the future and the organization's potentialities. Managers focus on the present and try to make the best of things as they occur.

Leaders are also likely to get the best out of people by achieving a balance between the corporate vision and concern for the employees' well being. Indeed, the wise leaders don't settle for getting the subordinates to go along with their visions; they encourage subordinates to develop their own visions within the corporate context. Even further, they possess charismatic qualities which can still whip the rest of us into a frenzy as we work for some collective good.

But leaders, at least in these terms, don't seem to come along that often anymore.

Management Applications Questions

What are the different ways of looking at leadership? How do leaders and leadership differ from managers and management? And what implications does leadership have for individuals, groups, and organizations?

PLANNING AHEAD

This chapter considers a number of different aspects of leadership. The learning activities of the chapter will make you familiar with the following topics:

Leadership and Managerial Behavior
Approaches to Studying Leadership
Leader Traits and Behaviors
Situational Contingencies and Leadership
Symbolic Leadership
Substitutes for Leadership
Practical Leadership Applications

Mention the word "leadership" and what comes to mind? As in the chapter opener, many people think of it as an almost mystical quality that some have and others do not. Some say they cannot define it, but they know it when they see it. Others tend to treat it more specifically, arguing, for example, that "good" leaders behave more considerately toward their subordinates or supervise their subordinates loosely rather than closely.

Regardless of the way leadership is viewed, most managers consider it so important that library shelves are replete with books on the subject, and millions of dollars a year are spent on leadership training. Let us see if we can strip away some of the mystique in the concept of leadership and relate it to other aspects of OB.

The first part of Chapter 15 was devoted to various forms of power and influence. A natural extension of this discussion is the subject of leadership. We define **leadership** as a special case of interpersonal influence that gets an individual or group to do what the leader wants done. It is a special case because it has long been a topic of special interest and has developed its own literature.

The chapter opener notes that leadership is often identified with things like charisma and vision. This "breed apart" way of looking at leadership catches the fancy of the popular press. And, as we show later in the present chapter, this view has also attracted the interest of some behavioral researchers. It is, however, only one of a number of ways of looking at leadership. It is also a view that can be put in better perspective after these other approaches have been examined.

LEADERSHIP AND MANAGERIAL BEHAVIOR

To begin, it is important to separate leadership from managerial behavior. Henry Mintzberg reminds us that a manager's job is a broad one that includes at least 10 different roles.[2] You should recall from Chapter 1 that only one of these roles is that of a leader. Thus, in addition to leadership, a manager engages in many other activities, ranging from ceremonial roles to monitoring and disturbance handling roles, among others. The same distinction is apparent when one looks at the four traditional management functions—planning, organizing, *leading,* and controlling. Leading is only one of a broader set of responsibilities identified from this vantage point. An organizational manager will probably be involved with planning a budget. Even though such planning is an important managerial activity and has an impact on subordinates, it is not leadership. It is important for you to keep this distinction between leader/manager and leadership/management in mind.[3]

Within organizations, it is also important to note that leadership occurs in two forms. **Formal leadership** is exerted by persons appointed to or elected to positions of formal authority in organizations. **Informal leadership** is exerted by persons who become influential because they have special skills or resources that meet the needs of others. While we typically think of the formal aspects of leadership, most work situations also contain informal leaders. Research suggests, as you might expect, that when subordinates see their supervisors as inadequate in important ways, an informal leader will step in to fill the vacuum. Both formal and informal leadership are important. But if one category is more important than the other, the dominant one is likely to be formal leadership.[4]

APPROACHES TO STUDYING LEADERSHIP

Over the last 80 years or so, a number of different theories or approaches to studying leadership have been developed. We use a causal attribution perspective (related to our discussion of attribution in Chapters 3 and 13) to create four categories of leadership approaches as shown in Table 16.1. The theories in each category share slightly different perspectives on the relationship between leadership and the key results of task performance and human resource maintenance. The categories and their underlying assumptions regarding leadership are[5]

1. *Leader traits and behaviors.* The individual leader is the key determinant in causing the outcomes of performance/human resource maintenance.
2. *Situational contingencies and leadership.* The leader and situational contingencies in combination are the key determinants in causing the outcomes of performance/human resource maintenance.
3. *Symbolic leadership.* The leader may, indeed, have very little to do with performance/human resource maintenance. Instead, leadership may be a *result* of performance/human resource maintenance or may be an attribution

TABLE 16.1 Leadership Approaches Categorized by Causal Attributions of Performance/Human Resource Maintenance Outcomes	
I. Leader traits and behaviors Great man/trait theory Leadership behavior theory Leader reward and punishment theory House's charismatic theory Bass' transformational/transactional theory	**III. Symbolic leadership**
II. Leader situational contingencies Fiedler's leadership contingency theory Fiedler's cognitive resource theory House's path goal theory Situational leadership theory	**IV. Substitutes for leadership**

Source: The general idea for this table was suggested by James C. McElroy, "Alternative Schemes for Teaching Leadership," *The Organizational Behavior Teaching Review,* Vol. 11, No. 2, 1986–87, p. 91.

used to explain outcomes after the fact. A common example is the almost ritualistic firing of a baseball manager when the team is not doing well. In this case, failure is attributed to the manager in a symbolic way after the fact.

4. *Substitutes for leadership.* Many individual, task, and organizational characteristics have the capacity to substitute for hierarchical leadership in causing performance/human resource maintenance. Thus, subordinates with much experience might need much less leadership than a brand new subordinate (experience serves as a leadership substitute).

LEADER TRAITS AND BEHAVIORS

The theories falling in the *leader traits and behaviors* category all attribute performance/human resource maintenance outcomes, in one way or another, to selected characteristics and/or activities of the leader. Other variables are considered to have a minor impact. Among the five theories, however, differences exist in terms of the specific attributions or explanations for leadership results.

Great Man/Trait Theory

This approach is the earliest used to study leadership and dates back at least to the turn of the century. The early studies attempted to identify those traits that differentiated the great persons in history from the masses.[6] This led to a research emphasis that tried to identify traits that would separate leaders from nonleaders or more effective from less effective leaders. Table 16.2 lists some of the traits used in this research tradition.

TABLE 16.2 Illustrative Traits that Researchers Considered in Separating Leaders from Nonleaders	
Height	Knowledge
Weight	Insight
Physique	Originality
Energy	Adaptability
Health	Dominance
Appearance	Initiative
Fluency of speech	Persistence
Intelligence	Ambition
Scholarship	Self-confidence

Source: Developed from Ralph M. Stogdill, *Handbook of Leadership* (New York: Free Press, 1974), Chapter 5.

You may recall from Chapter 3 that we discussed a number of psychological characteristics—such as problem-solving style or locus of control—and indicated that if the characteristics were carefully matched with job requirements that they could help explain job success for a person. Applying that notion to the trait theory of leadership, a manager would try to determine a set of leader traits or characteristics that would relate to performance/human resource maintenance for leaders in which he or she was interested. The manager would assume that the traits were stable enough so that once they were identified they could be used to help select a leader for a particular leadership position.

Leadership Behaviors

The leadership behavior approach, like the great man/trait approach, again assumes that the leader is the primary cause of performance/human resource maintenance. This time, however, instead of dealing with underlying traits like those shown in Table 16.2, behaviors or actions are used. Two classic research programs at the University of Michigan and Ohio State University provide useful insights into leadership behaviors.

Michigan Studies

A key set of early leader-behavior studies was conducted by University of Michigan researchers. They divided leader behaviors into employee-centered and production-centered. Employee-centered supervisors are those who place strong emphasis on the welfare and motivation of subordinates. Production-centered supervisors tend to place a stronger emphasis on getting the work done than on the welfare and motivation of the employees. In general, employee-centered as opposed to production-centered supervisors were found to have more productive work groups.[7]

These behaviors may be viewed on a continuum, with employee-centered at one end and production-centered at the other. Sometimes the more general terms human relations-oriented and task-oriented are used to describe these alternative leader behaviors.

Ohio State Studies

Another important research program at Ohio State University investigated two similar dimensions of leader behavior—consideration and initiating structure.[8] A highly considerate leader is sensitive to people's feelings and tries to make things pleasant for followers. A leader high in initiating structure is concerned with spelling out task requirements and clarifying other aspects of the work agenda. These dimensions are similar to those used above and to what people sometimes refer to as socioemotional and task leadership, respectively. They also encompass what we discussed in Chapter 8 as group maintenance and task activities.

At first, it looked to the Ohio State researchers as if being high on consideration or socioemotional warmth resulted in a leader having more highly satisfied and/or better performing subordinates. Later results, however, indicated that leaders should be high on both consideration and initiating structure behaviors. A key point here is that consideration and initiating structure are *not* seen as being on a continuum. That is, rather than a leader necessarily being low on one dimension when high on the other, the leader could be high on both, low on both, or high on one and low on the other.

Managerial Grid

One of the more popular outgrowths of this latter perspective is the managerial grid concept described by Robert Blake and Jane Mouton.[9] They attempt to measure a manager's concern for people and concern for task, and then plot the results on the managerial grid shown in Figure 16.1. Once it is determined where you, for example, would fall on the grid, a training program would be designed to help shift your leadership style in the preferred direction of high concern for task and high concern for people. In Blake and Mouton's terminology, this ''9-9'' leader is a person whose leadership behavior is that of a ''team manager''—one who is able to integrate task and people concerns to the benefit of the organization and its members.

Leader Reward and Punishment

Leader reward and punishment theory is based on the reinforcement concepts discussed in Chapter 5, where the leader is seen as someone who manages reinforcements for subordinates.[10]

Recent research examines the following four leader behavior dimensions in this context:

1. *Performance-contingent reward behavior.* The degree to which a leader administers positive reinforcers such as acknowledgments, recognition, and so on, contingent on high subordinate performance.
2. *Contingent punishment behavior.* The extent to which a leader administers

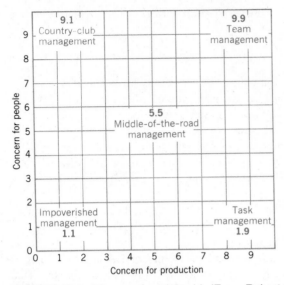

FIGURE 16.1 The managerial grid. (From Robert R. Blake and Jane Syrgley Mouton, "The Developing Revolution in Management Practices," *Journal of the American Society of Training Directors,* Vol. 16, no. 7 (1962), pp. 29–52. Used by permission.

punitive measures such as reprimands and disapproval contingent on poor subordinate performance.

3. *Noncontingent reward behavior.* The extent to which a leader rewards a subordinate regardless of how well the subordinate performs.
4. *Noncontingent punishment behavior.* The degree to which a leader uses punitive measures, regardless of how well a subordinate performs.

Results indicate that performance-contingent reward behavior is generally associated with higher levels of subordinate performance and satisfaction. Results for contingent punishment and noncontingent reward behavior are mixed, and, as you probably predicted, noncontingent punishment behavior is often negatively associated with performance and satisfaction. Thus, the leader exchange and reinforcement relationship is clearest and most positive for performance-contingent reward behavior.

House's Charismatic Theory

Robert House's charismatic theory uses both traits and behaviors. He defines **charismatic leaders** as those "who by force of their personal abilities are capable of having a profound and extraordinary effect on followers."[11]

Basically, House sees the charismatic leader with developed traits of self-confidence, dominance, and a conviction in the moral rightness of his or her beliefs. These traits are linked to such charismatic behaviors as role modeling, image building, goal articulation (the more simple and dramatic the goal the better), exhibiting high expectations, showing confidence, and arousing motives. As before, these traits and behaviors are believed to have a key impact on performance and human resource maintenance.

Bass's Transformational and Transactional Theory

A recent and related approach is Bernard Bass's transformational and transactional leadership theory.[12] Bass divides leadership into two basic categories: transactional and transformational. In **transactional leadership** the leader exerts influence during daily leader–subordinate exchanges without any special emotional inputs or considerations. The leader gets the subordinate to do what he or she wants by exchanging something the subordinate wants for the subordinate's obedience.

There are two important dimensions involved in transactional leadership: contingent reward and management-by-exception. The contingent reward dimension involves aspects similar to the leader reward and punishment theory mentioned earlier. Essentially, contingent reward is concerned with providing rewards in exchange for appropriate subordinate behavior.

Management-by-exception involves leaving the subordinate alone if the old ways are working or if the subordinate is meeting mutually accepted performance. Bass argues that transactional leadership is appropriate for effective performance of daily tasks. However, to get subordinates to go beyond routine accomplishment of daily tasks, transformational leadership is needed. **Transformational leadership** broadens and elevates the goals of subordinates and gives them the confidence to go beyond their expectations. Transformational leadership consists of three dimensions: charisma, individualized consideration, and intellectual stimulation.

Charismatic behavior is that which instills pride, faith, and respect and effectively articulates a sense of vision. A recent study asking people to rate presidents on charisma based on their biographies ranked John F. Kennedy and Franklin D. Roosevelt highest in terms of charismatic leadership.[13] That was consistent with their general reputation. Also, General George Patton and Malcolm X received very high charismatic ratings among those who were not presidents. While charismatic behavior is important for transforming subordinate expectations, it is not enough by itself. It gets subordinates excited and activated but does not provide the necessary follow-through for successful goal accomplishment. Individualized consideration and intellectual stimulation are needed to provide the follow-through.

Individualized consideration involves delegating tasks to stimulate and create learning, recognizing the individual needs of each subordinate and respecting each subordinate as an individual. Not surprisingly in the previously mentioned study, Adolph Hitler was found to score the lowest on individualized consideration. Eleanor Roosevelt and Ralph Nader received among the highest scores.

Intellectual stimulation involves introducing and encouraging new ideas as well as rethinking traditional methods, with emphasis on the many angles in performing a

NEWSLINE 16.1 / SUPERLEADERS

Why do people work hard for one boss and loaf under another?

Dr. Warren Bennis, professor of management at the University of Southern California, says it is a matter of whether the boss can imbue his office with a sense of mission.

Bennis set out a few years ago to determine what makes a superleader. In so doing, he interviewed 90 CEOs, university presidents, consistently winning coaches, and the like. He and a colleague, Burt Nanus, wrote a top selling book, *Leaders*, based on the results of these interviews.

Superleaders were found to have five traits in common:

- *Vision:* the ability to create a compelling picture of a desired state of affairs that inspires individuals to perform.
- *Communication:* the capacity to portray the vision clearly to develop support of constituents.
- *Persistence:* the capacity to stay on course regardless of obstacles.
- *Empowerment:* the ability to develop a structure to harness the energies of people to achieve a desired result.
- *Organizational ability:* the capability to monitor group activities, learn from mistakes, and use that knowledge to improve the organization.

Reported in *The Avalanche Journal*.

---

job. In this dimension, General George Marshall and Ralph Nader scored quite high whereas Henry Ford II and President Gerald Ford scored quite low in the previously mentioned study.

It is the charismatic transformational individual who is often thought of when people speak of ''leaders.'' Such a person was called a ''leader'' in the chapter opener. Those who emphasize transactional leadership would be considered as the ''managers'' in the chapter opener. Interestingly, based on their data, Bass and his associates argue that, rather than being a mystical gift rarely seen, charisma may be normally distributed and that all leaders possess varying degrees of it.

Newsline 16.1 nicely summarizes the previous discussion by characterizing a number of superleaders in terms of traits or behaviors ranging from vision to persistence.

SITUATIONAL CONTINGENCIES AND LEADERSHIP

Among all the theories just discussed, a common attribution is that the leader's traits and behaviors are the primary causes of performance/human resource maintenance outcomes. Now, we turn to a second category of approaches that view the traits and behaviors as acting in conjunction with *situational contingencies* (that is, other important things in the leadership situation) to determine these outcomes.

Fiedler's Leadership Contingency Theory

The first situational contingency approach we consider is one by Fred Fiedler, since his work essentially commenced the situational contingency era.[14] His theory clearly demonstrates the discipline of situational thinking. Such thinking is very important if you are to be able to make the most of what situational contingency approaches have to offer.

Fiedler's object is to predict work-group task performance or effectiveness. His theory holds that group effectiveness depends on a successful match between the leader's style and the demands of the situation. Specifically, Fiedler is interested in the amount of control the situation allows the leader. **Situational control** is defined as the extent to which a leader can determine what the group is going to do, and what the outcomes of its actions and decisions are going to be. For example, where there is high control, leaders can predict with a great degree of certainty what will happen when they want something done.

Leadership Style, Situational Control, Behavior and Performance

Fiedler uses an instrument called the least preferred co-worker (LPC) scale to measure a person's basic leadership style. The people completing the scale are asked to describe the person with whom they have been able to work least well (least preferred co-worker or LPC). Fiedler argues that leaders with high LPC scores have a relationship motivated style and leaders with low LPC scores have a task-motivated style.

He considers this task- and relationship-motivation to be a trait that leads to different leadership behaviors (directive or nondirective) depending on the amount of situational control the leader has. In turn, the match between these directive and nondirective behaviors and situational control influences group performance. Figure 16.2 summarizes Fiedler's predictions of the effective style in high, moderate, and low-control situations. In general, task-motivated leaders perform best in situations of high leadership control and low leadership control. Relationship-motivated leaders are at their best in moderate control situations.

FIGURE 16.2 Predictions from Fiedler's contingency theory of leadership.

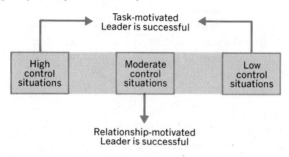

Fiedler sees task-motivated leaders as business before pleasure types. They crave tangible, measurable evidence of performance. They are highly motivated to accomplish any task to which they commit, regardless of extrinsic rewards.

Task-motivated leaders like clear guidelines. When these are missing, as in low-control situations, these leaders will behave in a directive manner and try to develop them. In so doing, they do not worry much about subordinates' feelings. Once these leaders are in control, however, they tend to be considerate and to behave in a non-directive manner. In moderate-control situations, these leaders have problems. Here, they attempt to take control by being directive and may thus ignore group-member needs and conflicts that arise. Thus, performance may suffer. High-control situations, by contrast, are made to order for these leaders, as they provide the structuring with which these leaders are most comfortable. Hence, these leaders tend to behave *non-directively* and this enhances performance.

Relationship-motivated leaders are also concerned with doing a good job, but their primary orientation is toward good interpersonal relations with others. These leaders tend to tolerate different viewpoints and are good at dealing with complex problems that require creative and resourceful thinking.

In low-control situations, group support is so important that the leader tends not to push group members to do necessary job requirements. In other words, the relationship-motivated leader tends to be *nondirective* where such direction is needed. Hence, performance suffers. Similarly, these leaders are not at their best in high-control situations when they do not need to worry about their relations with the group and tend to behave in a pushy and *directive* manner. Thus, relationship-oriented leaders are at their best in moderate control situations where their concern with interpersonal relations is most appropriate to deal with problems that occur.

Diagnosing Situational Control

While the prior discussion is a useful summary of Fiedler's theory, the question remains how we diagnose or measure the amount of situational control. Fiedler relies heavily on three dimensions: leader–member relations, task structure, and position power. *Leader–member relations* (good/moderate/poor) is concerned with the extent that group members support the leader. *Task structure* (high/medium/low) is concerned with the degree that task goals, procedures, and guidelines the leader is responsible for in the group are spelled out (the what and how of the task). *Position power* (high/moderate/low) is concerned with the extent to which the position gives the leader authority to reward and punish group members.

Figure 16.3 shows how these three variables relate to one another in eight combinations to create different amounts of situational control for a leader. The basic characteristics of high-, moderate-, and low-control situations are now presented along with examples also highlighted in the figure.

High-Control Situations

During high-control situations, the leader has a great deal of control illustrated by good leader–member relations, a highly structured task, and high position power. An

Situational Characteristics

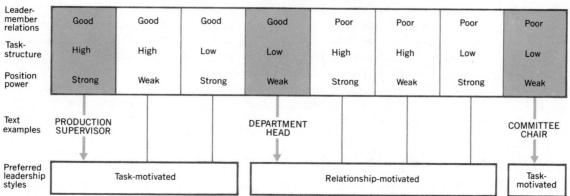

Leader-member relations	Good	Good	Good	Good	Poor	Poor	Poor	Poor
Task-structure	High	High	Low	Low	High	High	Low	Low
Position power	Strong	Weak	Strong	Weak	Strong	Weak	Strong	Weak
Text examples	PRODUCTION SUPERVISOR			DEPARTMENT HEAD				COMMITTEE CHAIR
Preferred leadership styles	Task-motivated			Relationship-motivated				Task-motivated

FIGURE 16.3 Summary of Fiedler's situational variables and their preferred leadership styles.

experienced supervisor of a production line with nonunion, highly supportive workers serves as an example. Supportive subordinates mean good leader–member relations. The structure of the task is high, and the leader has considerable experience so there is high task structure. Likewise, the nonunion nature of the job tends to provide the leader with the authority to reward and punish and hence provides high position power. This is a high-control situation.

Moderate-Control Situations

During moderate-control situations, the leader is typically presented with mixed problems—perhaps good relations with subordinates *but* a low structured task *and* low position power; or the opposite, poor relations but a structured task and high position power. An example might be a well-liked university department chair with a high proportion of tenured faculty and responsible for enhancing the teaching, research, and service missions of the department. There are good leader–member relations, but task structure is low since the "how" of the task is not very clear. The leader's position power is also not very high vis-à-vis the tenured faculty members.

Low-Control Situations

During low-control situations, the leader encounters poor leader–member relations and *neither* the task nor position provide control for the leader—a challenging situation indeed. An example might be the chair of a student council committee of volunteers who are not happy about this particular person being the chair. The committee is to organize a "Parents' Day" program to improve university–parent relations. The "what" is clear, but the "how" is not. Who can say exactly which activities will improve relations? Because the volunteers can readily quit, the leader also has low position power.

The Research

The roots of Fiedler's contingency theory go back more than 25 years and have been thoroughly researched. As with virtually any well-tested theory in the management or behavioral science fields it is easy to find research that is both pro and con. One example of controversy concerns what it is exactly that Fiedler's LPC instrument measures. Some question Fiedler's interpretation of the instrument in terms of behavior. To help answer this and other questions Fiedler and others have conducted extensive research over the years, making the contingency theory the most thoroughly researched of all leadership theories.

Fiedler's Cognitive Resource Theory

One of the outgrowths of this research has been a newly developed approach by Fiedler called the cognitive resource theory.[15] It is linked to Fiedler's contingency theory as shown by the shaded area in Figure 16.4 and as summarized here. The key variables in cognitive resource theory are: (1) directive/nondirective leader behavior; (2) leader stress; (3) leader and subordinate cognitive resources or abilities; (4) leader experience; and (5) group support of the leader.

Cognitive resource theory starts with two assumptions. First, that bright leaders (leaders higher in cognitive resources or abilities) develop more effective plans, decisions, and action strategies than do less bright leaders who are lower in cognitive resources. Second, leaders communicate these plans, decisions, and action strategies through directive leader behavior. As we pointed out previously, the extent to which the leader is directive or nondirective may come about through his or her task/relationship motivation and situational control. That is the linkage between Fiedler's contingency theory and cognitive resource theory.

Given the two preceding assumptions, we can start with the left side of Figure 16.4. If the leader is directive and not under stress, his or her cognitive abilities will be communicated via directive behavior and predict group performance for those group tasks that require cognitive resources. However, if a directive leader, with a task requiring cognitive resources, is under stress, his or her experience rather than cognitive abilities will predict group performance.

The reason for the previous statement is that a leader will tend to reduce stress and this will distract the leader from the task. Furthermore, brighter leaders tend to be better at these stress reducing activities than their less bright counterparts and will be diverted even further from the task. At the same time, under stress, leaders will tend to revert to previously learned behaviors; hence leader experience will be related to group performance.

However, not all tasks require cognitive resources. Moving a piece of heavy furniture, for example, does not call for much in the way of cognitive skills. Also, a socially-oriented group is more likely to call for interpersonal rather than cognitive skills. Of course, for groups such as these the leader's cognitive abilities tend to be irrelevant.

Bright, directive leaders, not diverted by stress can have an impact on group performance for tasks requiring cognitive resources. However, Figure 16.4 shows that

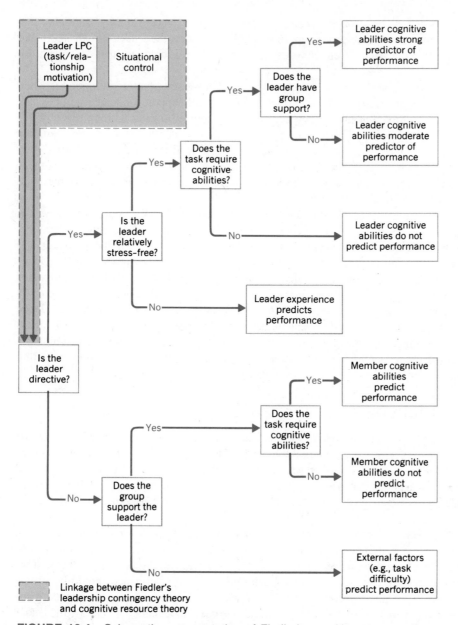

FIGURE 16.4   Schematic representation of Fiedler's cognitive resource theory (modified from Fred E. Fiedler and Joseph E. Garcia, *New Approaches to Effective Leadership,* New York: John Wiley, 1987, p. 9).

this impact will be stronger where the group members accept the leader than when they do not. Supportive groups are more likely to support the leader's goals and make it easier for the leader's directiveness and cognitive resources to have an impact on performance.

Now looking at the lower branch of Figure 16.4 we see what Fiedler predicts when the leader is nondirective. First, if the group does not support the leader and the task calls for cognitive resources, then neither group member nor leader cognitive abilities are likely to predict performance. Since the leader is nondirective, group members will tend to take charge of the planning and direction. If they are nonsupportive they are likely to have their own agendas not related to the task that has been assigned. Hence, external factors rather than leader or group member cognitive resources, are expected to predict group performance.

On the other hand, if the leader is nondirective, the task requires cognitive resources, and the group is supportive, then member abilities will predict performance. The leader's nondirectiveness allows members to take charge of the planning and direction, and allows for their cognitive resources to be directed toward performance.

A major contribution of cognitive resource theory is that it specifically recognizes the leader's cognitive abilities along with other aspects of leadership. The theory is so recent that it is only beginning to be systematically tested. There is evidence supporting parts of the theory and, indeed, Fiedler developed the theory from such evidence. For now we can consider the approach to be useful because of its emphasis on cognitive resources in combination with leadership. It also has an important link with Fiedler's leadership contingency theory.

House's Path-Goal Leadership Theory

Another well known approach to situational contingencies is one developed by Robert House; based on the earlier work of others.[16] This theory has its roots in the expectancy model of motivation that we discussed in Chapter 4. The term "path-goal" is used because of its emphasis on how a leader influences subordinates' perceptions of work goals and personal goals, and the linkages or paths found between these two sets of goals.

The theory assumes that a leader's key function is to adjust his or her behaviors to complement situational factors, such as those found in the work setting. House argues that when the leader is able to compensate for things lacking in the setting, subordinates are likely to be satisfied with the leader. Performance should benefit as the paths by which effort leads to performance (expectancy) and performance leads to valued rewards (instrumentality) become clarified. Redundant behavior by the leader will not help and may even hinder performance. People do not need a boss telling them how to do something that they already know how to do!

Details of the Theory

The details of House's approach are summarized in Figure 16.5. The figure shows four types of leader behaviors and two categories of situational contingency variables. The leader behaviors are adjusted to complement the situational contingency variables

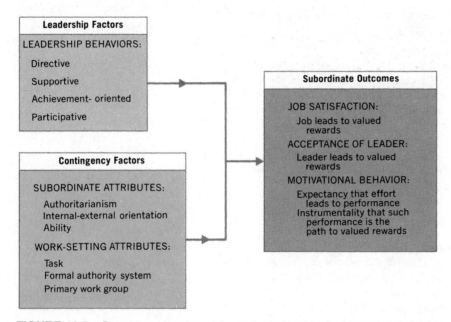

FIGURE 16.5 Summary of major path–goal relationships in House's leadership approach. (Adapted from Richard N. Osborn, James G. Hunt, and Lawrence R. Jauch, *Organization Theory: An Integrated Approach.* New York: John Wiley & Sons, 1980, p. 464.)

in the work setting to influence the motivation for task performance and satisfaction of subordinates.

Details concerning each aspect of the four leader behavior dimensions are shown in Table 16.4. The contingency variables include subordinate attributes and the work setting. Important subordinate characteristics are authoritarianism (close-mindedness, rigidity), external–internal orientation, and ability. The key work setting factors are the nature of the subordinates' tasks, the formal authority system, and the primary work group. The most well-researched issues deal with how clear cut and repetitive tasks are as compared with being ambiguous and nonrepetitive.

Predictions from the Theory

Leader directiveness is predicted to have a positive impact on subordinates when the task is ambiguous and to have just the opposite effect for clear tasks. When task demands are ambiguous, leader directiveness is needed to compensate for the lack of structure. When task clarification is otherwise available, directiveness is viewed as a hindrance by subordinates. In addition, the theory predicts that ambiguous tasks being performed by highly authoritarian and close-minded subordinates call for even more directive leadership than do ambiguous tasks alone.

Leader supportiveness is predicted to increase the satisfaction of subordinates who work on highly repetitive tasks or on tasks considered to be unpleasant, stressful, or

---

TABLE 16.4 Leader Behavior Dimensions in House's Path–Goal Approach

Leader directiveness

Letting subordinates know what is expected.

Providing specific guidance as to what should be done and how.

Making the leader's part in the group understood.

Scheduling work to be done.

Maintaining definite standards of performance.

Leader supportiveness

Showing concern for status and well-being of subordinates.

Doing little things to make the work more pleasant.

Treating members as equals.

Being friendly and approachable.

Leader achievement-orientedness

Setting challenging goals.

Expecting subordinates to perform at their highest level.

Showing a high degree of confidence in subordinates.

Constantly emphasizing excellence in performance.

Leader participativeness

Consulting with subordinates.

Soliciting subordinate suggestions.

Taking these suggestions seriously.

Source: Developed from Robert J. House and Terence R. Mitchell, "Path–Goal Theory of Leadership," *Journal of Contemporary Business* (Autumn 1974), pp. 81–97.

---

frustrating. The leader's supportive behavior helps to compensate for these adverse conditions.

Leader achievement orientedness is predicted to cause subordinates to strive for higher performance standards and to have more confidence in their ability to meet challenging goals. For subordinates in ambiguous nonrepetitive jobs, achievement-oriented leadership should increase subordinates' expectancies that effort will lead to desired performance.

Leader participativeness is predicted to promote satisfaction on nonrepetitive tasks which allow for the ego involvement of subordinates. On repetitive tasks, open-minded or nonauthoritarian subordinates will also be satisfied with a participative leader.

The Research

The research so far supports the path–goal model in general and the above predictions in particular. However, if you turn back to Figure 16.5, you will note some contingency variables that are not included in these predictions—namely, subordinates' internal–external orientation and ability, and the nature of the work group. So far there is no available evidence concerning the place of these variables in the theory, but they do seem intuitively important. Why, for example, do you think ability might be important? (*Answer:* Because it can help provide task clarity.) What about the role of internal–external orientation? (*Answer:* Because those with high internal orientation, who feel in charge of their own destiny, should respond better to participation.)

In summary, even though not all of the contingency variables have been tested, path–goal theory is a promising avenue of inquiry for the continued study of leadership.

Situational Leadership

The situational leadership theory developed by Paul Hersey and Kenneth Blanchard, agrees with the other situational approaches that there is no single best way to lead.[17] They focus on the ''maturity'' of followers as a contingency variable deserving attention. Hersey and Blanchard feel that ''situational'' leadership requires adjusting the leader's emphasis on task behaviors (i.e., giving guidance and direction) and relationship behaviors (i.e., providing socioemotional support) according to the maturity of followers in performing their tasks. *Maturity* in this sense is defined as the ability and willingness of people to take responsibility for directing their own behavior in relation to a specific task.

Figure 16.6 displays the essence of this model of situational leadership. The figure identifies four leadership styles: delegating, participating, selling, and telling. Each

FIGURE 16.6   Hersey and Blanchard model of situational leadership. (From Paul Hersey and Kenneth H. Blanchard, *Management of Organizational Behavior,* Prentice-Hall, Englewood Cliffs, N.J., 1982, p. 152. Used by permission.)

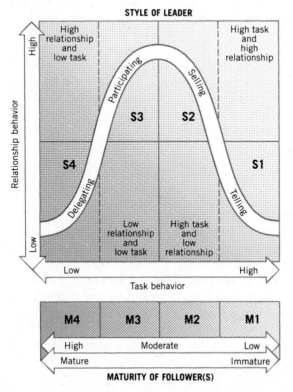

represents a different combination of emphasis on task and relationship behaviors by the leader. As you can see, the figure also suggests the following situational matches as the best choice of leadership style for followers of each of four maturity levels.

A "telling" style is best for low follower maturity. The direction provided by this style defines roles for people who are unable and unwilling to take responsibility; it eliminates any insecurity about the task that must be done.

A "selling" style is best for low to moderate follower maturity. This style offers both task direction and support for people who are unable but willing to take task responsibility; it involves combining a directive approach with explanation and reinforcement to maintain enthusiasm.

A "participating" style is best for moderate to high follower maturity. Able but unwilling followers require supportive behavior to increase their motivation; by sharing in decision making, this style helps to enhance the desire to perform a task.

A "delegating" style is best for high maturity. This style provides little in terms of direction and support for the task at hand; it allows able and willing followers to take responsibility for what needs to be done.

This approach requires that a leader develop the capability to diagnose the demands of situations, and then to choose and implement the appropriate leadership response. The theory gives specific attention to followers and their feelings about a task or job to be done. It also suggests that an effective leader reassess situations over time, with special attention being given to emerging changes in the level of "maturity" among people involved in the work. Again, Hersey and Blanchard advise that leadership style should be adjusted as necessary to remain consistent with actual levels of follower maturity. They suggest that leader effectiveness should improve as a result. In terms of research support, the theory has not been tested systematically enough to say much about its validity. Thus, the approach remains an intuitively-appealing one that still requires systematic empirical substantiation.[18]

SYMBOLIC LEADERSHIP

In contrast to the leader traits and behaviors and the situational contingencies approaches, stands a third category of theorizing we call *symbolic leadership*. This perspective recognizes that leadership may have very little to do with causing performance/human resource maintenance. Rather, leadership may be a result instead of a cause of performance/human resource maintenance. Or, it may be used symbolically as an attribution to explain outcomes after the fact.

With regard to the former, there is a fair amount of evidence suggesting that leader behavior is influenced by outcomes.[19] For example, a leader would be more supportive and do less structuring for high performing as opposed to low performing subordinates.

NEWSLINE 16.2 /
SHAKEUP AT PENN CENTRAL

Penn Central, once a railroad, is now a smattering of businesses, ranging from guidance control to telecommunications. Recently the company announced that the President and CEO Alfred W. Martinelli was being replaced along with three other top executives.

When a *Business Week* reporter talked about the shake-up with several knowledgeable people, they indicated that Martinelli was considered a top-notch manager and asset seller. However, he wasn't a good asset buyer. "Various deals came before the board and they weren't too brilliant. They didn't get done and thank God they didn't."

According to Carl H. Lindner, former board chair and the newly appointed chair *and* CEO, Martinelli couldn't come up with ideas that he (Lindner) liked, so Martinelli was dumped. The board is ready to pursue a new strategy.

Reported in *Business Week*.

This evidence raises the question of whether leadership is a necessary prerequisite for performance/human resource maintenance at all.

Jeffrey Pfeffer's work illustrates the symbolic aspects of leadership.[20] He cites research finding little evidence of the effects of leadership on performance. He argues that leaders are generally very constrained in what they can do. Even so, people accept and proclaim the belief of the leader as a causal agent because it serves to maintain the social order. Leadership becomes an attribution used to explain things after the fact. Here, the successful leader can attach himself or herself to successes and disassociate himself or herself from failures.

We mentioned earlier the firing of a baseball manager. Frequently this has been a scapegoating effort to send a clear message to organizational members and the public at large that previously held attitudes and behaviors are no longer acceptable. We can make the same argument in many cases for the firing of a chief executive officer and his or her staff. Newsline 16.2 illustrates these points.

Let us briefly look at how a subordinate might attribute leadership to a manager.[21] Subordinates may use actual observations, "hearsay" descriptions, or "inferred" observations. For example, if a manager responds quickly to a message left by you, this may be inferred as "decisive" behavior. As a subordinate you might then use this observation as evidence of "leadership" on the part of your supervisor.

Subordinates may also make inferences about whether the causes of observed behaviors are internal (e.g., the leader is basically a considerate person) or external (e.g., the leader is considerate because the boss requires it) to the leader. If these causes coincide with the subordinates' implicit views about what makes a good leader or ways in which "real leaders" would act in a given situation, then the supervisor will be seen as exhibiting "leadership." Whether the person in a leadership role is seen in this way or not can have a substantial impact on his or her relations with subordinates and key outcomes in the work unit.

SUBSTITUTES FOR LEADERSHIP

Standing in contrast to all three of the prior categories of leadership approaches, is the **substitutes for leadership** perspective of Steven Kerr and John Jermier.[22] They argue that frequently organizational and/or individual or task situational variables substitute for leadership in causing performance/human resource maintenance. Figure 16.7 shows several elements in this leadership approach.

Let us briefly discuss some of these substitutes as represented in the figure. As terms of the subordinate, ability, experience, training, and knowledge can be at a high enough level so that a person needs very little if any task-oriented leadership. Even here, however, relationship-oriented leadership is expected to be important. For example, a highly skilled tool and die maker does not need much task-oriented leadership, though he or she would still like a pat on the back. If someone has a strong professional-orientation, that person will probably tend to rely heavily on his or her

FIGURE 16.7 Substitutes for leadership. (Suggested by Steven Kerr and John Jermier, "Substitutes for Leadership: Their Meaning and Measurement," *Organizational Behavior and Human Performance,* Vol. 22 (1978), p. 378.

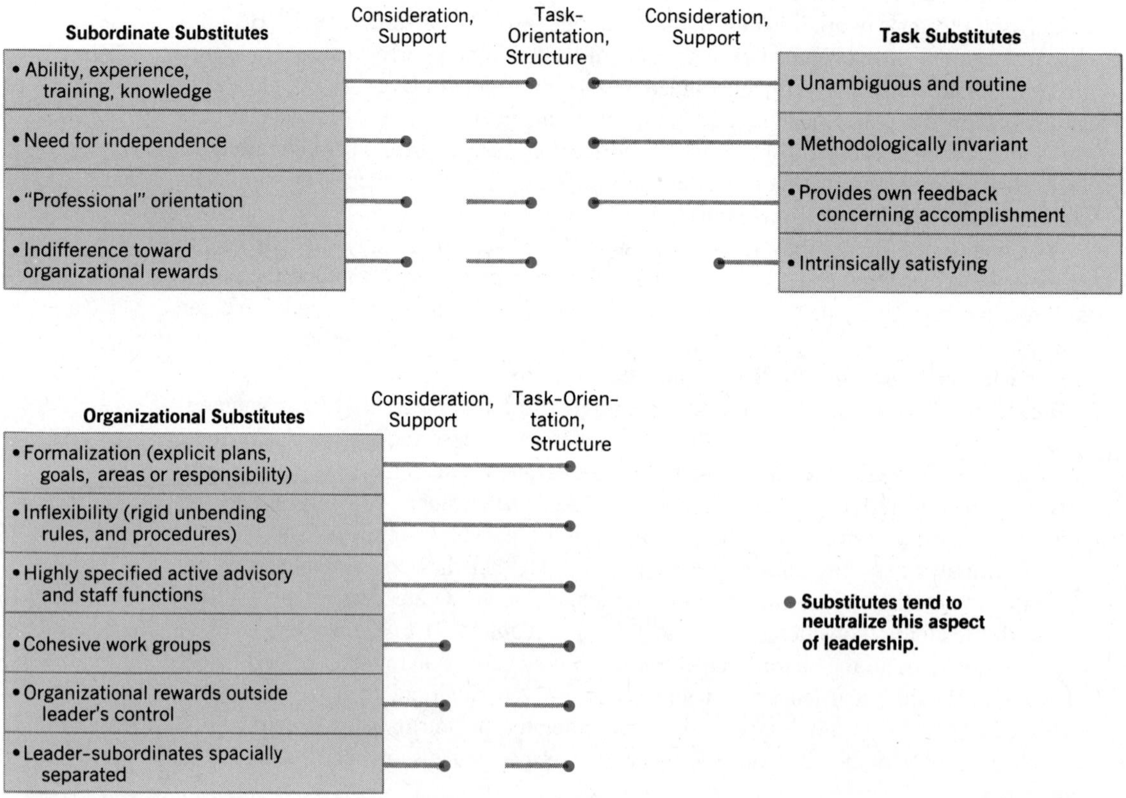

education, training, peers, and outside people and organizations for much of his or her job guidance. That person is also likely to look at these same sources for much of the interpersonal comfort that supportive leaders provide.

In terms of the task, machine paced work, such as that found on traditional automotive assembly lines, possesses the methodologically invariant characteristic shown in Figure 16.7. Screwing a nut on a bolt as 100 pieces per hour come down a moving assembly line does not require much direction from a leader. However, the tedium of the task is likely to make leader supportiveness important for most people. Again looking at task substitutes for leadership, performance feedback from the work itself can operate to minimize feedback needed from a task-oriented leader. Remember the impact of feedback as part of job enrichment in Chapter 6. Similarly, an intrinsically satisfying task can mean that leader supportiveness may not be needed. In terms of the organization, cohesive, interdependent work groups and active advisory and staff personnel can also reduce the need for a leader's performance feedback. Recall, especially from Chapters 8 and 9, the powerful impact that norms and cohesion can have on work guidance and performance.

PRACTICAL LEADERSHIP APPLICATIONS

Let us now look at how you as a manager might go about applying your newly gained leadership knowledge. To do that we divide the theories into two new categories: selection or placement, and training.[23] The assumption is that the individual leadership theories have quite different uses for managers. Some theories help explain selection or placement decisions (i.e., putting the right person in a leadership role). Other theories provide a means for justifying training programs designed to develop people into more effective leaders. Still others allow for either selection/placement or training. Table 16.5 categorizes the theories according to use.

TABLE 16.5   Leadership Theories from a Use Perspective

Useful for Selection/Placement	Useful for Training
Great Man/Trait Theory	Leader Behavior Theories
House's Charismatic Theory	Leader Reward and Punishment Theory
Fiedler's Leadership Contingency Theory	House's Charismatic Theory
Fiedler's Cognitive Resource Theory	Transformational/Transactional Theory
	House's Path-Goal Theory
	Situational Leadership Theory
	Fiedler's Leadership Contingency Theory
	Fielder's Cognitive Resource Theory
	Symbolic Leadership
	Substitutes for Leadershp

Source: Developed from James C. McElroy, "Alternative Schemes for Teaching Leadership," Vol. 11, 1986–87, p. 91.

Selection or Placement

If a trait approach is used, then the traits must be validated to show which ones actually have the strongest impact on performance/human resource maintenance. Recall that we discussed this in Chapter 3 on individual differences. Once the traits are validated, leaders are selected with the most appropriate level of those traits.

House's charismatic theory uses both specific traits and specific charismatic behaviors. Individuals with the most appropriate level of the traits would be selected. Then the specific behaviors could be emphasized in a training program.

For Fiedler's leadership contingency theory, leaders would be selected on the basis of their match or task or relationship motivation. For Fiedler's cognitive resource theory, leaders would be selected on the basis of their match on task or relationship motivation and cognitive abilities with the demands of the situation, as described earlier in the chapter.

Training

In leader behavior theory, leaders need to be trained to behave in more considerate and structuring ways. If other behaviors are considered important, then leaders would be trained to behave in those ways as well.

For transformational/transactional theory, leaders would be trained to use the appropriate transformational and transactional behaviors. The same kind of training is appropriate for the behavioral aspects of House's charismatic approach and for the leader reward and punishment approach.

The training involved in Fiedler's leadership contingency theory and cognitive resource theory is quite different from the preceding.[24] He basically believes that trying to change behavior with training is harder than selection, placement, or changing the situation to fit the leader's task or relationship-motivation style. Where he believes training is useful is in teaching leaders to diagnose the situation within which they are operating. For Fiedler's contingency theory, the diagnosis involves deciding ways to change situational control variables (where this is possible) to fit leadership style or to select or place a leader with the appropriate style to fit the situation. He and his associates have developed a training program called "Leader Match" to deal with the preceding issues for this contingency leadership model.

Diagnostic training is also appropriate for situational leadership theory, House's path–goal theory, and substitutes for leadership. For situational leadership and path–goal theory, diagnostic training is probably most useful in combination with training to behave in the ways indicated by the approaches.

So much for the previous approaches, which assumed that leadership caused performance/human resource maintenance or that situational variables substituted for leadership. What about symbolic leadership? For symbolic leadership it is important to sensitize leaders to the importance of symbolic leadership and to some of the behaviors that might cause subordinates to attribute leadership to them after the fact.

SUMMARY

This chapter began by defining leadership as a special case of interpersonal influence that gets an individual or group to do what the leader wants done. We also differentiated between leadership and managerial behavior, and between formal and informal leadership.

We then categorized a number of the best-known leadership theories into a four-cell matrix in order to facilitate their understanding and use. This matrix differentiated leadership theories on the basis of the degree to which a manager believes that: (Cell I) the leader is the key determinant in causing outcomes of performance/human resource maintenance; (Cell II) the leader and situational contingencies in combination cause a resultant of performance/human resource maintenance or are used to explain outcomes after the fact; (Cell III) leadership is a resultant of performance/human resource maintenance or is used to explain outcomes after the fact; and (Cell IV) the individual and/or organizational situational variables substitute for leadership in causing performance/human resource maintenance.

Trait, behavioral, leader reward/punishment, charismatic, and transformational approaches were illustrative of Cell I. Several situational contingency theories such as those by Fiedler and House exemplified Cell II. Substitutes for leadership was the label given to Cell III while Kerr and Jermier's substitutes for leadership approach illustrated Cell IV.

We concluded by regrouping the various leadership theories on the basis of whether they could be implemented through selection or placement (i.e., leaders are selected or placed based on appropriate traits) or training (i.e., leaders are trained to diagnose situations, adjust behaviors as appropriate, or to be sensitive to symbolic and attributional aspects of leadership). We argued that selection/placement was most applicable for trait theory, and for Fiedler's leadership contingency and cognitive resource theories. Training was most applicable in those theories that use behavior. These ranged from leader behavior theories through substitutes for leadership and symbolic leadership.

THINKING THROUGH THE ISSUES

1. Describe how leadership is related to the broader concepts of power and politics treated in Chapter 15.
2. Think of a work situation and describe at least one instance of informal leadership.
3. Describe the difference between leadership traits and behaviors and the implication of these differences for understanding current leadership theories.
4. Compare and contrast the assumptions regarding leadership underlying each of the four cells of the causal attributions of performance/human resource maintenance matrix found in Table 16.1.
5. Explain the basic elements in: (1) Fiedler's leadership contingency theory and (2) Fiedler's cognitive resource theory. Give examples of good leader

situation matches for persons with strong relationship-motivation and task-motivation, respectively.

6. Describe a situation you experienced where leadership was inferred from performance/human resource maintenance, or where it was used attributionally after the fact to explain good or poor performance/human resource maintenance.

7. Show the similarities and differences in Fiedler's contingency theory and House's path–goal theory.

8. Think of a work situation, apply one of the leadership theories and briefly explain how you would use selection/placement, training, or some combination to enhance performance/human resource maintenance.

CASE: THREE LEADERS

Read and think about the leaders and leadership situations described in each of the following examples.[25]

Quality Circle Chair

There are 10 people in the chairperson's quality circle (QC). The QC chair is also a supervisor within a department. He chooses the QC members by placing the names of volunteers into piles, by department, so that there will be a cross-section from all departments. Then he draws one name from each pile. Thus, he has his own plus other people in the QC.

The QC chair makes sure things keep moving rather than getting bogged down. He does not want to call himself a QC supervisor because he does not want to impose his feelings on the circle. He likes to think of himself as a member like the others. He wants decisions to be made by the QC, not by him, and if the circle wants his recommendations he wants members to ask for them because of his experience and expertise.

The leader and members work with the QC facilitator who sits in on all the meetings. The facilitator is a liaison with other units and helps obtain cooperation when necessary.

To develop members, the QC chair uses an alphabetical system to assign a new session leader from the members every week. Then the chair sits back and watches the circle move. If the group gets bogged down, he intercedes to keep it moving. He also serves as a mediator, suggesting ways to deal with problems. He wants members to solve problems with their own techniques rather than to use his to please him.

When the circle makes presentations to management, the chair introduces the presentation and the rest of the members are present. There are many practice runs first. The chair feels the circle is helping people grow by giving them experience in problem solving and decision making. The chair feels the circle broadens him and exposes him to technical areas he previously knew little about. He also feels that he deliberately gives up much of his supervisory power in the circle. He spends many unpaid hours at night working with the members on presentations.

The chair indicates that he can be freer in the QC than in his regular group, since there are no deadlines in the QC and almost constant ones in the regular group.

However, he feels some of his QC kind of leadership has carried over to his regular group. Now, when time is available and there is a question he asks his people what they think.

The QC chair sees QCs as having an impact on the leadership of those above him. He claims his superiors have become more participative. In summary, he thinks both his and his superiors' styles have changed.

Airline Field Manager

The airline field manager is a walking, talking ball of fire perhaps in her mid-thirties in age. She dresses professionally in what is not quite a uniform. She works for a major airline and is responsible for her firm's ticket counter, sky captains in the airport, and security.

Her performance is judged on delays. Do late passengers delay the plane? If her loading times are too late, she is called on the carpet. If there is one delay, it backs up other flights. Everything is supposed to be on time.

Her boss goes through monthly computerized charts showing lateness statistics and then gives her feedback. Lots of paperwork from above causes her additional stress. She would rather be with her people on the floor than doing paperwork but the paperwork is required.

She also gets lots of pressure from below. She must make sure her lines run as fast as feasible. Thus, she has to get enough staffing to handle passengers for a given time of day. She always tries to be out front as a visible member of management— especially when there are weather delays and missing connections. When there is a long line at the ticket counter she moves in and helps out.

Sometimes men do not like taking orders from her. She typically says something like, "you can spend eight hours a day being miserable or you can spend the time doing your job."

If a baggage belt breaks she will be right in the middle straightening out the bags. She frequently is dependent on other airports to deal with late passengers. Thus, she has to try to get cooperation when she has no direct authority over these airports.

She does not want to be too friendly with subordinates. She is their boss, not their buddy. If there is a passenger an agent cannot deal with, she handles the passenger. If the agent was correct she tells the passenger that. If the agent was wrong she apologizes for the agent's behavior and talks to the agent later. She also arbitrates between skycaps and passengers and skycaps and agents. She works hard to train agents to be polite to customers.

Heart Transplant Surgeon

This heart transplant surgeon directs between one and three assistant surgeons, two cardiac anesthesiologists, a scrub nurse, a circulating nurse, a profusionist (operates the heart-lung machine), and an intensive care team of physicians and nurses. About 98% of this team's patients' health has been improved and about 85% have been cured.

The surgeon meets the patient and relatives after a cardiologist has diagnosed the problem. Then, if called for, either a transplant or less extensive surgery is done. Once the patient and family have made a decision to have the surgery, and the operating room is scheduled, the surgeon has conferences with his surgical team, the cardiologist, and the intensive care people. He tries to make sure everything is thoroughly planned and potential problems anticipated. He also has tests conducted to make sure there are no contraindications for conducting the operation. Again, he goes over the operation with the patient and family and yet again with the patient immediately before the operation.

The patient is then taken to the operating room, put to sleep, and inserted with catheters for fluids, medications, and monitoring. The patient is then hooked up to a heart-lung machine.

The surgeon monitors what is happening: in the operating field—with the anesthesiologists at the head of the table, at the heart-lung machine, and with the circulating and scrub nurses. This monitoring involves coordination and the reduction of stress. He anticipates the next moves and makes sure his team is ready for them.

After the operation is completed, the patient is taken to intensive care. Those helping the patient there are under the surgeon's direction. He then discusses the operation with the relatives. He debriefs the team and asks each member how he or she thinks the operation went. He also tells team members how he thinks it went. He goes beyond depending on their professionalism to provide positive feedback and provides it himself.

By and large, team members are aware of mistakes and will work to correct them. The surgeon tries to get the most competent person on a given task to correct the error. He does not criticize in front of others. After the operation he talks with the person making the mistake and they try to work out procedures to keep it from happening again. The surgeon also encourages feedback on his own errors. He uses the team's mistakes as a foundation for improvement. Whenever possible, he allows team members to draw conclusions rather than imposing his own. He tries to lower the level of stress in the operating room. He encourages healthy patients after the operation to visit his team and the team in intensive care so that these people can see how well the patient is doing.

When there is a heart transplant, there are additional logistics to which the surgeon must attend. For example, he must obtain a donor heart and the like.

Death is a constant possibility that can affect the morale of his team. He reminds the team of its good record and he and its members carefully assess what happened to see if it was avoidable or not. In spite of his team always doing its best, deaths sometimes do occur.

Questions

1. Using three of the theories discussed in the text, compare and contrast the leader behaviors or leadership styles of the three leaders.
2. Discuss the extent to which you think the described leader behaviors are appropriate for the situations faced by each of the leaders. How would you go about deciding such appropriateness?
3. Describe how you might use the practical leadership applications discussed in the chapter to provide the appropriate leadership for each of these positions.

EXERCISE: SUBSTITUTES FOR LEADERSHIP

Purpose:
To develop your skill in applying substitutes for leadership to a real leadership situation.

Time:
50 minutes in class, plus at-home preparations.

Procedure:
1. Do the following before coming to class:
   a. Review substitutes for leadership as discussed in the chapter and as summarized in Figure 16.7.
   b. Think of a current or recent assignment in which you or someone you know is functioning or has functioned as a leader.
   c. Following the format in Figure 16.7, write down subordinate, task and organization leadership substitutes that you think neutralize leader consideration and structure. Be specific in identifying these for the particular group or organization in which your chosen leader functions.
   d. Given the above, estimate the overall importance of your leader's consideration and structure for performance/human resource maintenance.
   e. Indicate how you might use the above information to train the leader to diagnose how much consideration and structure he or she would need to provide appropriate leadership.
   f. Bring the results of (a) through (e) with you to class.
2. Form groups in class as assigned by your instructor.
3. Share, discuss, and summarize the preceding results for each member of your group.
4. Have a spokesperson prepared to report to the class on the summary in question 3 based on the individual results obtained for question 1.
5. Reconvene as a total class to hear reports and discuss implications of the exercise.

THE MANAGER'S VOCABULARY

Charismatic Leaders   Those leaders who by force of their personal abilities are capable of having a profound and extraordinary effect on followers.

Contingency Approach   A view that the relationship between leadership and the task performance and human resource maintenance of followers depends on selected contingency variables.

Formal Leadership   Exercising influence from a position of formal authority in an organization.

Informal Leadership   Exercising influence through special skills or resources that meet the needs of other persons.

Leadership   A special case of interpersonal influence that gets an individual or group to do what the leader wants done.

Situational Control   The extent to which leaders can determine what their group is going to do, and what the outcomes of their actions and decisions are going to be.

Substitutes for Leadership   Organizational, individual or task situational variables which substitute for leadership in causing performance/human resource maintenance.

Symbolic Leadership   Leadership may be a result, rather than a cause of performance/human resource maintenance, or may be used symbolically as an attribution to explain outcomes after the fact.

Transactional Leadership   Where the leader exerts influence during daily leader–subordinate exchanges without much emotion.

Transformational Leadership   Where the follower's goals are broadened and elevated, and they gain confidence to go beyond their expectations.

IMPORTANT NAMES

Bernard Bass   Developed a transformational approach to leadership.

Fred Fiedler   Developed the cognitive resource and contingency theories of leadership effectiveness.

Robert House   Developed charismatic and path-goal theories of leadership effectiveness.

NOTES

[1]Developed from Walter Keichal III, *Fortune* (May 30, 1983), pp. 135–140 and *Fortune* (July 21, 1986), pp. 127–128.

[2]Henry Mintzberg, *The Nature of Managerial Work* (New York: Harper & Row, 1973).

[3]See, for example, Abraham Zalenznik, "Managers and Leaders: Are They Different?" *Harvard Business Review,* (May–June, 1977), pp. 67–78.

[4]D. Katz and R. L. Kahn, "Human Organization and Worker Motivation," in L. R. Tripp (ed.), *Industrial Productivity* (Madison, Wis.: Industrial Relations Research Association, 1952).

[5]This perspective is based on James C. McElroy, "Alternative Schemes for Teaching Leadership," *The Organizational Behavior Teaching Review,* Vol. 11 (1986–87), pp. 87–94; and James C. McElroy and J. David Hunger, "Leadership Theory as Causal Attributions for Performance", in J. G. Hunt, B. R. Baliga, H. P. Dachler, and C. A. Schriesheim (eds.), *Emerging Leadership Vistas* (Lexington, MA: Lexington Books, in press, 1987).

[6]Ralph M. Stogdill, *Handbook of Leadership* (New York: Free Press, 1974).

[7]Rensis Likert, *New Patterns of Management* (New York: McGraw-Hill, 1961).

[8]Stogdill, *Handbook of Leadership, loc. cit.,* Chap. 11.

[9]Robert R. Blake and Jane S. Mouton, *The New Managerial Grid* (Houston: Gulf, 1978).

[10]See Henry P. Sims Jr., "The Leader as a Manager of Reinforcement Contingencies: An Empirical Example and a Model," In J. G. Hunt and L. L. Larson (eds.), *Leadership Frontiers* (Kent, Ohio: Comparative Administration Research Institute, Kent State University, 1977); and P. M. Podsakoff, W. D. Toder, R. A.

Grover, and V. L. Huber, "Situational and Personality Moderators of Leader Reward and Punishment Behaviors: Fact or Fiction?" *Organizational Behavior and Human Performance* Vol. 34 (1984), pp. 810–821.

[11]This section is based on R. J. House, "A 1976 Theory of Charismatic Leadership," in J. G. Hunt and L. L. Larson (eds.), *Leadership: The Cutting Edge* (Carbondale, Ill.: Southern Illinois University Press, 1977).

[12]This section is based on Bernard M. Bass, Bruce J. Avolio, and Laurie Goodheim, "Biography and the Assessment of Transformational Leadership at the World-Class Level," *Journal of Management,* Vol. 13 (1987), pp. 7–19 and Bruce J. Avolio and Bernard M. Bass, "Transformational Leadership, Charisma and Beyond," in J. G. Hunt, B. R. Baliga, H. P. Dachler, and C. A. Schriesheim, (eds.), *Emerging Leadership Vistas* (Lexington, Mass.: Lexington Books, in press, 1987).

[13]See Bass, Avolio and Goodheim.

[14]This section is based on Fred E. Fiedler and Martin M. Chemers, *The Leader Match Concept* (2nd ed.), (New York: John Wiley, 1984).

[15]This section is based on Fred E. Fiedler and Joseph E. Garcia, *New Approaches to Effective Leadership* (New York: John Wiley, 1987).

[16]This section is based on Robert J. House and Terrence R. Mitchell, "Path-Goal Theory of Leadership," *Journal of Contemporary Business* (Autumn 1977), pp. 81–97.

[17]See the discussion of this approach in Paul Hersey and Kenneth H. Blanchard, *Management of Organizational Behavior* (Englewood Cliffs, NJ: Prentice-Hall, 1982), pp. 150–175.

[18]For some criticisms, see Claude L. Graeff, "The Situational Leadership Theory: A Critical View," *Academy of Management Review,* Vol. 8 (1983), pp. 285–291.

[19]For example, see A. Lowin and J. R. Craig, "The Influence of Level of Performance on Managerial Style: An Experimental Object-Lesson on the Ambiguity of Correlational Data," *Organizational Behavior and Human Performance,* Vol. 3 (1968), pp. 440–458.

[20]Jeffrey Pfeffer, "The Ambiguity of Leadership," *Academy of Management Review,* Vol. 2 (1977), pp. 104–112.

[21]See Arthur Jago, "Leadership: Perspectives in Theory and Research," *Management Science,* Vol. 28 (1982), pp. 315–336.

[22]The discussion in this section is based on Steven Kerr and John Jermier, "Substitutes for Leadership: Their Meaning and Measurement," *Organizational Behavior and Human Performance,* Vol. 22 (1978), pp. 375–403.

[23]This general idea was suggested by McElroy, *loc. cit.*

[24]See Fiedler and Garcia, and Fiedler and Chemers, *loc. cit.* for a discussion of training.

[25]Adapted from Jim Wall, *Bosses* (Lexington, Mass: Lexington Books, 1986), pp. 129–133, 142–150, 256–260.

PART SIX
MANAGING IN
A DYNAMIC
ENVIRONMENT

This is the final part of the book. It is written to help bring closure to your introductory study of OB. It is also written to stimulate you to think about your future career as a manager and the contemporary environment within which that career will unfold. We want you to look ahead and ask "Where do I go from here?" "What special challenges am I likely to encounter along the way?" and "How can this knowledge of OB help me succeed?" The following case and Chapters 17 and 18 will help you to develop appropriate answers to these and related questions.

CAREER PLANNING CONTRASTS CASE

Harlan Cleveland achieved success as an executive.[1] He views career planning for managers in the following perspective.

> A career as an executive is not something you plan for yourself. It's a series of accidental changes of job and shifts of scenery on which you look back later, weaving through the story retroactively some thread of logic that was not visible at the time.
>
> If you try too carefully to plan your life, the danger is that you will succeed—succeed in narrowing your options and closing off avenues of adventure that cannot now be imagined, perhaps because they are not yet technologically possible. When a student asks me for career advice, I can only suggest that he or she opt for the most exciting "next step" without worrying where it will lead, and then work hard on the job in hand, not pine for the one in the bush. When your job no longer demands of you more than you have, go and do something else. Always take by preference the job you *don't* know how to do.

William O. Grabe also achieved success as an executive. Some of his views on career planning follow.

> An aspiring executive should not make the personal investment in a career without some basic planning. Career planning is more art than science and highly individualized. Nonetheless, some form of plan can greatly enhance the evaluation of various opportunities and enable you as a manager to make better career decisions. A career plan allows you to identify how to use your basic strengths to maximum advantage, set major career objectives, and establish immediate milestones to measure personal development and advancement.
>
> A fundamental requirement of successful career planning is self-awareness—the ability to bring out your own best effort. The path to the top can be hard. So you as a manager should assess your physical and mental strengths and your willingness to concentrate on the fulfillment of your career plan.

QUESTION

Which approach to career planning do you favor—Cleveland's or Grabe's? Why?

OUR VIEWPOINT   Cleveland and Grabe have very contrasting perspectives on career planning. While Cleveland suggests one should let his or her career develop in a random and opportunistic way, Grabe sees a career as something to be programmed and planned very rationally. Interestingly enough, each seems to have found executive success in his own way.

It may be best not to see the two points of view as "either–or" alternatives. In fact, each of us may end up doing some of what each suggests. A well-thoughtout plan can point you in a general career direction; an eye for opportunity can fill in the details along the way.

The essence of any successful career, no matter how well planned, is for a person to be good at his or her work. It is through a record of accomplishment that the potential to advance arises. Thus, we refer you back once again to the study of OB. First and foremost, it is intended to help you become good at being a manager.

SUMMARY

There are only two chapters in this final part of the book. Their titles speak for themselves—Challenges of Change and Stress and Managerial Futures, OB, and You. The ideas contained in these chapters will help you to summarize and integrate your thinking about OB in the context of today's dynamic and very challenging environment. They also offer opportunities for you to examine further some of the problems and prospects of achieving true success in a managerial career.

---

[1]These viewpoints are reported in the Summer 1975 issue of the *Advanced Management Journal*. See also Harlan Cleveland, *The Future Executive* (New York: Harper & Row, 1972).

CHAPTER 17
CHALLENGES OF CHANGE AND STRESS

In the face of constant change, our overriding challenge is to recruit change as an ally.

American Express Company Annual Report

THE CHANGING APPROACH
TO ORGANIZING WORK

The world of work has changed in the 1980s and it will continue to do so through the 1990s and beyond. Among the key trends are changes in[1]

What Managers Assume About Workers:

Old way Workers want nothing but pay, dislike responsibility, must be closely controlled.

New way Workers want challenge on the job, will seek autonomy and responsibility if allowed.

How Jobs are Defined:

Old way Work is deskilled and narrow, focusing on individuals who do, but don't think.

New way Work is multiskilled and team oriented. Doing and thinking are combined.

How Wages are Determined:

Old way Pay based on the job not the person, and determined by job evaluations.

New way Pay is based on skills acquired, and includes group evaluations and incentives.

How Organizations are Structured:

Old way Strict hierarchy with many levels, and top–down use authority.

New way Flatter structures with fewer levels, and room for lower-level participation.

The Nature of Labor Relations:

Old way Incompatible interests emphasized, leads to more conflict.

New way Mutual interests are emphasized, leads to more cooperation.

Management Applications Question

These are just a few examples of emerging trends that may well influence your work life and any managerial responsibilities it entails. How well prepared are you to handle the challenges of the change and stress characteristic of a dynamic work environment?

PLANNING AHEAD

The reading and other learning experiences offered in
this chapter will acquaint you with the following
important topics.

Change
Managing Planned Change
Organization Development (OD)
OD in a Managerial Perspective
Stress
Sources of Stress
Effective Stress Management

Megatrends and *Re-Inventing the Corporation* are two popular best-selling books whose titles alone serve as useful reminders of the ever-changing world in which we all live. Their author, John Naisbitt, does a remarkably fine job of communicating the many basic changes that affect our lives and the organizations in which we work. He begins *Megatrends* with this statement.[2]

> As a society, we have been moving from the old to the new. And we are still
> in motion. Caught between eras, we experience turbulence. Yet, amid the
> sometimes painful and uncertain present, the restructuring of *America*
> proceeds unrelentingly.

We have highlighted the word ''America'' in the last sentence for a reason. Naisbitt could have replaced it with the name of any country, state, city, or *organization*. The statement and its implications would ring just as true.

Yes, we clearly do live in a time of rapid, continual, and sometimes even unpredictable change. These newspaper and news magazine headlines should give you a sense of what we mean.

BUSINESS FADS: WHAT'S IN—AND OUT
—Business Week

MAKING A CASE FOR UNMANNED FACTORIES
—The Wall Street Journal

SPECIAL REPORT: THE *1990s*
—Fortune

What these headlines, the chapter opening example, and the things you read and hear about in the daily news add up to is this—*it is a new era for management!* For you and others like you, succeeding as a manager in this "new era" means being able to cope with and prosper under the influence of such driving, and sometimes conflicting, forces as

- *The growth of high technology.* Continuing advances in microprocessors and related computer technologies are calling for radical changes in the traditional nature of work, be it manufacturing, clerical, or managerial.
- *An information explosion.* The new technologies are giving people access to more data than ever before, and create new pressures for the use of electronic information processing for decision making.
- *Increased accountability for decision making.* The public at large is demanding that organizations and their managers act within prevailing ethical and moral standards, and that they do so with a sense of greater social responsibility.
- *A global economy.* Ever increasing world-wide competition for resources and markets creates pressures for responsive organizations with enhanced productivity and the capacity to successfully innovate.
- *Shifting values.* "Baby-boomers" who grew up in the 1960s are exerting their expectations that the workplace respect their needs for "autonomy," "participation," and "individuality" . . . and do the same for their children.

Considerably more about these and other important trends in the contemporary environment will be discussed in Chapter 18. For now, it is sufficient to recognize that times are indeed changing. And as they do, the modern manager must be comfortable and skilled at participating in and helping to manage the process of change. This manager must also be comfortable and skilled at coping with the stress that inevitably accompanies change—and be capable of helping others do the same.

CHANGE

"Change" is certainly a part of our lives. And, as the chapter opening example shows, it is especially characteristic of organizations as they seek to survive and prosper in the dynamic and uncertain environment of the late twentieth century. A **change agent** is a person or group taking responsibility for changing the existing pattern of behavior of another person or social system. It only makes sense, therefore, that part of every manager's job is to act as a change agent in the work setting. This means being alert to situations or people needing change, open to good ideas, and able to support the implementation of new ideas into actual practice. As change agents, managers facilitate creativity and innovation in organizations.

Planned and Unplanned Change

Not all change in organizations happens at a change agent's direction. **Unplanned change** occurs spontaneously or at random and without a change agent's attention. These changes may be disruptive, such as a wildcat strike that results in a plant closure, or beneficial, such as an interpersonal conflict that results in a new procedure or rule being established to guide interdepartmental relations. The appropriate goal in managing unplanned change is to act immediately once the change is recognized and, thus, minimize any negative consequences and maximize any possible benefits.

We are particularly interested in **planned change** that happens as a result of specific efforts by a change agent. Planned change is a direct response to someone's perception of a **performance gap**—that is, a discrepancy between the desired and actual state of affairs. Performance gaps may represent problems to be resolved or opportunities to be explored. In each case, managers as change agents should spot performance gaps and initiate planned changes to close them.

Consider the following analysis of a change situation reported in a *Wall Street Journal* article.[3]

Scene—Jerry Hathaway and his family are driving their camper toward a weekend outing in the country. But it's a Friday and Jerry is supposed to be at work at a New Hampshire packaging plant—his wife called in "sick" for him so they could all get away early.

Performance gap—The plant at which Jerry works suffers an abnormally high absenteeism rate.

Significance—In its legitimate and not-so-legitimate forms, absenteeism annually costs U.S. industry over $20 billion in lost pay alone. Another $10 billion or more gets spent in sick pay; $5 + billion goes for benefits which continue in the workers' absences. Once when Jerry and six co-workers failed to report for their evening shift, his plant lost 20 percent on its targeted production run.

Manager's response—The plant manager Eli Kwartler initiated a problem-solving and planned change effort in response to the perceived performance gap. Workers were surveyed to determine their feelings about work schedules. The data showed clear preferences among evening workers for a four-day week of 10-hour shifts Monday through Thursday instead of the 8-hour shifts. The company changed work schedules to a "4-40" compressed work week on the evening shifts.

Results—Absences fell and shift production climbed 9 percent. Even Jerry took fewer days off . . . he no longer had to skip work on Fridays to make a long weekend with his family.

This case illustrates how a planned change in working hours was initiated by management to resolve a performance gap in one company. It is useful to think of most planned changes as problem-solving efforts initiated by managers to resolve performance gaps to the benefit of the organization and its members.

Organizational Targets for Change

Organizational change involves modification in any of the various components that constitute the essence of an organization. These targets of change, as shown in Table 17.1, include organizational purpose and objectives, culture, strategy, tasks, technology, people, and structure. Newsline 17.1 indicates that these targets are sometimes addressed mistakenly by management "fads" offered by consultants and adopted by managers without much thought for the real situation and/or people involved. The logic of truly *planned* change, by contrast, requires a managerial willingness and ability to address problems concretely and systematically, and to avoid tendencies toward an easy but questionable "quick fix."[4] At the very least, you must recognize that the various targets of planned organization change are highly intertwined. For example,

A change in the basic *tasks* performed by an organization—that is, a modification in what it is the organization does—is almost inevitably accompanied by a change in *technology*—that is, a modification in the way in which tasks are accomplished. Changes in tasks and technology usually require alterations in the *structure* of the organization, including changes in the patterns of authority and communication as well as in the roles of members. These technological and structural changes can, in turn, necessitate changes on the part of *members*—the basic components of the organization. For example, members may have to acquire additional knowledge and develop new skills to perform their modified roles and to work with the new technology.[5]

TABLE 17.1   Organizational Targets for Change and Methods for Dealing with Them

Targets	Possible Change Methods
Purpose and objectives	Clarify overall mission; modify existing objectives; use management by objectives
Culture	Clarify, modify, and/or create core beliefs and values to help shape behavior of individuals and groups
Strategy	Modify strategic plans; modify operational plans; modify policies and procedures
Tasks	Modify job designs; use job enrichment and autonomous work groups
Technology	Improve equipment and facilities; improve methods and workflows
People	Modify selection criteria; modify recruiting practices; use training and development programs; clarify roles and expectations
Structure	Modify job descriptions; modify organizational design; adjust coordination mechanisms; modify distribution of authority

NEWSLINE 17.1 / BEYOND THE QUICK FIX—WATCH OUT FOR MANAGEMENT FADS

Managers may be far too prone to latch onto any management idea or technique that looks like a "quick fix" for their problems. Take what happened to Allan Kennedy, co-author of the best-seller *Corporate Cultures,* as a case in point. After delivering one of his $5000-for-90 minutes speeches to a group of senior executives from a large corporation, he was taken aback by the audience's enthusiasm. Later, the chairperson of the company raved about his ideas during dinner. "This corporate culture stuff is great," he told Kennedy. Then, turning to his president he said: "I want a culture by Monday."

This executive never got below the surface of Kennedy's ideas. He altogether missed the point that cultures take time to build— they can't be put into place overnight. The list of recently popular management concepts that run similar risks includes "quality circles," "intrapreneurship," "restructuring," "Theory Z," and many others. There's not a panacea in the lot . . . but they're not just gimmicks either. The key is to view them not as "fads," but as possible response to real problems for which they offer the best potential solutions.

Reported in *Business Week.*

MANAGING PLANNED CHANGE

Many of the ideas discussed elsewhere in this book represent potential planned changes in one or more aspects of an organization. They include changes in reward systems, job designs, group dynamics, work flow technology, and organizational structure, among others. Regardless of the specific focus, however, any change is a complicated and uncertain process, at the heart of which lies people. Consider these rather different but interesting historical illustrations of the difficulties of introducing planned organization change.

From the History of England[6]

The Royal Artillery was giving a demonstration to some visiting Europeans on Salisbury Plain in the 1950s. Visitors were most impressed with the speed and precision of the light artillery crew, but one asked about the duty of the man who stood at attention throughout the demonstration.

"He's number six," the adjutant explained.
"I, too, can count. But why is he there?"
"That's his job. Number six stands at attention throughout."
"But why then do you not have five?"

No one knew. It took a great deal of research through old training manuals, but finally they discovered his duty. He was the one who held the horses.

From the American Automobile Industry

H. Ross Perot left the board of directors of General Motors Corporation in late 1986 after a stormy relationship with CEO Roger Smith. A frustrated Perot once remarked, ''It takes five years to develop a new car in this country. Heck, we won World War II in four years.''

The organizations in each situation show tendencies toward the status quo when change is clearly needed. They highlight the tendency of people and organizations to act habitually in stable and predictable patterns over time. As a manager, you will need to recognize such inertia and learn how to deal with it to be successful in implementing planned changes.

Phases of Planned Change

Kurt Lewin, a famous psychologist, recommends that any change effort be viewed as a three-phase process: unfreezing, changing, and refreezing.[7] This process is diagrammed in Figure 17.1.

Unfreezing is the stage of preparing a situation for change. Unfreezing involves disconfirming existing attitudes and behaviors to create a felt need for something new. It is facilitated by environmental pressures, declining performance, the recognition of a problem, and awareness of a better way, among other things. Many changes are never tried or fail simply because situations are not properly unfrozen to begin with. Ross Perot, in the prior example, was citing the difficulty of getting the industrial giant GM moving at a time when change was desperately needed. Large systems seem particularly susceptible to the so called ''boiled frog phenomenon.''[8] This refers by analogy to a classic physiological experiment, which demonstrated that a live frog will immediately jump out when placed in a pan of hot water. When placed in cold water that is then heated very slowly, the frog will stay until it boils to death. Organizations, too, can fall victim to similar circumstances. When managers fail to monitor their environments, don't recognize the important trends, and sense no need to change, the consequences of the status quo can be disastrous.

Changing involves the actual modification in people, task, structure, and/or tech-

FIGURE 17.1   Three phases of planned change in organizations.

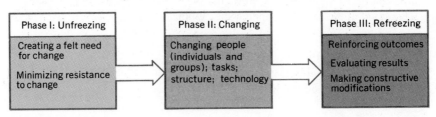

Phase I: Unfreezing	Phase II: Changing	Phase III: Refreezing
Creating a felt need for change Minimizing resistance to change	Changing people (individuals and groups); tasks; structure; technology	Reinforcing outcomes Evaluating results Making constructive modifications

nology. Lewin feels that many change agents enter this stage prematurely, are too quick to change things, and therefore end up creating resistance to change in a situation that is not adequately unfrozen. *Refreezing* is the final stage in the planned change process. Designed to maintain the momentum of a change, refreezing tactics include positively reinforcing desired outcomes and providing extra support when difficulties are encountered. Evaluation is a key element in this final step. It provides data on the costs and benefits of a change and offers opportunities to make constructive modifications in the change over time. Improper refreezing results in changes that are abandoned or incompletely implemented.

Planned Change Strategies

Managers use various means for exerting influence to get other persons to adopt a desired change. We summarize these means in Figure 17.2 as force-coercion, empirical-rational, and normative-reeducative change strategies.[9]

Force-Coercion

A **force-coercive strategy** uses legitimacy, rewards, and punishments as primary inducements to change. The change agent acts unilaterally to try to "command" change through the formal authority of his or her position, to induce change via an offer of special rewards, or to bring about change via threats of punishment. People respond to this strategy mainly out of the fear of punishment or desire for reward.

FIGURE 17.2 Power bases, change strategies, managerial behavior, and predicted change outcomes.

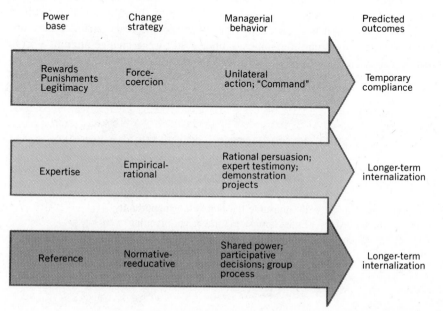

Compliance is usually temporary in nature and will continue only so long as the change agent remains visible in his or her legitimate authority, or so long as the opportunity for rewards and punishments remains obvious.

Empirical-Rational

Change agents using an **empirical-rational strategy** attempt to bring about change through persuasion by special knowledge and rational argument. Use of this strategy assumes that rational people will be guided by reason and self interest in deciding whether or not to support a change. Expert power is mobilized to convince others that the cost–benefit value of a proposed change is high; that the change will leave people better off than before. When successful, this strategy results in a longer-lasting more internalized change than does the force-coercion strategy.

Normative-Reeducative

A **normative-reeducative strategy** identifies or establishes values and assumptions so that support for a proposed change naturally emerges. This strategy builds essential foundations such as personal values, group norms, and shared goals to support change. Managers using normative-reeducative approaches emphasize personal reference and share power by allowing other persons to participate in change planning and implementation. Given this high level of involvement, the strategy is likely to result in a longer lasting and internalized change.

Resistance to Change

"Resistance" is usually viewed by change agents as something to be overcome in order for change to be successful. Consider, though, the viewpoint that resistance to change is really feedback that can be used constructively by the astute change agent.[10] The essence of this notion is to recognize that when people resist change, they are defending something important that appears threatened by the change attempt.

Shown in Table 17.2 are examples of why people might resist the introduction of

TABLE 17.2   Potential Sources of Resistance to a New Management Practice and Suggested Change Agent Responses

Sources of Resistance	Suggested Response
Fear of the unknown	Offer information and encouragement
Need for security	Clarify intentions and methods
No felt need to change	Demonstrate the problem or opportunity
Vested interests threatened	Enlist key people in change planning
Contrasting interpretations	Disseminate valid information and facilitate group sharing
Poor timing	Delay change and await a better time
Lack of resources	Provide supporting resources and/or reduced performance expectations

a new management practice. A manager's subordinates, for example, might resist the introduction of personal computers at their work stations because

- They had never before used a computer and were apprehensive that they could learn to use them successfully.
- They sensed the manager was forcing the computers on them without discussing their feelings on the matter first.
- They felt they were doing their jobs fine and didn't need the new computers.
- They were really busy at the present time and didn't want to try something new until the work slackened a bit.
- They weren't sure "why" the change was being made and wondered if the manager just wanted to "get rid" of them.

These and other viewpoints often create resistance to even the best and most well-intended planned changes. To better deal with these forces, managers often find it useful to separate such responses into resistance to change directed toward the change itself, the change strategy, and the change agent as a person.

Resistance to the Change

People may reject a change because it does not appear as something worth their time, effort, and/or attention. To minimize such resistance, you should be careful to ensure that any changes that you sponsor as a manager

1. Have a positive relative advantage; that is, their benefits are clearly apparent to the persons you are asking to change.
2. Are compatible with existing values and experiences.
3. Are not too complex, that is, they are easy to understand and to learn how to use.
4. Can be tried on an incremental or experimental basis before a total commitment has to be made.

Resistance to the Change Strategy

Resistance is sometimes focused on the strategy rather than on the change itself. Attempting change via force-coercion, for example, may create resistance among persons who resent management by "command" or the use of threatened punishment. People may also resist an empirical-rational strategy in which expertise is not clearly demonstrated, and a normative-reeducative strategy that appears manipulative and insincere.

Resistance to the Change Agent as a Person

Resistance may also reflect inadequacies in the personality of the change agent. Change agents who are isolated from other persons in the change situation, who appear self-centered, and who have a high emotional involvement in the change are especially prone to such problems. Research also indicates that change agents who are different from other key persons on such dimensions as age, education, and socioeconomic factors are likely to experience greater resistance to change.[11]

Dealing with Resistance to Change

Table 17.2 also shows that an informed change agent can take steps to deal with such resistance constructively, if it is recognized early enough in the change process. All things considered, six general approaches for dealing with resistance can be identified.[12]

1. *Education and communication.*   Use of one-on-one discussions, presentations to groups, memos, reports, and demonstrations to educate people beforehand about a change and to help them see the logic of the change.
2. *Participation and involvement.*   Allowing others to help design and implement the change; asking individuals to contribute ideas and advice, or forming task forces or committees to work on the change.
3. *Facilitation and support.*   Providing socioemotional support for the hardships of change, actively listening to problems and complaints, providing training in the new ways, and helping to overcome performance pressures.
4. *Negotiation and agreement.*   Offering incentives to actual or potential resistors; working out trade-offs to provide special benefits in exchange for assurance that the change will not be blocked.
5. *Manipulation and co-optation.*   Use of covert attempts to influence others; selectively providing information and consciously structuring events so that the desired change receives maximum support.
6. *Explicit and implicit coercion.*   Use of force to get people to accept change; threatening resistors with a variety of undesirable consequences if they do not go along as planned.

The advantages and disadvantages of these approaches are further described in Table 17.3. Managers using them must understand that resistance to change is something to be recognized and constructively addressed instead of feared. The presence of resistance typically suggests that something can be done to achieve a better ''fit'' among the change, the situation, and the people the change will affect. A manager should ''listen'' to such feedback and act accordingly.

ORGANIZATION DEVELOPMENT (OD)

Behavioral scientists have been working since the early 1960s with a comprehensive approach to planned change that is designed to improve the overall effectiveness of organizations. Called **organization development (OD),** this planned-change approach is defined as the application of behavioral science knowledge in a long-range effort to improve an organization's ability to cope with change in its external environment and increase its internal problem-solving capabilities.[13] Stated differently, OD is a

TABLE 17.3 Methods for Dealing with Resistance to Change			
Approach	Commonly Used	Advantages	Drawbacks
Education and communication	Where there is a lack of information or inaccurate information and analysis.	Once persuaded, people will often help with the implementation of the change.	Can be very time consuming if lots of people are involved.
Participation and involvement	Where the initiators do not have all the information they need to design the change, and where others have considerable power to resist.	People who participate will be committed to implementing change, and any relevant information they have will be integrated into the change plan.	Can be very time consuming if participants design an inappropriate change.
Facilitation and support	Where people are resisting because of adjustment problems.	No other approach works as well with adjustment problems.	Can be time consuming, expensive, and still fail.
Negotiation and agreement	Where someone or some group will clearly lose out in a change, and where that group has considerable power to resist.	Sometimes it is a relatively easy way to avoid major resistance.	Can be too expensive in many cases if it alerts others to negotiate for compliance.
Manipulation and co-optation	Where other tactics will not work, or are too expensive.	It can be a relatively quick and inexpensive solution to resistance problems.	Can lead to future problems if people feel manipulated.
Explicit and implicit coercion	Where speed is essential, and the change initiators possess considerable power.	It is speedy, and can overcome any kind of resistance.	Can be risky if it leaves people mad at the initiators.

Source: Reprinted by permission of the *Harvard Business Review*. Excerpt from ''Choosing Strategies for Change'' by John P. Kotter and Leonard A. Schlesinger, Vol. 57 (March–April 1979), p. 111. Copyright © 1979 by the President and Fellows of Harvard College. All rights reserved.

comprehensive approach to improving the overall effectiveness and health of an organization by making changes in the operations of its component system.

In concept, OD quite clearly belongs in our study of planned change in organizations. This point is evident in the following example of OD in practice.

Illustrative Case: OD in a Large Federal Agency

A new district director of a large federal agency was appointed following the retirement of the previous director.[14] The new director found that operations appeared inefficient and lethargic, with low performance. After discussion and diagnosis using an outside consultant, the director felt that team building directed toward improving task accomplishment might be helpful.

The first step was to hold a three-day meeting with all 36 managers of the district. The meeting objectives were to identify current operating processes, identify desired ways of operating, and develop improvement plans. The first day was primarily devoted to preparing general written procedures for the conduct of future performance reviews to be used as one way of motivating subordinates. The next day groups met to identify additional issues and problems facing the district, including the development of specific action plans for specific problems. The third day of the meeting, the district director and group members discussed recent administrative actions and the reasoning behind them. The discussion was open and candid.

Six months later, a one-day followup conference was held to review progress and to deal with new items. The groups discussed what action had been taken on the issues raised in the first meeting, and shared reports on improvement plan achievements. Some action had been taken on all issues, but they agreed that there was considerable room for improvement in working in a collaborative mode and in further problem solving.

Additional problems mentioned by the group were listed on the blackboard. Subgroups each took two of the listed problems, analyzed them, and proposed alternative courses of action. The total group reviewed these analyses and alternatives, and agreed on plans to resolve the problems. Although considerable progress had already been made during the previous six months, the group decided to meet again in three months to report on the implementation of action plans and decide upon further action.

The director had begun a continuing series of collaborative problem-identification and problem-solving activities. Not only were better operating procedures developed, but all of the district managers were involved in a team effort to revitalize district operations. The director was convinced that productivity and efficiency had improved to a satisfactory level.

The Goals of OD

Against this case illustration as background, we can now look more specifically at what OD is—and what it is *not!* First, OD is *not* a panacea or surefire cure for all that ails an organization and/or its members. What OD does offer, however, is a systematic approach to planned change in organizations that addresses both process and outcome goals. Briefly,

> *process goals* include achieving improvements in such things as communication, interaction, and decision making among an organization's members. They focus on how well people work together.
>
> *outcome goals* include achieving improvements in task performance. They focus on what is actually accomplished through individual and group efforts.

OD is designed to help organizations and their members better achieve process and outcome goals by[15]

- Creating an open problem-solving climate throughout an organization.
- Supplementing hierarchical authority with that based on knowledge and competence.
- Moving decision-making and problem-solving to points where relevant information is located.
- Building trust and maximizing collaboration among individuals and groups.
- Increasing the shared sense of "ownership" over organizational objectives among all members.
- Allowing people to assume more self-direction and self-control over their work.

Principles Underlying OD

The strong human resource focus of OD is evident in the prior list. As a framework for planned change, OD is designed to improve the contributions of people to organizational goals. But, it seeks to do so in ways that respect them as mature adults who need and deserve high-quality experiences in their working lives. The foundations for achieving change in this manner rest with a number of well-established behavioral science principles shared with the field of OB as described in this book. They include[16]

1. *Principles regarding* **individuals**
   - Individual needs for growth and development are most likely to be satisfied in a supportive and challenging work environment.
   - Most people are capable of assuming responsibility for their own actions and of making positive contributions to organizational performance.
2. *Principles regarding* **groups**
   - Groups help people satisfy important needs.
   - Groups can be either helpful or harmful in supporting organizational objectives.
   - People can increase the effectiveness of groups in meeting individual and organizational needs by working in collaboration.
3. *Principles regarding* **organizations**
   - Changes in one part of an organization will affect other parts as well.
   - The culture of the organization will affect the nature and expression of individual feelings and attitudes.
   - Organizational structures and jobs can be designed to meet the needs of individuals and groups as well as the organization.

OD IN A MANAGERIAL PERSPECTIVE

OD is an exciting application of behavioral science theory to management practice. It includes a set of tools with which any manager concerned about achieving and maintaining high levels of productivity will want to be familiar. Because of its comprehensive nature and scientific foundations, OD is frequently done with the aid of an external consultant or internal professional staff member.

Still, the basic concept of OD as a comprehensive approach to planned change can and should be routinely used by managers to help guide daily problem-solving activities. Just as "human resource development" must be a continuing management concern, so too must "organizational development." There are times when every organization or subunit needs to reflect systematically on its strengths and weaknesses—and on the problems and opportunities it faces. The concepts and ideas of OD can assist managers to do just that.

A General Model of OD

Figure 17.3 depicts a general model of OD and shows its relationship to the phases of planned change. The OD process begins with *diagnosis,* that is, gathering and analyzing data to assess a situation and set appropriate change objectives. From a planned-change perspective, good diagnosis helps to unfreeze an existing situation as well as pinpoint appropriate action directions. Diagnosis leads to active *intervention* wherein change objectives are pursued through a variety of specific activities. This equates to the changing phase of the planned-change process. In the *reinforcement* stage of OD, changes are monitored, reinforced, and evaluated. Refreezing of change occurs at this point, and the foundations for future replication of similar diagnosis–intervention–reinforcement cycles are set.

For one business firm the three stages in the general model of OD evolved as follows:

FIGURE 17.3   The organization development and planned-change processes.

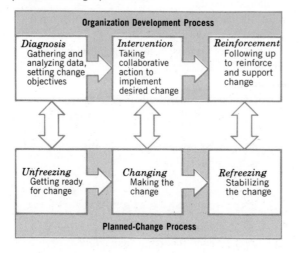

1. *Diagnosis*.   Management perceived a performance gap and hired a consultant. The consultant interviewed key people and planned a workshop where managers could analyze the interview results in a problem-solving format.
2. *Intervention*.   The workshop was held. Participants were coached on how to analyze the data and determine appropriate action directions; they also received advice on the effectiveness of the group process.
3. *Reinforcement*.   The consultant continued to meet periodically with the group to review progress; additional help was given when things ''bogged down''; problem-solving workshops became annual events for the firm.

Although OD is a planned-change process, the example suggests that it is also something more. Think of OD as ''planned change *plus*'' if you'd like. That ''plus'' is the goal of creating change in a way that organization members develop a capacity for continual self-renewal by learning how to implement similar diagnosis–intervention–reinforcement cycles in the future. True OD, therefore, seeks more than the successful accomplishment of one planned change. OD seeks to achieve change in such a way that organization members become more active and confident in taking similar steps to maintain longer-run organization effectiveness. A large part of any OD program's success in this regard rests with the strength of its action-research foundations.

Action Research

Action research is a process of systematically collecting data on an organization, feeding it back to the members for action planning, and evaluating results by collecting and reflecting on more data after the planned actions have been taken. It is a data-based and collaborative approach to problem solving and organizational assessment. Action research helps to identify action directions that may enhance organization effectiveness.

A typical action-research sequence is diagrammed in Figure 17.4. The sequence is initiated when someone senses a performance gap and decides to analyze the situation systematically for the problems and opportunities it represents. The process continues with data gathering, data feedback, data analysis, and action planning. It continues to the point where action is taken and results are evaluated. The evaluation or reassessment stage may or may not generate another performance gap. If it does, the action-research cycle begins anew.

Data gathering is a major element in the action-research process. Table 17.4 describes several methods available for this, including the major advantages and problems associated with each. Interviews and written questionnaires are common means of gathering data in action research. Formal written surveys of employee attitudes and needs are growing in popularity, and many of those available have been tested for reliability and validity. Some have even been used to the extent that ''norms'' are available so that one organization can compare its results with those from a broader sample of organizations.

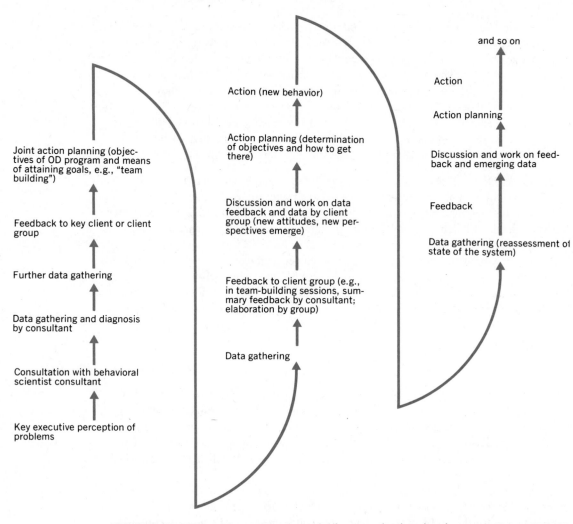

FIGURE 17.4   An action-research model for organization development. (Copyright 1969 by the Regents of the University of California. Reprinted from *California Management Review,* Vol. XII, no. 2, p. 26, Figure 1, by permission of the Regents.)

OD Interventions

OD interventions are activities initiated by consultants or managers in support of a comprehensive OD program. They are ways of facilitating the action-research process and ways of taking action in response to the problems and opportunities it brings to the surface. A list of popular OD interventions focusing on the individual, group, and organizational levels of action follows. The various interventions reflect management theories and concepts discussed throughout this book. Some, like team building and

TABLE 17.4   A Comparison of Different Methods of Data Collection

Method	Major Advantages	Major Potential Problems
Interviews	1. Adaptive—allow data collection on a range of possible subjects 2. Source of "rich" data 3. Empathic 4. Process of interviewing can build rapport	1. Can be expensive 2. Interviewer can bias responses 3. Coding/interpretation problems 4. Self-report bias
Questionnaires	1. Responses can be quantified and easily summarized 2. Easy to use with large samples 3. Relatively inexpensive 4. Can obtain large volume of data	1. Nonempathic 2. Predetermined questions may miss issues 3. Data may be overinterpreted 4. Response bias
Observations	1. Collect data on behavior rather than reports of behavior 2. Real-time, no retrospective 3. Adaptive	1. Interpretation and coding problems 2. Sampling is a problem 3. Observer bias/reliability 4. Costly
Secondary data/unobtrusive measures	1. Nonreactive—no response bias 2. High face validity 3. Easily quantified	1. Access/retrieval possibly a problem 2. Potential validity problems 3. Coding/interpretation

Source: David A. Nadler, *Feedback and Organizational Development: Using Data-Based Methods,* p. 119. Copyright © 1977 Addison-Wesley, Reading, Mass. Reprinted with permission.

management by objectives, are techniques with which you are already familiar; others are new. In all cases, the interventions are resources that managers can use comprehensively as part of the formal OD process or selectively to solve specific problems and accomplish specific goals in the work setting. A brief synopsis of the intervention techniques is provided to give you a feel for the range of ways OD interventions can be utilized in actual practice.

1. OD interventions to improve individual effectiveness
   - *Sensitivity training (T-groups).* Unstructured group sessions where participants learn interpersonal skills and increased sensitivity to other persons.
   - *Management training.* Structured educational opportunities for developing managerial skills and capabilities.
   - *Role negotiation.* Structured interactions to clarify and negotiate role expectations among persons who work together.
   - *Job redesign.* Realigning task components to better fit the needs and capabilities of the individual.
   - *Career planning.* Structured advice and discussion sessions to plan for career development.
2. OD interventions to improve group effectiveness
   - *Team building.* Structured experiences to help group members set goals, improve interpersonal relations, and become a better functioning team.
   - *Process consultation.* Third-party observation of critical group processes

(e.g., communication and decision making) and giving advice on how to improve these processes.

- *Intergroup team building*. Structured experiences to help two or more groups set shared goals, improve intergroup relations, and become better coordinated and mutually supportive.

3. OD interventions to improve organizational effectiveness

- *Survey feedback*. Comprehensive and systematic data collection to identify attitudes and needs, analyze results, and plan for constructive action.
- *Confrontation meeting*. One-day intensive meeting of a sample of employees to gather data on their attitudes and needs, analyze results, and plan for constructive action relevant to the organization as a whole.
- *Structural redesign*. Realigning the organization structure to meet the needs of environmental and contextual forces.
- *Collateral organization*. A parallel structure that permanently supports the formal organization by allowing participatory assessment, problem-solving and planning activities.
- *Management by objectives*. Formalizing an MBO framework throughout the organization so that individual–subunit–organizational objectives are clearly linked to one another in means–ends chains.

The various OD interventions are often used in combination with one another. This can result in an integrated and comprehensive program of planned organization change. Figure 17.5 gives you a final example of what a comprehensive OD effort can look like when done throughout the organization. Note the involvement of all organizational levels along with the use of data feedback, T-groups, team building, and management training sessions. As this illustration shows, organization development is an important integrating resource for managers interested in working comprehensively, collaboratively, and regularly over time to introduce planned changes and improve organizational productivity.

STRESS

Change of any sort in organizations is often accompanied by increased stress for the people involved. It is time now to develop a further understanding of "stress" as something with which all managers must successfully cope.[17] Read and think about the following experiences of three people—Mary, Bob, and Ray. Although working in different managerial jobs and organization settings, each shares the problem of accommodating high levels of job-related stress.[18]

1. *Mary*. Mary, a recent Wharton MBA holder, spent a sleepless night contemplating her first presentation before the executive committee of her new employer. She had spent much of the last six months preparing the report for her presentation and felt that it was the first real test of her managerial potential. Mary's presentation lasted 5 minutes and was followed by about

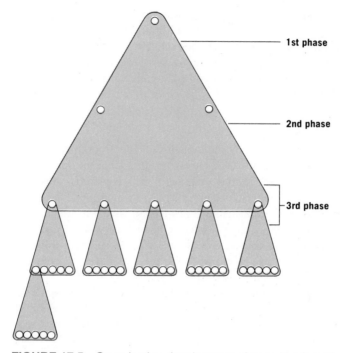

1st Phase. Data gathering, feedback, and diagnosis—consultant and top executive only.

2nd Phase. Data gathering, feedback, and revised diagnosis—consultant and two or more key staff or line people.

3rd Phase. Data gathering and feedback to total top executive team in "team-building" laboratory, with or without key subordinates from level below.

4th and Additional Phases. Data gathering and team-building sessions with second or third level teams.

Subsequent Phases. Data gathering, feedback, and interface problem-solving sessions across groups.

Simultaneous Phases. Several managers may attend "stranger" T-Groups; courses in the management development program may supplement this learning.

FIGURE 17.5 Organization development phases in a hypothetical organization. (Copyright 1969 by the Regents of the University of California. Reprinted from *California Management Review*, Vol. XII, no. 2, p. 27, by permission of the Regents.)

10 minutes of questions from committee members. Mary was thanked for making a fine presentation and dismissed from the meeting by the firm's president. She quickly went to the nearest lounge and in a release of tension shook uncontrollably.

2. *Bob.*   Bob's wife, Jane, is becoming increasingly worried about her husband. Several months ago Bob was passed over for a promotion to plant supervisor that he felt he deserved after 15 years of loyal service to the company. Bob used to come home from work tired but cheery and would spend an hour or so playing with their two boys. Lately, however, Bob walks into the house, grabs a can of beer, and plops down in front of the television. Except for dinner, he spends his evenings watching television and drinking beer. He has little to do or say to either Jane or the kids. Jane is at her wit's end. She has begged Bob to go to the doctor, but he says, "Nothing is wrong with me. It's your imagination."

3. *Ray.*   Ray, a successful advertising account executive, was finishing his typical "two-martini" lunch with a potential client, but Ray's mind was not on business as usual. He was thinking about the pain in his stomach and the diagnosis the doctor had given him yesterday. Ray's doctor had told him he

had a spastic colon induced by his life-style. Ray, recently divorced, knows that his gin consumption, smoking habit, and 12-hour workdays are not good for him, but his job is now the most important thing in his life, and the advertising business just happens to be highly stressful. He decides not to worry about his health and to concentrate on selling his luncheon partner one fantastic contract.

The Concept of Stress

Stress is a state of tension experienced by individuals facing extraordinary demands, constraints, or opportunities. In Mary's case, stress resulted from an opportunity to make an important presentation. Bob's stress emerged from a constraint—inability to gain promotion. Ray is torn between the demands of a doctor's advice and the potential opportunity of a successful business luncheon. Stress, again, is the result.

Any look toward your managerial future would be incomplete without confronting stress as something you are sure to encounter along the way. For a start, think about this statement by a psychologist who works with top-level managers having severe drinking problems: "All executives deal with stress. They wouldn't be executives if they didn't. Some handle it well, others handle it poorly." If you understand stress and how it operates in the work settings, you should be more likely to handle it well. This goes both for the personal stress you may experience and for the stress experienced by persons you supervise.

Stress and Performance

This preliminary discussion and even your personal views may give the impression that stress always acts as a negative influence on our lives. There are actually two faces to stress, as shown in Figure 17.6—one constructive and one destructive.

Constructive stress acts in a positive way for the individual and/or the organization. The figure shows that low to moderate levels of stress act in a constructive or energizing way. Moderate stress can increase effort, stimulate creativity, and encourage diligence in one's work. You may know such stress as the tension that causes you to study hard before exams, pay attention in class, and complete assignments on time. The same positive results of stress can be found in the workplace.

Destructive stress, on the other hand, is dysfunctional for the individual and/or the organization. Whereas low to moderate levels of stress can enhance performance, excessively high stress can overload and break down a person's physical and mental systems. Performance can suffer as people experience illness brought on by very intense stress and/or react to high stress through absenteeism, turnover, errors, accidents, dissatisfaction, and reduced performance.

Managers seek the positive performance edge offered by constructive stress. But, they must also be concerned about destructive stress and its potential to impact people and their work performance adversely. One of the most difficult tasks here is to find the optimum stress points for yourself and for the persons you supervise. The challenges of finding and maintaining the tricky balance between too little and too much stress are illustrated in Newsline 17.2.

NEWSLINE 17.2 /
THE CUSTOMER IS STILL KING AT NORDSTROM'S

Many frustrated American consumers are wondering where the service went. It is being said that personal service has become a rare commodity in the marketplace . . . a chilling comment about the service industries, which have provided almost 85 percent of the new jobs created since 1982. But at the 45 Nordstrom department stores in six western states, the customer is still king. Top management of this rapidly growing chain drills its staff with an incessant theme—"The customer is always right." And right they are, the company sales per square foot of space is about double the industry average and the chain continues to expand.

"Heroic" performances are the rule, not the exception for Nordstrom sales clerks. One paid for a customer's parking ticket when her car was towed away; another personally delivered purchases to a shut-in; still another ironed a customer's newly-bought shirt so it could be worn away to a meeting. This is the type of service expected from staff employed by this still closely-controlled family firm. But even though the sales force is smiling, as expected, it's also under pressure. Clerks work on commission and are expected to sell as much as $125 worth of goods per hour. Many can't keep up. Nordstrom's turnover is the highest in the industry, with 7–10 percent of their full-time employees leaving each year. Those who stick it out have good prospects for advancement since the company promotes only from within. Still, "the stress is intense" says one former clerk who walked off the job in the middle of a sale.

Reported in *Newsweek* and *Time*.

FIGURE 17.6 The relationship between stress intensity and individual performance.

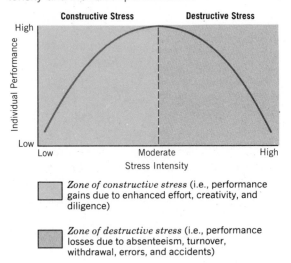

Zone of constructive stress (i.e., performance gains due to enhanced effort, creativity, and diligence)

Zone of destructive stress (i.e., performance losses due to absenteeism, turnover, withdrawal, errors, and accidents)

Stress and Health

There is no doubt that stress impacts the health of an individual. Stress is a potential source of both anxiety and frustration, each of which, in turn, is capable of breaking down the body's physiological and/or psychological well-being over time.[19] Excessive stress can lead to several health problems in the form of heart attack, stroke, hypertension, migraine headache, ulcers, drug–alcohol–tobacco abuse, overeating, depression, and muscle aches, among others.

Managers should be alert to signs for excessive stress in themselves and persons with whom they work. The symptoms are multiple and varied. When it comes to habits and feelings, here are some things to watch for.[20]

- Change in eating habits.
- Unhealthy feeling—aches and pains.
- Restlessness, inability to concentrate.
- Tense, uptight, fidgety, or nervous feelings.
- Increase in drinking or smoking.
- Feelings of being disoriented or overwhelmed
- Sleeping problems.
- Depression or irritability.
- Upset stomach.
- Dizziness, weakness, lightheadedness.

When it comes to observable work behaviors the key things to look for are *changes* from normal patterns. Among the things that may indicate increased and potentially destructive stress, for example, are

Changes from . . .	. . . to
regular attendance	absenteeism
punctuality	tardiness
diligent work	careless work
positive attitude	negative attitude
openness to change	resistance to change
being cooperative	being hostile

The prior emphasis on being alert to behaviors indicating excessive stress for you *and* others is deliberate and important. It is increasingly the case, and rightly so, that modern managers are asked to display greater concern and accept more responsibility for job-related influences on the health of their colleagues and subordinates. This position is defended on the basis of the following arguments.[21]

1. *Humanitarianism*.   To the extent that managerial awareness and action can enhance employee health, managers have a humanitarian responsibility to do so.
2. *Productivity*.   Healthy employees are absent less, make fewer errors, and must be replaced less frequently than less healthy ones.
3. *Creativity*.   Persons in poor health are less creative and less prone to take reasonable risks than are their healthy counterparts.
4. *Return on investment*.   Organizations invest substantial amounts of time and money in the development of employees; poor health decreases the return on this human resource investment.

SOURCES OF STRESS

Stressors are the things that cause stress. It is important for a manager to understand and be able to recognize stressors because they cause job-related stress, which influences work attitudes and behavior. Figure 17.6 shows three categories of stressors that can act in this fashion—work, nonwork, and personal factors. We will examine the managerial significance of each in turn.

FIGURE 17.7   Three categories of stressors and their potential consequences.

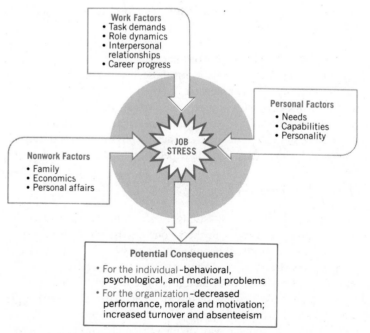

Work-Related Stressors

Of the stressors depicted in the figure, the work factors have the most obvious potential to create stress. Such stress can result from excessively high or low task demands, role conflicts or ambiguities, poor interpersonal relations, or career progress that is too slow or too fast. A look back to the examples of Mary, Bob, and Ray shows how these factors can act alone or in combination to cause job stress.

Among the various work related-stressors you should be especially aware that

- *Unrealistic task demands may create stress*. People asked to do too much for available time and/or for their abilities may suffer role overload. This can result in anxiety and high stress. Role underload, having too little to do or having insufficient challenge, may also be stressful.
- *Role ambiguities may create stress*. Not knowing what you are expected to do and/or not knowing the standards by which your work will be evaluated can be stressful. People with low tolerances for ambiguity are most prone to such reactions.
- *Role conflicts may create stress*. Feeling that you are unable to satisfy the multiple and potentially conflicting performance expectations of other people can create stress. Facing a situation where two or more people are expecting you to do different things at the same time is one example.
- *Interpersonal conflicts may create stress*. Conflicts caused by emotional antagonisms and personality conflicts can be very upsetting to the people involved. Negative side effects may even occur for other people who have to work with them.
- *Career developments may create stress*. Career progress that comes too fast can bring the pressures of having to work extra hard to perform up to expectations. Lack of progress can also be stressful for those who want to advance in their career but are blocked for some reason.
- *Physical aspects of the work environment may create stress*. People are sometimes bothered by noise, overcrowding, temperature, and air pollutants among other aspects of their environments. To the extent that the physical work setting contains such noxious elements, stress can be expected.

Nonwork Factors and Stress

Another important—but perhaps less obvious—source of stress for people at work is the "spill-over" of stress caused by factors in their nonwork lives. Such things as family events (e.g., birth of a new child), economic difficulties (e.g., sudden loss of a big investment), and personal affairs (e.g., facing a divorce) can add substantially to the overall stress experienced by a person. Since it is often difficult to completely separate one's work and nonwork lives, stress of this sort can affect the way people feel and behave on the job as well as away from it. The Social Readjustment Rating Scale presented in Table 17.5 is a popular way of measuring the amount of stress experienced by people from their basic life circumstances.

TABLE 17.5   The Social Readjustment Rating Scale

Life Event	Mean Value
1. Death of spouse	100
2. Divorce	73
3. Marital separation from mate	65
4. Detention in jail or other institution	63
5. Death of a close family member	63
6. Major personal injury or illness	53
7. Marriage	50
8. Being fired at work	47
9. Marital reconciliation with mate	45
10. Retirement from work	45
11. Major change in the health or behavior of a family member	44
12. Pregnancy	40
13. Sexual difficulties	39
14. Gaining a new family member	39
15. Major business readjustment	39
16. Major change in financial state	38
17. Death of a close friend	37
18. Changing to a different line of work	36
19. Major change in the number of arguments with spouse	35
20. Taking out a mortgage or loan for a major purchase	31
21. Foreclosure on a mortgage or loan	30
22. Major change in responsibilities at work	29
23. Son or daughter leaving home	29
24. In-law troubles	29
25. Outstanding personal achievement	28
26. Wife beginning or ceasing work outside the home	26
27. Beginning or ceasing formal schooling	26
28. Major change in living conditions	25
29. Revision of personal habits	24
30. Troubles with the boss	23
31. Major change in working hours or conditions	20
32. Change in residence	20
33. Changing to a new school	20
34. Major change in usual type and/or amount of recreation	19
35. Major change in church activities	19
36. Major change in social activities	18
37. Taking out a mortgage or loan for a lesser purchase	17
38. Major change in sleeping habits	16
39. Major change in number of family get-togethers	15
40. Major change in eating habits	15
41. Vacation	13
42. Christmas	12
43. Minor violations of the law	11

Source: T. H. Holmes, and R. H. Rahe, ''The Social Readjustment Rating Scale,'' *Journal of Psychosomatic Research,* Vol. 11 (1967). pp. 213–18. Reprinted with permission of Pergamon Press and Thomas H. Holmes, M.D. Copyright 1967, Pergamon Press, Ltd.

Complete the Social Readjustment Rating Scale for yourself or a person familiar to you. Circle the mean value for each event that has affected you or the other person. Total them to obtain a final stress score. Think seriously about how easily stress from general life events can build up, and how it may subsequently affect a person's attitudes and behavior at work.

Research with the Social Readjustment Rating Scale suggests that life event stress totals of 150 or less indicate generally good health, scores of 150 to 300 indicate a 35–50 percent probability of stress-related illness, and scores of 300+ indicate an 80 percent probability. An understanding of the potential impact of such ''life'' events on the individual's overall well-being can help to moderate and even control their harmful consequences.

Personal Factors and Stress

The final set of stressors includes personal factors such as individual needs, capabilities, and personality. These are properties of the individual that influence how one perceives and responds to stress emanating from work and nonwork sources. Stress can reach a destructive state more quickly, for example, when experienced by highly emotional people and those having low self-esteem. People who perceive a good fit between job requirements and personal skills have a higher tolerance for stress than those who feel less competent because of a person–job mismatch.[22]

Basic aspects of personality, as introduced in Chapter 3, also cause some people to experience more stress than others in similar situations. The Type A behavior pattern is a good example.

You should recall the **Type A personality** as one for which stressful behavior patterns like the following are commonplace.[23]

- Always moves, walks, and eats rapidly.
- Feels impatient with the pace of things, hurries others, dislikes waiting.
- Does several things at once.
- Feels guilty when relaxing.
- Tries to schedule more and more in less and less time.
- Uses nervous gestures such as clenched fist, banging hand on table.
- Does not have time to enjoy life.

The achievement orientation, impatience, and perfectionism of individuals with Type A personalities often creates stress in work circumstances that other persons find relatively stress-free. Type A's in this sense, bring stress on themselves.

There are some interesting issues regarding the relative advantages and disadvantages of Type A personalities in the workplace. On the one hand, the Type A personality may be beneficial for early and mid-career managerial success. That is, the characteristics and perhaps the performance edge gained by stress associated with Type A personalities may help people to advance through the ranks to the senior executive levels in organizations. When it comes to success at the top, however, the implications may change and Type A characteristics could lose their beneficial impact. Top managers with these personalities may lack the patience required to exhibit balanced reasoning, satisfy multiple or even conflicting performance demands, and deal with inevitable time delays. Their success, in turn may depend on being able to modify or at least control their Type A behavior to meet the different requirements of a chief executive role. The ability to manage stress is certainly critical to this flexibility. It is also essential to the maintenance of personal health and performance accomplishment at all steps in a managerial career.

EFFECTIVE STRESS MANAGEMENT

You can see that the role of stress in the work setting is complex. We know that constructive stress may facilitate individual task performance, but it is also true that destructive stress can reduce performance and even impair a person's health. Thus a good manager will find a healthy fit among the individual, the work environment, and the amount of job stress it involves. A *healthy fit* is one that stimulates productivity without damaging health. It is achieved through effective stress management, which includes the ability to (1) prevent stress, (2) cope with stress, and (3) maintain personal wellness.

Stress Prevention

It is always best to manage stress by preventing it from reaching excessive levels in the first place. Stressors emerging from personal and nonwork factors must be recognized so that action can be taken to prevent them from adversely affecting the work experience. Persons with Type A personalities, for example, may exercise self-discipline; managers of Type A employees may try to model a lower-key, more relaxed approach to work. At another level, family difficulties may be relieved by a change of work schedule, or the anxiety they cause may be reduced by knowing that one's supervisor understands. Work stressors such as role ambiguities, conflicts, and overloads can be prevented by good supervisor–subordinate communication, a willingness of subordinates to "speak up" when role dynamics are creating difficulties, and sensitivity by supervisors to behaviors or other symptoms indicating that subordinates are experiencing problems.

Stress Coping

We have already identified some of the symptoms indicating that excessive stress may already be affecting an individual at work. These include uncharacteristic irritability, nervousness or hostility, complaints of spontaneous illnesses, as well as any deviation from customary behavior patterns. When these symptoms are recognized, it is time to take action to maintain the desired healthy fit. Among the suggested guidelines individuals may follow to cope with stress by maximizing its benefits and minimizing its destructive effects are the following.[24]

1. *Control the situation.*   Avoid unrealistic deadlines. Do your best, but know your limits. You cannot be everything to everyone. Learn to identify and limit your exposure to stressors that trigger a strong stress response within you.

2. *Use time management techniques.*   Avoid the trap of trying to do too many things at once—and subsequently failing to accomplish much, if anything at all. Set realistic goals, and plan and manage your day in line with the time available. Effective supervisory behavior can be successful in preventing or, at least, minimizing these sources of stress. A good manager is supportive in setting a climate of trust and respect, but also provides goal clarification and adequate task directions to alleviate uncertainty and confusion in performance expectations.

3. *Pace yourself.*   Plan your day on a flexible basis. Do not try to do two or more things at the same time. Counter unproductive haste by forcing yourself to slow down. Think before reacting to negative situations or people. Live on a day-to-day basis instead of a minute-by-minute basis.

4. *Open up to others.*   Freely discuss your problems, fears, frustrations, and sources of uptightness with those who care about you. When in doubt, smile! A sincere smile can often defuse emotion and build a bridge of goodwill.

5. *Exercise and relax.*   Engage in regular noncompetitive physical activity such as jogging, swimming, riding a bike, or playing tennis, handball, or racquetball. (See your doctor when in doubt about your physical condition.) When feeling uptight, practice the ''relaxation response.'' Relax for a few minutes by following these simple steps: (a) sit comfortably with eyes closed in a quiet location, (b) slowly repeat a peaceful word or phrase over and over to yourself in your mind, (c) take complete but comfortable breaths, inhaling through the nose and exhaling through the mouth, and (d) avoid distracting thoughts by keeping a passive mental attitude.

Personal Wellness

Personal wellness is a term used to describe the pursuit of one's physical and mental potential through a personal health promotion program.[25] This concept recognizes individual responsibility to enhance and maintain wellness through a disciplined approach to physical and mental health. This requires attention to such things as smoking, weight, diet, alcohol use, and physical fitness. The essence of personal wellness is a life-style that reflects a true and comprehensive commitment to health.

Because stress has the potential to impact health, personal wellness makes a great deal of sense as a preventive stress management strategy. The manager who aggressively maintains his or her health should be better prepared to deal with the inevitable stressors that accompany the managerial role. This manager should also be able to take constructive advantage of stress that would otherwise take on destructive characteristics.

More generally, however, the managerial role also includes responsibility for the personal wellness of subordinates. A supervisor can impact personal wellness within the work unit through positive example, encouragement, and sensitivity and by practicing the basic concepts and techniques of human resource management presented throughout this book. When the manager is successful in creating a "healthy" work climate and environment, everyone should benefit from the increased capacity of people in this environment to handle successfully the change and stress that inevitably accompanies their lives at work.

SUMMARY

This chapter addressed the challenges of managing change and stress in organizations. The significance of these issues is high in a contemporary environment, characterized by many new trends and forces that impact people at work. Because both change and stress can facilitate creativity and innovation and thereby help organizations to adapt to changing environmental circumstances over time, good managers understand the two processes and know how to ensure that they operate to good advantage in the work setting.

Managers have the responsibility to act as change agents bringing about planned changes in their work settings. To be successful at change, managers must be aware of the unfreezing, changing, and refreezing phases of change as well as the force-coercion, empirical-rational, and normative-reeducative change strategies. Resistance frequently occurs during any change effort and should be carefully handled to minimize its disadvantages. The process of planned change is extended to the total system level in the form of organization development (OD), a comprehensive approach to implementing change and fostering organizational effectiveness. Based on action research foundations and drawing on a wide range of possible interventions, OD is a relatively new and promising application of behavioral science principles to management practice. Its basic goal is to help organizations keep pace with their environment and achieve productivity while maintaining high-quality work lives for their members.

Stress, the state of tension that accompanies exposure to extraordinary demands, constraints, and opportunities, is also commonplace in the managerial role and more generally among people at work. Managers must learn to tolerate frequently high levels of personal stress; they must also be capable of helping others to recognize and deal with stress that affects their work performance. Although stress can and does have a destructive side, even to the point of adversely affecting a person's health, it also has a positive and constructive side. The good manager is able to work well with stress and maintain its constructive potential at a healthy level in the work setting.

THINKING THROUGH THE ISSUES

1. Why is a manager a change agent? What can happen when a manager fails to fulfill this responsibility?

2. What are Lewin's three phases in the planned-change process? Give examples of what managers can do to accomplish each stage successfully.

3. Define the three basic change strategies and give examples of how a manager might use them in practice.

4. Describe how action research works as a foundation element in organization development (OD).

5. List and give examples of two OD interventions that address problems at each of the following levels of action: (1) individual, (2) group, (3) organization as a whole.

6. What is job stress and what are some of the potential stressors that may cause it to occur?

7. How can stress prove constructive for the individual? For the organization?

8. What can a manager do to cope successfully with the daily demands of high-pressure work responsibilities?

CASE: WARNER MANUFACTURING COMPANY

For the past year Pat Lee had been acquainted with Ron Carbone, Director of Human Resources for the Warner Manufacturing Company. Ron once attended a seminar on the management of planned change and organization development for which Pat served as the instructor. Since then he called several times seeking Pat's advice on some new training and development programs being developed for the company. Most recently, Ron asked Pat to conduct a six-day management training workshop for the top managment team and key middle managers of the company, a total of 14 persons.

The workshop was held a week ago. From all reports, it was well received by the participants. During the six sessions, Pat covered such topics as motivation, job design, group dynamics, perception, decision making, communication, conflict, leadership, and management by objectives. The last topic seemed to really turn the group on. Several persons spontaneously brought up their beliefs that the company suffered from a lack of clear-cut objectives. After some discussion, but without reaching any consensus on the issues, the group moved on to another workshop topic.

During the final session, Pat asked the participants to consider what follow-up activities, if any, were in order. They asked to meet once again in two weeks to review the workshop further with Pat and develop more specific ideas about future actions.

Yesterday Ron called and asked Pat to a meeting over lunch. At that time he expressed his concern that many of the persons attending the workshop felt the company's overall management practices could be changed for the better. However, he also indicated that an informal poll of the group showed that most of the dissatisfaction was felt by the middle managers. They felt, in turn, that nothing really constructive could happen until top management agreed with them that something must be done. "Finally," Ron said, "the problem is best summed up this way. The President (Marc Wilson) thinks the only problem facing the company is the inability of the Operations Vice President (Everett Morgan) to meet production schedules. Everett thinks the problem is Mark's lack of leadership. And, the Director of Finance (Alice Yates) doesn't seem to think there's any problem at all.''

The day-long evaluation session with the entire top and middle managment group is scheduled one week from now. Ron is looking toward you for suggesions on how to initiate a long-term planned change and organization development program for the company.

Questions

1. How do Lewin's three phases of planned change apply to this case? What are the implications for Pat Lee as a potential change agent?
2. To what extent is resistance to change an important issue for Pat to consider? What resistance might be expected for any comprehensive change effort and what might be done in advance to minimize this resistance?
3. How should Pat approach this situation in order to accomplish true organization development? Be specific and complete in addressing the full range of OD issues relevant to this situation.

EXERCISE: THE MANAGER AS CHANGE AGENT

Purpose:

To practice using alternative change strategies and to examine their respective advantages and disadvantages for the manager acting as a change agent.

Time:

50 to 75 minutes.

Procedure:

1. Form work groups as assigned by your instructor.
2. Each group will be assigned one of the following change strategies: A, B, or C.[27] Read and study your assigned strategy. Carefully discuss *how* to implement it in actual practice.

Change Strategy A.

As a change agent you believe that people are inherently rational and are guided by reason in their actions and decision making. Once a specific course of action is demonstrated to be in a person's self-interest, you assume that reason and rationality will cause the person to adopt it. Thus you approach change with the objective of communicating through information and facts the essential ''desirability'' of change from the perspective of the person whose behavior you seek to influence. If this logic is effectively communicated, you are sure that the person(s) will adopt the proposed change.

Change Strategy B.

As a change agent you believe that people who run things are basically motivated by self-interest and what situations offer in terms of potential personal gains or losses. Since you feel that people change only in response to such motives, you try to find out where their vested interests lie and then put the pressure on. If you have formal authority you use it; if not, you resort to whatever possible rewards and punishments you have access to and do not hesitate to threaten others with these weapons. Once you find a weakness, you exploit it and are always wise to work ''politically'' and by building supporting alliances wherever possible.

Change Strategy C.

As a change agent, you believe that people have complex motivations. You feel that people behave as they do as a result of sociocultural norms and commitments to these norms. You also recognize that changes in these orientations involve changes in attitudes, values, skills, and significant relationships, not just changes in knowledge, information, or intellectual rationales for action and practice. Thus when seeking to change others, you are sensitive to the suporting or inhibiting effects of any group pressures and norms that may be operating. In working with people, you try to find out their side of things and to identify their feelings and expectations.

3. Choose one group member to implement the assigned strategy in a role play with the instructor. Assume that the following situation exists.
   a. *You* as manager/change agent want your subordinates (each of whom supervises five workers) to begin a management by objectives (MBO) program in their respective work units.
   b. *Your instructor* as one of these supervisors has previously expressed to you some reluctance about starting an MBO program.
   c. *You* have called a meeting with the instructor/''supervisor'' in which you hope to get agreement to start the MBO program in motion right away.
4. Role plays of this situation will proceed at the instructor's direction.
5. During each role play, members of groups not participating in the role play should decide *what* change strategy is being attempted. Members of *all* groups should take notes on what happens and why.
6. At the conclusion of the role plays, the instructor will solicit feedback from the role players and other group members. Discussion on the change strategies and their respective advantages and disadvantages will follow.

THE MANAGER'S VOCABULARY

Action Research   The process of systematically collecting data on an organization, feeding it back for action planning, and evaluating results by collecting and reflecting on more data.

Change Agent   An individual or group that takes responsibility for changing the existing pattern of behavior of a person or social system.

Constructive Stress   Stress that acts in a positive way for the individual and/or the organization.

Destructive Stress   Stress that acts in a dysfunctional way for the individual and/or the organization.

Empirical-Rational Change Strategy   A strategy that attempts to bring about change through persuasion by special knowledge and rational argument.

Force-Coercion Change Strategy   A strategy that uses legitimacy, rewards, and punishments as primary inducements to change.

Normative-Reeducative Change Strategy   A strategy that attempts to bring about change by identifying or establishing values and assumptions such that support for the change naturally emerges.

Organization Development (OD)   The application of behavioral science knowledge in a long-range effort to improve an organization's ability to cope with change in its external environment and increase its internal problem-solving capabilities.

Organization Development (OD) Interventions   Activities initiated in support of an OD program and designed to improve the work effectiveness of individuals, groups, or the organization as a whole.

Performance Gap   A discrepancy between an actual and a desired state of affairs.

Planned Change   Change that happens as a result of specific efforts in its behalf by a change agent.

Stress   A state of tension experienced by individuals facing extraordinary demands, constraints, or opportunities.

Stressors   Things that cause stress (e.g., work, nonwork, and personal factors).

Type A Personality   A personality type characterized by impatience, perfectionism, and achievement orientation of the level sufficient to induce stressful behavior patterns.

Unplanned Change   Change that occurs at random or spontaneously, and without a change agent's direction.

IMPORTANT NAMES

Kurt Lewin   A social psychologist who identified unfreezing, changing, and refreezing as the three phases of planned change.

NOTES

[1]Developed from "Management Discovers the Human Side of Automation," *Business Week* (September 29, 1986), pp. 70–79.

[2]John Naisbitt, *Megatrends: Ten New Directions Transforming Our Lives* (New York: Warner, 1982). See also John Naisbitt and Patricia Aburdene, *Re-Inventing the Corporation* (New York: Warner Books, 1985).

[3]Developed from James Robins, "Firms Try Newer Approaches to Slash Absenteeism as Carrot and Stick Fail," *The Wall Street Journal,* March 14, 1979.

[4]See, for example, Ralph H. Kilmann, *Beyond the Quick Fix* (San Francisco: Jossey-Bass, 1984); and, Noel M. Tichy and Mary Anne Devanna, *The Transformational Leader* (New York: John Wiley, 1986).

[5]Robert A. Cooke, "Managing Change in Organizations," in Gerald Zaltman, ed., *Management Principles for Nonprofit Organizations* (New York: American Management Association, 1979). See also David A. Nadler, "The Effective Management of Organizational Change," pp. 358–369 in Jay W. Lorsch, editor, *Handbook of Organizational Behavior* (Englewood Cliffs, N.J.: Prentice-Hall, 1987).

[6]Reported in Anthony Jay, *Management and Machiavelli: An Inquiry into the Politics of Corporate Life* (New York: Holt, Rinehart and Winston, 1967), p. 96.

[7]Kurt Lewin, "Group Decision and Social Change," in G. E. Swanson, T. M. Newcomb, and E. L. Hartley, eds., *Readings in Social Psychology* (New York: Holt, Rinehart and Winston, 1952), pp. 459–473.

[8]Tichy and Devanna, op cit., p. 44.

[9]Robert Chin and Kenneth D. Benne, "General Strategies for Effecting Changes in Human Systems," in Warren G. Bennis, Kenneth D. Benne, Robert Chin, and Kenneth E. Corey, eds., *The Planning of Change,* 3rd

ed. (New York: Holt, Rinehart and Winston, 1969), pp. 22–45.

[10]Donald Klein, "Some Notes on the Dynamics of Resistance to Change: The Defender Role," in Bennis et al., eds., *The Planning of Change,* pp. 117–124.

[11]See Everett M. Rogers with F. Floyd Shoemaker, *Communication of Innovations,* 2nd ed. (New York: The Free Press, 1971).

[12]John P. Kotter and Leonard A. Schlesinger, "Choosing Strategies for Change," *Harvard Business Review,* Vol. 57 (March-April 1979), pp. 109–112.

[13]See Wendell L. French and Cecil H. Bell, Jr., *Organization Development,* 2nd ed. (Englewood Cliffs, N.J.: Prentice-Hall, 1978); Edgar F. Huse and Thomas G. Cummings, *Organization Development and Change,* 3rd ed. (St. Paul: West, 1985; and, W. Warner Burke, *Organization Development* (Reading, Ma.: Addison-Wesley, 1987).

[14]Huse and Cummings, op cit., p. 6. Copyright © 1985, West Publishing Company. All rights reserved.

[15]Warren Bennis, "Using Our Knowledge of Organizational Behavior," pp. 29–49 in Lorsch, op cit.

[16]Edgar F. Huse and Thomas G. Cummings, *Organization Development and Change,* 2nd ed. (St. Paul: West, 1980), pp. 8–9.

[17]Portions of this treatment of stress developed from John R. Schermerhorn, Jr., *Management for Productivity,* 2nd ed. (New York: John Wiley, 1986), pp. 635–641. See also Robert I. Sutton and Robert L. Kahn, "Prediction, Understanding, and Control as Antidotes to Organizational Stress," pp. 272–285 in Lorsch, op cit.

[18]From Arthur P. Brief, Randall S. Schuler, and Mary Van Sell, *Managing Job Stress,* pp. 6–7. Copyright © 1981 by Arthur P. Brief, Randall S. Schuler, and Mary Van Sell. Reprinted by permission of Little Brown and Company.

[19]Meyer Friedman and Ray Roseman, *Type A Behavior and Your Heart* (New York: Alfred A. Knopf, 1974).

[20]See John D. Adams, "Health, Stress, and the Manager's Life Style," *Group and Organization Studies,* Vol. 6 (September 1981), pp. 291–301.

[21]See John M. Ivancevich and Michael T. Matteson, "Optimizing Human Resources: A Case for Preventive Health and Stress Management," *Organizational Dynamics,* Vol. 9 (Autumn 1980), pp. 6–8.

[22]See Orlando Behling and Arthur L. Darrow, *Managing Work-Related Stress* (Chicago: Science Research Associates, 1984), pp. 14–16.

[23]Friedman and Roseman, *Type A Behavior and Your Heart.*

[24]Adapted from Robert Kreitner, "Personal Wellness: It's Just Good Business," *Business Horizons,* Vol. 25 (May–June 1982), pp. 28–35. Copyright 1982 by the Foundation for the School of Business at Indiana University. Reprinted by permission. See also Behling and Darrow, *Managing Work-Related Stress,* pp. 27–31.

[25]Kreitner, "Personal Wellness: It's Just Good Business."

[26]This is for a new case.

[27]The change strategies are developed from an exercise reported in J. William Pfeiffer and John E. Jones, *A Handbook of Structured Experiences for Human Relations Training,* Vol. II (La Jolla, Calif.: University Associates, 1973).

CHAPTER 18
MANAGERIAL FUTURES, OB, AND YOU

The qualities we encourage—ingenuity—dedication—a willingness, even eagerness, to chance risk.

H. J. Heinz Company Annual Report

HOW MANAGERS WILL MANAGE
IN THE 1990S

If present trends continue, forces such as the following will change the nature of managerial work in the 1990s and beyond.[1]

- *Pressures of increased competition* are causing many organizations to be "downsized" in the quest for greater productivity. Whole layers of the managerial pyramid are being removed; organizations cannot afford to employ people to crunch numbers and shuffle papers alone.

- *Advances in computer and communications technologies* are having similar effects. Machines can now do many traditional chores more cheaply than people; middle managers devoted to filling out forms, writing reports, and performing other information filtering functions just won't be needed.

- *Rapid growth of the service sector* is attracting a growing share of the managerial talents. More managers are working for small- to medium-sized service firms; the Bureau of Labor Statistics estimates that 74.3 percent of U.S. jobs will be in the services by 1995, and it may reach 88 percent by the year 2000. About one-sixth of the new jobs will be for managers.

The 1990s will be the decade of the "value added" manager—someone whose efforts tangibly improve an organization's products and bottom-line performance. Value added managers will find their jobs riskier and more demanding, but also rewarding. One such manager is Kate McDonough who gave up a job with a large bank for one at a small public relations firm. She sums it up this way: "I can take more risks. Boredom is way down. I'm making a contribution to the bottom line, and if I don't, there's no place to hide."

The 1990s will also see more emphasis by major employers on cultivating their managerial talent. GE and IBM are two firms noted for their success in developing outstanding managers. Don Laidlaw, IBM's Director of Executive Resources, says: ". . . having the right people at the right place at the right time, properly prepared . . . doesn't happen by chance." The strategies used by these and other progressive companies for meeting this challenge include

- identifying "high potential" people as early in their careers as possible—ideally within the first ten years.
- closely integrating job assignments with continuing education.
- filling many of the top jobs from within.

Management Applications Questions

The managers of tomorrow must be prepared to face new problems and opportunities. What lies ahead in your managerial career? How can a knowledge of OB help you achieve *both* performance success *and* personal satisfaction?

PLANNING AHEAD

The reading and learning activities provided in this final chapter will help you to review the field of OB and integrate your thinking around the following topics

The Manager's Changing World
Career Planning and Development
Managing Organizational Behavior: A Recap

OB is a knowledge base used by managers to effectively utilize individuals and groups as the human resources of organizations. When this goal is achieved, the manager can feel satisfied with a job well done. We think the many previous topics and learning experiences offered in this book will help you to become a fine manager. Now it is time to pull things together and point you in the direction of this exciting future!

THE MANAGER'S CHANGING WORLD

The following words from Charles Dickens's great novel *A Tale of Two Cities* will be remembered forever among the classics of western literature. His words describe the world of 1775.[2]

It was the best of times, it was the worst of times, it was the age of wisdom, it was the age of foolishness, it was the epoch of belief, it was the epoch of incredulity, it was the season of Light, it was the season of Darkness, it was the spring of hope, it was the winter of despair, we had everything before us, we had nothing before us.

Robert Fulmer, a noted management theorist, points out that Dickens's words may apply equally well today.[3]

Dickens saw the marked contrasts that surrounded the early days of the Industrial Revolution. Today, as we near the end of the Industrial Revolution, we find our world marked by contrasts equally as dramatic. An analysis of the probabilities associated with this decade reveals that it is indeed both the best of times and the worst of times.

While it may be easy to agree with Fulmer's statement, it is harder to guarantee just what the 1990s and the years beyond will offer to managers of the future. Still, those who think seriously about the future find themselves in general agreement on a number of trends, particularly those in the environment, people, and technology.

Trends in the Environment

The general environment was defined in Chapter 11 as a set of background educational–political–economic–cultural forces with the potential to influence organizations and their members. Even though we have explored throughout this book many environmental factors of major significance to managers, the modern manager must be prepared to master the challenges of tomorrow as well as those of today. John Naisbitt used the title *Megatrends* for his popular book dealing with the major changes in contemporary society,[4] and *future shock* is a phrase popularly used to describe the discomfort that comes about in times of rapid and uncertain change. Yet we do and will continue to live in a world well characterized as one of constant "change." This is a world in which "future shock" is more the rule than the exception.

A manager's responsibility, accordingly, extends into the willingness and ability to anticipate and deal with changing environmental circumstances over time. As you consider the environment of the future, it can help to identify at least six emerging challenges that will likely characterize the world of work well into the 1990s and even beyond.

The Internationalization of Management

No one can doubt that we live in an international environment in which the countries and economies of the world are increasingly interdependent. At the very least, hardly one of us can go a day without using, buying, or admiring a consumer product imported from another country. Then, too, not many nights pass without some international event, or crisis, being highlighted on the evening television news. What may not be quite as apparent, however, is the growing importance of direct foreign investment in the U.S. economy. For example, more Americans than ever before are working for "foreign" employers in their local communities. In an article entitled "Where the Jobs Are," *Newsweek* estimated that nearly 250,000 were employed by Japanese firms alone in 1986.[5] The number continues to grow as the influence of business firms from Canada, Europe, and Asia in particular continues to proliferate.

Into this truly international world steps the modern manager, and into the practice of management steps a growing recognition that managers around the world can learn from one another. The most visible case in point is still continuing interest in Japanese management practices, largely prompted in the early 1980s by two popular books—*Theory Z: How American Business Can Meet the Japanese Challenge* by William Ouchi, and *The Art of Japanese Management: Applications for American Executives* by Richard Tanner Pascale and Anthony G. Athos. But as examples used in this book from other countries like Korea, Switzerland, and Sweden have shown, good management and good ideas about managing are not confined to one or two countries alone. We all have things to share and learn from one another. So while researchers continue to analyze and compare management practices throughout the world, we can and should use the emerging insights to help develop critical thinking about how we do things, and to consider whether or not we could be doing them better.[6]

A Changing Job Mix in the Economy

Forecasts of where jobs will be in 1990 generally anticipate that plenty will be available, but as noted in the chapter opener they will be distributed differently. Many of these new jobs will go to persons in the service industries and high-technology areas building on developments in computers and electronic information processing. Among the 14.5 million new jobs expected in the service sector of the U.S. economy by 1990, for example, about one-sixth will be managerial positions. The fastest growing areas will include *business services* (e.g., management consulting, public relations, advertising, and lobbying), *professional services* (e.g., law, accounting, and engineering), *specialized services* (e.g., maintenance and repair of computers, copiers, and communications equipment), and *financial services* (e.g., banking, insurance, and brokerage).[7]

There are other forces besides ''service'' and ''high tech'' at work in the economy. *Big* business has been steadily losing jobs since the early 1970s. Job creation, present and future, thus includes *small-* and *medium-sized* businesses that stress entrepreneurship and innovation. The manager of tomorrow may be asked to work and perform in such industries where personal creativity and ''small'' organizational size are the norms. Interestingly, too, a major source of new jobs may rest largely on ''low-tech'' or ''no-tech'' foundations like restaurant chains and recreation.

Times of Economic Decline as Well as Growth

Beginning with the oil embargo and energy crisis of early 1970s, the world economy suffered a force very powerful and for many of us very new in its demands on organizations and their members—the reality of economic decline as opposed to growth. Up until this point in time management researchers, in particular, had let the phenomenon of growth predominate in capturing their attention. Now, however, changing times have brought appropriate attention to organizational decline as well as growth.[8]

The emphasis on ''downsizing,'' ''restructuring,'' and ''demassing''—all which became business buzzwords in the late 1980s—is sure to be with us for some time. And even though we do not offer the prospects of organizational retrenchment and decline as undeniable facts of a future manager's life, we can and do support the view that tomorrow's managers must be prepared to succeed in both the peaks and valleys of changing economic times. Among the special challenges in managing decline are the increased stress and increased conflict within and between organizations and their subunits that accompany decline. Significant, too, are the associated demands for increased adaptation and change, including the need for work-force adjustments and alternative organizational structures.

No longer can the scholar or manager be content to view the management of growth as a predominant concern. Learning to live with, cope with, and manage in situations of decline are now equally significant sources of challenge and concern. Perhaps the world of decline may even test the manager to the ultimate as a sponsor of ''productivity'' in the broadest use of the term.

Renewed Focus on Productivity as a Criterion of Work Accomplishment

''Productivity'' has reemerged in the vocabulary of management as the watchword of the 1980s and 1990s. This focus on productivity as a criterion of work accomplishment is not only appropriate, it is sure to be an anchor point for management long into the future. Figure 18.1 illustrates the positive balance between performance effectiveness, a measure of goal attainment, and performance efficiency, a measure of resource utilization, that high productivity requires.

Productivity is a summary measure of the quantity *and* quality of work performance with resource utilization considered. In the context of OB, productivity reflects a broad performance criterion that includes a measure of success or failure in the use of resources. In today's and tomorrow's economy, it is no longer sufficient to be effective in getting the job done (i.e., in accomplishing the task). It is necessary to do so efficiently in the use of resources, both material and human, as well.

The chapter opener highlights the **value-added manager** as one whose efforts tangibly improve an organization's products or services, *and* bottom-line performance results. As the example indicates, a major part of the modern manager's job is being defined to include specific responsibilities for establishing and maintaining the conditions necessary to ensure workplace productivity. High productivity, in turn, de-

FIGURE 18.1   Productivity and the relationship between performance effectiveness and performance efficiency.

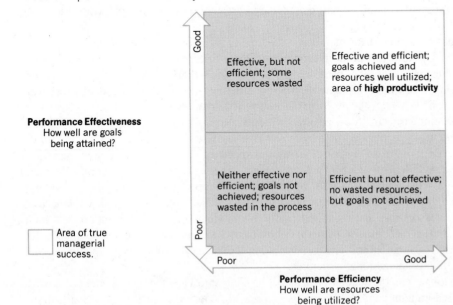

pends on achieving a total performance system in which individuals, groups, and the entire complex organizational system function well together. This is the criterion of success that society now demands of its organizations. This is the ultimate test of managerial competence that you will be called on to master.

Growing Complexity in the Ethical and Legal Environment of Work

Managerial ethics are standards and principles that guide the actions and decisions of managers and determine if they are "good or bad" or "right or wrong" in a moral sense. Ethical managerial behavior, accordingly, conforms not only to the mere dictates of law, but also to a broader moral code common to society as a whole. In today's complex and international world, managerial ethics are increasingly challenged to enhance and guarantee the desired social impact of organizations.

The modern manager is increasingly held up to public and even judicial scrutiny for his or her actions at work. These are times when the power of corporations to impact our physical well-being through pollution and poor safety practices is well known. These are times, too, when society is intolerant of unethical and/or illegal acts committed in the interest of personal or organizational gain, or both. Sensational recent examples include the insider-trading scandals of the U.S. securities industry; alleged illegal stock manipulation by top executives of Guinness, the large British brewer and distiller; and the "Iranscam," whose intricacies included the illegal diversion of U.S. government funds.

The legal environment of work is growing increasingly complex in this same context. **Corporate social responsibility,** defined as an obligation to perform in ways that serve both organizational and public interests, is a fact of managerial life more than ever before. A socially responsible organization delivers safe and reasonable products and/or services to its customers; a socially responsible organization fulfills its obligations, moral and legal, to its employees in a positive and complete way. What this means to the individual manager translates into a commitment to act in ethical ways that support both the quest for productivity and the burden of social responsibility. Among the social issues of substantial recent concern is drug abuse, both on and off the job. Newline 18.1 summarizes some of the controversy surrounding the issue—one that will surely remain important for quite some time to come.

Increased Emphasis on the Quality of Working Life

The surging focus on productivity highlights the role of human resource utilization in the performance process. Ideally, productivity is achieved along with a sense of personal satisfaction by the people doing the work. Both high performance *and* high satisfaction should result from a manager's efforts to work with individuals and groups in organizations to achieve productivity.

Quality of working life, or QWL for short, is a term that has gained deserving prominence as an indicator of the overall quality of human experiences in the workplace. It expresses a special way of thinking about people, their work, and the organizations in which it is accomplished. Indeed, QWL activities apply the various concepts and theories of OB with the following distinctive emphases:[9]

NEWLINE 18.1 / DRUG TESTING IN THE WORKPLACE

Consultant's estimate that 35–40 percent of Fortune 500 firms are testing job applicants or current employees for drugs, many in combination with company sponsored education and rehabilitation programs. But whose rights take precedence—the employer's or the employee's? This explosive question summarizes growing debate over corporate responses to a growing problem—drug and substance abuse by people at work.

On the employer's side of the issue stands the high cost and risk of inferior products and/or services being created by people whose capabilities are impaired. An executive of a major investment bank that implemented drug testing says: "Our program isn't designed to get rid of people. What we want to do is influence them toward working in our way, which is drug free. We can't afford to risk whatever results from [even] casual use . . . security in an industry dealing with billions of dollars demands that."

On the employee's side of the issue stands the view that such measures are unnecessary and even unconstitutional invasions of individual privacy. "For us it just doesn't make good business sense to police our employees' private lives," says the vice president of a small instrumentation firm. He continues, "We've considered testing and totally rejected it. One reason is the accuracy problem. Our only concern is job performance. But drug testing isn't a job performance test."

Reported in *The Wall Street Journal*.

- *Participative problem solving*. Getting people at all levels of responsibility involved in decision making, such as is found in quality circles and employee group meetings.
- *Work restructuring*. Rearranging the jobs people do and the work systems and structures surrounding them, such as is found in job enrichment and autonomous work groups.
- *Innovative reward systems*. Creating new ways of making rewards available for contributed work performance, such as is found in the Scanlon Plan and skills-based pay.
- *Improved work environments*. Making the work setting more pleasant and responsive to individual needs, such as in alternative work schedules and better physical conditions.

Just as machines that are poorly maintained break down and eventually wear out altogether, so too do the human resources suffer from neglect and adverse working conditions. Over the long term, the human resources of organizations must be well maintained if their continued performance contributions are to be ensured. Managers are increasingly expected, and rightfully so, to facilitate productivity for the organization while maintaining the quality of working life for its members. Literally, this entire book deals with QWL issues. It is written in the expectation that managers of the future will face increasing pressures to help others achieve and maintain a high quality of life at work. You, for example, must understand and accept the fact that those persons you may someday supervise will expect to live and work in conditions that protect, foster, and respect the dignity of the human being. This includes expanded opportunities for participation in the workplace and protection of rights, as well as freedom from physical or mental harm at work or from the by-products of work (e.g., industrial waste).

Manager of the future will have to address and respect people as the human resources of organizations in the social and legal context of a mature society. The successful and respected managers will be the ones best able to cope with and find opportunity in pressures such as those just reviewed. The successful and respected organizations will reflect the accomplishments of their managerial staffs.

Trends in People

Trends in the general environment can be associated with more specific and complementary trends among people in the work force. Given the challenges pointed out in the preceding discussion, it is clear that managers of the future will have to deal with new demands and concerns in their human resource management activities.

To begin with, labor force demographics are changing. Current estimates reveal that nine out of every 10 new jobs created in the U.S. economy during the 1990s will be filled by women, minorities, and immigrants. Hispanic women, mostly Mexican, are already one of the fastest growing groups in the American labor force. By 1995, roughly one out of every five teenagers seeking work will be from a minority.[10] There is also a growing emphasis on "part-time" employment. For example, a *Wall Street Journal* survey of some 60,000 households reports that "moonlighting" (i.e., working more than one job) is on the increase.[11] The same survey indicates that many people would like to work more hours to earn more money. Then, too, we note that work and leisure are both important to most people, even though the "get ahead" ambitions of younger workers in particular sometimes make it difficult for them to balance work and family.

These and related trends create new pressures for change in the traditional relationships between supervisors and their subordinates. Managers in the future must be increasingly well prepared to deal with:[12]

1. *Pressures for self-determination.* People will seek greater freedom to determine *how* to do their jobs and *when* to do them. Pressures for increased worker participation in the forms of job enrichment, autonomous work groups, flexible working hours, and compressed workweeks will grow.
2. *Pressures for employee rights.* People will expect their rights to be respected on the job as well as outside of work. These include the rights of individual privacy, due process, free speech, free consent, freedom of conscience, and freedom from sexual harassment.

3. *Pressures for equal employment opportunity.*   People will expect and increasingly demand the right to employment without discrimination on the basis of age, sex, ethnic background, or handicap. Among these demands will remain a concern for furthering the modest but dramatic gains made in recent years by women in the workplace. "Progress" will be recognized but not accepted in replacement for true "equality." As survey reports continue to come in the facts remain.[13]
   - Most women work in predominately female occupations.
   - Women's average wages are less than men's.
   - Men working in female-dominated fields average higher earnings than women.
   - Female managers average up to 50 percent less salary than their male counterparts.

4. *Pressures for equity of earnings.*   People will expect to be compensated for the "comparable worth" of their work contributions. What began as a concern for earnings differentials between women and men doing the same jobs will be extended to cross-occupational comparisons. Questions such as why a nurse receives less pay than a carpenter and why a maintenance worker is paid more than a secretary will be asked with increasing frequency. They will require answers other than the fact that certain occupations (such as nursing) have traditionally been dominated by women, whereas others (such as carpentry) have been dominated by men.

5. *Pressures for security.*   People will expect their security to be protected. This includes their physical well-being in terms of occupational safety and health matters, and their economic livelihood in terms of guaranteed protection against layoffs and provisions for cost-of-living wage increases.

Trends in Technology

Another undeniable aspect of our work environment is the emergence of high technology as a dominant force in our lives. "With computers and high technology," as the saying goes, "work won't be the same again!" This theme has emerged several times throughout this book. Without doubt, the greatest technological pressures of the present decade are the computer, electronic information processing, and the robot. Each, in its own way, has the capability to transform work of the future radically.

Even today we live in a time when *expert systems* are increasingly using techniques of artificial intelligence to facilitate complex diagnosis and decision making for businesses; we live in a time when organizations are creating new top management jobs for a position called "chief information officer"; and, we live in a time when managerial work stations are being constructed around one or more personal computers to serve a variety of functions. At a minimum, the modern manager has access through desk-top computing to[14]

- Spreadsheet programs for analyzing relationships among multiple variables.

- Wordprocessing programs for preparing, rewriting, and printing letters, memos, and reports.
- Database management programs for filing and organizing data for quick recall and repetitive uses.
- Graphics programs for creating and printing graphs, tables, and charts for reports and presentations.
- Electronic mail programs allowing messages to be sent and received between computers.
- Networking programs which allow data and programs to be shared among computers.

As the technology continues to develop and as the pace of changes in the nature of work itself quickens, the results will be revolutionary indeed. Managers of the future must be prepared to utilize and adapt successfully to the opportunities made available by continuing advances in computer, robot, and electronic information processing technologies. This challenge includes helping with the adjustment of employees who must work at the interface with these complex machines.

CAREER PLANNING AND DEVELOPMENT

The phrase that seems most appropriate to summarize the prior discussion of the manager's world of the future is an "age of transition." And, although no one can say for sure what will lie ahead, we have been able to identify a number of emerging trends in the environment, people, and technology that should be carefully considered for their managerial implications. Among these implications, a most important and relevant one relates to your personal career planning and development.

A **career** is a sequence of jobs and work pursuits constituting what a person does for a living. For many of us, a career begins on an anticipatory basis with our formal education. From there it progresses into an initial job choice and any number of subsequent choices that may involve changes in task assignments, employing organizations, and even occupations. A **career path** is a sequence of jobs held over time during a career. Career paths vary between those that are pursued internally within the same organization and those that involve changes among employing organizations over time. In today's day and age, with all the corporate restructuring that is taking place, the number of "one-company executives" is on the decline. The likelihood is that most managers will hold jobs with more than one company during their careers. Yet, many organizations encourage internal career paths by making long-term career opportunities available to their employees. The chapter opening example indicates that internal career paths are still significant as a source of top management talent in large corporations such as GE and IBM.

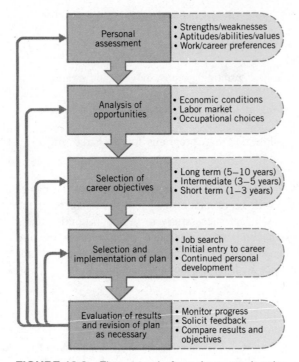

FIGURE 18.2   Five steps in formal career planning.

Career Planning

Careers and career paths inevitably mix together the needs of people and organizations. One noted theorist and consultant states,

> Organizations are dependent on the performance of their people, and people are dependent on organizations to provide jobs and career opportunities. . . . The problem for society, for organizations, and for people is how to match their respective needs, not only at the point of entry into the organization, but also throughout the career or life history of the person in the organization.[15]

A person's career is an important component of their total life experience. The following quotes from a study about people and their careers should cause you to think about your career, as well as the careers of those persons who will some day become your subordinates.[16]

> ''Years ago I made a bad mistake, and now I'm paying for it; I'm trapped in this job.''

"I should have found out how this firm was run before taking their offer. I had other good prospects at the time."

"They led me down the garden path, and I was damn fool enough to be taken in."

Such pessimistic statements suggest that everyone should think seriously about their careers, and think ahead!

Figure 18.2 summarizes a basic framework for formal career planning. It has a lot in common with the process of decision making covered in Chapter 13. The five steps in the framework begin with personal assessment and then progress through analysis of opportunities, selection of career objectives, and implementation of strategies, until the point of evaluation of results is reached. Then the process is recycled as necessary to allow constructive revision of the career plan over time. Success in each of these steps entails a good deal of self-awareness and frank assessment. The message is clear—a successful career begins with sufficient insight to make good decisions about matching personal needs and capabilities with job opportunities over time.

The manager's responsibility in respect to career planning is two-fold. It includes both the responsibility to plan and manage a personal career and the responsibility to assist in the career planning and development of subordinates. Some ideas on meeting each set of responsibilities follow.[17]

1. *To take charge of his or her personal career, a manager should*
   - Establish a personal career plan; be willing to modify this plan as opportunities develop.
   - Take and maintain a personal skills inventory; try to match job responsibilities and skills.
   - Set specific personal development objectives.
   - Maintain a career-oriented dialogue with higher-level managers.
   - Take advantage of all training and development opportunities.
   - Evaluate and constructively modify personal development efforts over time.
2. *To assist in the career planning and development of subordinates, a manager should*
   - Establish a human resource plan for the work unit.
   - Take and maintain a human resource inventory for the work unit.
   - Establish human resource development objectives for the work unit.
   - Maintain a career-oriented dialogue with subordinates.
   - Encourage and support subordinates' participation in training and development activities.
   - Evaluate and constructively modify all efforts to meet the development needs of subordinates over time.

Many things will command your attention over time as you grapple with the problems and prospects of a managerial career. Three issues of special interest are initial entry, adult transitions, and dual-career families.

Initial Entry to a Career

Choosing a job and a work organization are difficult decisions to make. They inevitably exert a lot of influence over our lives. Whenever a job change is contemplated, the best advice is to know yourself and learn as much about the new job and new organization as you can. This helps to ensure the best person–job–organization match. It is the point where one begins to form the important psychological contract that we first discussed in Chapter 3. By working hard to examine personal needs, goals, and capabilities, gather relevant information, share viewpoints, and otherwise make the recruitment process as *realistic* as possible, you can help get a new job started on the best possible note.

Table 18.1 is a sample checklist of things to be considered when contemplating a possible job change. Giving such careful and thoughtful attention to the critical joining-up decision can help in the successful implementation of a career plan.

Adult Life Cycles

As people mature, they pass through adult life stages that present somewhat different problems and prospects. It is helpful for you to recognize these transitions and to prepare to face them in the course of your managerial career. It is also useful to recognize the effects of these transitions on other people with whom you work. Understanding their special problems and pressures can help you to work with them better in a leadership capacity.

TABLE 18.1 Sample Items for a "New Job" Balance Sheet	Gain?	Loss?
What are the tangible gains and losses for *myself?*		
• salary and fringe benefits	————	————
• work hours and schedules	————	————
• use of skills and competencies	————	————
• development of skills and competencies	————	————
• status inside the organization	————	————
• status outside the organization	————	————
• out-of-town travel requirements	————	————
• chances for further advancement	————	————
What are the tangible gains and losses for *others* who are important to me?		
• income available for family needs	————	————
• time available for family/friends	————	————
• spill-over effects of my work stress	————	————
• pride in my accomplishments	————	————
• personal development opportunities	————	————
• leisure time activities	————	————
• overall life styles	————	————

Daniel Levinson's ideas about personality development as a series of life stages were introduced in Chapter 3. You should recall his basic point that life unfolds with a number of key transitions or stages having quite different implications for work and personal aspects of one's life.[18] Three transitions relevant to our present interest in careers are: early adulthood, mid-life, and later adulthood. Each transition involves special challenges as described in the following list.

The move to early adulthood	This is a period of completing one's education, entering an occupation, and becoming married. Parenthood follows, with new family and job responsibilities. It is a time of vitality, self-determination, and perhaps one or more job changes.
Mid-life transition	In the late thirties and early forties, the career is all important. Family complications stress this orientation, and personal crisis can occur. Some frustrations in the career may occur and bring with them added questions of confidence, goals, and identity. For the first time health and age become relevant concerns.
The move to later adulthood	Settling in begins here, with a knowledge of the ''system'' and a mellowing of goals. Concerns turn toward making a real impact at work, being a mentor to others, and balancing goals and reality. This is a time of consolidating personal affairs and accepting career limitations. The next step is retirement and, perhaps, a new career.

OB research reflects growing interest in the area of adult development as it relates to occupational experiences. One survey of over 600 executives who had changed jobs found that the decision criteria used in making the job changes varied in importance depending on the life stage of the individual making the decision.[19] Criteria such as opportunity for greater responsibility, experience for future assignments, and increased promotion potential were at their peak in the ''settling down'' period (ages 35 to 39); criteria of geographic location, state and local tax structures, and cost of living peaked with the ''mid-life transition'' and ''entry to middle adulthood.'' Such research highlights the requirement for any career or human resource planning system to match successfully the needs of the organization with those of the individual. As Table 18.2 shows, this responsibility must include an awareness that both task and socioemotional needs tend to vary across adult life stages.

Dual-Career Couples

One clear trend in the U.S. workforce is the growing proportion of **dual-career couples,** that is families in which both adult partners are part of the workforce.[20] By

TABLE 18.2 Developmental Needs in Early, Middle, and Late Career

Stage	Task Needs	Socioemotional Needs
Early career	1. Develop action skills. 2. Develop a specialty. 3. Develop creativity, innovation. 4. Rotate into new area after 3–5 years.	1. Support. 2. Autonomy. 3. Deal with feelings of rivalry, competition.
Middle career	1. Develop skills in training and coaching others (younger employees). 2. Training for updating and integrating skills. 3. Develop broader views of work and organization. 4. Job rotation into new job requiring new skills.	1. Opportunity to express feelings about mid-life (anguish, defeat, limited time, restlessness). 2. Reorganize thinking about self (mortality, values, family, work). 3. Reduced self-indulgence and competitiveness. 4. Support and mutual problem-solving for coping with mid-career stress.
Late career	1. Shift from power role to one of consultation, guidance, wisdom. 2. Begin to establish self in activities outside the organization (start on part-time basis).	1. Support and counseling to help see integrated life experiences as a platform for others. 2. Acceptance of one's one and only life cycle. 3. Gradual detachment from organization.

Source: Careers in Organizations by Douglas T. Hall (p. 90). Copyright © 1976 by Goodyear Publishing Co., Inc. Reprinted by permission.

1986 the Labor Department was reporting that 46 percent of all couples fell into this category; only 23 percent of American families had an adult male as the sole wage earner. This is an important issue for employees and employers alike, since both partners in these dual-career couples typically want rewarding careers—and family satisfactions. Balancing these often conflicting demands is not always easy. Separate surveys by *The Wall Street Journal* and *Fortune* revealed the following:[21]

- One of every 10 executive's spouses was employed full-time outside the home.
- Among them, 18 percent reported the wife or husband turned down a promotion or job offer within the past two years—most often due to possible conflicts with the other spouse's career.
- About 42 percent of those who experienced such conflicts said the career with the highest compensation and/or greatest long-term potential received priority.
- Fathers are as likely as mothers to admit that their jobs interfere with family life.
- About 25 percent of men and women had sought less demanding jobs in order to spend more time with their families.
- Almost 40 percent of men and 60 percent of women had missed at least one workday in the last three months due to family needs.

NEWSLINE 18.2 /
A SAMPLER OF HOW SOME ORGANIZATIONS ARE TRYING TO HELP

More and more companies are offering special employee benefits aimed at easing the stress felt by women workers and dual-career couples who combine full-time jobs with family responsibilities. A sample includes

Campbell Soup Company. Converted part of a warehouse into a day care center. It pays 60 percent of the operations cost and employees pay the rest.

IBM. Gives 30 minutes leeway at either end of the work day. Offers a spouse assistance program, which helps pay the cost of job placement, resumes, and counseling for spouses of transfered employees.

Mellon Bank. Gives more opportunities for flexible hours and work at home as well as job sharing—in one case two women split their work week and $30,000 a year pay as analysts.

Mutual Life Insurance Co. of New York. Allows parents to work some time at home in a "variable work site" program. Offers a flexible work hours program.

Procter and Gamble. Lets workers buy more vacation time or put money away for child care in a flexible benefits program.

Zayre Corporation. Gives child care reimbursements of up to $20 per week to headquarters employees with pre-schoolers.

Reported in *Business Week* and *Fortune*.

A dual-career issue of considerable recent visibility relates to child care. Newsline 18.2 indicates how some organizations are trying to help their employees manage families as well as jobs. Employers are realizing that the growing proportions of women employees and dual-career couples require new management responses in order to maintain morale and productivity. Programs such as those depicted in the newsline are initial steps in a direction that should gain further momentum over time.

Another important dual-career issue is the "trailing spouse" problem, or need to find employment for the partner of a person being newly recruited or asked to transfer to a new location. Without extra assistance for the trailing spouse, such as described for IBM in the newsline, many people are unwilling to commit to new opportunities that may result in a career sacrifice for their partners. It is further significant that the trailing spouse is often the woman. Wives still tend to relocate for the benefit of their husbands' careers, and one reason is that the couple follows the route of higher compensation. Even though women have made recent strides in gaining equal employment and career opportunity, we have already pointed out that the pay of women managers still generally lags behind that of their male counterparts.

Chances are that these and other dual-career problems and opportunities may come your way someday. They add additional complexity to career planning and development in the contemporary environment.

MANAGING ORGANIZATIONAL BEHAVIOR: A RECAP

Throughout this book we have been talking about managers, people to whom one or more other persons report in organizations. We have highlighted the importance of managers being able to work with subordinates, individually and in groups, to encourage high levels of task performance and provide for human resource maintenance. **Organizational behavior,** defined as the study of individuals and groups in organizations, is a body of knowledge that can help informed managers achieve success within this action framework.

The preceding sections of this chapter focused your thinking on the problems and opportunities of succeeding as a manager in the dynamic and complex environment of today—and tomorrow! It is hoped that our discussion of this contemporary milieu further sensitized you to the need to develop and maintain a full range of managerial competencies. As one resource available to help you in this quest, *Managing Organizational Behavior* can now be recapped in a summary perspective. Before we begin, though, think once again about the situation depicted in Figure 18.3. Serious attention to your course, this book, and the entire field of OB, can help you master this ''manager's challenge'' in whatever occupational specialization you may choose and in any organizational setting in which you may work—large or small, public or private.

FIGURE 18.3   Every manager's basic challenge.

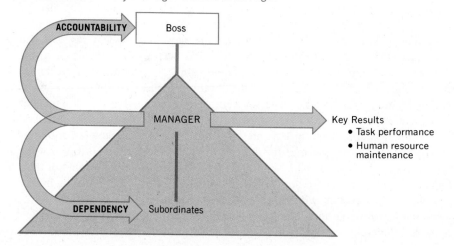

Managerial Responsibilities

At the beginning of this book, we identified the manager's responsibility to fulfill the functions of planning, organizing, leading, and controlling. These functions, in turn, were associated with a number of specific managerial roles and the need for a variety of managerial skills. We hope you feel increasingly confident about your abilities to perform effectively in these capacities. Table 18.3 offers a further reminder on the personal foundations for success in managing human behavior in organizations.

OB: The Manager's Knowledge Base

Throughout this book we have argued that

$$\text{OB is a knowledge base} \xrightarrow[\text{by}]{\text{used}} \text{managers} \xrightarrow[\text{achieve}]{\text{to}} \text{good human resource utilization}$$

That is, knowledge of the various topics falling within the purview of OB can help you develop essential skills and enact managerial roles in ways that facilitate high levels of both task performance and human resource maintenance in the work setting. The book has been organized and presented on this basis. Let us briefly review the discussions in each major part of the book on these fundamental OB topics.

TABLE 18.3   Selected Foundations for Success in Managing Human Behavior in Organizations

Interpersonal relations—Ability to enter into and maintain effective relationships with other persons in the work setting.

Leadership—Ability to deal with subordinates, to motivate and train, to help, and to deal with authority and dependency problems.

Conflict-resolution—Ability to mediate between conflicting parties, resolve disturbances, and negotiate differences with others.

Information processing—Ability to collect information, organize information for decision-making purposes, and disseminate information.

Decision making—Ability to know when a decision is needed, diagnose situation, plan an approach, search for solutions, evaluate potential consequences, and select an alternative.

Resource allocation—Ability to distribute physical, financial, human, and personal resources among competing demands.

Entrepreneurism—Ability to recognize problems, implement solutions, and take advantage of opportunities for constructive change.

Introspection—Ability to understand one's job and staff and to learn through self-study and awareness.

Source: Developed from Henry Mintzberg, *The Nature of Managerial Work* (New York: Harper & Row, 1973), pp. 188–193; and Robert L. Katz, "Skills of an Effective Administrator," *Harvard Business Review,* Vol. 42 (September–December 1974), pp. 90–102.

Introduction

Our introduction to OB in Part One began with an initial look in Chapters 1 and 2 at managers, organizations, and people at work. We explored the nature and meaning of work for individuals and used the psychological contract to emphasize the importance of a balance between the work contributions of people and the inducements they receive from the organization. Task performance and human resource maintenance were then introduced as key results sought by managers. After detailed consideration of the "job satisfaction–performance controversy," it became obvious that the statement "satisfied workers are productive workers" is an oversimplification. At the very least, managers must strive to create both satisfaction and performance within their areas of responsibility.

Managing Individuals in Organizations

Part Two of the book provides a knowledge of individuals. Chapter 3 presented the individual performance equation and noted how differences in individual attributes combine with effort and organizational support to influence task performance and human resource maintenance. The individual performance equation looked like this.

$$\text{Performance} = \frac{\text{individual}}{\text{attributes}} \times \frac{\text{work}}{\text{effort}} \times \frac{\text{organizational}}{\text{support}}$$

The next three chapters concentrated on various motivation theories and the management of rewards, learning, reinforcement, and job designs. These topics contain insights that can help managers derive maximum work efforts from subordinates and provide them with personally satisfying work settings.

Managing Groups in Organizations

Part Three showed that another important part of OB as a knowledge base is the study of groups. Chapter 7 discussed the major types of groups in organizations and presented a model of group behavior. Chapter 8 went on to discuss the major dimensions of group dynamics including norms, cohesion, membership roles, and intergroup relations. Finally, Chapter 9 showed how these concepts could be applied in group development and creative work-group designs to help meet the challenges of managing groups at work.

Managing Organizations

Part Four of the book focused on a knowledge of organizations as work settings. Organizations are work instruments that require managers if they are to achieve success. Chapter 10 reviewed basic concepts and attributes of organizations, and discussed alternative organizational perspectives. Chapter 11 introduced an open systems view of organization, stressing environment, technology, and size as important influences on organizational dynamics. Chapter 12 then took these ideas and applied them to designing organizations for effective mission accomplishment.

Managing the Processes of OB

In Part Five of the book, a number of basic processes in OB were covered in detail. It is through these processes that managers enact their day-to-day roles and responsibilities. It is also through these processes that managers put their knowledge of individuals, groups, and organizations to work. The processes include perception, decision making, communication, conflict, power, politics, and leadership. Special attention has been given to the subject of leadership, an all-encompassing and frequently talked about managerial skill. This is an important concept, and a number of key theories were discussed to stimulate your thinking.

Managing in a Dynamic Environment

The two chapters in Part Six focused on managerial challenges in the contemporary environment. Chapter 17 examined the challenges of change and stress, while Chapter 18 has focused on the challenges of environmental trends and managing a managerial career. As you hopefully embark on such a career, we want you to recognize a continuing need to learn throughout this career about OB and its managerial applications. Simply put, you must become a life-long learner to ensure long term success as a manager.

Final Advice

Many problems and prospects await you in a managerial career. The issues discussed here merely set the stage for what is yet to come. As you look ahead to an exciting future, remember your study of OB and these final career commandments.[22]

1. *Perform.*   The basic foundation of success in any job is good performance. A record of high performance will please your superiors, earn respect from your peers and subordinates, and call attention to you as a person of high potential.
2. *Stay visible.*   Do not hesitate to make sure that others recognize your hard work and the performance results achieved. This is a public relations task to be done in a professional manner and without becoming known as a braggart. When the performance record is there, project memos, progress reports, and even requests for more frequent evaluation and feedback sessions with superiors can enhance the visibility of your success.
3. *Be willing to move.*   Do not get locked into a job that you have already mastered and/or that is narrow and limited in the visibility or opportunity it offers. Take advantage of promotion opportunities within the organization. Be willing to change organizations for similar reasons. Do not be afraid to nominate yourself when appropriate for new and challenging changes of assignment.
4. *Find a mentor.*   It is always beneficial to have a senior executive who acts as a mentor from whom you can learn and who sponsors your career interests.

Ideally, this will be a person who can create mobility and opportunity for you as his or her own career progresses over time.

5. *Manage your career.* Stay active in thinking seriously and systematically about your career. Prepare and maintain a career plan even if it is only a broad frame of reference for directing your efforts and evaluating opportunities as they arise. Do not let success at any one stage distract you from taking advantage of new appointments with further growth potential. Take charge of your career, and stay in charge.

6. *Continue your education.* Life-long learning is both a responsibility and a prerequisite of long-term managerial success. In today's dynamic and challenging environment, the manager who fails to continue to learn and develop appropriate skills will not succeed. Maintain the "yearn to learn"—that is, make a commitment to take advantage of all opportunities for continuing education and personal managerial development that come your way.

SUMMARY

The future offers unlimited potential for growth, achievement, and satisfaction for good managers. Today's dynamic environment requires people and organizations to be highly productive to meet successfully the challenges of the late twentieth century. Everywhere we turn, concern is expressed about solving problems and taking advantage of the opportunities in our world. Managers are cornerstones in the quest for productivity, a quest that should include a concern with facilitating both high performance and satisfaction within the work unit and organization as a whole. Trends suggest that managers of the 1990s and beyond will be held accountable for achieving productivity in an extremely challenging environment. We look ahead to a world whose pressures include environmental trends such as the internationalization of management, increased attention to managerial ethics, and quality of working life, among many others. Individual trends for greater security, equality, and personal rights, plus the ever-changing world of technology, add further complexity to the future with which managers most successfully deal.

In this complicated work environment, career planning and development emerges as an important managerial responsibility. Managers must take charge of their personal careers to ensure success. This can involve deliberate and close adherence to a formal career plan, or it may involve having a clear sense of career direction, but being ready and able to respond to unforeseen opportunities as they occur. Because of a manager's supervisory responsibilities, he or she will also be involved in assisting subordinates in their career planning and development activities. Looking ahead to a managerial career involves anticipating such things as the pressures of initial entry to a career, dual-career families, and transitions through various adult life stages. Through it all, good managers will remain aware of how their needs and those of others must inevitably work in harmony with those of the organization.

We hope that you have gained a lot from this study of OB. We hope, too, that this learning experience will help you be truly successful in a managerial career.

THINKING THROUGH THE ISSUES

1. Identify three environmental trends that can be predicted for the future. Why do you think they are important to managers?
2. Identify three trends in people that will affect management in the future. How do you think they will impact managerial work?
3. What will the growing revolution in high technology mean to managers of the future?
4. Which of the foundations for managerial success listed in Table 18.3 is most difficult for you to master? Why? What do you plan to do about it?
5. What is the advantage of a systematic approach to career planning?
6. List the responsibilities of individuals and organizations in career planning and development.
7. Choose persons with whom you are familiar and who are at early, middle-, and late adult transitions. What are their special problems, needs, and concerns? How would you handle each of these people as their manager?
8. Summarize the most important managerial implications that you derived from (a) Part Two: Managing Individuals in Organizations; (b) Part Three: Managing Groups in Organizations; (c) Part Four: Managing Organizations; and (d) Part Five: Managing the Processes of Organizational Behavior. Explain why they will be important in the next managerial position you expect to hold.

CASE: JOURNEY TO THE TOP

When he became chief executive of a newly independent International Playtex, Inc., Joel E. Smilow also became his own boss.[23] This marked the end of a journey originally charted in a career path he had set upon graduation from the Harvard Business School in 1958. The chart identified the positions and salaries he wanted to achieve by certain ages. The last entry showed him as chief executive of an independent company. On August 5, 1986, he finally "checked" it off as a mission accomplished!

Joel's drive for success was evident in his college years at Yale. He spent summers working as a sales clerk in a department store to help pay his way. After graduating in 1954, he married, did a two-year stint in the U.S. Navy, and then went to Harvard. There he earned an MBA "with distinction" and accepted an offer to join Procter & Gamble in Cincinnati. He says he learned "strategy" at Harvard and "execution" at P&G.

One thing the brash young marketer kept in mind was his career plan. Whenever he felt he was slipping behind, he let his superiors know. Colleagues from his early days at P&G describe him as "incredibly smart" and very ambitious. He rose quickly and became brand manager for a number of winning products, and a couple of losers. But he felt limited by the institutional pace and the nature of the job. With a tendency to be "short" with people less capable than he, his personality wasn't a great fit with the brand manager's job of little authority but lots of responsibility. After being passed over for a promotion in 1965 he quit to join a small consulting firm. From there he was asked to join Playtex as a vice president—an offer he rejected as beneath his abilities. The company hired him as president in 1969. Overnight, Joel went from supervising 18 people at the consulting firm to managing 12,000 at Playtex.

Joel thrived under the freedom to run his own show. He acquired rights to promising new products, and diversified the product lines. He also built a reputation as a no-nonsense demanding boss about whom one observer says: "He wants people to work seven days a week, or at least a solid six." Some of his top managers quit along the way. One comments: "It's not his intellect I fault . . . it's the human dimension—or lack of it." Joel responds by stressing his honesty in dealing with others. "I've never in my life misled an executive as to his future. Maybe when you tell them the truth, you're considered tough."

When Playtex was bought by Beatrice, Joel quit in just four months. After spending the next 18 months looking at, but always refusing, a variety of top jobs, he joined a group seeking to take Beatrice private. Ultimately, he and a group of executives bought Playtex for $1.25 billion.

Questions

1. What are the potential benefits and risks of a career planning approach such as that taken by Joel Smilow?
2. Is Joel an effective manager in terms of the foundations for managerial success listed in Table 18.3? . . . in terms of his use of OB as a knowledge base for achieving a good utilization of human resources? Be specific in your answers.
3. Would you want to work for Joel? Explain your answer.

EXERCISE: PERSONAL CAREER PLANNING

Purpose:
To help you look ahead and establish the foundations for a career plan.

Time:
30 to 40 minutes in class; 1 hour at home.

Procedure:
A. Home Preparation
1. Write down your responses to the following questions:
   a. Where would I like to be in five years as a manager? (Be as specific as possible and list job title, name, and/or type of organization, and geographical location.)
   b. What salary do you hope to earn in the above position?
2. Think carefully about your answers in Question 1. List your current (a) strengths and (b) limitations in achieving these goals.

3. For each strength, write a plan of action for maintaining and/or increasing it over a five-year period.
4. For each weakness, write a plan of action for removing or reducing it over a five-year period.
5. Make a summary list of the people who you feel will need to help you if you are to succeed during this five-year time period.

B. In Class
1. Convene in small groups of three to five persons to share career goals and action plans.
2. Have a spokesperson ready to report to the class the goals of persons in the group, the salaries expected, and some highlights from the various action plans.
3. The instructor will lead a discussion of the values and limitations of career planning.

THE MANAGER'S VOCABULARY

Career A sequence of jobs and work pursuits representing what a person does for a living.

Career path A sequence of jobs held over time during a career.

Corporate Social Responsibility An obligation to perform in ways that serve both organizational and public interests.

Dual-Career Couple A family in which both adult partners are part of the workforce.

Managerial Ethics Standards and principles that guide the actions and decisions of managers and determine if they are "good or bad" or "right or wrong" in a moral sense.

Organizational Behavior The study of individuals and groups in organizations.

Productivity A summary measure of the quantity and quality of work performance with resource utilization considered.

Quality of Working Life A term used to indicate the overall quality of human experience in the workplace.

Value-Added Manager A manager whose work efforts tangibly improve an organization's bottom-line performance results.

NOTES

[1]Developed from Peter Nulty, "The Economy of the 1990s: How Managers Will Manage," *Fortune* (February 2, 1987), pp. 47–50; and, James Brahm, "Cultivating Tomorrow's Execs," *Industry Week* (July 27, 1987), pp. 33–38.

[2]Charles Dickens, *A Tale of Two Cities,* in the Words of Charles Dickens (New York: P.F. Collier, 1880), p. 343.

[3]Robert M. Fulmer, "Eight Paradoxes for the 1980s," working paper #0-003, School of Business Administration, Emory University, Atlanta, Georgia.

[4]John Naisbett, *Megatrends: Ten New Directions Trans-*

forming Our Lives (New York: Warner, 1982).

[5]"Where the Jobs Are," *Newsweek* (February 2, 1987), pp. 42–47.

[6]For a review of the issues see Nancy J. Adler, *International Dimensions of Organizational Behavior* (Boston: Kent Publishing, 1986).

[7]Nulty, op cit.; and, "Help Wanted," *Business Week* (August 10, 1987), pp. 48–53.

[8]See David A. Whetten, "Organizational Decline: A Neglected Topic in Organizational Science," *Academy of Management Review,* Vol. 5 (October 1980), pp. 577–588.

[9]David A. Nadler and Edward E. Lawler III, "Quality of Work Life: Perspectives and Directions," *Organizational Dynamics,* Vol. II (Winter 1983), pp. 22–136.

[10]Micheal Brody, "The 1990s," *Fortune* (February 2, 1987), pp. 22–24.

[11]Cathy Trost, "All Work and No Play? New Study Shows How Americans View Jobs," *The Wall Street Journal* (December 30, 1986), p. 17.

[12]Based in part on George Strauss, "Personnel Management: Prospects for the Eighties," in K. M. Rowland and G. R. Ferris (eds.), *Personnel Management* (New York: Allyn & Bacon, 1982), pp. 504–513; and Naisbitt, *Megatrends.*

[13]See *The American Woman 1987–88: A Report in Depth* (Washington: The Woman's Research and Education Institute, 1987).

[14]Henry C. Lucas, Jr., "Utilizing Information Technology: Guidelines for Managers," *Sloan Management Review,* Vol. 28 (Fall 1986), pp. 39–47.

[15]Edgar H. Schein, *Career Dynamics: Matching Individual and Organizational Needs* (Reading, Mass.: Addison-Wesley, 1978), p. 1.

[16]Irving Janis and Dan Wheeler, "Thinking Clearly About Career Choices," *Psychology Today* (May 1978), p. 67.

[17]Summarized in part from a discussion by Kae H. Chung and Leon C. Megginson, *Organizational Behavior: Developing Managerial Skills* (New York: Harper & Row, 1981), pp. 539–540, as based on Schein, *Career Dynamics,* pp. 189–199.

[18]Daniel J. Levinson, *The Seasons of a Man's Life* (New York: Alfred A. Knopf, 1978). See also Douglas T. Hall, *Careers in Organizations* (Santa Monica, Calif.: Goodyear, 1975).

[19]Raymond E. Hill and Edwin L. Miller, "Job Change and the Middle Season's of a Man's Life," *Academy of Management Journal,* Vol. 24 (1981), pp. 114–127.

[20]For a review see Uma Sekaran, *Dual-Career Families* (San Francisco: Jossey-Bass, 1986).

[21]Frank Allen, "Mobile Managers Get Greater Pay, Especially if They Join New Firms," *The Wall Street Journal* (October 6, 1980), p. 31; Fern Schumer Chapman, "Executive Guilt: Who's Taking Care of the Children?," *Fortune* (February 16, 1987), pp. 30–37.

[22]Based on Ross A. Webber, "13 Career Commandments," *MBA* (May 1975), p. 47; Alan N. Schoonmaker, *Executive Career Strategy* (New York: American Management Association, 1971).

[23]Developed from "Joel Smilow Finds the End of his Rainbow," *Business Week* (August 25, 1986), pp. 67–71.

HISTORICAL FOUNDATIONS OF ORGANIZATIONAL BEHAVIOR

One of the delightful aspects of contemporary society is a reawakening interest in our past. Many people are investigating their ancestries and trying to learn as much as possible about their "roots." To understand better what OB is today, it is also useful to identify its roots from the past. The significance of this historical inquiry is well expressed by Paul Lawrence in an introduction to his recent overview of the discipline.[1]

> Organizational behavior is a young and rapidly growing area of systematic inquiry. It is therefore not surprising that professionals in the field are often preoccupied with its present and future, and seldom reflect on its past. Yet an understanding of that past and an awareness of how knowledge and expertise have gradually accumulated can enrich the field's identity and add meaning to current efforts.

SCIENTIFIC MANAGEMENT

In 1911, Frederick W. Taylor published a short book called *The Principles of Scientific Management*.[2] This classic book is one you will still find to be provocative (and quick) reading today. The book begins with the following statement.

> The principle object of management should be to secure maximum prosperity for the employer, coupled with the maximum prosperity for the employee.

Taylor goes on to offer managers four principles of **scientific management** as guidelines for meeting this managerial responsibility.

1. Develop a "science" for every job. This science should include such things as rules of motion, standardized work implements, and proper working conditions.
2. Carefully select workers who have the right abilities for the job.
3. Carefully train these workers to do the job; then offer them proper incentives to cooperate with the job science.
4. Support the workers by taking responsibility for work planning and by smoothing the way as they go about their jobs.

Taylor's Pig Iron Study

Taylor reported a pig iron study conducted at the Bethlehem Steel Company to illustrate these principles. The year was 1899, and the company had a problem. There were 80,000 tons of iron to be loaded on freight cars for shipment. This iron was in the form of 92-pound "pigs" that workers hand carried up inclined planes to freight cars. A worker typically loaded 12½ tons of pig iron to earn a daily wage of $1.15. There were 75 persons in the loading gang available to do the work.

Taylor determined that it was possible for one worker to load 47½ tons per day if the principles of scientific management were followed. To prove his point, a study was conducted.

The principal actor was a man Taylor called "Schmidt." He was described as a person

> observed to trot back home for a mile to so after his work in the evening about as fresh as when he came trotting down in the morning . . . upon wages of $1.15 a day he had succeeded in buying a small plot of ground, and he was engaged in putting up the walls of a little house for himself in the morning before starting work and at night after leaving . . . he also had a reputation of . . . placing a high value on a dollar."

Taylor reports that under scientific management, Schmidt earned $1.85 per day while loading 47 tons and never failed to work at the new pace during a three-year period. One worker after another was picked out of the gang and similarly trained.

Implications

Over the years Taylor's work has been expanded, modified, and criticized, even to the point of questioning whether or not Taylor's reported data were really fiction or fact.[3] Edwin A. Locke, however, has offered a very thorough analysis of Taylor's basic arguments and the criticisms commonly lodged against them.[4]

Locke begins by noting that an essential element of Taylor's philosophy of management was the "scientific approach." By this, Taylor meant that something must be based on proven fact rather than on tradition, rule of thumb, guesswork, precedent, personal opinion, or hear say. Locke considers this philosophical foundation for Taylor's thinking directly consistent with the trend of modern management theory that emphasizes similar scientific rigor. He goes on to critique several of the major techniques recommended by Taylor. For your convenience, each of the techniques is briefly reviewed here in terms of Locke's evaluation.

1. *Time and motion study.* Taylor advocated breaking work down into its constituent elements or motions to eliminate inefficiencies and wasted effort. What we now know as "time study" is used routinely in industrial settings. Even though worker resistance to time study continues to exist, the methodology is generally accepted as standard management practice today.
2. *Standardized tools and procedures.* Taylor advocated standardization in the design and use of tools. This principle is also accepted today and includes the science of human engineering.
3. *The task.* Taylor felt that workers should be assigned specific amounts of work based on time study. This assigned quota he called a "task"; it is the equivalent of what we now refer to as a work "goal." Locke notes that virtually every contemporary theory or approach to motivation, including

organizational behavior modification and management by objectives, includes goal setting as an important component.

4. *The money bonus.* Taylor felt that money was a significant incentive to workers. Although money continues to be attacked by some social scientists for the primacy of its role in the latter sense, Locke acknowledges that the large variety of monetary incentive schemes have been developed since Taylor's time.

5. *Individualized work.* Taylor advocated individual as opposed to group tasks. He believed that group work and group rewards would undermine individual productivity. Locke quotes Taylor as writing, "Personal ambition always has been and will remain a more powerful incentive to exertion than a desire for the general welfare." This view of Taylor's is in some opposition to the current trend of management theory that emphasizes group tasks. Locke notes that this trend exists even though the evidence is not conclusive one way or the other that the group or individual level of task and reward is superior. He leaves this issue for future research to resolve and suspects that outcomes will depend on such situational factors as the nature of the task.

6. *Management responsibility for training.* Taylor was concerned that workers should not learn their skills haphazardly from other cohorts in the work setting. Rather, he felt that they should learn the proper way in which to perform the task from management experts. Management theory and practicing managers of today accept training as a substantial supervisory responsibility.

7. *Scientific selection.* Taylor advocated the selection of only "first-class" persons as defined in terms of high aptitude. Contemporary management theory emphasizes rigorous and scientific employee selection techniques as a means of ensuring that persons of correct ability are hired to fill jobs. Locke feels that Taylor's work was a substantial impetus to what is now known as the fields of industrial psychology and personnel management.

Managerially speaking, Locke is redirecting the attention of theorists and practitioners back to Taylor's work as one initial impetus to what we now know and respect as contemporary management theory. He cautions against premature dismissal of Taylor's ideas and/or preoccupation with criticisms that he feels are largely unjustified or misdirected. Locke concludes his paper with a statement that seems an appropriate summary to this brief look at Taylor's place among the historical roots of OB.[5]

Considering that it has been over 65 years since Taylor's death and that a knowledge explosion has taken place during these years, Taylor's track record is remarkable. The point is not, as is often claimed, that he was "right in the context of his time" but is now outdated, but that *most of his insights are still valid today.* The present author agrees with those who consider Taylor a genius.

THE HAWTHORNE STUDIES

Not long after Taylor's book was published, in 1924 to be exact, the Western Electric Company began a study of individual productivity in its Cicero (a suburb of Chicago) plant known as the Hawthorne Works.[6] The company was interested in the effects of physical working conditions on output. This concern reflects a direct interest in Taylor's first principle of scientific management.

Illumination Studies

Between 1924 and 1927, a series of studies was conducted to determine how various levels of illumination affected the output of workers. After varying the intensity of light for different work groups, measuring changes in output, and then analyzing the results, the researchers were disappointed. They failed to find any relationship between level of illumination and production. In some groups, output moved up and down at random; in others it increased steadily; and in one, it increased even as illumination was reduced to the level of moonlight! Perplexed by these results, the researchers concluded that unforeseen "psychological factors" had somehow interfered with the experiments.

Relay Assembly Test Room Studies

In 1927, a new group of researchers from Harvard University led by Elton Mayo began another series of studies. Their objective was to establish the effects of worker fatigue on productivity. Care was taken to design a test of this relationship that would be free of the "psychological effects" thought to have confounded the illumination studies.

Six operators who assembled relays were isolated for intensive study in a special test room. The operators were subjected to various rest pauses, lengths of workday, and lengths of workweek, while their production was regularly measured.

Once again, the Hawthorne researchers were unable to find any direct relation between changes made in physical working conditions and worker outputs. Overall, the productivity of the relay assemblers increased over time and regardless of the specific changes made in the work setting by researchers.

Mayo and his colleagues concluded that the new "social setting" created in the test room accounted for the increased productivity. Two factors were singled out as having special importance in this regard. First, there was a positive group development in the test room. The operators shared both good social relations with one another and a common desire to do a good job. Second, supervision was more participative than that otherwise experienced by the operators. Operators in the test room were made to feel important, given a lot of information, and frequently consulted for their opinion on what was taking place. This was not the case in their normal work situation.

Further Studies

Until worsening economic conditions forced their termination in 1932, Mayo and his group of researchers continued their Hawthorne studies. After the relay assembly test room experiments, however, their interest shifted from physical working conditions to such aspects of the "social setting" of work as employee attitudes, interpersonal relations, and group relations.

Two further studies were conducted. In one, 21,126 Western Electric employees were interviewed to learn what they liked and disliked about their work. The researchers felt that this knowledge could help management to make changes that would improve productivity. The interviews also yielded "complex" and "baffling" results that led researchers to conclude that the same thing (e.g., work conditions, wages) can be sources of satisfaction for some people and dissatisfaction for others. In other words, people are different! Interestingly enough, this thesis was also advanced by Frederick Taylor.

The second of the final Hawthorne studies was conducted in the Bank Wiring Room. This time the researchers specifically set out to examine the behavior of the work group. One of their "surprises" was to find individuals willing to sacrifice pay that could be earned by increasing output, that is, to restrict their output, to avoid the displeasure of the group. This finding complemented the earlier relay assembly study and suggested that the work group can have strong negative, as well as positive, influences on individual productivity.

Implications

The Hawthorne studies shifted the attention of managers and researchers away from physical work planning and the application of monetary incentives toward the social setting of workers and their individual attitudes. They gave birth to a body of literature now referred to as the "Human Relations Movement," a movement characterized by its concern for the creation of good human relationships between managers and their subordinates.[7] Many of the more humanistically oriented writers whose theories are well studied in the management fields received stimulation from this time in OB's history. They include Abraham Maslow, Chris Argyris, Douglas McGregor, Rensis Likert, and Frederick Herzberg, among others.

The Hawthorne studies have been criticized for their scientific methods.[8] A common concern is summarized in the **Hawthorne effect,** a term now used to describe situations in which persons who are singled out for special attention end up performing as anticipated only because of the expectancies created by the special situation. This term is a constant reminder that Mayo's test room operators may have improved their performance, not because of any subtle group dynamics or supervisory practices, but simply because they felt increased output was what the researchers and the company wanted.

Like Taylor's work, it is what the Hawthorne studies led to in terms of future research rather than what they actually achieved as research, that counts most. They represent an important historical turning point that allowed the field of management a new way of thinking about people at work. They extended the thinking of researchers beyond concerns for physical and economic considerations alone, and clearly established the managerial significance of the psychological and sociological aspects of people as *human* beings. As a result, the Hawthorne studies have had a major impact on what we study as part of OB. This legacy includes an interest in

- The group as an important force in the work setting.
- The sources of individual job satisfaction and dissatisfaction.
- Different "styles" of supervision, with a special emphasis on employee participation.
- The need for good interpersonal skills of managers.
- The importance of social relationships as a determinant of individual behavior at work.

THE MANAGEMENT FUNCTIONS

Perhaps you have already had a course or done some reading in an area called "management" or "administrative theory." If so, you are familiar with the classical axiom: good managers will do five things well: planning, organizing, staffing, directing or leading, and controlling. These "functions" of management derive from another important root of OB. This root includes a body of early literature that does not pretend to rigorous scientific foundations but is derived from the systematic reflections of practicing managers on their work experiences. This "grass-roots" approach to management is often criticized for being based on "armchair" rather than scientific evidence. We have discussed this problem more generally in a section on scientific thinking in Chapter 1. Nonetheless, the ideas of these early writers on management and administration have also had a significant impact on OB.

The classics among these works were written by Henri Fayol, Mary Parker Follett, James Mooney, and Lyndall Urwick.[9] We will limit our attention to Fayol, a successful executive in French industry.[10] In 1916, he published *Administration Industrielle et Generale* outlining his reflections on the proper management of organizations and the people within them.[11] His book offered the five "rules" listed in Table A.1. These rules, as shown in the table, have led to the formulation of what are now known as functions of management—planning, organizing, staffing, directing or leading, and controlling.

OB AND THE BEHAVIORAL SCIENCES

The three components of science deal with physical, biological, and behavioral phenomena, respectively. The behavioral sciences are particularly concerned with the study of human behavior. They would like to predict how people will behave in various settings. OB is an applied behavioral science that has a special interest in human behavior in organizations.

TABLE A.1   Henri Fayol's Rules for Managers and Their Relationship to the Functions of Management

Fayol's Rules	Management Function
Foresight. To complete a plan of action; to scheme for the future.	Planning
Organization. To provide the resources needed to implement the plan; to mobilize effort in support of the plan.	Organizing
Command. To get the best out of people working toward the plan; to lead; to properly select and evaluate workers.	Leading
Coordination. To ensure that the efforts of subunits fit together properly; that information is shared and any problems solved.	Controlling
Control. To verify progress; make sure things happen according to plan; take any necessary corrective action.	Controlling

Source: Developed from M. B. Brodie, *Fayol on Administration* (London: Lyon, Grant, and Green, 1967), pp. 12–14.

Figure A.1 shows that OB is closely related to three behavioral sciences: psychology and its concern for the individual, sociology and its concern for people in interaction with one another, and anthropology and its concern for people in their respective cultural settings. The Hawthorne studies, for example, can be viewed from the perspective of each of these disciplines. A psychologist would look at the relay assembly test room and be most interested in the feelings and behavior of the individual operators; a sociologist would be studying the group of six operators as they interacted and worked with one another; an anthropologist would be looking at the social system created by the test room environment and the behaviors of the operators and observers within it.

There is a natural bridge between OB and these behavioral sciences, as well as other allied social sciences like economics and political science. As a result, OB is an interdisciplinary body of knowledge that draws insights from many scientific sources and vantage points. OB is unique, however, in applying and integrating these diverse insights to better understand human behavior in organizations.

FIGURE A.1   The heritage of OB as an academic discipline.

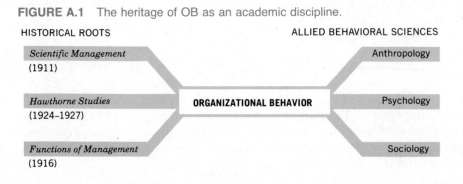

HISTORICAL ROOTS

ALLIED BEHAVIORAL SCIENCES

Scientific Management (1911)

Anthropology

Hawthorne Studies (1924–1927)

ORGANIZATIONAL BEHAVIOR

Psychology

Functions of Management (1916)

Sociology

THINKING THROUGH THE ISSUES

1. It is possible to criticize the work of Frederick W. Taylor and the Hawthorne studies. What impact do you feel these criticisms of OB's "roots" have had on the field of OB as it exists today?
2. How would you differentiate among the responses Frederick Taylor, Elton Mayo, and Henri Fayol would give to the question: "What should a manager do to ensure a high level of work unit performance?"

EXERCISE: THE GREAT OB HISTORY DEBATE

Purpose:

To increase your understanding of the historical "roots" of OB and to provide an opportunity to examine critically these roots for their managerial implications.

Time:

50 minutes.

Procedure:

1. Form work groups as assigned by your instructor.
2. Each group will be assigned or allowed to choose one of the following responses to the question: What should a manager do to ensure a high level of work unit performance?

   Response A: "Frederick Taylor offers the best insight into this question. His advice would be to . . ." (advice to be filled in by the group),

   Response B: "The Hawthorne studies are the true source of insight into this question. They suggest that a manager should . . ." (advice to be filled in by the group).

   Response C: Henri Fayol is the best source of insight into this question. His advice would be to . . ." (advice to be filled in by the group).

3. Each group will have 20 minutes to prepare a 5-minute response for oral presentation to the rest of the class.
4. The instructor will reconvene the class and a debate will take place according to the following format:
   a. Each group makes an opening statement.
   b. Each group is allowed to ask questions and/or offer rebuttals to the other groups.
   c. Each group makes a final 1-minute closing statement.
5. After time is called, the instructor will lead an open discussion on the three responses. This discussion will end with confrontation of the question: "Where does OB go from here?"

THE MANAGER'S VOCABULARY

Hawthorne Effect   Situations in which persons singled out for special attention end up performing as anticipated because of the expectancies created by the "special" situation.

Scientific Management   Frederick Taylor's four principles for systematically designing jobs, planning work, and selecting and training people to do them.

IMPORTANT NAMES

Henri Fayol   The author of the book *Administration Industrielle et Generale,* in which the functions of management were described.

Elton Mayo   The head researcher in the Hawthorne studies.

Frederick W. Taylor   The author of the book *The Principles of Scientific Management.*

NOTES

[1] Paul R. Lawrence, "Historical Development of Organizational Behavior," pp. 1–9 in Jay W. Lorsch (ed.) *Handbook of Organizational Behavior* (Englewood Cliffs, N.J.: Prentice-Hall, 1987).

[2] Frederick W. Taylor, *The Principles of Scientific Management* (New York: W. W. Norton, 1967), p. 9. (The original version of this book was published in New York by Harper, 1911.)

[3] Charles D. Wrege and Amedeo G. Perroni, "Taylor's Pig-Tale: A Historical Analysis of Frederick W. Taylor's Pig-Iron Experiments," *Academy of Management Journal,* Vol. 17 (March 1974), pp. 6–27.

[4] Edwin A. Locke, "The Ideas of Frederick W. Taylor: An Evaluation," *The Academy of Management Review,* Vol. 7 (1982), pp. 14–24. See also Edwin A. Locke, "Job Attitudes in Historical Perspective," pp. 5–11 in Daniel A. Wren and John A. Pearce II (eds.), *Papers Dedicated to the Development of Modern Management: Celebrating 100 Years of Modern Management* (Academy of Management, 1986).

[5] Ibid., p. 24.

[6] The Hawthorne studies are described in detail in F. J. Roethlisberger and William J. Dickson, *Management and the Worker* (Cambridge, Mass.: Harvard University Press, 1966); and G. Homans, *Fatigue of Workers* (New York: Reinhold, 1941). Both sources were used in preparing the synopsis. See also Ronald G. Greenwood and Charles D. Wrege, "The Hawthorne Studies," pp. 24–35 in Wren and Pearce, op cit.

[7] For a representative of this school of thought, see Willart E. Parker and Robert W. Kleemeier, *Human Relationships in Supervision: Leadership in Management* (New York: McGraw-Hill, 1951).

[8] Alex Carey, "The Hawthorne Studies: A Radical Criticism," *American Sociological Review,* Vol. 32 (June 1967), pp. 403–416. See also Greenwood and Wrege, op cit.

[9] For representatives of this school of thought see Henry C. Metcalfe and L. Urwick (eds.), *Dynamic Administration: The Collected Papers of Mary Parker Follet* (New York: Harper & Brothers, 1940); James D. Mooney, *The Principles of Administration,* rev. ed. (New York: Harper & Brothers, 1947); and L. Urwick, *The Elements of Administration* (New York: Harper & Brothers, 1943).

[10] The primary source for this discussion of Fayol's work is M. B. Brodie, *Fayol on Administration* (London: Lyon, Grant and Green, 1967).

[11] Available in the English language as Henri Fayol, *General and Industrial Administration* (London: Sir Isaac Pitman & Sons, 1949).

SCIENTIFIC FOUNDATIONS OF ORGANIZATIONAL BEHAVIOR

The field of OB takes care to ensure that the knowledge base from which you will derive managerial applications is built by acceptable scientific methods.

THE SCIENTIFIC METHOD

The **scientific method** involves four steps:[1]

1. Observations are made regarding real-world events and occurrences.

   Example Company officials become concerned that productivity in a plant is not as high as possible.

2. An explanation for the events and occurrences is formulated.

   Example These officials agree that productivity probably suffers because the physical working conditions are not as conducive to high production as they could. One aspect that seems especially important is the level of illumination in the work place.

3. Statements are made that use the explanation to predict future events and occurrences.

   Example Company officials and a team of researchers predict that changes made in levels of illumination will directly affect work output. As illumination increases, output should increase; as illumination decreases, output should decrease.

4. The predictions are verified by an examination conducted under systematic and controlled conditions.

   Example Two groups of workers are selected for study and their existing levels of output measured. In one group, light intensity is increased; in the other, it is held constant. Output is measured again for both groups. The prediction that illumination will directly affect output is tested against the data.

The previous example shows how the scientific method was followed as company officials moved from an initial observation that a problem may exist, to the point of eventually testing a plausible explanation for the problem and/or a means of resolving it. In actual practice, OB research is sometimes criticized because of the inability of researchers to completely meet the requirements set forth in step 4. It is very difficult to conduct a true experiment when the subjects are people working in organizations. Consequently, when you evaluate an OB research study and the managerial insights it claims to offer, you must have a basic understanding of the strengths and weaknesses of various research designs.

RESEARCH DESIGNS

A **research design** is the step-by-step approach used to study systematically a phenomenon in question.[2] The three basic research designs are experimental, quasi-experimental, and nonexperimental. Through good choice and use of a given research design, a researcher seeks to gather and interpret data in a scientifically defensible fashion. Two very important criteria in the selection of a research design are[3]

1. *Internal validity*   the strength of the design in establishing a definitive test of the research question (e.g., does X cause Y?)
2. *External validity*   the strength of the design in its ability to generate findings generalizable to other people and situations (e.g., will X cause Y somewhere else?)

Experimental Research

The best way to verify an explanation of the type "an increase in illumination will cause an increase in productivity" is to perform a true experiment. A **true experiment** exists when the subjects of a research investigation are randomly assigned to one or more treatment and control groups. The key to the prior statement is the word "random." Unless a subject has an equal chance of being assigned to the treatment group (for example, the one where light intensity is varied) and the control group (for example, the one where light intensity remains the same), a variety of explanations alternative to the one advanced by researchers could account for any changes observed. Randomization equalizes the chances and simplifies the process of drawing conclusions.

Consider the following diagrammatic example of a true experiment. In the diagram the "R" stands for random assignment of subjects, "O" for measures taken (e.g., production output), and "X" for the treatment being investigated (e.g., increased illumination).

$$R \quad O \quad X \quad O \quad \text{treatment}$$
$$R \quad O \qquad\quad O \quad \text{control}$$

Most true experimental research in OB is accomplished in the laboratory setting. Because it is hard to randomize subjects in the real-world work situation, "field" studies are most often not true experiments. This lack of true experimentation can lead to problems in drawing research conclusions and establishing "cause–effect" relationships.

In the illumination study discussed earlier there was no randomization in the assignment of subjects to treatment and control groups. Suppose in the study that output actually increased only in the treatment group as the researchers originally predicted.

Would that have meant that increased light intensity caused an increase in productivity? Not necessarily. In addition to the possibility that the results were due to increased illumination, one or more of the following explanations could have accounted for the observed differences in productivity.

- The workers in the treatment group might have been better workers than those in the control group to begin with.
- Something may have occurred in the treatment group that facilitated higher output—for example, new workers added, change in machinery, salary increased, and so on.
- Something may have occurred in the control group that inhibited higher output—for example, loss of workers, change in machinery, salary decrease, and so on.

Whenever a true experiment is not done, alternative explanations such as those just given should always be carefully ruled out. Then, and only then, can observed support for the original explanation be accepted as a basis for decision making and action.

Quasi-Experimental Research

It is possible to approximate true experimental conditions in field settings. In the illumination studies, for example, nonrandom treatment and control groups were formed, measures were taken before and after the treatment was administered, and the results were then analyzed systematically. This is a good research approach, but its strength relies very heavily on the ability of researchers to deal with alternative explanations.

A typical quasi-experimental design is diagrammed next. Although treatment and control groups exist, they are not created by randomization. This lack of random assignments makes them easier to do in work settings than true experiments. With good attention given to rival explanations, the quasi-experimental design can make a fine contribution to OB knowledge.

O   X   O   treatment
O   O   control

Nonexperimental Research

The least rigorous research designs are nonexperimental. In them, researchers simply observe events or occurrences of interest and then draw conclusions from the results. Still, nonexperimental designs are a source of OB knowledge. They exist in the form of case studies, questionnaire surveys, and reports on systematic interviews. When well accomplished and interpreted, nonexperimental research can be as insightful as research accomplished with the more rigorous designs. The burden of proof, however, is on the investigator to demonstrate that truly logical and defensible interpretations are being made from the research.

One of the most common of the nonexperimental designs is for data to be gathered from a number of persons. Then correlational statistics are used to establish the empirical relationships in the data. In such cases, researchers rely on the strength of statistical argument to overcome the built-in weaknesses of the research design. Much OB research is conducted using this method.

THE VOCABULARY OF SCIENCE

The previous discussion sets up the necessary groundwork for you to understand the OB research we discuss throughout the book. To further help you to become comfortable with the scientific vocabulary of OB, the following terms are introduced with clarifications as how we use them.[4]

Variable
A measure used to describe a real-world phenomenon.

> *Example*   Researchers counted the number of parts produced by workers in a week's time as a measure of their individual productivity.
>
> *Clarification*   How well variables are measured is an important criterion of good research. Measures are often criticized and debated; good measures get used repeatedly by many researchers. You need to be able to judge how well researchers have measured their variables. It is far easier to count the number of parts produced and call that productivity than it is to measure how the worker feels about the job and call that job satisfaction.

Hypothesis
A tentative explanation about the relationship between two or more variables.

> *Example*   One historical hypothesis of OB researchers was that an increase in the number of rest pauses allowed workers in a workday would increase productivity. Confirmation of this hypothesis would lead to the action implication: If you want to increase individual productivity in a work unit, give the subordinates more frequent rest pauses. This hypothesis has not been confirmed by scientific research.
>
> *Clarification*   A hypothesis is what becomes formulated during step 3 of the scientific method. Hypotheses are ''predictive'' statements. Once verified through empirical research, an hypothesis can be a source of direct action implications. Hypotheses are sometimes called ''propositions.''

Dependent Variable
The event or occurrence expressed in an hypothesis that indicates what the researcher is interested in explaining.

> *Example*   In OB research, individual performance is often the dependent variable of interest; that is, researchers try to determine what factors cause increases in performance. One hypothesized relationship between a causal factor and this

dependent variable is

$$\text{Increased rest periods} \xrightarrow[\text{to}]{\text{lead}} \text{increased performance (dependent variable)}$$

Independent Variable

An event or occurrence that is presumed by hypothesis to affect one or more other events or occurrences as dependent variables.

Example   In the previous example, increased rest periods was the independent variable.

Intervening Variable

An event or occurrence that provides the linkage through which an independent variable is presumed to affect a dependent variable.

Example   It is sometimes hypothesized that participative supervisory practices (independent variable) improve worker satisfaction (intervening variable) and therefore increase performance (dependent variable). This relationship would be depicted as

$$\text{Participative supervision} \longrightarrow \text{improved satisfaction (\textit{intervening variable})} \longrightarrow \text{increased performance}$$

Moderator Variable

An event or occurrence that specifies the condition under which an independent variable affects a dependent variable.

Example   The previous example hypothesizes that participative supervision would lead to increased productivity. It may well be that this relationship will hold only when the employees feel their participation is real and legitimate (a moderator variable). This role of a moderator variable can be diagrammed as

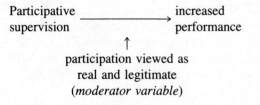

Theory

A set of systematically interrelated concepts, definitions, and hypotheses that are advanced to explain and predict phenomena.[5]

Example   One current theory of leadership effectiveness argues that task-oriented leaders will have more effective work groups when the leader has very much or very little situation control, and that relationship-oriented leaders will have more effective work groups when the situation affords the leader an intermediate amount of control.[6]

Clarification   Theories tend to be abstract and to involve multiple variables. They usually include a number of hypotheses, each of which would be based on clearly articulated concepts and definitions. Most, if not all, of the previously discussed kinds of variables would probably be involved. We should also note that many things called "theories" in OB do not strictly meet the definition above. Actually, they represent viewpoints, explanations, or perspectives that have logical merit and that are in the process of being scientifically verified. Theories are frequently referred to as "models" in OB.

Empirical Research

The use of objective measurements of research variables as a basis for investigating and verifying theories and hypotheses.

Example   Researchers collected data on the output of a work unit on a daily basis. These were objective "facts" because the same results would have been obtained by anyone who used the same measuring procedures. These "facts" are quite different from the "opinion" of an observer who may have watched the workers perform and then made a purely personal judgment regarding their accomplishments.

SCIENTIFIC RESEARCH IN REVIEW

The scientific method as depicted in Figure B.1 is an important criterion used to evaluate research contributions to OB. Ultimately you need to become a good consumer of other people's research. A familiarity with the scientific method, alternative research designs and the vocabulary of science are helpful first steps on the way. Important, too, is an awareness of increasing attention within the field of OB to the practicality of research.

Five dimensions of research relevance have been proposed to represent the key needs of practitioners with respect to the utilization of organizational science knowledge.[7] These five dimensions or properties of relevant research are briefly summarized as follows:

1. *Descriptive relevance*   is the accuracy of research findings in capturing phenomena encountered by the practitioner in his or her organizational setting
2. *Goal relevance*   is the correspondence of outcome or dependent variables in a theory to things the practitioner actually wishes to influence
3. *Operational validity*   is the ability of the practitioner to implement action implications of a theory by manipulating its causal or independent variables

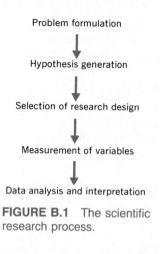

Problem formulation

↓

Hypothesis generation

↓

Selection of research design

↓

Measurement of variables

↓

Data analysis and interpretation

FIGURE B.1 The scientific research process.

4. *Nonobviousness* is the degree to which a theory meets or exceeds the complexity of common sense theory already used by a practitioner
5. *Timeliness* is the requirement that a theory be available to practitioners in time to use it to deal with problems

For managers to benefit in actual practice from OB research, theories must be high in practical relevance. To achieve this goal, organizational scientists are increasingly recognizing their responsibility to make research relevant, that is, to make sure that the work they do satisfies the five dimensions just described—descriptive relevance, goal relevance, operational validity, nonobviousness, and timeliness. You should find a good correspondence between these criteria and the various theories and findings discussed in this book. You should also find that the emerging OB research as reported in the scholarly literature is responsive to similar tests of practicality and meaningfulness for managers and people at work.

THINKING THROUGH THE ISSUES

1. Because their subject is human behavior in organizations, OB researchers are often unable to perform true experiments. What alternative research designs can be used in their place?
2. Use each of the terms in The Vocabulary of Science section as they might be found in a work conversation between two managers.

CASE: TRAINING SUPERVISORS AND CONVINCING MANAGEMENT

Shane Alexander is the personnel director of the Central State Medical Center. One of her responsibilities is to oversee the hospital's supervisory training programs. Recently, Shane attended a professional conference where a special "packaged" training program was advertised for sale. The "package" includes a set of videotaped lectures by a distinguished management consultant plus a workbook containing readings, exercises, cases, tests, and other instructional aids. The subjects covered in the program include motivation, group dynamics, communication skills, leadership effectiveness, performance appraisal, and the management of planned change.

In the past, Shane felt that the hospital had not lived up to its supervisory training goals. One of the reasons for this was the high cost of hiring external consultants to do the actual instruction. This packaged program was designed, presumably, so that persons from within the hospital could act as session coordinators. The structure of the program provided through the videotapes and workbook agenda was supposed to substitute for a consultant's expertise. Because of this, Shane felt that use of the packaged program could substantially improve supervisory training in the hospital.

The cost of the program was $3500 for an initial purchase of the videotapes plus 50 workbooks. Additional workbooks were then available at $8 per copy. Before purchasing the program, Shane needed the approval of the senior administrative staff.

Upon returning from the conference, Shane proposed such a purchase at the next staff meeting. She was surprised at the response. The hospital president was noncommittal, the vice president was openly hostile, and the three associate administrators were varied in their enthusiasm. It was the vice president's opinion that dominated the discussion. He argued that to invest in such a program on the assumption that it would lead to improved supervisory practices was unwise. "This is especially true in respect to the proposed program," he said. "How could such a package possibly substitute for the training skills of an expert consultant?"

Shane argued her case and was left with the following challenge. The administrators would allow $1,000 to be spent to rent the program with 30 workbooks. It would be up to Shane to demonstrate through a trial program that an eventual purchase would be worthwhile.

There were 160 supervisors in the hospital. The program was designed to be delivered in eight 2½-hour sessions. It was preferred to schedule one session per week, with no more than 15 participants per session.

Shane knew that she would have to present very strong evidence to gain administrative support for the continued use of the program. Given the opportunity, she decided to implement a trial program in such a way that conclusive evidence on the value of the "packaged" training would be forthcoming.

Questions

1. If you were Shane, what type of research design would you use to test this program? Why?
2. How would the design actually be implemented in this hospital setting?
3. What would be your research hypothesis? What variables would you need to measure to provide data that could test this hypothesis? How would you gather these data?

4. Do you think the administrator's request for "proof before purchase" was reasonable? Why or why not?

THE MANAGER'S VOCABULARY

Dependent Variable   The event or occurrence, expressed in an hypothesis, that indicates what a researcher is interested in explaining (e.g., work performance or job satisfaction).

Empirical Research   The use of objective measurement of research variables as a basis for investigating and verifying theories and hypotheses.

External Validity   The strength of a research design in its ability to generate findings generalizable to other people and situations.

Hypothesis   A tentative explanation about the relationship between two or more variables.

Independent Variable   The event or occurrence that is presumed in the statement of an hypothesis to affect one or more other events or occurrences.

Internal Validity   The strength of a research design in establishing a definitive answer to the research question.

Intervening Variable   An event or occurrence that provides the linkage through which an independent variable is presumed to exert an effect on a dependent variable.

Moderator Variable   An event or occurrence that specifies the condition under which an independent variable affects a dependent variable.

Research Design   A step-by-step approach used to study systematically a phenomenon in question.

Theory   A set of systematically interrelated concepts, definitions, and hypotheses that are advanced to explain and predict phenomena.

True Experiment   When the subjects of a research investigation are randomly assigned to one or more treatment and control groups.

Variable   A measure used to describe a real-world phenomenon.

NOTES

[1]Developed from Eugene Stone, *Research Methods in Organizational Behavior* (Santa Monica, Calif.: Goodyear, 1978), p. 8.

[2]For a good review of research designs, see Donald T. Campbell and Julian C. Stanley, *Experimental and Quasi-Experimental Designs for Research* (Chicago: Rand-McNally, 1969); and Stone, *Research Methods in Organizational Behavior*.

[3]See Stone, *Research Methods in Organizational Behavior*, for a good discussion of threats to internal and external validity.

[4]Ibid.

[5]C. William Emory, *Business Research Methods*, rev. ed. (Homewood, Ill.: Richard D. Irwin, 1980).

[6]Fred E. Fiedler, Martin M. Chemers, and Linda Mahar, *Improving Leadership Effectiveness: The Leader Match Concept* (New York: John Wiley, 1976).

[7]Kenneth W. Thomas and Walter G. Tymon, Jr., "Necessary Properties of Relevant Research: Lessons from Recent Criticisms of the Organizational Sciences," *Academy of Management Review*, Vol. 7 (1982), pp. 345–352.

PERFORMANCE APPRAISAL FOUNDATIONS OF ORGANIZATIONAL BEHAVIOR

A concern for performance, a key result of the efforts of people at work, underlies a manager's interest in the field of Organizational Behavior.[1] Accordingly, one major responsibility shared by all managers is to facilitate high levels of individual and group performance accomplishment. It is in this action context that our study of OB, and its many concepts and theories, takes meaning.

An important foundation for the managerial application of OB in the workplace is the process of performance appraisal. Formally defined, **performance appraisal** is a process of formally evaluating performance and providing feedback on which performance adjustments can be made. Essentially, performance appraisal works on the basis of the equation: Desired performance − actual performance = need for action. To the extent that desired levels exceed actual levels, a performance variance requiring special attention exists. And only when actual performance is accurately measured is a manager well prepared to apply a knowledge of OB to analyze the performance situation, identify problems and/or opportunities involved, and take appropriate action.

Although most managers will be involved with performance appraisal at the individual and group levels, we'll restrict our attention here to the appraisal of individual performance. Many of the issues, problems, and principles that can be identified at this level of action also apply to the others. It is useful in this respect to recall our Chapter 1 discussion of means–ends chains. This logic suggests that each person should perform tasks that are the "means" for higher-level objectives (i.e., "ends") to be achieved. When such means–ends linkages are made throughout an organization and across all levels, organizational performance in the form of mission accomplishment should be facilitated.

Beginning with this notion of interlocking means–ends chains, we can say (1) that jobs are created to fulfill specific purposes within the framework of organizational objectives, (2) those specific job duties/responsibilities that define each of the many jobs that get created should point to what is expected of people at work, and (3) that these specific duties/responsibilities become the focus of evaluating one's performance. Performance appraisal, therefore, plays a key role in completing the means–ends linkages of work activities and goals throughout an organization.

PURPOSES OF PERFORMANCE APPRAISAL

Any performance appraisal system is central to an organization's human resource management activities. The major functions of performance appraisal are to:[2]

1. *Define* the specific job criteria against which performance will be measured.
2. Accurately *measure* past job performance.
3. *Justify* the rewards given to individuals, thereby discriminating between high and low performance.
4. *Define* the development experiences the employee needs to both enhance performance in the current job and prepare for future responsibilities.

These four functions include two general purposes served by good performance-appraisal systems: evaluation and development. For the manager this means that fulfilling both judgmental (serving evaluation purposes) and counseling (serving developmental purposes) roles are essential to the performance-appraisal process. From an evaluative perspective, performance appraisal lets people know where they stand relative to objectives and standards. As such it is an input to decisions that allocate rewards and otherwise administer the personnel function of the organization. From a counseling perspective, performance appraisal facilitates decisions relating to planning for and gaining commitment to the continued training and personal development of subordinates.

Administrative Decisions

Administrative decisions are concerned with such issues as promotions, transfers, terminations, and salary increases. Where these decisions are made on performance criteria as opposed to some other basis (e.g., seniority), some sort of performance appraisal system is necessary. Performance appraisal information is also useful for making selection and placement decisions, where performance results are matched against individual attributes and selection dimensions to determine which are most related to performance. Also, if one were to identify specific aspects of performance which are inadequate, the performance appraisal process may lead to improved training and development programs. Then, too, appraisals form the basis of any performance-contingent reward system. As discussed in Chapter 5, such systems depend on good performance appraisals to make them work.

Managers make a wide variety of these and other administrative decisions relating to the performance of people at work. The quality of these decisions depends directly on the quality of the performance information collected. Therefore, effective management action requires good performance appraisal information.

Employee Feedback and Development Decisions

Another use of performance appraisals is to let employees know how they stand in terms of management expectations and performance objectives. Performance appraisal feedback should involve a detailed discussion of the employee's job-related strengths and weaknesses. This feedback can then be used for developmental purposes. In terms of the expectancy motivational approach in Chapter 4, feedback can help to clarify the individual's sense of both instrumentality and expectancy.

Performance appraisal feedback can also be used as a basis for individual coaching or training by the manager to help the employee overcome performance deficiencies. In one recent survey, approximately 65 percent of the sampled firms were found to be using performance appraisals for developmental purposes.[3]

DIMENSIONS AND STANDARDS
OF PERFORMANCE APPRAISAL

The ease or difficulty of establishing performance dimensions and standards makes a difference in the way performance appraisal systems are established. In addition to performance outcomes, the behaviors or activities that result in these outcomes are frequently important to performance appraisal. Thus, it is essential to discuss both output measures and activity measures as key components of the performance appraisal process.

Output Measures

A number of production and sales jobs provide ready measures of work output. For example, an assembler may have a goal of 50 completed units of a product per hour. The number of assembled units is easily measurable, and it is possible for the organization to set standards concerning how many units should be completed per hour. Here, the performance dimension of interest is a quantitative one—50 completed units per hour. However, the organization may also introduce a performance quality dimension as well. The employee may be evaluated not only in terms of the number of units per hour but the number of units that pass a quality control inspection per hour. Now, *both* quantity and quality are important, and the worker cannot trade one for the other. In other words, assembling 60 units per hour will not do if only 40 pass inspection. Neither will having a larger proportion of units pass inspection if only 35 units are assembled per hour.

In addition, management may also be interested in other performance dimensions, such as downtime of the equipment used for assembling. Thus, a worker would be evaluated in terms of the performance dimensions of quantity and quality of assembly output and equipment downtime. In this way, management could make sure not only that a desirable product was assembled at a desirable rate but that the worker was careful with the equipment.

Activity Measures

In the preceding example, the output measures were straightforward as was the measure of equipment downtime. Often, however, output measures are difficult, if not impossible, to obtain for a single individual over a period of time and unsuitable for providing appropriate appraisal and feedback. Rather than using output measures, activity or behavioral measures may be called for. For a sales representative, for example, number of units sold during a given time period represents output, whereas techniques used to obtain sales, such as number of calls made, would be activity measures of performance.

Activity measures are typically obtained by some sort of observation and rating on the part of the evaluator. Output measures, on the other hand, are often directly obtained from written records or documents (e.g., production records). While difficulty of obtaining output measures may be one reason for using activity measures, some activity measures are more useful for employee development and counseling than are output measures alone.

Where jobs lend themselves to systematic analysis, the activities can be inferred from a job analysis. Job analyses typically result in written descriptions of job duties and responsibilities (job descriptions) and specification of personal requirements to perform the duties (job specifications).[4] These documents are used in many organizations as the basis for selection and training, as well as for other aspects of wage and salary administration.[5]

MEASUREMENT ERRORS IN PERFORMANCE APPRAISAL

In addition to concern with the purpose of the appraisal system and its dimensions and standards, it is important to be concerned about those things that can threaten the reliability and validity of a performance appraisal system. To be meaningful, an appraisal system must be both **reliable** (i.e., provide consistent results each time it is used) and **valid** (i.e., actually measure people on relevant job content). A number of measurement errors can threaten performance appraisals from each perspective.[6]

Deficiency and Contamination Errors

Systematic job analyses define the domain of key job duties/responsibilities, and as a result, help prevent two common errors in measuring performance—*deficiency* and *contamination*. Deficiency occurs where elements important to job success are left out. For example, a job description for a secretary that failed to consider ''dealing with others'' would be a deficiency in most such jobs. Careful job analysis would help avoid such deficiencies, and thus help ensure that the performance evaluation would cover *all* relevant dimensions of work.

The opposite of deficiency is contamination. Here, dimensions extraneous to job success are included in the performance measure. This might take several forms, from measuring specific behaviors that are not truly a part of the job to having the measures reflect common judgmental errors or even bias as a part of the evaluation. Thus, a measure of ''leadership'' might be a contaminating dimension for a salesperson. However, it would not be a contaminating factor for a managerial job. This is why systematic analysis is so important. In like manner, raters often commit one or more judgmental or rating errors (described below) that are reflected in their evaluations of others. This important source of contamination must be guarded against if useful performance information is to be collected.

Halo Errors

Halo error results when a person rates another person on each of several different dimensions and gives a similar rating for each dimension. Here, a sales representative considered to be a ''go-getter'' (and thus rated high on ''dynamism'') would also be rated high on dependability, tact, and whatever other performance dimensions were used. The rater fails to discriminate between the person's strong and weak points, and thus a ''halo'' carries over from one dimension to the next. As you can see, this can create a problem where each of the performance dimensions is considered to be an important and relatively independent aspect of the job.

Leniency/Strictness Errors

Just as some professors are known as easy ''A's,'' some managers tend to give relatively high ratings to virtually everyone under their supervision. Sometimes the opposite also occurs, where some raters tend to rate everyone low. A key problem is that there is very little discrimination between the good and poor performers. Leniency errors involve a tendency to lump them all together.

Central Tendency Errors

In contrast to a tendency to rate all subordinates as very good or very bad, central tendency errors occur when the manager lumps them together around the ''average'' or middle category. This gives the impression that there are no very good or very poor performers on the dimension being rated. No true performance discrimination is made.

Recency Errors

A different kind of error from those just noted occurs when a rater lets recent events influence a performance rating more than earlier ones. Take, for example, the case of an employee who is usually on-time but shows up one hour late for work the day before a performance rating is made. She is rated low on ''promptness'' because the one incident of tardiness overshadows her usual promptness. Recency errors can easily occur in the performance appraisal process.

Personal Bias Errors

In addition to the preceding kinds of errors, raters sometimes allow specific biases to enter into performance evaluations. For example, a given rater may intentionally give higher ratings to white than nonwhite ratees, thereby having the performance appraisal reflect a racial bias. Managers must reflect carefully on their personal biases and guard against their interference with ratings of subordinates that are supposed to be performance based.

PERFORMANCE APPRAISAL METHODS

A number of methods are commonly used in performance appraisal. As a part of the discussion, we include a brief treatment of some strengths and weaknesses of these methods in terms of purpose, dimensions and standards, and rating errors. The methods are divided into two general categories: comparative methods and absolute methods.[7]

Comparative Methods

Comparative methods of performance appraisal seek to identify the relative standing among those being rated. That is, they would like to establish that Bill is better than Mary who is better than Leslie on a performance dimension. Comparative methods can indicate that one person is better than another on a given dimension, but not how much better. They also fail to indicate whether the person receiving the better rating is "good enough" in an absolute sense. It may well be that Bill in our example is merely the best of a bad lot. Three comparative performance appraisal methods are ranking, paired comparison, and forced distribution.

Ranking

Ranking is the simplest of all the comparative techniques. It consists of merely rank ordering each individual from best to worst on each performance dimension being considered.

Paired Comparison

In a paired comparison method, each person is directly compared with every other person being rated. The frequency of endorsement across all pairs determines one's final ranking. Every possible paired comparison within a group of ratees is considered as shown here. (Underlines indicate the person rated better in each pair):

<u>Bill</u> vs Mary   <u>Mary</u> vs Leslie   <u>Leslie</u> vs Tom
<u>Bill</u> vs Leslie   <u>Mary</u> vs Tom
<u>Bill</u> vs Tom

Number of times Bill is better $= 3$
Number of times Mary is better $= 2$
Number of times Leslie is better $= 1$

Overall, the best performer in this example is Bill, next comes Mary, then Leslie, and last of all is Tom. The paired comparison method becomes tedious when there are lots of people to compare.

Forced Distribution

Here a small number of performance categories are used (e.g., very good, good, adequate, poor, very poor). Each rater is instructed to rate a specific proportion of employees in each of these categories (e.g., 10 percent must be rated very good, 20 percent must be rated good, etc.). This *forces* the rater to use all the categories and not to rate everyone as outstanding or poor or average or the like.

Summary

Comparative methods force the evaluator to differentiate among ratees. A halo error can still occur since comparisons may be similar across all dimensions, although this is less likely with paired comparisons. These methods are not especially good for individual feedback or counseling since they do not reveal much about how close to standard a given employee is. Comparing one employee unfavorably with another is also likely to make the person receiving this feedback defensive. Finally, it may be hard to anchor the performance in terms of expected standards and to compare employees in one group with those of another. It is hard to determine, for example, if the highest ranked person in one group is an equivalent performer to the highest ranked persons in other groups.

On balance, then, comparative techniques are primarily useful for administrative purposes. Two strengths are the forced discrimination they provide and their relative simplicity. A key shortcoming is the lack of an absolute performance standard for comparison purposes.

Absolute Methods

Absolute methods of performance appraisal specify precise measurement standards. For example, tardiness might be evaluated on a scale ranging from "Never tardy" to "Always tardy." Four of the more common absolute rating procedures are (1) graphic rating scales, (2) critical incident diary, (3) behaviorally anchored ratings scales, and (4) management by objectives approach.

Graphic Rating Scales

This method lists a variety of dimensions thought to be related to high-performance outcomes in a given job, and that the individual is accordingly expected to exhibit. The scales allow the manager to assign the individual scores on each dimension. These ratings are sometimes given point values to allow a summary numerical rating of performance to be given. An example is shown in Figure C.1 found in the case at the end of this module.

The primary appeal of graphic rating scales is that they are relatively easy to do, are efficient in the use of time and other resources, and can be applied to a wide range of jobs. Unfortunately, they are also subject to halo errors and because of generality may not be linked to job analysis or other specific aspects of a given job. This can be corrected by ensuring that only relevant dimensions of work based on sound job analysis procedures are rated.

Critical Incident Diary

In this method, supervisors record incidents of each subordinate's behavior that led to either unusual success or failure in a given performance aspect. These are typically recorded in a diary-type log kept daily or weekly under predesignated dimensions. In a sales job, for example, followup of sales calls and communicating necessary customer information might be two of the dimensions. Descriptive paragraphs can then be used to summarize each salesperson's performance for each dimension as they are observed.

This approach is excellent for employee development and feedback. Since it consists of qualitative statements rather than quantitative information, however, it is difficult to use for administrative decisions. To provide for such information, the critical incident technique is sometimes combined with one of the other methods.

Behaviorally Anchored Ratings Scales (BARS)

This is a performance appraisal approach that has received increasing attention. The procedure for developing this type of scale starts with the careful collection of descriptions of observable job behaviors. These descriptions are typically provided by managers and personnel specialists and include both superior and inferior performance. Once a large sample of behavioral descriptions are collected, each is evaluated to determine the extent to which it describes good-versus-bad performance. The final step is to develop a rating scale where the anchors are specific critical behaviors, each reflecting a different degree of performance effectiveness. An exmaple of a BARS is shown in Table C.1 for a retail department manager. Note the specificity of the behaviors and the scale values for each. Similar behaviorally anchored scales would be developed for other dimensions of the job.

As you can see, the BARS approach is detailed and complex. It requires much time and effort to develop. A separate BARS is required for each job, and thus the method is most cost efficient where there are many similar jobs subject to the same appraisal.

The BARS provides specific behaviors useful for counseling and feedback combined with quantitative scales useful for administrative comparative purposes. Initial results with BARS suggested that they were less susceptible to common rating errors than more traditional scales. Later evidence suggests that the scales may not be as clearly superior as originally thought, especially if an equivalent amount of developmental effort is put into other types of measures. Nevertheless, these scales are likely to have a lower level of contamination and deficiency than most other methods. They represent state-of-the-art notions concerning appraisal procedures, and there is strong rationale supporting their use.[8]

Management by Objectives

Of all the appraisal methods, the management by objectives (MBO) procedure is most directly linked to means–ends chains and goal setting.[9] Where an MBO system is used, subordinates work with their supervisor to establish specific task-related objectives that fall within their domains and serve as means to help accomplish the supervisor's higher-level objectives. Each set of objectives is worked out between a supervisor and subordinate for a given time period. The establishment of objectives is similar to a job analysis, except that it is directed toward a particular individual in his or her job rather than toward a particular job type alone. The increased discretion of the MBO approach means that each specific person is likely to have a custom tailored set of work goals, while still working within the action context of organizational means–ends chains.

MBO is the most individualized of all the appraisal systems and tends to work well for counseling if the objectives go beyond simply desired outputs and focus on important activities as well. In comparing one employee with another, a key concern is the ease or difficulty of achieving the goals. If one person has an easier set of objectives to meet than another, then comparisons are unfair. Since MBO tends to rely less heavily on ratings than do the other appraisal systems, rating errors are less likely to be a problem. Contamination is less likely and deficiency can also be low, depending on the comprehensiveness of the objectives.

TABLE C.1   Example of a Behaviorally Anchored Rating Scale Dimension

Supervising Sales Personnel

Gives sales personnel a clear idea of their job duties and responsibilities; exercises tact and consideration in working with subordinates; handles work scheduling efficiently and equitably; supplements formal training with his or her own "coaching"; keeps informed of what the sales people are doing on the job; and follows company policy in agreements with subordinates.

Effective	9	Could be expected to conduct full day's sales clinic with two new sales personnel and thereby develop them into top sales people in the department.
	8	Could be expected to give his or her sales personnel confidence and strong sense of responsibility by delegating many important jobs to them.
	7	Could be expected *never* to fail to conduct training meetings with his or her people weekly at a scheduled hour and to convey to them exactly what is expected.
	6	Could be expected to exhibit courtesy and respect toward his or her sales personnel.
	5	Could be expected to remind sales personnel to wait on customers instead of conversing with each other.
	4	Could be expected to be rather critical of store standards in front of his or her own people, thereby risking their developing poor attitudes.
	3	Could be expected to tell an individual to come in anyway even though he or she called in to say he or she was ill.
	2	Could be expected to go back on a promise to an individual whom he or she had told could transfer back into previous department if he or she did not like the new one.
Ineffective	1	Could be expected to make promises to an individual about his or her salary being based on department sales even when he or she knew such a practice was against company policy.

Source: J. P. Campbell, M. D. Dunnette, R. D. Arvey, and L. V. Hellervik, "The Development and Evaluation of Behaviorally Based Rating Scales," *Journal of Applied Psychology*, Vol. 57 (1973), pp. 15–22. Copyright 1973 by the American Psychological Association. Reprinted/adapted by permission of the publisher and author.

IMPROVING PERFORMANCE APPRAISALS

The prior section summarizes a number of strong and weak points for various performance appraisal methods. As with most other issues in organizational behavior, there are trade-offs that managers must recognize in setting up and implementing a performance appraisal system. In addition to the pros and cons already mentioned for each method, some specific things to keep in mind to reduce errors and improve appraisals include[10]

1. Train supervisors so that they understand the evaluation process rationale and can recognize the various sources of measurement error.
2. Make sure that supervisors observe subordinates on an ongoing, regular basis or do not try to limit all their evaluations to the formally designated evaluation period (e.g., every six months or every year).
3. Do not have the supervisor rate too many subordinates. The ability to identify performance differences drops and fatigue sets in where the evaluation of large numbers of people is involved.
4. Make sure that the performance dimensions and standards are clearly stated and that the standards are as noncontaminating and nondeficient as possible.
5. Try to avoid terms such as ''average'' and the like since different evaluators tend to react differently to the terms.
6. Remember that appraisal systems cannot be used to discriminate against employees on the basis of age, sex, race, and so on. To help provide a legally defensible system in terms of governing legislation, the following recommendations are useful.[11]
   - Appraisal must be based on an analysis of job requirements as reflected in performance standards.
   - Appraisal is appropriate only where performance standards are clearly understood by employees.
   - Clearly defined individual dimensions rather than global measures should be used.
   - Dimensions should be behaviorally based and supported by observable evidence.
   - If rating scales are used, avoid abstract trait names (e.g., loyalty) unless they can be defined in terms of observable behaviors.
   - Rating scale anchors should be brief and logically consistent.
   - The system must be validated and be psychometrically sound as must the ratings given by individual evaluators.
   - There must be an appeal mechanism if the evaluator and ratee disagree.

THINKING THROUGH THE ISSUES

1. Define and give examples of two types of (a) comparative performance appraisal methods and (b) absolute performance appraisal methods, as they might be applied to jobs with which you are familiar.
2. Explain steps you might take as a manager to improve the performance appraisal process and help ensure that it is legally defensible.

CASE: ALLEGED SEX DISCRIMINATION IN PERFORMANCE APPRAISAL

Jayne Burroughs and John Watson are both employed as technicians in the pathology lab of Central Catholic Hospital, a major medical center in the core of a major city. They both hold specialist degrees and are licensed pathologist's assistants. Both have been employed in their jobs for five years.[12]

Last month, Dr. Clarence Cutter, the chief pathologist and supervisor of the lab, decided to reorganize his operation. He decided that supervising the work of both assistants was taking up too much of his time. He reasoned that if he were to promote one of them to a midlevel supervisory position, he could reduce the time he spent in direct supervision. Dr. Cutter presented his argument to Fred Wunderlich, the hospital's director of personnel. Wunderlich agreed and added that Dr. Cutter could probably use even more help in the lab. He suggested that either Burroughs or Watson be promoted to a new job titled Administrative Assistant to the Pathologist and that a new person be hired to fill the vacated lab technician position. Thus, a new structure was developed for the department in which two lab technicians reported to an administrative assistant, who in turn reported to the chief pathologist.

The next task for Dr. Cutter was to decide which of his lab technicians to promote to the new position. In order to make the decision, he pulled the latest six-month performance evaluations he had made on Burroughs and Watson. Figure C.1 reproduces their performance review results. On the basis of the performance reviews, he promoted John Watson to the administrative assistant position.

Upon learning of Watson's promotion, Burroughs went·to Dr. Cutter and demanded that he justify why he promoted Watson instead of her. This explanation did not satisfy Burroughs, and she filed a formal complaint alleging sex discrimination in a promotion decision, both with Mr. Wunderlich, the personnel manager, and Robyn Payson, the Hospital's Equal Employment Opportunity officer.

A hearing was scheduled by Wunderlich to resolve the issues. Wunderlich and Payson constituted the review board at the hearing, and Cutter and Burroughs were invited to present their cases. In the hearing, Burroughs opened the case by presenting her formal complaint: Both she and Watson have identical credentials for their jobs and have equal tenure on the job (five years). In addition, it is her belief that she and Watson have performed equivalently during this period of time. He told her that he was not obligated to present a justification to her; that he was perfectly within his rights as chief pathologist to make such a decision and that she should rest assured that his decision was made on grounds that were fair and equitable to her and Watson. Therefore, according to her charge, the only reason Dr. Cutter could possibly have had for promoting Watson over her would be her sex. She noted that a decision of that nature is in clear violation of Title VII of the Civil Rights Act of 1964, which reads in part:

It shall be an unlawful employment practice for an employer to fail to refuse

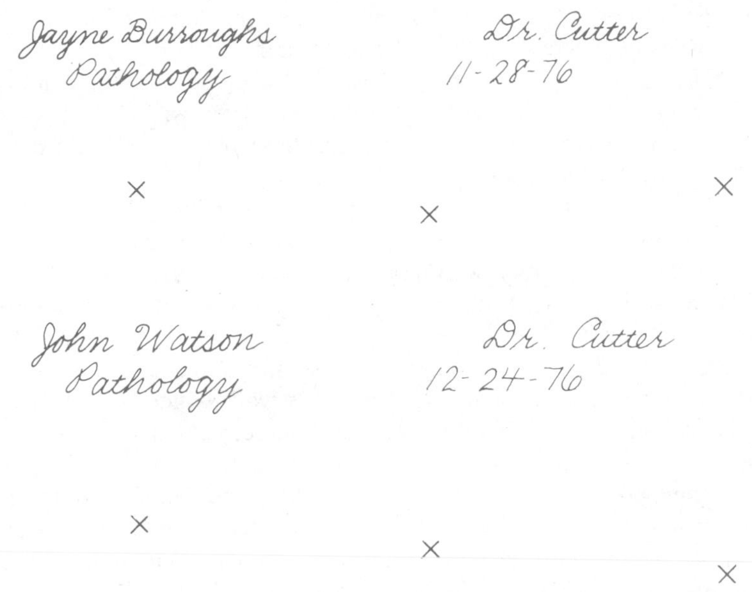

Jayne Burroughs
Pathology

Dr. Cutter
11-28-76

X   X   X

John Watson
Pathology

Dr. Cutter
12-24-76

X   X   X

FIGURE C.1   Six-Month Performance Reviews for Burroughs and Watson

to hire or to discharge, or otherwise to discriminate against any individual with respect to his compensation terms, conditions, or privileges of employment because of such individual's race, color, religion, sex, or national origin. (Title VII, Sec. 703, Par. a-1 of the Civil Rights Act of 1964, as amended by P.L. 92-261, effective March 24, 1972.)

Dr. Cutter countered by justifying his decision on the basis of actual performance review data. He argued that sex had nothing whatsoever to do with his decision. Rather, he presented to the board the latest six-month performance evaluations, which showed Watson to be performing better than Burroughs on three performance dimensions: (1) work quantity; (2) work quality; and (3) cooperation (see Figure C.1).

The performance results served to anger Burroughs further. She requested that the hearing be adjourned and reconvened after she had had a chance to review the results and prepare her case further. Wunderlich and Payson agreed and rescheduled a second hearing two weeks later.

At the second hearing, Burroughs presented the following list of grievances with regard to the promotion decision and the information on which it was based:

1. The decision is still in violation of Title VII of the Civil Rights Act because the way the performance evaluation was carried out discriminated against her on the basis of sex. Her reasoning on this point included the following charges:

    (a) Dr. Cutter is biased against females, and this factor caused him to rate males in general above females in general.

    (b) Dr. Cutter and Mr. Watson are in an all-male poker group that meets on Friday nights, and she has systematically been excluded. Thus, ties of friendship have developed along sex lines, which created a conflict of interest for Dr. Cutter.

    (c) Dr. Cutter has said to her and to others on several occasions that he doubts females can carry out managerial tasks because they must constantly be concerned with duties at home and they get pregnant.

2. The measuring device itself failed to include a number of activities she carries out that are critical to the functioning of the lab. For example, while Dr. Cutter and Watson are talking over coffee, she is frequently cleaning up the lab. She says that, although Mr. Watson's work is good, he tends to concentrate only on visible work outcomes, and leaves much of the "invisible work," like cleaning up, to her.

3. The timing of the performance review was bad. She charged that it was unfair to her to base the decision on only one six-month evaluation. Dr. Cutter has a total of 10 performance reviews for each of them. Why didn't he base his decision on all 10, rather than on just the latest review?

4. Also with respect to timing, Ms. Burroughs pointed out that her review has been made a month earlier than Mr. Watson's. She charged that December 24 was Christmas Eve and the day of the lab's office party. She charged that the spirits of the occasion (liquid and other) tended to shade Dr. Cutter's judgment in favor of Watson.

Questions

Put yourself in the position of Mr. Wunderlich and Ms. Payson. Decide whether there is any justification to Ms. Burroughs' charges, or if Dr. Cutter is justified in his decision. In making your decision, address yourself to the following questions:

1. Are issues of reliability, validity, and measurement error involved in this case? If so, what sources of error must you consider in making a judgment?

2. Is the measuring instrument itself at issue in this case? Why or why not? What recommendations would you make for changing the instrument?

3. What general changes would you recommend in this case? Why?

THE MANAGER'S VOCABULARY

Behaviorally Anchored Rating Scales (BARS)   A performance appraisal method that uses descriptions of critical job behaviors to anchor different levels of effectiveness along a performance scale.

Contamination Error   An error condition that occurs where dimensions extraneous to job success are included in performance measurement.

Critical Incident Diary   A performance appraisal method wherein incidents are recorded for each employee that lead to success or failure on a given performance aspect.

Deficiency Error   An error situation that occurs when elements important to job success are left out of performance measurement.

Forced Distribution   A performance appraisal method that involves fitting a specific proportion of employees into each of several performance categories.

Halo Error   An error that occurs when a person rates another person on each of several dimensions and gives the same rating for each dimension.

Leniency/Strictness/Central Tendency Errors   Errors that occur when a rater's tendency is to give relatively high, relatively low, or relatively average ratings to virtually everyone rated.

Management by Objectives (MBO)   Supervisors and subordinates work together to establish specific task-related objectives falling within the subordinate's task domain and that serve as a means to help accomplish the supervisor's higher-level goals.

Paired Comparison   A performance appraisal method involving a comparison of each employee on a one-on-one basis against every other employee.

Performance Appraisal   A process of formally evaluating performance and providing feedback on which performance adjustments can be made.

Personal Bias Error   An error that occurs when a rater allows specific biases to enter into performance evaluations.

Ranking   A performance appraisal method involving the rank ordering of all individuals from best to worst on a performance dimension.

Recency Error   An error that occurs when a rater lets recent events influence a performance rating more than earlier ones.

Reliability   In performance appraisal, the degree to which one obtains consistency of results from a measure each time it is used.

Validity   In performance appraisal, extent to which a measure actually measures people on actual job content.

NOTES

[1]We especially thank Dr. Lawrence Peters, Texas Christian University, for his fine critique of this module in its draft form and the many useful suggestions provided.

[2]Charles J. Fombrun and Robert L. Laud, "Strategic Issues in Performance Appraisal, Theory and Practice," *Personnel*, Vol. 60 (November–December 1983), p. 24.

[3]Ibid., pp. 23–31.

[4]See Gary P. Latham and Kenneth N. Wexley, *Increasing Productivity Through Performance Appraisal* (Reading, Mass.: Addison-Wesley, 1981), pp. 48–51.

[5]See David L. Devries, Ann M. Morrison, Sandra L. Shullman and Michael L. Gerlach, *Performance Appraisal on the Line* (Greensboro, NC: Center for Creative Leadership), 1986 Ch 3, 6.

[6]For discussion of a number of these errors see *ibid*, Ch 3.

[7]For more detail, see Latham and Wexley, *Increasing Productivity Through Performance Appraisal,* and Stephen J. Carroll and Craig E. Schneier, *Performance Appraisal and Review Systems* (Glenview, Ill.: Scott, Foresman, 1982).

[8]See R. Jacobs, D. Kafry, and S. Zedeck, "Expecta-

tions of Behaviorally Anchored Ratings Scales," *Personnel Psychology,* Vol. 33 (Autumn 1980), pp. 595–640, Frank J. Landy and James L. Farr, "Performance Rating," *Psychological Bulletin,* Vol. 87 (1980), pp. 72–107, Shullman and Gerlach op cit, Ch. 3 and Devries, Morrison, for current pro and con discussions of BARS.

[9]See Steven J. Carroll and Henry L. Tosi, *Management by Objectives: Application and Research* (New York: Macmillan, 1976); and, Anthony P. Raia, *Managing by Objectives* (Glenview, Ill.: Scott, Foresman, 1974), for a detailed discussion of MBO.

[10]Based on J. J. Bernardin and C. S. Walter, "The Effects of Rater Training and Diary Keeping on Psychometric Error in Ratings," *Journal of Applied Psychology,* Vol. 61 (1977), pp. 64–69; see also R. G. Burnask and T. D. Hollman, "An Empirical Comparison of the Relative Effects of Sorter Response Bias on Three Rating Scale Formats," *Journal of Applied Psychology,* Vol. 59 (1974), pp. 307–312.

[11]Based on W. F. Cascio and H. J. Bernardin, "Implications of Performance Appraisal Litigation for Personnel Decisions," *Personnel Psychology,* Vol. 34 (1981), pp. 211–212. See also Devries, Morrison, Shullman and Gerlach, op cit, for a discussion.

[12]Andrew D. Szilagyi, Jr. and Marc J. Wallace, Jr., *Organizational Behavior and Performance,* 3rd ed. (Glenview, Ill.: Scott, Foresman, 1983), pp. 393–394. Used by permission.

NEWSLINE CREDITS

Newsline 1.1: "McWorld?," *Business Week* (October 13, 1986), pp. 78–86, and "From Singapore to Sao Paulo, a Network of True Believers," *Business Week* (October 13, 1986), pp. 80–81.

Newsline 1.2: "Getting Man and Machine to Live Happily Ever After," *Business Week* (April 20, 1987), pp. 61–62.

Newsline 2.1: "Can U.S. Workers Compete?," *U.S. News & World Report* (September 2, 1985), pp. 40–44.

Newsline 2.2: Edward C. Baig, "America's Most Admired Corporations," *Fortune* (January 19, 1987), pp. 18–31.

Newsline 3.1: *U.S. News & World Report* (September 2, 1985), p. 46, and *The Wall Street Journal* (March 5, 1987), pp. 1, 19.

Newsline 3.2: Amal Kumar Naj, "The Human Factor," *The Wall Street Journal* (November 10, 1986), pp. 36D–37D; Hank Gilman, "The Age of Caution," *The Wall Street Journal* (June 12, 1987), pp. 23D, 28D.

Newsline 4.1: Ruth Walker, "Knowing What Co-Workers Earn: Some Say Office Openness Can Be Helpful," *Christian Science Monitor* (November 3, 1983), pp. 14, 15. Reprinted by permission from the *Christian Science Monitor* © 1983, The Christian Science Publishing Society. All rights reserved.

Newsline 5.1: "Paying Employees Not to Go to the Doctor," *Business Week* (March 21, 1983), p. 150; "Giving Goodies to the Good," *Time* (November 18, 1985), p. 98; and "Incentive Plans Spur Safe Work Habits, Reducing Accidents at Some Plants," *The Wall Street Journal* (January 27, 1987), p. 1.

Newsline 5.2: "Companies Turn to Incentives," *The New York Times* (July 19, 1985), p. 1E; Bruce G. Posner, "Pay for Profits," *Inc.* (September 1986), pp. 57–60; and "Ford Schedules Profit-Sharing Payments for '86, Averaging Over $2100 a Worker," *The Wall Street Journal* (February 19, 1987), p. 20.

Newsline 6.1: "Boldly Going Where No Robot Has Gone Before," *Business Week* (December 22, 1986), p. 45; "Limping Along in Robot Land," *Time* (July 13, 1987), pp. 46–47.

Newsline 6.2: "Now a Soviet Manager Can Start Thinking for Himself," *Business Week* (November 11, 1985), p. 93.

Newsline 7.1: "How (and Why) to Run a Meeting," *Fortune* (July 11, 1983), pp. 132–133. © 1983 Time Inc. Courtesy of Fortune Magazine. Used by permission.

Newsline 7.2: Takashi Oka, "Managers at Honda's Hub: Casual But Purposeful," *Christian Science Monitor* (October 18, 1983), pp. 17, 18. Reprinted by permission from the Christian Science Monitor © 1983 The Christian Science Publishing Society. All rights reserved.

Newsline 8.1: Gene Bylinski, "America's Best-Managed Factories," *Fortune* (May 28, 1984), p. 19. Used by permission. © 1984 Time Inc. Courtesy of Fortune Magazine.

Newsline 8.2: *The Wall Street Journal* (May 11, 1984), p. 25. Reprinted by permission of *The Wall Street Journal,* © Dow Jones & Company, Inc., 1984. All rights reserved.

Newsline 9.1: Tom Peters and Nancy Austin, *A Passion for Excellence,* New York: Random House. (1985); Tom Peters and Nancy Austin, "A Passion for Excellence," *Fortune* (May 13, 1985) pp. 20–32.

Newsline 9.2: "Quality Circles: Rounding Up Quality at USAA," AIDE Magazine (Fall 1983), p. 24. Used by permission.

Newsline 10.1: Joseph A. Raelin, *The Clash of Cultures: Managers and Professionals.* Boston: Harvard Business School Press, and R. N. Osborn and C. Baughn, "New Patterns in the Formation of U.S./Japanese Cooperative Ventures: The Role of Technology,'' Columbia Journal of World Business, in press. For a related discussion see Richard L. Daft, *Organization Theory and Design.* St. Paul: MN, West Publishing, pp. 273–279.

Newsline 10.2: William M. Bulkeley, ''The Right Mix: New Software Makes the Choice Much Easier,'' *The Wall Street Journal* (March 27, 1987), p. 17.

Newsline 11.1: C. Q. Gelertner, ''When Employees Run Department as Their Own Separate Business Firms Find Profits Rising,'' *The Seattle Times* April 1, 1984, pp. C-1 and C-2. Used by permission.

Newsline 11.2: Bill Saporito, ''IBM's No-hands Assembly Line,'' *Fortune* (September 15, 1986), pp. 105–108.

Newsline 13.1: ''Judging by Looks Isn't Only Unfair—It's Unprofessional,'' *Chicago Tribune* (November 8, 1983), p. 3; and Walter Kiechel III, ''Beauty and the Managerial Beast,'' *Fortune* (November 10, 1986), pp. 201–202.

Newsline 13.2: Michael M. Miller and Patricia Bellow Gray, ''Why Businesses Often Sink in 'Decisional Quicksand','' *The Wall Street Journal* (December 15, 1986), p. 25.

Newsline 14.1: Walter Kiechel III, ''Memo Punctilio,'' *Fortune* (September 15, 1986), pp. 185–186.

Newsline 14.2: '' 'Japan, U.S.A.,' The Difference Japanese Management Makes,'' and ''At Sanyo's Arkansas Plant the Magic Isn't Working,'' both in *Business Week* (July 14, 1986), pp. 45–46, 47–50, 51–52, respectively; and ''Where the Jobs Are,'' *Newsweek* (February 2, 1987), pp. 42–46.

Newsline 15.1: Walter Kiechel III, ''Summoning Managerial Courage,'' *Fortune* (January 19,

1987), pp. 149–152.

Newsline 15.2: William G. Scott and Terrence R. Mitchell, ''Markets and Morals in Management Education,'' *Selections* (Autumn 1986), pp. 308; Paul S. Abbott, ''Schools Branded 'Moral Failures','' *Albuquerque Journal* (November 25, 1986), p. 5, Section B. Myron Magnet, ''The Decline and Fall of Business Ethics,'' *Fortune* (December 8, 1986), pp. 18–31.

Newsline 16.1: Steven Fox, ''Superleaders Able to Inspire Employees to Perform,'' *Avalanche Journal* (Lubbock, TX), November 19, 1982; Warren Bennis and Burt Nanus, *Leaders* (New York: Harper & Row), 1985.

Newsline 16.2: Russell Mitchell, ''With Lindner in Charge, Penn Central is on the Prowl,'' *Business Week* (April 20, 1987), pp. 80–81.

Newsline 17.1: ''Business Fads: What's In And Out,'' *Business Week* (January 20, 1986), pp. 52–61.

Newsline 17.2: ''Nordstrom's High Style,'' *Newsweek* (January 5, 1987), p. 43; ''Where the Customer is King,'' *Time* (February 2, 1987), pp. 56–67; and ''Pul-eeze! Will Somebody Help Me?'' *Time* (February 2, 1987), pp. 48–54.

Newsline 18.1: Michael Waldholz, ''Drug Testing in the Workplace: Whose Rights Take Precedence?,'' *The Wall Street Journal* (November 11, 1986), p. 35; and Cathy Trost, ''For Firms that do Test, the Pitfalls are Numerous,'' *The Wall Street Journal* (November 11, 1986), p. 35.

Newsline 18.2: Alex Taylor III, ''Why Women Managers are Bailing Out,'' *Fortune* (August 18, 1986), pp. 16–23; Fern Schumer Chapman, ''Executive Guilt: Who's Taking Care of the Children?,'' *Fortune* (February 16, 1987), pp. 30–37; and ''Should Business be Forced to Help Bring up Baby?'' *Business Week* (April 6, 1987), p. 39.

PHOTO CREDITS

NAME INDEX

SUBJECT INDEX